Russian Culture in War and Revolution, 1914–22.
Book 2: Political Culture, Identities, Mentalities, and Memory

Russia's Great War and Revolution

Vol. 1, bk. 1
Murray Frame, Boris Kolonitskii, Steven G. Marks, and Melissa K. Stockdale, eds., *Russian Culture in War and Revolution, 1914–22: Popular Culture, the Arts, and Institutions* (2014)

Vol. 1, bk. 2
Murray Frame, Boris Kolonitskii, Steven G. Marks, and Melissa K. Stockdale, eds., *Russian Culture in War and Revolution, 1914–22: Political Culture, Identities, Mentalities, and Memory* (2014)

Series General Editors: Anthony Heywood, David MacLaren McDonald, and John W. Steinberg

RUSSIAN CULTURE IN WAR AND REVOLUTION, 1914–22
BOOK 2: POPULAR CULTURE, IDENTITIES, MENTALITIES, AND MEMORY

EDITED BY

MURRAY FRAME
BORIS KOLONITSKII
STEVEN G. MARKS
MELISSA K. STOCKDALE

Bloomington, Indiana, 2014

SLAVICA

Each contribution © 2014 by its author. All rights reserved.
Cover design by Tracey Theriault.

Cover: Sergei Chekhonin, cover illustration to N. N. Glebov-Putilovskii, ed., *Oktiabr': Foto-ocherk po istorii velikoi oktiabrskoi revoliutsii (1917–1920 gg.)* (Peterburg [sic]: Vsemirnoe Biuro Khudozhestvennoi Propagandy 3-go Internatsionala, 1921).

Library of Congress Cataloging-in-Publication Data

Russian culture in war and revolution, 1914-22 / edited by Murray Frame, Boris Kolonitskii, Steven G. Marks, Melissa K. Stockdale.
  volumes cm -- (Russia's Great War and Revolution ; volume 1)
  Includes bibliographical references.
  Contents: Book 1. Popular culture, the arts, and institutions -- Book 2. Political culture, identities, mentalities, and memory.
  ISBN 978-0-89357-423-9 (book 1) -- ISBN 978-0-89357-424-6 (book 2)
  1. Popular culture--Russia--History--20th century. 2. Popular culture--Soviet Union--History. 3. Political culture--Russia--History--20th century. 4. Political culture--Soviet Union--History. 5. World War, 1914-1918--Social aspects--Russia. 6. Soviet Union--History--Revolution, 1917-1921. 7. Russia--Intellectual life--1801-1917. 8. Soviet Union--Intellectual life--1917-1970. 9. Russia--Social conditions--1801-1917. 10. Soviet Union--Social conditions--1917-1945. I. Frame, Murray. II. Kolonitskii, B. I. III. Marks, Steven G. (Steven Gary), 1958- IV. Stockdale, Melissa Kirschke.
  DK264.8.R87 2014
  947.084'1--dc23
                              2014014607

Slavica Publishers
Indiana University
1430 N. Willis Drive
Bloomington, IN 47404-2146
USA

[Tel.] 1-812-856-4186
[Toll-free] 1-877-SLAVICA
[Fax] 1-812-856-4187
[Email] slavica@indiana.edu
[www] http://www.slavica.com/

In memory of Richard Stites, generous friend and inspirational scholar

Contents

From the Series Editors xi

Preface xix

Political Culture

Melissa K. Stockdale

    Mobilizing the Nation: Patriotic Culture in Russia's
    Great War and Revolution, 1914–20 3

Boris Kolonitskii

    Russian Leaders of the Great War and Revolutionary
    Era in Representations and Rumors 27

Corinne Gaudin

    Circulation and Production of News and Rumor
    in Rural Russia during World War I 55

Oleg V. Riabov

    The Symbol of "Mother Russia" Across Two Epochs:
    From the First World War to the Civil War 73

Svetlana Malysheva

    Mass Urban Festivals in the Era of War and Revolution, 1914–22 99

Steven G. Marks

    The Russian Experience of Money, 1914–24 121

Identities and Mentalities

Dan Healey
    Love and Death: Transforming Sexualities in Russia, 1914–22 151

Christine Ruane
    Fashion in Russia's War and Revolution 179

Christopher A. Stroop
    Thinking the Nation through Times of Trial:
    Russian Philosophy in War and Revolution 199

Rebecca Mitchell
    Music and Russian Identity in War and Revolution, 1914–22 221

Martin A. Miller
    Psychiatric Diagnosis as Political Critique:
    Russia in War and Revolution 245

Myths and Memory

Karen Petrone
    The Great War and the Civil War in Russian Memory 259

Alexandre Sumpf
    The Great War in Soviet Interwar Films: How to Forget (or Not) 273

Aaron J. Cohen
    Russian Monuments to the First World War:
    Where Are They? Why Are They? 297

Frederick C. Corney
    Twentieth-Century Apocalypse" or a "Grimace of Pain"?
    The Vanishing Traces of October 313

Conclusions

William G. Rosenberg

    Summing Up: Culture(s) in a Time of Crisis 343

Aviel Roshwald

    The Great War and Russian Culture in Comparative Perspective 357

Notes on Contributors 369

From the Series Editors

Origins of the Project

Since its inception in 2006 *Russia's Great War and Revolution, 1914–22* has taken shape through the collaboration of an international community of historians interested in the history of World War I's understudied eastern theater. Timed to coincide with the centenary of the Great War—and, by extension, the revolutions it helped unleash—this series responds to several developments in the historiography of the Russian Empire, its Soviet successor, and the Great War as a whole.

During a century of scholarly and popular discussion about the First World War, the "Russian" part of the conflict received little sustained attention until after 1991. In the former USSR, the war stood in the shadow of the revolutions of 1917 and the subsequent Civil War that resulted in the formation of the Soviet Union; most of all, it was eclipsed by the apotheosization after 1945 of the Great War of the Fatherland, the victory over Nazi Germany, as the defining moment in Soviet history. As a result, the First World War appeared as the final folly of an outmoded bourgeois-noble autocracy, doomed to collapse by the laws of history. Non-Soviet scholars, often hampered by restricted access to archival collections, downplayed the Russian war experience for other reasons. Specialists in the history of the late empire or early Soviet order tended to see the war as either the epilogue to the former or the prologue to the latter. Western historians often focused on the war experience of their own states— most often Britain and its imperial possessions, France, or Germany—or on a welter of issues bequeathed by the outbreak of the war in 1914 and the peacemaking in the years following 1918. These issues included most notably the vexed question of Germany's "war guilt," encoded in Article 231 of the Versailles Treaty, which has continued to provoke a lively and contentious discussion in the intervening 100 years.

The disintegration of the Soviet Union by the end of 1991 cast the history of the Soviet state and the late empire in a different light. Long-closed archives— particularly for military and international history—became relatively accessible to post-Soviet and Western scholars. As important, opportunities opened quickly for collaboration and dialogue between historians in Russia and their colleagues abroad, fostering new research and interpretations that would have been impossible or inconceivable before the late 1980s. Likewise, the dramatic

---

Russian Culture in War and Revolution, 1914–22, Book 2: Political Culture, Identities, Mentalities, and Memory. Murray Frame, Boris Kolonitskii, Steven G. Marks, and Melissa K. Stockdale, eds. Bloomington, IN: Slavica Publishers, 2014, xi–xvii.

changes of the era led scholars in- and outside the former USSR to re-examine long-held assumptions about the Soviet state and its origins, accompanied by renewed debate over the viability of the Russian Empire as it adapted to the challenges of modernity. As part of this general re-evaluation, Russia's Great War became a subject of study in its own right. By the early 21st century, the war years came to be seen as what Peter Holquist termed "a continuum of crisis." Rather than an abrupt rupture between juxtaposed imperial and Soviet orders, the war now appears not just as a powerful force of disruption, but also a period of intense mobilization—as in the other combatant states—that produced the modes and the "gaze" of statecraft, mass culture, and social control often associated with the totalitarian/authoritarian states of the interwar and Cold War years. Such practices include the nationalization of economies, the increasing application of technology to surveillance, reaching farther than before into the "private" sphere, but also such issues as displaced or refugee populations, racialized nationalist ideologies, and the development of such means as mass propaganda in support of building a utopia in our time.

All of these contexts have been brought into sharp focus by the centenary of the Great War. This occasion has engendered a great deal of scholarly and popular interest, attested by the gathering stream of books, exhibits, and memorials that will, over the coming years, mark the milestone anniversaries in the conflict's history: the war's outbreak in the summer of 1914 and key moments enshrined in the historical memories of the combatant states. All of the one-time enemies will honor the millions of dead, wounded, incapacitated, and displaced by the first "war to end all wars." For the first time, Russians will take part in these rites of commemoration. At the end of 2012, the Russian Federation declared August 1 the annual "Day of Remembrance for the Victims of the First World War" (Den' pamiati zhertv Pervoi mirovoi voiny), first observed in 2013. Similarly, having long been consigned to the margins of the dominant narratives on the First World War, Russia's part in and experience of the Great War has become the focus of a substantial body of new scholarship. This collection forms part of that new contribution to the international understanding of that conflict.

If the concept behind *Russia's Great War and Revolution* reflects recent trends in the historiography on the war's meaning for Russian history, its form draws on earlier examples of the sort of international collaboration that have become increasingly possible since the late 1980s. Each of the general editors and many members of the editorial collective had participated in similar partnerships, albeit on a smaller scale. Such projects included two volumes on Russian military history that enlisted the best specialists from the international community. Eric Lohr and Marshall Poe edited *The Military and Society in Russia* (Brill, 2002), while *Reforming the Tsar's Army* (2004), edited by Bruce Menning and David Schimmelpenninck van der Oye, appeared with the Wilson Center and Cambridge University Press in 2004. Other participants in this project had taken part in two other similar collections. In 2005, Routledge published *The Russian Revolution of 1905: Centenary Perspectives*, co-edited by Jonathan Smele and Anthony Heywood. That year also saw the publication by Brill of volume 1 of *The Russo-Japanese War in Global Perspective: World War Zero*; volume 2 came out two years later. Both were overseen by Menning, Schimmelpenninck, and John W. Steinberg. Each of these collections provided instructive examples of how to organize and produce the broad collaborative effort that has led to the appearance of *Russia's Great War and Revolution*.

Aims

Recognizing both the growing scholarly interest in Russia's Great War and the occasion presented by the successive centenaries of the First World War and the Russian revolutions, the editors of this collection have sought to assemble the best current international scholarship on the conflict. Ideally, they have oriented this collection toward several audiences. For those in the academy—scholars, undergraduates and graduate students—we offer a series of edited collections, varying in format and approach, that will provide a "snapshot" of the current state of the field. As a reflection of existing scholarly interests and debate, these materials will by default indicate those topics and issues demanding further attention. Editorial teams agreed on the optimal structure, periodization, and approach taken in their respective volumes. As a consequence, depending on the topic covered, some volumes provide a largely narrative treatment of events—for instance, military operations and engagements—or of developing issues, as occurs in the volume on international relations. Others, most often dealing with the "home front" or Russia as an empire, will present chapters that examine specific problems, groups, or regions.

In addition to addressing our academic communities, the editors seek also to engage non-professional readers in the general public, including secondary school students. To this end, as a supplement to the books in this collection, the larger editorial collective have created a dedicated website with such supporting materials as maps, illustrations, sound files, and moving images. Further, the editors plan to house on the web-site special sections devoted to summaries of the published findings and instructional guides to aid teachers in developing school and lesson plans. Finally, alongside its appearance in book form, the series will also be available on the internet through the Project MUSE scholarly database. Readers with access to that platform will be able to conduct searches in and download entire books or individual chapters as they require. In addition to benefiting scholars interested in Russia during the Great War and revolutions, the MUSE edition will provide instructors with a ready trove of materials which can provide specific readings, as well as a valuable research resource for their students.

Conceptualization and Organization

The volumes in this collection reflect the current state of scholarship on Russia's experience of the "long" Great War, spanning the First World War, the revolutions, and the Russian Civil War. Editors have sought to cover all the significant aspects of Russia's history during 1914–22, so far as current expertise permits, under a series of thematic rubrics. These cover a wide range of subjects, including the experience of the soldiers involved, as well as of the urban and rural populations on the "home front"; the course of international relations, both formal and non-governmental; the implications of war and revolution for the empire as a polity incorporating a broad variety of national and confessional populations bound to the imperial "center" by distinctive administrative and legal regimes; and the impact of prolonged "total war" on the cultural, religious, and intellectual life of the region. Looking outward beyond the territories of the Russian Empire/USSR themselves, other volumes address the perspectives of the Central Powers during the Great War, the effects of war and civil war in Siberia and the Far East, the lengthening "arc of revolution" through the peripheries of the former empire and beyond to the global south and New World in the years following 1917, and, finally, the repercussions of total wars and revolution on ideas about and performance of gender, sexuality, and the sphere of intimacy in Russian society. Of course, throughout, the use of the term "Russia" and its inflections connotes, unless otherwise stated, the territory and populations housed within the boundaries of the Russian Empire in 1914.

Given the breadth of the subject matter and the renewed interest of historians in Russia's Great War, this collection does not aspire to offer a comprehensive narrative history of the war, nor is it meant to serve as an encyclopaedia of issues, events, and persons associated with the war and revolutions. Rather, it seeks to provide clear representation of current scholarly interests and debates, while indicating areas in need of more research. Thus, readers will find relatively few articles on the economic history of either the war or the Civil War. Likewise, many areas of international relations remain uncovered, not least the formation of policy-making institutions in the successor states to the Russian Empire. Those interested in the revolutionary period will find the "workers' movement" far less prominent in this collection than would have been the case for much of the late 20th century, while the peasantry and Russia's regions have begun to receive comparatively greater attention.

As noted previously, an underlying aim of this series is to encourage further research into areas as yet insufficiently covered in current scholarship. Thus, despite the increasing prevalence of the "imperial turn" in our historiography, the impact of the war, revolutions, and Civil War in Russia's imperial borderlands has only begun recently to command the interest that it warrants. By the same token, like their counterparts for the history of other countries, specialists on 20th-century Russia have yet to delve deeply into the manifold aspects of religion and religiosity in the wartime Russian Empire, from popular or folk religion and religious practice, through the high politics of spiritual institutions, to the effects of war and turmoil on currents in theology and religious philosophy that had begun to run so strong during the "Silver Age."

Finally, throughout the long process that led to the appearance of this series, the editorial teams have sought to avoid the imposition of an explicit interpretive agenda, in the interests of conveying a sense of current areas of debate and consensus in our historical literature. Thus, while the periodization of 1914–22—i.e., the years spanning the Russian Empire's entry into war through two revolutions, civil war, and the formation of the Soviet state—has taken hold with many historians, others continue to maintain that such an approach risks flattening or downplaying the significance of 1917 and its consequences for the area's subsequent history. In the interest of providing as clear as possible a reflection of the current "state of play," these volumes house a variety of interpretations and periodizations, inviting readers to draw their own inferences and conclusions from the evidence and arguments on offer.

Process

From the beginning, editors have viewed *Russia's Great War and Revolution* as a truly global project, incorporating perspectives from historians across Europe, North America, Russia, Asia, and Australia. In addition to the subject matter treated in the volumes' contents, this global approach informed the composition of the editorial teams that oversaw the production of each volume. Each of these groups included members from North America, Russia, and the United Kingdom or continental Europe. Where the contents required it—for instance, in the book dealing with Asia, scholars from elsewhere joined the editorial team. In the interests of reaching the broadest possible international audience, the editors agreed on English as the language for the series, with the intention of publishing a parallel Russian-language edition when feasible. The articles in these volumes consist both of submissions in response to a widely circulated open call and invited contributions. Papers were selected in a two-stage process involving initial vetting by editorial team-members, then evaluation by the full editorial board. Throughout, editors strove for the greatest possible inclusiveness, with the result that the articles in the series represent a broad variety of scholars, ranging from graduate students through all ranks of the academic *cursus honorum*.

The project and its publication took shape through a series of editorial-board meetings that began at the University of Aberdeen in the summer of 2008. A meeting at the University of Wisconsin-Madison the following summer resulted in agreement on the thematic areas to be addressed by separate volumes, in addition to provisional topical headings for each volume. At Uppsala University in 2010, board-members refined outlines of desired contents for each volume, leading to a public call for papers the following autumn. From that point forward, editors pursued submissions, while project representatives participated in the presentation of project overviews and draft articles at the annual conventions of the Association for Slavic, East European, and Eurasian Studies (ASEEES), the Study Group of the Russian Revolution, the British Association for Slavonic and East European Studies (BASEES), the Southern Conference on Slavic Studies, and the 2010 Stockholm meeting of the International Council for Central and East European Studies (ICCEES).

The chapters contained in the volumes comprising *Russia's Great War and Revolution* have undergone an intensive multi-stage review process, overseen collectively by the 30-odd members of the full editorial board. The publisher also solicited a peer assessment of the project description and design; the resulting review yielded important and helpful suggestions, as did consultation with the project's advisory board. Next, editorial teams for individual volumes jointly assessed contributions. To select papers for inclusion in individual volumes and to prepare the latter for publication, the editorial board adopted a two-tier review exercise. Editorial teams were paired according to areas of overlapping interest or approach. Each of the teams would read and critique the contents for the other's volume, followed by a general discussion involving the entire editorial board. Finally, after the completion of revisions, that volume's editorial team sent it on to the general editors, who solicited anonymous peer reviews for final review. Once the volume editors addressed any critiques or suggestions from these last reviews, the general editors submitted the volume to the publisher for production.

Acknowledgments

In the eight years from its origins to the first appearance of its results, this project benefited immeasurably from the support of many people and institutions. The editorial board owes a special debt of gratitude to Alice D. Mortenson from Minneapolis, Minnesota for her unstinting support of and generosity to this undertaking, not least through the Alice D. Mortenson/Petrovich Chair of Russian History. This resource proved indispensable in making possible several successive editorial meetings. Special thanks are also due to Scott Jacobs of Houston, Texas, who provided significant support to this project for more than five years. His contributions helped ensure the success of the summer editorial meetings at the University of Wisconsin-Madison in 2012. Both donors also made possible many of the translations in the collection.

The editorial board also benefited from the support of several universities and departments. Significant financial support was provided by the University of Aberdeen, Scotland, through the School of Divinity, History and Philosophy, the College of Arts and Social Sciences, and the

Principal's Interdisciplinary Fund to facilitate our inaugural board meeting at Aberdeen in 2008 and our fifth full meeting in 2014. The Department of History at the University of Wisconsin-Madison hosted the 2009 and 2012 editorial-board meetings; Nicole Hauge played a key role in arrangements for the visitors to Madison on both occasions. In addition, we benefited from the support of the university's Anonymous Fund and the office of the Dean of the College of Letters and Science. Our colleagues in the Department of History at Uppsala University in Sweden gave us the use of their facilities and meeting-space in the summer of 2010, providing an excellent and hospitable environment for our discussion. Many of the home institutions of the editorial board also contributed travel costs and meeting-space for the compilation of several volumes in this collection; some helped underwrite some translation costs as well.

Several other groups and institutions played an important role in the gestation of this series. The Kennan Institute of the Woodrow Wilson International Center Scholars, particularly Associate Director William Pomeranz, has actively supported the project since its outset. Grants to support our editorial meetings were provided by the British Academy, BASEES, and the Great Britain Sasakawa Foundation. The German Historical Institute in Moscow very kindly sponsored the translation into English of chapters written in German. The Study Group on the Russian Revolution served as an important venue for the development of many of the chapters, particularly from British and European contributors, that appear in these volumes. George Fowler and Vicki Polansky of Slavica Publishers have proven the ideal partners in this lengthy process, offering sage counsel, clear deadlines, exemplary patience, professionalism, and rigor, all of which have made the production process run with an enviable dispatch and smoothness.

Finally, the editorial board expresses its heartfelt thanks to more than 200 contributors, who offered their skills, effort, insight, and scholarship to *Russia's Great War and Revolution*. At the risk of tautology, it must be said that this series could not have come to fruition without them. Their efforts—and patience with an extended production schedule—allowed us to present our readers with strong evidence for the enduring importance and complexity of this eight-year span in the history of Central and Eastern Europe and Asia, the consequences of which continue to shape our world in ways that we are still witnessing.

Anthony Heywood
David MacLaren McDonald
John W. Steinberg
June 2014

Preface

This book is the second of a two-part collection of essays on the cultural history of Russia between 1914 and 1922, both of which form part of a larger series on Russian history during the Great War, Revolution, and Civil War.[1] The two books that comprise the culture "volume" of the series are intended to complement each other, and they are published separately only for reasons of space. The general aim of the umbrella project to which the culture volume belongs is to consider Russia's experience of war and revolution as a "continuum of crisis"—in Peter Holquist's apt phrase[2]—from the outbreak of conflict in 1914 to the formation of the Soviet Union in 1922. The merits of this approach are at least two-fold: it focuses attention on the history of Russia during the First World War—until recently a largely neglected area—and it connects that history to the early years of the Bolshevik regime, thereby transcending the often artificial partition of 1917 in the historiography of modern Russia. Contributors to this volume were therefore asked to address an aspect of Russian cultural history during the 1914–22 period. Some have taken a slightly broader perspective, and a few are focused predominantly on the years prior to 1917, but all of them advance our understanding of Russia's experience of the Great War, its relationship to the early Soviet period, and the complex memory of the "continuum of crisis."

Definitions of culture and cultural history are now so expansive and protean that the subject matter of these two books is potentially enormous. Emmet Kennedy has defined culture as "any symbolic representation of value, particularly of values that are perpetuated in time through the educational process (schools, churches, press, theater),"[3] and Peter Burke has described cultural history as "a concern with the symbolic and its interpretation."[4] These two statements highlight the difficulty of distinguishing too strictly between traditional understandings of culture as the arts and sciences, and more

---

[1] Details of the larger series, "Russia's Great War and Revolution," can be found at http://russiasgreatwar.org/index.php

[2] Peter Holquist, *Making War, Forging Revolution: Russia's Continuum of Crisis, 1914–1921* (Cambridge, MA: Harvard University Press, 2002).

[3] Emmet Kennedy, *A Cultural History of the French Revolution* (New Haven: Yale University Press, 1989), xxii.

[4] Peter Burke, *What is Cultural History?* (Cambridge: Polity Press, 2004), 3.

Russian Culture in War and Revolution, 1914–22, Book 2: Political Culture, Identities, Mentalities, and Memory. Murray Frame, Boris Kolonitskii, Steven G. Marks, and Melissa K. Stockdale, eds. Bloomington, IN: Slavica Publishers, 2014, xix–xxiii.

recent approaches that imply almost anything can have a "cultural history" (since all objects and behaviors may be read for their symbolic content). Accepting that cultural history has few, if any, boundaries—a liberating yet potentially bewildering condition—we have not aimed for encyclopaedic coverage of the subject, for inclusion of every conceivable topic. Instead, the contents of the two books reflect the work of scholars whose current or recent research falls broadly into the category of Russian cultural history during the late imperial and early Soviet periods. The result is a diverse and stimulating array of original essays on subjects that range from the experience of cultural institutions and the arts, to aspects of identity and memory in popular culture. Many of the topics have rarely, if ever, been explored for this period of Russian history.

Through their close focus on diverse aspects of cultural life in Russia, the essays collectively demonstrate that cultural responses to war and revolution were far from uniform, and they defy simple generalizations. Nevertheless four broad observations can be made. The first is that, despite the traumatic upheaval that Russia experienced between 1914 and 1922, cultural life appears to have persisted with undiminished energy, even accelerating in some spheres—witness, for instance, the exponential growth in native film production from 1914 to 1917, or the myriad proletarian culture projects launched during the Civil War. The reasons for this "cultural acceleration" were complex and varied: patriotic mobilization; commercial demand; the thirst to comprehend global conflict and domestic revolution; the impulse to escape from reality; and notably the political conviction that culture had agency, that it was a tool capable of reshaping society. These factors help to explain why cultural activity was barely disrupted, even when basic material resources were in desperately short supply.

Secondly, according to the findings of several contributors, popular culture manifested greater signs of Russian national integration during the First World War than hitherto assumed. It was not simply that patriotic sentiment prompted a ban on German films or fueled attacks on European clothing fashions, for example, important though such developments were, especially during the first year of the conflict. Rather, a much wider spectrum of the empire's population increasingly engaged with a national public culture—especially through newspaper war reportage and efforts of civil society to organize patriotic work—and this may reflect a level of national unity not ordinarily associated with the final few years of tsarism.

The third observation is that—perhaps inevitably—consideration of the 1914–22 period as an integrated continuum reveals as many continuities as it does discontinuities, with the consequence that 1917 appears less prominent as a turning point in Russian cultural history (at least within the confines of this discrete period). The vibrant cultural experimentation of the Civil War years—the subject of many studies—conveys an impression of rapid cultural transformation under the Bolsheviks. Yet when that story is considered in the context of the Great War, the sense of a sharp disjuncture in the cultural sphere is less obvious. To cite a few examples that are elaborated in the volume's chapters: the attitudes of state and intelligentsia towards culture remained fundamentally similar across the revolutionary divide; changes in sexual mores, often associated with the Revolution, were already underway before 1917; and the history of popular holidays and festivals indicates how traditional cultural forms persisted beneath the veneer of new ideological content. This serves as a reminder that whilst some aspects of a culture—signs, symbols, and names, for example—can be replaced quickly, others—like deep-seated assumptions, values, and conditioned behavior—evolve at a different pace from the welter of military and political events. In that sense, the rhythms of cultural history do not correspond neatly to the chronological parameters of this volume. This does not mean that culture was impervious to the pressures of war, revolution, and civil war—on the contrary, they left indelible imprints on Russian culture—but it suggests that cultural change was less rapid or all-encompassing than political, social, and economic transformations, and that it might be more apposite to think of the period as a transitional rather than a revolutionary one for culture.

Finally, the essays suggest that cultural life was not only tightly intertwined with its social and political contexts, but that the wider history of Russia's Great War and Revolution cannot be fully comprehended without due attention to culture in its broadest sense. Cultural activity was one of the central mechanisms for circulating information, promoting patriotism, exchanging views, attacking hierarchies, exploring alternatives, and escaping reality. Even after the fall of the autocracy, cultural activity was the principal way in which most ordinary people connected with public life: through reading, viewing, listening, and socializing in a variety of cultural settings. More broadly, popular culture—the values and attitudes of ordinary people—set limits to what was adapted, ignored, embraced, or resisted. It was for these reasons that the Bolsheviks, as much as their tsarist predecessors, placed great emphasis on the importance of cultural policy (the short-lived Provisional Government paid less attention to this matter).

The chapters are arranged into sections that reflect certain thematic synergies. They are bracketed by an introduction (in book 1) that discusses the broader context of cultural policy in late imperial and early Soviet Russia, and by two concluding essays (both in book 2) that draw together the volume's themes from both a Russian and a wider European historical perspective. Given the mercurial nature of culture and cultural history, there is an inevitable element of overlap between some topics and sections, and certain chapters could have appeared in different sections, but ultimately we think it is more helpful to have some subdivision of the chapters than to present them without any attempt at classification. A few topics that readers might expect to find under the heading of "culture" are treated elsewhere in the wider project on Russia's Great War and Revolution: the intelligentsia, for instance, is discussed as a social category in the Home Front volume, although many of its representatives certainly appear throughout this volume. Moreover, the emphasis in these two books is largely Russo-centric, providing a degree of focus for an otherwise diverse range of subjects. Other nationalities of the tsarist and early Soviet polities feature more prominently in other volumes of the project (albeit not necessarily from a cultural perspective).

ଔ ଵ

Unless otherwise noted, all dates before February 1918 are given in the Old Style (Julian) calendar, which was 13 days behind the New Style (Gregorian) calendar used in the West. The New Style calendar was adopted by the Russian government in February 1918. Russian names and terms have been transliterated according to the Library of Congress system (with exceptions for rulers' names and a few others that are widely known in their anglicized forms). Russian patronymics (full name or initial) have been included for individuals who are not well-known or readily identifiable (except where their patronymics are unknown). Places of publication of books cited in the footnotes have been included, except where unknown.

ଔ ଵ

We would like to express our gratitude to the many people who have helped make this volume possible: to the contributors, especially for their patience and professionalism; to the General Editors of the volume's umbrella project, Russia's Great War and Revolution 1914-22 (RGWR), Tony Heywood, David McDonald, and John Steinberg, for their unfailing support and encouragement; to the RGWR Editorial Board—too large to name individually—for all kinds of help and advice, but especially for their tremendous collegiality and friendship, both during and after the RGWR editorial conferences in Aberdeen (2008), Uppsala (2010), and Madison (2009 and 2012); to the translators of the chapters that were originally in Russian or French, Joan Bridgwood, Kirsty McCluskey, Diana Statham, Victoria Steinberg, Hannah Zinn, and Josephine Von Zitzewitz; to the generous sponsors of the translations, David Finkelstein and the School of Humanities, University of Dundee, Gerald Sonnenfeld and Clemson University, and David McDonald and the University of Wisconsin-Madison; to Véronique Wechtler for additional translation advice; to the anonymous volume reviewer for helpful suggestions; and to Vicki Polansky for being such an exemplary editor.

One of the greatest pleasures in preparing this volume was the opportunity to "workshop" the chapters at several events, where contributors discussed themes and shared ideas arising from their research. We were fortunate to be able to hold two volume-based conferences whilst work on the chapters progressed, the first at the European University at St. Petersburg in summer 2011, and the second at Clemson University in fall 2011, for which we would like to acknowledge the support of Tom Kuehn and Gerald Sonnenfeld at Clemson University, and David McDonald. We would also like to thank Joye and Hubert Shuler and Louise and John Allen of Charleston, South Carolina, for their unforgettable hospitality. Volume-based panels were also held at the ICCEES World Congress, Stockholm (2010) and the ASEEES annual convention, Boston (2013). We thank all the contributors to—and organizers of—these events for helping to enhance the volume in such an amicable and stimulating manner.

Murray Frame
Boris Kolonitskii
Steven G. Marks
Melissa K. Stockdale
December 2013

Political Culture

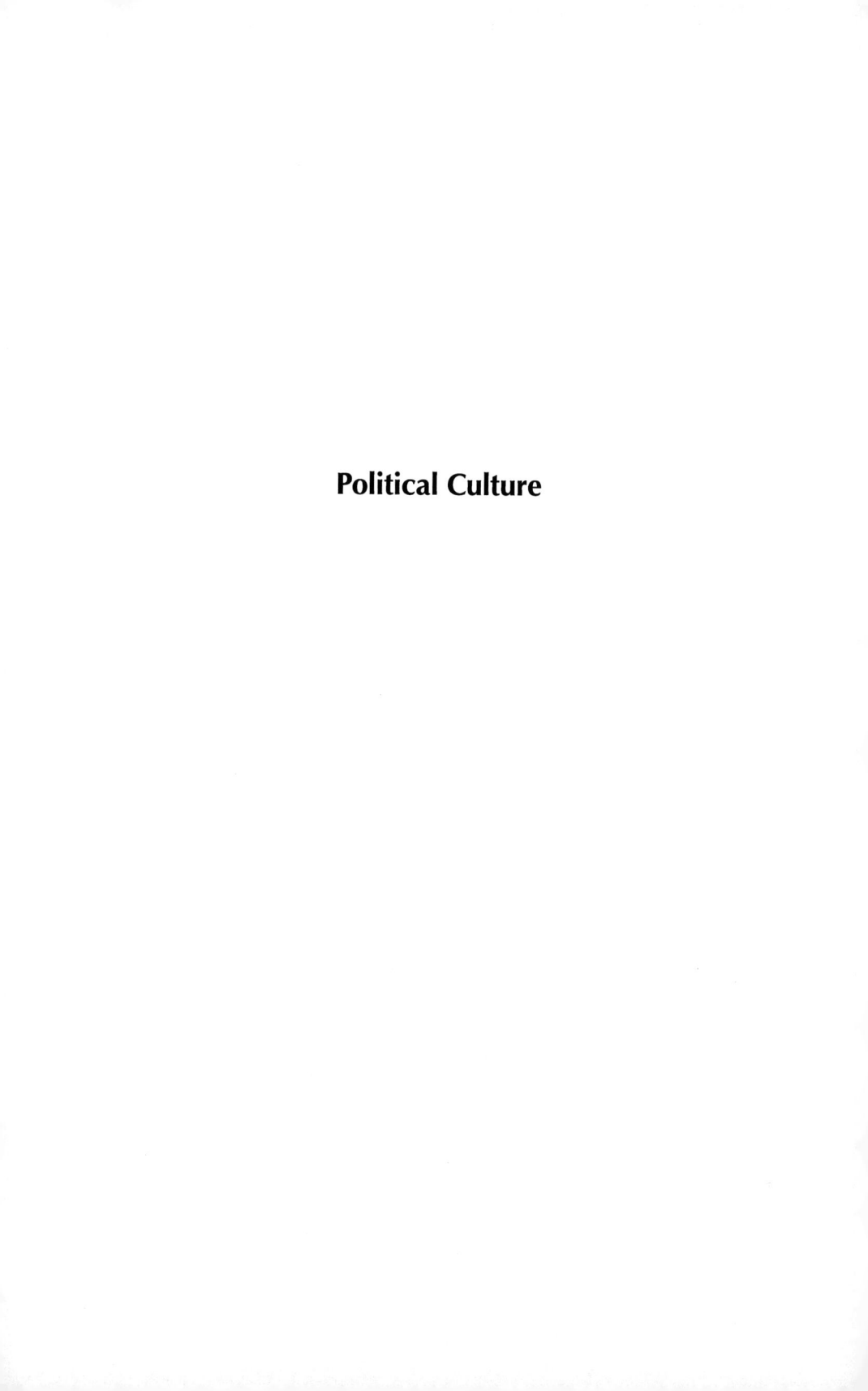

Mobilizing the Nation: Patriotic Culture in Russia's Great War and Revolution, 1914–20

Melissa K. Stockdale

When Russians learned they were at war with Germany, an enormous surge of patriotism swept the country. Massive strikes gripping the capital had already quietly ended. On 20 July on Palace Square, where some 200,000 citizens of every class and occupation had gathered in hopes of seeing the tsar, the huge crowd dropped spontaneously to its knees and began singing the national anthem when he appeared on a balcony before them.[1] (See fig. 1 in the gallery of illustrations following page 178.) In Moscow, 20,000 people gathered on Red Square before the statue of the heroes Minin and Pozharskii to hold a patriotic demonstration; similar demonstrations occurred in cities great and small across the empire.[2] And on 26 July 1914, at the historic one-day session of the legislature, deputy after deputy—representing Russia's national minorities and major political parties—rose to declare loyalty, unity, and willingness to sacrifice for Russia. Representatives of Latvians and Estonians, Poles and Lithuanians, characterized their constituents as "ardent patriots of Russia." Pavel Miliukov, leader of the largest opposition party in the Duma, declared his party's suspension of parliamentary struggle for the duration: "We are united in this struggle; we set no conditions and demand nothing...."[3]

These patriotic manifestations of national unity impressed contemporaries deeply; in Russia, as elsewhere, a "sacred union" (*sviashchennoe edinenie*) was proclaimed at the start of the Great War.[4] As one paper enthused, "Here is that psychological moment which defines historic events, the fate of peoples and

---

[1] There are many contemporary descriptions; a secondary account is W. Bruce Lincoln, *Passage through Armageddon: The Russians in War and Revolution, 1914–1918* (New York: Simon and Schuster, 1986), 41–43.

[2] *Letopis' voiny*, no. 2 (30 August 1914): 30; *Rech'*, 23 July 1914, 4; and *Kievlianin*, 24 July 1914, 4.

[3] *Gosudarstvennaia Duma. Stenograficheskii otchet* (hereafter *GDSO*) IV, 2, special session (26 July 1914), cols. 22–28.

[4] On "l'union sacrée" in France, see Leonard V. Smith, Stéphane Audoin-Rouzeau, and Annette Becker, *France and the Great War, 1914–1918* (Cambridge: Cambridge

Russian Culture in War and Revolution, 1914–22, Book 2: Political Culture, Identities, Mentalities, and Memory. Murray Frame, Boris Kolonitskii, Steven G. Marks, and Melissa K. Stockdale, eds. Bloomington, IN: Slavica Publishers, 2014, 3–26.

of states... A sacred flame has been kindled, towards which every Russian will strive—without distinction of tribe, faith, or condition—and gather in a united, mighty, and boundless force."[5] People expressed the same sentiments in letters, diaries, and other writings not tailored for publication: "The mood in Moscow is amazing! And I repeat—woe to the Germans, the outburst is colossal, a unity such as history will remember." "The unity and fervor of Russian society so gladdens me... Say what you like, though Russia might be wretched ... still there is no Russian soul who would not stand up for the fatherland."[6]

Yet three and a half years later, Russia's war had ended disastrously. Trying to make sense of humiliating defeat, many Russians concluded that the patriotic outburst of the early war had been deceptive, that in fact the population did not love their country enough to sustain the fight to the end. Often, this deficiency was represented as a consequence of the common people's inability to think of themselves as a nation. Such were the views of a number of prominent and oft-cited generals. In the 1920s General Anton Denikin claimed that the illiterate masses went to war without a perception of the "necessity to sacrifice": they did not understand "abstract national principles."[7] General Aleksei Brusilov blamed this state of affairs directly on an inept imperial government which had failed to teach the people to know their own country: "How could they acquire that patriotism which would inspire them with love for their great Russia?"[8]

Scholars, too, have contended that the mass of the population did not think of itself as a nation. The government is said to have conceived of Russia in traditional, imperial terms, while the common people's imagined community,

---

University Press, 2003), 27–29. The phrase "United Russia" was also used; see A. Peshekhonov, "Edinaia Rossiia," *Russkoe bogatstvo* (September 1914), esp. 297–300.

[5] Litovchenko, "Sobiraites', russkie liudi—v edinenii sila," *Kievlianin*, 22 July 1914, 1.

[6] Gosudarstvennyi arkhiv Rossiiskoi Federatsii (GARF) f. 102, op. 265, d. 990 (Department of Police; perlustrated letters, 1914), l. 974, letter from "Kolia," Moscow, 21 July, and d. 992, l. 1104, letter from "Tvoia Katia," Nizh. Rybinsk, 30 July.

[7] Anton Denikin, *The Russian Turmoil: Memoirs Military, Political, and Political* (London: Hutchinson and Co., n.d.), 21–22. A rare example pre-dating Russia's defeat is General N. N. Ianushkevich's assertion that the masses failed to grasp the idea of defending the nation: a person from Tambov "is ready to stand to the death for Tambov province, but the war in Poland seems strange and unnecessary to him." Quoted in Michael Cherniavsky, ed., *Prologue to Revolution: Notes of A. N. Iakhontov on the Secret Meetings of the Council of Ministers, 1915* (Englewood Cliffs, NJ: Prentice-Hall, 1967), 22–23 "The Meeting of 24 July 1915."

[8] A. A. Brusilov, *A Soldier's Notebook, 1914–1918* (London: Macmillan and Co., 1930), 38–40. See also Nicholas N. Golovine, *The Russian Army in the World War* (New Haven: Yale University Press, 1931), 244–45; and Iu. N. Danilov, *Rossiia v mirovoi voine: 1914–1915 gg.* (Berlin: Slovo, 1924), 112, 115–16.

to use Benedict Anderson's phrase, was decidedly local. A number of scholars contend that prior to the Bolshevik revolution, "a critical mass consciousness based on nation or nationality did not develop in Russia."[9] Noting the importance of heroic narratives of the past for consolidating modern national communities, some argue that prior to the 1930s Russians lacked "a sense of a common heritage and an awareness of a glorious history." Speaking directly of the war, some believe that because print media were still mainly urban prior to the war, patriotic culture did not extend to the peasantry; others see this wartime patriotic culture as largely negative: Russians knew what they were fighting *against*, "but not for whom and for what."[10] In contrast, historians who suggest that by 1917 the masses of the population did conceive of themselves as members of a nation—thanks in part to the experience of the war—remain a minority.[11]

There were, admittedly, problems in promoting patriotism and national cohesion in Russia's Great War. For many citizens, uniting in support of the war effort was complicated by distrust of a repressive government, ideological divisions, deeply-felt class antagonisms, or ethnic tensions and prejudices. The transitional nature of the period following the 1905 revolution was another complication: while Russia had ceased to be an absolutist regime, one in which the person of the tsar embodied the nation, it had not yet worked out its new basis of "nationhood." And, since more than half the empire's population was not ethnically Great Russian, articulating a shared "Russian" national identity could be highly problematic. Nonetheless, it is possible to document

---

[9] Astrid S. Tuminez, *Russian Nationalism since 1856: Ideology and the Making of Foreign Policy* (Lanham, MD: Rowman and Littlefield, 2000), 38–39. See also Richard Pipes, *The Russian Revolution* (New York: Knopf, 1990), 109–11, 203–04, who writes that the Russian soldier was "a virtual stranger to the sentiment of patriotism"; and Vera Tolz, *Russia* (New York: Oxford University Press, 2001), 6–7, 180–81.

[10] David Brandenberger, *National Bolshevism: Stalinist Mass Culture and the Formation of Modern Russian National Identity, 1931–1956* (Cambridge, MA: Harvard University Press, 2002), 10–16. Scholars who see patriotic culture as an urban phenomenon include Hubertus F. Jahn, *Patriotic Culture in Russia during World War I* (Ithaca, NY: Cornell University Press, 1995), 109, 172–74; O. S. Porshneva, *Krest′iane, rabochie i soldaty Rossii nakanune i v gody Pervoi mirovoi voiny* (Moscow: ROSSPEN, 2004), 86–91, 260–62; and Leonid Heretz, *Russia on the Eve of Modernity: Popular Religion and Traditional Culture under the Last Tsars* (Cambridge: Cambridge University Press, 2008).

[11] Aaron B. Retish, *Russia's Peasants in Revolution and Civil War: Citizenship, Identity, and the Creation of the Soviet State, 1914–1922* (Cambridge: Cambridge University Press, 2008), especially 4–7, 22–63, argues that the war pushed peasants to "embrace the national polity." See also Joshua A. Sanborn, *Drafting the Russian Nation: Military Conscription, Total War, and Mass Politics, 1905–1925* (DeKalb: Northern Illinois University Press, 2003), 18–19; and Melissa K. Stockdale, "United in Gratitude: Honoring Soldiers and Defining the Nation in World War I Russia," *Kritika: Explorations in Russian and Eurasian History* 7, 3 (Summer 2006): 459–85.

vigorous mass campaigns during the war to promote and mobilize patriotism and a positive sense of national community.

In Russia as in all the belligerent states, no entity had a monopoly on patriotic discourse. Governmental, civic, and private organizations engaged in efforts to define and appeal to the patriotic national community, as did individual citizens. The diversity of voices and values precluded the possibility of a single master narrative. Alongside love of and loyalty to one's country—that is, traditional, state-based patriotism—there could be patriotism that was local, chauvinistic, pacifistic, or social.[12] A strong current of aspirational patriotism emphasized fighting for a fairer, more democratic future, rather than in defense of putative "age-old traditions."[13] But contestations over the meaning and content of patriotism, and efforts to rethink who was included in the national community, should not be mistaken for the absence of certain powerful shared themes and myths. Also important for understanding patriotic culture is the way various sectors of the population expected to advance their interests through shaping and buying into the narrative of "sacred union."[14]

One short chapter cannot explore every manifestation of patriotic culture, or every debate about the national community across war, revolution, and civil war. Here, I will confine my discussion largely to the Great War itself, with particular interest in the creation and mass diffusion of positive images and narratives depicting a far-flung, inclusive, and united Russian (*rossiiskii*) community worthy of citizens' love and sacrifice. I will then consider counter-narratives identifying people deemed disloyal or otherwise unworthy of membership in the nation, ending with a brief discussion of the shifting and contested patriotic landscape after October 1917.

---

[12] Helpful discussions of patriotism include Rogers Brubaker, "In the Name of the Nation: Reflections on Nationalism and Patriotism," in *The Many Faces of Patriotism*, ed. Philip Abbott (Lanham, MD: Rowman & Littlefield, 2007), 37–51; E. J. Hobsbawm, *Nations and Nationalism since 1870: Programme, Myth, Reality* (Cambridge: Cambridge University Press, 1990), 86–93; Eugene Weber, *Peasants into Frenchmen: The Modernization of Rural France, 1870–1914* (Stanford, CA: Stanford University Press, 1976), 95–114; and Hugh Cunningham, "The Language of Patriotism, 1750–1914," *History Workshop Journal*, no. 12 (1981): 8–33.

[13] Marxist Georgii Plekhanov, for example, argued that German victory would strengthen the old order, while Russian victory would aid the "liberation movement." G. V. Plekhanov, *O voine*, 2nd ed. (Petrograd, [1915]), esp. 25–32. On "aspirational patriotism," see David Monger, *Patriotism and Propaganda in First World War Britain: The National War Aims Committee and Civilian Morale* (Liverpool: Liverpool University Press, 2012), 95.

[14] Linda Colley, *Britons: The Forging of the Nation, 1707–1837* (New Haven: Yale University Press, 1992), 54–56, 93–94, argues that different classes and interest groups came to see the new "British" nation as "a usable resource, as a focus of loyalty which would also cater to their own needs and ambitions."

A United and Giving People

In the first months of war, Russians displayed a voracious appetite for patriotic images and stories. Publishers, filmmakers, and other entrepreneurs rushed to supply this profitable demand, as Hubertus Jahn shows in his pioneering study of early wartime culture. *Lubki*—popular broadsides—enticed both rural and urban buyers. Ranging in style from crude cartoons to full-color artistic renderings, they typically depicted exciting battles, barbaric or ridiculous enemies, or popular heroes like Cossack Koz'ma Kriuchkov, who single-handedly killed 11 Germans with his lance. (See fig. 2.) Citizens purchased hundreds of thousands of war-themed pamphlets and maps of the various fronts, and sent millions of patriotic postcards. Enthusiastic crowds turned out for circus pantomimes featuring fantastically staged air and land battles, clowns mocking the enemy, and grand patriotic finales with flags and the symbolic figures of Russia and her allies. However, Jahn suggests that by the end of the first year of war, interest in caricatures of the Kaiser and flag-waving entertainment had waned: war-weary audiences came to prefer escapist fare.[15]

A more durable and participatory component of patriotic culture was giving money, goods, or labor to the war effort. A number of institutions already existed, such as the Society for Aid to Soldiers and their Families, with over 800 local chapters on the eve of the war.[16] Hundreds of new organizations sprang into being, the largest and most famous of which were the so-called "public organizations," the Union of Zemstvos and Union of Cities. The latter had 630 member towns by September 1917, and over 54,000 full-time employees—22,000 of them women—as well as legions of volunteers.[17] Initially established to help the Red Cross deal with sick and wounded soldiers, their mandate soon extended to helping supply the army with foodstuffs and boots, fighting the spread of epidemics on the home front, and even sponsoring lectures on "War and Culture." With their unprecedented size and scope, and reputed energy and competence, the Union of Zemstvos and Union of Cities deeply impressed Russia's citizens. While the myth of their success may have exceeded the reality—of which ultra-conservatives were bitterly certain—the perceived accomplishments of the progressive public organizations became an important strand of the patriotic narrative.[18]

---

[15] Jahn, *Patriotic Culture*, 39, 86–90, 100–02, 158.

[16] An overview of the main entities for aiding soldiers is N. Beliavskii, "Pomoshch' soldatam i ikh sem'iam," *Russkii invalid*, 30 September 1914, 3; and 1 October 1914, 3–4.

[17] Paul P. Gronsky and Nicholas J. Astrov, *The War and the Russian Government* (New Haven: Yale University Press, 1929), 186–87, 193–96.

[18] Historians, too, have some doubts about the public organizations, though a full-scale history remains to be written; see William E. Gleason, "The All-Russian Union of Towns and the Politics of Urban Reform in Tsarist Russia," *Russian Review* 35, 3 (1976): 290–302.

Another new organization, the semi-official Tat'iana Committee, exemplifies the "we are one family" dimension of the sacred union. Named in honor of its patron, the emperor's second daughter, the focus of the Tat'iana Committee was assisting Russia's millions of refugees. Since many refugees came from the borderlands and were not ethnically Great Russian, the committee's local chapters often included representatives of national minority organizations, making it diverse in membership as well as clientele.[19] A good illustration of its familial rhetoric comes from the appeal for its nation-wide charitable collection in May 1915. The text speaks movingly of the enemy's devastation of Russia's borderlands, but begins with a proud assertion of multiethnic solidarity:

> the spirit of the Russian land is not weakening, its unity grows stronger, consciousness grows that all the peoples populating Russia are brothers in spirit, in culture, in love for the great Russia that unites us…. Russians, Poles, Latvians, Lithuanians, Jews, Armenians, Tatars stand staunchly, a bulwark of the strength and greatness of Russia in the struggle for right and justice.[20]

Thanks to the vigorous publicity for the Tat'iana Committee's collection, these inclusive words were "repeated a million times throughout the country," a columnist for *Gazeta-kopeika* approvingly noted, and "are meeting a fervent response." Donations to this collection alone exceeded three million rubles.[21]

War relief involved large and diverse sectors of the population in the roles of organizers, makers, or givers. In any given city, hundreds or even thousands of volunteers took collection boxes around streets, railway stations, and amusement spots. Every donor was given a small pin or souvenir, enabling them to display their patriotism. Tiny national flags of Russia and its allies were particularly popular, and many locales held a "National Flags Day."[22] Another fundraising technique that promoted national consciousness was war-related exhibits of art or artifacts. In July 1916, the Committee on St. George Cavaliers launched a traveling exhibit of trophies of the war, in part to raise awareness of "the importance of concern for the Fatherland's most glorious defenders." The exhibit stopped at 44 towns along the Volga, also featuring popular lectures on the feats of heroes and the screening of films

---

[19] Peter Gatrell, *A Whole Empire Walking: Refugees in Russia during World War I* (Bloomington: Indiana University Press, 1999), 40–42, 60–61, 67, 77, 118.

[20] "Rossiia—razorennym okrainam," *Kievlianin*, 23 May 1915.

[21] *Gazeta-kopeika*, 23 May 1915, 1; the figure comes from I. I. Tolstoi, *Dnevnik v dvukh tomakh* (St. Petersburg: "Liki Rossii," 2010), 2: 763 (diary entry of 11 June 1915).

[22] *Gazeta-kopeika*, 21 August 1914, 3; *Kievlianin*, 5, 6, and 13 September 1914, 2, 4, and 3, respectively, and "Kak otozvalis' krest'iane na voinu," *Derevenskaia gazeta*, 21 October 1914, 11–12.

about the war. The exhibit drew enormous crowds, raising 200,000 rubles through collections and modest entry fees, and stimulating local organization of public prayer services, parades, and patriotic rallies.[23]

Over the course of the conflict, virtually every national minority group organized war relief or services, undertakings that also helped demonstrate their membership in the Russian patriotic community. Readers of various periodicals thus learned about generous Mennonite donations to the Red Cross, gifts from the *inorodtsy* of Akmolinskaia oblast' to the Union of Cities, and fundraising for soldiers and refugees by Siberian Poles.[24] Jewish Committees in Riga, Kiev, and elsewhere raised large sums to outfit clinics, purchase gifts for frontline troops, and in other ways show their commitment to the national cause.[25] Many contemporaries were sure that by proving their loyalty, civic maturity, and willingness to sacrifice, Russia's national minorities—as well as other groups enjoying only "second-, third-, or even fourth-class" rights—would win at war's end the full citizenship they deserved.[26]

No comprehensive figures exist for wartime giving, but considerable anecdotal evidence documents a national outpouring of aid. For example, newspaper editorial offices often acted as collection points for war causes; since many papers published accounts of donations received, we can glean from them some sense of the nature of giving. In March 1915, for instance, the nationalist organ *Kievlianin* published a list of 14,973 rubles in donations sent to its offices for 15 wartime causes over a seven-month period. The givers appear fairly diverse in occupation; donations made by individuals were mostly in the range of 1 to 5 rubles. Many contributions were made collectively, such as those by the employees of a business, or a group of brick makers. Much the same picture comes from the mass circulation daily *Russkoe slovo* and the penny press, though donations to the latter were often measured in kopecks rather than rubles.[27]

Whatever the sums or labor donated, wartime giving and the publicity it received made three significant contributions to patriotic culture. The mas-

---

[23] Rossiiskii gosudarstvennyi istoricheskii arkhiv (RGIA) f. 29 (Chancellery of the War Ministry), op. 3, d. 2549, ll. 8--9, 77; on the exhibit, see *Sel'skii vestnik*, 16 April 1916, 3.

[24] *Russkie vedomosti*, 10 January 1915, 6, and 15 May 1915, 4; *Kievlianin*, 26 July 1914, 3; "Irkutskii pol'skii komitet," *Voina*, no. 3 (1914): 77–78.

[25] "Dlia armii," *Voina i evrei*, no. 1 (1915): 16; and "Rizhskaia evreiskaia obshchina," *Voina i evrei*, no. 2 (1915): 14.

[26] For example, M. Slavinskii, "Voina i natsional'nyi vopros," *Chego zhdet Rossiia ot voiny: Sbornik statei* (Petrograd: Kn-vo "Prometei," 1915), especially 103–08, 116–20, and speech by Duma deputy A. I. Chkhenkeli, *GDSO*, IV, 4, session 53 (9 June 1916), cols. 5054-55.

[27] *Kievlianin*, 5 March 1915, 4; *Russkoe slovo*, 26 November 1915, 6. *Gazeta-kopeika* sometimes published the notes accompanying donations: *Gazeta-kopeika*, "Podarok voinam ot chitatelei 'Gazety-Kopeiki,'" 22 December 1914, 2.

sive reporting on war relief in the periodical press helped tie the national community together spatially, providing a positive image of generosity and service occurring everywhere in Russia. Besides its encompassing geographic dimension, this compassionate generosity was shown to be organized from below as well as from above, and to come from different classes and national groups.[28] It therefore contributed powerfully to the narrative of a patriotic citizenry that was not only united but conscious and competent. (See fig. 3.) The portrayal of unstinting generosity also presented a positive national image that had deep cultural roots. As Adele Lindenmeyr notes in her study of charity in Imperial Russia, the Russian Orthodox Church fostered "a self-conscious ideology of Russians' exceptional benevolence, which it linked to a vision of national identity." Russians practiced true compassion for the unfortunate; theirs was a culture of giving.[29] During the Great War, that benevolence was shown as characteristic of all patriotic Russians, in the broad (*rossiiskii*) rather than ethnic (*russkii*) sense of the word.

Communicating with the People: Publicizing Patriotism

From the very outset of war, writers, philosophers, and educators hastened to explain to the public its causes, the consequences of victory or defeat, and how patriotic citizens could help in this struggle. And the generals' postwar complaints notwithstanding, the imperial authorities also expended much time and money in trying to shape popular opinion, particularly that of the peasantry. In July 1914, the Chief Administration for Press Affairs, under the Ministry of Internal Affairs, created a Committee for Popular Publications. It quickly made its top priority communicating with rural people about the war and its significance for Russia. In August the Committee requested 150,000 rubles to improve the government-subsidized rural newspaper *Sel'skii vestnik*, publish a series of pamphlets on the war, and create small libraries of suitable readings for wounded soldiers at hospitals and clinics. Ministers promptly funded this proposal, noting that "printing matters are in the highest degree useful and important."[30]

The Committee for Popular Publications tackled its mission energetically. Within its first 18 months of existence it published 14 pamphlets in editions of one to two million each, distributing them free of charge to soldiers, field hospitals, zemstvos, and some 22,000 primary schools. (Committee members

---

[28] Contemporaries were especially struck by the generosity of the peasantry, which could be interpreted as proof that they cared about state interests. A. Borisov, "Vnutrennie dela i voprosy," *Russkie zapiski*, no. 2 (December 1914): 336–75.

[29] Adele Lindenmeyr, *Poverty Is Not a Vice: Charity, Society, and the State in Imperial Russia* (Princeton, NJ: Princeton University Press, 1996), 7–8.

[30] RGIA f. 1276 (Council of Ministers), op. 10, d. 1090 (Committee for Popular Publications, 1914), l. 1. The Committee received another 400,000 rubles in 1915.

noted that demand for the pamphlets exceeded supply.) Maps and other graphic images were also popular. A map of Europe showing the various military theaters—including Russia's—was distributed free of charge to subscribers of *Sel'skii vestnik*. Some 178 zemstvos also requested copies, inspiring a second printing priced for sale at a modest 5 kopecks each; in all, 130,000 copies of the European map were published, soon followed by others.[31]

The first pamphlet produced by the Committee for Popular Publications, "The Great War" (August 1914), managed to instruct, vilify, and inspire in just four pages. Clearly written in easy-to-read language, it explained that the war was entirely the fault of the arrogant and perfidious Germans, who had long desired Russia's land for themselves. But the Germans were sadly mistaken in imagining they would easily beat their intended victim: Russia was strong and had strong allies, her tsar was resolute, and her people united. Above all, God was on Russia's side.[32] Another pamphlet—embellished with gruesome photos—chronicles German atrocities. "War with Turkey" describes an enemy that is contemptible and beatable, historically humbled by Russia in every conflict. "Our Glory" celebrates the sturdy heroism of the soldier, the son of the common people, from the days of Suvorov's 18th-century triumphs over the Germans to the 1812 Fatherland War to the present. But in insisting, too, on the heroism of the noble officers, this pamphlet reminds readers that *all* social estates in Russia love their country and willingly sacrifice for her.[33]

The success of the government-subsidized paper *Sel'skii vestnik* illustrates both the importance attached to reaching rural dwellers and peasant appetite for news about the war.[34] The Committee for Popular Publications invested great effort in improving this daily newspaper, since it considered it "the most important and reliable instrument for influencing the rural reader." It expanded its reporting on the war; provided all sorts of free supplements to subscribers, such as war-related maps and posters (fig. 4); and attentively covered the situation of rural soldiers' families. These changes brought in a slew of new subscribers. In summer 1914, *Sel'skii vestnik*'s circulation stood at 34,053; by May 1915 it had grown to 86,731 paid subscriptions, and by early

---

[31] RGIA f. 1276, op. 11, d. 1418 (1915), ll. 1–4, 74. The figure on state schools comes from Jeffrey Brooks, *When Russia Learned to Read: Literacy and Popular Literature, 1861–1917* (Princeton, NJ: Princeton University Press, 1985), 41.

[32] "Velikaia voina," in RGIA f. 1276, op. 11, d. 1418, ll. 10–12.

[33] "Nasha slava," l. 21, "Voina s Turtsiei," l. 34, and "V plenu u nemtsev," l. 74, all in RGIA f. 1276, op. 11, d. 1418.

[34] On the war's stimulation of peasant interest in the wider world, see Corinne Gaudin's chapter in this book, 55–71; and Scott J. Seregny, "Zemstvos, Peasants, and Citizenship: The Russian Adult Education Movement and World War I," *Slavic Review* 59, 2 (Summer 2000): 290–315.

1916 circulation was expected to exceed 150,000 (including free subscriptions delivered to the army and hospitals).[35]

Sel'skii vestnik was in many respects quite traditional in its representation of Russian patriotism. Articles from the initial weeks of war spoke of devotion to Faith, Tsar, and Fatherland. A slight variant to this theme stated that "We are defending the Motherland, the Tsar, our wives and daughters, we are defending our entire existence."[36] Sel'skii vestnik also emphasized the widespread support for the war, thanks to the justness of the cause. The patriotic demonstrations that occurred in numerous cities and the success of the general mobilization were offered as further proof of popular support.[37] And almost every article reminded readers that Germany had attacked Russia, that Russia's war was a defensive one.[38]

The most important theme in Sel'skii vestnik during the first year of the war, as with most periodicals in the empire, concerned the sacred union: a united resolve to defend the country that transcended class, faith, nationality, and party. Drawing the parallel so often noted between the 1812 "Fatherland War" and the current conflict, the paper editorialized that "Entering into the second Fatherland War, Russia meets it as she did the first. All classes of Russian society, the entire Russian people, have merged into a single spirit."[39] Articles about the historic session of the legislature on 26 July celebrated the end of divisions by party: "All have become fiery sons of our common, great Motherland." The paper also stressed the national minorities' display of unity in the Duma: representatives of Baltic Germans, Poles, Muslims, and Jews made speeches declaring themselves "profoundly loyal to the Motherland, prepared for any sacrifice for her."[40]

---

[35] RGIA f. 1276, op. 11, d. 1418 (1915), ll. 4–5. The most popular daily at this time, *Russkoe slovo*, saw its circulation climb to 750,000, but no other publication approached these figures. On the popular press, see Louise McReynolds, *The News Under Russia's Old Regime: The Development of a Mass Circulation Press* (Princeton, NJ: Princeton University Press, 1991), 228–44.

[36] *Sel'skii vestnik*, 22 July 1914, 4; 17 July 1914, 1; 23 July 1914, 1 ("we stand strongly, all as one, for Faith, Tsar, and Fatherland"); and 13 August 1914, 3.

[37] *Sel'skii vestnik*, 15 July 1914, 1; and 17 July 1914, 1. See also 18 July 1914, 2; and 19 July 1914, 3.

[38] *Sel'skii vestnik*, 22 July 1914, 4; see also 24 July 1914, 3, where Duma Deputy N. L'vov of Saratov remarks that "in general, war with the Germans is extraordinarily popular."

[39] *Sel'skii vestnik*, 23 July 1914, 1; the parallels with the Napoleonic War of 1812, when "every social estate responded with high patriotic feeling and gave their all for defense of the Motherland," were noted again on 30 May 1915, 1.

[40] *Sel'skii vestnik*, 29 July 1914, 2 and 3–4.

The picture of patriots and patriotism presented in *Sel'skii vestnik* was a remarkably durable one.[41] Patriots were full of love for Faith, Tsar, and Fatherland and for their families and land: that which was familiar, dear, handed down from old times. Patriots' loyalties were thus founded on the past and present, rather than on hopes for a better future (in contrast to the aspirational trope stressed by progressive society and national minorities). Patriots were of course strong and brave, and gave unstintingly of their labor, goods, and even their lives. Thus, steadfast service and generous sacrifice were patriots' defining features. Equally important, patriots were to be found among all classes and every national group in Russia—all were, at least potentially, true "children" of the motherland. This theme of unity of the peoples of Russia (fig. 5), which was by its nature an inclusive construction of the patriotic national community, one depending on loyalty to a common geographic territory and ruler rather than on race, social estate, or religion, persevered despite the obvious fracturing of national unity from summer 1915 onwards.[42]

The Orthodox Church and the Language of Sacrifice

On 20 July 1914 the Holy Synod of the Russian Orthodox Church issued a proclamation calling on the faithful to unite in a national effort to defend "Faith, Tsar, and Fatherland" from German aggression. It exhorted all Orthodox people to put aside their differences, unite around the throne, and "go willingly and robustly to the defense of the Fatherland ... remembering that shame and death will fall on the head of the lazy, self-seeking, and traitors, while eternal glory is in store for those who put their property and their life on the altar of the Fatherland."[43] This proclamation, legitimizing the war as a righteous cause enjoying God's favor, was to be read aloud by every priest in every parish at Sunday services, thus speedily reaching tens of millions of Orthodox churchgoers.

The Russian Orthodox Church had always supported the modern state's military ventures, and the Great War was no exception. The particular ardor with which the church embraced this war effort, however, was striking, as were the multiple ways in which the church sanctified the national cause. We know how significant this legitimizing function of the Orthodox Church was for Soviet authorities in the Second World War, when the church declared

---

[41] These themes are presented, for example, in issues of 21 July 1915, 2; 24 July 1915, 1; and 16 January 1916, 4.

[42] The striking exception to this harmonious picture is the paper's treatment, from summer 1915 onwards, of Russian Germans, especially the German colonists, who did not "consider themselves Russian" and had proved to be traitors. See, for example, *Sel'skii vestnik*, 4 September 1916, 3.

[43] The text is reproduced in S. G. Runkevich, *Velikaia otechestvennaia voina i tserkovnaia zhizn': Istoricheskie ocherki* (Petrograd, 1916), 19.

the fight against the German invaders a "Holy War."[44] But there has been little exploration of the church's patriotic activities in the First World War, important though these were.

The Holy Synod marshaled the church's vast resources to help the Red Cross, funded a large military hospital, and instituted a regular collection for soldiers after every divine service. With the goal of helping the families of mobilized soldiers, the church greatly expanded its network of parish guardianship councils; within a year 36,118 out of Russia's 40,590 parishes had these bodies. Composed of elected members of the laity, the councils distributed aid to needy soldiers' families and assisted them with the harvest. They also took a lead role in organizing donations for the army.[45] This mobilization of rural charitable impulses was a tangible way of involving thousands of small, scattered communities in the collective national war effort.

The Orthodox Church also developed war-related prayers and rituals. Besides daily prayers for the health of the emperor, tsarevich, and supreme commander, and prayers for victory, there were added more novel supplications for wounded soldiers and POWs. From 2 September 1914, the synod decreed that a requiem (*panikhid*) was to be held every Saturday in church for the fallen. The church became involved in the memorialization of fallen soldiers in other ways as well, through construction of monuments and special fraternal cemeteries. It directed every parish school to erect a tablet inscribed with the names of its former teachers or pupils who had died serving their country in the war; women's patriotic sacrifice was not overlooked, since guidelines stipulated that Sisters of Mercy be listed as well as soldiers.[46]

Special national observances could unite all the faithful in thanksgiving, entreaty, or acts of sacrifice. From October 1914, major victories were celebrated with all-Russian services of thanksgiving and the daylong ringing of church bells.[47] A different kind of national observance was on 8 July 1915, the day celebrating the Kazan' Icon of the Mother of God, which the Orthodox Church designated as an All-Russian day of prayer for the troops. A description of one local observation of this national day of prayer depicted a cathedral illuminated by hundreds of candles and overflowing with worshipers. The prayers were repeated four times, since this parish had sent four rounds of men to the army; with each cycle of prayers the troops of each separate call-up were individually named. The priest evoked a cathartic torrent of sobbing

---

[44] See Steven Merritt Miner, *Stalin's Holy War: Religion, Nationalism, and Alliance Politics, 1941–1945* (Chapel Hill: University of North Carolina Press, 2003), 69, 76–83, 93–114.

[45] From 1915, parish guardianship councils were required to report on their war work monthly; they apparently remained active into 1917: RGIA f. 796 (Chancellery of the Holy Synod), op. 198, d. 329, otd. 1, st. 5 (1917), "Ob okazanii pomoshchi na voennye nuzhdy (o popechitel'nykh sovetakh)," ll. 5–6, 10.

[46] Runkevich, *Velikaia otechestvennaia voina*, 82–83, 124–25.

[47] Opredelenie No. 8480, reported in *Prikhodskii listok*, 15 October 1914, 2.

with his heartfelt, impromptu sermon: "Brothers and Sisters! Today we are carrying out the national day of prayer for our dear troops. All Russia is praying for them!... Remember your wounded brothers and refrain from evil. They're dying on the field of battle and we should not forget this. We must help the sick, widows, and orphans.... Let us do everything like sincere Christians, loving each other."[48]

Church authorities, like the secular ones, appreciated the power of the printed word during the war. Besides publishing war-related tracts and devotional literature for distribution to soldiers, the synod launched an ambitious national publication, its first-ever daily newspaper. Debuting in September 1914, *Prikhodskii listok* (Parish News) was cheaper and livelier than existing diocesan weeklies, and aimed at a much broader audience. Its goal, the editors explained, was to provide readers with accurate information and discussion about current events "on a church and state foundation."[49] The size of print runs was large, averaging 46,000 copies a day, enough to allow every parish in the country to receive at least one copy.[50]

The front page of each issue of *Prikhodskii listok* was devoted to news about the war. Other regular features included "The Clergy and the War," "The War and School," and "The War and the Parish." Here was the real heart of the paper: news from and about the wartime activities and needs of parishes all over the empire. Priests, teachers, and others were urged to send in accounts of events organized in their village, and peasants' responses to them.[51] In this way, *Prikhodskii listok* provided clergy with vignettes for sermons, information teachers and clerics could disseminate to pupils and congregants hungry for news, and models for charitable and patriotic undertakings. This publication also reinforced readers' sense of belonging to a far-flung national-religious, patriotic community. They could see that the problems they confronted were faced by others, or be reminded that the same prayer services for the troops that they took part in were simultaneously being enacted everywhere in Russia.

---

[48] G.P., "Kak narod molit'sia vo dni voiny," *Prikhodskii listok*, 22 July 1915, 3. At the local level, pilgrimages were organized to sacred places to pray for wounded soldiers and for victory. Good examples are a pilgrimage in Vladimir province with some 4,000 participants, and one in Petrograd with more than 20,000. Palomnik, "Narodnoe molenie," *Prikhodskii listok*, 7 July 1915, 3; and "Krestnyi khod," *Gazeta-kopeika*, 17 May 1915, 3. Benedict Anderson, *Imagined Communities: Reflections on the Origin and Spread of Nationalism*, rev. ed. (London: Verso, 1991), 54–56, notes the role of pilgrimage in creating communities, including secular-national ones.

[49] *Prikhodskii listok*, 1 September 1914, 2.

[50] RGIA f. 800, op. 1, d. 590, "O pechatanii "Prikhodskogo listka," l. 12, 20, 50, 113.

[51] "Ot redaktsii," *Prikhodskii listok*, 1 September 1915, 4; the editors reminded correspondents to provide the name of their village and of all people mentioned in their articles.

Besides offering collective rituals of support, the church more explicitly legitimized the conflict. One strand of its narrative was that God had sent it in punishment for sin; conversely, repentance and renewed faith could save the nation.[52] In January 1916, A. Volynets, a regular contributor to *Prikhodskii listok,* reminded readers that St. Serafim of Sarov had foretold both the war and Russia's eventual victory, one that ultimately depended not on force of arms but on spiritual purity. His message was reassuring: "The Lord will give Russia victory for its Orthodox faith."[53] The purely spiritual-moral message often merged with more secular, nationalist views that represented the conflict as a clash between the Teutonic and Slavic peoples and their respective civilizations. For example, in August 1914 Archimandrite Lavrentii explained, "Clearly, in this great struggle Divine Providence has allotted to our dear Motherland a high mission and purpose: to become the liberator of all Slavic tribes in general from centuries-old German oppression and violence. What a great and glorious cause is in store for Holy Rus' to accomplish in the world war that has begun!"[54]

Sacrifice was perhaps the central theme of Orthodox writing and preaching on the war. (See fig. 6.) The synod's July 1914 phrase about "bringing any sacrifice" reverberated widely, as in the 1916 secret circular of Tikhon, Archbishop of Kursk, instructing his clergy to tell their flocks that "in wartime, every citizen should be prepared to bring any sacrifice to the altar of the fatherland, not excluding his own life; that the trials currently being experienced by the entire Russian people, both personal and economic, should be borne by all uncomplainingly." People who acted otherwise were traitors.[55] Such phrases effectively effaced boundaries between the spiritual and the temporal, by making the state—and, arguably, the nation—an object of veneration and a sacred site.

In this way, the Orthodox Church also provided to anyone discussing the war, whether in secular or religious vein, a "language of sacrifice," a vocabulary and diction that were simultaneously elevated but familiar and comprehensible to churchgoers.[56] Adrian Gregory has made this point in discussing Britain's experience of the war, suggesting that one reason the

---

[52] *O voine: Vnebogosluzhebnaia beseda Petrogradskogo mitropolita Vladimira 1914 g., avgusta 15 dnia* (Moscow: Tip. T. Dortman, 1914), 10–12, 16–18, 24–25. See also D. B-ov, "Do okonchatel'noi pobedy!" *Prikhodskii listok,* 20 July 1916, 2.

[53] A. Volynets, "Sila dukha," *Prikhodskii listok,* 3 January 1916, 2.

[54] Arkhimandrit Lavrentii, "Pouchenie po sluchaiu voine," *Prikhodskoe chtenie,* no. 6 (August 1914): 190–91.

[55] RGIA f. 797, op. 86, otd. 3, st. 5, d. 17, ll. 1, 2–4. Special Instruction of Tikhon, Archbishop of Kursk, to his clergy, 3 February 1916.

[56] A secular example is V. M. Purishkevich's Duma speech honoring "the sacrifices the Polish people have placed on the altar of our common fatherland." *GDSO,* IV, 4, zas. 4 (1 August 1915), col. 246.

revivalist-inspired patriotic rhetoric of a Lloyd George resonated so effectively was that "the grammar and vocabulary of the language of sacrifice were deeply familiar to a Bible-reading and hymn-singing public."[57]

Identifying the Enemies Within

While unity, service, and generous sacrifice were the main tropes of patriotic narrative, there were also more exclusionary counternarratives that identified selfish, disloyal individuals or groups who posed a danger to the national community. In the first months of the war, popular fears about spies could generate accusations of aiding the enemy or make it dangerous to speak German in public–or even what *sounded* like German (as Latvian and Yiddish speakers learned to their sorrow). In 1915, the search for internal traitors escalated, a development related to panic over the unfolding disaster at the front, widespread demands for an explanation of its causes, and the need to deflect anger away from the authorities.[58] But the hunt for enemies within was not solely a function of red herrings and scapegoats. Military debacles and their accompanying ordeals invited a national sorting and closing of ranks, a reckoning of who were the "true" patriotic sons and daughters of the nation, willing to serve and sacrifice even at the nadir, and who were not.

Notwithstanding the patriotic service of some 350,000 Jewish soldiers at the front, Jews were particularly vulnerable. Besides the strain of anti-Semitism in Russian culture, there was the simple problem of proximity: the majority of Jews were confined to residence in the Pale of Settlement, located in the western borderlands where much of the fighting took place. When things went badly for the Russian army, the Jews were on hand to blame. By March 1915, military authorities were summarily cleansing entire Jewish communities from areas in or near the theaters of war, thousands were taken hostage as guarantors against "further Jewish espionage," and looting and pogroms directed at Jews by Cossacks, soldiers, and local civilians assumed terrible proportions.[59] Besides causing widespread misery, these brutal policies hampered conduct of the war against the external enemy, thus incurring

---

[57] Adrian Gregory, *The Last Great War: British Society and the First World War* (Cambridge: Cambridge University Press, 2008), 152–56.

[58] See William J. Fuller, *The Foe Within: Fantasies of Treason and the End of Imperial Russia* (Ithaca, NY: Cornell University Press, 2006).

[59] GARF f. 102, DL, 1915, op. 73, d. 72, "Report of 26 August 1915 from Governor of Kovno to Department of Police," l. 11. Estimates of the number of Jews expelled range from 500,000 to 1,000,000; see Oleg Budnitsky, *Russian Jews between the Reds and the Whites, 1917–1920*, trans. Timothy J. Portice (Philadelphia: University of Pennsylvania Press, 2012), 73. The fullest eyewitness account is S. An-ski, *The Enemy at His Pleasure: A Journey through the Jewish Pale of Settlement in World War I*, ed. and trans. Joachim Neugroschel (New York: Metropolitan Books/Henry Holt and Co., 2002).

the ire of civilian authorities as well as outraging significant portions of the Russian public.[60]

Anger at the German aggressor and long-simmering resentment of German economic dominance quickly spilled over onto Russian Germans. As Eric Lohr demonstrates, from early 1915 radical measures were directed against naturalized Russian subjects of German origin, among them the so-called "German colonists" (many of whom were Mennonites). The colonists' distinct culture and German heritage aroused suspicions, while their rich farm lands excited envy. New laws compelled tens of thousands of Russian Germans to sell their lands for a pittance, others had their shares in businesses liquidated, and thousands were deported into the country's interior.[61] Adherents of Christian sects deemed to be "German"—which included Baptists—were also persecuted. The press, led by the influential conservative daily *Novoe vremia*, played a prominent role in fanning anti-German hysteria.[62]

Unworthy or disloyal members of the national community were not identified solely on ethnic or religious lines. By the second half of 1916, as shortages and rising prices exacerbated social tensions, military censors reported growing numbers of letters equating speculators and profiteers with internal enemies. As one soldier wrote in August 1916, "It seems to me that before you can dream about victory you must destroy the internal enemies, namely: speculators, merchants, and other such harmful egoists who have forgotten the motherland and play into the hands of enemies." Similarly, a letter from an officer complained that while husbands and fathers suffered at the front, in the rear their families were being "robbed by these damned profiteers and internal enemies, who are vastly more dangerous than the external enemy."[63] Most dangerously for the legitimacy of the dynasty, as Boris Kolonitskii demonstrates, by late 1916 rumors about the supposed treason of the imperial family—or at least of the "German" Empress—in cahoots with Rasputin and "dark forces" at court, were being embraced at every level of society.[64] A unifying belief that there was treachery at the top constituted a terrible inversion of sacred union.

---

[60] The Council of Ministers discussed the problems caused by army "excesses" towards the Jews; notes of these meetings are in Cherniavsky, *Prologue to Revolution*, 57–71.

[61] Eric Lohr, *Nationalizing the Russian Empire: The Campaign against Enemy Aliens during World War I* (Cambridge, MA: Harvard University Press, 2003), 76–82, 95–111.

[62] For example: *Novoe vremia*, 31 July 31 1914, 2; 1 November 1 1914, 13, 14; and "Obzor 1914 god," 1 January 1915, 12.

[63] Rossiiskii gosudarstvennyi voenno-istoricheskii arkhiv (RGVIA) f. 2003, op. 1, d. 1486, "Svodka otchetov voennykh tsenzorov shtabov armii" (1916), ll. 186, 226–27.

[64] See Kolonitskii's chapter in this book, 27–54.

"For Freedom and the Fatherland!" Patriotic Discourse in Revolutionary 1917

Monarchy formally ended in Russia on 2 March 1917, but Russia's involvement in the Great War did not. The Provisional Government resolved to honor Russia's commitment to her allies and continue the fight until victory. The Petrograd Soviet, though more insistent on renouncing annexations and indemnities and more open to the possibility of a negotiated peace, was similarly committed to defending "free Russia" from German militarism. The soldier was now a soldier-citizen, proclaimed to be defending freedom *and* the fatherland. Initially, the great majority of the population shared the commitment to defense. But as the country's economic situation continued to worsen, national unity and the common people's willingness to stay in the war speedily eroded. Trying to rekindle patriotism on a new foundation, to offer new and compelling explanations of why Russia's people must continue the fight, necessarily consumed much of the new authorities' energies and resources, as well as those of groups across much of the political spectrum.

One innovative means by which the Provisional Government sought to define and nourish revolutionary patriotism was its Committee on Social-Political Enlightenment.[65] Shortly after February, a non-governmental body involved with providing technical assistance for the war effort created the "Bureau for Organizing Morale" (Biuro organizatsii dukhy); its object was to raise the patriotic consciousness of the revolutionary citizenry. In July, this bureau was renamed the Committee on Social-Political Enlightenment and brought into Aleksandr Kerenskii's newly formed Political Cabinet of the War Minister. Among its members were prominent socialists who supported a defensive war effort shorn of imperialist goals, including Plekhanov and Soviet executive committee member Vladimir Voitinskii.[66]

One of the Committee's main goals was to develop popular awareness of the need to defend Russia's new freedom, which meant continuing the "struggle with German militarism." Another goal was to disseminate understanding of unity, discipline, and the defense of spiritual values (*dukhovnye tsennosti*) as "the basic factors of state organization."[67] This kind of cultural or educational work, directed at popular audiences and especially soldiers, was a pressing concern for many people in 1917. Organizations engaged in such efforts in the

---

[65] On the new regime's cultural projects, see Daniel Orlovsky, "The Provisional Government and Its Cultural Work," in *Bolshevik Culture: Experiment and Order in the Russian Revolution*, ed. Abbott Gleason, Peter Kenez, and Richard Stites (Bloomington: Indiana University Press, 1985), 39–56; on the Committee, see Peter Holquist, *Making War, Forging Revolution: Russia's Continuum of Crisis, 1914–1921* (Cambridge, MA: Harvard University Press, 2002), especially 3–6, 143–44, 211–17.

[66] GARF f. 9505 (Committee on Social-Political Enlightenment), op. 1, d. 1, "Report," l. 4; and f. 1788 (Provisional Government, Ministry of Internal Affairs), op. 1, d. 14, l. 3.

[67] GARF f. 9505, op. 1, d. 1, l. 9.

capital included the Central Committee of the educational commissions of the Petrograd garrisons and the cultural-educational organs of various political parties. Liberal nationalist Petr Struve launched the "League of Russian Culture," to counter class antagonisms by promoting a sense of common national destiny.[68]

Besides organizing mass public meetings in May and June on the theme of "Consciousness and Responsibility," the Committee on Social-Political Enlightenment sponsored free lectures for soldiers on topical issues. It ran courses in "Political Literacy" to train future lecturers on diverse social, political, and cultural topics, and set up a people's club with a tearoom and library. In an effort to reach civilians outside the capitals, it opened 16 branches in the provinces and sent 25 lecturers on tour.[69] Continuing in the tradition of the tsarist "Committee on Popular Publications," it assembled 300,000 minilibraries (*bibliotechki*) of carefully vetted texts, which were distributed at the front and rear. The content of libraries varied according to the presumed "preparedness" of their intended readers, but each one included Tat′iana Bogdanovich's "Great Days of the Revolution." This pamphlet combined key texts from the February days with a simple narrative featuring the Duma and the "entire people," on the one hand, who were patriotically united to help Russia win the war, versus the tsar and his bad advisers, on the other, who cared more about preserving their power than they did about Russia.[70]

The Committee also took part in the effort to popularize the "Liberty Loan" (*zaem svobody*), one of the largest and most concerted patriotic campaigns of 1917. The Liberty Loan, authorized on 27 March 1917 at 5 percent interest, was Russia's seventh domestic loan of the war. The Provisional Government hoped to match or exceed earlier subscription campaigns, since the war effort urgently needed the funds.[71] Moreover, war loan campaigns—in

---

[68] On enlightenment activities in 1917 see T. N. Zakharova, "Vlianie kul′turnogo faktora na obshchestvennoe soznanie mass v Petrograde v 1917 godu," in *Revoliutsiia 1917 goda v Rossii: Sbornik nauchnykh statei,* ed. O. A. Polivanov and V. I. Startsev (St. Petersburg: Tret′ia Rossiia, 1995), 153–60; and P. V. Volobuev et al., *1917 god v sud′bakh Rossii i mira: Fevral′skaia revoliutsiia. Ot novykh istochnikov k novomu osmysleniiu* (Moscow: Institut rossiiskoi istorii RAN, 1997), 218–21. On Struve, see Richard Pipes, *Struve: Liberal on the Right, 1905–1944* (Cambridge, MA: Harvard University Press, 1980), 234–39.

[69] GARF f. 9505, op. 2, d. 2 ("Otchety, doklady i plany deiatel′nosti"), ll. 18, 30, 38; op. 1, d. 1, l. 6; and op. 2, d. 3 ("Tezisy lektury"), ll. 21–22. Some 1500 people took the training courses for lecturers.

[70] T. Bogdanovich, *Velikie dni revoliutsii: 23 fevralia–12 marta 1917 g.* (Petrograd, 1917); GARF f. 9505, op. 1, d. 7 ("Spravka o deiatel′nosti Literaturnoi komissii"), ll. 1, 8, 11–13; d. 1 ("Polozhenie o komitete"), l. 4; and d. 3 ("Pis′mo"), l. 23. In all, the Committee managed to make available 10 million copies of pamphlets and leaflets.

[71] GARF f. 9505, op. 1, d. 1, l. The classic treatment of Russia's war loans is Paul N. Apostol, "Credit Operations," in Alexander M. Michelson et al., *Russian Public Finance*

every combatant nation—were as much about involving civilians in their country's war effort as they were about raising revenue. Subscribing to the loan, just like collecting scrap metal or planting a victory garden, invested even the most humble citizen in the struggle, allowing them to act as patriots and demonstrate their membership in the national community.

In 1917, as before, propagandizing the loan was a broad-based effort. The Ministry of Finance coordinated efforts to enlist government employees, the clergy, and people working in the financial and commercial sectors in the project. The Soviet of Workers' and Soldiers' Deputies supported the loan and urged "the citizens of free Russia" to follow its example. Clubs and societies formed special groups to popularize the loan. Most of the Russian press took an active part in the campaign, publishing full-page appeals, reporting major loan-related events, and printing weekly subscription totals coming in from all over the country.[72]

The effort to sell the loan featured a revamped patriotic message, as is apparent in the handsome loan posters produced in large quantities. One complex composition, showing a soldier and worker united, melds traditional and more revolutionary motifs—peasant huts and a church with factory smokestacks and a red banner. The slogan similarly joins old and new by saying, "The motherland and freedom are in danger. Give money to the state for the struggle with the enemy." Boris Kustodiev's mature, bearded peasant soldier, standing atop a podium with bayonet in his hands, is the epitome of dignified resolve. (See fig. 7.) The top of the poster reads simply "Liberty Loan," but the inscriptions on the red banners being borne by the marching crowds underline the message that "war until victory" and defense of revolutionary liberty are two sides of the same coin: "Don't let the enemy take away the freedom you've won."[73]

Many cities held a Liberty Loan holiday to energize support. An innovative mobilization of art and artists characterized Petrograd's "Day of the Liberty Loan" on 25 May 1917, which was orchestrated by the Union of People in the Arts.[74] Events included a big public meeting at the Mariinskii Theater featuring speeches by enlisted men and political luminaries, concerts and shows performed at dozens of indoor and outdoor sites, and a grand parade. The enormous crowds that turned out enjoyed themselves vastly and the

---

During the War: Revenue and Expenditure (New Haven: Yale University Press, 1928), 249–52, 263–77; see also V. V. Strakhov, "Vnutrennie zaimy v Rossii v pervuiu mirovuiu voinu," *Voprosy istorii*, no. 9 (2003): 8–43.

[72] Apostol, "Credit Operations," 271; and *Russkie vedomosti*, 1 June 1917, 4; *Rech´*, 2 June 1917, 4 and 22 June 1917, 6; and *Den´*, 8 April 1917, 1.

[73] The posters are featured in the excellent catalog by N. I. Baburina, *Russkii plakat Pervoi mirovoi voiny* (Moscow: Iskusstvo i kul´tura, 1992), 109–12, 117–19.

[74] A brief description of the Petrograd celebration is in James von Geldern, *Bolshevik Festivals, 1917–1920* (Berkeley: University of California Press, 1993), 19–20.

festive event was deemed a terrific success.[75] For Samarkand's "Day of the Liberty Loan" in July, a special edition newspaper spoke of the need for a new Minin and Pozharskii to emerge from the people and save Russia, just as those heroes had saved her during the Time of Troubles. It then proceeded to cast Kerenskii as a latter-day Pozharskii and urged every citizen to be like Minin, which meant "supporting comrade Kerenskii" by buying into the loan. The article concluded, "Subscription to the Liberty Loan is a sort of exam one passes to receive the title of 'free citizen.'"[76]

After a strong start, subscriptions to the Liberty Loan began to falter, slowing irrevocably in July. Some contemporaries, and subsequently some historians, have seen in the disappointing denouement to the Liberty Loan not only a clear sign of popular disillusionment with the war, but also a failure to "pass the exam" of conscious citizenship. But material difficulties also played a major role. As Steven Marks shows in his contribution to this book, citizens experiencing runaway inflation and an imploding economy had reason to fear tying up their money in any long-term investment. One could argue that attracting in such conditions more than four billion rubles in subscriptions—an amount nearly double what the biggest previous loan had yielded—was not all that bad a showing.[77]

Of course, the new freedoms which citizens were urged to defend included the freedom to speak *against* the war. Some people had opposed Russia's participation in the war from the outset. Others subsequently turned against it, for a variety of reasons: the belief that its goals had ceased to be just ones, that no victory could make up for its continued horrible costs, or that the humbler classes bore a disproportionate share of the sacrifice. Thanks to the near absence of censorship in Russia in 1917—one way in which Russia's experience of the war differed sharply from all other belligerents'—the population was now exposed to every conceivable critique of the war, and of the government and society conducting it. Particularly potent were class-based arguments that contended soldiers' sacrifices were wasted on unworthy ends, or that denied any meaningful foundation for "national unity" given the opposing interests of the propertied classes and the working masses. For example, the influential Bolshevik newspaper for soldiers, *Okopnaia pravda* (Trench Truth), consistently denounced the imperialist nature of the war and the slaughter of millions of peasants and workers for the interests of Russian

---

[75] *Rech'*, 26 May 1917, 6; and 27 May 1917, 6.

[76] "Zaem svobody ili zaem rabstva?" *Den' zaima svobody* (Samarkand, July 1917), 2–3.

[77] Figures come from *Vestnik vremennogo pravitel'stva*, cited in Robert Paul Browder and Alexander F. Kerensky, eds., *The Russian Provisional Government. Documents*, vol. 2 (Stanford, CA: Stanford University Press, 1961), 490; see also Peter Gatrell, *Russia's First World War: A Social and Economic History* (Harlow, UK: Pearson/Longman, 2005), 201–02, 209. Inflation makes it impossible to determine the relationship of the 1917 figures to those of 1916.

and international capital. Its provocative slogan was "Burzhuis [bourgeoisie] to the trenches!"[78]

Weak censorship constraints also allowed even more discussion of who was *not* a loyal member of the national community. The mass edition pamphlet "The Traitors and Betrayers of Russia," for example, ascribes Russia's many defeats prior to the revolution to government incompetence and internal enemies; the latter supposedly created artificial shortages and inflation to sabotage the war effort. Traitors big and small "worked for the death of Russia. They robbed it and drank its blood."[79] This kind of inflammatory language had become so common, Maksim Gor'kii ironically observed in June 1917, that "the word 'traitor' is heard just as often as the call 'Waiter!' was heard in the taverns of the old days."[80]

The Bolshevik seizure of power, draconian peace of Brest-Litovsk in March 1918, and expanding Civil War further fractured and divided patriotic narratives. With much of the former empire gone, and control of other regions contested, the question of *where* was Russia was no more settled than the question of *what* Russia would be. Both the Bolsheviks and their opponents cast themselves as legitimate leaders and stewards of this inchoate fatherland. They sought to devise symbols, slogans, rituals, and heroic myths to appeal to the population (or their own followers), engage their loyalties, and mobilize them to fight.

The anti-Bolshevik forces always considered themselves the real Russian patriots, but were nonetheless rather ineffectual in propagating a patriotic narrative. Internal divisions and lack of a coherent and agreed upon political program hampered them profoundly, making it difficult to generate positive, unifying themes. What became the main slogan of the Whites in South Russia, "Russia, one and indivisible," did not have the appeal of the myth of "sacred union": it was less flexible and more backward looking, lacking the fulfillment of subaltern groups' aspirations implied in the wartime patriotic narrative. Peasants could not be sure of keeping the lands they had acquired, minorities could not be sure of equal rights and cultural autonomy, and Jews could expect humiliation and violence. The Whites' strongest appeal was religious, representing themselves as defenders of Orthodoxy and the restorers of "Holy Russia," versus Russia's betrayers, the atheist Bolsheviks (or "Jew-Bolsheviks"), bought and paid for with "German gold." The Orthodox

---

[78] Allan K. Wildman, *The End of the Russian Imperial Army*, 2: *The Road to Soviet Power and Peace* (Princeton, NJ: Princeton University Press, 1987), 52–54.

[79] Evgenii Gorets, *Izmenniki i predateli Rossii* (Moscow: Izd. Sytina, 1917), 5–6, 21, 25.

[80] "Untimely Thoughts," *Novaia zhizn'*, no. 61 (29 June 1917), in Maxim Gorky, *Untimely Thoughts: Essays on Revolution, Culture, and the Bolsheviks, 1917–1918*, trans. Herman Ermolaev (New York: P. S. Eriksson, 1968), 70.

Church not only strongly supported the Whites but also provided them the means of communicating with millions of believers.[81]

Ironically, when Marxist Georgii Plekhanov supported Russia's war effort in 1914, repudiating the Communist Manifesto's famous claim that "the worker has no fatherland," Lenin had savagely attacked this "chauvinism." Once in power, however, the Bolsheviks proved willing to use tropes familiar from pre-October patriotic narratives. On 21 February 1918, as the German army resumed its offensive in Russia, the Council of People's Commissars issued Lenin's decree "The Socialist Fatherland is in Danger!" It summoned workers and peasants to revolutionary defense of the country, declaring that it was their "sacred duty" to defend the Republic of Soviets against the bourgeois-imperialist German hordes. Point 8 of the decree played chillingly to fears of enemies within, stipulating that "enemy agents, profiteers, marauders, hooligans, counterrevolutionary agitators and German spies are to be shot on the spot."[82]

In the Civil War, Bolshevik propaganda emphasized the Whites' subordination to their imperialist foreign allies; White generals were depicted as snarling dogs, their leashes held by figures representing the United States, France, and Britain (fig. 8). Another example showing the Soviet government as the true defender of Russia's independence comes from the Soviet-Polish War. In May 1920, invading Polish armies captured Kiev, regarded by many Russians as the birthplace of their culture. Newspapers called upon the population to join the army and "defend the fatherland" from the Polish aggressors. ROSTA windows cartooned a Polish officer devouring a peasant woman (*baba*). According to Orlando Figes, the Bolsheviks were stunned by the strength of the public response. Some 14,000 officers joined the Red Army to fight the Poles, thousands of civilians volunteered for war work, and there were mass patriotic demonstrations. Grigorii Zinov'ev, head of Petrograd's soviet executive committee, admitted, "We never thought Russia had so many patriots."[83]

---

[81] On anti-Bolshevik views and propaganda, see Paul F. Robinson, "Always with Honour: The Code of White Russian Officers," *Canadian Slavonic Papers* 41, 2 (1999): 121–41; Peter Kenez, *The Birth of the Propaganda State: Soviet Methods of Mass Mobilization, 1917–1929* (Cambridge: Cambridge University Press, 1985), 63–69; and Oleg Riabov's chapter in this book, 73–97.

[82] Plekhanov, *O voine*, 23–27; and V. I. Lenin, *Collected Works* (Moscow: Progress Publishers, 1965), 27: 30–33, including reproduction of the Russian text.

[83] On Civil War depictions of the Whites, see Victoria E. Bonnell, *Iconography of Power: Soviet Political Posters under Lenin and Stalin* (Berkeley: University of California Press, 1997), 194–99; Orlando Figes, *A People's Tragedy: A History of the Russian Revolution* (New York: Viking, 1996), 697–700.

Conclusions

As Eric Hobsbawm reminds us, historians must be careful not to assume that the views of the nation disseminated by governments and elites are the views held by the common people. The opinions of the latter can be difficult to discover.[84] While the sources make it possible to analyze large-scale efforts to promote patriotism and a sense of national community in Russia, they shed less light on how these efforts were perceived by the common people, or the meanings ordinary individuals assigned to them. But the evidence does require that we rethink our assumptions about the feebleness of efforts to foster mass patriotism in World War I Russia.

Instead, we see enormous state, public, and private efforts to mobilize popular support for the war effort and help to cultivate love of and loyalty to the nation. Mass edition pamphlets and posters explained the war's causes, and why Russia would and must win. An unprecedented outpouring of giving and serving on the home front, organized from below as well as from above, actively involved tens of millions of people in aid of the nation's war effort and their fellow citizens. New or expanded national newspapers informed the population of these efforts occurring simultaneously all over Russia, and connected them to it. Widely disseminated maps of Russia and the fronts, and images of heroes and leaders, allowed people to visualize their community and those defending it. New prayers, rituals, and commemorative days sacralized the struggle and helped unite the national community in collective acts of sacrifice, thanksgiving, and mourning.

Besides uniting the population in hatred and fear of the enemy (fig. 9), wartime patriotic culture offered compelling positive images and narratives. Russians were people of steadfast service and sacrifice; a nation united without distinction of class, faith, ethnicity, or region; and a people of compassionate generosity. This was a broad, civically-grounded construction of the national community, including all those who lived in and were loyal to this shared territorial entity, rather than being based on the more traditional markers of religion, ethnicity, or descent. Everyone could prove full membership in this community, at least theoretically, by demonstrating their patriotism. This patriotic narrative also provided inspiring examples of popular heroes and victories from days past—above all, in 1613 and 1812—reminding the population that Russians had prevailed over seemingly indomitable aggressors before. Most of the population had ample incentive to buy into this construction of the patriotic nation, since proving one's patriotism laid a basis for various groups to try to enhance or protect their claims to rights and benefits. However, there were also more exclusionary narratives, which identified scapegoats and internal enemies to make sense of defeats or shortages. The

---

[84] Hobsbawm, *Nations and Nationalism*, 11.

measures taken against groups construed in this way could be radical and harsh.

Though the tropes of service, unity, and sacrifice persisted after February 1917, there were also changes in patriotic narrative. Monarchy was gone, and with it the triadic formula of "faith, tsar and fatherland." Now a joined pair—"freedom and the fatherland" or "the motherland and the revolution"—became the precious objects of defense. The near absence of censorship from March to November in 1917 also allowed greater contestation over the meaning of patriotism, and even more reference to internal enemies. After the October coup, and especially Brest-Litovsk, the objects of patriotic loyalty and the boundaries of the national community became still more confused. But both Reds and Whites would appeal to love of country and things held "sacred," as well as inciting fear and hatred of both foreign and internal enemies.

Despite the generals' postwar lament that the common people had failed to conceive of a nation or been willing to sacrifice for it, one is struck by the endurance of soldiers and civilians, and the generosity of the entire population, through years of hardship and staggering losses. It is quite possible to conclude that the war experience helped consolidate in the population a sense of membership in a great national community, rather than being a test of patriotism that they failed. But by late 1916, apparent incompetence and rumors of treason—particularly at the very top—increasingly made this sacrifice seem to have been in vain. A further source of anger among ordinary citizens was the perceived *inequality* of sacrifice, a feeling that for all the talk of unity and love of the fatherland, the common people were bearing most of the burdens of the war.

Russian Leaders of the Great War and Revolutionary Era in Representations and Rumors

Boris Kolonitskii

Images of political leaders and statesmen are an important resource for political mobilization. This resource acquires considerable significance in times of acute political crisis and military conflict: those who are actively involved in politics during times of crisis often seek to identify themselves with leaders—with heads of state and/or leaders of public movements. The study of the formation, circulation, and reception of images of Russian political figures during the Great War and revolutionary era is therefore exceptionally important for our understanding of the political developments of that time. Examining cultural forms of political representation furthers our understanding of political cultures.

This theme has already been reflected in the works of various historians. Richard Wortman, in his remarkable book devoted to the various representations of the Russians tsars, gave consideration to the modification of Nicholas II's image during the Great War.[1] The story of how these images were received by the tsar's subjects, however, remained beyond the boundaries of that study. Richard Abraham has written the fullest biography of A. F. Kerenskii, the most popular figure of the February Revolution.[2] The author could not ignore the emerging cult of the leader of the Revolution. Various aspects of the "Kerenskii cult" have been considered by A. G. Golikov and G. L. Sobolev.[3] It nonetheless appears that a fresh assessment of the multi-

---

[1] Richard S. Wortman, *Scenarios of Power: Myth and Ceremony in Russian Monarchy*, 1: *From Peter the Great to the Death of Nicholas I* (Princeton, NJ: Princeton University Press, 1995), and 2: *From Alexander II to the Abdication of Nicholas II* (Princeton, NJ: Princeton University Press, 2000). Translations of these two volumes were published in Russia in 2002 and 2005.

[2] Richard Abraham, *Alexander Kerensky: The First Love of the Revolution* (London: Sidgwick & Jackson, 1987).

[3] A. G. Golikov, "Fenomen Kerenskogo," *Otechestvennaia istoriia*, no. 5 (1992): 60–73; G. L. Sobolev, comp., *Aleksandr Kerenskii: Liubov´ i nenavist´ revoliutsii. Dnevniki, stat´i, ocherki i vospominaniia sovremennikov* (Cheboksary: Izd-vo Chuvashskogo Universiteta, 1993).

Russian Culture in War and Revolution, 1914–22, Book 2: Political Culture, Identities, Mentalities, and Memory. Murray Frame, Boris Kolonitskii, Steven G. Marks, and Melissa K. Stockdale, eds. Bloomington, IN: Slavica Publishers, 2014, 27–54.

farious images of the "revolutionary leader" present in propaganda, art, and in the collective consciousness of the revolutionary period will allow us to broaden our understanding of the activity of Kerenskii and his opponents, while also enabling us to draw some conclusions about the development of a revolutionary political culture.

The cult of Lenin has received the most interest from scholars—suffice it to mention the books of N. Tumarkin, B. Ennker, and O. Velikanova.[4] However, in focusing on the key stages of the development of the Lenin cult—the assassination attempt (August 1918), the jubilee celebrations for the leader's 50th birthday in 1920, his death, his embalmment, the posthumous commemorative practices—these authors touch only fleetingly upon the events of 1917. Yet this period of acute, competitive political struggle was immensely important for establishing cultural forms of perception of charismatic leaders and the ways in which they were represented.

Although an examination of the Stalin cult does not altogether fit within the chronological framework of the present subject, the investigative approaches and methods, conclusions and observations of historians are of considerable interest. Among works of this sort, particular mention should be made of Jan Plamper's book.[5] In addition, when studying how political figures were represented, one should not confine oneself to analyzing the texts and actions of the objects of political cults and those of their supporters. In history it is often the case that the adversaries of statesmen and political actors inadvertently assist the quest for new cultural forms of glorification of their enemy leaders; occasionally they assist in circulating these cultural forms, and sometimes—against their will—they have a hand in their creation. The context of a political struggle is extremely important for restructuring the processes of political and cultural creativity: adversarial political leaders, together with their supporters, require competitive and creative efforts for the furthering of "their" political cult.

In addition, cults of the "leading figures" are frequently accompanied by the creation of supporting cults of second-rank leaders, "sub-cults." The formation of a "pantheon of leaders," an unstable and dynamic structure in which different leaders are apportioned different functions, can have an unpredictable impact on the cult of the main leader.

---

[4] Nina Tumarkin, *Lenin Lives! The Lenin Cult in Soviet Russia* (Cambridge, MA: Harvard University Press, 1983) (published in Russian in 1997); Benno Ennker, *Die Anfänge des Leninkults in der Sowjetunion* (Cologne: Böhlau Verlag, 1997) (published in Russian in 2011); Olga Velikanova, *Making of an Idol: On Uses of Lenin* (Göttingen: Muster-Schmidt-Verlag, 1996); Velikanova, *Obraz Lenina v massovom vospriiatii sovetskikh liudei po arkhivnym materialam* (Lewiston, ME: Edwin Mellen Press, 2001).

[5] Ian Plamper [Jan Plamper], *Alkhimiia vlasti: Kul't Stalina v izobrazitel'nom iskusstve* (Moscow: Novoe literaturnoe obozrenie, 2010), published in English as Jan Plamper, *The Stalin Cult: A Study in the Alchemy of Power* (New Haven: Yale University Press, 2012).

Finally, it is worth reconstructing how the proffered images of leaders have been received: at times the "interpretation" of messages by their audiences might not have corresponded at all to the intentions of a cult's creators, nor to the political goals of its object. Images of leaders, as they gained ground, were no longer controlled by their creators (and that includes by the leaders themselves). When studying the various perceptions of leaders over time, one should examine the mass demand for these, or other, images; an investigation into leader cults is impossible without considering the history of their consumption.

ଓ ଓ

Russia's entry into the war required from Nicholas II a significant reworking of his own image, and this was manifested in his speeches, actions, gestures, and portraits.[6] Nicholas himself played an important role in this, although his correspondence with the empress shows clearly that Aleksandra Fedorovna also played the part of "image-maker." The Ministry of the Imperial Court, having subjected all publications containing pictures of the royal family and any corresponding texts to censorship, also had an influence on the circulation of images of members of the imperial household. The role of commercial publications and publishing houses was an important one; they circulated what they considered to be the more fortuitous images and words of the tsar, while suppressing those that they thought unfavorable or irrelevant.

In his attempts to influence the processes of patriotic mobilization, Nicholas II was guided by the tradition of the symbolic presentation of military conflicts in Russia. At times, he replicated the actions and gestures of his predecessors. Thus, he repeated several measures taken by Alexander I during the Patriotic War of 1812. The memory of that conflict, of exceptional importance for Russia's historical memory, was actualized in 1912, when the war's jubilee was widely celebrated. The tsar was not alone in turning to events that occurred 100 years earlier: many Russian propagandists, writers, and artists used elements of cultural memory about the 1812 war in order to comprehend the present military conflicts. It is not surprising that, in 1914, the war was referred to as the Second Patriotic and even the Great Patriotic War.

There was another contextual element that Nicholas II could not ignore: the strategies for self-representation employed by other European monarchs, who were also modifying their images during the war, striving to promote patriotic mobilization and, at the same time, strengthen their political positions. Photographs in illustrated publications kept readers abreast of the new ways in which the heads of European states were being depicted. A well-known rivalry for bellicosity and masculinity existed between the monarchs of the

---

[6] For an examination of the ways in which the tsar and several representatives of the dynasty were portrayed, see B. I. Kolonitskii, *"Tragicheskaia erotika": Obrazy imperatorskoi sem'i v gody Pervoi mirovoi voiny* (Moscow: Novoe literaturnoe obozrenie, 2010).

belligerent countries: they would dress in their army's military field uniform and pay visits to theaters of military operations. This was meticulously captured on film for use as military propaganda by the countries in question, and it was also echoed in their enemies' press. The bar was set unattainably high by the "king knight" Albert I, king of the Belgians, who even took to the skies in an aeroplane.

Nicholas II was obliged to act within the confines of his own "scenario of power." Richard Wortman has demonstrated persuasively that images of the "Muscovite" tsar, the "pilgrim," and the "crowned toiler" were especially important for the last tsar.[7] During the war, the development of this "scenario" led to the emergence of a militarized simplification of the tsar's image: he appeared as a simple officer of the Russian army, and the soldier's tunic (*gimnasterka*) became his permanent mode of dress. The image of the emperor dressed in the field uniform of a Russian officer, singled out by his modesty against the background of his sparkling entourage, demonstrated solidarity with the regiments of the Russian infantry, who were enduring the primary ordeals of war.

The heir to the throne, 11-year-old Grand Duke Aleksei Nikolaevich, who had accompanied Nicholas II on trips to the front since autumn 1915, dressed in the uniform of a simple Russian soldier. Such simplifying measures that corresponded to the religious and aesthetic views of both the tsar and the tsarina, who sought a mystical link to the "ordinary people," were intended to promote the patriotic mobilization of the population—in every country, the war, which required the active and conscious participation of millions of people, was a unique kind of "democratizer," a fact that the Russian autocrat could not ignore. Propagandists wrote with tenderness about the "simple" countenance of the tsar, in which the imperial couple took such pride. However, one can hardly consider these strategies of "simplification" wholly successful: even some confirmed monarchists were disappointed by the ordinary countenance of the "unsightly colonel."[8] Other compatriots of the tsar preferred to see not the "simplification" of the emperor, but rather the democratization of Russia.

Still less successful was the promotional project of Empress Aleksandra Fedorovna. If the tsar adopted the role of a "simple officer," then the empress assumed the role of a "simple sister of mercy." Together with her two eldest daughters she undertook a preparatory course and passed the examination necessary to qualify as a nurse. The tsarina and tsarevnas worked in a hospital and even assisted during surgical operations. Posters and postcards acquainted the population with these activities; in official portraits the empress

---

[7] R. Uortman [Wortman], "Nikolai II i obraz samoderzhaviia," in *Reformy ili revoliutsiia? Rossiia 1861–1917. Materialy mezhdunarodnogo kollokviuma istorikov*, ed. D. Gaier [Dietrich Geyer] and V. S. Diakin (St. Petersburg: Nauka, 1992), 18–30; R. S. Uortman [Wortman], *Stsenarii vlasti: Mify i tseremonii russkoi monarkhii*, 2: *Ot Aleksandra II do otrecheniia Nikolaia II* (Moscow: Ob"edinennoe gumanitarnoe izdatel'stvo, 2004), 656.

[8] Kolonitskii, *"Tragicheskaia erotika,"* 72–240.

and her daughters were depicted wearing the modest uniforms of Red Cross nurses. At the outset of the war, the tsarina's popularity grew somewhat; over time, however, negative images increasingly circulated.

A notable proportion of the tsar's subjects—even those well-disposed towards the monarchy—considered that the tsarina, with the help of her "advisors" (primarily G. E. Rasputin), was, in fact, the country's ruler, and had pushed her husband away from power. These rumors did not correspond to reality, although from August 1915, when the emperor became the supreme commander in chief of the Russian army, the empress's involvement in politics definitely increased.

Rumors that the tsarina held pro-German views spread widely. Moreover, she was accused of preparing a separate peace and even conducting espionage on behalf of the enemy. Historians have not found convincing evidence to support these unlikely rumors. The tsarina herself, however, facilitated the circulation of gossip, conducting correspondence with relatives in Germany without appropriate discretion. The letters contained not only news of family affairs: in April 1915, the tsarina received a letter proposing a discussion of conditions for the termination of war (the German emperor was, allegedly, unaware of this initiative).[9] Many representatives of the political elite became aware of the empress's correspondence, and this affected her reputation.

Finally, there was talk among both representatives of "high society" and the common people that the tsarina was deceiving her husband. Rumors named a number of her alleged male and female lovers, but Rasputin was mentioned especially often. These rumors were completely groundless. The tsar and tsarina, however, were victims of their own piety in this situation: public opinion did not shake their confidence in the special mission being conducted by the exotic "elder" (*starets*).

Imprudent actions on the tsar's and, particularly, the tsarina's part encouraged the spreading of rumors, yet the empress also became a victim of her own promotional project: patriotic images of the tsarina and her daughters were received and "interpreted" in a most unpredictable manner. Thus, with time, the image of the "simple sister of mercy" became a great problem for the royal family. Many confirmed monarchists were unpleasantly taken aback by the fact that the tsarina was performing the role of a "simple handmaiden": this was regarded as sufficient in itself to damage the prestige and dignity of imperial rule. "The ermine mantle suited the Empress better than the dress of a sister of mercy."[10]

---

[9] Joseph T. Fuhrmann, ed., *The Complete Wartime Correspondence of Tsar Nicholas II and the Empress Alexandra (April 1914–March 1917)* (Westport, CT: Greenwood Press, 1999), 119.

[10] A. A. Mosolov, *Pri dvore poslednego imperatora (Zapiski nachal'nika kantseliarii ministerstva dvora)* (St. Petersburg: Nauka, Sankt-Peterburgskoe otdelenie, 1992), 98–99; A. I. Spiridovich, *Velikaia voina i Fevral'skaia revoliutsiia, 1914–1917*, bk. 3 (New York: Vseslavianskoe izdatel'stvo, 1962), 74.

Moreover, for many people of that time the assistance of the tsarevnas in dressing wounds and in medical operations was highly dubious. Photographs and reports that got past the censor of the Ministry of the Imperial Court confirmed that the young unmarried women were coming into contact with the naked bodies of men. This could constitute persuasive "evidence" to confirm the rumors about the supposed debauchery of the royal family.

During the war, the image of the sister of mercy itself underwent a substantial change. Initially it was a sign of patriotic mobilization, a symbol of the country: women in uniform bearing a red cross demonstrated what the ideal gender role of the female patriot and Christian should be in wartime. The nurse's uniform became a popular fashion in high society, and this was copied by other strata of the population. But over time the sister of mercy became a symbol of the frivolity and even debauchery of a home front that had forgotten the hardships suffered by its frontline soldiers. Rumors of genuine and imagined scurrilous tales began to emerge; moreover, professional prostitutes began to use the beautiful and popular "patriotic" uniform bearing the red cross, and at times female fraudsters would also wear it.[11] For the frontline soldiers the sister of mercy became both an object of sexual fantasies and the personification of an amoral internal enemy. In this context, any poster, postcard, or newspaper illustration that depicted the tsarina and tsarevnas in the uniform bearing the red cross "confirmed" the most unlikely rumors about the repulsive orgies and artful deceptions that supposedly took place in the tsar's palace.

Negative images of the tsarina also affected the way various portrayals of Nicholas II were received: a true sovereign cannot tolerate in his home a wife who deceives him both as husband and ruler. This is also reflected in the various charges brought against people who had insulted the tsar during the war. Sometimes the tsar himself was accused of betraying Russia, of acting in collusion with the enemy. But more often he was portrayed as a unique kind of sacrifice: as a "weak" sovereign, unaware of how his unfaithful wife and cunning advisors manipulated him. Those who insulted the tsar more often than not called him an "idiot," and this reflected their political conclusions: owing to a lack of necessary personal qualities the sovereign was simply unable to execute his professional sovereign duties.

The "weak tsar" image was also affected by portrayals of other members of the royal family, above all Grand Duke Nikolai Nikolaevich, who in 1914 became the supreme commander in chief of the Russian army. He had the reputation of a harsh, ruthless, decisive, and coarse general. His political significance increased greatly during the war; this was linked to the fact that the commander in chief enjoyed very extensive rights—in certain situations even

---

[11] On images of the sisters of mercy, see Kolonitskii, *"Tragicheskaia erotika."* On the ambivalence of the image of the sister of mercy in the culture of war, see Magnus Hirschfeld, *Sittengeschichte des Ersten Weltkrieges* (Hanau am Main: Schustek, 1965), 129–38.

the civilian authorities were subordinate to him. This led to an administrative muddle; even before the Revolution there was talk in the country of "dual power."

The peculiarities of wartime propaganda also tell of the grand duke's popularity. The army and the whole country were supposed to believe in their commander in chief; it followed that one should glorify the grand duke's accomplishments—both genuine accomplishments and those only attributed to him. The tsar himself wanted to strengthen the authority of his military commander and relative, and the highest honors were therefore bestowed upon the grand duke, who was glorified by imperial manifestos and decrees. Various journalists and political actors participated in the circulation of images of the grand duke, including representatives of the opposition. Some wanted to have the ever more influential military commander on their side; others sought to place him in opposition to the "weak" tsar and his ineffective bureaucracy. Still others believed that glorifying the commander in chief would encourage the patriotic mobilization of the country. Sometimes these motives overlapped. Commercial organizations also played a part in circulating the grand duke's image: he became a sought-after brand, and the production of postcards and posters, photographs and sketches dedicated to the commander in chief became commonplace.

The cult of the country's main military commander took shape under the influence of a series of factors; as well as patriotic propaganda, folklore played a significant role. Grand Duke Nikolai Nikolaevich began to feature in all kinds of legends and rumors: at the most unexpected moments, the courageous commander supposedly appeared in critical frontline regions and, with his decisive actions, saved the army, dispatching any traitors. One might assume that various popular prints and "folk" posters that depicted the grand duke in the thick of battle, on a dashing steed, lent credence to such rumors. More "realistic" rumors—which were still nonetheless far from the truth—spread in educated circles. Legends about "good old Mikola" (a popular way among peasants to pronounce the name "Nikolai," especially in southern Russia and Ukraine) were reflected even in literature.[12] It is impossible not to notice a certain stylistic link between these rumors and the published depictions of the grand duke: frequently artists deliberately stylized his portraits, making reference to the 1812 era.[13]

The development of Grand Duke Nikolai Nikolaevich's image was also influenced by the fact that in German and Austro-Hungarian propaganda he was the face of the enemy. It was precisely the commander in chief and not

---

[12] A. I. Ivanov, *Pervaia mirovaia voina v russkoi literature 1914–1918* (Tambov: Izd-vo TGU imeni G. R. Derzhavina, 2005), 119–20.

[13] Contemporaries were already writing about the stylization of wartime "popular prints" and how they were linked to rumor. See V. Denisov, *Voina i lubok* (Petrograd, 1916), cols. 2, 3, 28. It is revealing that the author alludes to depictions of the commander in chief.

the Russian emperor who came to personify the opponent in German and Austrian propaganda. At different stages of the war the political elites of Germany and Austria-Hungary did not rule out a separate peace with Russia, and similar sentiments were also characteristic of public opinion in these countries. In such a situation it would have been unwise to denounce Nicholas II too severely; at the same time, the brutal grand duke, who even before the war had not concealed his anti-German convictions, became the ideal personification of the sworn enemy. Even in frontline German propaganda, pamphlets addressed to Russian soldiers exposed the fierce "warmonger," Nikolai Nikolaevich, and placed him in opposition to the "peace-loving" tsar, who had to submit to the evil will of his belligerent relative. Assertions of this sort underscored Nicholas II's reputation as a "weak tsar." The effect of such propagandist activity did not at all correspond to the designs of the German politicians and generals: in the minds of many Russian soldiers, peasants, political figures, and intellectuals, the authority of the strong and "patriotic" military commander was opposed to the indecisive and "unpatriotic" emperor.

This opposition between commander in chief and sovereign circulated increasingly widely in Russian society. If initially the cult of the commander in chief, the "supreme leader," was supposed to fulfil the role of a supporting cult that strengthened the authority of the emperor, the "sovereign leader," over time the popularity of Nikolai Nikolaevich grew ever more dangerous for Nicholas II. In a way this is reminiscent of the German situation: the cult of von Hindenburg soon began to present a symbolic threat to Wilhelm II.[14] In Russia, the situation was even more complex: the commander in chief was a representative of the ruling dynasty, and therefore the cult of the military commander presented an immediate political threat to Nicholas II. Throughout the country people started to talk about the desirability of replacing the "weak" tsar with his "strong" relative; corresponding speculations about "Nicholas III" were no secret to the tsar and tsarina.

Not only the defeat suffered by the Russian army, but also fear of political competition from his popular relative influenced Nicholas II's decision in August 1915 to remove Nikolai Nikolaevich from the post of commander in chief (he became a viceroy of the tsar in the Caucasus and led the troops on the Caucasian front). The emperor assumed general command of the Russian forces. This in itself overcame the "dual power" between military and civilian authority, and an important rival was eliminated. At the same time, however, the monarch's authority suffered a blow: the removal of the grand duke, whom

---

[14] O. S. Nagornaia, "Tannenberg, 1914–1934: Natsional'nyi mif i politicheskaia kul'tura Germanii" (Candidate diss., Cheliabinsk, 2002), 78. On the cult of Hindenburg, see J. Von Hoegen, *Der Held von Tannenberg: Genese und Funktion des Hindenburg-Mythos (1914–1934)* (Cologne: Böhlau Verlag, 2007).

a large proportion of the population still considered a "strong" and "patriotic" leader, confirmed the improbable rumors about the tsar and tsarina.[15]

In his book devoted to patriotic mobilization in Russian mass culture during the First World War, Hubertus Jahn argues that while writers, artists, theater directors, and cinematographers succeeded in creating images of an external enemy, images depicting positive political integration were lacking.[16] It is possible to agree only in part with this important assertion. Indubitably, the tsar did not become a symbol of patriotic unity. However, the image of Grand Duke Nikolai Nikolaevich became, for a time, such a symbol; for a variety of reasons, several social and political forces played a part in its creation. But this popularity also began to present a danger to the regime. It was not possible to keep the tsar's relative in his post, but his removal was a blow to the tsar's authority.

The cultural developments that occurred during the war had serious political consequences. The obsession with espionage and the anti-German sentiment that were characteristic of Russian militaristic propaganda were reflected in literature and art; they were evident in the collective consciousness and influenced the reception of decisions made by the main political participants.[17] Another characteristic trait of wartime propaganda and culture was the use of images of the monarchs of enemy countries in order to personify the foe. These were primarily the rulers of Germany and Austria-Hungary—Wilhelm II and Franz-Josef. For this purpose, unfavorable images of monarchs established in a rich, European, anti-monarchic cultural tradition were used: the culture of patriotic mobilization in different countries contained a hidden but powerful anti-monarchic device. This also impacted upon attitudes towards the institution of monarchy in Russia.

The multifarious rumors that circulated were an important cultural feature of the war years. Military censorship of the press and private correspondence, while complicating regular correspondence, actually facilitated the circulation of rumors—this was common to all belligerents; but only in Russia did it have especially serious political consequences.

Prominent politicians, officers of the General Staff, foreign diplomats and aristocrats, including members of the imperial family, all participated in the

---

[15] It is revealing that legends about Grand Duke Nikolai Nikolaevich continued to circulate even in Soviet times. Thus, in the spring of 1924, a rumor in Odessa suggested that "Nikolai Nikolaevich's manifesto was circulating" in Moscow, that he was apparently on his way to the capital "with an army," and that "he had been recognized by all countries." V. A. Savchenko, *Neofitsial'naia Odessa epokhi NEPa (mart 1921–sentiabr' 1929)* (Moscow: Rossiiskaia politicheskaia entsiklopediia, 2012), 41.

[16] Hubertus F. Jahn, *Patriotic Culture in Russia during World War I* (Ithaca, NY: Cornell University Press, 1995), 172–74.

[17] See K. F. Shatsillo, "'Delo' polkovnika Miasoedova," *Voprosy istorii*, no. 4 (1967): 103–16; W. C. Fuller, Jr., *The Foe Within: Fantasies of Treason and the End of Imperial Russia* (Ithaca, NY: Cornell University Press, 2006).

spreading of rumors. In some cases it could be said that those responsible for spreading the rumors sincerely believed them. In this way, intimations were taken to be expert appraisal, which was then taken into consideration when making political decisions.

The most improbable rumors united the "upper" and "lower" strata of society: aristocrats and intellectuals occasionally circulated the same rumors as illiterate soldiers and peasants. This created a situation that had a dangerous political resonance: the rumors united representatives of different levels of society—people of varied viewpoints, who all believed that the tsar was an incompetent ruler and that his wife had sympathies with, or even collaborated with, the enemy. These ideas were formulated by people of varied political persuasions, from revolutionaries to monarchists. The rumors played an important integrating role in uniting feuding politicians against the "dark forces"—against the variegated image of an enemy that was in part represented by members of the royal family.

Some researchers believe that these rumors were deliberately fabricated by the tsar's adversaries, by his internal opponents and/or external enemies, and that only later did they spread to popular circles. In some instances this was certainly the case. However, some rumors that proliferated among the "lower strata" of Russian society were radically different from the rumors that spread throughout educated circles; for example, all kinds of rumors circulated among the peasants about the widowed Empress Mariia Fedorovna, but these rumors were encountered very rarely in other sections of society. (In cases where insult had been caused to members of the royal family, it was not uncommon for rumors to circulate about the supposed licentious behavior of the tsar's mother and her betrayal of Russia, while in diaries, letters, and memoirs—sources that speak for the consciousness of educated circles—rumors about Mariia Fedorovna virtually do not exist.) Obviously, the appearance of rumors was frequently a spontaneous reaction of the common people to unexpected provocations of the war era.

Public life after the overthrow of the monarchy in 1917 cannot be conceived without the condition of extreme politicization of culture. This being the case, rumors of the prerevolutionary period formed the basis of stage plays and cinema screenings, cartoons and satirical poems, quasi-historical novels and publications, all of which professed historical accuracy. Many contemporaries spoke indignantly of the "pornography" that gained currency once censorship had been lifted. The erotic images and texts can hardly be described as pornographic; in any case, they are far more modest than the "political pornography" from the days of the French Revolution. It is revealing, however, that they were received as "pornographic." In a number of countries, the war gave rise to a multitude of compositions in which obsession with espionage and eroticism fused with xenophobia and representations of high society. "Political pornography" of the Russian revolutionary era developed this genre (and in some cases this was done by the very same artists and writers).

The collapse of the monarchy gave rise to a completely new political and cultural situation. Not only was it necessary to create new institutions, but a new political rhetoric and new forms of political culture also had to be formulated. The new situation necessitated the creation of new ways of representing political leaders, as well as the reshaping of attitudes towards them. Republican and democratic projects anticipated not only a change in the regime; they also sought to formulate a new political language. The personification of political life—unavoidable in any regime—had to become fundamentally different. Writers and artists participated in the creation of a new political language, together with leading political figures and influential publicists. But many of the ordinary participants in the political process were testing the waters, proposing their own descriptions of the revolutionary leaders and attitudes towards them, accepting or discarding portrayals of the new authorities.

In this context, sacralizing images of the political process and prescriptive types of emotional attitudes towards political leaders were of considerable significance. The language of the monarchy consciously sacralized the head of state, but it also promoted a particular manner in which subjects should relate to their sovereign; not only must he be respected, he must also be loved.

In the context of revolution, many conceptions of monarchical language became taboo. Even the word "state" sometimes appeared suspicious: poorly educated participants in the political process could not imagine the state without the sovereign (*gosudarstvo bez gosudaria*). In the context of revolution, several Romanovs—namesakes of the former tsar—renounced their family name. The name Nikolai also decreased in popularity, although it had been the most popular male Russian name until the collapse of the monarchy.

In the creation of these new political cultural forms, those involved in politics were forced to improvise, drawing upon any symbolic and rhetorical techniques available to them.

One of the first "freedom leaders" was M. V. Rodzianko.[18] The chairman of the Provisional Committee of the State Duma was initially perceived as an important hero of the Revolution; such ideas were particularly widespread in the provinces. Thus, deputies of the Ekaterinoslav Diocesan Conference came to the following decision: "The money previously raised for the construction of a monument in honor of the house of the Romanovs is to be directed towards the building of a 'monument to the liberation of the Russian Orthodox Church from state oppression.'" The central element of the composition was intended to be a statue of Rodzianko.[19] Already in the middle of March, resolutions glorified the "leaders of the revolutionary movement"—Rodzianko, Kerenskii, and

---

[18] A. B. Nikolaev, *Revoliutsiia i vlast': IV Gosudarstvennaia duma 27 fevralia–3 marta 1917 goda* (St. Petersburg: Izd-vo Rossiiskogo gosudarstvennogo pedagogicheskogo universiteta imeni A. I. Gertsena, 2005).

[19] *Russkii invalid* (Petrograd), 8 March 1917.

Chkheidze. Sometimes the list changed: Rodzianko, L'vov, and Kerenskii.[20] However, Rodzianko's popularity was short-lived, the renaming of streets in his honor was a transient phenomenon, and projects for the construction of impressive monuments were not realized. Nevertheless, the various forms of glorification of Rodzianko provide an insight into the immediate reaction to the Revolution of relatively conservative members of the Russian population.

Relatively soon Kerenskii became the most important "leader of the Revolution." In the first Provisional Government he held the position of minister of justice; however, his influence was already significant by March–April 1917. An important contributing factor in the creation of his cult was the rich political culture of the revolutionary underground. A highly important element of this was the cult of the "freedom fighters," which, after February, virtually became the state political cult of new Russia. A fantastic speaker and improviser, the artistic Kerenskii actively developed his own image, assisting in the formation of a revolutionary political culture. His collaborators monitored the press and kept a close watch on how the minister's actions were received by the public. At the same time, various political forces—sometimes at odds with one another—strove to use the authority of the popular politician to their own ends and circulated his texts and images. In the context of the hyperpoliticized first few months of the Revolution, Kerenskii's image also became a profitable brand that attracted commercial interests: people were glad to purchase brochures and portraits of Kerenskii, sculpted busts and insignias bearing his picture.

An important factor in defining the authority of the leader of the Revolution was Kerenskii's prerevolutionary biography: his background and path through life, which were in accordance with the canons of a revolutionary political culture, were supposed to confirm his special status. Not surprisingly, in public addresses the "revolutionary minister" himself referred to his past, while his supporters published a few biographies of the young minister—some of these might be described as "revolutionary hagiographies." In such publications, some episodes of Kerenskii's life were passed over; at the same time, the biographers aimed to strengthen his revolutionary status. In keeping with this, biographies did not, for example, draw attention to the fact that the leader's father had had an impressive administrative career. It was not mentioned that his mother's maiden name was Adler, and that her father had held the rank of a general: against the backdrop of war with Germany and revolution against the monarchy, a background such as this would not help to promote his political career. Meanwhile, the earliest manifestations of opposition—his arrest during the Revolution of 1905, his career as a defense lawyer for alleged political offenders, his fervent speeches in the State Duma

---

[20] *Rabochaia gazeta*, 15 March 1917.

and, finally, his decisive actions in February—were recorded meticulously in Kerenskii biographies.[21]

One is struck by a number of stylistic similarities between several biographies of Kerenskii published in 1917 and the standard Soviet biographies of Lenin. Certain aspects of his childhood point towards the particular mission for which the future leader was destined (it is not surprising that several biographies published photographs from Kerenskii's childhood—the boy on his mother's knees). Both Kerenskii and Lenin were born in Simbirsk, on the Volga, and much was made of this in their biographies. The tradition of popular protest, which was very much alive in folk songs and tales, had an impact upon the personalities of the two future leaders. One should not assume that Soviet writers, when compiling biographies of Lenin, immediately looked to Kerenskii's life history. It would be more accurate to say that they had a common source: the biography of an exemplary "freedom fighter." The canon of this genre was developed within the Russian revolutionary tradition long before 1917.

Kerenskii made use of the revolutionary tradition in other ways. He openly emphasized his friendly relations with E. K. Breshko-Breshkovskaia, a veteran of the liberation movement, whom Socialist-Revolutionary (SR) propaganda called the "grandmother of the Russian Revolution." In the SR Party there was a genuine cult of the "grandmother," and the circulation of propagandist clichés against the backdrop of revolution led to the appearance of new stock phrases; young supporters of the party called themselves the "grandmother's grandchildren." Within this metaphorical framework, Kerenskii was the "favourite grandchild." This was evident both in the concrete political support that Breshko-Breshkovskaia offered Kerenskii and in the transfer of the "freedom fighter" cult onto the young politician. Moreover, at times Kerenskii was included in the pantheon of "freedom fighters." Thus, for example, a series of cards entitled "A Portrait Gallery of Revolutionary Figures" was released by the M. Snopkova SR publishing house. Kerenskii's portrait was included alongside those of various veterans and martyrs of the Populist movement and the SR Party, such as S. V. Balmashov, Breshko-Breshkovskaia, G. A. Gershuni, I. P. Kaliaev, N. K. Mikhailovskii, E. S. Sazonov, and V. N. Figner.[22]

The official role of the minister of justice affected the presentation of the cult of Kerenskii; he was known as "the minister of people's justice." The political amnesty and several other popular measures adopted by all members of the Provisional Government occasionally were attributed to Kerenskii alone. Moreover, he was sometimes regarded as the principal opponent of any prison system. For example, one publishing house released a series of

---

[21] For more information, see B. I. Kolonitskii, "Legitimatsiia cherez zhizneopisanie: Biografiia A. F. Kerenskogo (1917 god)," in *Istoriia i povestvovanie*, ed. G. V. Obatnin and P. Pesonen (Moscow: Novoe literaturnoe obozrenie, 2006), 246–78.

[22] *Delo naroda* (Petrograd), 29 June 1917.

postcards dedicated to various figures in the Provisional Government, in which each minister was shown in front of a scene that symbolized his sphere of activity; Kerenskii was depicted against the background of a burning prison. The significance of this image becomes clear if one takes into account the cultural and political context of the period: during the February Revolution, an array of prison buildings were destroyed and burnt, and many of those involved genuinely believed that in their "new life" there would be no need for prisons and other such institutions.[23] Kerenskii was accredited with initiating the utopian project, of which in reality he was not a proponent. However, in the circumstances, the revolutionary leader himself was in no hurry to refute the popular myth.

Kerenskii was known as the "genius of free Russia," and such a title had several facets. Gifted in political improvisation and sensitive to the mood of an amicable audience, Kerenskii demonstrated substantial creativity. His opponents justifiably called him a "political impressionist," but it was thanks to these qualities that, while contriving new rhetorical manoeuvres and new strategies for self-representation, he keenly perceived the needs of his audience and personally assisted in forming the political style of the period.

The politicization of leisure activities was a feature of public life after February: people who had "woken up" to political life were ready to use their free time and their own money in order to participate in various political and politicized events. This phenomenon was also characteristic of mass culture of that time: the reader and spectator wanted politics, preferably engaging politics, and so writers and artists, theater and cinema directors, publishers and entrepreneurs tried to meet this demand. One of the clearest examples of such a fusion of art and politics were the "rally-concerts," which were particularly popular in spring 1917. Addresses made by influential politicians alternated with choral performances of revolutionary songs; speeches made by veterans of the liberation movement were followed by recitations of poetry. Kerenskii was a real star of these rally-concerts; he transformed his political speeches into entertaining spectacles. In his youth, the future leader had dreamed of a career as an opera singer, and in 1917 he appeared on the stages of the best theaters in Russia. Kerenskii's most famous appearance was his renowned speech in the Moscow Bol'shoi Theater on 26 May. After this speech Kerenskii's adversaries mocked the form of his address; Lenin, for example, called him the "minister of revolutionary theatricality."[24] But at the same time many of Kerenskii's supporters would have regarded this assessment as a compliment to their beloved leader.

---

[23] B. I. Kolonitskii, *Simvoly vlasti i bor'ba za vlast': K izucheniiu politicheskoi kul'tury Rossiiskoi revoliutsii 1917 goda*, 2nd ed. (St. Petersburg: Liki Rossii, 2012), 31–36.

[24] V. I. Lenin, "K s"ezdu Sovetov," in V. I. Lenin, *Polnoe sobranie sochinenii*, 55 vols. (Moscow: Politizdat, 1967–70), 32 (1969): 447.

The minister was regarded as the symbol of new Russia: "the honorable symbol of the honorable February Revolution," or as another observer put it,

> Kerenskii's name has already become an appellation. Kerenskii is a symbol of truth, a guarantee of success; Kerenskii is that lighthouse, that beacon, towards which swimmers, exhausted of all energy, reach out, and from this fire, from his words and invocations, they receive an influx of new strength for the arduous struggle.[25]

Both in propagandist texts and addresses made by various groups, Kerenskii was referred to as "the Sun of freedom," "the Sun of Russia." This letter from a "group of working women" from Tver', composed on 10 March, is revealing:

> Kerenskii's name long ago became dear and beloved in all corners of our motherland. In the darkest ... days of the recent past ... we keenly seized upon any resonances of Kerenskii's words and thoughts ... and now this name, this personality—A. F. Kerenskii—has become the Sun of Russia, the Conscience of free citizens...
>
> We grandmothers, mothers, sisters and daughters, caring Marthas, ask you, brothers, you who are standing nearby—care for his life, care for his time, ensure that he sleeps and eats well, at least, ... so that the strengths of the Sunshine of New Russia do not rupture, ... our regards to the Conscience and Heart of the free citizens of Russia, A. F. Kerenskii...[26]

Already by spring, streets that had previously carried "tsarist names" were being renamed in honor of Kerenskii, and when surnames were being changed in 1917, several people began to choose new ancestral names in honor of the popular politician Kerenskii.[27]

In April, the Ministry of Justice received a telegram from Tomsk province (*guberniia*), addressed to the minister and "Citizen Kerenskii." It said that the popular assembly in the Sergiev-Mikhailovskii *volost'* had resolved unanimously to revoke the name of the *volost'* that had been "given in honor of a grand duke of the hated house of the Romanovs." The Minister was informed that:

---

[25] V. V-vii, *A. F. Kerenskii* (Petrograd, 1917), 3; O. Leonidov, *Vozhd' svobody Kerenskii* (Moscow, 1917), 4.

[26] *Vestnik Tverskogo gubernskogo Ispolnitel'nogo komiteta*, 16 March 1917.

[27] *Izvestiia Petrogradskogo Soveta*, 24 May 1917; Abraham, *Alexander Kerensky*, 202; *Kievlianin*, 3 June 1917; A. M. Verner, "What's in a Name? Of Dog-Killers, Jews and Rasputin," *Slavic Review* 53, 4 (1994): 1070.

the assembly ... has decided to rename the *volost* in your name, that is to say, the name of the greatest citizen of free Russia. It will be a reminder of you, the indefatigable warrior for liberation of the oppressed and the abused, for land and for freedom, which is sacred not only to the citizens of what shall henceforth be called the Kerenskii *volost'*, but also for every citizen of the free Russian Democratic Republic. Our warmest thanks to you, for all that you have done! Here's to the good health of citizen Kerenskii for many years to come![28]

After the April crisis, Kerenskii assumed the role of military and naval minister, in May 1917. He tried to instill discipline in the armed forces on new "democratic" foundations and prepared a frontline offensive; for this he adjusted his rhetoric and representational strategies. Kerenskii encouraged the soldiers of the Russian army to follow the example of the revolutionaries, soldered together by an "iron discipline." The minister militarized his own image and dressed in a khaki uniform without any distinguishing features. In this way he simultaneously created for himself the image of both a military and a democratic leader. The new tone of the leader's speeches was in keeping with his constant call to create an "iron discipline"; his contemporaries could discern "steel notes" in his speeches.

This image attracted a sizeable number of supporters and the military minister began to be perceived as a unique type of leader and savior, a Leader with a capital "L." Kerenskii's special status was discernible in many speeches: the minister's supporters assured him that "only he" could save Russia now. The appeals from a series of prominent representatives of the artistic intelligentsia are revealing: their texts resemble the eulogistic appeals addressed to Soviet leaders in the 1930s.

Kerenskii's political style also became popular. Several members of various committees began to dress in paramilitary field jackets and copied the rhetoric of the "revolutionary minister," delivering speeches "à la Kerenskii." D. A. Furmanov, who subsequently became the stereotypical image of the Bolshevik commissar, was no exception (noted in Furmanov's diary on 29 May 1917).[29] The leader of the Ukrainian national movement, S. V. Petliura, was described in the following manner: "From the outside he is a genuine replica of Kerenskii: clean-shaven, a field jacket, sometimes abrupt movements."[30]

But the call to "iron discipline" resulted, for the first time, in serious political attacks on Kerenskii from left-wing socialists. Until May, Lenin and

---

[28] Rossiiskii gosudarstvennyi istoricheskii arkhiv (RGIA) f. 1405, op. 538, d. 177, ll. 49–50.

[29] P. V. Kupriianovskii, *Neizvestnyi Furmanov* (Ivanovo: Ivanovskii gosudarstvennyi universitet, 1996), 61.

[30] Cited in V. P. Buldakov, "Krizis imperii i revoliutsionnyi natsionalizm XX veka," *Voprosy istorii*, no. 1 (2000): 38.

other Bolsheviks refrained from directing open criticism at Kerenskii: not for nothing did they fear the reaction of the Russian soldiers, who were prepared to use force to protect their idol.[31] However, his attempts to discipline the army and his continued preparations for a frontline offensive resulted in a number of soldiers altering their attitudes towards the socialist head of the War Ministry. Bolshevik propagandists, sensing a favorable atmosphere, began a campaign directed personally against Kerenskii and his "penal injunctions."

This campaign was not unsuccessful. Herein could be seen the polarization of political life, which had pushed the idea of "nationwide unification" into the past, an idea which had been so popular after February. But it was precisely this polarization that resulted in Kerenskii simultaneously gaining new supporters: if, for the opponents of "iron discipline," he had come to personify the revival of the "old regime," for many patriots he fulfilled the role of savior of the state. Talk of "Napoleon," "Bonaparte," and "Bonapartism," widespread at the time, is revealing. Some regarded Kerenskii as the "grave-digger of the Revolution," while others dreamed about the appearance of a formidable and belligerent national leader who would overcome the crisis. Not all of Kerenskii's supporters considered it important or possible to compare him with Napoleon, but many genuinely regarded him as a unique leader-cum-savior.

The June offensive—the "Kerenskii offensive"—initially boosted the minister's popularity. It is revealing that demonstrators who welcomed the offensive in various cities across Russia used a similar political language. They glorified Kerenskii and carried his picture with them. Still more interesting is the fact that the portrait of the army leader was attached to both the red and tricolor national flags.[32] For a time Kerenskii's image served to unite a number of moderate socialists, several liberals, and even groups of nationalists.

The failure of the offensive might have had a severe impact on Kerenskii's popularity, but this did not happen: the July crisis fundamentally altered the country's political situation, and the attack on authority undertaken by the Bolsheviks and their allies was repulsed. Kerenskii and his supporters attributed the failure of the frontline military operation to internal enemies—first and foremost to the Bolsheviks, who had made a stand against the government. At the same time, the success in suppressing Bolshevik activity was attributed primarily to Kerenskii.

---

[31] Even Lenin, after his arrival in Russia, refrained from openly criticizing Kerenskii. However, he made use of images from 1848 to describe the situation in Russia, and readers of Marx were able to discern a number of hidden critical messages. See B. I. Kolonitskii, "A. F. Kerenskii kak Lui Blan [Louis Blanc]: Obraz 'revoliutsionnogo ministra' v propagande bol'shevikov (March–April 1917)," in *Con amore: Istoriko-filologicheskii sbornik v chest' Liubovi Nikolaevny Kiselevoi* (Moscow: OGI, 2010), 231–42.

[32] P. K. Kornakov, "1917 god v otrazhenii veksillologicheskikh istochnikov (Po materialam Petrograda i deistvuiushchei armii)" (Candidate diss., Leningradkii gosudarstvennyi universitet, 1989), 173.

In July 1917, Kerenskii was the leader of the Provisional Government, and he made the Winter Palace his residence. Many of his supporters continued to regard him as a unique leader-savior, and depictions of him were sometimes taken to be symbols of new Russia. Thus, those who had paid significant sums of money to acquire Liberty Loan bonds (not less than 25,000 rubles) became the recipients of small busts of Kerenskii.[33]

Kerenskii, the "minister-cum-democrat," was referred to as the "symbol of democracy": "For us Kerenskii is not a minister, neither is he an orator for the people, he has ceased to be a simple human being. Kerenskii is a symbol of revolution," wrote his admirers, subjectively considering themselves disciples of democracy—such was the content of a pamphlet published in 1917.[34]

At the same time, Kerenskii's monopoly as a national leader was contested by other political forces, and several of his supporters did not regard him as a universally acknowledged leader. After February Kerenskii declared his membership of the SR Party. Several SR leaders used Kerenskii's popularity; however, at the elections for the Central Committee of the SR Party at the June 1917 congress, Kerenskii did not receive the required number of votes. This was evidence of the schism that was occurring in the party: if the right-wing SRs supported Kerenskii unconditionally, the left-wingers openly criticized him. This was a consequence of political differences, and a reaction to the cult of the "revolutionary leader": the old SR leaders were not ready to regard Kerenskii, the "March SR" (i.e., someone who had joined the party after the February Revolution), as the country's unique leader-savior. The deepening schism within the SR Party was linked not only to political differences, but also to attitudes towards various cultural traditions.

On the other hand, the status of the unique leader-savior was questioned by other forces as well. The number of people in the country who were prepared to seek salvation in military dictatorship was multiplying. Initially the preferred candidate for the role of dictator was Admiral A. V. Kolchak, commander of the Black Sea Fleet, but later the popularity of General L. G. Kornilov, who had become commander in chief in July 1917, began to increase.

It is impossible not to observe that both Kolchak and Kornilov could have become political figures on a national scale by virtue of the fact that both skilfully adapted to the new political environment and actively made use of revolutionary symbolism and rhetoric. Kolchak, for example, while commander of the Black Sea Fleet, appealed to the revolutionary tradition of the fleet as he strove to strengthen discipline among its sailors. It is not surprising that he contributed to the development of the cult of Lieutenant Shmidt, the

---

[33] *Birzhevoi kur'er*, 28 July 1917; E. Iu. Smirnova, "Iazyk revoliutsii v finansovykh periodicheskikh izdaniiakh," 5 (typescript). I am grateful to E. Iu. Smirnova for communicating this information to me.

[34] Gosudarstvennyi muzei politicheskoi istorii Rossii (St. Petersburg) f. 2, no. 10964. See also A. Kulegin and V. Bobrov, "Istoriia bez kupliur," *Sovetskie muzei*, no. 3 (28 July 1990): 5–6.

hero of the 1905 Revolution, and several of the admiral's supporters even referred to him as the "perpetuator of Shmidt's work."[35] Kornilov's supporters lauded him as a "democrat," the "first people's commander in chief," while the creators of the Kornilov Shock Regiment, named in honor of the general, used revolutionary symbolism when forming this elite unit.

The rivalry between Kerenskii and Kornilov was a rivalry between two unique leader-saviors. Of course, the conflict between the head of the Provisional Government and the commander in chief had many causes. The cultural images used for the glorification of the two leaders, however, had considerable political significance: a compromise between the two "unique leader-saviors" was difficult, as their active supporters would not have expected such steps from either Kerenskii or Kornilov. In a sense, the general and the "revolutionary minister" were both hostage to their image.

The political defeat of the commander in chief as a result of the "Kornilov affair," which culminated in the general's arrest, was not a political victory for Kerenskii. His opponents "on the right" became his self-confessed enemies, while at the same time the Bolsheviks and other left-wing socialists strengthened their position, increasingly launching personal attacks against Kerenskii. At the same time, the "revolutionary minister" lost support among groups in the center and left-of-center who previously had supported him. It is revealing that the parties which formed the last coalition of the Provisional Government did not include their prominent leaders. Their support was ever more conditional; if the Kadets criticized Kerenskii "from the right," then "from the left" he was attacked by prominent Mensheviks and SRs.

It marked a change in the general political situation. Kerenskii, who was not the leader of a major party, previously personified a compromise that both liberals and moderate socialists strove for. In these circumstances, "supra-partisanship" and ideological ambiguity constituted a peculiar kind of political trump card. In the context of political polarization, however, Kerenskii's position obviously was weakened.

The political isolation of Kerenskii occurred with the help of well-defined images that exerted a certain influence on political developments. This sometimes involved recoding images that were already established and widely distributed. And so the unique leader-savior was transformed into the principal and only culprit of a deepening crisis. This attitude towards the head of the Provisional Government united people of diverse political viewpoints, from right and left, but it was also common among several of Kerenskii's former supporters. The writer Z. N. Gippius, for instance, who in spring 1917 believed that "only Kerenskii" could save Russia, claimed by autumn that "he alone" was guilty in the developing catastrophe. People of varied political persuasions, particularly those who had become disillusioned with Kerenskii, accordingly referred to him as a "phony leader." They used various images to

---

[35] See B. I. Kolonitskii, "Pamiat' o pervoi rossiiskoi revoliutsii v 1917 godu: Sluchai Sevastopolia i Gel'singforsa," *Cahiers du monde russe* 48, 2/3 (2007): 519–37.

construct the "phony leader"; some of these were reproduced only by clearly-defined political forces, while others were shared by people of diverse political positions.

Political actors with differing viewpoints often referred to Kerenskii as a "traitor." Supporters of Kornilov accused the head of the Provisional Government of betraying the general, after having cunningly violated the agreement with the commander in chief. Lenin and his supporters declared that Kerenskii was a traitor to the Revolution who was prepared to hand over revolutionary Petrograd to the Germans (it was sometimes asserted that this was part of an international plan that concealed an agreement between the British and German imperialists). Rumors of this sort were evident in popular culture. The text of this *chastushka* (folk poem) is revealing:

On the table stands a bowl,
Full of grapes ready to pick,
Kerenskii sold off Petrograd,
After Russia was sold by Nic.[36]

The far right openly declared that the head of the Provisional Government was acting in the interests of anti-Russian forces. The image of "Kerenskii the traitor" was present in all kinds of conspiracy theories. Finally, many former supporters of Kerenskii also believed that the "revolutionary minister" had "betrayed" their expectations.

Various images helped to confirm the "traitor's" reputation; in this process, several images of the "revolutionary leader" were turned on their heads. Thus, the image of the "poet of the Revolution" who prophesied on theater stages acquired another meaning: a person who is forever wearing different masks is constantly altering his political role, and this does not inspire trust. Kerenskii the "actor" was condemned from both left and right: if the leader's artistry had served earlier as persuasive evidence of his political creativity, by autumn 1917 it had become a sign of so much flexibility as to suggest the absence of a clear political position.

Adherents of various political views emasculated Kerenskii and deprived him of his manliness. This was demonstrated most clearly in the feminization of the "revolutionary leader's" image. Aleksandr Fedorovich Kerenskii became known as "Aleksandra Fedorovna," a reference to images of the last empress and qualities attributed to her: debauchery and betrayal. Gippius, in autumn 1917, referred to her former friend as a "petticoat revolutionary."[37] G. V. Plekhanov was accredited with the following characterization of Keren-

---

[36] "Na stole stoit tarelka, / A v tarelke vinograd, / Nikolai prodal Rossiiu, / A Kerenskii—Petrograd." V. Bilyi, "Koroten'ky pisni ('chastushky') rokiv 1917–1925," *Etnografichnyi visnyk*, bk. 1 (Kyiv, 1925), 30.

[37] Otdel rukopisei Rossiiskoi Natsional'noi biblioteki f. 481, op. 1, d. 3, ll. 272, 275. In the printed version, the description is attenuated: "a feminine revolutionary." Z. N.

skii: the "Sarah Bernhardt from Tsarevokokshaisk."[38] By the same token the founder of Russian Marxism identified three commonly acknowledged characteristics of Kerenskii: his capacity for acting, his femininity, and his provincialism.

Kerenskii's "femininity" subsequently surfaced in a popular rumor that circulated in 1917: he was reputed to have fled the Winter Palace dressed in a nurse's uniform (this unlikely rumor, which was widely circulated in Soviet culture, was first recorded in right-wing circles). One is compelled to recall, in this connection, the context that influenced the reception of Empress Aleksandra Fedorovna's image: the sister of mercy as a symbol of corruption and debauchery.

In right-wing circles, people increasingly talked about Kerenskii's Jewish background. For Russian monarchists, "the Jew," living in tsarist repose, was the most salient personification of the "phony leader." If several conservatives previously referred to Kerenskii as "Pozharskii" or "Minin," by autumn 1917 he was increasingly known as "False Dmitrii," the usurper. Hatred directed towards the head of the Provisional Government in right-wing circles was so great that the Petrograd newspaper *Groza*, which in contrast to other Black Hundred publications survived the February Revolution, even welcomed the "Yid" Kerenskii's fall from grace.[39]

The characterization of Kerenskii as a Napoleonic figure acquired new significance. Increasingly he was described as a phony Napoleon, a politician who was trying to play the role of Napoleon while lacking the necessary political and personal qualities (his reputation as an "actor" reinforced this). Trotskii gave Kerenskii no credit for his independent political role; he referred to him as a political function, calling him the "mathematical center of Russian Bonapartism." The demeaning of Kerenskii's image was also treated in Trotskii's article "Bonapartists."

Negative images of Kerenskii, which were circulated by both left- and right-wingers and which functioned in both "high" and "low" culture, are critical to our understanding of the situation in October. Across the country many people were dissatisfied with the activities of the Bolsheviks and their allies, but virtually no one was prepared to defend Kerenskii, who personified

---

Gippius, *Siniaia kniga: Peterburgskii dnevnik, 1914–1918* (Belgrade: Russkaia biblioteka, 1929), 231.

[38] R. B. Gul', *Ia unes Rossiiu: Apologiia emigratsii*, 2: *Rossiia vo Frantsii* (Moscow: B. S. G. Press, 2001), 96. Compare with the descriptions of Kerenskii in Plekhanov's newspaper: V. I. Startsev, *Krakh kerenshchiny* (Leningrad: Nauka, Leningradskoe otdelenie, 1982), 145–46.

[39] For more information, see B. I. Kolonitskii, "Aleksandr Fedorovich Kerenskii kak 'zhertva evreev' i 'evrei,'" in *Jews and Slavs*, 17: *The Russian Word in the Land of Israel, the Jewish Word in Russia* (Jerusalem: Hebrew University of Jerusalem, Center for Slavic Languages and Literatures, 2006), 241–53.

the power of the Provisional Government. Even among the troops that he had initially managed to assemble, Kerenskii was not very popular. Circulated images of the head of the Provisional Government are very important for our understanding of the initial stages of the Civil War. The politician who had personified the idea of domestic political compromise was used by opposing sides as a negative image for the structuring of their identities. In this way, the ideology of the White movement, which was ambiguous in its early stages, proposed first and foremost the disavowal of "Kerenskii politics." At the same time, Bolshevik propaganda labeled their opponents "Kornilovtsy" and "Kerentsy" (supporters of Kornilov and Kerenskii).

By June 1917 the opposition between "Lenintsy" and "Kerentsy" (supporters of Lenin and Kerenskii) could already be observed in various conflicts. The names of these leaders were sometimes signs of self-identification, but at other times they were pejorative labels used by political opponents. This latter circumstance is very important for understanding the early stages of the Lenin cult. The terms "Leninstvo" (Leninism) and "Lenintsy" were used very widely by opponents of the Bolshevik Party. Support for the leader's authority within the Bolshevik Party had earlier led to the creation of a distinctive cult, and other Social Democrats called Lenin's supporters "Lenintsy." This term had been used by police officers when classifying trends in the Russian Social Democratic Workers' Party. But these terms were injected with new life in 1917.

These terms had negative connotations and were also applied to those political and public movements and figures, who, at the time, were in no way supporters of Lenin. Thus, for example, the language of the Revolution was widely used during conflicts within the Russian Orthodox Church. If those who favored radical reform of the church referred to their opponents as "Rasputintsy" (supporters of Rasputin), the "dark forces" and the "bourgeois," conservatives used the concepts of "Church Bolshevism" and even "Church Leninstvo" (Church Leninism).[40] Plekhanov, who in 1917 stood on the defensive, used the term "poluleninstvo" (semi-Leninism) in order to describe the position of the leading centers of Mensheviks and SRs.[41]

"Lenin," "Leninstvo," "Lenintsy"—these words were used widely by various opponents of the Bolshevik Party when describing the most diverse conflicts. Moreover, excessive use of such terms encouraged discussions about Lenin, which furthered the fame of the best-known Bolshevik. Already by mid-April, the SR leader V. M. Chernov made this point: "I think that Lenin can only thank his enemies for their zeal. I think that it is in Lenin's chief in-

---

[40] P. G. Rogoznyi, "'Tserkovnyi Bolshevizm': K izucheniiu iazyka bor'by za vlast' v Rossiiskoi Pravoslavnoi Tserkvi (aprel' 1917–mart 1918 g.)," in *Politicheskaia istoriia Rossii pervoi chetverti 20 veka: Pamiati professora V. I. Startseva* (St. Petersburg: D.A.R.K., 2006), 329–40.

[41] *Edinstvo*, 7 July 1917.

terests to make himself into a 'bugbear' for the bourgeoisie, to dominate their imagination." But his party newspaper also wrote about "Lenintsy"...[42]

Meanwhile, several supporters of the Bolshevik Party at the time were not at all content with the proposed self-appellation. "We are not Lenintsy," declared several participants in the demonstrations organized by the party at the time of the April crisis and June demonstration. Some turned it into a joke: "I'm a Smolenskii." It is revealing that this information was also printed in *Pravda*: it is possible that certain activists were unenthusiastic about this personification of the party line.[43] One can confidently suggest that those members of the *Pravda* editorial office who sanctioned a publication of this sort were not anxious to use the term "Lenintsy" in order to denote party members. There could be a number of reasons for this. Firstly, Lenin's ideas initially seemed excessively radical even to some members of the Bolshevik leadership. They did not want to be "Lenin's supporters," let alone "Lenintsy." Secondly, certain members of the Bolshevik ranks who had joined the party after February were convinced, at times, by the arguments of "anti-Lenin" propaganda. In May, several of these activists even sympathized with Kerenskii. Thirdly, many socialists deemed the very idea of a leader cult and personifications of the party line to be unacceptable (it is revealing that even Lenin himself at times shied away from this concept). Moreover, several old Social Democrats who had joined the Bolshevik Party in 1917 had a history of serious conflict with Lenin and were not prepared to identify themselves with the "leader."

In these circumstances it was precisely the personification of propagandist attacks against the Bolsheviks from Lenin's political opponents that furthered his renown: everyone in the country found out about "Lenintsy," although they sometimes understood the term in different ways.

Propagandist attacks from opponents provoked reactions: already during the April crisis protesters accused of "Leninstvo" began, by way of response, to proclaim the slogan "Long live Comrade Lenin!" and hold up corresponding posters.[44] The Bolshevik Party press soon came definitively to Lenin's defense. This was manifested in the publication of his first biographies in the Bolshevik press, for example in the Moscow newspaper *Sotsial-demokrat*, which on 26 May printed an article by M. Ol'minskii, and in the Petrograd newspaper *Soldatskaia Pravda*, in which an article appeared on 13 May by N. K. Krupskaia (corrected by Lenin himself). These publications constituted a distinctive reaction to the propagandist attacks of Lenin's political opponents.

After the April conference, Lenin's position in the party became considerably stronger. At the same time attacks on Lenin became dangerous for the

---

[42] V. Chernov, "Lenin," *Delo naroda* (Petrograd), 16 April 1917.

[43] "Aprel'skie dni 1917 goda v Petrograde," ed. P. Stulov, in *Krasnyi arkhiv* 2 (33) (1929): 39, 56; *Pravda*, 28 May, 20 June 1917.

[44] "Aprel'skie dni 1917 goda v Petrograde," 56, 73.

party. Its leadership and activists were compelled to defend Lenin; at times the identity of "Lenintsy" was simply imposed by his political opponents, who forced all Bolsheviks to identify with Lenin. Finally, some members of the party leadership had their own particular reasons for glorifying Lenin and furthering his popularization among the masses.

The activity of G. E. Zinov'ev in this period has been poorly investigated and insufficiently appraised. Nonetheless, the merit for devising several successful slogans of Bolshevik propaganda can be attributed chiefly to him. *Pravda* printed several resolutions that lauded, first and foremost, Lenin and Zinov'ev. It could be said that Zinov'ev, more than anyone else, contributed to the creation of Lenin's positive image, while simultaneously strengthening his own position in the party. Subsequently, his slogans were reproduced at the periphery. Bolsheviks of the Twelfth Chemical Detachment, for instance, wrote in *Okopnaia Pravda*: "Long live our valiant leaders of the Russian people, comrades Lenin and Zinov'ev."[45] The fact that Zinov'ev went into hiding with Lenin after the July Days gave him an aura of "party martyr" and created for him the symbolic position of someone close to the first party leader. Thus, on 3 October 1917 a group of soldiers from the Kyshtym factory sent their greetings to the "leaders of the proletariat," Lenin, Zinov'ev, and the Central Committee of the Party.[46] However, Zinov'ev was unable to control the structure of the Bolshevik Party's "pantheon of leaders" and the hierarchy within it. And in this case, propagandist attacks from opponents and political repression furthered the popularity of other party leaders. Thus, Trotskii's arrest in July 1917 triggered waves of resolutions in his support.

At the same time, Lenin made use of his very particular status within the party. The activity of the Bolsheviks' book-publishing industry in 1917 corroborates Lenin's exceptional place among Bolshevik leaders. He was a very popular author. It is also revealing that the party's provincial publishing houses, which often issued Lenin's works, almost never printed the works of other leaders. This distinguished them from Bolshevik publishing houses in Petrograd and Moscow that printed brochures by Zinov'ev, Kamenev, and Trotskii. For provincial Bolsheviks, it was Lenin who personified the party.

After coming to power the Bolsheviks immediately started using state resources for their own ends, yet quite some time elapsed before the images of leaders began to play a significant role (in this respect the cult of Kerenskii in 1917 developed far more quickly, although the process of its creation was not centralized). It is true that as early as May 1918 several sections of the Red Army were already named in his honor. The situation altered substantially after the attempt on Lenin's life on 30 August 1918. Brochures dedicated to

---

[45] *Okopnaia pravda*, 18 June 1917.

[46] *Rabochii put'*, 18 October 1917. Nina Tumarkin hints at the particular role of Zinov'ev in the glorification of Lenin, but she looks at a later period. N. Tumarkin, *Lenin zhiv! Kul't Lenina v Sovetskoi Rossii* (St. Petersburg: Akademicheskii proekt, 1997), 74.

the Bolshevik leader were printed in vast quantities. Already in 1919, sculpted busts of Lenin were bound for dozens of towns and were erected with great ceremony. Various institutions, streets, and settlements were named in honor of Lenin—by 1919 the town "Leninsk" had appeared.[47]

It is interesting to note, however, that depictions of Lenin on Bolshevik propaganda posters initially used the genre of harmless caricature, although his official portraits were already widely used. This is also true of several posters by M. M. Cheremnykh (1919) and of the renowned poster by V. N. Deni, "Comrade Lenin cleanses the earth of filth" (1920). In addition, during the Civil War the image of the leader was used in posters relatively infrequently.[48]

A genuine cult of Trotskii emerged during the Civil War (the small town of Trotsk had already appeared by 1919, and a village was renamed in his honor as early as 1918).[49] His popularity among the Reds was aided in no small measure by his enemies: it was Trotskii—sometimes depicted as a sinister cosmopolitan Jew, sometimes as the devil, sometimes as a bloodthirsty subhuman—who became for them an important personification of Bolshevism (Lenin appeared less frequently on White propaganda posters, sometimes alongside Trotskii). At the same time, in Red propaganda Trotskii was depicted as a socialist Saint George, slaying the dragon of capitalism (the corresponding illustration by Deni appeared on a Soviet calendar). Propagandists of the Red Army, led by Trotskii, played a significant role in this.[50] And, in the given context, the poster-cartoon was the first step towards the creation of a poster iconography of the leader; one might suppose that Bolshevik propagandists deliberately painted images of their leaders with friendly irony, anticipating reproaches about the creation of the leader cult.

Lenin and Trotskii became the most important Bolshevik leaders. In his memoirs, Trotskii repeatedly—and not without pride—mentioned that his portrait hung everywhere next to Lenin's (his testimony is confirmed by other sources; on several postcards of that period we can see rooms adorned with portraits of Lenin and Trotskii). The assertion of the memoirist itself testifies to the fact that the leader cult in Bolshevik political culture was already an important and constant element. Trotskii wrote—not without reason—that the two names often went together in conversation, in articles, in poetry, and

---

[47] Tumarkin, *Lenin zhiv!*, 80–92; B. B. Ennker, *Formirovanie kul'ta Lenina v Sovetskom Soiuze* (Moscow: ROSSPEN, 2011), 51–54; Velikanova, *Obraz Lenina*, 166, 192–93.

[48] Stephen White, *The Bolshevik Poster* (New Haven: Yale University Press, 1988), 24, 25, 69; Victoria E. Bonnell, *Iconography of Power: Soviet Political Posters under Lenin and Stalin* (Berkeley: University of California Press, 1997), 141–42, 146.

[49] Velikanova, *Obraz Lenina*, 193.

[50] David King, *Trotsky: A Photographic Biography* (Oxford: Blackwell, 1986), 110, 111, 121; White, *Bolshevik Poster*, 7.

in *chastushki*.[51] In 1921, the Menshevik leader L. Martov wrote that in Soviet Russia "authentic Bolshevik fanaticism" and adoration of Lenin and Trotskii were widespread phenomena. This fanaticism went hand in hand with "hysterical hatred" of their opponents.[52]

There were even rumors that the peasants spoke of a new tsar called Lenintrotskii, who wished to revive Holy Russia. At times the two Bolshevik leaders stood in opposition to one another; participants in several uprisings and protests placed "bad" Trotskii against "good" Lenin.[53] But reverse scenarios also occurred.

Moreover, the list of Bolshevik leaders was not restricted to Lenin and Trotskii. Streets and establishments were also named in honor of other leaders. This list of the most important leaders could be different in different contexts, and the hierarchical composition within this group could vary, but Lenin and Trotskii were always present. And Lenin occupied a special position; local political leaders were sometimes "measured against Lenin." It is revealing that F. Khodzhaev was called the "Lenin of Bukhara" and I. Smirnov—the organizer of the anti-Kolchak guerrilla movement—was known as the "Siberian Lenin." Lenin's name was used especially frequently in the development of "revolutionary" Russian names; Trotskii's name followed closely behind. Sometimes the names of important leaders were combined: Trolen (Trotskii, Lenin), Malentro (Marx, Lenin, Trotskii). Some Armenian boys were given the name Lentrosh (Lenin, Trotskii, Shaumian).[54]

The development of a leader cult was also evident in the mass consumerism of the early Soviet period: rings and medallions bearing Lenin's portrait appeared, and all kinds of goods were decorated with his picture—cigarette packets, cups, and even baked goods.[55] Women were offered shawls that bore the portraits of the five most important leaders (Trotskii, of course, was subsequently removed from these). At the same time the immoderate commercialization of the leaders' images was subject to criticism (kitsch testified to popularity but undermined their sanctity); their circulation was subject to control, in order to correspond with established canons. This was very much

---

[51] L. D. Trotskii, *Moia zhizn': Opyt avtobiografii* (Moscow: Kniga, 1990), 2: 239, 250; *Kollektsiia pochtovykh kartochek sovetskogo perioda s 1917 po 1945 god iz kollektsii M. Voronina: Katalog* (St. Petersburg: Welcome, 2009), 1: 209, 210.

[52] Gregor Aronson, ed., *Martov i ego blizkie* (New York, 1959), 53.

[53] Tumarkin, *Lenin zhiv!*, 102–04.

[54] B. Kolonitskii, "'Revolutionary Names': Russian Personal Names and Political Consciousness in the 1920s and 1930s" (trans. S. Smith), *Revolutionary Russia* 6, 2 (1993): 210–28.

[55] Tumarkin, *Lenin zhiv!*, 187; Ennker, *Formirovanie kul'ta Lenina*, 318–20; Velikanova, *Obraz Lenina*, 170–71.

reminiscent of the censorship imposed by the Ministry of the Imperial Court in prerevolutionary Russia.

CO ɞ

The essentially new political situation that arose during the Great War and revolutionary period called for new forms of political personification. Leader cults of the Soviet period are frequently connected, in historiography, with longstanding and deep-rooted state and/or religious traditions (of particular note is the work of N. Tumarkin). Some works of historians and political scientists convey a distinctive kind of cultural determinism: Russia, they suggest, is doomed to have an authoritarian form of government that gives rise to leader cults or their imitations.

It appears, however, that the development of Soviet political culture was heavily influenced by the experience of the Great War and particularly the February Revolution. The various forms of the cult of the military leader—the leader of the Revolution, the "leader of democracy"—that appeared had a notable impact upon the cults of Soviet leaders. Kerenskii struggled with the Soviet regime all his life, but nonetheless he can be regarded as one of the unacknowledged inventors of the Soviet political tradition. Trotskii spoke of Kerenskii with disdain, but this did not prevent him from using some elements of the "revolutionary minister's" strategies for self-representation.

It is important to consider the aggregate of emotions with respect to the political leader, which are attributed to different political regimes. The requirement of political supervision over statesmen, which corresponds to the republican form of government, does not sit easily with the monarchical requirement of adoration for the head of state. Incidentally, a number of participants in the antimonarchical revolution, who considered themselves democrats, sensed the need to love their political elect. It is not surprising that Kerenskii was called the "first love of the Revolution." The need to love one's leader also developed in Soviet political culture.

All the same, the Russian Revolution's "first love" was neither its most important nor its last love. The word "love" (love of the party, love of one's leaders) was used often in Soviet political language. One should not assume that the requirement to love the leader found no echo with the Russian people. It is revealing that in the 1920s, 1930s, and 1940s the name Vladimir was the most popular name given to boys. Specialists in the study of names attribute this to the development of the Lenin cult. As might be expected, in 1924 (the year of Lenin's death) there was a sharp rise in the popularity of this name.[56]

One can identify several elements that were used consistently in this watershed period in the formation of leader cults—"sovereign leaders," "supreme leaders," and "revolutionary leaders." These cults are often military

---

[56] Kolonitskii, "'Revolutionary Names.'"

and always militaristic; their legitimacy is founded upon battles and victories. An absence of victories is sometimes compensated by developing images of the leader's cunning counterparts who personify the image of the enemy: through their cunning behavior they steal victory from the leader. In these circumstances, suppression of the enemy constitutes victory. The language used to legitimize the leader changed substantially after the Revolution (and here the period of the Kerenskii cult was extremely important), yet the language of delegitimization retained its component parts: xenophobia and the emasculation of political leaders, who lay claim to the status of supreme leader. Anti-German sentiment and anti-Semitism were the most widely used forms of xenophobia, and the act of symbolically depriving leaders of their intrinsic masculinity was manifested in images of the "weak ruler" (Nicholas II) and direct feminization (Kerenskii). Various political and cultural ideological forms were superimposed upon the structures of authoritarian and patriarchal consciousness.

Translated by Diana Statham

Circulation and Production of News and Rumor in Rural Russia during World War I

Corinne Gaudin

> The Austrian is in Izhor—the Turk on the White Sea!
> Don't babble such nonsense—Smoke *Solomkoi* [cigarettes].[1]

This ditty, like many others composed as part of the Shapashnikov tobacco company's wartime advertisement campaign—implying that their cigarettes would inure the smoker to alarmist rumors—displayed a humor quite atypical of the times. Journalists and rural activists, police and administrators hardly deemed rumors in time of war to be a laughing matter, even less so when they circulated through Russia's hinterland. For the former, uneducated peasants' predilection to spin "popular fantasies" was patent proof of the urgent need to intensify enlightenment work in the village. For authorities, rumors were even more alarming, the work of revolutionary or enemy agitators who exploited the low cultural level of the population in order to sow anxiety and discord. Yet, rural Russia during World War I was not unusual in the propensity of its inhabitants to pass on fanciful information. Russia's highly educated ministers, intellectuals, and journalists were no less actively circulating fantastic stories of court shenanigans and high-level treason.[2] It was neither lack of information, nor the unique gullibility of a population on the margins of literacy that begot rumors, but the war itself. Germany, Britain, France, and Austria were each awash with their own stories about fifth columnists, the arrival of improbable allies, or the sinister motives of privileged superiors bent on extending the war for profit.[3] What most analysts at the time failed to recognize was that rural Russians were integrated in overlapping official

---

[1] "Ne zapugaiut! (Vzdornye slukhi)," advertisement in *Rech'*, 1 January 1916, 4.

[2] B. I. Kolonitskii, "*Tragicheskaia erotika*": *Obrazy imperatorskoi sem'i v gody Pervoi mirovoi voiny* (Moscow: Novoe literaturnoe obozrenie, 2010); William Fuller, Jr., *The Foe Within: Fantasies of Treason and the End of Imperial Russia* (Ithaca, NY: Cornell University Press, 2006).

[3] Adrian Gregory, *The Last Great War: British Society and the First World War* (Cambridge: Cambridge University Press, 2008); Maureen Healy, *Vienna and the Fall of the Habsburg Empire: Total War and Everyday Life in World War I* (Cambridge: Cambridge University

and unofficial information networks fed as much by printed news and official communiqués as by oral rumor.

The war confronted peasants with an unprecedented amount of information coming from outside, information that they avidly absorbed and used. Villagers exhibited an ostensibly insatiable appetite for news from the war: observers throughout the countryside described assailed press kiosks, and crowds at every arrival of mail. Exchange of war news became part of village sociability, as any chance meeting began with ritual exchange of bits gleaned from readings and conversations. Hubs of information exchange proliferated, as people gathered periodically at mobilization centers, for livestock requisitions, at overcrowded railway stations, and at taverns that subscribed to newspapers. Soldiers on leave were questioned by their compatriots, and POWs traveling through rural districts attracted groups of curious onlookers.

Despite growing recognition that the war brought an unprecedented intrusion of the outside world into the village, it remains unclear how the widespread gathering and recycling of information transformed the ways in which villagers positioned themselves in society. On the one hand, a growing number of recent studies have convincingly shown peasants mobilizing national arguments when they appealed the fairness of draft laws and taxes, or reached out to demand services.[4] Other studies, on the contrary, depict a peasantry—and a peasant soldiery—interpreting the war through a fatalistic and religious lens, largely locked in local concerns over land and agriculture.[5] This view has been bolstered by research suggesting that ineffective propaganda never found the language to reach villagers who remained indifferent until the burdens of mobilization awakened anti-war

---

Press, 2004); Jeffrey Verhey, *The Spirit Of 1914: Militarism, Myth and Mobilization in Germany* (Cambridge: Cambridge University Press, 2000).

[4] See especially Scott Seregny, "Zemstvos, Peasants, and Citizenship: The Russian Adult Education Movement and World War I," *Slavic Review* 59, 2 (2000): 290–315; Joshua Sanborn, *Drafting the Russian Nation: Military Conscription, Total War, and Mass Politics, 1905–1925* (DeKalb: Northern Illinois University Press, 2003); Aaron Retish, *Russia's Peasants in Revolution and Civil War: Citizenship, Identity, and the Creation of the Soviet State, 1914–1922* (Cambridge: Cambridge University Press, 2008), 22–63.

[5] O. S. Porshneva, *Krest'iane, rabochie i soldaty Rossii nakanune i v gody pervoi mirovoi voiny* (Moscow: ROSSPEN, 2004); Leonid Heretz, *Russia on the Eve of Modernity: Popular Religion and Traditional Culture under the Last Tsars* (Cambridge: Cambridge University Press, 2008), 191–233; A. V. Astashev, "Russkii krest'ianin na frontakh pervoi mirovoi voiny," *Otechestvennaia istoriia*, no. 2 (2003): 72–86. Some of the behaviors presented in these works as being characteristic of a fatalistic, tradition-bound Russian peasant are hardly exceptional. Miraculous apparitions and other religious rumors also emerged on the Western front, and concern for the state of their farms was as much a common theme in the letters of French and German soldiers.

sentiment.[6] General Anton Denikin's famous phrase that the peasant recruit defined himself not as Russian, but as "from Tambov; the Germans won't reach us" continues to be cited as emblematic not only of Russian soldiers' lack of civic and patriotic understanding, but of the parochial outlook of Russia's peasantry as a whole.[7] This only highlights a problematic tendency to try to understand peasants by relying on sources generated by and about soldiers, without consideration of the potentially transformative experience of soldiering.[8] It is also misleading to try to identify an overarching peasant opinion about the war. For every villager investigated for talking about the futility of the war there was another denouncing him. If some villagers proceeded to slaughter livestock before a rumored requisition, there were others ready to turn them in to the authorities. Some spoke of omens of the coming of end times or visions of the Mother of God, while others more pragmatically fed expectations that peasant soldiers would be rewarded with land after the war. Villagers' attitudes towards the war were as varied as those of the rest of society.

The purpose of this chapter is to examine the effects of the circulation of intersecting written and oral communication. The world of village rumor was not a world apart from urban and official Russia, and a number of themes and leitmotifs omnipresent in the press were absorbed to become part of the language of rumors, petitions, and denunciations. Each of these intersecting forms of communication was increasingly structured around two overarching questions that also happened to be prominently featured in the press: who was sacrificing most to the war effort, and who was the enemy. These two questions, when posed in the Russian heartland, where there were few national minorities or foreigners to bear the brunt of the hunt for the enemy within, and no German colonists from whom to take land, could be deeply

---

[6] E. S. Seniavskaia, *Psikhologiia voiny v XX veke: Istoricheskii opyt Rossii* (Moscow: Rosspen, 1999); Hubertus Jahn, *Patriotic Culture in Russia during World War I* (Ithaca, NY: Cornell University Press, 1995). On the lack of patriotism among rural recruits, see W. Bruce Lincoln, *Passage through Armageddon: The Russians in War and Revolution, 1914–1918* (New York: Simon and Schuster, 1986), 45–6, 143; Allan K. Wildman, *The End of the Russian Imperial Army*, 1: *The Old Army and the Soldiers' Revolt (March–April 1917)* (Princeton, NJ: Princeton University Press, 1980), 76–79; Vladimir Buldakov, "Soldiers and Changes in the Psychology of the Peasantry and Legal and Political Consciousness in Russia, 1914–1923," *The Soviet and Post-Soviet Review* 27, 2–3 (2000): 217–40.

[7] For instance V. A. D'iachkov and L. G. Protasov, "Velikaia voina i obshchestvennoe soznanie," in *Rossiia i Pervaia mirovaia voina: Materialy mezhdunarodnogo kollokviuma*, ed. N. N. Smirnov (St. Petersburg: Dmitrii Bulanin, 1999), 65; Nicolas Werth, "Paysans-soldats et sortie de guerre de la Russie en 1917–18," in *Encyclopédie de la grande guerre, 1914–1918*, ed. Stéphane Audoin-Rouzeau and Jean-Jacques Becker (Paris: Bayard, 2004), 827.

[8] I. V. Narskii, "Frontovoi opyt russkikh soldat: 1914–1916 gody," *Novaia i noveishaia istoriia*, no. 1 (2005): 199–202.

divisive. The manner in which peasants positioned themselves in the national discussion about the war had the potential to upend the processes of local politics, tying village-level conflicts and rivalries into nationally adjudicated notions of fairness.

 septembre;

Police and press reports were unanimous in noting peasant avidity for printed news from the war. One rural correspondent remarked that "each piece of published paper is treated like manna from heaven." Another reported that public readers omitted nothing, dutifully reciting papers from beginning to end. Villagers circulated old papers until they were "worn out with holes," and when market goods were wrapped in newsprint, peasants read that.[9] While demand outstripped supply, authorities and publishers did much to alleviate what rural activists called the "newspaper hunger." Over 400 new papers were established just in the second half of 1914, while the total print run of some 600 pamphlets and brochures exceeded 11 million copies.[10] Circulation of the country's largest newspaper, *Russkoe slovo*, more than doubled, reaching 1.2 million by 1917, and it became the most popular paper for collective subscriptions. Local police and zemstvo reports suggest that much of this increase in print was being absorbed by the countryside, subscription rates in individual villages growing to three, four, in places even ten times prewar rates.[11]

Raw circulation numbers understate the extent of press penetration in the countryside where publications fed into oral networks of communication. The

---

[9] Quotation from "Voina i derevnia," *Russkie vedomosti*, 20 August 1914 [no. 190], 4; Rossiiskii gosudarstvennyi istoricheskii arkhiv (RGIA) f. 1291 (Land Section, Ministry of Internal Affairs), op. 54, 1915, d. 62, ll. 4, 49, 107 (press clippings from *Russkie vedomosti* [December 1914], *Peterburgskie vedomosti* [June 1915], and *Utro* [October 1915]).

[10] A. F. Berezhnoi, *Russkaia legal'naia pechat' v gody pervoi mirovoi voiny* (Leningrad: Izd-vo Leningradskogo universiteta, 1975), 27; Eric Lohr, "The Russian Press and the 'Internal Peace' at the Beginning of World War I," in *A Call to Arms: Propaganda, Public Opinion, and Newspapers in the Great War*, ed. Troy Paddock (Westport, CT: Praeger, 2004), 91–113. See also Melissa K. Stockdale's chapter in this book.

[11] "Voina i naselenie Moskovskoi gubernii v 1914–1915 gg.," *Statisticheskii ezhegodnik moskovskoi gubernii za 1915 g.* (Moscow: Moskovskoe gubernskoe zemstvo, 1916), pt. 2, 95–101; Kostromskaia gubernskaia zemskaia uprava, *Voina i Kostromskaia derevnia (po dannym ankety statisticheskogo otdeleniia)* (Kostroma: Tip. Kh. A. Gelina, 1915), 73–75; Gosudarstvennyi arkhiv Riazanskoi oblasti (GARO) f. 5 (Governors' chancellery), op. 4 (1915), d. 5667, ll. 3–14; d. 5748, l. 130 (police reports on village reading); "Sibirskaia derevnia i voina," *Russkoe slovo*, 21 March 1915, 4; "Interes k voine," *Riazanskaia zhizn'*, 21 January 1915 [no. 21], 4.

editor of *Russkoe slovo* estimated that each issue averaged seven readers.[12] In villages, the number might have been higher. Papers were read aloud and discussed in groups anywhere people gathered. Numerous zemstvo and police reports remarked upon the growing popularity of collective subscriptions by communes and taverns. Subscribers who lived far from *volost'* centers complained that issues regularly arrived late and ragged, having stopped in villages along the way. Some peasants who lived on the margins of networks of information exchange complained of isolation: Samara farmsteaders who had separated their fields during the Stolypin agrarian reforms, for instance, told a visiting correspondent that their main regret was that distance from the village precluded the sharing of news and letters that invariably accompanied the arrival of the post.[13] The press, whether consumed first or second hand, had become central to rural social life.

It is difficult to gauge, however, how much peasants actually knew: access to the press was intermittent, and the reading fragmented. The telegraph did ensure that some news traveled quickly. The fall of Przemyśl', for instance, was announced in the most distant district capitals within hours, allowing the peasant diarist A. A. Zamaraev in his village in Vologda province to inscribe the victory into his journal the next day.[14] On the other hand, the vast majority of villagers did not subscribe to papers or journals, so picked up single issues and pamphlets, caught the news on a visit to the tavern, or heard stories second-hand that had been read by others. One observer noted that ubiquitous discussions about the war centered less on what was read in papers, than about what was said was read in papers.[15] Even Zamaraev, who tried to read the press when he could, prefaced most of his diary entries with "it is said that…" What he had heard was of varying accuracy and timeliness: rumors (quickly confirmed) of the fall of Belgrade and of Turkey's declaration of war appeared with a week's delay, news of Belgium was vague ("Belgium is all destroyed," he wrote). Meanwhile, an October 1916 entry noting that

---

[12] Louise McReynolds, *The News under Russia's Old Regime: The Development of a Mass-Circulation Press* (Princeton, NJ: Princeton University Press, 1991), 256.

[13] N. Tirlianskii, "V voinu na khutorakh," *Ezhemesiachnyi zhurnal*, no. 3 (1915): 117–19.

[14] "Otkliki pobedy," *Russkoe slovo*, 10 March 1915, 3; A. A. Zamaraev, *Dnevnik Totemskogo krest'ianina A. A. Zamaraeva: 1906–1922 gody*, ed. V. V. Morozov and N. I. Reshetnikov (Moscow: Rossiiskaia akademiia nauk, Institut etnologii i antropologii im. Miklukho-Maklaia, 1995), 102.

[15] Vsevolod Vzorov, "Voina i derevnia," *Ezhemesiachnyi zhurnal*, no. 8 (1915): 104–07. Also Krest'ianin, "Iz derevni," *Severnye zapiski*, no. 2 (1915): 208–16; N. Ulianov, "Pamiatniki sovremennoi voiny: Pochtovyi den' v sele," *Istoricheskii vestnik*, no. 8 (1916): 456–66.

police were henceforth subject to the draft was a false rumor that had been circulating at least since summer 1915.[16]

Many of the capital city newspapers were ill-designed for such fragmented reading. Articles were typically written with the assumption that the reader was following a conversation, so pursued previous threads without recapping. For instance, when an August 1916 article in *Rech'* rhetorically accused the Kaluga provincial governor of reintroducing serfdom, it was commenting on a criticism first leveled in a *Novoe vremia* piece that had condemned the governor for "artificially inflaming passions" and undermining the unity necessary to defeat the Teutonic invasion. The issue was picked up by other papers, but few bothered to describe the governor's decree at the root of the polemic, which had proposed to draft refugees and peasants to work on private estates.[17] Such articles were just another bit thrown into a cauldron where the mere whiff of labor and livestock requisitions could provoke slaughter and selloffs, as well as rumors that women were to be conscripted for trench work. In Kaluga itself, a labor levy for trench work six months earlier had led to flight, grumbling that labor was not levied on towns, and rumors that women would be taken and that corrupt elders could be bought off.[18] While there is no direct evidence of a link between press and rumor in this case, the fears of peasants and the hyperbolic comments in the press fed into the same world of suspicion over the intent of provincial authorities.

The distinct popularity of *Russkoe slovo*—besides its low cost—may have lain in the fact that it privileged self-contained vignettes. These were short factual reports and anecdotes from around the country, easily understood and adapted to fragmented reading. In some ways, these vignettes were structured and functioned like rumors: usually unsourced (sometimes even introduced by a passive "it is said") and un-contextualized, they stood in lieu of explanation. This pattern is best illustrated by the ubiquitous topic of shortages and prices. *Russkoe slovo*, like many provincial dailies, wrote regularly about artificial shortages allegedly caused by corrupt and unpatriotic speculators. Only speculation, for instance, could explain that Russia, with the suspension of exports, should lack eggs when it produced at least 250 million per month. Only speculation could explain that when the Riazan' provincial zemstvo needed railway cars to transport food, there were none to be had,

---

[16] Zamaraev, *Dnevnik*, 92, 95, 145; GARO f. 5, op. 4 (1915) d. 5702, ll. 2, 6, 9, 11 (Gendarme investigation of rumors); GARF f. 102 (Department of Police), 4 d-vo (1915) d. 108, ch. 10, l. 8; ch.72, ll. 1, 8 (Vladimir and Tambov governors' mood reports).

[17] RGIA f. 1291, op. 31, 1916, d. 271, ll. 20, 32–33 (newspaper clippings).

[18] Similar rumors had spread through Moscow province in the same period, and a year earlier in Smolensk and Podolia. GARF f. 102, 4 d-vo, op. 124, d. 108 (1915), ch. 26, l. 2 (Kaluga governor's report on popular mood); ch. 42, l. 28ob. (Moscow mood report); "Golosa iz derevni," *Russkie vedomosti*, 8 February 1915 [no. 31], 6.

but for malt and hops they magically appeared.[19] Almost every issue from early 1915 included brief reports about the sudden disappearance of a product in a locality, of hidden stocks of sugar or meat discovered in a basement or warehouse, of unknown people making rounds of stores to buy up the last of salt or shoes. Most of these entries were presented without comment or analysis. But there was no need, since they were embedded in a well-established explanatory framework: their very specificity was emblematic proof of the harmful activities of internal enemies.

The near universal acceptance that speculation was to blame for Russia's economic woes increasingly worried government officials by mid-1915. Police and governors' mood reports remarked that anger over prices was tarnishing the government. In September, the Nizhegorod governor wrote to the Department of Police that he feared disturbances because of an undercurrent of rumors, fanned by the press, about the inability of authorities to deal with artificially inflated prices. Similar assessments came from the offices of the Tver' police and the Vladimir governor. The governor of Moscow province was further convinced that harmful individuals were gaining influence over peasants under false pretences of fighting speculation.[20] The authorities were absolutely correct to connect the world of print with the world of talk, but they somewhat naively assumed it was peasants' special gullibility that led them to blindly believe what was written.

Villagers did not merely consume news, but positioned themselves within the flow by choosing what to repeat and what to overlook. Alternative explanations of inflation and shortages existed, but they were hardly acceptable, as they implied that peasant producers were benefiting unduly from increases in the price of grain. Least admissible was the opinion that "the village is wealthy," making frequent appearance by 1916 in the very same newspapers that also harped about speculators. Minister of Internal Affairs Aleksei Khvostov in January 1916 told *Rech'* that he had seen how villagers in Tula were living so well that they were fixing their houses and eating chocolate. *Russkoe slovo* published data on the rise of deposits in banks, and on the increase of meat and sugar consumption. Sketches from the hinterland then functioned to support that storyline. Articles told of peasant women in new calico dresses, of villages filled with shiny new samovars, and of roads

---

[19] "Dorogovizna," *Russkoe slovo*, 17 March 1915, 6; "Prichiny krizisa," *Russkoe slovo*, 6 March 1916, 4.

[20] GARF f. 102, 4 d-vo, d. 108, ch. 43, ll. 12–13 (Nizhegorod governor's mood report); ch. 42, l. 28 (Jan. 1916 Moscow report); ch. 11, ll. 2–4, 9, 11 (Vladimir); ch. 42, l. 42; ch. 26, l. 11 (Kaluga); ch. 72, l. 2 (Tambov); Gosudarstvennyi arkhiv Tverskoi oblasti (GATO) f. 927 (Gendarme administration, Tver' province), op. 1, d. 1892, ll. 208–09, 242 (September–October 1915 district police reports).

crowded with peasant carts brimming with new furniture.[21] Much of this reporting was anecdotal, again sometimes little better than rumor. The story of a peasant woman who prayed that the war would never end, since she had never lived so well, was repeated in numerous contexts: in newspaper reports and journal "sketches from the countryside," in the August 1916 issue of the Tambov zemstvo's journal, in the Tula governor's June 1916 mood report, and in an April 1915 peasant complaint against the excessive privileges enjoyed by soldiers' families.[22]

The semi-official *Sel'skii vestnik*, a Ministry of Internal Affairs daily targeting the rural population, was most assiduous in promoting the counternarrative that the village was benefiting from the war. In early 1916 it published a special supplement to explain that the giant needs of the war, and not evil people were the cause of inflation. The pamphlet reminded readers that trade was not only legal, but vital: some grow grain, others have to distribute it for the general good, it explained. But the core of the pamphlet's argument was a chiding exhortation for peasants to stop complaining—their letters to the front were demoralizing the troops—and to consume less. Villagers were living better, the authors asserted. Prohibition and stipends to soldiers' families had brought money into the village, so that villagers now ate more meat, sugar, and white bread. The author scolded: "those who went in bast shoes now want boots, those who only drank tea in a tavern now want a samovar and pastries every day."[23] *Sel'skii vestnik* was contributing to a growing subnarrative that pitted urban consumers against rural producers. It told readers that workers were suffering more, and that peasants had a duty of frugality towards the soldiers.

There is some evidence that such talk of village wealth was noticed and resented. One group of soldiers sent an anonymous—and unpublished—letter to *Sel'skii vestnik* in 1915 denying that family benefits left the village awash with cash: "you write much, but you know little; [you should] write less and work more... Someone is lying. Who is the soldier to believe ... your announcements,

---

[21] "Beseda s A. N. Khvostovym," *Rech'*, 11 January 1916, 4; "Ogranichenie potreblenie miasa," *Russkoe slovo*, 10 March 1916; "Sakharnaia kompaniia," *Russkoe slovo*, 3 March 1916, 4; "V ural'skoi derevne," *Rech'*, 5 January 1916, 5; I. Ivaniuzhenov, "Okolo zemli," *Novoe vremia*, 2 November 1915; RGIA f. 1291, op. 54, 1915, d. 62, ll. 38, 92 (clippings from *Petrogradskie vedomosti* and *Birzhevye vedomosti*).

[22] A. Faresov, "Narod bez vodki," *Russkaia budushchnost'*, no. 1 (1915): 14; GARF f. 102, 4 d-vo, 1916, d. 78, ch. 9, l. 1ob. (Tula governor's report); RGIA f. 1292 (MVD: Administration of Obligatory Military Service), op. 7, d. 264, l. 21 (April 1915 complaint letter); *Tambovskii zemskii vestnik* (August 1916), quoted in M. D. Karpachev, "Derevnia i paradoksy voennogo vremeni: Sotsial'no-politicheskaia situatsiia v Voronezhskoi gubernii nakanune padeniia monarkhii," *Istoricheskie zapiski*, no. 11 (2005): 16.

[23] *Voina i derevnia* (Petrograd: Tip. Sel'skogo vestnika, 1916), 5.

or our beloved families?"[24] But even while soldiers emphasized their families' unique vulnerabilities, in the village these families were sometimes the ones perceived to be exceptionally privileged and therefore to blame for false ideas about rural wealth. According to one Riazan´ zemstvo employee, talk of village wealth darkened the mood by ignoring the exhaustion of maintaining the family farm and that "the only ones with money are childless soldiers' wives (*soldatki*) who work outside for wages."[25] The suspicion that *soldatki* were the ones living better was commonly invoked in 1915 communal refusals to help soldiers' families complete fieldwork.[26]

What most captured peasants' attention were the prices of consumer goods. "Everywhere you turn," wrote one peasant official, "talk is about prices, wages, food, and envious discussion of soldiers' benefits," an observation repeated in numerous accounts and police reports.[27] The unjust enrichment of merchants, which turned the terms of trade against peasants, was the preferred storyline. "Why aren't there fixed prices on nails?... It's become that with a full *desiatina* of grain you can't buy shoes," one peasant told a correspondent in 1916. Similar comparisons, expressed in cow–firewood or other equivalents, appeared in denunciations of merchants sent to the Riazan´ police that same year.[28] The story of speculation made sense of many peasants' experience of inflation in a way that other narratives did not.

The fact that prices on consumer goods were uncontrolled clearly rankled and fed the opinion that the city was protected to the detriment of the countryside. Zamaraev recorded almost weekly in his diary the prices of goods like nails, salt, tobacco, sugar, and flour. Already in August 1914 he wondered whether inflation was due to the war or the greed of merchants. By 1915, he was

---

[24] RGIA f. 1291, op. 51, 1914, d. 128a, ll. 89–90 (unpublished letter to *Sel´skii vestnik*).

[25] T. Mikheev, "K derevenskim nastroeniiam," *Vestnik Riazanskogo zemstva*, no. 1 (1917): 63–65.

[26] For more on the decline of communal aid in 1915, see Corinne Gaudin, "Rural Echoes of World War I: War Talk in the Russian Village," *Jahrbücher für Geschichte Osteuropas* 3 (2008): 409–13. On conflicting stereotypes of *soldatki*, see Emily Pyle, "Village Social Relations and the Reception of Soldiers' Family Aid Policies in Russia, 1912–1921" (Ph.D. diss., University of Chicago, 1997), 196–224.

[27] S. Matveev, "V glubokom tylu," *Russkie zapiski*, no. 11 (1915): 191; also B. Iur´evskii, "Derevenskie zametki," *Russkaia budushchnost´*, no. 18 (1915): 15–16.

[28] I. Solov´ev, "Tverdye tseny i zakupka khleba," *Russkaia budushchnost´*, no. 37 (1916): 16; GARO f. 5. op. 4, d. 5729a, ll. 67, 229. For a recent overview of the economic impact of the war on peasants, see Peter Gatrell, *Russia's First World War: A Social and Economic History* (Harlow, UK: Pearson, 2005), 72–76, 144–46. On the importance of terms of trade in fueling peasant discontent, see A. M. Anfimov, *Rossiiskaia derevnia v gody pervoi mirovoi voiny: 1914–fevral´ 1917* (Moscow: Izd. Sotsial´no-ekonomicheskoi literatury, 1962), 313–17; A. A. Kurenyshev, "Krest´ianstvo Rossii v period voiny i revoliutsii 1917–1922 gg.," *Voprosy istorii*, no. 4–5 (1999): 148–56.

clearly leaning towards the latter. At the end of 1916, he recounted rumors of a trial of sugar speculators in Kiev, adding that "there is a lot of corruption." And a few weeks later, after mentioning "scandals on the railroad," he concluded that "disorder and waste" was a main cause of suffering. Zamaraev also picked up on another theme that was getting increasing press, the unwillingness of the wealthy to share in the burden of war. *Russkoe slovo* periodically carried these stories, describing for instance that city restaurants and cabarets were full, and that trade in luxury goods was thriving.[29] Such accounts struck the Vologda diarist, and his 23 January 1917 entry summarized a *Russkoe slovo* article about the English elite's renunciation of luxuries, regretting that his compatriots did not do the same. The final step of his disillusionment came on the eve of the February Revolution: after reporting that peasants could not buy rationed goods (such as flour and sugar), he rued that "the village is left to its own devices."[30]

It would be an error, however, to see in such talk a growing sense of peasant identity, such as Benjamin Zieman has suggested emerged from rural–urban tensions in Germany.[31] The overarching themes of internal enemies and unequal sacrifice could support conflicting and divisive narratives within the village. The need to economize and contribute to the war effort was a new argument that could be mobilized to justify village assembly efforts to lower the salaries of peasant elected officials.[32] Soldiers' sometimes vehement claims that they were exempt from all taxes clashed with the narrative that it was soldiers' wives—not the countryside as a whole—that were indulging in newfound wealth. Even the most unlikely of spy rumors could escalate private disputes into accusations of disloyalty. One such rumor from 1915, for instance, asserted that Germans were training Russian German and Jewish arson instructors to disrupt the harvest with the aid of special crop-burning machines. The Department of Police probably did its bit in disseminating this rumor by passing it on to district police offices with the injunction to be especially vigilant. Thus, in July 1915 one peasant from a district of Riazan'

---

[29] Bukva [I. F. Vasilevskii], "Sredi obyvateli," *Russkoe slovo*, 1 April 1916, 6; Baian, "Krov' i brillianty," *Russkoe slovo*, 3 March 1916, 2.

[30] Zamaraev, *Dnevnik*, 125, 130, 147, 150–51, 154. Unfavorable comparisons of Russia's wealthy with those abroad were published in a wide range of provincial publications as well. See, for instance, V. Vsteselovskii, "Evangel'skii pritochnyi bogach i nashi materialisty," *Orlovskie eparkhalnie vedomosti*, no. 43 (1915): 1019–23; A. V. Matankin, "Spekulatsiia," *Staryi Vladimirets*, 24 January 1917, 2.

[31] Benjamin Ziemann, *War Experiences in Rural Germany, 1914–1923* (Oxford: Berg, 2007).

[32] On reducing salaries, see Gosudarstvennyi arkhiv Vladimirskoi oblasti (GAVO) f. 704 (Vladimir gendarme administration), op. 1, d. 1454, l. 366 (petition to governor); RGIA f. 1291, op. 54, 1915, d. 62, ll. 12, 46 (press clippings from *Saratovskii listok* [June 1915] and *Russkoe slovo* [January 1915]).

province where there were neither Germans nor Jews wrote to the police that a neighbor, after receiving secret funds from Germany, had recruited 14 fellow villagers to form a party dedicated to crop burning.[33] The endless stories about espionage and treachery even within the army fed accusations against rank-and-file soldiers and their families. So when a Tver' villager in January 1916 noticed that his neighbor, a soldier's wife, received money from the front, he told police that it was "probably money from illegal activity, like spying."[34] Accusers were not only appropriating themes developed in the press; they further fed the extraordinary suspiciousness of both local and central police authorities. The Department of Police itself in September 1915 had instructed local authorities to keep their eyes open for families who received suspiciously large amounts of goods or money from soldiers.[35] The origins of rumors of crop-burning machines or of soldiers "lying around the trenches for German money" matter less than the process of amplification that came from mutual reinforcement. The highest official to the lowliest peasant was caught up in a single web of suspicion, but the lines of division could simultaneously cut between village and city, and within the village.

The multiplicity of overlapping resentments over perceived inequitable levels of sacrifice came through most strongly in complaints about the draft. Villagers echoed a judgment circulating widely among soldiers and discussed in the press that the rich were buying themselves out of the draft. In April 1915, a rumor swept through Vladimir province that the number of exemptions for factory workers in war industries had been set by German sympathizers. By October 1916, such rumors had escalated along with the number of draftees who simply did not show up. According to a peasant writing to his father at the front, when the draft orders came to his village, "[recruits] all ran away to Voronezh." According to the police, the widespread opinion that "they now only take the poor to defend the motherland" and that factory owners were selling exemptions to get cheap labor was responsible for growing difficulties in locating fleeing recruits. By December 1916, Vladimir police and military authorities had lost control of the situation: an astonishing 7,792 men—43 percent of those called up—were absent for unknown reasons.[36] This figure should be contrasted with official statistics for 1916 that reported an average of 5,800 desertions per month for the entire country. In the absence of fine-

---

[33] GARO f. 641 (Riazan' circuit court), op. 1 , d. 6551, ll. 3–3ob., 6–6ob., 46, 48–49 (police investigation).

[34] GATO f. 927, op. 1, d. 1892, ll. 14–15 (1915); also GAVO f. 704, op. 1, d. 1175, l. 46 (letters to police).

[35] GATO f. 927, op. 1, d. 1892, l. 213 (Department of Police circular).

[36] GAVO f. 704, op. 1, d. 1175, l. 213 (report to Department of Police); l. 39 (letter seized by military postal censorship); op. 2, d. 27, ll. 478, 499–500 (7 January 1917 gendarme report on recruitment). On draft evasion by the wealthy, see, for instance, "Okolo voiny," *Russkoe slovo*, 12 January 1915, 4.

grained studies on draft evasion, it is difficult to know whether recruits were only temporarily able to evade the draft, or whether the situation in Vladimir was unusual. Until then, perhaps we should not be so quick to dismiss as "veritable fairy tales" (in the words of General B. T. Gurko) the rumors that some one or two million men were roaming the rear and in hiding.[37]

What is clear is that the perception that the connected and the wealthy could avoid the draft was widespread. Zamaraev in Vologda, lamenting another mobilization in March 1916, also concluded that "they do not take the rich." He confirmed his verdict by recording talk of one neighbor whose two sons had been inexplicably bypassed and that, indeed, "something there is not clean."[38] The suspicion that the exempted had bribed their way out of service drove petitioners to indignant demands: "if you do not demand that Shilov be sent to where he should go, then I will go to someone over your head," wrote an irate villager in November 1914. Another anonymous denunciation from Tver′ named two peasants "who live here as if the law of mobilization does not concern them. And why does the local leadership take no measures?"[39] The police rarely found evidence to support such charges, uncovering instead disputes on unrelated matters or longstanding webs of enmity between accused and accuser. It is impossible to know whether expressed indignation was real or feigned. The strategic use of legal or moral arguments in petitions with authorities against rural rivals had long constituted an integral part of prewar village politics.[40] The arguments deployed, however, were quite new, linking as they did local reputations or misdeeds with larger loyalties and relative levels of sacrifice and service to the nation.

Villagers not only broadened their arsenal of arguments, but sought to go beyond the well-worn path of two-way communication with authorities, appealing to a broader audience by writing to the press. This practice also was not entirely new: the Ministry of Internal Affairs's *Sel′skii vestnik* had encouraged and published readers' letters since the 1880s, but topics had

---

[37] Gurko argued that the rumor arose from an optical illusion caused by more generous leave policies. N. N. Golovine, *The Russian Army in the World War* (New Haven: Yale University Press, 1931), 123. On desertion, and the difficulties of establishing reliable statistics, see Wildman, *The End of the Russian Imperial Army*, 362–65; A. B. Astashov, "Desertirstvo i bor′ba s nim v tsarskoi armii v gody Pervoi mirovoi voiny," *Rossiiskaia istoriia*, no. 4 (2011): 44–52.

[38] Zamaraev, *Dnevnik*, 130.

[39] GATO f. 985 (Ves′egonsk district military service administration), op. 1, d. 152, ll. 82, 591–92ob., 857 (denunciation letters). Also GARO f. 5, op. 4, d. 5620, ll. 67–68ob., 181; d. 5729a, ll. 67–68ob.; f. 1292 (Riazan′ province gendarme administration), op. 1, d. 990, l. 142 (denunciation letters). See also Sanborn, *Drafting the Russian Nation*, 37–38.

[40] Corinne Gaudin, *Ruling Peasants: Village and State in Late Imperial Russia* (DeKalb: Northern Illinois University Press), chap. 3.

been prescribed to serve the newspapers' didactic mission.[41] Other papers had published submissions by rural correspondents, self-styled fighters for progress and enlightenment "from the benighted village." Both these types of writings from the countryside continued to be published during the war, but now they were supplemented by submissions complaining about private concerns. The press was a new actor intervening in what had previously been a two-way conversation between peasants and authorities, more firmly embedding private grievances into public debate.

The language and substance of these letters suggest they served a range of purposes. Some letters seemed to be testing rumor: one villager from Samara wrote to *Russkoe slovo* that "we heard from the papers that merchants petitioned for the end of prohibition on beer in order to raise the price of grain." The story had indeed been published, and here the newspaper simply published the letter without comment, further fanning the flames of suspicion about the influence of selfish grain merchants.[42] A few simply reflected a desire to be heard. A group of Vladimir peasants anonymously asked for *Russkoe slovo* to publish an article answering the following question: "If Russia is the breadbasket of Europe, and prices increase because of speculation, then does it not follow that the death penalty should be applied with confiscation to the benefit of families of wounded and killed?"[43] Clearly, the writers already knew what the answer to their question should be.

More often, the press was just another avenue to petition. One common topic covered complaints about benefits paid to soldiers' families, that they were being paid late, that village officials played favorites, or that they skimmed money under the guise of service fees. For instance, one reader complained to *Golos Moskvy* that the local *volost'* elder was withholding taxes from stipend payments to soldiers' families (except for his daughter-in-law), adding that the "other son is at home with a health exemption, but in fact he's completely healthy."[44] Some papers published long excerpts, others periodically summarized the gist of a group of letters under such titles as "The Tears of Soldiers' Wives," attacking the unpatriotic indifference of rural officials and driving home the message that soldiers' families deserved respect.[45] Even ostensibly petty matters such as *volost'* handling of mail could

---

[41] James Krukones, *To the People: The Russian Government and the Newspaper Sel'skii vestnik, 1881–1917* (New York: Garland, 1987), 13–16.

[42] RGIA f. 1291, op. 54, 1915, d. 62, l. 3 (clipping from *Russkoe slovo*, January 1915); "Trezvyi skhod," *Russkoe slovo*, 19 January 1915, 4.

[43] GARF f. 102, op. 265, d. 1006, l. 53 (intercepted letter, June 1915).

[44] RGIA f. 1291, op. 51, 1914, d. 128a, ll. 54, 61 (newspaper clipping and subsequent investigation).

[45] "Soldatskie slezy," *Novoe vremia*, 18 December 1914; "Zaderzhka posobie," *Russkoe slovo*, 15 November 1914; "Zloupotreblenie sel'skikh vlastei," *Russkoe slovo*, 12 February

be grounds for accusations of unpatriotic behavior: arguments that mail was delayed, that corrupt officials withheld letters for payments, or that they stole newspapers could be rallied to tarnish local reputations.[46] Although many of these accusations seem to have been founded on no more than hearsay, they reflected an awareness that the audience for local gossip reached far beyond the village.

Letters also demonstrated a clear expectation that the press, by giving voice, could accomplish results. One writer to *Sel'skii vestnik* asked that it publish his request for verification of the draft process in his district "since many of those who are exempted are healthy as bulls."[47] Such expectations that letters would prompt official action had some foundation. The Ministry of Internal Affairs reviewed press reports, and sent relevant clippings to provincial governors with orders to investigate the allegations. Even some unpublished letters were forwarded to the ministry, not only by *Sel'skii vestnik*—which had long done so by virtue of its official status—but by independent papers as well. A mere 19 lines in *Gazeta-kopeika* alleging that one women who received payments as a soldier's wife while her husband in fact worked in Petrograd triggered two months of investigation, and a governor's summary report of four tightly typed pages.[48] Not infrequently, investigations uncovered longstanding disputes between those publicly accused and those who wrote "under the guise of journalists shedding light on events in the farthest corners of the Russian village," as an exasperated Novgorod governor put it.[49] The act of appealing to the press suggests more than a mere desire to elicit official remedy; by arguing that a delayed newspaper was an attempt to keep peasants in the dark, that an instance of petty corruption (real or not) insulted those who give their "lives to free holy Russia from the German regime," or that the *volost'* elder as richest peasant in the district had not even filed others' requests for seed aid from the zemstvo,[50] writers were impugning the patriotism of local rivals, appropriating national symbolic capital in local battles.

ଓ ଅ

1915.

[46] RGIA f. 1291, op. 54, 1915, d. 62, ll. 44–45 (clipping and investigation of *Saratovskii vestnik*, March 1915); ll. 70, 77 (*Staryi vladimirets* and *Utro Rossii*, January 1915); op. 51, 1914, d. 128a, l. 191 (unpublished letter to *Vechernee vremia*, September 1914).

[47] RGIA f. 1291, op. 51, 1914, d. 128a, ll. 91–92.

[48] Ibid., ll. 31–36ob.

[49] RGIA f. 1291, op. 54, 1915, d. 62, ll. 8–9 (investigation of "Iz perepiski s chitateliam," *Sovremennoe slovo*, August 1915).

[50] Ibid., l. 66 ("Ot chitatelei," *Vechernee vremia*, August 1915); op. 51, 1914, d. 128a, ll. 110 ("Neuriaditsa," *Utro Rossii*, February 1915), 191.

Letters to the press, denunciations, even rumoring were participatory acts. They made claims to speak and write and judge in the name of community well-being, and as such joined the argument about the place of each in the war. Villagers from the farthest reaches of provincial society were actively engaged in the circulation and interpretation of news and information. The press provided tools to translate eminently local, personal conflicts into something relevant to the fate of the nation. But peasants did not merely consume and reproduce interpretations and stories they gleaned from the press. Some narratives that cast the peasants as beneficiaries of higher prices on agricultural products were ignored, rejected, or deflected onto minorities within the village (allegedly wealthier households of soldiers' wives or those with subsidiary income from factory work). Storylines about corruption, spies, and profiteers served not only to question the level of exactions demanded of peasants, but to frame the alleged misdeeds of local rivals. By doing so, petitioners were not merely extending previous practices of conducting village politics by appealing to stronger, outside forces. They were attacking not just specific acts, but presenting those acts as a way of being that was inimical to the demand of shared sacrifice. Villagers were linking personal fates to larger forces—translating private problems into social considerations—which is what politics is about.

Rural inhabitants' ability to position themselves within a national argument—whether or not it was strategic—makes sense of their widespread engagement with the new politics unleashed in 1917. Historians have long remarked upon the speed with which petitions, village assembly resolutions, and local court proceedings appropriated the language of citizenship and equality after February, even if there remains disagreement over the extent to which peasants understood this language.[51] The increasing frequency with which the diarist Zamaraev jotted down bits from his press readings throughout 1917 conforms to a familiar pattern. He immediately adopted new political vocabulary and categories, attending a meeting of "citizens" the day after Nicholas II's abdication, recording with evident approval how "Romanov Nikolai" had been placed on ordinary rations, and later condemning the behavior of deserting soldiers as treachery by the "unconscious masses."[52] Until the middle of 1918, the same events that alarmed city opinion elicited comment from the Vologda diarist: salacious revelations of Rasputin's alleged influence at court, the closing of opposition press, the dissolution of the Constituent Assembly, the assassination of two former prominent liberals

---

[51] Retish, *Russia's Peasants*, 64–94; Sarah Badcock, *Politics and the People in Revolutionary Russia: A Provincial History* (Cambridge: Cambridge University Press, 2007); Jane Burbank, *Russian Peasants Go to Court: Legal Culture in the Countryside, 1905–1917* (Bloomington: Indiana University Press, 2004), 228–30; Orlando Figes and Boris Kolonitskii, *Interpreting the Russian Revolution: The Language and Symbols of 1917* (New Haven: Yale University Press, 1999).

[52] Zamaraev, *Dnevnik*, 155–56, 165.

in the Provisional Government in their hospital beds, the "shameful peace" of Brest-Litovsk.[53] More remarkable was a 23 April entry announcing the opening of a people's house (*narodnyi dom*) "with many newspapers and books. Now there is freedom, people feel good and happy. Now no one is afraid of discussion."[54] Whether or not the explicit connection drawn here between reading and talking, and the heady hopes of those "truly historic" times was shared by others is a question that has barely been touched upon in the historiography.

If February 1917 intensified the mobilizing effects of the war, the years of civil war, dominated by a struggle for survival (not to mention lack of paper), had precisely the opposite effect. Informational networks stretching from the capitals to the village frayed until they broke completely by 1919. This development clearly distressed Zamaraev: "there are no telegrams or papers," "the news is poor, we know little," "no news from Petrograd," peppered his diary from late 1917 through spring 1918, after which the lack of papers became unremarkable. There was still news—usually hearsay—in the diary, but it was predominantly local. Zamaraev's horizons shrank to the boundaries of his district and the daily routine of work. Unable to know the price of goods in Tver′, or the availability of merchandise in Petrograd, the diarist was left with little option but to turn inward, his experience refracted through the prism of repeated requisitions and extraordinary levies.[55] The point here is not to present this single peasant diarist as typical. His struggles to make sense of the world around him, however, stand as a warning of the dangers of trying to understand rural Russia in these turbulent years without considering the transformations wrought by earlier engagement with the war and the February Revolution. Were one to encounter this peasant only during the Civil War years, or through the more common route of a petition or complaint, one would find the traits so often attributed to peasant mentality or psychology, his passivity and narrow focus on local and material concerns read not as a reaction to extreme circumstances, but as confirmation of an allegedly essential peasant characteristic.[56] Neither can Zamaraev's silence be read as archaization: he fed his curiosity—even in the darkest hungry months of 1920—by reading books in the new *narodnyi dom*, jotting down such things

---

[53] Ibid., 165, 178–80, 183. On the concerns of Petrograders, see S. V. Iarov, *Gorozhanin kak politik: Revoliutsiia, voennyi kommunizm i NEP glazami Petrogradtsev* (St. Petersburg: Dmitrii Bulanin, 1999).

[54] Zamaraev, *Dnevnik*, 158.

[55] On the marginalizing and demobilizing effect of the "struggle for existence" in 1920–22, see I. V. Narskii, *Zhizn′ v katastrofe: Budni naseleniia Urala v 1917–1922 gg.* (Moscow: ROSSPEN, 2001).

[56] The work that has most explicitly interpreted the Revolution and Civil War through the prism of peasant mass consciousness is V. P. Buldakov, *Krasnaia smuta: Priroda i posledstviia revoliutsionnogo nasiliia* (Moscow: ROSSPEN, 1997).

as the size of the British parliament building, the misfortunes of the John Franklin North Pole expedition, or the features of Austrian cities.[57] Even as he disconnected with Russia, he sought connections with the past and with the world through books on geography and history. What Zamaraev's laconic entries suggest is that the news famine of the Civil War years played its role—alongside the real famine—in marginalizing, depoliticizing, and demobilizing Russian villagers. The extent of this role remains to be studied.

---

[57] Zamaraev, *Dnevnik*, 197, 204, 219. For critique of the concept of archaization, see Steven Smith, "Nebesnye pis'ma i rasskazy o lese: 'Sueveriia' protiv bol'shevizma," *Antropologicheskii forum*, no. 3 (2007): 280–305; I. V. Narskii, "Samoobol'shchenie nadezhdoi: Slukhi na Urale v 1917–1920 kak sotsiokul'turnyi fenomen," *Problemy Rossiiskoi istorii*, no. 1 (2002): 195–206.

The Symbol of "Mother Russia" Across Two Epochs: From the First World War to the Civil War

Oleg V. Riabov

As much research of the last two decades has shown, gender discourse played a significant role in the propaganda of all belligerent nations during the First World War.[1] Both male and female national personifications—Britannia, Germania, Columbia, Marianne—were widely represented in wartime discourse. "Mother Russia," one of the best-known symbols of Russianness at home and abroad, also occupied an important place in this story. Russia's maternal metaphor can be regarded as a weapon of war. "Metaphors can kill": George Lakoff's words illustrate the importance of discourse in wartime.[2] Gender discourse occupies a particular role in this context. In her analysis of Cold War history, Cynthia Enloe writes about a series of contests over the definitions of masculinity and femininity.[3] Gender discourse is indeed a field of heated battle in any conflict—the intended audience also intervenes, labeling given models of masculine and feminine behavior canonical or deviant. Images of

---

[1] George L. Mosse, *Nationalism and Sexuality: Respectability and Abnormal Sexuality in Modern Europe* (New York: Howard Fertig, 1985); Margaret H. Darrow, *French Women and the First World War: War Stories of the Home Front* (Oxford: Berg, 2000); Kimberly Jensen, *Mobilizing Minerva: American Women in the First World War* (Urbana: University of Illinois Press, 2008); Allison S. Belzer, *Women and the Great War: Femininity under Fire in Italy* (New York: Palgrave Macmillan, 2010); Suzanne Evans, *Mothers of Heroes, Mothers of Martyrs: World War I and the Politics of Grief* (Montreal: McGill-Queen's University Press, 2007); R. Margaret et al., eds., *Behind the Lines: Gender and the Two World Wars* (New Haven: Yale University Press, 1987); Billie Melman, ed., *Borderlines: Genders and Identities in War and Peace 1870–1930* (New York: Routledge, 1998); Neil R. Storey and Molly Housego, *Women in the First World War* (Oxford: Shire Publications, 2010); Helen Sims, "Posters and Images of Women in the Great War," in *Representations of Gender from Prehistory to the Present*, ed. Moira Donald and Linda Hurcombe (New York: St. Martin's Press, 1999).

[2] George Lakoff, "Metaphor and War: The Metaphor System Used to Justify War in the Gulf," http://www2.iath.virginia.edu/sixties/HTML_docs/Texts/Scholarly/Lakoff_Gulf_Metaphor_2.html

[3] Cynthia H. Enloe, *The Morning After: Sexual Politics at the End of the Cold War* (Berkeley: University of California Press, 1993), 18–19.

men and women are effective "symbolic border guards," serving as markers of inclusion and exclusion and participating in the formation of collective identity, in the demarcation of Us from Them, and in valuing the former more highly than the latter. The relationship of gender discourse with relations of power and subordination is another factor in its usefulness to wartime propaganda. The hierarchical relations between, and within, genders are used as a sort of blueprint to legitimize other forms of social inequality. It is precisely because gender theory is implicated in power relations that it becomes an essential part of the discourse of war and violence in general.

Gender discourse takes on a special meaning in the context of the war propaganda of the modern era. This is connected with the role it plays in nationalism. As Anne McClintock observed, "Nationalism is constituted from the very beginning as a gendered discourse, and cannot be understood without a theory of gender power."[4] The interaction of gender and national discourse facilitates their mutual support and legitimization. Comparing the nation to the family is an effective way to position a given community as natural and organic. It is precisely this that explains the broad dissemination of female, and especially maternal, national personifications. The nation-family comparison is used actively in political mobilization, and in the legitimization and delegitimization of power: political opponents are frequently labeled as internal enemies of the nation, as renegades who have betrayed their familial bonds.

This chapter, based on an analysis of textual and visual sources, aims to explore the development of the "Mother Russia" image in the transitional period between 1914 and 1920. First of all, it will analyze the representations of Us and Them in the gender discourse of the First World War, in order to illustrate the context in which this image was employed; it will then consider the various meanings of "Mother Russia," which allowed this image to form part of wartime discourse; finally, it will trace the image's development in the process of the legitimization and delegitimization of power, and in the discourse of various political factions during the Revolution and Civil War.

"Mother Russia" and the First World War: Maternal Metaphor as Weapon

"This great surge of patriotic feeling, of love for the Motherland and of loyalty to the Crown, sweeping like a hurricane through Our land, is a guarantee in My eyes—yes, and I think, in yours—that our great Mother Russia will bring this war, sent to her by the Lord God, to its desired conclusion."[5] These words,

---

[4] Anne McClintock, "'No Longer in a Future Heaven': Nationalism, Gender, and Race," in *Becoming National: A Reader*, ed. Geoff Eley and Ronald G. Suny (New York: Oxford University Press, 1996), 261.

[5] See V. Kuz'min-Karavaev, "Voprosy vnutrennei zhizni," *Vestnik Evropy*, no. 8 (1914): 416.

from the speech given by Nicholas II on 26 July 1914 before the members of the State Council and the Duma, demonstrate that the image of "Mother Russia" was actively employed in the discourse of the First World War from its very beginning.

Starting with her appearance as "Mother Earth" (*Mat'-syra zemlia*) in pagan times, the maternal image has been present in Russian culture throughout its whole history.[6] "Mother Russia" has been a noticeable element of war propaganda since at least the 18th century; to serve "Mother Russia" is a theme of Aleksandr V. Suvorov's Science of Victory.[7] The first attempts to visualize Russia in female form also emerged in the 18th century, in particular the triumphal arch project designed in 1762 by the architect Aleksei Uvarov, proposed for construction on Nevskii Prospekt on the occasion of Russia's victory in the Seven Years' War but rejected by Peter III. The arch was to have been crowned with a tented roof featuring a female figure personifying Russia.[8] Russia also appears in female form on the alto-relievo *The Establishment of the Russian Navy* (*Zavedenie flota v Rossii*) (by the sculptor Ivan I. Terebenev, 1812), on the attic of the lower cube of the Admiralty tower. In those years of national enthusiasm, Fedor P. Tolstoi created a series of medals dedicated to the events of the 1812 war. *The People's Volunteer Corps* (*Narodnoe opolchenie*) (1816) depicts Russia arming her sons (see fig. 10 in the gallery of illustrations following page 178). Slavophile and nationalist texts—and, above all, their representation of the Slavs as feminine, as opposed to the masculine Teutons—further fueled the perceptions of artists who made use of the "Mother Russia" image.[9]

By the end of the 19th century, "Mother Russia" had become a commonplace image, appearing on medals, calendars, advertisements, and the interiors of mansions. The use of the image on banknotes is particularly notable in its transformation into an element of everyday life, of "banal nationalism" in the phrase of Michael Billig.[10] The 25-ruble note from 1899 depicts a woman in royal garb, wearing the crown of Monomakh; she carries an orb and sceptre, and leans on an ancient Russian shield (fig. 11). In addition, similar images were used on 5- and 10-ruble banknotes in 1894–95, and on 500-ruble bonds released in 1912.[11]

---

[6] O. V. Riabov, *"Matushka-Rus'": Opyt gendernogo analiza poiskov natsional'noi identichnosti Rossii v otechestvennoi i zapadnoi istoriosofii* (Moscow: Ladmomir, 2001).

[7] Aleksandr V. Suvorov, "Nauka pobezhdat'," http://militera.lib.ru/science/suvorov/index.html

[8] A. G. Raskin, *Triumfal'nye arki Leningrada* (Leningrad: Lenizdat, 1977), 52–53.

[9] Riabov, *"Matushka-Rus'*," 57–59.

[10] Michael Billig, *Banal Nationalism* (London: Sage Publications, 1995).

[11] A. I. Malyshev, V. I. Tarankov, and I. N. Smirennyi, *Bumazhnye denezhnye znaki Rossii i SSSR* (Moscow: Finansy i statistika, 1991), 60–61.

The Russo-Japanese War (1904–05) was highly significant in terms of the popularization of the "Mother Russia" image, in particular a drawing with the highly suggestive title *In Recognition of Righteousness and Strength*, published at the very start of the conflict. Russia's pre-eminence—both moral and military—was represented by the figure of a woman with a dove of peace in her right hand and a sword in her left. The perfidy and barbarity of the enemy were symbolized by a half-naked samurai creeping up behind.[12]

Russian authors considered the First World War to be first and foremost a confrontation between Russia and Germany. This was interpreted not only as a military conflict but as a metaphysical one.[13] In the discourse of propaganda, "We" was defined as the bearers of those qualities that assured global leadership, now or in the future, while "They" embodied every fault. These distinctions were regarded as eternal and inevitable, and this sort of essentialized contradiction could be constructed by various methods. Thus, it became popular to refer to the Slavic and Teutonic epics, an appeal to historical "facts" which supposedly demonstrated the primordial opposition of the two peoples.[14] Another method was the use of gendered symbols, metaphors, and images. Clearly, the interpretation of Russian-ness and German-ness as two opposite principles made it possible to view them through the lens of gender dichotomy.

It should be explained that the idea of female messianism—the redeeming mission of woman or the feminine principle—was widely disseminated in the culture of the Silver Age, due to the influence of Sophiology.[15] In philosophical essays, Russia's femininity was interpreted as a sign of her messianic calling, the source of her unique character and a factor in her pre-eminence over other cultures. Similar sentiments could be found in geopolitical discourse, in discussions of Russia's relationship with the West (primarily with Germany). Particularly revealing are the arguments of Vasilii Rozanov, who shed light on this question in his article "About the 'Russian Idea.'" In Germany, he writes, the Russians are widely held to be innately feminine, and this, "in combination with the manly Teutonic race, will bring forth wonderful

---

[12] A. Kudriavtsev, "V soznanii pravoty i sily," *Niva*, no. 10 (1904): 193. It has also been reproduced in O. V. Riabov, *"Rossiia-Matushka": Natsionalizm, gender i voina v Rossii XX veka* (Stuttgart: Ibidem-Verlag, 2007),260.

[13] Ben Hellman, *Poets of Hope and Despair: The Russian Symbolists in War and Revolution (1914–1918)* (Helsinki: Institute for Russian and East European Studies, 1995), 98. See, for example, V. F. Ern, "Mech i krest," in *Sochineniia* (Moscow: Pravda, 1991), 297.

[14] M. O. Men'shikov, "Zolotoe serdtse," in *Pis'ma k russkoi natsii* (Moscow: Moskva, 1999), 497; V. V. Rozanov, *Voina 1914 goda i russkoe vozrozhdenie* (Petrograd: Tip. T-va A. S. Suvorina; "Novoe vremia," 1915), 86–87.

[15] O. V. Riabov, *Russkaia filosofiia zhenstvennosti (XI–XX veka)* (Ivanovo: Iunona, 1999), 184–85.

material for history."[16] He remarks: "The man is the head of the household … but woman is its mistress.… And, ultimately, she governs the man himself.… That's what we can tell Wilhelm and Bismarck in response to their insinuation about the 'feminine' Slavic character."[17] Rozanov agrees that Russia is "a woman, forever seeking her bridegroom, her master, her husband,"[18] but he also emphasizes that female softness and pliancy are signs of strength. Woman first enters a man's home with kindness and tenderness, but, the very next moment, she becomes mistress of the house. "The 'feminine' entwines itself around the masculine, absorbing it"; water—one of the symbols of the feminine principle in Silver Age philosophy—"wears away the stone." Thus, the Europeans would find themselves conquered by Russian femininity; they themselves would yield to the Russian principle, rejecting "the very essence of the European principle: hubris, acquisition, dominance."[19]

Of course, with the start of the war, when Germany was transformed from "love-hate object" into Public Enemy No. 1, the old images of the "mystical love affair"—Sergei Bulgakov called it "erotic hypnosis"[20]—appealed to few. As in the propaganda of other belligerent nations, images of "Us" emphasized the masculine; the idea of Russia as feminine was viewed now as an "invention of German imperialism." Rozanov himself now wrote that it was the Germans who created "an entire theory about the incapacity of the Slavic tribes, including the Russian, for education and culture"; in their opinion "the Slavs are too soft and feminine, and they cannot and will not be independent." Only "in combination with the manly Teutonic tribes can they produce a wonderful crossbreed, capable of engaging in culture and politics. This means that the Slavs can be excellent slaves to the Germans, and learned Germans even derive the name 'Slav' from the Latin 'sclavi': slave." But, exclaims the author, "now this 'bland' and 'feminine" Russian muzhik has arisen, to show his neighbors that he is not such a 'woman' as His Excellency, the Prussian Junker, considers him to be."[21]

In the argument of the publicist Mikhail O. Men'shikov, not only the "German" idea of Russian femininity was subject to criticism; he also deconstructed the most commonplace image of the Russian soul, which itself facilitated the association of Russia with femininity. He cited the words of one French poet, addressed to members of the Duma: "The golden Slavic

---

[16] V. V. Rozanov, "Vozle 'russkoi idei,'" in *Sochineniia* (Moscow: Sovetskaia Rossiia, 1990), 322.

[17] Ibid., 325–26.

[18] Ibid., 329.

[19] Ibid., 333.

[20] S. N. Bulgakov, *Voina i russkoe samosoznanie (publichnaia lektsiia)* (Moscow: Tip. T-va I. D. Sytina, 1915), 16.

[21] Rozanov, *Voina 1914 goda*, 30–31.

heart will come together with the reason of the West to form a valuable alloy; from this alloy shall be cast a bell, which will ring the birth of the new civilization, when justice will be heard as clearly as love." A similar line of argument is also characteristic of Russian messianism: the feminine Russian heart complements masculine Western reason. To Men'shikov, however, this characterization does not seem flattering: it turns out that "we have only our good, golden heart, while they have reason."[22] He notes that it is reminiscent of Bismarck's characterization of the Slavic race, i.e., that the Slavs are an innately feminine tribe, while the Germans are a masculine one; the German is a manly type, while the Slav is always somewhat womanish. It is permissible to speak of the golden heart of a woman; but to extol a man in the same terms is to somehow undermine him in an important sense. Having befriended a Russian, Men'shikov continues, it is very easy to exploit him, to condition him to serve you without any demand for recompense. The first of the Europeans to discover this dear, golden quality of the Russian heart were the Germans, who always despised Russia "as only a vulgar man can despise a woman."[23]

In war propaganda, various images were used to establish the supremacy of Russian masculinity. In one caricature, the leaders of Germany, Austria-Hungary, and Turkey are depicted as mischievous children being punished by a Russian muzhik.[24] The invocation of the "Russian bear" by propagandists was a curious means of masculinizing Russia's image. This was rare in previous conflicts, insofar as Russian propaganda was sensitive to the predominantly Russo-phobic nature of this image. But now, as the "Russian bear" became aligned with the Western powers, the image acquired positive connotations, which made possible its "rehabilitation" in Russia. In the course of the First World War, no fewer than 20 caricatures appeared in Russian satirical journals depicting the bear as a symbol of Russian masculinity: peace-loving and fair, on the one hand, and powerful and merciless on the other.[25] (See fig. 12.)

This emphasis on the masculine nature of Russianness was reinforced by the symbolic emasculation of the enemy, which took various forms. One in particular was used widely in posters, caricatures, and lubki, in which Russian women emerged as stronger than enemy men, for example in the drawing *The Austrian Went to Radziwillow (Shel avstriets v Radzivili)* by Kazimir Malevich (fig. 13).[26] Another topic of visual propaganda—the enemy troops

---

[22] Men'shikov, "Zolotoe serdtse," 530.

[23] Ibid., 531.

[24] "Iz-za lesa, iz-za gor vykhodil diadia Egor," *Bich* (Baku) 43 (1914).

[25] Andrzej de Lazari, Oleg Riabow and Magdalena Żakowska, *Europa i Niedźwiedź* (Warszawa: Centrum Polsko-Rosyjskiego Dialogu i Porozumienia, 2013).

[26] Further examples include *Avstriiskaia logika, Zhalo,* no. 21 (1915): 4; Aleksandr Radakov, "Kinematograf 'Satirikona,'" *Novyi satirikon,* no. 2 (1915): 9; and the lubok *V plenu u baby,* in V. Slavenson, "Voina i lubok," *Vestnik Evropy,* no. 7 (1915): 106. See also

hiding behind their women—served as a further means of depicting the opponent's behavior as unmanly.[27]

The impotence metaphor was another form of emasculation. The caricature *On the Separation of Austria and Hungary* depicts the state system of the Habsburg empire as a family. Austria is represented by Franz Joseph, shown as a senile old man; his wife, Hungary, tells him: "Come on, out you get, out of bed, you old boot—I'm sick of you!"[28]

Depicting the enemy as a woman was a popular way to emasculate him,[29] and this was used widely on the Russian side.[30] Sometimes this was accompanied by use of the prostitution metaphor: the titles of caricatures aimed at Germany—*The Loose Woman, A Lost But Entirely Unlovely Creature*—speak for themselves.[31] The most popular target was Ferdinand I, the king of Bulgaria, whose entry into the war on the side of Germany was viewed as stemming from his corruptibility.[32] The satirical journals were full of caricatures depicting Ferdinand in a woman's dress,[33] emphasizing his servility and his lack of subjectivity, autonomy, and other masculine qualities (see, for example, fig. 14).[34]

The gendering of another enemy state—Turkey—indicated the influence of Orientalism. Edward Said demonstrated that the relationship between the Western individual and the East is both sexualized and gendered: *homo occidentalis* is represented as male, while Eastern culture is represented as fe-

---

Karen Petrone, "Family, Masculinity, and Heroism in Russian War Posters of the First World War," in *Borderlines*, 105.

[27] *V Bel'gii, Oskolki*, no. 39 (1915): 1. See also Aleksandr Radakov, *Vsegda dzhentl'meny, Novyi satirikon* 34 (1914): 2.

[28] *K otdeleniiu Vengrii ot Avstrii, Zhalo*, no. 16 (1915): 4.

[29] Joshua S. Goldstein, *War and Gender: How Gender Shapes the War System and Vice Versa* (Cambridge: Cambridge University Press, 2001), 362.

[30] Petrone, "Family, Masculinity, and Heroism," 105–06. See also Klaus Vashik, "Metamorfozy zla: Nemetsko-russkie obrazy vraga v plakatnoi propagande 30–50-kh godov," in *Obraz vraga*, ed. Lev Gudkov (Moscow: OGI, 2005), 196.

[31] *Bludnitsa, Oskolki*, no. 11 (1916): 8; Re-mi, *Pogibshee i vovse ne miloe sozdanie, Novyi satirikon*, no. 41 (1914): 5.

[32] See, for example, the caricature *The Bulgarian Judas* (*Bolgarskii Iuda*), in which Ferdinand vainly tries to wash off the Slavic blood that covers him. *Bich* (Baku), no. 31 (1915): 8.

[33] For example: *Ne torguisia, ne skupis', Zhalo*, no. 27 (1915): 4; *Frederika Koburgskaia: Znamenitaia bolgarskaia soderzhanka, Zhalo*, no. 33 (1915): 4; Re-mi, *Shansonetnyi dukh, Novyi satirikon*, no. 32 (1915): 9; Ivan Maliutin, *Slabost', Budil'nik*, no. 39 (1914): 1.

[34] See also *My est' Ferdinand I, Bozhei i Frantsa-Iosifa milost'iu, Bich* (Baku), no. 41 (1914): 10; *Khoziain i sluga (K mobilizatsii v Bolgarii), Bich* (Baku), no. 39 (1915): 1.

male.[35] The East is associated with sensuality, with desire, sexual promise, the invitation to penetrate and to impregnate.[36] Russian caricatures mock the cowardice of Turkish troops.[37] Turkey is frequently depicted as a woman.[38] Note, particularly, the caricature *At Tsargrad*, in which Russian sailors bear off the sultan's harem as a trophy.[39] The inability to defend one's women is a widespread trope of symbolic emasculation, the extreme form of which is the practice of mass rape in time of war.[40]

Thus, the tendency to feminize Them and masculinize Us—emphasizing the weakness of the first and the inevitable victory of the latter—is fairly evident in the Russian view of the war. And yet the feminization of Russia, set against the masculinization of the enemy, could also be observed; this became the context in which the maternal personification of Russia could enter the discourse of the First World War. In the course of its long history, the "Mother Russia" image acquired a multitude of meanings, which now found new life in wartime discourse. This polyvalency allowed the image to contribute to various crucial functions, including: military mobilization; commemoration; establishing moral superiority; demonstrating military power; legitimizing Russia's entry into the war; reinforcing imperial unity; and establishing the natural, organic nature of a friendly relationship with the Entente powers.

First of all, it was the image of a suffering, violated, desecrated Motherland that featured as a tool of mobilization. Besides the cult of heroism, strength, and ruthlessness as masculine attributes, the representation of the soldier as defender was a crucial discursive practice, making war an attractive option.[41] Therefore, images of "Our" women's suffering (or the sufferings of the nation, as represented by a female, maternal figure) were widely used in wartime discourse as an appeal to the gender identity of Russian men.[42] A characteristic

---

[35] Edward Said, *Orientalism* (New York: Pantheon Books, 1978).

[36] Reina Lewis, *Gendering Orientalism: Race, Femininity and Representation* (New York: Routledge, 1996), 5.

[37] *Vot edinstvennyi sluchai, kogda odin turok idet na dvoikh*, Bich (Baku), no. 9 (1915): 2.

[38] For example: *Mogut voiti*, Bich (Baku), no. 39 (1914): 1; *Na stsene vostochnogo teatra*, Bich (Baku), no. 50 (1914): 8; *Novoe turko-germanskoe tango*, Bich (Baku), no. 4 (1915): 5.

[39] *U Tsar'grada*, Bich (Baku), no. 18 (1915): 1. Incidentally, a similar theme was employed in the Russian satirical art of the Russo-Turkish war, for example, *Vozvrashchenie turok iz plena na rodinu*, Budil'nik, no. 40 (1878): 1.

[40] Nira Yuval-Davis, "Nationalism, Feminism, and Gender Relations," in *Becoming National*, 129; Goldstein, *War and Gender*, 362.

[41] J. Ann Tickner, *Gendering World Politics: Issues and Approaches in the Post–Cold War Era* (New York: Columbia University Press, 2001), 57; Nira Yuval-Davis, *Gender and Nation* (London: Sage Publications, 1997), 15.

[42] Yuval-Davis, *Gender and Nation*, 94.

method used in such representations involved creating images of the dishonor or sexual violence suffered by women at the hands of the Enemy. The enemy as sexual aggressor is a constant presence, both in stories about individual women and in representations of the Motherland disgraced.[43]

This type of discourse was widely used by the propaganda machines of all belligerent countries, including Russia.[44] From the very start of the war, images of disgrace or sexual violence suffered by Russian women at the hands of the male enemy occupied an important place in descriptions of "German brutality." The theme of the lascivious enemy is elaborated in essays,[45] satirical art,[46] film,[47] and belles lettres.[48] The defense of honor, both that of Russian women and of the Motherland, is a key motif of the mobilization discourse. For example, I. Kudriashov—a village elder from Kaluga province—writes in a letter that "We shall not let the enemy insult our Mother Russia..."[49] "Mother Russia" is also present in commemorative practice: images of the inconsolable sorrow of the nation for her fallen troops emerge as an indispensable element

---

[43] See, for example, Sam Keen, *Faces of the Enemy: Reflections of the Hostile Imagination* (San Francisco: Harper & Row, 1986).

[44] One of the most famous images in the history of war propaganda is that of Belgium as a young woman raped by the Germans at the start of the First World War, from Ellsworth Young's poster "Remember Belgium!" See Walton Rawls, *Wake Up, America! World War I and the American Poster* (New York: Abbeville Press, 1988), 65. For further examples of the rape metaphor in First World War propaganda, see Billie Melman, "Introduction," in *Borderlines*, 10–11.

[45] For example: Rozanov, *Voina 1914 goda*, 62–65, 74; B. I. Imshenetskii and A. Bogdanov, eds., *Voina i zhenshchina* (Petrograd: Tip. I. V. Leont'eva, 1914), 8–10.

[46] See, for example, the caricatures *Stranichka iz germanskoi istorii: Nashestvie gunnov 20 veka*, *Oskolki*, no. 15 (1915): 8; *Novaia mifologiia*, *Oskolki*, no. 2 (1916): 1; *Otsenka dobychi (kul'turtregery)*, *Bich* (Baku), no. 32 (1915): 10 and passim.

[47] One example is *The Disgrace of the Twentieth Century, or The Antichrist* (*Pozor XX Veka ili Antikhrist*). See Hubertus F. Jahn, "Russkie rabochie, patriotizm i Pervaia mirovaia voina," in *Rabochie i intelligentsiia v epokhu reform i revoliutsii, 1861–fevral' 1917*, ed. Sergei I. Potolov (St. Petersburg: RAN, Otdelenie istorii, 1997), 385. Another example is *The Horrors of Rheims* (*Uzhasy Reimsa*). See Hubertus F. Jahn, *Patriotic Culture in Russia during World War I* (Ithaca, NY: Cornell University Press, 1995), 165.

[48] These include the works of Lidiia Alekseevna Charskaia, Ol'ga Mikhailovna Bebutova, and Nikolai Nikolaevich Breshko-Breshkovskii. See Ben Hellman, "Pervaia mirovaia voina v lubochnoi literature," in *Rossiia i Pervaia mirovaia voina*, ed. N. N. Smirnov (St. Petersburg: Dmitrii Bulanin, 1999), 311.

[49] "Rossiiskaia liubov': Otkliki voiny," *Niva*, no. 7, encl. (1915): 3.

of wartime culture. Thus, S. A. Vinogradov's poster *From Moscow to the Russian Prisoners of War* expresses Russia's mourning for her sons.[50]

Moreover, peace-loving and selfless, "Mother Russia" also served to illustrate the just character of the war. To represent one's country with images of pure, chaste womanhood is a common practice of war propaganda, intended to illustrate both the purity of the state's intentions and the rightness of its participation in the conflict.[51] This is hardly surprising, since the Victorian concept of femininity supports the interpretation of morality (identified, above all, with selflessness and the spirit of sacrifice) as feminine.[52]

It should be noted that this idea held a particular attraction in Russia: Russian identity was often specified by emphasizing Russia's sacrifice and selflessness,[53] and this was employed in prowar propaganda. In particular, the poster *On Russia's War with Japan* (*K voine Rossii s Iaponiei*), printed in April 1904, asserted that Russia's participation in the war was purely defensive, "sacrificing herself for the world."

As we know, an obligatory element of war propaganda was the dehumanization of the enemy. In this case, it is remarkable that dehumanization was achieved through the enemy's masculinization, by rendering the "sins of Teutonism" explicitly gendered, or relating them to qualities consistently associated with the masculine principle. The image of Russia, meanwhile, was full of contrasting—feminine—qualities.

One manifestation of the supposedly "bestial manliness" of Germany was its cruelty and cult of strength, contrasted with the apparent natural kindness, meekness, and mildness of the Russian soldier.[54] Establishing his thesis about the peaceful nature of the Russians and the aggression of the Germans, Men'shikov invoked the epics of both cultures, contrasting Iaroslavna with the "bloodthirsty and grasping" Kriemhild:[55] the opposition of the "feminine" Russian woman and her "masculine" German counterpart reinforces the idea of the Teutonic pathology. In propaganda, German women were portrayed as lacking femininity in both appearance and character. The image of the cruel and heartless German Sisters of Mercy became a popular theme in anti-

---

[50] S. A. Vinogradov, *Moskva russkim voinam v plenu 31 okt.–1 noiabr 1915*, in Nina Baburina, *Russkii plakat Pervoi mirovoi voiny* (Moscow: Iskusstvo i kul'tura, 1992), 49.

[51] Mosse, *Nationalism and Sexuality*, 90.

[52] Jean B. Elshtain, *Public Man, Private Woman: Women in Social and Political Thought* (Princeton, NJ: Princeton University Press, 1981).

[53] Riabov, "*Matushka-Rus'*," 87–89.

[54] M. O. Men'shikov, "Vechno-zhenstvennoe," in *Pis'ma k russkoi natsii*, 516.

[55] Men'shikov, "Zolotoe serdtse," 497.

German propaganda.[56] Not just caricaturists,[57] but also entirely respectable authors were affected by the idea that German women were mannish and physically unattractive.[58] And, as for German men, cruelty, aggression, and the cult of strength were interpreted by Russian authors as excessive. German masculinity was considered to be overabundant, and therefore abnormal and bound for defeat. Nikolai Berdiaev writes of the "tragedy of Teutonism" as the "tragedy of overweening will ... too exclusively masculine."[59]

A soulless rationalism, manifested in the worship of technology, was one more characteristic of "Teutonism" and one with distinctive gendered connotations. In the partly animated film *The Lily of Belgium*, directed by Władysław Starewicz (1915), living nature is contrasted with German machinery to create an association with the "rape of Belgium."[60]

The accusation of "idolatry of Man" or "man-God" (*chelovekobozhie*) was a particular way to dehumanize the enemy.[61] The term "hubris" was used traditionally by many Russian authors to characterize the West in general, and Germany in particular. Russia, in contrast, was represented as humility incarnate.[62] Meanwhile, the sin of hubris was designated "satanic" and associated with the masculine principle. Accusations of treating with the forces of evil—with Hell—are traditionally involved in constructing the image of the enemy; and equating Teutonism to the Satanic principle was a crucial factor in its dehumanization.[63]

---

[56] Re-mi, *Nemetskie sestry miloserdiia dobivaiut ranenykh*, *Novyi satirikon*, no. 40 (1914): 12; *V Konstantinopole*, *Zhalo*, no. 37 (1914): 1; Aleksandr Radakov, *Poslednii krik berlinskoi mody*, *Novyi satirikon*, no. 24 (1915): 12; *V germanskom lazarete*, *Oskolki*, no. 41 (1915): 8; *Razuchilis' byt' sentimental'nymi*, *Oskolki*, no. 50 (1915): 1; Re-mi, *Sovsem bezvykhodnoe polozhenie*, *Novyi satirikon*, no. 20 (1916): 9. A parallel theme appeared on the famous British poster by D. Wilson, *Red Cross or Iron Cross?* in Charles Roetter, *The Art of Psychological Warfare, 1914–1945* (New York: Stein and Day, 1974).

[57] For example, *Stranichka voiny*, *Oskolki*, no. 16 (1916): 4.

[58] For example, S. L. Frank, "Sila i pravo," *Russkaia mysl'*, no. 1 (1916): 11.

[59] N. A. Berdiaev, *Sud'ba Rossii* (Moscow: Filosofskoe obshchestvo SSSR, 1990), 171. Later, in *The Russian Idea*, Berdiaev even characterized Germany's excessive masculinity as a "monstrosity" which "will lead to nothing good" (1948). See N. A. Berdiaev, "Russkaia ideia: Osnovnye problemy russkoi mysli XIX veka," in *O Rossii i russkoi filosofskoi kul'ture: Filosofy russkogo posleoktiabr'skogo zarubezh'ia* (Moscow: Nauka, 1990), 267.

[60] Jahn, *Patriotic Culture*, 165.

[61] S. N. Bulgakov, "Chelovechnost' protiv chelovekobozhiia: Istoricheskoe opravdanie anglo-russkogo sblizheniia," *Russkaia mysl'*, no. 6 (1917).

[62] See Riabov, "*Matushka-Rus'*."

[63] See, for example, M. O. Men'shikov, "Dushi narodov," in *Pis'ma k russkoi natsii*, 506; Ern, "Mech i krest," 328.

Additionally, the "Mother Russia" image testified not only to Russia's moral superiority, but to its military pre-eminence: in the form of an all-powerful fighter and protector, "Mother Russia" served to establish the inevitability of victory over the enemy. The poster *Russia for Justice* (*Rossiia—za pravdu*) shows her as a forceful young woman. Clad in an ancient Russian helmet and chainmail, a sword in her right hand and a shield depicting St. George in her left, she stands over the defeated dragon; its three heads symbolize Germany, Austria-Hungary, and the Ottoman Empire (fig. 15). We should note that this representation of the nation as a warrior woman was employed in the propaganda of many countries.[64] A more specific expression of the perceived strength of the Motherland is the lubok *Russia and Her Warrior* (*Rossiia i ee voin*). In the accompanying text, Germany's technological pre-eminence is represented as proof of a weak spirit, while the Russian soldiers' bond with their Mother Earth is represented as favoring their victory. Additionally, this lubok stands out for being, in all likelihood, one of the very few depictions of "Mother Russia" together with her sons (evidently so, as she is depicted here as a mature woman relative to the majority of other portrayals of the period) (fig. 16).

Another function of this symbol was to legitimize Russia's entry into the war. The defense of Serbia, or even the unification of the Slavs, was often represented as a fundamental cause and main aim of the Great War. Thus, at the very start of the conflict, in his welcome speech to Nicholas II on the occasion of the imperial family's visit to the ancient capital, the mayor of Moscow pronounced the following words: "The Slavic question must be solved by the unification of all Slavic peoples under the protection of Russia, the mother of the Slavs."[65] In one caricature, published in August 1914 in *Zhalo*, Serbia is depicted as a harmless but mischievous little boy, threatened with serious punishment by Austria-Hungary and Germany. In such a situation, Russia—portrayed as a woman—simply cannot hold back from defending Serbia, her child (fig. 17).

And indeed, the maternal metaphor was often invoked to represent Russia's special relationship with the Slavic countries. This allowed Russia's policy towards these countries to be represented as founded on selfless, motherly concern, endowing her both with certain rights and duties. It is hardly surprising that Bulgaria's position, for example, was assessed in the following terms: "Born of Russian blood shed for the liberation of the Slavic peoples, Bulgaria

---

[64] Maurice Rickards, *Posters of the First World War* (New York: Walker, 1968).

[65] "Istoricheskaia letopis'," *Istoricheskii vestnik*, no. 9 (1914): 28. During the Galicia offensive of August 1914, an appeal was published from the commander in chief, Grand Duke Nikolai Nikolaevich, addressed to "The Russian People": "Freed Russian brothers! There is a place for all of you in the bosom of Mother Russia!" See A. Petrishchev, "Khronika vnutrennei zhizni," *Russkoe bogatstvo*, no. 9 (1914): 236.

betrayed the Slavs and took up arms against Mother Russia together with our historic enemies."[66]

We should note that the image of Russia's relationship with her "Slavic children" was also attractive to the propaganda of the Central Powers. In a caricature published in the German magazine *Ulk*, Russia is depicted as a haughty matron, and the "Last of the Serbs" looks more like her serf than her son (fig. 18). The Asiatic elements of "Mother Russia"'s appearance also catch the eye, contrasting as they do with the idealized Slavic features attributed to her by Russian artists.

Furthermore, the "Mother Russia" image formed part of an imperial discourse, with Russia as the mother of all the peoples of the empire, collected into a state that is underpinned by the maternal care and protection attributed to it. The image of Russia as universal mother served to reinforce imperial unity. "The Pole, the Russian, the Jew, the Latvian, the Georgian, and the Tatar stand shoulder to shoulder. Here there is not Greek and Jew. All are the children of one Motherland," wrote Vasilii Nemirovich-Danchenko (brother of the famous theater director).[67] Propaganda persistently emphasized that the representatives of all nations feel "filial love and loyalty to Russia";[68] the Pole had come to understand that she was his mother, not his stepmother;[69] many of them "called Russia 'Mother' for the first time."[70] The Declaration of Russian Germans, made at the beginning of the war, stated: "We, German settlers in Russia, have always considered her our mother and our motherland...."[71] However, as we know, by no means everyone trusted in the loyalty of the "internal Germany"; Russian Germans often were portrayed as "unfaithful children." The caricature *The Fruits of Russian Kindness and Credulity* depicts them as serpents threatening their adoptive mother, Russia. She can only regret her own short-sightedness and carelessness: "Lord! Whom have I nurtured!" (fig. 19).

The "Mother Russia" image was also used to establish the "natural" character of Russia's allied relationships: her allies were often rendered female. In the poster *Concord*, three female figures represent Russia (Faith), England (Hope), and France (Love), symbolizing the irreproachable morality

---

[66] "Bolgarskoe predatel'stvo: (Politicheskoe obozrenie)," *Niva*, no. 39 (1915): 720.

[67] Vasilii I. Nemirovich-Danchenko, "Vchera i segodnia," in *Velikaia voina Rossii za svobodu i ob˝edinenie slavian*, ed. D. I. Tikhomirov (Moscow, 1914), 95.

[68] "Voina i gosudarstvennaia duma," *Niva*, no. 7 (1915): 123–24.

[69] A. Korinfskii, "Izgnanniki voiny," *Niva*, no. 36 (1915): 677.

[70] "Otkliki voiny: Voina i russko-pol'skie otnosheniia: Voprosy vnutrennei zhizni," *Niva*, no. 34 (1916), supplement: 3.

[71] "Istoricheskoe zasedanie Gosudarstvennoi Dumy," in *Velikaia voina Rossii*, 78.

of the aims and motives of the Entente powers' war efforts.[72] In the interests of public opinion, it was important to show that the configuration of power within Europe was entirely appropriate, and therefore enduring. As we know, from the time of Peter I onwards, the West had been the most significant Other in the construction of Russian identity. Now it emerged, as the philosopher Vladimir Ern remarked, that the "old antithesis of Russia and Europe is shattered by real war";[73] the powers fighting arm-in-arm with Russia against Germany were "one hundred percent" European. In this context, Russian authors turned to the idea of the "two Europes" previously set out by Dostoevskii.[74] Germany personified everything that was negative in Europe as a whole. It became clear that Russia had been divided from Europe by the very things that "now became so forcefully real in armed Teutonism."[75] Ern even wrote of the "anti-Europe," Europe and "her twin."[76] And yet there was another Europe, the "land of holy miracles," the Europe of "great deeds and heroism," "faith and sacrifice," "nobility and sincerity."[77] It was with precisely this Europe that Russia enjoyed the "most profound inner unity," "a shared reverence of the sacred."[78] National, confessional, and gender markers were closely interrelated. Comparing Catholic France, Belgium, Poland, and Orthodox Russia, on the one hand, to Protestant Germany on the other, the author emphasizes:

> In different tongues but with one liturgical impulse we sing to the Most Pure and Immaculate Mother of Lights. In Belgium, France and Poland are Her altars, Her relics, Her miraculous images and icons. We are drawn together, not just by outrage on behalf of our common worship, but by something higher, more radiant.[79]

He writes of the "profound disorder of what we might call the sexual moment of [German] collective national life," which

---

[72] "Soglasie," 1914 (Rossiiskaia natsional'naia biblioteka), in Jahn, *Patriotic Culture*, 26.

[73] V. F. Ern, "Vremia slavianofil'stvuet: Lektsiia pervaia," in *Sochineniia*, 372.

[74] Ben Hellman, "Kogda vremia slavianofil'stvovalo: Russkie filosofy i pervaia mirovaia voina," in *Studia russica helsingiensia et tartuensia: Problemy istorii russkoi literatury nachala XX veka*, ed. Liisa Byckling and Pekka Pesonen (Helsinki: Helsinki University Press, 1989), 218.

[75] Ern, "Vremia slavianofil'stvuet," 381.

[76] Ibid., 373.

[77] Ibid., 382.

[78] Ibid., 381.

[79] Ern, "Mech i krest," 337–38.

enshrined in dogma the anomaly of abstract masculinity and the negation of a healthy feminine essence ... Martin Luther ... cut off the living spiritual nourishment to the German body, the heavenly femininity of the Most Holy and Immaculate Virgin Mother. Ever since then the German soul has been tragically lost, from the *Critique of Pure Reason* to the current proud undertaking: to seize power over all peoples, to take over the world by force of violence and the purely satanic, abstract, and masculine technology of their culture. The question of whether Earth will allow her rapist to take possession of her sacred essence will be answered on the field of battle.[80]

However, this complex line of argument was directed primarily at a "highbrow audience." The broad masses were more likely to understand the use of images corresponding to a traditional hierarchy of gender relations. The caricature *On Shrovetide* (*Na Maslenoi*) depicts England and France as sweet young ladies in the masterful embrace of a Russian merchant (fig. 20). The very same perception of Russia as head of the Entente comes across in the lubok *Our Numbers Have Grown* (*A nashego-to polku pribylo*),[81] with the Russian soldier depicted as much bigger physically than his allies; and in *Concord*, as we have seen already, with Russia occupying the central place among her allies.

"Mother Russia" in the Revolutions and Civil War

Even the February Revolution began with a reference to "Mother Russia." The telegram prepared for Nicholas II by Mikhail Rodzianko, chairman of the State Duma, contained the following words: "There is no sacrifice I would not make for the active good and salvation of our dear Mother Russia. Therefore I am prepared to renounce the throne...." (2 March 1917).[82]

Throughout its history, the "Mother Russia" image has actively been employed in the discourse of legitimization and delegitimization of national political systems, as well as in political mobilization. The government frequently invoked the concept of hierogamy—the sacred marriage between the ruler and his land—well known from the political mythology of the ancient Near East.[83] In medieval texts, the prince is represented as the defender of Russia's

---

[80] Ibid., 325.

[81] Andrew M. Nedd, "Segodniashnii Lubok: Art, War, and National Identity," in *Picture This: World War I Posters and Visual Culture*, ed. Pearl James (Lincoln: University of Nebraska Press, 2010), 259.

[82] See Aleksandr I. Spiridonovich, *Velikaia voina i Fevral'skaia revoliutsiia: 1914–1917 gg.* (New York: Vseslavianskoe Izd-vo, 1960–62), 3: 296.

[83] Ernst H. Kantorowicz, *The King's Two Bodies: A Study in National Political Theology* (Princeton, NJ: Princeton University Press, 1957).

soil and keeper of her honor;[84] echoes of hierogamy can also be found under Nicholas II.[85] The representation of political opponents as internal enemies aiming to destroy "Mother Russia" also strengthened the legitimacy of the government.

The opposition, in turn, invoked the image of the Motherland suffering under the arbitrary rule of an unjust government. This probably dates as far back as the 16th century, in connection with the appearance of the concept of Holy Rus'. Prince Andrei Kurbskii wrote of Ivan the Terrible's allies: "They have gnawed through the belly of their mother, the sacred Russian land, who gave birth to them and raised them, to her own misfortune and ruin!"[86] In the discourse of the *narodnik*s (revolutionary populists) during the 19th century, "Mother Russia" was a symbol of opposition to the state, which embodied the paternal principle and which, following the reforms of Peter I, was often associated with something alien and essentially Western.[87]

The discourse of the first revolution (1905–07) manifested a similar polarization of views about the relationship of people and state: Mother Russia and our Father, the Tsar. The government appealed to the mythology of hierogamy, attempting to represent itself as acting in the interests of the nation as a whole.[88] In far-right discourse, "Mother Russia" also appeared in a favorite role, namely symbolizing both Russia's strength[89] and its suffering at the hands of "troublemakers," defining "trouble" (*smuta*) as an inherently un-Russian phenomenon.[90] Yet in revolutionary discourse, Russia was depicted as a woman oppressed by tsarism. This image appears in numerous satirical publications: the drawing *Golgotha*, for instance, published in *Sekira* following

---

[84] L. A. Chernaia, "'Chest'": Predstavleniia o chesti i bezchestii v russkoi literature XI–XVII vv.," in *Drevnerusskaia literatura: Izobrazhenie obshchestva*, ed. A. S. Demin (Moscow: Nauka, 1991). Echoes of the idea of a sacred marriage between "our Father the Tsar" and "Mother Russia" can also be found in the rituals of Muscovite Rus'. See Joanna Hubbs, *Mother Russia: The Feminine Myth in Russian Culture* (Bloomington: Indiana University Press, 1988), 188–89.

[85] Riabov, "*Rossiia-Matushka*," 129–30.

[86] Andrei Kurbskii, "Istoriia o velikom kniaze Moskovskom," in *Pamiatniki literatury Drevnei Rusi: Vtoraia polovina XVI veka*, ed. L. A. Dmitriev and D. S. Likhachev (Moscow: Khudozhestvennaia literatura, 1986), 319; see also 271.

[87] Riabov, "*Matushka-Rus'*," 108–10.

[88] For example, in the Supreme Manifesto of 6 August 1905. See *Niva*, no. 32 (1905): 637.

[89] For example: "Sviataia Rus'," in *Sviataia Rus': Bol´shaia entsiklopediia Russkogo naroda. Russkii patriotizm*, ed. O. A. Platonov (Moscow: Institut russkoi tsivilizatsii, 2003), 702; "Izbavi nas ot lukavogo," *Pliuvium*, no. 15 (1907): 1 and passim.

[90] See, for example, Sof´ia I. Smirnova, *Chernaia sotnia* (St. Petersburg: Tip. A. S. Suvorina, 1906). See also the caricatures *Vkolachivanie v grob zazhivo*, *Pliuvium*, no. 43 (1907): 2; [No title] *Medved'*, no. 4 (1906): 1.

the suppression of the December uprising in 1905, depicts Russia as a woman re-enacting the Stations of the Cross.[91] The image of the suffering motherland was also found in revolutionary poetry.[92]

The *narodnik* discourse of the February Revolution actively employed the image of the oppressed "Mother Russia" in order to subvert the old regime and legitimize the new. As one publication stated:

> Why did A. F. Kerenskii come to love his Mother Russia? Above all, he came to love her with a fierce filial love because of the sufferings inflicted on our Mother Russia for centuries by her ancestral tormentors, the autocratic tsars and their guard dogs, the oprichniks.[93]

Here we see the fundamental tropes of the *narodnik* discourse: "Mother Russia"'s sufferings, her "tormentors," the "filial love" of her liberators. In this case, the hero's role is filled by Kerenskii; his depiction as an all-powerful savior and leader[94] is constructed, among other things, on the image of his special relationship with "Mother Russia."

The idea of hierogamy also served the delegitimization of power. Insofar as the tsar's model masculinity—as the symbolic spouse of the nation—conditioned his political leadership, and vice versa, revolutionary propaganda attempted to emasculate him in order to desacralize the government. Elizabeth Hemenway analyzes one political fairytale, published in the summer of 1917, which begins with the following words: "Once upon a time there was a wealthy widow with a pretty face and a healthy body. She was not old and not young,

---

[91] *Golgofa, Sekira,* no. 7 (1905): 5. See also the depictions of the suffering "Mother Russia" in the magazines *Nagaechka,* no. 4 (1905): 10; ibid., no. 2 (1905): 8; *Gvozd´,* no. 5 (1906): 1, 5; *Vampir,* no. 1 (1906): 1; *Ovod,* no. 5 (1906): 1; *Shut,* no. 43 (1907): 1 and passim.

[92] See, for example, Iurii Kramol´nik, "Rodine," *Nagaechka,* no. 4 (1905): 5. Curiously, even the magazine *Skandal,* which mostly carried openly erotic material, evidently considered it necessary to publish material dedicated to the revolutionary liberation of "Mother Russia." See, for example, "L.K."'s poem *Rodine* (To the Motherland), *Skandal,* no. 2 (1906): 7.

[93] V. Kir´iakov, "A. F. Kerenskii," *Niva,* no. 19 (1917): 287. This image was also used in German propaganda for criticizing Russia. In the magazine *Russkii vestnik,* published in Germany for Russian POWs and intended to create antiwar and anti-Entente feeling, the "anti-bourgeois" mood of the revolutionary Russian masses was also taken into account following the February Revolution. In particular, a letter from a soldier was published that contained the words: "We do not want millions of people like us to die at the whim of our capitalists! We do not want foreigners to cling to Mother Russia and suckle at her bosom, while we consume their sops." B. I. Kolonitskii, "Zanimatel´naia anglofobiia: Obrazy 'Kovarnogo Al´biona' v gody Pervoi mirovoi voiny," *Novoe literaturnoe obozrenie* 1 (41) (2000): 76.

[94] Boris Kolonitskii, "'Russkaia ideia' i ideologiia Fevral´skoi revoliutsii," *Toronto Slavic Quarterly,* no. 21 (2007), http://www.utoronto.ca/tsq/18/kolonitsky18.shtml.

and she was called Mother Russia."[95] In this tale, "Kol′ka the Publican," like "Proshka the Bolshevik" and "Proshka the Menshevik," is merely a son of "Mother Russia," and in no way her husband.[96]

The apparent inability of Nicholas II to be a worthy husband to his empress also served to demonstrate his unsuitability as spouse to the sacred body of the people, "Mother Russia." The rumors of Aleksandra Fedorovna's affair with Rasputin reinforced this idea.

> By the time of the revolution, numerous obscene pictures were in circulation all over Russia. One of these scribbles was *The Family* (*Sem′ia*): a bearded man (Rasputin) and, in his embrace, two sharp-hipped beauties (the tsaritsa and Ania [Anna A. Vyrubova]) ... and all this against a background of shameless dancing girls (the Grand Duchesses).[97]

Meanwhile, Russia was now represented as a woman breaking her chains: either alone, tearing them asunder—as in the drawing *The Radiant Revival of Russia* from *Budil′nik*[98]—or being freed by a revolutionary—as depicted on the banner carried on one of the March demonstrations by the workers of the Izhora plant (fig. 21).

Russia was also depicted as an exultant victress, crowning the liberating heroes (fig. 22).[99] As P. K. Kornakov remarks, together with Liberty, the allegorical figure of Russia-as-woman was the most popular figure in the visual discourse of the February Revolution.[100] The popularity of the "Mother Russia" image can also be gauged by the many ways in which it appeared: on

---

[95] Elizabeth J. Hemenway, "Mother Russia and the Crisis of the Russian National Family: The Puzzle of Gender in Revolutionary Russia," *Nationalities Papers* 25, 1 (1997): 103.

[96] Ibid., 103. On the feminization of Nicholas II's image in revolutionary discourse, see ibid., 109. As Boris Kolonitskii remarks, it is possible to deduce from cases of *lèse-majesté* brought during the war that the insult "old woman tsar" (tsar′-baba) was very widely used. B. I. Kolonitskii, *"Tragicheskaia erotika": Obrazy imperatorskoi sem′i v gody Pervoi mirovoi voiny* (Moscow: Novoe literaturnoe obozrenie, 2010), 211.

[97] Edvard Radzinskii, *"Gospodi ... spasi i usmiri Rossiiu": Nikolai II. Zhizn′ i smert′* (Moscow: Vagrius, 1993), 133. For other examples of similar drawings, see Khersonskii, *O Tsare Durake, o Tsaritse Bludnitse i o Grishke-Rasputnoi shishke* (Petrograd: Elektropechatnia "Uspekh," 1917); L. A. Evstigneeva, *Zhurnal "Satirikon" i poety-satirikontsy* (Moscow: Nauka, 1968), 137; Kolonitskii, "Tragicheskaia erotika," 319.

[98] *Svetloe Rossii voskresenie*, *Budil′nik*, no. 14/15 (1917): 8–9. See also D. Mel′nikov, *Vpered! Budil′nik*, no. 19 (1917): 9.

[99] P. K. Kornakov, "Simvolika i ritualy revoliutsii 1917 g.," in *Anatomiia revoliutsii: 1917 god v Rossii. Massy, partii, vlast′*, ed. V. Iu. Cherniaev (St. Petersburg: Glagol, 1994), 360.

[100] Ibid.

the banners of revolutionary organizations; on military banners; on medallions (see fig. 23); on magazine covers.[101] Finally, it appeared on the agitational posters of various political parties, for example, the Kadets.[102]

Meanwhile, "Mother Russia" also had her place in the symbolic system of those who opposed overthrowing autocracy. The perception of the February Revolution among monarchists in April 1917 can be gauged by these lines of the poet Sergei S. Bekhteev: "Let posterity curse / Those sons who, with such criminal perfidy / Dared to betray/ Their helpless mother!"[103]

Over time, the charm of the revolution faded even for its supporters, and to all appearances the image of "Mother Russia"'s liberation was no longer an inspiration.[104] The "eternal feminine" had abruptly turned out to be "eternally womanish," and there is a degree of misogyny detectable in the reactions of many. The caricature *The Maiden, Revolution* illustrates this disenchantment. The object of dreams, imagined as a beautiful young maiden, turns out in fact to be a vulgar old "baggage."[105] Perhaps the most scandalous version of this depiction of Russia-as-woman was Aleksandr S. Roslavlev's poem "The Naked Woman," which appeared in "naked print" in *Novyi satirikon* in early 1918: "Obscenely gleeful / Dirty and uncombed / "Rusha" stands naked / Right at the window."[106]

Opposition to the Bolsheviks spawned a new impulse in the development of Russia's maternal metaphor. The image of "Mother Russia" under Bolshevik threat is a central one in leaflets from the autumn of 1917.[107] The Bolsheviks were depicted as "Mother Russia's oppressors," "hirelings of the Kaiser," and "executioners"; satirical art made good use of these themes. One caricature, dated July 1917, depicts the Bolsheviks subjecting Russia to torture.[108] Curi-

---

[101] Ibid., 358.

[102] A. F. Maksimov, *Golosuite za Partiiu Narodnoi svobody (Vashik i Baburina, Real'nost' utopii: Iskusstvo russkogo plakata XX v.)* (Moscow: Progress-Traditsiia, 2004), 55.

[103] S. S. Bekhteev, "Rossiia," http://soulibre.ru/Была_Державная_Россия_(Сергей_Бехтеев) (accessed March 2014).

[104] One sketch by Isaak Babel' might serve as indirect proof of weariness, not just with the Revolution, but also with the use of the "Mother Russia" image. Recalling an appearance by Kerenskii in June 1917, Babel' described it thus: "Aleksandr Fedorovich gave a speech about his wife and mother, Russia. The crowd suffocated him with the sheepskins of his own passions." Isaak Babel', "Liniia i tsvet," in *Miniatiury*, http://lib.ru/PROZA/BABEL/miniatures.txt_with-big-pictures.html.

[105] M. Bobyshov and Boris Antonovskii, "Deva Revoliutsiia," *Bich* (St. Petersburg), no. 28 (1917): 1, 16.

[106] Aleksandr Roslavlev, "Golaia," *Novyi satirikon*, no. 4 (1918): 3.

[107] Hemenway, "Mother Russia," 115–16.

[108] N. Nikolaevskii, "Pochesti i uslugi, okazannye bol'shevikami materi Rossii," *Bich* (St. Petersburg), no. 26 (1917): 12.

ously, the idea of hierogamy also plays a role in anti-Bolshevik discourse. Boris I. Antonovskii's caricature *Lenin's Affair with Russia*, published in *Novyi Satirikon* in those same July days, depicts Lenin persistently wooing a portly woman in Russian national costume; the child who results from this union is born wearing a Pickelhaube (see fig. 24).

After the October Revolution (and particularly the Brest-Litovsk Treaty) the "Mother Russia" image became even more prominent in the discourse of national treason. Consider this letter written by a Russian peasant (the style and mistakes of the original are preserved here):

> I, a Great Russian native of Orlov province, a peasant of Mtsensk district, write these curses on 10 January 1918.
> TO YOU
> Rulers, robbers, tyrants, devastators, Usurpers and Oppressors of mother Russia and the Russian Citizen, Trotskii, Uritskii, Zinov'ev, Spiridonova, Antonov, Lunacharskii, Krylenko and Co.
> Let me ask you: how long are you going to jeer at the many Millions of Russia at a tired and tormented people? instead of peace you signed a truce with the enemy and gave a big advantage to our opponent and you declared war on Russia the troops you deceived you sent to the Russian-Russian front You started a fratricidal war, your mercenary Red Guards are looting, killing, raping everywhere; all mother Russia is in flames, We conscientious Great Russians send you hangmen mercenaries of the Kaiser our curse may you be cursed anathema hangmen mercenaries of the Kaiser you don't know the Russian people will come to sober up and your end will come.[109]

The motif of the struggle against Bolshevism as a conflict with the enemies of Russia, with "aliens," "German spies," and so on, was exploited in the discourse of the White movement. A characteristic example is the poster *Sacrificed to the International* (*V zhertvu Internatsionalu*), depicting Russia as a bound woman surrounded by a group of Bolshevik leaders, with Kerenskii joining them.[110] The Bolshevik Revolution is portrayed as the murder of Russia-as-woman in the poster *Lenin and Trotskii: Doctors to the Ailing Russia*.[111]

The crucifixion of Russia was a popular theme and one which, evidently, also expressed the religious impulses of revolution.[112] A drawing in *Novyi Satirikon* depicted Russia as a woman nailed to the cross by a German officer

---

[109] http://www.yale.edu/annals/Steinberg/Documents/Steinberg128.htm.

[110] Waters, "The Female Forms," 331.

[111] "Lenin i Trotskii–vrachi bol'noi Rossii," *Rodina*, no. 3 (2008): 60. http://upload.wikimedia.org/wikipedia/ru/1/10/Ленин_и_Троцкий_-_врачи_больной_России.jpg

[112] On religious impulses in the February Revolution, see Kolonitskii, "'Russkaia ideia.'"

and a Russian traitor.[113] The idea of Russia crucified found expression in the poetry of Bekhteev, which was popular among White supporters: "And the host of the 'Red Star' / Having sealed her fate / Nails the unhappy Motherland, / Reviling her, to the cross!" ("Russian Golgotha," 1920).[114]

Depicting the enemy as a rapist was another common tool in the propaganda of mobilization. In General Petr Vrangel''s appeal to the military specialists of the Red Army, former Imperial Army officers, "Mother Russia" is presented not only as "ruined, stained by the blood of her brothers," but also as "dishonored."[115] Incidentally, a similar image of the revolution as the undoing of "Mother Russia" appears in the allied media. For example, in Bernard Partridge's caricature in *Punch*, the Bolshevik is represented as a procurer, bringing Russia by force to be violated by the kaiser: "Come on; come on and be kissed by him" (fig. 25).

Meanwhile, the White movement represented itself as "Mother Russia"'s redeemer. The motif of liberating the motherland is a prominent one in the rhetoric of the White leadership, from Ataman Dutov to General Vrangel'.[116] In the Volunteer's Oath, the aim of the White movement is defined as "to defend and free our tired and tormented Motherland." One mobilization leaflet from 1919 is illustrated with a soldier breaking the shackles of a young woman ("The volunteer army, like an epic hero, frees Russia from the Bolsheviks"); the text calls "all loyal sons of the Motherland" to join the ranks of the Whites.[117]

By virtue of its multiplicity of meanings, "Mother Russia" is one of the few symbols to unite such a politically heterogeneous phenomenon as the White movement. Its use on banknotes testifies to the degree to which it fulfilled a need: it can be seen on the "Don government" paper notes, the banknotes of the High Command of the Armed Forces of South Russia, and the treasury notes of the Provisional Siberian Government under Ataman Semenov (see fig. 26).[118]

---

[113] Kazimir Grus, "Legkaia rabota," *Novyi satirikon*, no. 5 (1918): 1. See also, for example, Aleksandr Radakov, "Poslednee zavoevanie revoliutsii," *Novyi satirikon*, no. 43 (1917): 16.

[114] S. S. Bekhteev, "Russkaia Golgofa," http://soulibre.ru/Сбылось_предсказание_Мессии_(Сергей_Бехтеев) (accessed March 2014).

[115] V. G. Cherkasov-Georgievskii and General P. N. Vrangel', *Poslednii rytsar' Rossiiskoi imperii: Dokumental'noe zhizneopisanie* (Moscow: Tsentrpoligraf, 2004), 314.

[116] For example: O. G. Goncharenko, *Beloe dvizhenie: Pokhod ot Tikhogo Dona do Tikhogo okeana* (Moscow: Veche, 2007), 136; Nikolai G. Ross, *Vrangel' v Krymu* (Frankfurt am Main: Posev, 1982), 246.

[117] "Edinaia, Velikaia i svobodnaia Rossiia—vot za chto boretsia Dobrovol'cheskaia Armiia" (Rossiiskaia gosudarstvennaia biblioteka).

[118] M. V. Khodiakov, *Den'gi revoliutsii i Grazhdanskoi voiny: Denezhnoe obrashchenie v Rossii, 1917–1920 gg.* (St. Petersburg: Piter, 2009), 116–27; I. S. Shikanova, "Denezhnye

The "Mother Russia" image is found yet again on the medal created by order of General Anton Denikin on 25 November 1918 to commemorate the 1200-verst march undertaken by a detachment under Colonel Mikhail Drozdovskii.[119] This medal is remarkable in its visualization of the idea that the greatest aim and ideal of the Volunteer Army is a "Unified, Indivisible, Great" Russia. Russia is depicted as a woman in ancient Russian dress, standing above a precipice with a sword held out in her right hand. Russian soldiers scale the cliff towards her, symbolizing the endeavour to rebuild the government.

As for the Bolsheviks, they hardly ever used this image in a positive sense. We know of only a few cases from the Civil War period in which Bolshevik propaganda personified the nation as female: Bessarabia, for example, is depicted on one poster as an imprisoned woman.[120] Particularly interesting is the familiar theme employed in one poster by Viktor Deni (Denisov) from the time of the Polish-Soviet War: a "Polish gent," together with Hetman Petliura, crucifies a young woman symbolizing Ukraine.[121]

However, in terms of the depiction of the Russian nation as a woman, there are no examples to be found in the Bolshevik propaganda of the period. This absence might be explained by any number of factors. Above all, it was the critics of Bolshevism who identified with the "Mother Russia" image: from the monarchists to the Mensheviks and Socialist Revolutionaries.[122] In their analysis of the ways in which contenders for government fought for the right to control the symbolic system of the revolution, Orlando Figes and Boris Kolonitskii suggest distinguishing the "language of inclusion" from the "language of exclusion" in Russia during 1917:[123] the first being characteristic of *narodnik* discourse, the second of Bolshevik discourse. Evidently, the Bolsheviks had no need of "Mother Russia" as a symbol of popular unity. In the opinion of Victoria Bonnell, the most important symbol of Bolshevik collective identity was the worker.[124] Furthermore, Soviet identity in the 1920s was formed along class lines; the nihilistic attitude to national identity characteristic

---

znaki atamana G. M. Semenova v sobranii ON GIM: Numizmaticheskii sbornik GIM," *Trudy GIM* 16, 138 (2003): 347.

[119] Kornakov, "Simvolika i ritunaly," 358.

[120] Victoria E. Bonnell, "The Representation of Women in Early Soviet Political Art," *Russian Review* 50 (July 1991): 275.

[121] Viktor Deni, *Palachi terzaiut Ukrainu: Smert´ palacham!* (1920) (Rossiiskaia natsional´naia biblioteka), in Boris S. Butnik-Siverskii, *Sovetskii plakat epokhi grazhdanskoi voiny, 1918–1921* (Moscow: Vsesoiuznaia knizhnaia palata, 1960), 608.

[122] Waters, "The Female Forms," 331.

[123] Orlando Figes and Boris Kolonitski, *Interpreting the Russian Revolution: The Language and Symbols of 1917* (New Haven: Yale University Press, 1999), 116.

[124] Bonnell, *Iconography of Power*, 24.

of some Bolsheviks manifested itself in playing down the significance of the "maternal" aspect of the nation.[125]

In addition, the Bolshevik revolution was not conceived as anti-European; rather, it was directed against the "backward Asiatic" aspects of Russian society.[126] Iver Neumann suggests that the Bolsheviks added the idea of the "two Europes" to their armory; the dichotomy between the "real Europe" and the "false" was fundamental to their identity strategies until the end of the 1920s, and they saw themselves as leaders of the former.[127] "Mother Russia," "Russia, the fat-bottomed baggage," was a symbol of backwardness in the eyes of the Bolsheviks; a symbol of that which the revolutionary transformation was supposed to eradicate.[128] This attitude is expressed very eloquently in a poem printed in *Pravda* with the suggestive title "Rus' and the USSR":

Rus'! Did you rot? Perish? Croak?
Well! Rest in peace!
You did not live, only sighed
In a dim, cramped hut.
You creaked and shuffled on crutches,
Smeared your lips in the icons' soot,
Cawed, like a crow, across distances
Slept heavily for centuries
Hey, old crone, blind and stupid!
Your grandchild has pulled down your shack...[129]

---

[125] In an article of 1934 dedicated to the differences between the Soviet motherland and the "Mother Russia" of the "old-regime," Mikhail Kol'tsov cites the words of a certain Father Arkadii, a teacher of religion at a *realschule*: "We will keep our impeccable mother country from the unclean touch of aliens, internal and external. Love our Orthodox Motherland as she loves you ... nurturing you at her breasts, under the sceptre of the beloved monarch and the Imperial family." Meanwhile, the students—including Kol'tsov himself—could not rid themselves of the feeling that landowners, merchants, and industrialists clung to those "breasts." "The words 'Motherland' and 'Fatherland' stood alongside repellent, strange words, like 'autocracy,' 'gloria,' 'he met his maker,' 'Most August,'" he concluded. Mikhail Efimovich Kol'tsov, "Naidennaia Rodina," *Pravda*, 19 June 1934.

[126] Iver B. Neumann, *Uses of the Other: "The East" in European Identity Formation* (Minneapolis: University of Minnesota Press, 1999), 100; Neumann, "Constructing Europe: Russia as Europe's Other," in *Political Symbols, Symbolic Politics: European Identities in Transformation*, ed. Ulf Hedetoft (Aldershot, UK: Ashgate, 1998), 239.

[127] Iver B. Neumann, *Russia and the Idea of Europe: A Study in Identity and International Relations* (London: Routledge, 1996), 117.

[128] See A. I. Solzhenitsyn, *Rossiia v obvale* (Moscow: Russkii put', 1998), 134.

[129] V. Aleksandrovskii, "Rus' i SSSR," *Pravda*, 13 August 1925.

Finally, the Bolshevik worldview was built on a distrust of feminine values. The one, collective body of the new class was a self-sufficient male colossus to whom femininity was extraneous.[130] Attempts were made to represent this new class as one big family, rendering the traditional family obsolete.[131] This is unsurprising: the values that inspired Bolshevik adherents ("scientific socialist" rationalism, willpower, organization, discipline) are traditionally perceived as male attributes.[132] Clearly, such a concept of the gender norms of the new epoch could hardly allow for a maternal national image.

The watershed came with an incident—an important one, in terms of understanding the logic of the further development of Russia's maternal metaphor—in which the Bolshevik propaganda of the period was obliged to "turn for help" to "Mother Russia." On 30 May 1920, when the Red Army was fighting the forces of Josef Piłsudski, an appeal "to all former officers, wherever they may be" was printed in *Izvestiia*, signed by the military specialists of the Red Army, headed by general Aleksei Brusilov. This appeal stated, in part:

> In this critical historical moment of our national life, we, your old comrades-in-arms, appeal to your feelings of love for and loyalty to the Motherland and turn to you with an urgent request to forget all grievances, whoever and whatever may have caused them, and to join the Red Army willingly and with every eagerness and self-sacrifice … in order to fight for our beloved Russia, whatever may come, with your honest service and without sparing your life, and not to let her be plundered, for in that case she may be lost forever; and then our descendants will justly curse us and rightly denounce us because we, out of egotistical feeling, did not make use of our military expertise and experience, forgot our own Russian people and brought ruin to our Mother Russia.[133]

Conclusion

Noting the importance of the "Mother Russia" image to war propaganda, it should be emphasized that the belligerent countries of the First World War all made similar use of female national personifications as a symbol of collective identity, as a weapon of war, and a means of mobilization. The "Mother Russia"

---

[130] Eric Naiman, *Sex in Public: The Incarnation of Early Soviet Ideology* (Princeton, NJ: Princeton University Press, 1997), 74. See also Riabov, *Russkaia filosofiia zhenstvennosti*, 264–69.

[131] For more detail about views on the family, see Riabov, *Russkaia filosofiia zhenstvennosti*, 271–72.

[132] Waters, "The Female Forms," 228.

[133] *Izvestiia*, 30 May 1920, 1.

image fulfilled all these functions, although its anti-Western connotations and association with the ideas of Russian messianism were the source of a range of particularities, especially the concept of the maternal nature of the native land as the source of both military and moral strength. "Mother Russia" was even more in demand during the period of the February Revolution, becoming one of the most important symbols of collective identity. This image took part in processes of political mobilization and the legitimization and delegitimization of governments; various political systems employed it, using the most diverse means of mass agitation. It played a significant role in the propaganda of the White movement, which in many ways inherited the experience of the First World War. Images of "Mother Russia" suffering or disgraced formed part of the discourse of mobilization; pictures of Russia armed, or honoring her heroes, embodied the greatness and strength of the White movement. The "Mother Russia" image distinguished Us from Them, allowing the enemy to be marked out; it acted as a symbol of unity and of the indivisibility of the body of the state.

One consequence of the Bolshevik revolution was a break with the previous perception of the "Mother Russia" image; in Soviet ideology of the 1920s and the first half of the 1930s, Russia's maternal personification was used as a symbol of all that was archaic and backward. Only in the mid-1930s was "Mother Russia" reborn, in the form of the Soviet motherland;[134] the symbol's relatively speedy restoration testified to its deep roots in the "mytho-symbolic complex" of Russian culture.[135]

Translated by Kirsty McCluskey

---

[134] Riabov, "*Rossiia-Matushka,*" 183–201.

[135] The term is Anthony Smith's: Anthony D. Smith, *The Ethnic Origins of Nations* (Oxford: Blackwell Publishers, 1986), 15–30.

Mass Urban Festivals in the Era of War and Revolution, 1914–22

Svetlana Malysheva

The tendency to consider mass celebrations as powerful instruments of political and economic domination—as tools of manipulation—has become increasingly prevalent in the theoretical arsenal of researchers in recent decades.[1] The development of a cultural-historical paradigm for research has made it possible to include the important issue of the influence of mass festivals on the mentality and psychology of social groups, on the formation of national (or supranational) identities.[2] The tradition of study of Russian festivals during the First World War and the early Soviet era also lies within this investigative context.[3] Studying the festivals of this "time of catastrophe"

---

[1] For the classification of theoretical approaches to the study of festivals, see Michael Maurer, "Feste und Feiern als historischer Forschungsgegenstand," *Historische Zeitschrift* 253, 1 (1991): 102–03.

[2] See, for example, Ute Schneider, *Politische Festkultur im 19.Jahrhundert: Die Rheinprovinz von der französischen Zeit bis zum Ende des Ersten Weltkrieges (1806–1918)* (Essen: Klartext-Verlag, 1995); and Sabine Behrenbeck and Alexander Nützenadel, eds., *Inszenierungen des Nationalstaats: Politische Feiern in Italien und Deutschland seit 1860/71* (Cologne: SH-Verlag, 2000).

[3] See, for example, Christel Lane, *The Rites of Rulers: Ritual in Industrial Society—the Soviet Case* (Cambridge: Cambridge University Press, 1981); James von Geldern, *Bolshevik Festivals, 1917–1920* (Berkeley: University of California Press, 1993); Karl Schlögel, *Jenseits des Großen Oktober: Das Laboratorium der Moderne. Petersburg, 1909–1921* (Berlin: Siedler Verlag, 1988); Richard Stites, *Revolutionary Dreams: Utopian Vision and Experimental Life in the Russian Revolution* (New York: Oxford University Press, 1989); Stefan Plaggenborg, *Revolutionskultur: Menschenbilder und kulturelle Praxis in Sowjetrussland zwischen Oktoberrevolution und Stalinismus* (Cologne: Böhlau, 1996); V. V. Glebkin, *Ritual v sovetskoi kul'ture* (Moscow: Janus-K, 1998); Orlando Figes and Boris Kolonitskii, *Interpreting the Russian Revolution: The Language and Symbols of 1917* (New Haven: Yale University Press, 1999); Richard S. Wortman, *Scenarios of Power: Myth and Ceremony in Russian Monarchy*, 2: *From Alexander II to the Abdication of Nicholas II* (Princeton, NJ: Princeton University Press, 2000); B. I. Kolonitskii, *Simvoly vlasti i bor′ba za vlast′: K izucheniiu politicheskoi kul′tury rossiiskoi revoliutsii 1917 g.* (St. Petersburg: Dmitrii Bulanin, 2001); Choi Chatterjee, *Celebrating Women: Gender, Festival Culture*

allows us to concur with the idea that Russian military-patriotic discourse and Soviet discourse[4] represent a continuum and to highlight some of their common traits.

The history and specific character of Russian mass festivals in the era of war and revolution are related, to a large extent, to the processes which preceded this time. The post-reform period in Russia was characterized by a significant increase in interest in history among the educated public. In principle, this interest began at the beginning of the 19th century and is rightly associated with the rise of temporal consciousness in this period. Changing notions of time and temporal order—the emergence of calculated time, and the assertion of a new order of time which constricted previous cyclical time systems related to nature, the agricultural cycle, and also religious cyclical rituals such as hours of prayer,[5] and religious holidays—were among the most important moments in the transformation of European culture. New, modern notions of time in Europe and later in Russia signified a turn in consciousness, which was also reflected in semantics.[6] Basically, replacing "fixed" cyclical time by a linear system (with its calculated, measured time) created the perspective for the temporalization, or if you will, the "historicization" of consciousness.[7] This historicization is partially reflected as well in the realization of the "state-building" function within 19th-century historiography, which is "an integral part of the project of the formation of the nation, responding to questions about the historical origin and purpose of the national community, thus providing its identity."[8]

Specific to Russia was the dissemination, beginning in the 18th century, of modern temporalization "from above," by the state, rather than its gradual development "from below" through urban bourgeois culture, as in Western

---

and Bolshevik Ideology, 1910–1939 (Pittsburgh: University of Pittsburgh Press, 2002); Frederick C. Corney, *Telling October: Memory and the Making of the Bolshevik Revolution* (Ithaca, NY: Cornell University Press, 2004); Malte Rolf, *Das sowjetische Massenfest* (Hamburg: Hamburg Edition, 2006).

[4] See, for example, Karen Petrone, *The Great War in Russian Memory* (Bloomington: Indiana University Press, 2011), 29.

[5] See Gerhard Huck, "Freizeit als Forschungsproblem," in *Sozialgeschichte der Freizeit*, ed. Huck (Wuppertal: Hammer, 1980), 13–14.

[6] See V. M. Zhivov, "Zametki o vremeni i dosuge," in *Sokrovennye smysly: Slovo. Tekst. Kul'tura. Sbornik statei v chest' N. D. Arutiunovoi*, ed. Y. D. Apresian (Moscow: Iazyki slavianskoi kul'tury, 2004), 745.

[7] The term "historicization" is used here not in the sense of "historical problematization or problematization as an historical problem" but in the sense of "an awareness of historicity, the presence of temporal retrospective."

[8] B. I. Rovnyi, *Vvedenie v kul'turnuiu istoriiu: Uchebnoe posobie* (Cheliabinsk: Kamennyi poias, 2005), 57.

Europe.[9] Of course, the historicization of the population's consciousness was also an objective process. Thus, the Fatherland War of 1812 and the rise of patriotic feeling and social consciousness intensified and strengthened the "historical" mood and interest in the country's history.[10]

The 19th century in Russia was marked by broad public celebration of the anniversaries of various events and prominent figures; these were initiated, organized, and carried out predominantly by official government agencies, the army, and the church.[11] Official agencies also played a prominent role in these events. During the second half of the 19th century the number of celebrations grew, with their frequency and scope increasing from the end of the 19th century and reaching their peak after 1907, when defeat in the Russo-Japanese War induced the authorities to claim (or construct) the memory of an heroic past to heal wounded national pride.[12] On the eve of the First World War, grandiose celebrations swept Russia, crowning a century of mass public celebrations and anniversaries: the 200th anniversary of the Great Northern War,[13] the 100th anniversary of the Fatherland War of 1812, and the 300th anniversary of the Romanov dynasty.[14]

The festivals of the 19th and early 20th centuries created a "historicized" mass consciousness and kept the imperial myth of the emperor updated, developing and presenting it in relevant scenarios.[15] Until the end of the 19th century, Russian political symbolism and mythology had a somewhat weak "national subtext," given that it was permeated by the idea of exalted foreign

---

[9] On this, see Zhivov, "Zametki o vremeni i dosuge," 745–54.

[10] See, for example, V. P. Kozlov, *Rossiiskaia arkheografiia v kontse XVIII–pervoi chetverti XIX veka* (Moscow: Rossiiskii gosudarstvennyi gumanitarnyi universitet, 1999), 170–230.

[11] K. N. Tsimbaev, "Fenomen iubileemanii v rossiiskoi obshchestvennoi zhizni kontsa XIX–nachala XX vv.," *Voprosy istorii*, no. 11 (2005): 100.

[12] Ibid., 99.

[13] *Prazdnovanie 200-letiia pobedy Petra I nad shvedami pri derevne Lesnoi: 1708–1908* (Vil'na, 1908); *Tsar' na Poltavskikh prazdnestvakh: 26–27 iiunia 1909 g.* (St. Petersburg, 1909).

[14] N. N. Vinogradov, ed., *Prazdnovanie 300-letiia tsarstvovaniia Doma Romanovykh v kostromskoi gubernii: 19–20 maia 1913 g.* (Kostroma: Izd. Kostromskoi gubernskoi uchenoi arkhivnoi komissii, 1914; repr., Kostroma: Gosudarstvennoi arkhiv Kostromskoi oblasti i Mezhdunarodnyi istoriko-khudozhestvennyi festival' "Vekhi," 1993).

[15] The scenario, according to the concept of Richard S. Wortman, is understood as an individual method of presentation of the imperial myth—the narrative—which dramatizes the difference between rulers and mere mortals. See Richard S. Wortman, *Stsenarii vlasti: Mify i tseremonii russkoi monarkhii*, 1: *Ot Petra Velikogo do smerti Nikolaia I: Materialy i issledovaniia* (Moscow: OGI, 2002), 20, 22.

rulers and elites.[16] Still, to a certain extent they helped in forming the identity of the inhabitants of Russia, their conception of the commonality of one's own fate with the fate of the country and empire, and creation of a complex of patriotic and loyal sentiments.[17] Small wonder, then, that the beginning of the First World War was characterized by such a powerful burst of patriotic feeling. It was thanks to the "preparation" of mass consciousness through the historicizing processes of the 19th and early 20th centuries that it became possible to call the First World War the "new Fatherland" and even the "Great Fatherland" war.

However, very soon the word "fatherland" was dropped from these titles. The military situation and the deterioration of sociopolitical and economic conditions on the home front both contributed to the rapid decline of patriotism. An important role in this decline was also played by the population's weak historical grounding and superficial patriotic feelings, among members of so-called "educated society" and not just the uneducated masses. Stabilization of patriotic and loyal sentiment was hindered as well by the fact that in a series of holiday and anniversary festivals at the turn of the century were rooted rudimentary themes that were "alternative" and "oppositional" to the official governmental myth. The liberal public, going against the general governmental "trend" in celebratory discourse by shunning any reference to the transformational processes of the past, often celebrated anniversaries of reforms and progressive Russian figures.[18] Revolutionary holidays originating in and gaining popularity in the work environment[19] also played a destructive role, especially the May Day holiday.

Patriotic feelings at the beginning of World War I were distinguished by certain detrimental features[20] appearing during collective holiday-carnival activities, sometimes as a "mass psychosis under the device of the 'unity of

---

[16] Ibid., 20–21.

[17] K. N. Tsimbaev, "Pravoslavnaia Tserkov' i gosudarstvennye iubilei Imperatorskoi Rossii," *Otechestvennaia istoriia*, no. 6 (2005): 42–51.

[18] See Tsimbaev, "Fenomen iubileemanii," 103.

[19] The May Day holiday was so popular that in some cases it was even included in the calendar of weekends and holidays in factories and plants. Beginning in 1897, the Ministry of Trade and Industry and other regulatory authorities issued circulars ordering officials of factory inspections to exclude 1 May from the number of non-working days. See, for example, *Kamsko-Volzhskaia rech'*, 21 September 1913.

[20] Hubertus Jahn rightly observed that patriotism and nationalism in Russia in the period of World War I flourished in a situation of mass communication; therefore patriotic culture was predominantly an urban phenomenon since in cities the lines of communication were shorter, which allowed it to spread faster. See Hubertus F. Jahn, *Patriotic Culture in Russia during World War I* (Ithaca, NY: Cornell University Press, 1995), 172. However, we must keep in mind that these "flashes of patriotism" in mass communication—in part, festivals and demonstrations—could not be prolonged.

the tsar with the people'" and sometimes in the chauvinistic haze of anti-Germanism and the hysteria of spy mania.[21] Just a few years later, the government, having encouraged this mood with myths of the "internal enemy" and "national treason" (evoked to explain the failure of the military) found the mood turned against itself, transformed into myths about "dark forces" around the throne.[22] This "reversal of meaning" was largely possible because, as Hubertus Jahn accurately observes, for the Russian population the tsar and the monarchy were not generally recognizable points of identification, while the weakness of the national idea, the virtual absence of national symbols or their abstractness and vagueness, gave scope for a great many individual interpretations or their simple disregard.[23]

Superficiality, rootlessness, and a kind of "perversion" of patriotic and loyal sentiment among the lower classes was conditioned for many by the symbolic distancing from them on the part of the ruler and the elites in the scenarios played out in the festivals. But it was also a result of the physical exclusion of the "people" (*narod*) from prewar celebrations. Here we have in mind not only court ceremonies, a "theater of power" which by definition is played mainly for those who wield power.[24] We should not forget that despite the constant appeal to the "people" in the discourse of governmental ("royal" or "state ceremonial") festivals, frequently the "people" themselves were not present.

In reality, as seen in the official calendar of festivals recorded in the *Code of Laws of the Russian Empire*,[25] in addition to 52 Sundays (weekly holidays), there were 32 Orthodox holidays (the "Lord's" or "scheduled" festivals) and a minimum of 8 public holidays ("royal" or "state ceremonial"), which affected only a very small portion of the urban population.[26] Examples of

---

[21] Igor′ Arkhipov, "Patriotizm v period krizisa 1914–1917 godov," *Zvezda*, no. 9 (2009), http://magazines.russ.ru/zvezda (accessed 15 December 2011).

[22] Ibid.

[23] See Jahn, *Patriotic Culture*, 173.

[24] Wortman, *Stsenarii vlasti*, 20.

[25] *Svod zakonov Rossiiskoi imperii. Izdanie 1857*, 14: *Ustavy o pasportakh, o preduprezhdenii prestuplenii, o tsenzure, o soderzhashchikhsia pod strazheiu, i o ssyl′nykh. Ustav o preduprezhdenii i presechenii prestuplenii*. St. 29–30 (St. Petersburg, 1857), 8–9. This calendar of holidays remained unchanged until the February Revolution of 1917. See *Svod zakonov Rossiiskoi imperii. Izdanie 1916*, 14: *Ustav blagochiniia i bezopasnosti* (Petrograd, 1916), 9–10.

[26] On this, see S. Iu. Malysheva, "'Ezhenedel′nye prazdniki, dni gospodskie i tsarskie': Vremia otdykha rossiiskogo gorozhanina vtoroi polovini XIX–nachala XX vv.," *Ab Imperio: Issledovaniia po novoi imperskoi istorii i natsionalizmu v postsovetskom prostranstve=Studies of New Imperial History and Nationalism in the Post-Soviet Space*, no. 2 (2009): 225–66.

those enjoying these holidays were employees of civilian agencies and, in part, the students of educational institutions of the Ministry of Education. Time off for holidays for other urban groups was regulated by special laws or circulars of relevant ministries and departments. As a result, for example, employees in retail establishments almost everywhere in the Russian Empire (with the exception of some cities)[27] were actually deprived of Sundays and other festival days of rest, except for 3 days off a year at Easter, Pentecost, and Christmas. Craftsmen (in addition to Sundays) rested only on the 12 great feasts of the church.[28] The number of non-working festival days for workers (in addition to Sundays) was determined in 1897 as 14[29] and in 1902 as 17 Orthodox holidays.[30] This lack of uniformity within the holiday calendar calls attention to an interesting fact: if representatives of the urban "elites," the educated strata, so-called "white-collar society" (civil servants, high school students, college students, officers, etc.) rested and celebrated on both religious Orthodox and governmental holidays ("royal" or "state ceremonial days"), then the rest of the urban population—workers, artisans, clerks, and other employees of shops and offices—were categorically "cut off" from the celebration of state holidays, insofar as they were not, in general, eligible for time off on "royal days"! Similarly, days off on "irregular" state holidays (as well as other numerous anniversaries of various events and institutions), such as the celebrations of "victories of Russian arms" that began during the First World War, were enjoyed mostly by members of that same "white-collar society."[31]

---

[27] By 1902, in Tiumen', Tiflis, Pskov, Vladikavkaz, Georgievsk, Kremenchug, and Astrakhan', trading on holidays and Sundays was banned completely. See Natsional'nyi arkhiv Respubliki Tatarstan (NART) f. 98 (Kazanskii gubernskii ispolkom Soveta rabochikh, soldatskikh i krest'ianskikh deputatov), op. 6, d. 191, l. 101 (V Kazanskuiu gorodskuiu dumu—ot pravleniia Vspomogatel'nogo obshchestva prikazchikov g. Kazani, 30 aprelia 1902 g.). It appears, however, that the list was incomplete inasmuch as it left out some cities such as Smolensk, for example.

[28] *Svod zakonov Rossiiskoi imperii. Izdanie 1893*, 11, pt. 2: *Ustavy: Kreditnyi, o vekseliakh, torgovyi, sudoproizvodstva torgovogo, kolsul'skii i o promyshlennosti. Ustav o promyshlennosti. St. 430* (St. Petersburg, 1893), 77.

[29] *Sobranie uzakonenii i rasporiazhenii Pravitel'stva, izdavaemye pri Pravitel'stvuiushchem Senate*, no. 62, 13 June, St. 778 (1897), 2136–37.

[30] See n. 3 to article 198: *Svod zakonov Rossiiskoi imperii, poveleniem Gosudaria Imperatora Nikolaia Pervogo sostavlennyi*, 11, pt. 2: *Ustav o promyshlennosti fabrichno-zavodskoi i remeslennoi. Ustav o promyshlennom trude. Izdanie 1913* (St. Petersburg, 1913), 47.

[31] For example, the grand celebration of the 300th anniversary of the Romanov dynasty in 1913 virtually ignored the representatives of the workers and the urban poor. As pointed out by Malte Rolf, "in Petersburg they provided only neighborhood outdoor gatherings in order to prevent massive accumulation of the poor in the town center";

Thus, for a significant part of the urban population time off for holidays was linked to the traditional rural holiday calendar, which was associated with the religious (Orthodox) holiday tradition and also with the pagan traditions of the agricultural celebratory cycle. Therefore, it cannot be overemphasized how foreign, incomprehensible, and even unknown the loyal, secular monarchist mythology of the "state ceremonial days" seemed to them! Indeed, I believe this is one of the main reasons for the indifference with which the population of Russia (urban as well as rural) reacted to the decision of the Provisional Government of 16 March 1917 to remove "royal days" from the Russian holiday calendar.[32] For the majority of urban residents, these holidays were not days of rest.

The wild demonstrations of "Slavic unity" surrounding the outbreak of World War I, and the "patriotic carnival"[33] of 1914, stimulated widespread participation in secular festive events by the urban lower classes, who even struggled with their employers about their right to participate in these processions and thus get extra days off.[34] Shortly before the declaration of war, President of the State Duma Mikhail Rodzianko perplexedly asked, "Who are these people ... who walk the streets in crowds with national flags, singing the national anthem and holding patriotic demonstrations in front of the Serbian embassy?"[35] He was surprised to discover among them masses of urban workers. Similarly, the authorities and businesses tried to organize special, individual patriotic demonstrations of workers in appropriate areas of Petrograd and its suburbs, which began after work. Thus the demonstration of workers on 22 July (4 August) 1914 in honor of the name day of Dowager Empress Mariia Fedorovna (which occurred days after the declaration of war and thus spilled over into a patriotic event) began at six o'clock in the evening.[36] However workers, artisans, clerks, and servants were not all that keen to participate in the evening "ersatz demonstrations," preferring instead to spend the entire holiday in the center of the city, at worship services in the churches, and then among the tens of thousands of demonstrators on Nevskii Prospekt.[37]

---

he concludes that "the urban working class was left out of official celebrations." See Malte Rolf, *Sovetskie massovye prazdniki* (Moscow: RossPEN, 2009), 44.

[32] *Vestnik Vremennogo pravitel´stva* (Petrograd) 70, 116 (1917).

[33] Arkhipov, "Patriotizm v period krizisa 1914–1917 godov."

[34] See B. I. Kolonitskii, *"Tragicheskaia erotika": Obrazy imperatorskoi sem´i v gody Pervoi mirovoi voiny* (Moscow: Novoe literaturnoe obozrenie, 2010), 521–22.

[35] M. V. Rodzianko, *Krushenie imperii i Gosudarstvennaia Duma i fevral´skaia 1917 goda revoliutsiia: Pervoe polnoe izdanie zapisok Predsedatelia Gosudarstvennoi Dumy. S dopolneniiami E. F. Rodzianko* (Valley Cottage, NY: Multilingual Typesetting, 1986), 242.

[36] "Manifestatsiia rabochikh," *Novoe vremia*, 23 July (5 August) 1914.

[37] *Novoe vremia*, 1 (14) August 1914.

Nationwide church services and processions, carried out in cities all over Russia at the beginning of the war, very clearly demonstrated the results of the authorities' "celebratory policies" of the preceding decades. In the crowds walking the city streets, side by side with urban "bourgeois" suits, military and civilian uniforms, elegant women's gowns, hats, and umbrellas there were workers' shirts and village head scarves in abundance. Participants carried before them banners and icons of the Mother of God, St. George, and other saints. Images of the emperor, the heir, national flags—although they had their place—were far from occupying an "exclusive" or sometimes even central position in the processions.[38] Because the majority of townspeople had little experience of the celebration of secular, state holidays, mass acts of celebrating (or mourning) for members of the lower classes, and to some extent for urban "society," were associated above all with religious rituals. Similarly, the expression of patriotism and loyalty in the first days and months of the war took on religious forms. As Boris Kolonitskii points out, the writer Vasilii Rozanov had a reason for seeing parallels with the Easter celebration in patriotic demonstrations.[39] The same is true of the famous event on 20 July 1914 on Palace Square when, after the reading of the declaration of the beginning of the war and many hours of waiting, thousands of people fell to their knees as the tsar appeared on the balcony.[40] This was more a religious ritual than a secular act.

Again, it is important to note that secular, state holidays ("royal days") before the war were on the periphery of the celebratory culture of most of the urban classes (not to mention the rural population). Even in the structure of secular, state holidays themselves, religious forms usually took the primary position. Practically the only secular form in a secular festival was the military parade. As Tsimbaev notes, "Secular government was not able to and did not consider it necessary to organize non-military mass spectacles."[41] Most forms of celebration for both religious and secular holidays were religious—the requiem with the commemoration of deceased members of the dynasty, the solemn liturgy, the thanksgiving service, the sacred processions, reading in the churches, etc.—and were organized by the Orthodox Church, their order being determined by circulars issued from St. Petersburg. The imperial idea "for public consumption" was dressed in religious garb.

---

[38] This can be seen in the photograph of the procession in Kazan′ after the national prayer service on 20 July 1914, following news of the outbreak of the war with Germany. See S. Iu. Malysheva, *Sovetskaia prazdnichnaia kul′tura v provintsii: Prostranstvo, simvoly, istoricheskie mify (1917–1927)* (Kazan: Ruten, 2005), 33.

[39] Kolonitskii, *"Tragicheskaia erotika,"* 78.

[40] "Tsar′ i narod," *Novoe vremia,* 21 July (3 August) 1914. For this event in detail, see Kolonitskii, *"Tragicheskaia erotika,"* 73–82.

[41] Tsimbaev, "Fenomen iubileemanii," 104.

The outbreak of World War I prompted the government to rely on these religious forms of celebration in constructing the image of the pious tsar (*bogomolets*) in the process of nationalizing his image and creating the myth of the "unity of the tsar with the people."[42] However, at the beginning of the war, the holiday calendar was not systematically reworked.[43] Instead, events were spontaneously added, celebrating, for example, "Russian victory in arms" at the capture of Przemysl in 1915[44] and that of Erzerum and Trebizond in 1916.[45] But even these completely secular celebrations were clothed in the accustomed religious forms. Thus the celebration of the capture of Przemysl was marked by a thanksgiving prayer service at the Assumption Cathedral in the Moscow Kremlin before a large gathering of people, a magnificent and solemn procession through Red Square amidst the ringing of bells, public prayer at Lobnoe Mesto (the Place of Skulls), and numerous public prayer services in institutions, organizations, schools, and railway stations. It is interesting to note that the many grandiose, daylong, mass demonstrations for the occasion were also rather religious in character—the demonstrators performed "Lord, Save Thy People" almost as often as the national anthem, "God Save the Tsar," and even the military parade on Red Square was described by a newspaper as a "church parade with troops from the Moscow Garrison."[46] Celebrations of the capture of Erzerum and Trebizond (occurring around Easter) concluded with a solemn liturgy, a thanksgiving prayer service, and decoration of the city with flags and lights. Collections for wartime needs were also conducted within the framework of holiday events; these included the collection and distribution of Easter and Christmas gifts as well as feting of soldiers and wounded soldiers, and collection of funds to help "the war-ravaged Slavs" on "Serbian-Montenegrin Day" (11 January 1915) or "Slavic Day" (22 May 1916).[47]

In connection with the beginning of the war, adjustments were made to the official celebratory discourse. Visible in the official imperial manifestos of the summer and fall of 1914 were prescribed myths that had to be broadcast to the population through mass celebrations and events and which should have

---

[42] See Kolonitskii, "*Tragicheskaia erotika*," 81–98. In fact, the appeal to the popular religious festiveness can already be heard in the imperial manifesto of war: "Today is Elijah's Day, the great day...." See *Novoe vremia*, 21 July (3 August) 1914.

[43] It should be noted, however, that the government received suggestions to reduce the number of days off in connection with the war. See "O sokrashchenii prazdnikov: Oktiabristskaia formula perekhoda," *Russkoe slovo*, 8 (21) August 1915.

[44] "Molebstvie v Uspenskom sobore: Parad voiskam. Manifestatsii," *Russkoe slovo*, 11 (24) March 1915.

[45] See, for example, *Kamsko-Volzhskaia rech'*, 7 and 9 February, 10 April 1916.

[46] "Molebstvie v Uspenskom sobore: Parad voiskam. Manifestatsii."

[47] "Serbo-Chernogorskii den': Tseremonial," *Russkoe slovo*, 8 (21) January 1915; *Kamsko-Volzhskaia rech'*, 10 January, 7 and 9 February, 10 April, 22 May 1916.

contributed to the consolidation of the people, army, and the government, unifying the people under the "Orthodox Tsar" and thus positioning the protection of the country and Slavdom as a religious act, an act of defense of the faith. Thus, among the myths disseminated, the myth of unity was strengthened by the "kinship"-myth (*edinorodstvo*) of the government and the army: "I turn to My army ... one kindred spirit, strong as a granite wall, and give my blessing to its martial labors," proclaimed the emperor after the reading of the imperial manifesto on 20 July 1914.[48] The thesis of the unity of the Slavic and Orthodox peoples and the mission of Russia as their defender rang out in the same manifesto: "following our historical covenants, Russia, united in faith and blood with the Slavic people, has never looked upon their fate with indifference..."; and on 26 July: "the whole of Russia will rise up to a feat of arms with iron in its hand and a cross on its heart"; and in the imperial manifesto of 20 October, where Turkey's attack was characterized as a new blow against Russia by "the old oppressor of the Christian faith and all Slavic peoples."[49]

The last quote illustrates a feature of historical mythology at the time of the First World War (often found in times of war in general) which was also fully reflected in the celebratory narrative: xenophobia, enumerating the offenses that were inflicted by the enemy in the past in order to prove its present day "barbarism, "savageness," and other deviant traits. In like manner, the widespread celebration in 1916 of the 300th anniversary of the deaths of Kuz'ma Minin, William Shakespeare, and Miguel de Cervantes underscored the high status of Russian culture and its close relationship with European culture in the face of German "barbarism."[50] Articles proving the "harmfulness" of the enemy (for example, the German language being the source of thieves' cant)[51] were also manifestations of this phenomenon.

Xenophobic attitudes were formed in the course of numerous marches and demonstrations in support of Serbia and "Serbian-brothers" in the last weeks before Russia's entry into the war. Thereafter, the xenophobic enthusiasm of the demonstrators turned primarily against "Germanism" and "Teutonic barbarism," although in principle the object of hatred of an aggressive crowd of demonstrators could be any "foreign" national, religious, or other group.[52] Patriotic demonstrators in St. Petersburg and other cities in the first days of the war looted German shops, restaurants, and cafes, and on 22 July the German embassy was ransacked. With a view to preserving order in society, the

---

[48] *Novoe vremia*, 21 July (3 August) 1914.

[49] See *Novoe vremia*, 21 July (3 August) 1914; *Kazanskie gubernskie vedomosti*, 2 August and 28 October 1914.

[50] Tsimbaev, "Fenomen iubileemanii," 107–08.

[51] See "Spetsial'noe vliianie nemetskoi 'kul'tury,'" *Kazanskii telegraf*, 23 July 1916.

[52] See Arkhipov, "Patriotizm v period krizisa 1914–1917 godov."

government on 23 July banned all demonstrations in the capital and later in its province as well.[53] After some time, bans on processions and demonstrations were declared in other provinces. However, anti-German demonstrations sprang up in city after city. But official propaganda did not remove xenophobia from its arsenal, even though this weapon was increasingly turned toward the ruling dynasty—all strata of the population exaggerated the thesis of the German origin of the tsar and his family, with all its ensuing consequences.[54]

The overthrow of the autocracy was accompanied, oddly enough, by the same religious sentiments in mass celebrations as were present in the demonstrations at the start of the war. Spring festivals celebrating the overthrow of the autocracy organically combined revolutionary euphoria with the mood and rhetoric of Easter and the elements of Easter rituals.[55] One of the most colorful and distinctive celebrations was the All-Russian "Festival of Freedom," which was also called the "Festival of the Russian Revolution," the "Festival of the People's Freedom," etc., and was celebrated throughout the country on 15 March 1917. For example, in Kazan´ it began with a solemn public prayer and then continued with a military parade and grandiose mass demonstrations that took place throughout the city with numerous rallies and ended with a solemn requiem on the graves of the fallen freedom fighters.[56] A bright Easter mood permeated even such an essentially somber event as "the funeral of the victims of the Revolution" on 24 March 1917 in Petrograd: a magnificent funeral ceremony on the Field of Mars was accompanied by a ten o'clock procession of about 350,000 people, and a gun salute at the Peter and Paul Fortress for each one of the 184 coffins before they were lowered into a mass grave. Newspaper reports called it "a festival of rebirth" and "a national celebration."[57]

The February Revolution and the brief period of "Russian freedom" from February to October 1917 were characterized by an unprecedented abundance of festivals, which in a whimsical way combined the prerevolutionary religious splendor of religious acts, the rigor and solemnity of military parades, and the passionate transports of revolutionary demonstrations and illegal "May-Day meetings." These festivals represented a transitional stage towards Soviet post-October celebrations. Festivals were organized for the slightest occasion; the very political culture of the February Revolution has been characterized

---

[53] Kolonitskii, *"Tragicheskaia erotika,"* 82–83.

[54] On this, see ibid.

[55] Figes and Kolonitskii, *Interpreting the Russian Revolution*, 74, 81.

[56] "K narodnomu prazdniku," *Golos Kazani*, 15 March 1917; V. SH-kh, "Prazdnik Svobody: Den´ 15 March 1917 g.," *Golos Kazani*, 17 March 1917; "Prazdnik narodnoi Svobody," *Golos Kazani*, 17 March 1917.

[57] See "Pokhorony zhertv revoliutsii: Prazdnik vozrozhdeniia," *Novoe vremia*, 25 March (7 April) 1917.

by researchers as festive.[58] The relationships among the key organizers of the festivals, in general, mirrored the dynamics of the governmental processes and the heated fight for power in the country. If the commissions for festivals, in the capitals and at the local level, were often created through the joint efforts of the Soviets and the Committees for Public Safety (with the participation of other organizations), by summer 1917 the striving for "demarcation" and individual leadership of the festivals on the part of these agencies was becoming more evident.[59] The February Revolution, despite the abundance of one-day festivals, hardly shook the foundations of the official holiday calendar: the disappearance of the "royal days," as already mentioned, went virtually unnoticed and no attempt was even made to change religious holidays.

In contrast, in the year following the October Revolution the Bolsheviks formulated a new official calendar of holidays. "State ceremonial days," which had been abolished by the Provisional Government, were replaced from 1918 by "revolutionary Soviet holidays and memorial days," during which all citizens were prohibited from working. In the beginning there were six days; after the Civil War, the number grew.[60] The Soviet calendar of holidays, in this way, took on the structure of the prerevolutionary official calendar of holidays, preserving both its parts—religious and state holidays. However, the ratio between these two parts was no longer in "harmony." Having inherited a tradition of illegal workers' "May-Day meetings" and revolutionary marches and demonstrations, revolutionary holidays—state holidays which were now termed "civic"—dominated the calendar and the nascent Soviet celebratory culture. Religious holidays were only "tolerated." Bolsheviks, realizing that religious holidays were the main competition to "revolutionary" Soviet holidays, still preserved these "special days of rest" in the official calendar until the 1930s, however reluctantly, as "customary holidays for the majority of the population of a given locale."[61] They were gradually displaced from the calendar and the everyday practices of the population. Their number was

---

[58] Figes and Kolonitskii, *Interpreting the Russian Revolution*, 33, 38.

[59] Thus, in Kazan′ the All-Russian Festival of the People's Freedom on 15 March 1917 was organized jointly by the Commission of the Council of Workers' and Soldiers' Deputies and the Executive Committee of Public Safety; a few months later, the Council was already forming festival committees on its own. See *Golos Kazani*, 14 and 15 March 1917; NART f. R-98, op. 1, d. 18, l. 162 (Kul′turno-prosvetitel′nyi otdel Kazanskogo gubernskogo ispolkoma soveta rabochikh, soldatskikh i krest′ianskikh deputatov–Ia. A. Pozenu, 3 September 1917 g.).

[60] Malysheva, *Sovetskaia prazdnichnaia kul′tura v provintsii*, 29–58.

[61] They were thus designated in the "Pravila Sovnarkoma RSFSR o ezhenedel′nom otdykhe i prazdnichnykh dniakh" (2 December 1918), included in the first Soviet Codex of Labor Laws. See *Dekrety sovetskoi vlasti*, 4: *10 noiabria 1918–31 marta 1919 goda* (Moscow: Gospolitizdat, 1968), 124.

limited to ten days per year; in May 1925 reduced to eight;[62] and in 1927 to seven.[63] By 1930, religious holidays were completely excluded from the Soviet calendar.[64]

In addition, the creators of the Soviet calendar of festivals introduced to this model two significant innovations in order to democratize the very culture of festivals. First, the holidays on the Soviet calendar of festivals embraced all levels of the population. This "popular" celebratory calendar aroused protests among some of the leading figures of Proletkul't. For example, Nikolai Liashko rejected the possibility of not only nationwide, but also of "all-class" (that is, all groups of the working class) festivals. He insisted on catering the festival policies towards the most conscious part of the proletariat, its elite.[65] Curiously, implementation of this idea would have made Soviet revolutionary holidays more like "royal days," which had also been celebrated by a narrow layer of the empire's urban elite. At the same time, one of Liashko's proposals for the revolutionary calendar—a group of 12 holidays in which the Day of the October Revolution was crowned "the holiday of holidays"—could not but evoke associations with the Orthodox 12 great feasts and Easter in the prerevolutionary official calendar. As we can see, in this "Proletkul't version" the connection of the Soviet holiday calendar with the prerevolutionary model is even more apparent. However, the Bolsheviks did not support the idea of "narrow-class" holidays. "Popular" Soviet holidays were supposed to facilitate the indoctrination of large sections of the population by inculcating the historical mythology that was the content of the mass "revolutionary festivals." Second, the creators of the Soviet holiday calendar creatively used the idea of an "alternative," "parallel" holiday calendar which for the last 35 years of existence of the Russian Empire had been used to represent the non-Orthodox, mainly Muslim, population of the empire.[66] Local councils of trade unions (with the consent of the People's Commissariat of Labor) were given

---

[62] "Postanovlenie III sessii VTSIK XI sozyva ot 5 maia 1925 g. 'Ob izmenenii st. 112 Kodeksa zakonov o trude,'" *Sobranie uzakonenii i rasporiazhenii raboche-krest'ianskogo pravitel'stva TSSR*, no. 44 (Kazan', 1925), 493

[63] "Postanovlenie Prezidiuma TSIK SSSR "O prazdnichnykh dniakh, posviashchennykh godovshchine Oktiabr'skoi revoliutsii i ob osobykh dniakh otdykha". 26 oktiabria 1927 g.," *Sobranie uzakonenii i rasporiazhenii raboche-krest'ianskogo pravitel'stva TSSR*, no. 54 (Kazan', 1927), 648.

[64] See *Kodeks zakonov o trude RSFSR: Izdanie 1922 g. s izmeneniiami do 1 marta 1930 g.* (Moscow, 1930), 32.

[65] See Rossiiskii gosudarstvennyi arkhiv literatury i iskusstva (RGALI) f. 1230 (Tsentral'nyi komitet proletarskikh kul'turno-prosvetitel'nykh organizatsii [Proletkul't]), op. 1, d. 458, ll. 3–6 (doklad N. Liashko "Rabochie prazdnestva Proletkul'ta" [1921–22 gg.]).

[66] On the struggle for an "alternative" holiday calendar, see Malysheva, "Ezhenedel'nye prazdniki, dni gospodskie i tsarskie," 225–66.

the right to adjust the section on religious holidays in the religious calendar to include a few groups of religious festivals of different confessions, depending on the religious preferences of the largest groups in the local population. The right to choose the group of religious holidays which gave time off to one or another of the labor collectives was granted to the general meeting. Individual choice was excluded.[67]

Early Soviet festival politics in general were distinguished by the effort to promote the demonstration of national-cultural diversity in the shaping of holiday practices. Thus, in 1920 the instruction of the All-Russian Central Commission for Organizing the Celebration of the Third Anniversary of the October Revolution recommended including in the festival a "march of the Russian [*rossiiskie*] republics." "All nationalities in the characteristic costumes and symbols of their basic trade should approach the stage and flood it with their diversity. Ukrainians, Great Russians, the Caucasus, Kazan', Siberia, Turkestan, Kirghiz, Bashkirs—in a word, the whole multiethnic camp of the Russian plains joined together under the red banner."[68] Besides producing a number of festival events in local languages, national-regional features appeared in the outward staging of early Soviet festivals and the structures unveiled in conjunction with them. For example, working within the framework of October celebrations, alongside the ubiquitous monuments and busts of Lenin, Marx, and Engels, were monuments to local revolutionary figures. In Yerevan and other cities in Armenia, Stepan Shaumian and Melik Melikian (Melik—"Grandfather") were introduced; in Kazan'—Mullanur Vakhitov. Another example comes from festival installations, which were very popular in the early years of Soviet power, such as triumphant arches in the "Eastern style" (Kazan') or in the "Armenian style in the form of a semicircle, with a large and small Ararat at the head."[69] However, archival documents demonstrate a striking uniformity of form, events, order, and accounts of early Soviet festivals—from Khabarovsk to Kiev, from Yerevan to Murmansk—along the whole length of the vast country. This uniformity is difficult to explain as just a following of instructions "from above," especially in the absence of well-established and reliable channels of communication. It is perhaps largely due to reliance on previous holiday practices.

---

[67] See Malysheva, *Sovetskaia prazdnichnaia kul'tura v provintsii*, 29–58.

[68] Rossiiskii gosudarstvennyi arkhiv sotsial'no-politicheskoi istorii (RGASPI) f. 17 (TSK KPSS), op. 60 (Otdel agitatsii i propagandy), d. 5, l. 16 (Instruktsiia po organizatsii prazdnovania tret'ei godovshchiny Oktiabr'skoi revoliutsii, 1920 g.).

[69] RGASPI f. 17, op. 60, d. 300, ll. 27–28, 33ob. (doklad Agitpropotdela TSK KP (b) Armenii i Komissii po provedeniiu prazdnovaniia piatoi godovshchiny Oktiabr'skoi revoliutsii, 1922); d. 365, l. 27 (otchet Pervomaiskoi komissii pri TatTSIK o rabote ee po provedeniiu prazdnovaniia dnia 1 maia 1922 g.); NART f. R-732 (Tsentral'nyi ispolnitel'nyi komitet Soveta rabochikh, krest'ianskikh i krasnoarmeiskikh deputatov Tatarskoi avtonomnoi sovetskoi sotsialisticheskoi respubliki), op. 1, d. 126, ll. 33, 154.

The organizers of Soviet festivals practiced in general the same forms of celebrations as their prerevolutionary predecessors. The military parade, a favorite form of secular celebration in tsarist Russia, remained a "favorite" of the new government, having strengthened its position in the wave of militarization in the years of World War I, the Revolution, and the Civil War. During the Civil War, military parades, functioning as shows of force to reassure supporters as well as deter enemies at home and abroad, were carried out mainly on the anniversary of the October Revolution and on Red Army Day—that is, the day of the Bolshevik seizure of power and the day honoring their main fighting force. That the military parades were directed "outward," to a significant degree, including to foreign observers, is confirmed by the detailed instructions given in preparation for the October 1922 military parade on Red Square by the chairman of the Revolutionary Military Council, Trotskii, to the chairman of the Moscow Sovnarkhoz, Aleksandr I. Muralov; the chief of the Air Force, Andrei A. Znamenskii; Deputy Chairman of Sovnarkom and the Council of Labor and Defense, Lev Kamenev; and the Chairman of the Executive Committee of the Comintern, Grigorii Zinov'ev. Trotskii demanded that thorough consideration be given to the placing of the platform (*tribun*) on Red Square, "so that the idling Soviet public does not obstruct the whole picture for the foreigners." He ordered that only that which was worthy be taken out and shown. In particular, commanders were forbidden to show "dead cats" instead of healthy horses, or faulty equipment (he threatened punishment for every breakdown of an armored car or truck on the square). Particular responsibility was placed on the chief of the Air Force, who was ordered to "eliminate every risky operation, as some unfortunate adventure on Red Square or on Khodynka can cloud the entire holiday." Trotskii also paid close attention to the outward appearance of participants in the parade and demonstration. He directed that soldiers "if possible" have the same hats and shoes and particularly emphasized that this also applied to the commanders and commissars, "who sometimes appear in the parade in extremely pretentious clothes."[70]

If the military parades were supposed to show the awesome strength of the new government, then forms of celebration like demonstrations and rallies were supposed to emphasize the support of the working people for the government. Demonstrations and rallies were, perhaps, the most widespread and demanded forms of celebration. They not only continued the traditions of the revolutionary processions of the tsarist period but were also inversions of religious forms of celebration that were understandable and familiar to the

---

[70] RGASPI f. 17, op. 60, d. 163, ll. 51, 54, 55, 56, 57 (Lev Trotskii–A. I. Muralov and L. B. Kamenev, 8 September 1922; Lev Trotskii–A. A. Znamenskii, A. I. Muralov, and L. B. Kamenev, 8 September 1922; Lev Trotskii–L. B. Kamenev and A. I. Muralov, 11 September 1922; Lev Trotskii–G. E. Zinov'ev, L. B. Kamenev, and A. I. Muralov, 11 September 1922, Lev Trotskii–A. I. Muralov, 15 September 1922).

people, such as sacred processions and church services.[71] This connection was obvious even to peasants, who in the early years of Soviet power habitually crossed themselves in front of portraits of the leaders and, when participating in Soviet demonstrations, took them for sacred processions.[72] At the same time, demonstrations (conducted far more often than parades) fulfilled a very important function—the symbolic ordering of reality, the symbolic construction of a new social hierarchy.

Virtually all of the celebratory forms and rituals of the early Soviet period in one way or another borrowed from prerevolutionary festival practices, both secular and religious. Such an indispensable form of celebration as the ceremonial gathering of party-soviet activists with representatives of trade unions and worker collectives contained a very clear reference to prerevolutionary ceremonial gatherings in estate-based clubs (especially noble and military) of representatives of social estates, serving as a presentation and affirmation of the imperial myth. The ritual of taking the Red oath, timed to coincide with the celebration of May Day in 1922, borrowed elements from the military rituals of tsarist Russia. In the ritual honoring of the cavaliers of the first Soviet order—the Red Banner—during the celebration of the anniversary of the Red Army, we can discern elements of the honoring of recipients of former imperial orders or medals. Rituals renaming factories, barracks, and other establishments for the 1922 anniversary of the October Revolution demonstrated a "genetic" relationship with Orthodox rites of baptism and the procession of the cross.[73] Of course, all of these forms were now filled with other content and expressed other scenarios of power. But even those "new" festive forms that played a key role in indoctrination, such as the large-scale "revolutionary festivals"—the historical re-enactments during the period of war communism—took their cue not only from the celebration of the French Revolution, but also returned to their roots in the lush anniversary celebrations on the eve of the First World War. This feature of prewar tsarist celebrations —"openness ... in respect to the use of means for engendering mass culture" and the "previously unthinkable" presentation of power through mass media[74]—also largely shaped the body of work of future creators of Soviet revolutionary dramatizations: film directors, artists, and performers who

---

[71] Many researchers have pointed out this "kinship." V. V. Glebkin links such Soviet festive forms as the demonstration and rally meeting with the world view of the Russian peasantry, who expressed in these new cultural forms the social practices to which they were already accustomed. See Glebkin, *Ritual v sovetskoi kul'ture*, 69, 72, 77, 82.

[72] *Revoliutsionnye prazdniki v shkole pervoi stupeni: Po otchetam, sochineniiami dnevnikam pedagogov i detei shkol gorodskikh, derevenskikh i shkol pri proizvodstvakh* (Moscow: Novaia Moskva, 1926), 5–6, 56.

[73] See Malysheva, *Sovetskaia prazdnichnaia kul'tura v provintsii*, 298–300.

[74] Rolf, *Sovetskie massovye prazdniki*, 40–41.

saw in the Soviet festivals the opportunity to put into practice their artistic aspirations and experiments.

It appears that the Bolsheviks in the early Soviet period generously shared out the organization of festivities: with soviet organs (a festival commission created under soviet auspices and soviet organs positioned as the main organizers of Soviet holidays); with the trade unions (until 1927 they were the head "constructors" of festival columns and responsible for gathering workers for demonstrations); and with the military and other "power" organizations (they were responsible for the most important form of Soviet celebration—the military parade—and also fulfilled certain security functions in the organizing and carrying out of the festivals). The Bolsheviks also gave a role to the theatrical and creative intelligentsia, especially leftist orientations in art (their representatives arranged festival decorations, developed scripts and the production of large-scale theatrical performances during the revolutionary festivals); and even to the masses, whose initiative was persistently and regularly called upon by the festival commission. However, from the very beginning all the activities of these agencies and organizations were under the strict control of the party leadership, directed into the "necessary" channels, and censored. In other words, "soviet" leadership of Soviet holidays was very conditional. All-Russian Festival Commissions were created by the Central Committee of the Communist Party, while regional, provincial, and republic committees were created by the corresponding party committees, whose agitprops were supposed to lead and control all the work of organizing and holding festivals. But since direct party control of Soviet festivals was perceived as "inconvenient," party decisions about establishing festival commissions were "carried out" through the All-Russian Central Executive Committee and local soviet organs. Led by representatives of the festival committee of the soviets, officially the festivals were organized by the All-Russian Central Executive Committee and local soviet agencies.[75] In fact, in the first years of Soviet power, everything was already under the jurisdiction of party organs: the design of the commission; the creation of circulars for the conduct of festivals; the approval of plans for the festival; the composition of slogans and

---

[75] See, for example, the organization of the anniversary celebrations of the October Revolution in the country in 1920 and 1921: RGASPI f. 17, op. 60, d. 5, ll. 2– 2ob., 4, 6 (protokol soveshchaniia po voprosu o prazdnovanii Oktiabr'skoi godovshchiny, 5 oktiabria 1920; protokol no. 1 zasedaniia Vserossiiskoi Tsentral'noi komissii po provedeniiu Oktiabr'skikh torzhestv, 7 oktiabria 1920 g.; protokol ot 8 oktiabria 1920 g.), d. 38, l. 1, 2a, 5, 6, 8, 78 (Ob Oktiabr'skikh torzhestvakh vsem partiinym organizatsiiam RKP; Protokol no. 1 zasedaniia Komissii, sozdannoi po postanovleniiu Orgbiuro ot 23 sentiabria po voprosu o prazdnovanii chetvertoi godovshchiny Oktiabrskoi revolutsii, 27 sentiabria 1921 g.; Protocol no. 2 zasedaniia komissii, 29 sentiabria 1921 g.; Protokol no. 1 zasedaniia Komissii, sozdannoi po postanovleniiu Orgbiuro TsK RKP ot 23 sentiabria po voprosu o prazdnovanii chetvertoi godovshchiny Oktiabrskoi revoliutsii, 4 oktiabria 1921 g.; Postanovlenie TsK RKP po voprosu o kharaktere prazdnovaniia).

themes for the festivals; the content of reports, lists, and published celebratory literature; the content of festival performances; analysis of the quality of the festivals; and so on.

Determination of the content of festivals was the exclusive prerogative of the Bolshevik Party. The historicization of consciousness which was being effected on the eve of the Revolution, with help from mass public festivals and anniversaries, also turned out to be an excellent means of manipulation and indoctrination, which the Bolsheviks did not fail to use. They used early Soviet festivals to create and "advance" to the masses a new historical mythology which was designed to legitimize the seizure of power in October 1917.[76] Its main content became the representation of the struggle of the oppressed against the oppressors, the timeless "proletariat" against the timeless "bourgeoisie" (individual stories on the history of uprisings and revolutions were "extracted" from Russian and European history and staged in a simplified form and vulgarized to the level of an abstract struggle of "good" and "evil"). The October Revolution of 1917 was positioned as the logical conclusion, the culmination of this epochal battle.

With the help of historical mythology, early Soviet festivals made a strong attempt to adjust the collective memory of the inhabitants of the country concerning the events of the recent past, especially about the Revolution and the Civil War. These adjustments were not limited to concrete historical subjects.

The Bolsheviks used and creatively reworked several discursive practices of prerevolutionary festivals and rituals. In particular, they made ample use of a component of patriotic discourse of the First World War that seemed most "useful" for the task of fighting an internal and external enemy (and also legitimizing civil war)—namely, a destructive component, the strong xenophobic sentiment.[77]

Of course, much more was required for "social" and "political" xenophobia, even in the very first Soviet festive dramatizations, as clearly observed by the diametrically opposing trends in the representation of "friends" and "enemies." The deviance of the latter was highlighted by buffoonery and a joking manner of presentation, dehumanizing the images of "enemies." However, the values of internationalism, inscribed on the banners of the Bolsheviks, did not prevent them from playing the card of "national" xenophobia. Celebratory discourse was one of the most convenient channels

---

[76] On the content and storylines of early Soviet historical mythology, see James von Geldern, "Festivals of the Revolution, 1917–1920: Art and Theater in the Formation of Soviet Culture" (Ph.D. diss., Brown University, 1987); Schlögel, *Jenseits des Grossen Oktober*; Stites, *Revolutionary Dreams*; Geldern, *Bolshevik Festivals*; Corney, *Telling October*. For the historical mythology of early Soviet festivals in the provinces, see Malysheva, *Sovetskaia prazdnichnaia kul'tura v provintsii*.

[77] Incidentally, there were also attempts to utilize the constructive content of patriotic discourse—how else can we understand the famous slogan, "The Socialist Fatherland is in danger!"?

for its transmission. For example, in announcing the May Day 1920 holiday amnesty of prisoners, the leadership of one province publicly excluded from the number of those released—along with the counterrevolutionaries, criminals, and such—Polish prisoners, as "citizens of a state that launched an armed struggle against Soviet Russia."[78] Another striking example was the presentation of the official festive discourse of the events of the Civil War in the summer of 1918 in the Volga region: the Civil War in the region was portrayed as a "raid of Czechoslovaks" and subsequent liberation "from the Czechoslovak counterrevolutionary gangs."[79] Imposed on the collective memory was the image of the opposing side as alien, dark, "wild" forces, while the Civil War in the territory was portrayed as a type of foreign invasion. In this instance, exploiting the worst nationalistic feelings, even the xenophobia of the population, gave the Civil War additional legitimacy (not only as a form of class struggle but as a struggle against foreign domination). The unclaimed patriotic fervor of the World War was directed onto the opposition in the Civil War.

With the help of the festive discourse, other important points of collective memory were also corrected. Thus, the latter consolidated the sense of rupture brought about by the events of the World War, the Revolution, and the Civil War. The "starting point" of the new era in the collective memory was the era of catastrophe, which the World War began. However, in the official Bolshevik narrative, the leading role of conceptual foundation in the collective memory of the events of 1914–22 was assigned to the complex of myths and stories about the October Revolution. As a result, the First World War was artificially "overlaid" in the official Soviet discourse by the events of the Revolution. Thus in 1924, in the largest "revolutionary festival" performed in Kazan' province for the tenth anniversary of the beginning of the World War—a historical dramatization of the "imperialist war"—the events of the conflict itself, its beginning and end, were very typically "lost" in the continuum of class struggles of the "workers" and "ruling classes." This struggle was only briefly interrupted by a surge of patriotism at the beginning of the war. It is noteworthy that the events of the last year of the war were completely absent from the dramatization—it ended with a scene of the storming of the

---

[78] NART f. R-700 (Revoliutsionnyi komitet Tatarskoi ASSR), op. 1, d. 1, l. 5 (Tsirkuliarno: Pervomaiskaia amnistiia, 1920).

[79] NART f. P-732 (Tsentral'nyi ispolnitel'nyi komitet Soveta rabochikh, krestianskikh i soldatskikh deputatov TASSR), op. 1, d. 622, l. 199ob. (Rukopis' stati v Komissiiu po izdaniiu i redaktirovaniiu pechatnykh materialov v sviazi s piatoi godovshchinoi TASSR, iiun 1925 g.); d. 259, l. 80ob. (Plan prazdnovaniia tretei godovshchiny Tatarskoi Respubliki, mai–iiun' 1923).

Winter Palace and the October Revolution, which meant the culmination of the struggle of the "workers" and "bourgeoisie," the beginning of a new era.[80]

However, in "substituting" the October Revolution for the World War as the turning point in the collective memory, the Bolsheviks most certainly did not want to transfer the war's negative connotations, the sense of social and humanitarian disaster. But that is precisely the connotation that the events of October 1917 had for the mass of the population, even for those fully loyal to the new government. A typical characterization of this perception is found in the letter of the fairly well-educated worker Aleksei Smirnov: "The nightmarish horrors of the historic moment being experienced, the heady intoxication of the political struggle, the specific odor of blood and tears powerfully absorbed the whole soul of the citizen and plunged all his consciousness into a whirlwind of spontaneously inflamed passions."[81] Bolsheviks, in contrast, positioned the October Revolution as the beginning of an era of liberation.

The events of October 1917 were "emotionally recoded": feelings of disaster were emotionally replaced in the 1920s by a celebratory discourse of "joy." This recoding was predominantly carried out through large-scale, grandiose celebrations of the October anniversary. The official discourse of 1917 was instilled into the mass consciousness in the course of these festivals. That discourse was marked by an almost biblical language of liberation and the creation of a just kingdom, and—following Marxian dictums on the Revolution—as the holiday of the toilers. This image was consolidated in the memory of urban dwellers by the festive decorations around the city, the colorful demonstrations and re-enactment of revolutionary events, the fireworks and salutes, the free shows and entertainment, food, and the meetings and evenings of remembrance where the masses had explained to them the "true" picture of the events of October. "The huge holiday enthusiasm"[82] of the townspeople, recorded in all the reports about the celebrations, played a significant role in the actual transfer—through collective memory of those extraordinary euphoric sensations which celebrations of the beginning of the 1920s evoked in contemporaries—onto the assessment of the real events of the October coup. The culmination of this process of transformation of the collective memory of October came a few years later with the grand celebration of its ten-year anniversary under the slogans characteristic of this "discourse of joy": "To prepare for the tenth anniversary of October means to permeate everything and everyone with the sparkling joy of the October

---

[80] See *Stsenarii instsenirovki imperialisticheskoi voiny. Kazan´, 3 avgusta 1924 goda* (Kazan´, 1924).

[81] See NART f. R-98, op. 1, d. 18, l. 386 (Pis'mo rabochego A. Smirnova v Kazanskii gubernskii ispolkom soveta rabochikh, soldatskikh i krestianskikh deputatov, 7 dekabria 1917 g.).

[82] NART f. P-732, op. 1, d. 156, l. 23 (Otchet ob itogakh prazdnovaniia godovshchiny Oktiabr'skoi revoliutsii v Gorodskom raione g. Kazani v 1922 g., noiabr´ 1922).

victory!" "It is not enough to celebrate October for a few days in October. We have to create a sense of October long before the tenth anniversary...!" "The festival of October is not a holiday for the masses. It is the triumph of the masses themselves. Everyone prepare to meet the Great October days!"[83]

At the same time, propagation of the "discourse of joy," as well as the focus in the mid-1920s on entertainment and "the inculcation into daily life" of the mass Soviet holidays—accompanied by appropriate modifications in the forms of celebration—testified to the changing function of Soviet holidays. The time of "historic" festivals of the era of war and revolution had passed. They were replaced by the Soviet festival geared towards contemporary issues, the "topic of the day," the "here and now" of the time of the first Five-Year Plan.

In these various mass celebrations of the "extreme" era—World War I, the 1917 Revolution, and the Civil War—common characteristics are clearly seen. These concern not only the continuity and borrowing of models of the festive calendar and forms of celebration, or continuity in personnel—the use of "experts" who had produced prerevolutionary mass events (in the words of Malte Rolf) to organize Soviet holidays. Mass celebrations of the period under consideration were united by their "historical" content, their focus on historical retrospective. To some extent, they reflect the general trend from the mid-19th century of the "historicization" of social consciousness. At the same time, this appeal to subjects from the historical past, the urgent construction and inculcation of historical mythology, more than anything testifies to the lack of legitimacy of authority and the desire to substantiate or renew it. Whether we are talking about bolstering the status and prestige of an authority shaken by internal or external threats, or the legitimization of a newly founded and still fragile regime, the significance of festivals in general (and festivals with "historical content" in particular) as a most powerful and universal means of social-psychological influence on a population, of indoctrinating it, is magnified in times of transition. The greater the need, the more grandiose the festival, the more large-scale the historical parallels, and the more majestic the historical myths. This largely explains the riddle of staging "'feasts during the plague.'"[84] At the same time, "historical" celebration in an era of social and

---

[83] See, for example: NART f. P-732, op. 1, d. 1062, ll. 78, 80, 81 (Lozungi k prazdnovaniiu 10-I godovshchiny Oktiabrskoi revolutsii, podgotovlennye agitatsionno-zrelishchnoi podkomissiei Prazdnichnoi komisii, 1927).

[84] Thus, creating an uproar during the terrible famine of 1921–22, Soviet festivals seem like complete madness. At the same time, the same or a "related" Soviet power structure produced texts with shocking content. In a review by the Tatar Republic in April 1922, it was stated that the famine had reached such proportions that "cannibalism has become an everyday occurrence. In Kazan' corpses dead from hunger lie about the streets and they are not cleaned up sometimes for several days" (RGASPI f. 17, op. 60, d. 365, l. 93 [Pamiatka po Tatarskoi Respublike za aprel', 31 maia 1922 g.]). At this same time, a commission for the preparation of the May-Day

military disasters evoked a response and willingness to participate in these activities by a large part of the population, which is explained by a variety of social and psychological factors. Historical celebrations acted as a kind of "valve" for releasing the discontent, fear, and frustrations of those times. They "turned around" the frightening daily existence, becoming a kind of self-preservation in the madness of catastrophic daily life. The stabilization of power and the weakening of internal and external threats were accompanied in significant measure by a loss of interest in "historic" holidays and anniversaries.

Translated by Hannah Zinn

Festival, accustomed to decorating the city for the celebrations, rightly decided that "decorations in a limited measure be placed in the mall areas and squares.... Special decoration of buildings, gardens, and other places is too costly and because of the famine is not appropriate." At the same time, in order to bring troops to take their oath in conjunction with the May-Day holiday, complex structures were being built in the city (NART f. R-732, op. 1, d. 126, l. 2, 10 [Plan prazdnovaniia 1 Maia po gorodu Kazani, aprel' 1922 g.; Radiotelegramma vsem kantispolkomam, profbiuro, voenkomam, partkomam i politprosvetam o prazdnovanii 1 Maia, aprel' 1922 g.]).

The Russian Experience of Money, 1914–24

Steven G. Marks

"Is there really anything more important than money? No!" "Money is the key to a person's well-being, and gives you everything that is magnificent in life." "Money rules the world!" Those words, from a get-rich-quick pamphlet published in 1916, convey the upwardly-mobile aspirations of urban Russians in the late tsarist empire. An entire generation had grown accustomed to economic expansion undergirded by monetary stability; its hopes were a lustrous reflection of the strong ruble that had come into being when Minister of Finance Sergei Witte brought Russia onto the gold standard in 1897.[1]

The currency produced in the reign of Nicholas II looked and felt solid, with bills of substantial size, elegant designs, and the finest quality printing. Colloquially known as "Romanovs," they depicted strong Russian rulers— Peter the Great, Catherine the Great, Nicholas I, and Alexander III. Coins of copper, silver, or gold displayed, most commonly, the imperial double-headed eagle and the profile of the tsar. These "pictographs of power" were readily accepted as legal tender by the population at large, whether urban, rural, or ethnic.[2] Despite social tensions and centrifugal tendencies on the borderlands, monetary conditions in late imperial Russia suggested countervailing tenden-

---

For their invaluable comments on earlier drafts of this article I thank Jonathan Daly, Murray Frame, Boris Kolonitskii, Adele Lindenmeyr, Christopher Read, Aviel Roshwald, and Melissa Stockdale. My department chair, Thomas Kuehn, and the Clemson University Russian Area Studies Committee provided financial support for which I am grateful. For their assistance in Moscow, I am also deeply indebted to Nadezhda Kostrikova of the Russian State Archive of the Economy (RGAE); Arkadii Trachuk, director of Goznak; and Natal′ia Kuratnikova and her staff at the Goznak archive.

[1] Anonymous, *Den′gi i ikh dobyvanie* (Kiev: Imperial, 1916), 3. For the gospel of success in late imperial Russian popular fiction, see Jeffrey Brooks, *When Russia Learned to Read: Literacy and Popular Literature, 1861–1917* (Princeton, NJ: Princeton University Press, 1985), chap. 8.

[2] James Cracraft, "Pictographs of Power: The 500-Ruble Note of 1912," in *Picturing Russia: Explorations in Visual Culture*, ed. Valerie Kivelson and Joan Neuberger (New Haven: Yale University Press, 2008), 139–41; and Robert G. Papp, "Road to Chervonets: The Representation of National Identity in Russian Money, 1896–1924" (unpublished

Russian Culture in War and Revolution, 1914–22, Book 2: Political Culture, Identities, Mentalities, and Memory. Murray Frame, Boris Kolonitskii, Steven G. Marks, and Melissa K. Stockdale, eds. Bloomington, IN: Slavica Publishers, 2014, 121–48.

cies working toward integration of the populace in a unified polity.[3] But with the onslaught of war and revolution, the financial infrastructure collapsed, and it was not fully reconstructed until 1924.

Among its many characteristics, money is a symbolic representation of values. It can therefore be seen as a prism that refracts a society's ideals—to quote Ralph Waldo Emerson, "the coin is a delicate meter of civil, social, and moral changes."[4] Accordingly, scholars who are engaged in the "new economic criticism" view discourses about money (and economics in general) as a rich vein of source material to be mined with the same techniques of cultural analysis one would apply to art and literature.[5]

This article, too, approaches money as a cultural and intellectual phenomenon.[6] From discussions of money in diaries, memoirs, letters, newspapers, and government documents, as well as from the designs of currency notes and coins, I extract clues to Russian attitudes: above all what the citizenry felt about the tsarist and Soviet regimes, and how the leaders of those regimes envisioned the society they governed. These clues lead to the article's three overarching claims: 1) that the ruble's sinking value generated much of the popular opposition to the tsarist, Provisional, and Soviet governments in turn; 2) the flip side of the coin: only after the resurrection of a gold-backed hard currency, in 1924, was the populace ready to accept the passing of the old order and acquiesce to the new one; and 3) the Soviet financial administration presented an alternative to both Left Communism and Stalinism that, had circumstances been different, might have allowed for the long-term continuation of the market economy introduced with the New Economic Policy (NEP).

---

ms., American Numismatic Society, Summer Seminar 1996), 23–39; my thanks to the author for permission to photocopy his important work.

[3] E. A. Pravilova, *Finansy imperii: Den'gi i vlast' v politike Rossii na natsional'nykh okrainakh, 1801–1917* (Moscow: Novoe Izd–vo, 2006).

[4] From Emerson's essay "Wealth" (1860), quoted in *The Oxford Book of Money*, ed. Kevin Jackson (Oxford: Oxford University Press, 1995), 20.

[5] Martha Woodmansee and Mark Osteen, eds., *The New Economic Criticism: Studies at the Intersection of Literature and Economics* (London: Routledge, 1999); Marc Shell, *Money, Language, and Thought: Literary and Philosophical Economies from the Medieval to the Modern Era* (Berkeley: University of California Press, 1982).

[6] The subject of Russian money is largely absent from Western historiography. In Russia and the former Soviet Union, collectors have generated a vast and useful literature. Russian-language scholarship has tended to stress financial policy, but archival studies of money and monetary policy have appeared in increasing number (see footnotes below). Eric Helleiner, *The Making of National Money: Territorial Currencies in Historical Perspective* (Ithaca, NY: Cornell University Press, 2003), does not treat Russia, but is essential reading on the modern history of money, including its cultural dimensions.

The history of money thus helps us to map in a new way the experiences and mentalities of Russia's people and their rulers during the tumultuous decade that began in the summer of 1914.

World War I

At the onset of war the imperial government adopted a financial policy that ended up undermining social stability by flooding the nation with worthless currency.[7] During the conflict the Russian state budget was in deficit to about the same degree as in Germany and the UK. All of the belligerents covered military expenditures with some combination of loans, taxes, and/or currency emissions, but Russia (and the Ottoman Empire) relied more than any of the others on the printing press. The tsarist government suspended gold convertibility and issued treasury notes without regard for the old legal limit.[8] It did so initially to prevent the depletion of the nation's gold reserve, which was the basis of its once-stable currency. Besides, it promised to be a short, victorious war. As Minister of Finance Petr Bark explained on 1 August 1914, it was better to use paper money than gold to pay for supplies in the foreign territories the Russian army was sure to occupy.[9]

Out of dire necessity, the temporary expedient became permanent. The state lost its largest source of revenue (nearly a third of the budget) with the suspension of vodka sales at the start of hostilities; when crowds of binge-drinking peasants stole bottles of liquor they correctly proclaimed that they were liberating "the national wealth."[10] It turned out to be a long and expensive war, costing on average 40 million rubles per day in the first two years and twice that in 1917. To cover its costs the government had to print 20–30 million

---

[7] For more detail on this subject, see Steven G. Marks, "Russian War Finance, 1914–1917," in *1914–1918 Online* (Berlin: Freie Universität, 2014).

[8] Stephen Broadberry and Mark Harrison, "Economics of World War I: An Overview," in *Economics of World War I*, ed. Broadberry and Harrison (Cambridge: Cambridge University Press, 2005); Peter Gatrell, "Poor Russia, Poor Show," in ibid.; A. L. Sidorov, *Finansovoe polozhenie Rossii v gody Pervoi mirovoi voiny, 1914–1917* (Moscow: Izd-vo Akademii Nauk SSSR, 1960), 109–10; Arthur Z. Arnold, *Banks, Credit, and Money in Soviet Russia* (New York: Columbia University Press, 1937), 39–41. Foreign and domestic loans, including treasury bills designed as short-term bonds, provided 62 percent of Russian wartime revenues; 7 percent came from surpluses carried over from prewar budgets; and 31 percent from currency emissions (Gatrell, "Poor Russia," 247–48).

[9] B. D. Gal'perina et al., eds., *Sovet ministrov Rossiiskoi imperii v gody pervoi mirovoi voiny: Bumagi A. N. Iakhontova* (St. Petersburg: Dmitrii Bulanin, 1999), 29.

[10] *Novaia zhizn'*, 10 March 1918, cited in James Bunyan and H. H. Fisher, eds., *Bolshevik Revolution, 1917–1918: Documents and Materials* (Stanford, CA: Stanford University Press, 1934), 672.

rubles daily, or five–six times the amount before the war.[11] Only in retrospect did they realize that their dependence on the printing press was an addiction to a "sweet poison," in the words of the ex-president of the Duma, Mikhail Rodzianko.[12]

To make matters worse, the government imposed price caps on grain and other agricultural products for the purpose of calming price fluctuations, combating price-gouging, and ensuring that food remained affordable for the cities and armed forces.[13] Since the fixed prices took little account of production and transport costs, peasants sold to traders under the table at an illegally high mark-up or curtailed delivery to the market.[14] This, along with the ever-expanding number of banknotes in circulation, put upward pressure on prices. In general the cost of living more than doubled between 1914 and 1916, but in some places it rose much more than that: for example in Sarapul district, along the Kama River, the price of sugar multiplied 27 times. By February 1917 the purchasing power of the ruble eroded to about 30 kopecks in prewar money.[15]

Very quickly, in accordance with Gresham's Law, which holds that bad money drives out good, the populace hoarded gold, silver, and soon copper coins.[16] While using the depreciating paper money in market exchanges, they held onto metallic currency, depositing it in "land banks"—which is to say they buried coins in the ground or hid them "all across Mother Russia in money boxes and clay canisters, under the stove or in the bosom."[17]

---

[11] Rossiiskii gosudarstvennyi arkhiv ekonomii (RGAE) f. 7733 (USSR Ministry of Finance), op. 1, d. 166 (Interdepartmental correspondence of the state financial agencies; correspondence with regional authorities, 1918–22), l. 11; I. A. Mikhailov, *Voina i nashe denezhnoe obrashchenie* (Petrograd: Kaspari, 1916), 33. In England the increase in printed money was 0 percent, in France 100 percent, and in Germany 300 percent (Sidorov, *Finansovoe polozhenie*, 146). Turkey is harder to compare because very little paper money circulated before the war: Şevket Pamuk, "The Ottoman Economy in World War I," in *Economics of World War I*, 128–29.

[12] "Zapiska M. V. Rodzianko," *Krasnyi arkhiv*, no. 10 (1925): 82.

[13] Gal'perina, *Sovet ministrov*, 41, 44.

[14] V. Maklakov, "Kanun revoliutsii," *Novyi zhurnal* 14 (1946): 307.

[15] Arnold, *Banks*, 48–50; Tsuyoshi Hasegawa, *February Revolution: Petrograd, 1917* (Seattle: University of Washington Press, 1981), 84; Aaron B. Retish, *Russia's Peasants in Revolution and Civil War: Citizenship, Identity, and the Creation of the Soviet State, 1914–22* (Cambridge: Cambridge University Press, 2008), 58.

[16] In early 1914, 69.5 percent of the money in Russia was paper; by the end of the year it was 82 percent, and by late 1916 it was 100 percent. R. E. Vaisberg, *Den'gi i tseny* (Moscow: Izd-vo Gosplana, 1925), 16–17.

[17] Respective quotes in RSFSR. Vysshii sovet narodnogo khoziaistva (hereafter VSNKh), *Trudy I vserossiiskogo s"ezda sovetov narodnogo khoziaistva 25 maia–4 iiunia 1918*

For people who were not well-to-do, small change was all they had ever had. With the disappearance of coins, buying and selling things became harder. To ease the problem, the treasury produced paper surrogates for coins. In 1915, it printed postage stamps for that purpose from the 1913 Romanov tercentenary issue (without the adhesive), and in 1916 small rectangular paper kopecks which specified that they were the "equivalent of silver [or, for lower denominations, copper] coins."[18]

The psychological impact of those notes was enormous. To go from the solid coinage and currency of a generation to puny pieces of paper signified the sudden decline in national and personal fortunes.[19] People from all walks of life commented on the small-change drought and the inundation of paper money—and would do so for the next decade. Diarists began to report prices as they would the weather, and it was never sunny skies. In all the memoir literature one sees a growing preoccupation with prices and dismay at the ever-rising cost of staples.[20] According to a Russian who lived through it, it was like to trying to hold melting snow in your hands: the longer you kept your money, the less you had.[21]

Fearing hunger, people ate up rumors and hunted scapegoats. As a pamphleteer observed, most people did not understand the "basic laws" of market prices, let alone the causes of inflation.[22] They figured out for themselves who was responsible, whether true or not. Some blamed the peasants. Some blamed the workers. Accusations flew against shopkeepers. Conspiracy theories circulated widely, charging police and officials for corruption or for conniving with speculators to jack up prices for regular people.[23]

---

g. (Stenograficheskii otchet) (Moscow: Gos. tipografiia, 1918), 131; and E. Vladimirovich, *Pochemu desheveiut den'gi* (Odessa: Vlast' naroda, 1917), 16.

[18] A. V. Aliamkin and A. G. Baranov, *Istoriia denezhnogo obrashcheniia v 1914–1924 gg. (no materialam Zaural'ia)* (Ekaterinburg: Izd-vo ural'skogo gos. gornogo universiteta, 2005), 73–76.

[19] N. P. Okunev, *Dnevnik moskvicha (1917–1924)* (Paris: YMCA Press, 1990), 479, states this explicitly in 1921.

[20] Examples from different strata of the population include Okunev, *Dnevnik moskvicha*; Iurii Vladimirovich Got'e, *Time of Troubles: The Diary of Iurii Vladimirovich Got'e*, trans. and ed. Terence Emmons (Princeton, NJ: Princeton University Press, 1988); A. A. Zamaraev, *Dnevnik totemskogo krest'ianina, 1906–1922 gody* (Moscow: Rossiiskaia Akademiia Nauk, 1995).

[21] I. Kh. Ozerov, "O regulirovanii denezhnogo obrashcheniia," *Ekonomist*, no. 3 (1922): 77.

[22] Nikolai Morozov, *Kak prekratit' "vzdorozhanie zhizni"?* (Moscow: I. D. Sytin, 1916), 2–5.

[23] Barbara Engel, "Not by Bread Alone: Subsistence Riots in Russia during World War I," *Journal of Modern History* 69, 4 (December 1997): 696–721; Corinne Gaudin,

They also blamed "alien" ethnic groups: first, resident Germans, whom they suspected of treason.[24] Second, Jews.[25] Increasingly, though, as we know from studies of riots and protest marches, the populace saw the tsar as culpable for the financial crisis.[26] From the start of the war, police officials and government ministers were apprehensive about this "nervousness of the population." The sense of panic in the Council of Ministers paralleled the inflation rate. Already in 1915 Minister of Internal Affairs Nikolai Maklakov expressed concern that rising prices were "having an effect on the mood of the population of the capital, inciting it toward rebellion!" By early 1917, top officials were stating publicly that they "could not hide their alarm" at the disaster facing them.[27]

Left with few alternatives, the government sold war bonds with the dual purpose of raising revenues and sponging up the excess cash circulating in the country due to the printing of money. But subscriptions to the last four (of six) imperial issues were disappointing. The government was well aware of what this said about the political mood of the country: as Andrei Shingarev, a Kadet member of the Duma, stated in January 1917, the "government does not enjoy the confidence of investors or the workers."[28] Appeals to patriotism had grown ineffectual.

With the fall of the monarchy in March 1917 a wave of palpable optimism spread across the land. That, too, was expressed in terms of money. G. A. Kniazev of Petrograd noted in his journal that "our janitor's wife 'Aunt Pasha' believes that now everything will be cheaper. Bread, she expects, will go

---

"Circulation and Production of News and Rumor in Rural Russia during World War I," in this book.

[24] Gal'perina, *Sovet ministrov*, 321; Got'e, *Time of Troubles*, 32, 72, 89–90, 103.

[25] Pierre Pascal, *Mon Journal de Russie: À la Mission militaire française, 1916–1918* (Lausanne: L'Age d'homme, 1975), 72; Eric Lohr, "The Russian Army and the Jews: Mass Deportation, Hostages, and Violence during World War I," *Russian Review* 60, 3 (July 2001): 417. Accusations that Jewish currency manipulations were responsible for the inflation continued into the Soviet period; see Vladimir P. Buldakov, "Freedom, Shortages, Violence: The Origins of the 'Revolutionary Anti-Jewish Pogrom' in Russia, 1917–1918," in *Anti-Jewish Violence: Rethinking the Pogrom in East European History*, ed. Jonathan Dekel-Chen et al. (Bloomington: Indiana University Press, 2011), 76–77, 79; A. V. Kvashonkin et al., eds., *Bol'shevistskoe rukovodstvo: Perepiska, 1912–1927* (Moscow: ROSSPEN, 1996), 90–91; Got'e, *Time of Troubles*, 435, 440, 447.

[26] Engel, "Not by Bread Alone"; Iu. I Kir'ianov, "Massovye vystupleniia na pochve dorogovizny v Rossii (1914–fevral' 1917 g.)," *Otechestvennaia istoriia*, no. 3 (1993): 6.

[27] Sidorov, *Finansovoe polozhenie*, 162–63 (first and third quotes); Gal'perina, *Sovet ministrov*, 66, 124, 155 (second quote), 210, 267, 278, 337.

[28] Sidorov, *Finansovoe polozhenie*, 154–55, 160–63. Shingarev was not alone in this assessment; see also V. V. Strakhov, "Vnutrennie zaimy v Rossii v pervuiu mirovuiu voinu," *Voprosy istorii*, no. 9 (2003): 39–41.

back down to three kopecks, sugar, butter too.... Everyone expects the new order to produce supernatural changes and improvements to life.... And what will happen later on? It could not be worse than what we've already been through."[29]

But it was. Within a few months, state revenues plummeted as the bureaucracy disintegrated, hindering tax collection. The currency crisis worsened and the economy unraveled. That dashed the inflated hopes of the nation, which then withdrew support from the Provisional Government. In late May, Kniazev wrote that "now money has gone crazy. Money has lost all value."[30] "The ruble," another contemporary mourned, "is broken."[31] Even for wealthy aristocrats, times were hard, especially if their allowances were locked up in inaccessible foreign investments. Prince Andrei Lobanov-Rostovskii reminisced that with the loss of that income he could only afford to eat every other day; "on the off days I would sit through the dinner hour in one of the public parks [of Petrograd]. On one such occasion a beggar came up to me and was dumbfounded when I told him that I didn't have a penny in my pocket."[32] How well that suggests the world turned upside down, as it was in 1917.

A new double-headed eagle debuted on the paper money of the Provisional Government. The renowned artist Ivan Bilibin designed it after a 16th-century prototype, but shorn of the imperial crown and regalia—which led Russian wits to christen it the "naked" or "plucked" bird.[33] The notes that entered circulation in spring 1917 were called Duma money, or "dumki" after a picture of the Tauride Palace, the seat of the legislature, on the 1,000-ruble bill. Bilibin superimposed a swastika on the obverse as an ancient Oriental good-luck symbol. But it did not work. The treasury kept stoking the printing presses, and between February and October the ruble shrank in value from 30 to 6 or 7 prewar kopecks. No wonder the Russians bestowed disdainful nicknames on the Provisional Government's currency, like Kerenskii money, or "kerenki," the 20- and 40-ruble notes whose worthlessness they associated with the prime minister under whom they appeared; or, for the same shabbily

---

[29] G. A. Kniazev, "Iz zapisnoi knizhki russkogo intelligenta za vremia voiny i revoliutsii 1915–1922 g.," *Russkoe proshloe*, no. 2 (1991): 115, 124, 126.

[30] Ibid., 157.

[31] A. L. Sidorov et al., eds., *Ekonomicheskoe polozhenie Rossii nakanune velikoi oktiabr'skoi sotsialisticheskoi revoliutsii* (Moscow: Izd-vo Akademii Nauk SSSR, 1957), 2: 378–79.

[32] Andrei Lobanov-Rostovsky, *The Grinding Mill: Reminiscences of War and Revolution* (New York: Macmillan, 1935), 234–35.

[33] A. V. Aliamkin and A. G. Baranov, "Bumazhnye denezhnye znaki revoliutsionnoi Rossii," www.bonistikaweb.ru/INTERKRIMPRESS/banknoti-2006-3.htm (accessed 10 March 2014).

made notes, "kvas labels."[34] (See fig. 27 in the gallery of illustrations following page 178.) Another insult to the memory of the old ruble: kerenki were issued in unperforated sheets and had to be cut out with scissors.

Emissions of paper money continued unabated. A contemporary economist decried this "dance of the billions"; little could anyone imagine how much more frenzied the dance would become after the Bolshevik takeover.[35]

Bolshevik Revolution

Across the former empire, rival currencies and monetary surrogates sprang up like weeds as political boundaries fluctuated and national economic ties were torn asunder during the long years of war and revolution. What better indicator of that state of affairs than the circulation of up to 20,000 different types of money in a zone that before the first World War had one unified currency?[36]

As people perceived subtle spurts in values they shifted out of one kind of money and into another. The circumstances were such that "market women have to become professors of mathematics—as the people jestingly say—to find their way in this financial labyrinth."[37]

All of the breakaway ethnic regions printed their own money. So did every White army. In every part of the country, city governments, local soviets, branch offices of the State Bank or the People's Commissariat of Finance (Narkomfin) issued currency notes, mostly without Moscow's authorization. For regions that were loyal to the Kremlin but far away, especially in Central Asia, the Soviet government gave its permission to design and distribute their own money.[38] Foreign currencies also circulated widely in border regions—not German, Austrian, or Polish money, which was as weak as the ruble, but in the Caucasus Turkish lira, and in the Far East Chinese yuan, American

---

[34] M. V. Khodiakov, *Den′gi revoliutsii i grazhdanskoi voiny: Denezhnoe obrashchenie v Rossii, 1917–1920 gg.* (St. Petersburg: Piter, 2009), 22–33; A. A. Sidorov, *Russkaia grafika za gody revoliutsii 1917–1922* (Moscow: Dom pechati, 1923), 14; Papp, "Road to Chervonets," 45–47; B. I. Kolonitskii, *Simvoly vlasti i bor′ba za vlast′: K izucheniiu politicheskoi kul′tury rossiiskoi revoliutsii 1917 goda* (St. Petersburg: Liki Rossii, 2012), 91–92. Arthur Ransome, *Russia in 1919* (New York: B. W. Huebsch, 1919), 135, testifies to the scornful rather than playful nature of the term "kerenki" among the populace.

[35] Sidorov, *Finansovoe polozhenie*, 146.

[36] Khodiakov, *Den′gi*, 7–8.

[37] Alexander Berkman, *Bolshevik Myth (Diary 1920–1922)* (London: Pluto Press, 1989), 162.

[38] Aliamkin and Baranov, *Istoriia denezhnogo obrashcheniia*, 106ff, 182; Vaisberg, *Den′gi*, 13–23.

dollars, Mexican pesos, and especially Japanese yen, which Tokyo banks were aggressively distributing.[39]

Because prices were skyrocketing like "airplane flights,"[40] private firms, railroads, and cooperatives issued their own token money, which at least guaranteed that one could buy something at a fixed price in that establishment. Then those tokens, too, would circulate locally. In Vladivostok, to give but one of thousands of examples, the scrip of the Kunst and Albers department store was exchanged as regular money.[41] Doctors' prescriptions functioned the same way.[42] And the quantities multiplied through rampant counterfeiting.[43]

Meanwhile, within the space the Bolsheviks directly controlled, the government, for reasons we will see, was churning out astronomical sums of money: it distributed 900 billion rubles in 1920, 16 trillion in 1921, 1.9 quadrillion in 1922, and 223 quadrillion in 1923. By March 1924 there were an unfathomable 809 quadrillion rubles in Soviet notes in circulation.[44] "The time

---

[39] Alfred Nawrath, *Im reiche der Medea: Kaukasische Fahrten und Abenteuer* (Leipzig: Brockhaus, 1924), 65; A. I. Pogrebetskii, *Denezhnoe obrashchenie i denezhnye znaki Dal'nego Vostoka za period voiny i revoliutsii* (Harbin: Knizhnoe delo, 1924), 146; RSFSR. Upravlenie upolnomochennogo narodnogo komissariata finansov na Dal'nem Vostoke, *Otchet o deiatel'nosti finansovykh organov Dal'nego Vostoka za 1922-oi god* (Chita, 1923), 53–55; John J. Stephan, *The Russian Far East: A History* (Stanford, CA: Stanford University Press, 1994), 132.

[40] RSFSR, *Sotsial'naia revoliutsiia i finansy: Sbornik k III kongressu Kommunisticheskogo Internatsionala*, comp. O. Iu. Shmidt and S. M. Izmailov (Moscow: Pervaia moskovskaia fabrika zagotovleniia gos. znakov, 1921), 39.

[41] Lobanov-Rostovsky, *Grinding Mill*, 323; Stephan, *Russian Far East*, 132; Pogrebetskii, *Denezhnoe obrashchenie*, 26; Aliamkin and Baranov, *Istoriia denezhnogo obrashcheniia*, 184–85. For a sampling of privately issued monetary tokens from around the country, see Aleksandr Chashchin, *Sretensk: Stranitsy proshlogo* (Chita: Ekspress, 2009); M. M. Gleizer, *Bonistika v Petrograde — Leningrade — Sankt-Peterburge* (St. Petersburg: Aleksandr PRINT, 1998); Dmitri Kharitonov, *Jewish Paper Money in Russia* (Prague: Partner Praha, 2003); Vladimir Kozlov, *Bony i liudi: Denezhnoe obrashchenie Urala, 1840–1933 gg. Opty nestandartnogo cataloga* (Ekaterinburg: Bank kul'turnoi informatsii, 2000); and Evgenii Ovsiankin, *Arkhangel'skie den'gi*, 2d ed. (Arkhangel'sk: Pravda Severa, 2008).

[42] E. M. Almedingen, *Tomorrow Will Come* (Boston: Little, Brown, 1941), 183.

[43] M. B-n, *Kak otlichat' nastoiashchie den'gi ot fal'shivykh* (Kiev: Kondof, 1918); Pogrebetskii, *Denezhnoe obrashchenie*, 37; Khodiakov, *Den'gi*, 140, 142; Clemson University Special Collections, "Autobiography of Abe Wolfe Davidson," typescript ms., box 8, pp. 168, 178; Konstantin Paustovsky, *The Story of a Life*, trans. Joseph Barnes (New York: Pantheon Books, 1964), 587.

[44] Arnold, *Banks*, 184, 186–87; S. S. Katzenellenbaum, *Russian Currency and Banking, 1914–1924* (London: P. S. King, 1925), 59; L. N. Dobrokhotov et al., eds., *Denezhnaia reforma 1921–1924 gg.: Sozdanie tverdoi valiuty. Dokumenty i materialy* (Moscow: RossPEN, 2008), 738; L. N. Iurovskii, *Nashe denezhnoe obrashchenie* (Moscow: Finansovoe izd-vo NKF SSSR, 1926), 152–53.

is not far distant," remarked Gosplan (State Planning Committee) economist Vladimir Bazarov, "when the sum of those nominal rubles will exceed the number of all atoms or electrons of which our planet is composed."[45] The hyperinflation this fueled made the situation before 1917 seem like a trifle: between January and December 1923, the Russian commodity price index leaped from 21 million to 2.3 billion rubles, and peaked at 62 billion in March 1924—compared with 1 in 1913 and 18 in December 1917.[46] As historian Iurii Got'e noted in his diary, "prices are leaping upward so fast the mind can't keep up with them…. There is not enough money for anything."[47]

Lobanov-Rostovskii's memoir gives us a snapshot of an incident that occurred in Odessa in April 1919, but which applied millions of times over for every person living in the former tsarist empire in the years to come: there was a "somersaulting of prices, and nobody knew what the currency would be worth in an hour. I went into a barbershop for a shave and, while waiting, went around the corner to get a newspaper. By the time I was back the price of the shave had risen from five rubles to eight rubles."[48] Two years later, inflation had metastasized: a British visitor was astonished that a porter at the train station would reject a tip of 1,000,000 rubles: "'Mala! Mala!' [sic] (Little! Little!) he would say, holding out his hand for more."[49]

Idiomatic speech both lagged behind and kept pace with the mind-boggling changes in monetary values. Beggars on the streets of Moscow during the first years of the NEP still harassed passersby with the set phrase "give us a kopeck"—but kopecks had long ago become irrelevant.[50] By 1923, the basic official monetary unit was the 100-ruble note, renominated but worth a million 1921 rubles (fig. 28). With their irrepressible humor the Russians spoke of these "milliony" as "limony" (lemons): "A cabby tells you that he has to pay hundreds of 'lemons' for a sack of oats, … and has to spend so many 'lemons' a day to keep his body and soul together."[51]

Germany, Austria, Hungary, Poland, and Czechoslovakia all experienced hyperinflation in the wake of the war and the collapse of the old Eastern

---

[45] Alec Nove, *An Economic History of the USSR, 1917–1921* (London: Penguin, 1989), 81.

[46] Iurovskii, *Nashe denezhnoe obrashchenie*, 248; Katzenellenbaum, *Russian Currency*, 74–75. By comparison, the German wholesale price index maxed out in late 1923 at 127 trillion marks; see Thomas J. Sargent, "The Ends of Four Big Inflations," in *Inflation: Causes and Effects*, ed. Robert E. Hall (Chicago: University of Chicago Press, 1982), 75.

[47] Got'e, *Time of Troubles*, 282, 442–43.

[48] Lobanov-Rostovsky, *Grinding Mill*, 330.

[49] Fred A. MacKenzie, *Russia before Dawn* (London: T. Fisher Unwin, 1923), 211.

[50] Ilya Ehrenburg, *Men, Years-Life*, 3: *Truce: 1921–33*, trans. T. Shebunina (London: MacGibbon and Kee, 1963), 67.

[51] Michael S. Farbman, *Bolshevism in Retreat* (London: W. Collins and Sons, 1923), 187–88.

European empires. That circumstance has not prevented the perpetuation of a myth that the Bolsheviks launched hyperinflation in Russia deliberately and with ideologically-driven ill intent.[52] The myth originated with John Maynard Keynes, who wrote in *The Economic Consequences of the Peace* (1919) that "Lenin is said to have declared that the best way to destroy the Capitalist System was to debauch the currency. By a continuing process of inflation, governments can confiscate, secretly and unobserved, an important part of the wealth of their citizens."[53] But Keynes, who picked this notion up from a phony interview with Lenin he read in the British and American press, was wrong.[54]

Anyone who reads the Russian newspapers and documents from the period will have to acknowledge that most of the Bolsheviks were actually desperate to figure out a way to stop the printing presses—they simply had no choice but to keep them rolling. Revenue streams dried up when out of socialist euphoria the Soviet government made utilities and public transport free of charge.[55] In an oft-cited rhetorical flourish, the Bolshevik economist Evgenii Preobrazhenskii, a Left Communist, once proclaimed "Glory to the printing press!… In the archive of the great proletarian revolution, … occupying the place of honor will be the printing press, the machine gun of the Commissariat of Finance that launched a barrage of fire into the rear of the bourgeois system, overthrew its monetary laws, and turned them into the means of its destruction." But he was fantasizing: in reality, as he then and later stated, the simple reason the treasury printed money was to keep the government from collapsing.[56] Quite a few other Bolsheviks tried to find some advantage in it—including some who said uncontrolled currency emissions made it easier to finance electrification and the founding of new universities. But that is not the same as doing what Keynes charged.[57]

---

[52] Alec Nove, "Ideology, Planning, and the Market," *Critical Review*, no. 4 (1991): 562; William G. Rosenberg, "The Problem of Market Relations and the State in Revolutionary Russia," *Comparative Studies in Society and History* 36, 2 (April 1994): 379–81.

[53] J. M. Keynes, *The Economic Consequences of the Peace* (New York: Harcourt, Brace, and Howe, 1920), 235.

[54] Frank W. Fetter, "Lenin, Keynes, and Inflation," *Economica*, n.s., 44, 173 (February 1977): 77–80, showed that Lenin's remarks were apocryphal. In response to Fetter, Michael V. White and Kurt Schuler, "Retrospectives: Who Said 'Debauch the Currency': Keynes or Lenin," *Journal of Economic Perspectives* 23, 2 (Spring 2009): 213–22, found the likely source of Keynes' statement, but they take it at face value. In light of the evidence I have found, I believe their conclusion, that the fake interview reflected Bolshevik policy, is incorrect.

[55] Khodiakov, *Den'gi*, 34–40.

[56] Preobrazhenskii, *Bumazhnye den'gi v epokhu proletarskoi diktatury* (Moscow: Gos. izd-vo, 1920), 4; Narkomfin, *Sotsial'naia revoliutsiia*, 39.

[57] N. N. Shaposhnikov, "O putiakh ozdorovleniia denezhnoi sistemy," *Ekonomist*, no. 4–5 (1922): 51–52.

By far the greater number of high-ranking Soviets, including some Left Communists, thought that the severely devalued currency undermined the Bolshevik position by hurting the working class.[58] In Lenin's mind, "money, or those scraps of paper that now go by the name of money, are harmful and dangerous insofar as the bourgeoisie, in keeping stocks of these pieces of paper, retains its economic power." His solution, proposed in May 1918, was not to reduce the value of money by printing more of it, as per Keynes, but to require people to exchange their old banknotes for a new, redenominated currency.[59]

What is more, the government had to create money because it was, ironically, in chronic short supply. It was a time not of feast, but of "monetary famine."[60] That was a result of the steady depreciation of the currency. Throughout the Civil War the Red Army was constantly dunning the government for infusions of cash. When after 1921 the NEP revived the money-based economy, shortages of currency became even more severe, and firms and regions were begging Moscow for shipments of it by train or plane.[61] That same year, government expenditures grew more than 15 times as it spent hundreds of billions of rubles on aid to famine-stricken provinces.[62] For regular people, it was a "continuing crisis of impecuniousness" due to the inflation and the lack of banknotes. Got'e expressed the desperation of his contemporaries: "Again no one is getting paid anywhere; I need 'millions' and there is nowhere to get them."[63]

To compensate for the shortage of bills, from January 1918 the Soviet government allowed coupons from prerevolutionary bonds and mortgages to circulate as currency at their face value. Although they banned money issued by the White armies, they often had to reverse course and accept it as legal tender. The Soviet government continued to print dumki, kerenki, and even

---

[58] See, e.g., Iu. Larin, "Sekret denezhnogo potoka," *Ekonomicheskaia zhizn'*, no. 14 (22 January 1920): 1; Papp, "Road to Chervonets," 54–55.

[59] Iu. P. Bokarev, "Denezhnoe obrashchenie na territorii Rossii v gody oktiabr'skoi revoliutsii i grazhdanskoi voiny," in *Denezhnoe obrashchenie Rossii: Istoricheskie ocherki, katalog, materialy arkhivnykh fondov v trekh tomakh*, 1: *Istoricheskie ocherki: S drevneishikh vremen do nashikh dnei*, ed. G. I. Luntovsky, A. N. Sakharov, and A. V. Iurov (Moscow: Interkrim-Press, 2010), 239.

[60] VSNKh, *Trudy I vserossiiskogo s"ezda*, 172.

[61] RGAE f. 7733, op. 1, d. 166, ll. 1–2, 8–10, 12–13, 19, 22, 43, 61, 70, 99; f. 7733, op. 1, d. 5929 (Correspondence between regional and central financial authorities, 1921–24), ll. 1–10, 17, and passim; Aliamkin and Baranov, *Istoriia denezhnogo obrashcheniia*, 105; Khodiakov, *Den'gi*, 132.

[62] A. S. Sokolov, *Finansovaia politika sovetskogo gosudarstva, 1921–1929 gg.* (Moscow: Zvezdopad, 2005), 57–58.

[63] Got'e, *Time of Troubles*, 435.

tsarist money, and by the billions: it was easier than forging new templates, and the money was in demand both at home and in the border regions of the former Russian Empire.[64] But all that money was almost worthless. Peasants wallpapered their huts with sheets of kerenki.[65] At markets, littering the ground were 250- and 500-ruble notes that no one bothered to pick up.[66]

Showing signs of impending collapse as early as 1916, the money economy caved in after the Bolshevik Revolution. The Soviet government inherited the policy of grain requisitioning from the tsarist regime, but applied it with more concerted, and violent, effort. Shortages made it necessary to introduce rationing in the cities, and because money was lacking for salaries, "naturalization" of wages became common. By 1920 the average factory worker received 92.6 percent of his pay in goods and 7.4 percent in cash.[67] But the naturalization trend, in tandem with the deteriorating purchasing power of the ruble, brought forth a barter and black-market economy that characterized the period of "War Communism" from 1918–21. As government-issued currency had lost much of its ability to function as a means of exchange, natural money substitutes—bread, salt, milk, potatoes, rye flour, firewood, overcoats, or matches—took its place, and, according to a contemporary, "in the countryside anything could be [had] for moonshine." Their relative values and exchange rates were reported in newspapers and official publications, which functioned as a kind of price courant: in Kaluga on a certain day, 1 cart loaded with birch firewood bought 6.5 lbs. [sic] of kerosene, 10 lbs. of salt, or 1 overcoat; 24 glasses of milk bought 2 boxes of matches.[68]

Throughout the period the Soviet government agonized over how to "disentangle ourselves from the financial-economic mess."[69] Inside and outside the Bolshevik Party, a surprisingly wide array of opinions was expressed publicly, including calls by a few brave souls, in 1918, for a return to the market economy and the restoration of private entrepreneurship. For urging that approach, the prominent liberal economist Ivan Ozerov and others were outed as oppositionists, but given the number of "bourgeois specialists" at

---

[64] Aliamkin and Baranov, *Istoriia denezhnogo obrashcheniia*, 86, 97–98, 104–5, 213, 223–24; Khodiakov, *Den'gi*, 27–29, 40–41, 43, 57–70, 142–43, 152; Papp, "Road to Chervonets," 50; RGAE f. 7733, op. 1, d. 166, l. 93.

[65] Iu. P. Bokarev, "Rubl' v epokhu voin i revoliutsii," in *Russkii rubl': Dva veka istorii XIX–XX vv.*, ed. N. P. Zimarina (Moscow: Progress-Akademiia, 1994), 184.

[66] Sokolov, *Finansovaia politika sovetskogo gosudarstva*, 79.

[67] Khodiakov, *Den'gi*, 174–75.

[68] Vaisberg, *Den'gi*, 100–01, 110–11, 113; A. Iu. Davydov, *Nelegal'noe snabzhenie rossiiskogo naseleniia i vlast' 1917–1921 gg.* (St. Petersburg: Nauka, 2002), 285 (quote), 299, 302.

[69] VSNKh, *Trudy I vserossiiskogo s"ezda*, 146.

work in Narkomfin and its subsidiary the State Bank, this was not an isolated viewpoint.[70]

While sober commentators on all sides of the political spectrum bemoaned the "constant revolution in prices," for radicals it presented an opportunity.[71] In the early stage of War Communism, a squabbling group of socialist idealists, both Bolshevik and non-Bolshevik, promoted the abolition of money and the institutions responsible for it.[72] In some ways this was making a virtue of necessity, as money was growing more worthless by the hour.[73] But it was also the natural instinct for most socialists, who assumed that "if you have exchange and the circulation of money you cannot speak of socialism."[74] According to Aleksei Rykov, the chairman of the Supreme Council of the National Economy (VSNKh), only when money is extinct can we "begin to organize a communist society in earnest."[75]

The most persistent advocate for the abolition of money was Left Communist Iurii Larin. A member of the VSNKh presidium, Larin envisioned the full "naturalization" of the economy, in which barter became the basis of all trade. As he reasoned, peasants grow food and workers make things. All they had to do was swap. Monetary transactions would be unnecessary after the government succeeded in nationalizing all firms and farms, whose em-

---

[70] Ozerov, "O regulirovanii denezhnogo obrashchenii," 73–88; Evgenii Efimov, "Schastlivaia gor′kaia zhizn′ Ivana Ozerova," *BOSS*, no. 3 (2008), www.bossmag.ru/view.php?id=3364 (accessed 10 March 2014); Sokolov, *Finansovaia politika sovetskogo gosudarstva*, 50–54; V. I. Lenin, *Neizvestnye dokumenty 1891–1922* (Moscow: ROSSPEN, 1999), 545. This was also the position put forward by the leadership of the Menshevik and Socialist Revolutionary parties during War Communism; see Vladimir N. Brovkin, *The Mensheviks after October: Socialist Opposition and the Rise of the Bolshevik Dictatorship* (Ithaca, NY: Cornell University Press, 1987), 53–54, 77–84, 103–04; and Brovkin, *Behind the Front Lines of the Civil War: Political Parties and Social Movements in Russia, 1918–1922* (Princeton, NJ: Princeton University Press, 1994), 163–64, 175.

[71] VSNKh, *Trudy I vserossiiskogo s″ezda*, 171–72.

[72] For a survey of the major theories, see Robert Tartarin, "Le Blé, le temps, l'énergie: Théories soviétiques de l'abolition de la monnaie 1917–1921" (Ph.D. diss., University of Paris, 1980).

[73] Silvana Malle, *Economic Organization of War Communism, 1918–1921* (Cambridge: Cambridge University Press, 2002), 174–84.

[74] VSNKh, *Trudy I vserossiiskogo s″ezda*, 103.

[75] RSFSR. VSNKh, *Trudy II vserossiiskogo s″ezda sovetov narodnogo khoziaistva (19 dekabria—27 dekabria 1918 g.) (Stenograficheskii otchet)* (Moscow: Koop. izd-vo, 1919), 74. Nikolai Bukharin contributed only minimally to the debate over money, but during War Communism he, too, believed money would soon disappear. See Alec Nove, "Bukharin as an Economist," in *The Ideas of Nikolai Bukharin*, ed. A. Kemp-Welch (Oxford: Clarendon Press, 1992), 31; E. N. Sokolov, *Finansovaia politika sovetskoi vlasti (oktiabr′ 1917–avgust 1918 gg.)* (Riazan′: Riazanskii gosudarstvennyi universitet, 2008), 77–78.

ployees—the nation's entire workforce—would receive payment in kind. Then money, and with it capitalism, would wither away.[76]

Larin and many other Bolsheviks, including Lenin at first, assumed that the nationalized State Bank would facilitate the demise of money by functioning as the sole "accounting apparatus" for all individuals and nationalized enterprises. It would issue checks in limited quantities to control inflation, and would reconcile its books with non-monetary units of account. Exchanges of cash would cease altogether.[77] In line with these notions, in March 1919 the Soviet government put all of its firms on "budgetary financing" and forbade them from purchasing supplies on the free market. The same year it intentionally removed the term "money" from its currency, replacing it with "settlement token" (*raschetnyi znak*) (fig. 29). In that spirit the government shifted responsibility for all currency emissions to a Central Budgetary and Settlements Administration within Narkomfin, in effect shuttering the State Bank.[78] For Larin these were steps toward "liberating people's minds" from the "bygone truths" of bourgeois political economy and the "influence of a dead past."[79]

Most radicals, whether Bolshevik or not, agreed, but disputes emerged over the question of what should replace money as the standard of value in Soviet society. Their proposals followed the ideological fault lines across the Russian socialist movement. In a series of articles the neo-narodnik agrarian economist Aleksandr Chaianov postulated that, unlike capitalism, socialism would not reduce everything to monetary values. Instead of price indicators, he proposed "real-materials calculation" for a new kind of accounting that gauged social utility by balancing losses and gains in natural terms. For instance, socialist bookkeepers would substitute the following for capital expenditures: "Producing 1,000 puds of grain required 262 days of work by people, 162 days of work by horses, 12 units of input by simple machines, 21 units by complex machines, 1.5 canisters of fuel, etc."[80]

---

[76] Iu. Larin, "Udvoenie i naturalizatsiia zarabotnoi platy," *Izvestiia*, 10 September 1918, 3; Larin, "Naturalizatsiia zarabotnoi platy," *Izvestiia*, 14 September 1918, 2; VSNKh, *Trudy II vserossiiskogo s˝ezda*, 106, 139.

[77] L. Obolenskii, "Bezdenezhnye rasschety i ikh rol' v finansovom khoziaistve," *Narodnoe khoziaistvo*, no. 1–2 (1920): 7, 9, 11; VSNKh, *Trudy I vserossiiskogo s˝ezda*, 56–58, 89; VSNKh, *Trudy II vserossiiskogo s˝ezda*, 266–69, 277.

[78] Bokarev, "Denezhnoe obrashchenie na territorii Rossii v gody oktiabr'skoi revoliutsii," 266; Aliamkin and Baranov, *Istoriia denezhnogo obrashcheniia*, 289; RGAE f. 7733, op. 1, d. 166, l. 87.

[79] Iu. Larin, "Zakony denezhnogo obrashcheniia," *Ekonomicheskaia zhizn'*, no. 167 (31 July 1920): 1.

[80] A. V. Chaianov, "Problema khoziaistvennogo ucheta v sotsialisticheskom gosudarstve," *Ekonomicheskaia zhizn'*, no. 225 (9 October 1920): 1; ibid., no. 231 (16 October

Chaianov's rival was Stanislav G. Strumilin, a Menshevik economist who became a spokesman for rapid industrialization after joining the Bolshevik Party in 1923. Strumilin's arguments against Chaianov blazed one of the trails that led to the Soviet planned economy. His premise was that once socialism eradicated the free market, prices could no longer fulfill their function as an indicator of supply and demand. Money, as the expression of those cues, became irrelevant, so an alternative had to be created that would allow the central authority to determine how to distribute resources and goods.[81] In place of monetary valuations he suggested an equivalent based on labor effort, which he named the "trudo-edinitsa" (labor-unit), or "tred." Each tred corresponded to the expenditure of 100,000 kilogrammeters during a single workday of a single worker. 1,000 treds equaled 1 kilotred, and so forth. Kilogrammeters are a measure of work-energy performed by the human body; thus, the tred could be broken down into smaller units derived from caloric intake. The minimum daily need of the average person was 2,000 calories, which Strumilin designated the "dnevnoe dovol'stvie" (daily need) or "dov," 1,000 of which would be the "kilodov," etc. The dov would also be broken down into a smaller unit, the "utilizatsiia" (utilization), or the "ut."

The tred, dov, and ut were encapsulations of physical labor, which according to socialist theory played the predominant role in the production of wealth. And if prices under capitalism were the numerical manifestations of the exploitation of the workforce, under socialism their equivalent—the tred—would reflect the will of the people as embodied by the proletarian state. The government, therefore, would set all treds. Each enterprise would have a special "calculation office" that kept its accounts in units of treds, dovs, and uts and balanced out the amounts involved in its operations. On a monthly basis the central planning agency would publish those data along with materials used in production and work norms. Firms would then rely on the information to adjust inputs and outputs. That was the production side. On the consumer side, stores would mark goods not with prices, but with labels indicating "labor value," and customers would know how much they could afford to spend by checking the number of treds stamped in their "savings book."[82]

Chaianov and Strumilin, along with Larin, insisted that their proposals were pragmatic, but many Communists derided them as "wild and harmful

---

1920): 2; Chaianov, "Substantsiia tsennosti i sistema trudovykh ekvivalentov," *Ekonomicheskaia zhizn'*, no. 247 (4 November 1920): 1.

[81] For proposals made along these lines by other Soviet economists, see Malle, *Economic Organization*, 188–91. For their antecedents in 19th-century European socialism, see Tartarin, "Le Blé," chaps. 1–2.

[82] S. Strumilin, "Trudovoi ekvivalent," *Ekonomicheskaia zhizn'*, no. 167 (31 July 1920): 1–2; Strumilin, "Problema trudovogo ucheta," *Ekonomicheskaia zhizn'*, no. 237 (23 October 1920): 1; ibid., no. 14 (22 January 1921): 1–2.

fantasies."[83] As the debates continued into the early 1920s, the realists' arguments prevailed. Sounding like Friedrich Hayek, the Austrian laissez-faire economist, critics in the Bolshevik ranks doubted it would be humanly possible, without monetary valuation, to assess the constantly shifting worth of materials used in production or the quality of each worker's labor and each factory's output.[84] In any case, as Preobrazhenskii pointed out, the tred would end up circulating like money, and when it did supply and demand would set de facto prices even if in tred denominations.[85]

Lenin lent his weight to the pro-money forces. By spring 1918 he was coming to realize that his original intention to seize the banks and turn them into a centralized switchboard governing all economic activity was easier said than done.[86] In a speech of 1919 he could not have stated his position more clearly: "Can [money] be abolished at one stroke? No." Socialists wrote well before the Revolution that it would be a long time until that was feasible, which "our experience corroborates": in order to eliminate money we would need to be able to feed and supply hundreds of millions of people, but we are as yet technically and organizationally incapable of doing so.[87] Monetary affairs played a part in Lenin's battle for political legitimacy and survival. After introducing the NEP and allowing the return of limited market forces, he equated a strong ruble with the victory of the Bolshevik regime: "If we succeed in stabilizing the ruble for a long period, and then for all time, it will prove that we have won."[88]

The problem was that the currency was not strong. Instead, it was a daily reminder of the bankruptcy of the Soviet economy and a rebuke of Bolshevism.[89] Despite all the breaks with the past that had occurred since 1917, it was clear to everyone in the society that the tsarist ruble was worth more than "Sovznaki" (Soviet tokens; the generic term used for all forms of paper currency issued from 1918 to 1923). For government bureaucrats as much as for people on the streets, the tsarist ruble was still the abstract ideal that everyone had in mind when judging prices and the cost of living: "memories of the old prices" constantly penetrated the "thick fog brought in with the collapsing currency" and led the mind back to 1913.[90] This was a stunning

---

[83] Dobrokhotov, *Denezhnaia reforma*, 53.

[84] VSNKh, *Trudy II vserossiiskogo s"ezda*, 274–76.

[85] E. Preobrazhenskii, "Teoreticheskie osnovy spora o zolotom i tovarnom ruble," *Vestnik sotsialisticheskoi akademii*, no. 3 (February 1923): 76.

[86] V. I. Lenin, *Collected Works*, 4th ed. (Moscow: Progress, 1960–78), 27: 227–28, 384.

[87] Ibid., 29: 358.

[88] Ibid., 33: 422.

[89] Rosenberg, "Problem of Market Relations and the State," 384.

[90] Preobrazhenskii, "Teoreticheskie osnovy," 81–82.

admission of how hard it was to transform mindsets even after wrenching revolutionary upheaval. They had torn down the statues and insignias of the monarchy. They had killed off the royal family. But the old ruble was a symbol that stubbornly refused to die.

That was the case throughout the era of War Communism and into the NEP. City dwellers from Tambov went to the countryside looking to buy foodstuffs from Tatars and found that they only accepted "paper with the mug of the White tsar; without the mug we don't give you anything."[91] Orel railroad workers demanded payment in tsarist currency.[92] And peasants held out hope that the old money would be restored. In 1922, when financial reform was under discussion but inflation was worse than ever, a Communist sympathizer from Saratov province complained about how many of his fellow villagers were still attached to coins with those "cursed little eagles" on them.[93] All the while, the Soviet government struggled to erase the pessimistic popular assessment of its money. In 1918 anonymous critics of the regime circulated Soviet bills they had defaced by rubber-stamping them with slogans like "FAKE MONEY" and "MONEY FOR FOOLS."[94] Four years later, nearly everyone in the country would have agreed.

This was no way to run a dictatorship of the proletariat. Money is a tool and symbol of political power, and its weakness suggested to contemporaries that the Soviet government's hold on the country was still precarious.[95] Referring to the continuing circulation of Japanese money in the Far East, the Provincial Executive Committee in late 1923 explained that "not one government in the world, desiring independence and full authority over its territory, would tolerate within its borders the free movement of foreign currency." This was a matter of "protecting the dignity of the government, and its sovereignty."[96]

Grigorii Sokol'nikov, the Commissar of Finance from 1922–26, justified money in those very terms in a speech titled "Hard Currency, Hard Power." "During wartime," he said, "the fate of the government is decided by its army; in times of peace, the government's fate is decided by its currency." Strong money is "one of the attributes of state power." As Lenin knew, without stabilization of the ruble, Russia would be the weakest country in Europe. A new governing class, Sokol'nikov argued, could not achieve its goals with the

---

[91] A. L. Okninskii, *Dva goda sredi krest′ian* (Riga: Izd-vo Didkovskogo, 1936), 100.

[92] RGAE f. 7733, op. 1, d. 166, ll. 57–58.

[93] RGAE f. 396 (Letters to *Krest′ianskaia gazeta*), op. 2, d. 94, l. 89 (quote); RGAE f. 7733, op. 1, d. 166, ll. 255–58.

[94] Aliamkin and Baranov, *Istoriia denezhnogo obrashcheniia*, 194–95.

[95] V. Belenko, *Denezhnoe obrashchenie v 1914–1922 gg.* (Tashkent: Turkestanskoe gosudarstvennoe izd-vo, 1923), 16.

[96] Pogrebetskii, *Denezhnoe obrashchenie*, 400.

"empty coffers" inherited from the ideologists of War Communism.[97] Although Larin, Chaianov, Strumilin, and like-minded comrades continued to concoct schemes for the abolition of money through the early 1920s, Sokol'nikov's statism, with the support of Lenin, triumphed over their utopian dreams.

All of these preoccupations of the regime and the meanderings of its monetary policies were reflected in the designs of its currency.[98] Before Moscow was able to assert full, centralized control over monetary circulation, local Soviet financial authorities were left to their own devices and issued banknotes displaying nationalist symbols, above all landscapes—among them the "walrus" notes of Arkhangel'sk (1918) (fig. 30); the panorama of an old Central Asian town, presumably Tashkent, foregrounded by abundant native fruits on the bills of Soviet Turkestan (1918); and Mount Ararat on the money of Soviet Armenia (1922–23). These images struck an emotional chord in the hearts of the population at a time of political fragmentation—just as the paper money of the White armies and breakaway regions was intended to do when it featured the Tsar Bell on the notes of the Armed Forces of the South (1919); the statue of Minin and Pozharskii on the 100-ruble note dispensed by the Don Cossack host in Rostov (1919); or regional scenery on the gorgeous 1920 issues of the Far Eastern Republic (fig. 31).[99]

By contrast, the money of the Bolshevik central authority communicated an ideological message—as French revolutionary currency notes once did, and American banknotes still do.[100] In the Soviet case, this did not just bespeak doctrinal fervor but was also a practical consideration: Great Russian symbolism would have risked alienating the national minorities when they were being conquered and courted to form a union headed by Moscow. The only exception was an idyllic view of the Kremlin, the nerve center of Communist power, which appeared on the 10,000-ruble monetary note of 1923. But otherwise no specifically Russian nationalist symbols were to be found. Insisting that the currency convey the principles of the "new [Soviet] state," Narkomfin sought artists to design "proletarian credit" notes with an emblem representing "the factory and the countryside."[101]

---

[97] G. Sokol'nikov, "Tverdaia valiuta, tverdaia vlast'," *Sotsialisticheskoe khoziaistvo*, bk. 5 (1924): 6, 8, 11.

[98] The paragraphs on this subject all draw on Papp, "Road to Chervonets," 56, 73–83.

[99] A. E. Mikhaelis and L. A. Kharlamov, *Bumazhnye den'gi Rossii* (Perm': Permskaia pechatnaia fabrika Goznaka, 1993), 25–26. When Rostov money was adopted for use throughout the "White South," the original Cossack motifs were replaced with Russian ones; V. A. Lazarev and A. G. Baranov, "Istoriia vypuska donskikh denezhnykh znakov," *Numizmaticheskii al'manakh*, no. 1 (2006): 41.

[100] Helleiner, *The Making of National Money*, 101–06.

[101] RGAE f. 7733, op. 1, d. 166, ll. 59–60, 87, 91 (first quote); Khodiakov, *Den'gi*, 44–48 (other quotes).

It took a while before a distinctively Soviet public symbolism emerged. Regional officials still favored the double-headed eagle, and it figured prominently on many currency bills. In 1918, the Chita branch of the People's Bank, on the authority of the Siberian Soviets' Central Executive Committee, issued 50-ruble credit notes featuring a factory worker directing the viewer's gaze to the double-headed eagle breaking free of its chains; on the other side was a rather rococo ornamentation surrounding the hammer and sickle (fig. 32). That same year the central government outlawed the eagle because of its association with the White military governments, on whose money it was the predominant motif.[102]

The hammer and sickle logo was the ultimate visual expression of the Bolshevik pretension to leadership of the urban and rural working classes. It, too, went through numerous iterations on the currency, including versions with a hammer, sickle, and shovel (fig. 33). In ethnic regions it took on local color: cotton sickles in Central Asia, and in Azerbaijan traditionally dressed Azeris who awkwardly hold the implements. There were several variations of the hammer and sickle on the money of the RSFSR, until finally the design was concretized in Ivan I. Dubasov's tweaking of the Soviet crest, which began to decorate the notes of the USSR in 1924.

From then on the currency mirrored subtle shifts in the party line. Dubasov was leader of the artists' collective at Goznak (Gosudarstvennyi Znak, or State Insignia), the agency responsible for the production of government paper. In its studios busts made by the Soviet court sculptor Ivan Shadr (pseudonym of Ivan D. Ivanov) served as models for engravings of the worker, peasant, and Red Army soldier represented on different monetary notes of 1923.[103] The soldier disappeared from Soviet currency thereafter as the NEP emphasized reconstruction over revolutionary warfare. On Sokol'nikov's orders, in the next series of notes the "drawing should depict the worker and peasant together" as an expression of the new era's ideological agenda.[104]

But the bill that saved the day for Bolshevism was short on both ideology and national symbolism while designed to appeal to a population concerned with the loss of its wealth. That was the chervonets.

---

[102] Kolonitskii, *Simvoly vlasti*, 97–99; Pogrebetskii, *Denezhnoe obrashchenie*, illustrations passim.

[103] A. V. Trachuk and N. M. Nikiforova, *Ekspeditsiia zagotovleniia gosudarsvtennykh bumag. 1818–2008* (Moscow: IMA-Press, 2008), 172–81; A. V. Alekhov, "Patriarkh denezhnogo dela," www.bonistikaweb.ru/NUMALMAN/na3-1999dubasov.htm (accessed 10 March 2014); Mikhaelis and Kharlamov, *Bumazhnye den'gi*, 29. Unlike the soldier and peasant, the 1,000-ruble note featuring the worker never entered circulation.

[104] M. M. Gleizer, *Sovetskii chervonets* (St. Petersburg: Real, 1993), 23–24.

The Chervonets and Financial Reform

Once the Bolshevik leadership put paid to the notion of eliminating money, the discussion shifted to bolstering its value en route to reestablishing a hard currency. To do that they first had to resolve the question of which commodity would back the currency.

An inscription on the Soviet "settlement tokens" of 1919–21 asserts that they are "guaranteed by the full property of the state [or republic]." But this was hardly convincing coming from a regime that was in such woeful financial shape.[105] Government officials and monetary experts therefore elaborated plans for a currency covered by tobacco duties or reserves of salt or grain.[106] Bolshevik authorities in Semirech'e oblast' backed their paper money with opium, a valuable native crop which the Soviet Provincial Executive Committee in Vernyi (now Almaty) stockpiled like bullion. Banknotes stated it explicitly and were decorated with opium poppies (fig. 34).[107] These arrangements may have made sense locally, but were not an option for a government seeking to restore confidence in its national currency. The answer was gold.

On that issue Commissar of Finance Sokol'nikov faced tough opposition from leftists who advocated inflationary financing for rapid factory construction. One of them was Strumilin, who tarred the gold standard as a Western conceit in the "old Russian spirit," rather than the "new creative spirit of the Russian revolution."[108] But Lenin once again came down on the side of Sokol'nikov, endorsing the restoration of a hard currency backed by gold, on the grounds that it would transform the economy "from a system [thought up by] Communist fools ... into a base for socialism."[109]

Sokol'nikov supported a gold-based currency largely for the emotional force it would have at home and abroad. A gold ruble that achieved equality with the US dollar on world markets was necessary, he maintained, to stimulate foreign trade—but in his eyes it would also give bragging rights to his much-maligned nation for having mastered the premier tool of global finance.[110] For domestic purposes as well, he knew that Soviet money would only become

---

[105] Papp, "Road to Chervonets," 58, 60.

[106] Sokolov, *Finansovaia politika sovetskogo gosudarstva*, 55–56, 82–83, 127; A. A. Shchelokov, *Bumazhnye den'gi*, 3rd ed. (Moscow: Eksmo, 2009), 83–88, 208.

[107] A. Iu. Kuznetsov, *Opiumnye den'gi* (Moscow: Triada, 2010).

[108] S. Strumilin, "K finansovoi reforme," *Ekonomicheskaia zhizn'*, no. 120 (1 June 1922): 2.

[109] Sokolov, *Finansovaia politika sovetskogo gosudarstva*, 77.

[110] VSNKh, *Trudy I vserossiiskogo s"ezda*, 116–18; Dobrokhotov, *Denezhnaia reforma*, 371–73, 388–89, 397; Samuel A. Oppenheim, "Between Right and Left: G. Ia. Sokolnikov and the Development of the Soviet State, 1921–1929," *Slavic Review* 48, 4 (Winter 1989): 603.

hard currency when the peasants accepted it, and they would only accept it if it had gold backing.[111] On this point, if nothing else, Sokol'nikov agreed with Preobrazhenskii, who observed that the peasantry's wariness of the state's currency was more "psychological than economic" in nature.[112]

Sokol'nikov's solution was to put in place a quasi-gold standard involving a brand new currency called the "chervonets." These were banknotes each worth, on paper anyway, 10 tsarist gold coin rubles or 7.7 grams of pure gold. With reassurance of the public in mind, Narkomfin revived a vintage term used for gold coins dating to medieval Russia: the State Bank declared that "these notes were given the ancient name 'chervonets'" in order "to underline and emphasize" their distinctiveness from the Soviet ruble/Sovznak.[113]

The mass-persuasion function of the banknotes was further evident in their design: the words "Chervonets" and "Gold" were capitalized and printed in traditional Cyrillic lettering, which stood out from the plain cursive of the rest of the text. The size of the notes was larger than any other Russian currency issues, and the quality of the printing, paper, and the complex geometrically woven vignettes had not been seen since before the fall of the old regime. By intention, everything about the chervonets trumpeted the return of the gold standard (fig. 35).

But while Sokol'nikov wanted these to be "symbols of gold value"—in other words to represent gold—he was adamant that they not be exchangeable for it. He favored gold backing, but not free circulation of the precious metal: if that were allowed, then when people lost faith in paper money they would simply trade it in for gold coins to be hoarded as a hedge against inflation—which would once again drive the good money out of circulation and defeat the effort to create a hard currency.[114] As the chervonets notes stipulated on their face, the State Bank guaranteed them to be "exchangeable for gold ... as established by law"—an empty promise as the legislation was never enacted.[115] But even without true convertibility the *appearance* of a gold standard is what mattered.

---

[111] Sokol'nikov, "Tverdaia valiuta," 19.

[112] Narkomfin, *Sotsial'naia revoliutsiia*, 33 (quote); Katzenellenbaum, *Russian Currency*, 132–34.

[113] Cited in Papp, "Road to Chervonets," 67. See Helleiner, *The Making of National Money*, 108–10, for similar propagandistic motives in the naming of the French franc and British gold "sovereign."

[114] Dobrokhotov, *Denezhnaia reforma*, 265, 267.

[115] Vincent Barnett, "As Good as Gold? A Note on the Chervonets," *Europe-Asia Studies* 46, 4 (July 1994): 663–69. Lenin had come up with this idea. In a July 1918 memorandum about new currency notes, he instructed Commissar of Finance Gukovskii to retain "the old text about being exchangeable for gold (the exchange will be suspended by separate decrees)." See Lenin, *Collected Works*, 44: 116.

The government introduced the chervonets in 1922 as it groped its way toward monetary stabilization. For the next two years a parallel currency system existed in which the government used the chervonets to finance industry, while workers and peasants continued to use Sovznaki. The idea was to carve out a restricted sphere in which a hard currency issued in limited amounts (i.e., the chervonets) could operate until the budget deficit came under control and constant paper emissions were no longer necessary to cover it.[116]

Orchestrated by Sokol'nikov, the Bolshevik government engaged in free-market currency trading as part of its monetary strategy. In this as many other aspects of the chervonets and financial reform, we see the influence of "bourgeois specialists," most prominently Nikolai N. Kutler, a nobleman, tsarist minister of agriculture, and Kadet Duma deputy, who during the NEP joined the governing board of Gosbank as chief of its currency-emissions administration; and Leonid N. Iurovskii, an economics professor from a wealthy merchant family who served as deputy to the head of Narkomfin's hard-currency office.[117] It was under their guidance that representatives of the State Bank and Narkomfin worked to strengthen the chervonets vis-à-vis the Sovznak by buying and selling foreign and domestic paper money and precious metals on the Moscow "black bourse," the underground currency exchange that was semilegalized in early 1922, and on the commodity exchanges tellingly known as "amerikanki." On a daily basis, the State Bank released or withdrew chervontsy from the market as needed to maintain parity with gold prices and foreign hard currencies.[118]

These maneuvers may have been standard practice for central banks in the West, but for the secret police and the leftists in the party they smacked of an alliance with despised capitalist speculators. Despite Narkomfin, the police could not refrain from raiding the money markets, arresting dealers and at the same time often netting agents of the state currency administration.[119] Kutler and Iurovskii were also detained during periodic purges of old-regime elements; Sokol'nikov vociferously defended them and chided Soviet officials

---

[116] Dobrokhotov, *Denezhnaia reforma*, 13–15, 173–76.

[117] V. E. Iurovskii, "Arkhitektor denezhnoi reformy 1922–1924 godov," *Voprosy istorii*, no. 2 (1995): 140–42; M. G. Nikolaev, "Na puti k denezhnoi reforme 1922–1924 gg.: Chetyre aresta N. N. Kutlera," *Otechestvennaia istoriia*, no. 1 (2001): 84–85, 87, 89–90, 93–94; I. V. Bystrova, "Gosudarstvo i ekonomika v 1920-e gody: Bor'ba idei i real'nost'," *Otechestvennaia istoriia*, no. 3 (1993): 22–23. For capsule biographies of these and other individuals from the old regime working for the Soviet financial agencies, see Dobrokhotov, *Denezhnaia reforma*, 770–830 passim.

[118] Armand Hammer, *Hammer: Witness to History* (New York: Simon and Schuster, 1987), 157–58; Arnold, *Banks*, 165–66; Katzenellenbaum, *Russian Currency*, 84; Dobrokhotov, *Denezhnaia reforma*, 28; Yuri Goland, "Currency Regulation in the NEP Period," *Europe-Asia Studies*, no. 8 (1994): 1253–54, 1258–59.

[119] Dobrokhotov, *Denezhnaia reforma*, 54–55; Goland, "Currency Regulation," 1254.

for their exaggerated fears of the free market.[120] But that had no effect on Larin and other critics on the left, who denounced Sokol'nikov for being under the sway of "former tsarist ministers."[121]

In 1922 and 1923, the deficit continued to grow and hyperinflation ran wild with Sovznaki being printed in the quadrillions of rubles. Rampant price increases ate away at workers' salaries and created the "scissors" crisis, in which the cost of manufactured goods outstripped the peasants' ability to buy them. A visual epitome of the crisis was the 50-kopeck note of 1923, which was a picture of a coin printed on paper. The peasants were stuck with those and other worthless "milashki" (Sovznaki by the millions) and demanded payment in "cherviachki" (worms), their cynically comical diminutive for the chervonets. But the tight emission rules kept the latter in short supply. Once again the peasantry stopped shipping produce to the cities and threatened to withdraw from the market. The NEP's tentative reintegration of the rural and urban economies was at risk of coming undone. Cooperatives and stores went out of business as trade dried up. Factory workers went on strike over delayed wages.[122] The Soviet secret police sent reports to the leadership on the damaging effects the currency crisis was having on the loyalties of the rural and urban population throughout the country.[123]

Alarm at the revival of popular discontent prompted the monetary reform of February 1924—as Bolshevik leader Lev Kamenev acknowledged, it was an urgent political issue, rather than a technical one.[124] Alongside the chervonets, Narkomfin now issued new gold-backed treasury notes in small denominations of 1, 3, and 5 rubles, essentially small change to the large-denomination chervontsy. Exchangeable at the fixed rate of 10 for every 1 chervonets, the treasury notes marked the return of a unified hard currency. The government would protect the value of its new money by issuing it in "homeopathic doses" keyed to the number of chervontsy in circulation. And, as a Narkomfin official stated, indicating the psychological dimension once again, a key to their success in gaining the confidence of the populace would be the quality of the printing.[125] Likewise with the minting of copper, silver, and small amounts of gold coins, which Sokol'nikov explained as serving

---

[120] Dobrokhotov, *Denezhnaia reforma*, 373–75.

[121] E. H. Carr, *The Bolshevik Revolution, 1917–1923* (London, Macmillan, 1952), 2: 352 n. 1.

[122] Dobrokhotov, *Denezhnaia reforma*, 345; Arnold, *Banks*, 194–195; Sokolov, *Finansovaia politika sovetskogo gosudarstva*, 131–32, 137 (quotes), 138–39; Papp, "Road to Chervonets," 68.

[123] G. N. Sevostianov et al., eds., *"Sovershenno sekretno": Lubianka–Stalinu o polozhenii v strane (1922–1934 gg.)*, 2 vols. (Moscow: Institut rossiiskoi istorii RAN, 2001), passim.

[124] Dobrokhotov, *Denezhnaia reforma*, 562.

[125] Ibid., 439, 442, 740 (quote); RGAE f. 7733, op. 1, d. 5929, l. 97.

"demonstrative purposes."[126] The coins were decorated with the symbols of the revolutionary state and the NEP, but their size and weight were intended to remind their handlers of tsarist coins.[127] As the monopoly position of the chervonets was established, all preexisting currencies were demonetized and for a limited time accepted in exchange for the new notes.[128]

Accompanying its currency reform, the government floated a series of 5-6 percent bond issues in order to raise capital for industrial investment, make peasant savings available for public finance, and strengthen the interconnection between rural and urban realms.[129] Over the course of 1924, the money economy was restored in full. What Sokol'nikov, in a jab at the leftists, called the "denaturalization" of the state economy was completed when monetary taxes replaced taxes in kind. With these initiatives Narkomfin succeeded in balancing the state budget in 1923-24, and produced a surplus the following year.[130]

By any measure the reform was a phenomenal success. Communist revolutionaries brought an end to the Russian monetary crisis without the capital, functioning infrastructure, and American financial aid available to Berlin in its fight against hyperinflation. The government initiated a promotional campaign for the financial reform, but if the hymn to the "Sound of Silver" published in the magazine *Krasnaia niva* was any indication, the state's propaganda expressed the authentic mood of relief and triumph felt across the country. The Soviet press was thrilled that the ruble traded with the dollar on world currency markets.[131] Mossel'prom, the state agro-industrial agency, touted cigarettes named "Chervonets" with a slogan by Vladimir Maiakovskii: they "taste great and are as strong as pure gold currency."[132] Brimming with the pride and joy of a father of a healthy child—and a healthy currency—Sokol'nikov gave his newly-born second son Mikhail the last name "Chervonnyi."[133]

---

[126] Sokolov, *Finansovaia politika sovetskogo gosudarstva*, 108–09, 144–45.

[127] Papp, "Road to Chervonets," 78–82.

[128] RGAE f. 7733, op. 1, d. 5929, l. 97, 135, 140, 147; Gleizer, *Sovetskii chervonets*, 21, 28.

[129] RGAE f. 7733, op. 1, d. 166, l. 143; f. 7733, op. 1, d. 5929, ll. 136, 138; f. 396, op. 2, d. 94, l. 121.

[130] Dobrokhotov, *Denezhnaia reforma*, 377 (quote); Arnold, *Banks*, 207–10; Nove, *Economic History*, 82.

[131] Sokolov, *Finansovaia politika sovetskogo gosudarstva*, 146, 150–52.

[132] Mikhail Anikst, ed., *Soviet Commercial Design of the Twenties* (New York: Abbeville Press, 1987), 34.

[133] Fatekh Vergasov, "Girsh Iankelevich Brilliant—Grigorii Iakovlevich Sokol'nikov," www.pseudology.org/people/Sokolnikov.htm (accessed 10 March 2014).

The peasants, too, responded enthusiastically to the stabilization of the currency. A letter to the editor of *Krest'ianskaia gazeta* testified that the countryside was glad the new money replaced "all those worthless 'millions' and 'billions'" because it reminded his village of "the good old times."[134] Another wrote that the "peasant is now content—he is his own master and happy to be able to sell his surplus and receive money for it"—an opinion that was widespread according to secret-police intelligence gathered during the year.[135]

However, what was comforting for the peasant was bitter medicine for many Bolsheviks, who had not made a revolution to satisfy rural capitalists. The three-ruble treasury bill of 1924 depicted a reclining peasant holding a scythe and whetstone while resting his head on the shoulder of a reclining worker who reads to him (fig. 36). In popular parlance the bill was ridiculed as the "two lazybones."[136] Party leftists did not comment on the note's artwork, but they disliked its deeper meaning: opposed to the worker-peasant alliance that was the keystone of the NEP, they believed the peasantry would always hold the urban proletariat hostage by threatening to withhold grain from the market. Security agents monitoring the countryside stoked fears of a widening conspiracy funded by rich peasants with stocks of money that was now worth something.[137] What opponents of hard currency once predicted seemed to be coming to pass: the drive to stabilize prices had turned the government into a "good mama for the little kulaks."[138]

Resentment toward Sokol'nikov for his anti-inflationary policies was especially strong among advocates of central planning based in VSNKh and Gosplan, who were itching to industrialize. They blasted the fiscal conservatism of the Commissariat of Finance and the State Bank, which they claimed was restraining the growth of heavy industry on which all hopes for a communist future rested. At the 11th Party Congress in 1922 they hammered Sokol'nikov for turning the Dictatorship of the Proletariat into the "Dictatorship of Narkomfin," with its "anti-emissions ardor" and financial "hocus-pocus." His witheringly sarcastic reply: "Printing money is the opium of the people." Lenin consistently backed him, as did Trotskii, who diagnosed

---

[134] RGAE f. 396, op. 2, d. 94, ll. 92.

[135] Ibid., ll. 4–6 (quote); see also G. F. Dobronozhenka, ed., *VChK–OGPU o politicheskikh nastroeniiakh severnogo krest'ianstva 1921–1927 gody* (Syktyvkar: Syktyvkarskii gosudarstvennyi universitet, 1995), 71, 73; and Sokolov, *Finansovaia politika sovetskogo gosudarstva*, 146–47.

[136] Rostislav Nikolaev, "Real'nyi rabochii na kaznacheiskom bilete?" www.bonistikaweb.ru/petkoll/2002-4.htm (accessed 10 March 2014).

[137] Sevostianov et al., *"Sovershenno sekretno,"* 2: 299–305.

[138] Narkomfin, *Sotsial'naia revoliutsiia*, 10–11.

inflation as the "syphilis of the planned economy."[139] But Lenin was not long for this world, and Trotskii was soon to be isolated politically.

The demise of the financial reform and its chief architect came on the heels of their success. Despite Joseph Stalin's ostensible support for the NEP, the new ruler and his inner circle endorsed reliance on the printing press to speed-finance industry. Under pressure from his enemies, Sokol'nikov, who had openly opposed Stalin in the succession struggle, was forced out of office in January 1926. The balance of power shifted away from Narkomfin and toward the "productionists" of VSNKh and Gosplan. That year they reopened the currency-emissions tap, after which inflation began to reemerge. With the abandonment of fiscal orthodoxy, the Soviet Union could stop appeasing the peasantry and move toward the command economy.[140]

The chervonets was not, as the leftists alleged, a ransom paid to speculators and peasant traders. They could not comprehend that Sokol'nikov's financial reform, by bringing an end to a decade-long era of economic turmoil, firmly established the sovereignty of the Soviet Union and the authority of Moscow over the whole of its territory. It was not the introduction of the NEP that pulled the rug out from under popular discontent with Bolshevism. It was the stabilization of the ruble. That is what Sokol'nikov meant when he wrote the Politburo that "the restoration of our hard currency is … no less significant … than the victory of the Red Army."[141]

What I think Sokol'nikov's opponents did understand was that he represented a real alternative to their own vision of the future. He was open to the world market, prioritized fiscal responsibility over the planning fetish, favored consumers and peasants over heavy industry, and tolerated non-Bolsheviks in the ranks of officialdom. Sokol'nikov did not challenge the primacy of the Communist Party, but he believed that the monetary equivalent of the laws of gravity imposed limits on the state's ability to act.

Sokol'nikov's alternative to the command economy could be summed up in a phrase used by Lev S. El'iasson, a prerevolutionary economist and law professor who after 1917 worked for the State Bank and Narkomfin: the goal of the financial reform was to bring about a "normal economic life."[142] But nothing could have been more offensive for Bolshevik revolutionaries than those words. Aleksandr Rodchenko parodied precisely such mundane sen-

---

[139] Sokolov, *Finansovaia politika sovetskogo gosudarstva*, 85–86, 112–16, 157 n. 35.

[140] Andrea Graziosi, "Building the First System of State Industry in History," *Cahiers du monde russe et soviétique* 32, 4 (October–December 1991): 545–47, 549, 556–57, 559–61; Goland, "Currency Regulation," 1260–93 passim; Vladimir Mau, *Reformy i dogmy: 1914–1929. Ocherki istorii stanovleniia khoziaistvennoi sistemy sovetskogo totalitarizma* (Moscow: Delo, 1993), 137–52; Sokolov, *Finansovaia politika sovetskogo gosudarstva*, 357–58; Arnold, *Banks*, 254–57.

[141] Dobrokhotov, *Denezhnaia reforma*, 337.

[142] Ibid., 173–74.

timents in his design for a textile pattern on which he sequenced cartoons of the new 10-kopeck coins alongside those of snow boots, people farting, and bottles of beer.[143] A normal economic life governed by the normal rules of markets and money was tantamount to the victory of capitalism over the socialist state. And that was anathema to party radicals, including Stalinists, who yearned for the destruction of the old society and the creation of a new one.[144]

---

[143] Christina Kiaer, *Imagine No Possessions: The Socialist Objects of Russian Constructivism* (Cambridge, MA: MIT Press, 2005), 232 and plate 21.

[144] Bystrova, "Gosudarstvo i ekonomika," 27–28; Rosenberg, "Problem of Market Relations and the State," 394–96.

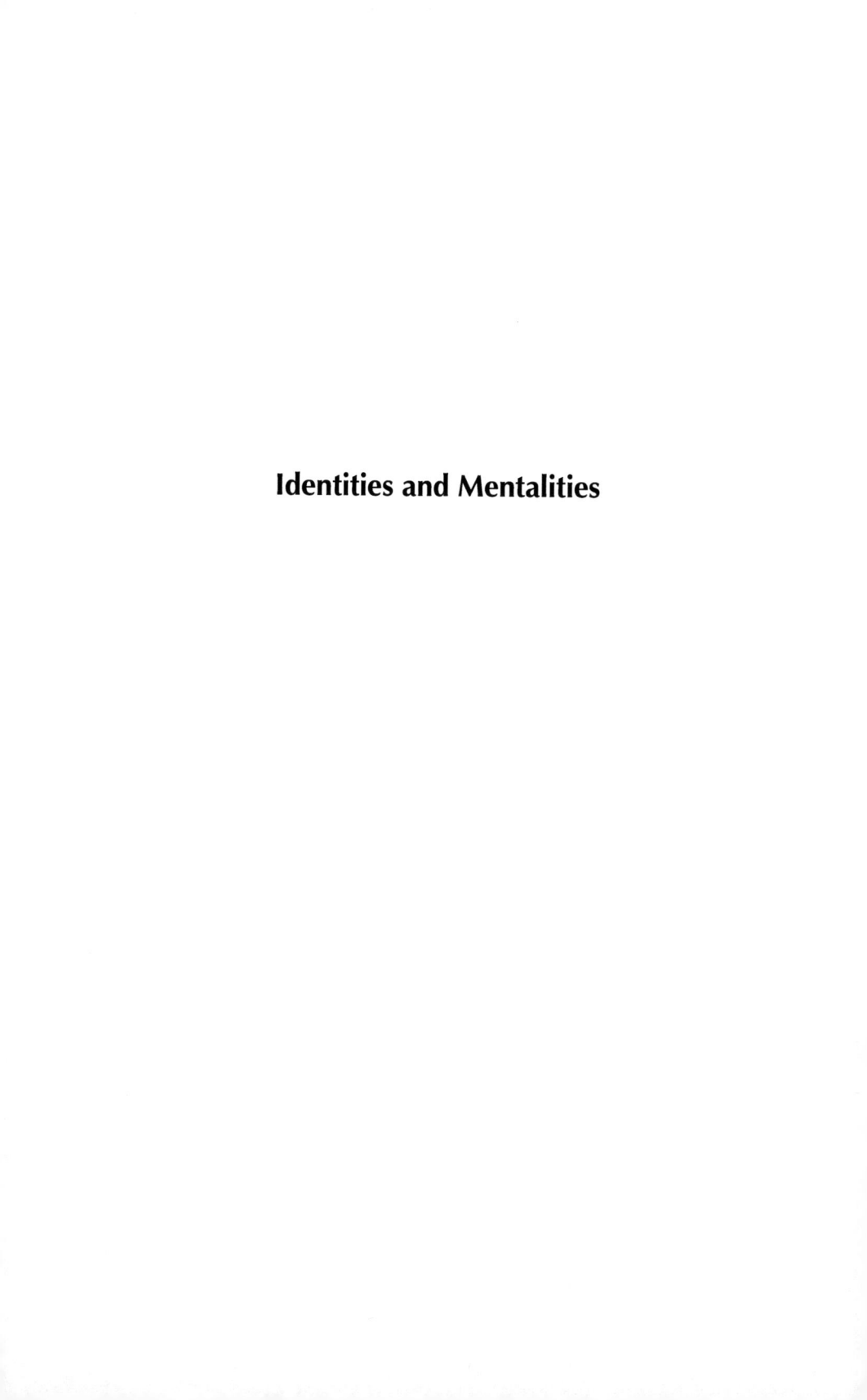

Identities and Mentalities

Love and Death:
Transforming Sexualities in Russia, 1914–22

Dan Healey

Historians have long viewed the Great War as an event that transformed sexualities, whether we understand "sexualities" to mean sexual experience and identities, or the discursive constructions that resulted when authorities attempted to regulate sex. The war brought mass mobilization, new occupational and economic opportunities, increasing women's activity in public arenas, and sharp challenges to private morality and practice. It also of course brought violence, death, and disease to millions on the European continent, heralding demographic collapse with its alarming consequences for national vigor during and after the conflict. While at first glance sexuality appears to be an issue of secondary importance when considering the Great War, the problems of population health and regeneration ("biopower"), and of national morale, relied in some degree on a "rational" sexual order and were far from trivial. Sexuality and its challenges directly undermined or underpinned national vigor.[1]

Russia's experience in 1914–22 distinguishes it from the Western European nations that are the typical focus of historians writing about the impact of the Great War on sexuality. Revolution, civil war, and famine in the Russian Empire radicalized and temporally extended the experience of violent conflict that more quickly subsided elsewhere in Europe. Russia's two wars—the "imperial" war of 1914–17 and the Civil War of 1918–21—and two revolutions—the February and October 1917 political ruptures—constituted a uniquely devastating "continuum of crisis," and the impact on sexuality and its regulation would be commensurate.[2] A much-heralded "sexual revolution" was said to accompany the Bolshevik takeover of 1917, and traditionally

---

[1] The literature on the history of sexuality in 20th-century Europe is very large, with the earliest attempt at an analysis of the impact of the Great War being Magnus Hirschfeld's *Sittengeschichte des Weltkrieges* (Leipzig: Schneider & Co., 1930). For recent discussions, see, e.g., Dagmar Herzog, *Sexuality in Europe: A Twentieth-Century History* (Cambridge: Cambridge University Press, 2011).

[2] Peter Holquist, *Making War, Forging Revolution: Russia's Continuum of Crisis, 1914–1921* (Cambridge, MA: Harvard University Press, 2002).

Russian Culture in War and Revolution, 1914–22, Book 2: Political Culture, Identities, Mentalities, and Memory. Murray Frame, Boris Kolonitskii, Steven G. Marks, and Melissa K. Stockdale, eds. Bloomington, IN: Slavica Publishers, 2014, 151–78.

historians of Russia have emphasized the ideologized socialist revolution in sexual relations as a major breakpoint with the past. Yet in many ways the continuum of imperial war and then the Civil War were a "formative experience" that tempered the socialist "sexual revolution," dictating solutions that did not always sit comfortably with Marxist thinking.[3] By tracing a history of Russian sexuality between 1914 and 1922 I argue that sexual change began well before the Bolsheviks took the Winter Palace; and I will contend that after that event, continuity merits our attention as much as the changes it brought. What happened in the Russian Empire and Soviet Russia in the sexual sphere during these years largely reflected legacies bequeathed by a restless and divided prewar society. I also argue for the transnational influence on Russian trends and events. Prewar legacies in this realm were greatly influenced by European strains of thinking about, and acting upon, sexuality, present before 1914, and they exerted even stronger influence thereafter.

To begin, part 1 examines what I will call "cultures of sexuality" during the period, focusing on the evolution of popular ideas about sex and gender relations, and attempting to trace the transformations people experienced in their intimate lives. Memoirs, diaries, the popular press, "ethnographic" and medical material, and popular literature furnish important sources for an excavation of wartime/revolutionary sexual cultures, and I rely on some excellent recent scholarship as well. Material for the study of sexuality in this context is hazardously diffuse, and some generalizations made here are based on frankly modest source bases and indirect readings. Few sources set out to address sex directly, and the constraints on explicit discussion of sex, even in private ego documents, require "against the grain" readings for allusions to sexuality.[4] Part 1 also explores gender crossings and confusions throughout the "continuum of crisis" to suggest how the rupture with traditional patterns of masculinity and femininity, associated with war or unleashed by revolution, had an impact on sexualities in culture and individual identity. Part 2 discusses attempts by authorities to regulate sexuality during the years of war and revolution, through legislation, propaganda, and internal debates about sex-related matters. Apparent is the increasing significance of medicine, with its transnational influence, as a biopolitical guide for those who would rule Russia. The Bolshevik medicalization of sexuality was radically materialist, attempting to deprive sex of sacred or transcendent value. Yet the Soviet bid to revolutionize sex confronted important limits from an uncomprehending population and religious opposition. Moreover, considerations of demography,

---

[3] Here I extend the argument made in Sheila Fitzpatrick, "The Civil War as a Formative Experience," in *Bolshevik Culture: Experiment and Order in the Russian Revolution*, ed. Abbott Gleason, Peter Kenez, and Richard Stites (Bloomington: Indiana University Press, 1985).

[4] On reading "against the grain" for histories of sexualities, see Ann Laura Stoler, *Race and the Education of Desire: Foucault's History of Sexuality and the Colonial Order of Things* (Durham, NC: Duke University Press, 1995).

hygiene, and military strength appeared to be at least as salient as ideological factors in determining some aspects of the "sexual revolution" proclaimed by the Bolsheviks.

Part I. Cultures of Sexuality

The work of Laura Engelstein and many other scholars has demonstrated that imperial Russian culture before 1914 was marked by sophisticated debates about sexuality that grew increasingly explicit, bringing sex into the public imagination in unprecedented ways.[5] Novels and films imagining women's sexual freedom, or spiritual and even political redemption through predatory and violent sexuality, utopias of sexual abstinence or gender fluidity, and dreams of homogenic comradeship and same-sex love were all fresh in the popular mind in August 1914.[6] These dreams were distinctively Russian in their origins, expression, and politicization; and at the same time they adapted and responded to transnational currents in literature and cinema, in women's emancipation, in the international campaigns against regulated prostitution, in pleas for homophile emancipation, the rise of Freudian challenges to psychiatric medicine, and much else.[7] The coming of war in 1914 had the potential to bring many of these blueprints for the erotic into the realm of experiment and experience.

---

[5] Laura Engelstein, *The Keys to Happiness: Sex and the Search for Modernity in Fin-de-Siècle Russia* (Ithaca, NY: Cornell University Press, 1992); see also, e.g., Olga Matich, *Erotic Utopia: The Decadent Imagination in Russia's Fin-de-Siècle* (Madison: University of Wisconsin Press, 2005); Dan Healey, *Homosexual Desire in Revolutionary Russia: The Regulation of Sexual and Gender Dissent* (Chicago: University of Chicago Press, 2001); and M. Levitt and A. Toporkov, eds., *Eros i pornografiia v russkoi kul´ture/Eros and Pornography in Russian Culture* (Moscow: Ladomir, 1999).

[6] Engelstein, *The Keys to Happiness*, 359–420; Eric Naiman, *Sex in Public: The Incarnation of Early Soviet Ideology* (Princeton, NJ: Princeton University Press, 1997), 48–52; John E. Malmstad, "Bathhouses, Hustlers, and a Sex Club: The Reception of Mikhail Kuzmin's Wings," *Journal of the History of Sexuality* 9, 1–2 (2000): 85–104; and John E. Malmstad and Nikolay Bogomolov, *Mikhail Kuzmin: A Life in Art* (Cambridge, MA: Harvard University Press, 1999). On cinema, see, e.g., Rachel Morley, "Gender Relations in the Films of Evgenii Bauer," *Slavonic & East European Review* 81, 1 (2003): 32–69.

[7] Engelstein, Naiman, Matich, and Malmstad cited above discuss transnational influences on literature and culture; for transnational influences on Russian discussions of prostitution, homosexuality, and psychoanalysis, see Laurie Bernstein, *Sonia's Daughters: Prostitutes and Their Regulation in Imperial Russia* (Berkeley: University of California Press, 1995); Linda Harriet Edmondson, *Feminism in Russia, 1900–17* (Stanford, CA: Stanford University Press, 1984); Healey, *Homosexual Desire*, 100–25; and Aleksandr Etkind, *Eros nevozmozhnogo: Istoriia psikhoanaliza v Rossii* (St. Petersburg: Meduza, 1993).

1914–1916: Sinister Foreplay

While many dreams of eros and violence were to be unleashed in August 1914, it is striking how, for that part of Russia's educated elite not exposed to war at the front, the conflict began and continued for some time with little apparent disruption of gender and sexual conventions. Diaries and memoirs predictably exude patriotic confidence and a sense of duty that conventionally meant sublimation of sexuality. The reactionary philosopher of sexuality Vasilii Rozanov, whose prewar reflections on the subject projected a distinctly Russian antirational understanding of eros in modern life, observed war's preparations with effusive admiration for the male warrior. Recalling a conversation in late July 1914, with a young artillery officer, Rozanov was charmed by his persuasive and calm bearing. Russia's lack of war-making equipment would be made up for by the enthusiasm of its army, and this officer was prepared to make the supreme sacrifice. "No complaint, no criticism, no hysterics. 'Yes, you're made of iron,' I thought about this youth."[8] Rozanov noted with satisfaction that Russian men were not the "'characterless' and 'feminine' … muzhiks" that "his highness, the Prussian Junker" had hastily imagined.[9] In an extraordinary diary entry from July 1916, Rozanov sang the praises of Russian virility as he meditated on the half-erect and generously proportioned penis of a bathhouse attendant who scrubbed him, an "Ivan" who was only 17, "but very masculine," strikingly fit, and due to be sent off to war within weeks. The philosopher mused at length that such an organ would keep "seven maidens" contented; and it saddened him that the attendant, whose brother was already at the front, might be killed in battle.[10]

Aristocratic diarist Catherine Sayn-Wittgenstein, just 19 when the war broke out, volunteered as a nurse with her sister in one of the capital's reception infirmaries for wounded soldiers. Sayn-Wittgenstein expressed her delight at their "colossal popularity" as the youngest sisters in the facility, and at the effusions of "love" that the soldiers directed her way.[11] Sayn-Wittgenstein's scrupulously conventional understanding of her sexuality, as directed exclusively toward motherhood within marriage, demonstrates her sense of propriety and duty, in line with the gendered expectations of her class; she did not muse explicitly about physical love, but only alluded to it when

---

[8] V. V. Rozanov, *Voina 1914 i russkoe vozrozhdenie* (Petrograd: Novoe vremia, 1915), 18–24, quoted at 22.

[9] Rozanov, *Voina 1914*, 31.

[10] V. V. Rozanov, *Poslednie list´ia. Poslednie list´ia 1916 god. Poslednie list´ia 1917 god. Voina 1914 goda i russkoe vozrozhdenie* (Moscow: Respublika, 2000), 177–79 (entry for 17 July 1916). I am grateful to Evgeny Bershtein for bringing this document to my attention.

[11] Catherine Sayn-Wittgenstein, *La fin de ma Russie: Journal 1914–1919* (Paris: Phebus libretto, 2007), 58 (entries for 17 and 28 November 1914).

considering if she would ever be ready to become a wife and mother.[12] Sayn-Wittgenstein's chaste experience of nursing was at odds with a rapidly developing anxiety about the behavior of the "sisters of mercy" (military nurses): one general wrote in 1915 to protest at their appearance in uniform in public, enjoying restaurant meals en masse, and even escorting soldiers to private apartments. It had been hoped that by recruiting upper-class women to army nursing, standards of propriety would be maintained.[13] Perceptions of the "sisters" worsened during the war; by 1916 the military censor noted how soldiers' letters expressed demoralized hostility toward nurses whose primary concern seemed to be chasing officers, not doing their professional duty.[14] Worse still were widely circulating accusations that "sisters of depravity" spread sexually transmitted diseases.[15] However much nurses' reputation deteriorated as the war continued, for prudent Sayn-Wittgenstein at this early stage of the imperial war nursing offered a respectable and evidently exciting means of interacting with men.

Another privileged upper-class Petrograd youth coming of age during these first years of conflict was Vladimir Nabokov, later the Russian emigration's most renowned novelist. His too was an apparently conventional sexual awakening for a young man of his class in 1914–16, although of course his memoirs are highly aestheticized. The 16-year-old wrote poetry about his first love, "Tamara," a girl he wooed and, we are told, won, during the summer of 1915 at the Nabokov dacha and later the following winter through the streets, museums, and cinemas of Petrograd. They "haunted museums," favoring deserted galleries in the Hermitage, its broom cupboards, and, when a "hoary, blear-eyed, felt-soled attendant would grow suspicious" they abandoned the city's great collections, seeking out ever-humbler museums for fumbling exploration.[16] The war seemed to intrude little on Nabokov's sexual debut, except perhaps to weaken adult supervision of the adolescent and facilitate a degree of freedom with the opposite sex.

The war soon did intrude, however, as the declining reputation of nurses, already mentioned, suggests; fears of ever bolder female sexuality and male

---

[12] Sayn-Wittgenstein, *La fin*, 95, 101.

[13] Joshua A. Sanborn, *Drafting the Russian Nation: Military Conscription, Total War, and Mass Politics, 1905–1925* (DeKalb: Northern Illinois University Press, 2003), 147–48; on training and recruitment of these nurses, see P. P. Shcherbinin, *Voennyi faktor v povsednevnoi zhizni russkoi zhenshchiny v XVIII–nachale XX v.: Monografiia* (Tambov: Iulis, 2004), 388–99.

[14] A. B. Astashov, "Seksual'nyi opyt russkogo soldata na Pervoi mirovoi i ego posledstviia dlia voiny i mira," *Voenno-istoricheskaia antropologiia: Ezhegodnik* (2005–06): 374–75.

[15] Shcherbinin, *Voennyi faktor v povsednevnoi zhizni russkoi zhenshchiny*, 404–05; Astashov, "Seksual'nyi opyt russkogo soldata," 373–75.

[16] Vladimir Nabokov, *Speak, Memory: An Autobiography Revisited* (London: Weidenfeld and Nicolson, 1967), 235.

promiscuity now colored perceptions. By the summer of 1916 in his aphoristic diary Rozanov commented insistently on the flagrant behavior of "prostitutes" on Petrograd's Nevskii Prospekt. "There is no doubt that some modest % go in for prostitution and are intoxicated with it … passing along Nevskii, virtually in a massive gang, throwing their heads up, striding confidently … with a 'Take us! Take us!'—for 5 or a maximum of 10 rubles (the war, prices are rising).…"[17] He saw something monstrous but admirable in these women's bold sexuality, at least, in his characteristic conceptualization, when contrasted with the "dry spirit" of the "fortress" of Christian marriage.[18] The growing commercialization of all heterosexual relations, and in particular woman's ability to extract a price in return for sexual favors, was a recurring theme in the bourgeois satirical journal *Novyi Satirikon*. An early 1916 cartoon (by an artist, Boris D. Grigor'ev, known for his erotic sketches) entitled "Her Profits" (see fig. 37 in the gallery of illustrations following page 178) showed a conversation between a well-heeled courtesan and a society gentleman:

"Have you heard, Margot, that income tax is going to be introduced?"
"Really, would I have to pay?"
"Well, what of it?"
"My God, I'd die of shame."[19]

Other cartoons of that year tied women's flagrant prostitution to black-marketing in scarce foodstuffs, and mocked bourgeois women as cunning deceivers and manipulators of foolish husbands.[20] The latter was a perennial theme of the war of the sexes, but in wartime the demasculinization of non-serving men, and the coarsening of the sexually knowing female, were typical pan-European tropes of life in the rear.[21] A woman lounging on a sofa asks her male partner to tell her a "spicy story" in a 1916 cartoon entitled "Surrogate"

---

[17] Rozanov, *Poslednie list′ia*, 181–85, quoted at 181 (entry for 22 July 1916).

[18] Ibid., 184.

[19] B. Grigor'ev, "Eia dokhody," *Novyi Satirikon*, no. 11 (1916): 4. Grigor'ev produced an erotic sketch-cycle, "Intimité," at this time, and he published it in Petrograd in 1918. On the artist and this series of sketches of café singers and prostitutes, see http://www.mishanita.ru/2011/07/16/11120/#eros (accessed 3 November 2012).

[20] For examples, see drawings by cartoonist Re-Mi, *Devushka 1916 goda*," *Novyi Satirikon*, no. 38 (1916): 12 (prostitution and black market); *Uzhasnyi sluchai*, *Novyi Satirikon*, no. 6 (1916): 9 (loose morals in a lawyer's office); *Vesennie bolezni*, *Novyi Satirikon*, no. 22 (1916): 10.

[21] Karen Petrone, *The Great War in Russian Memory* (Bloomington: Indiana University Press, 2011), 106–08.

(fig. 38). The price of rouge is so high that she cannot afford it; only dirty tales will bring color to her cheeks.[22]

Naturally, gender and social position determined how far one experienced these subtle shifts in elite propriety. In early 1916, Sayn-Wittgenstein noted with disgust how shameless female fans threw themselves at the opera singer Sobinov at Petrograd performances, and later that summer expressed contempt for "the flirting that prospers" at the socially mixed spa of Staraia Russa she visited with her family. It was with some relief that she recorded in August 1916 how, while traveling first class by train south to Kiev, and thence to the family estate near Mogilev in Podol'ia, close to the Austrian front, that the carriage was filled with officers returning to active duty, who acted "very correctly" in the presence of Catherine and her sisters.[23] Yet this privileged virgin's sense of security would soon be shattered by the unraveling of this public restraint in 1917. In the wartime rear, the "business-as-usual" operation of theaters, resorts, and railway travel is striking in itself as furnishing venues where sexuality seemed imminent, if contained.[24] The press, and later memoirists, carped bitterly about high living and pleasure seeking in the rear. By late 1916 and early 1917, the incongruity of elite indulgence during a time of national collapse was readily apparent to British spy R. H. Bruce Lockhart, who in his memoirs regretted his callow love of champagne and gypsy parties during these months in Petrograd and Moscow.[25]

Peasants and workers appear to have experienced sexuality in the early war as a similar mix of the familiar and the novel, although gaining access to their opinions and experiences is challenging. The detailed research of Aleksandr Astashov in military archives, particularly those of the postal censor, has yielded a compelling portrait of the sexual preoccupations of the Russian soldier in the imperial war.[26] Another important, but for the historian problematic, fund of sources comes from the wartime nurse Sof'ia

---

[22] A. Radakov, "Surrogat," *Novyi Satirikon*, no. 45 (1916): 8. For a similar cartoon on women's morals, see Miss, "Zhutkoe predpolozhenie," *Novyi Satirikon*, no. 50 (1916): 5. Rozanov wrote ambivalent commentaries on letters he received from sexually active bourgeois women requesting advice: *Poslednie list'ia*, 79–80 (22 March 1916).

[23] Sayn-Wittgenstein, *La fin*, 96–97, 99–100, 105.

[24] After some hesitation following the outbreak of war, theaters in St. Petersburg resumed productions of their prewar repertoire and enjoyed full houses. See Murray Frame, "Cultural Mobilization: Russian Theatre and the First World War, 1914–1917," *Slavonic & East European Review* 90, 2 (2012): 288–322.

[25] R. H. Bruce Lockhart, *Memoirs of a British Agent* (London: Putnam, 1932), 160–61, 165. On the press, see Richard Stites, "Days and Nights in Wartime Russia: Cultural Life, 1914–1917," in *European Culture in the Great War: The Arts, Entertainment, and Propaganda, 1914–1918*, ed. Aviel Roshwald and Stites (Cambridge: Cambridge University Press, 1999), 24; on memoirists' recollections, see Petrone, *The Great War*, 106–08.

[26] Astashov, "Seksual'nyi opyt russkogo soldata."

Fedorchenko's collection of the aphorisms she heard from soldiers as patients before and after 1917.[27] Fedorchenko's heavy-handed stylization, and Soviet censorship of her texts, suggests that we should read her material as memoir or documentary fiction rather than faithful ethnographic transcripts. Nevertheless, even Astashov, a careful historian, uses Fedorchenko to illustrate points confirmed in other sources, and here I follow a similar approach.[28]

Mobilization brought a raft of new experiences for many soldiers. Most were peasants from the village, and if 70 percent were young married men in 1914, attrition meant that only 30 percent were married by 1917; the unmarried recruits perhaps had little or no sexual experience. Astashov argues, citing folklore studies and contemporary observers, that their outlook was colored by a high degree of misogyny, the burden of patriarchal village culture. Young men resented patriarchal control over permission to marry and the choice of spouse, and they supposedly projected that resentment onto women in general.[29] Mobilization presented an opportunity to escape the tyranny of patriarchs, while simultaneously the loss of family surroundings compelled these men to consider their "family position" and its significance for their futures.[30] Fedorchenko's material encapsulated these dilemmas in pithy aphorisms and snatches of apparently recollected conversation. Young men might speak about women and sex in ways that were intensified by barracks living. One soldier commented how conversations before sleep with comrades seemed novel: "Nothing interrupts us; you start with God and you finish by talking about women… And there's nobody to talk to at home. You work like a dog, lie down, and expire. You'd never talk with the wife like that."[31] Although cross-class camaraderie seems to have been rare, men of the same ranks likely experienced homosocial companionship that captivated their emotions, compelling comparisons between the isolation of village family life

---

[27] S. Fedorchenko, *Narod na voine* (Moscow: Sovetskii pisatel', 1990), unfortunately reproduces censorship of some of the most sexually explicit material she gathered. On her book and its fate under Stalinism, see Petrone, *The Great War*, 235–38, 257–58. My thanks to Karen Petrone, and an anonymous reader, for advice on using Fedorchenko's material.

[28] For criticism of unreflective use of Fedorchenko, see E. S. Seniavskaia, "O. S. Porshneva. Mentalitet i sotsial'noe povedenie rabochikh, krest'ian i soldat v period Pervoi mirovoi voiny (1914–mart 1918 g.). Ekaterinburg: Uro Ran, 2000. 415 S. Tir. 500," *Otechestvennaia istoriia*, no. 1 (2001): 192–94.

[29] Astashov, "Seksual'nyi opyt russkogo soldata," 368. On peasant masculinity, the tyranny of the patriarch, and misogyny, see also Christine D. Worobec, "Masculinity in Late-Imperial Russian Peasant Society," in *Russian Masculinity in History and Culture*, ed. Barbara Evans Clements, Rebecca Friedman and Dan Healey (Houndmills, UK: Palgrave, 2002).

[30] Astashov, "Seksual'nyi opyt russkogo soldata," 369.

[31] Fedorchenko, *Narod na voine*, 55.

against the intimate bonds of frontline comradeship.[32] "In war I started to live as though war was my home, and soldiers became my comrades—together to the death. At home I was all alone even though my family surrounded me."[33] The love of comrades changed minds and fates, as another soldier reportedly said of a friend killed in battle: "I loved him like my own heart, only more [...] For about two years it's been painful for me to smile, and I've practically forgotten how to laugh anymore."[34] These emotions perhaps align with Astashov's view, based on analysis of popular song and verse, that in this war there would be no cult of the wife as friend waiting for the soldier to return, but instead a nagging anxiety for peasant soldiers that back in the village wives were betraying their husbands at the front.[35]

Astashov's research shows how disorderly and dangerous casual sexual activity reportedly characterized Russia's frontline districts from the outset of the war. Military authorities and local governors in provinces near the front such as Chernigov and Podol'sk complained about promiscuous relations between soldiers and local women and girls, whether they were service personnel, local inhabitants, or refugees.[36] Many impoverished and desperate women and girls turned to casual prostitution—or at the very least, the authorities saw them as potentially swelling the ranks of sex-workers. Such women allegedly offered their sexual services to soldiers and officers in heavily militarized districts behind the front, evidence of a supposed "collapse of morals" accompanying war.[37] Censors intercepted "love" letters from soldiers and officers to women of easy virtue near the frontlines, and noted how the theme of the sexually available army nurse frequently occurred in soldiers' correspondence.[38] Authorities were convinced that sexually transmitted disease was fast rising to epidemic proportions in these districts, more evidence of disorderly sexual activity. Military-medical experts reported alarming rates of infection for syphilis and gonorrhea in 1915–16, and in the summer of 1916 a group of 71 Duma deputies called for a debate on the STD epidemic.[39] Patriotic notes colored these discourses. Austro-Hungarian prostitutes were said to be de-

---

[32] On rare recollections of camaraderie between officers and men, see Petrone, *The Great War*, 87–89, 109–11.

[33] Fedorchenko, *Narod na voine*, 55.

[34] Ibid., 54.

[35] Astashov, "Seksual'nyi opyt russkogo soldata," 374, 376–77.

[36] Ibid., 369–70.

[37] Ibid., 370.

[38] Ibid., 372, 375.

[39] Ibid., 373–74.

liberately infecting Russian soldiers.[40] Russian medics meanwhile alleged that a good proportion of the peasant-army's syphilis was acquired non-sexually in the village—the "innocent" peasant had brought it with him when mobilized.[41] Still others remembered how cowardly men sought out diseased prostitutes to gain an infection that would result in their removal from active service.[42] Through such indirect evidence the inference that mobilization and war detached sexual behavior from traditional village constraints in the most militarized parts of the Russian Empire between 1914 and 1917 is inescapable.

Military men shared sexual violence, and even in the censored version of Fedorchenko's work, tales of these encounters remain unusual records of wartime rape and abuse.

> A fel'dsher examined her. How did you get this "dose"? My husband came home and gave me such a "reward." You're lying, a husband would never do this to his lawful wife. She started crying. You're right, an officer summoned me one night to come and collect his laundry. I went and three of them abused me all night, then they let me go and gave me three rubles. Since that time I've been sick… That was in ****, the officers there are too well off.[43]

Cossacks perpetrated, and were later often held to have been at the center of, the worst sexual violence inflicted on civilians. Postwar diaries recorded vicious rapes of young Polish, Jewish, and Russian women by groups of Cossacks, and Karen Petrone notes that while these texts constructed a Soviet demonization of the Cossack, they also had a considerable basis in fact.[44] Civilian women and girls lived in a heightened state of fear of violation when armed forces moved through their villages and towns, even before the Civil War unleashed soldiers' basest instincts.[45] The ideology of sexual violence was embedded in tsarist and later Soviet army speech, orders, and song: misogynist obscenity peppered commands from officers, and the songs sung by companies were so pornographic that officers had to order men to fall silent, or change the lyrics, when marching through populated areas.[46] Unsur-

---

[40] Ibid., 373.

[41] Ibid. On non-sexually transmitted syphilis as a diagnostic and cultural category in Russian medicine, see Engelstein, *The Keys to Happiness*, 165–211.

[42] Astashov, "Seksual'nyi opyt russkogo soldata," 373; Petrone, *The Great War*, 108.

[43] Fedorchenko, *Narod na voine*, 32. On this passage, see Petrone, *The Great War*, 149.

[44] Petrone, *The Great War*, 149–54; for examples, see Fedorchenko, *Narod na voine*, 41; Astashov, "Seksual'nyi opyt russkogo soldata," 371.

[45] Fedorchenko, *Narod na voine*, 43.

[46] Sanborn, *Drafting the Russian Nation*, 160.

prisingly, war amplified what was apparently already a significant degree of violence in relations between the sexes.

If sexual mores loosened as a result of war, one great condensing point for many of these themes was the Romanov dynasty and its collapsing authority. The many representations of the Romanovs as licentious playthings of the "mad monk" Grigorii Rasputin created a "political pornography" similar to that noted by historians of the French Revolution.[47] Peter Gatrell notes that the dynasty's dependence on the infamous spiritual advisor was particularly shocking because of his sexual excess: it contradicted every tenet of the loyal middle class's public code of discipline (even while the cartoonists of *Novyi Satirikon* proclaimed that this code was more honored in the breach).[48] Re-Mi's famous caricature of the "Russian Ruling House" on the cover of *Novyi Satirikon* in April 1917, with Rasputin enthroned and the craven Nicholas and treacherous Aleksandra by his side, was still a relatively desexualized depiction after the tsar's abdication; by this time far more scabrous images had circulated in cheap prints (*lubki*) for months.[49] The monarchy was vilified at all social levels. Boris Kolonitskii describes in detail how daring pamphlets and "smutty postcards" about the depravities of the ruling house circulated in tens of thousands of copies in Petrograd, and how cinema, cabarets and music halls all disseminated similar themes to wide audiences in 1916–17.[50] Fedorchenko provides extensive material, much of it in verse, about Rasputin's malign sexuality as seen through the eyes of the simple soldier. One aphorism proposed that the tsar and his monk fell out over the same Polish mistress, and the tsar had Rasputin killed. A ballad about "Grishka" alleged, "Girls and women—there were crowds of them / He lived, drank, fornicated like a hound / Living it up, shagging it up, to the bitter end."[51] Kolonitskii makes it clear that the image of depraved sexuality was an acid that destroyed Romanov claims to rule, by undermining popular respect for the autocracy, questioning the tsar's masculinity, and linking sexual disorder in the ruling house to treason. Even the tsar's wife and daughters could not escape; having been promoted

---

[47] Orlando Figes and Boris Kolonitskii, *Interpreting the Russian Revolution: The Language and Symbols of 1917* (New Haven: Yale University Press, 1999), 10; see also Kolonitskii, "Slukhi ob imperatritse Aleksandre Fedorovne i massovaia kul'tura (1914–1917)," in *Vestnik istorii, literatury, iskusstva. Otd-nie ist.-filol. nauk RAN* (Moscow: Sobranie, Nauka, 2005), 1: 362–78; Kolonitskii, *"Tragicheskaia erotika": Obrazy imperatorskoi sem'i v gody Pervoi mirovoi voiny* (Moscow: Novoe literaturnoe obozrenie, 2010).

[48] Peter Gatrell, *Russia's First World War: A Social and Economic History* (Harlow: Pearson Education, 2005), 102.

[49] Re-Mi, "Rossiiskii tsarstvovavshii dom," *Novyi Satirikon*, no. 13 (1917): 1; Kolonitskii, "Slukhi ob imperatritse"; note the caricature of Tsar Rasputin surrounded by a host of nude female angels in Hirschfeld, *Sittengeschichte des Weltkrieges*, ix.

[50] Figes and Kolonitskii, *Interpreting the Russian Revolution*, 11–12.

[51] Fedorchenko, *Narod na voine*, 87, 88.

as "sisters of mercy" their image suffered as the reputation of military nurses was battered.[52]

That this first stage of war destabilized peacetime understandings of sexuality, and loosened peacetime prohibitions on casual sexual behavior, is unsurprising and typifies what was happening across Europe.[53] For historians of Russia it is worth emphasizing the importance of continuities between "imperial war" and what followed. A "sexual revolution" in behavior and mores began before 1917 in mass mobilization, in the movement of soldiers, refugees and prisoners around the empire, in the new forms of sociability this brought, and in the challenges to traditional ways of thinking about sex. The "sexual revolution" also began in the less measurable undermining of patriarchal power, whether in the psyches of unmarried soldiers who expected, as Astashov notes by quoting one memorable soldier's letter from February 1916, that "the entire female sex would be shared out among the men" if the war dragged on much longer; or in the desacralization of autocracy soiled by sexual depravity.[54] Even if political revolution had never come to Russia in 1917, its sexual culture would still have been very different after the experience of 1914–16.

Violent Carnival, 1917–21

Revolution and Civil War brought an intensification of violence that left its mark on sexuality. The popular overturning of all authority of these years compelled many to speak more bluntly about sex, abandoning old restraints of morality or religious scruple. The young lesbian poet Anna A. Barkova, from an educated but poor family in Ivanovo-Voznesensk, wrote scornfully in her 1917 diary about the cult of a girl's "first love": "She is lying when she talks about feeling a wistful sweet emotion in her breast; it is not in her breast, but lower down." Long preludes to the sex act were a waste of time, and it would be far better if one could simply ask, "Are you in the mood?" and get down to it.[55]

Russia's upper and middle classes, harried by popular contempt and, with the advent of civil war, outright violence, imagined their personal torment and the nation's ordeal in terms of sexual violation. In January 1918 Sayn-Wittgenstein looked back on 1917 with the bitter realization that her sense of insecurity began with the end of monarchy. In March of that year, when at a street demonstration with girlfriends she had felt a moment's exaltation,

---

[52] Figes and Kolonitskii, *Interpreting the Russian Revolution*, 13–24.

[53] Herzog, *Sexuality in Europe*, 45–61.

[54] Astashov, "Seksual'nyi opyt russkogo soldata," 372.

[55] Anna Barkova, *Vosem' glav bezumiia: Proza, dnevniki* (Moscow: Fond Sergeia Dubova, 2009), 421–23.

it was a feeling of love for this faceless crowd, a desire to melt into it and to be recognized as part of it. The feeling did not last; it weakened when I noticed at closer range the brutal animal faces of the soldiers and the people in the crowd, and it disappeared completely under the hostile looks directed at us...[56]

Not long after these March 1917 events, her family retreated from the capital to their estate in Ukraine, unwittingly putting themselves in grave danger. Sayn-Wittgenstein wrote of their terrors as soldiers and peasants lay siege nightly to the manor house, in one diary entry imagining the mob's assault in chaste terms that require little imagination to see the underlying fear of sexual violation. "[T]hey will penetrate our home... If only they would shoot us right away, at least! From a distance, without touching us." A swift, impersonal death from a merciful bullet was preferable to the unspeakable torments of rape and death by beating or stabbing.[57]

The fears of the aristocracy and middle class were projected onto the national body, imagined as feminine, and violated by revolutionaries. Often the violence depicted in cartoon and other media was, like the entries in Sayn-Wittgenstein's diary, suggestive of rape without explicitly naming sexual violation. Nails and knives served as surrogate phalluses. Many images produced by the press in White-occupied regions showed Russia as a young woman, literally crucified at Golgotha, or stabbed by Bolshevik fanatics.[58] Anna Eremeeva has shown how many film plots and poems produced by both sides in the Civil War relied upon love-triangle scenarios that positioned a faithless or undecided woman between "our side" and "theirs." Vacillation brought degradation. In Aleksandr Blok's landmark verse *The Twelve* (*Dvenadtsat'*, 1918), the prostitute Kat'ka is caught fatally in the crossfire between Red Guard Pet'ka and his enemy Van'ka.[59] In a March 1918 issue caustically devoted to "The Nude," a cartoon in *Novyi Satirikon* contrasted the tastes of the prerevolutionary and contemporary eras: the nude of the "good old days" was a bourgeois woman in her boudoir, a servant removing her luxurious garments while a suitor looks on. The nude "of our days" was being stripped of her clothing in the street by three bestial men whose faces and positions suggested that rape would follow theft (fig. 39).

---

[56] Sayn-Wittgenstein, *La fin*, 196 (20 January 1918).

[57] Ibid., 148 (15 October 1917).

[58] Anna Eremeeva, "Woman and Violence in Artistic Discourse of the Russian Revolution and Civil War (1917–1922)," *Gender and History* 16, 3 (2004): 726–43, see 728–32. A Bolshevik plunges a knife into the stomach of a half-naked woman personifying the Russian Revolution in the cartoon by B. Antolovskii, "Ispolnenie slova," *Novyi Satirikon*, no. 2 (1918): 12.

[59] Eremeeva, "Woman and Violence," 736–38.

One of the books of Fedorchenko's stylized aphorisms, devoted to the Civil War on the Southern Front, appears to describe the fighting man's increasingly blunt view of sexual liaisons and their significance.[60] It is impossible to gauge how far this impression of greater popular sexual frankness is Fedorchenko's literary projection onto the men and the period, and how far her writing reflected lived experience. The views of these men in Fedorchenko's work plausibly extend and intensify the sexual behavior and thinking of soldiers described by Astashov for the pre-1917 era using military archival sources. Fedorchenko's material suggests Civil War soldiers viewed physical love through a cynicism about class and material exchanges for sex with women, a misogyny that Astashov documented for the era of "imperial war." "So what if we weren't lawfully married? I still showed my concern, even if we only lived together for three days," proclaimed one informant.[61] Another explained his philosophy of love as a series of short-term affairs that might cost financially, but never emotionally. Soldiers supposedly recognized their own actions as promiscuous and even base: "As many broads as you like, some passionately, some sweetly, but never genuinely."[62] Lower-class men resented middle- and upper-class lovers. One surreptitiously but deliberately trod on their feet at dances, expressing his resentment that the officers got all the pretty girls. Others felt disgust or hatred for such women's mercenary approach to love (a civilian might depend on the rations of a soldier passing through her village, for example).[63] Despite the apparent abundance of sexual opportunity, fear of sexually transmitted disease reportedly deterred some from casual sex, and one told of his shame at having to show his infected genitals to a nurse. Civil War experience of "one's own" women left a bitter taste; "I don't want to get married. Back in the village, I've got a wife, only I don't count that. The only thing that counts is my free emancipation [*voliu vol'nuiu*]."[64] Fedorchenko's memorialization of Civil War soldiers' cynical and misogynist attitudes appears to tap currents that were already well established during the 1914–17 conflict.

The scale of real sexual violence, so widely mobilized as metaphor in the contending Red and White press and fiction in the period, is impossible to quantify.[65] We have no satisfactory statistics for rape and sexual crime during the Civil War period, nor are comprehensive central figures likely to

---

[60] Fedorchenko, *Narod na voine*, "Kniga 3. Grazhdanskaia voina," 152–386.

[61] Fedorchenko, *Narod na voine*, 260.

[62] Ibid., 261.

[63] Ibid., 222, 267–68.

[64] Ibid., 263, 265.

[65] On rape as a cultural obsession (even if not a political problem) for early Bolsheviks and fellow-travelers, see Naiman, *Sex in Public*, 57–78; and Igal Halfin, "The Rape of the Intelligentsia: A Proletarian Foundational Myth," *Russian Review* 56, 1 (1997): 90–109. For the Whites, see Eremeeva, "Women and Violence."

exist; while authorities deplored rape, they seldom recorded it systematically. Courts and police operated sporadically, especially where power changed hands repeatedly, and when crimes were counted, rape was not generally among them. Reporting sexual assault and pursuing a case against a rapist, in the chaotic conditions of the era, required a woman to place enormous faith in officials who might be gone tomorrow.[66] Only five arrests for rape were registered by the nascent agencies of the People's Commissariat of Internal Affairs in the city of Petrograd in 1918, and complaints that did not lead to arrest must have been correspondingly rare.[67] Civilians were fearful of sexual violence regardless of which army's forces passed through their neighborhoods.[68] Sexual assault was an unacknowledged weapon of war, meant, when inflicted, to terrorize the "enemy," and when held up as a threat against "one's own women," to bolster the fighting zeal of frontline husbands, sons, and brothers on the battlefield.[69]

Prostitution reportedly flourished in Petrograd, Moscow, and other centers during the Civil War years, encouraged by the collapse of the conventional economy and both the Reds' and Whites' requisitioning of available foodstuffs and other commodities. For women lacking factory employment or a sinecure in a stable office job, the exchange of sex for a loaf of bread, a roof over one's head, or in the case of some "class enemies" to redeem a husband held hostage, acquired a brutal logic. Perhaps some women who might never have contemplated the practice before 1917 now had little choice.[70] The fact that the biggest cities had large numbers of comparatively well-fed mobilized soldiers moving through them offered opportunities to women prepared to sell sexual services. Sexually transmitted disease infections shot up. One Petrograd official estimated the number of the city's prostitutes in 1920—a year when the city's population plummeted to a fraction of its prewar level—at 17,000. A forced-labor camp established in late 1919 on the southern edge of

---

[66] For a discussion of rape statistics before and after 1917, see Dan Healey, *Bolshevik Sexual Forensics: Diagnosing Disorder in the Clinic and Courtroom, 1917–1939* (DeKalb: Northern Illinois University Press, 2009), 83–87.

[67] V. I. Musaev, *Prestupnost' v Petrograde v 1917–1921 gg. i bor'ba s nei* (St. Petersburg: Dmitrii Bulanin, 2001), 182. On Soviet police procedure for investigating sex crimes, see Healey, *Bolshevik Sexual Forensics*, 60–65.

[68] For comments from a White officer about Ukrainian peasant women and girls' terror, see V. A. Krivoshein, "Deviatnadtsatyi god: Glavy iz vospominanii," *Zvezda*, no. 10 (1996): 198–218, at 205.

[69] Petrone, *The Great War*, 154–64; Sanborn, *Drafting the Russian Nation*, 146–61.

[70] Two St. Petersburg historians contend that such exchanges scarcely qualify as "prostitution," but the diminished importance of cash during War Communism militates against this view; see N. B. Lebina, and M. B. Shkarovskii, *Prostitutsiia v Peterburge* (Moscow: Progress-Akademiia, 1994), 61–62.

Petrograd held 6,500 women, of whom 60 percent were suspected of living off prostitution.[71]

Violence, hunger, disease, a shrinking economy, and devastating political change: in these conditions the dreams imposed on sexuality by Russia's pre-1914 prophets of love were tested to destruction. Contemplating the physiological consequences alone, the officer and literary figure V. P. Shklovskii pointed out the obvious results of privation: "Men experienced virtually total impotence, and women stopped having their periods."[72] Whatever new order might prevail in the New Russia, it would inherit a physically and morally exhausted population.

Gender and Sexual Crossings, 1914–22

One of the striking features of Russia's "continuum of crisis" that historians have usually overlooked is the persistence of represented and real gender crossings and inversions throughout the period. These transgressions of the usual gender boundaries exposed important fractures in the sexual culture of Russia in turmoil. Often such fractures led to determined efforts to restore the existing gender order. Shocking representations of gender inversion dramatized the threat posed by "revolution," yet they could also ultimately serve to reinforce "traditional" masculinity or femininity. The shock of gender inversion often turned on the implicit or explicit heterosexual anxieties it invoked. An examination of gender crossings can also illuminate ways in which "queer" sexualities—which had rapidly acquired unprecedented visibility in prewar culture—claimed space in the revolutionary flood that accompanied imperial and civil war.

The best-known example of gender crossing in the period is the case of Russia's women soldiers, which has attracted attention in recent work by Russian and Western historians.[73] These historians demonstrate how the unprecedented if modest number of women who petitioned to join the

---

[71] Musaev, *Prestupnost′ v Petrograde*, 182–92.

[72] Ibid., 182.

[73] Melissa K. Stockdale, "'My Death for the Motherland Is Happiness': Women, Patriotism, and Soldiering in Russia's Great War, 1914–1917," *American Historical Review* 109, 1 (2004): 78–116; Laurie Stoff, *They Fought for the Motherland: Russia's Women Soldiers in World War I* (Lawrence: University Press of Kansas, 2006); Stoff, "They Fought for Russia: Female Soldiers of the First World War," in *A Soldier and a Woman: Sexual Integration in the Military*, ed. Gerard J. DeGroot and C. M. Peniston-Bird (Harlow, UK: Pearson Education, 2000); Sanborn, *Drafting the Russian Nation*; Richard Abraham, "Mariia L. Bochkareva and the Russian Amazons of 1917," in *Women and Society in Russia and the Soviet Union*, ed. Linda Edmondson (Cambridge: Cambridge University Press, 1992); Shcherbinin, *Voennyi faktor v povsednevnoi zhizni russkoi zhenshchiny*, 424–44; Iu. N. Ivanova, *Khrabreishie iz prekrasnykh: Zhenshchiny Rossii v voinakh* (Moscow: ROSSPEN, 2002), 89–120.

Imperial and the Soviet armies had the potential to unsettle a gender order that deemed soldiering as exclusively men's patriotic duty. The approximately 5,000 women who served in combat roles by the end of the Provisional Government regime were the first women in any country in the modern era to be granted state-sanctioned access to battle experience on equal terms with men.[74] One widely stated purpose of the recruitment of women, and the formation of women's battalions, was to shame male deserters into returning to their units, or to inspire men to volunteer for active duty. In this sense, as Joshua sSanborn's sophisticated analysis reveals, official women's battalions reinforced the norms of gender by deploying an extreme argument "to get men to behave according to the military-masculine ethic, not to create a gender-free army."[75] Men who refused to fight, or who were failures before the "military-masculine ethic" could be taunted as pseudo-women. A collective letter to a patronizing male soldier from a women's battalion in 1917 mocked such failure: "So allow us to give you some advice: dress yourself up in our sarafans, tie a kerchief on your head, cook the borshch, do the washing up, ... and wag your tongues."[76] Leaders of women's battalions said they were acting to do their patriotic duty, and rejected the notion that women combatants constituted a sexual provocation; yet their incursion into traditional male territory (symbolized most vividly by commander Mariia Bochkareva's visit with male comrades to a soldiers' brothel), baited an already demoralized and misogynist peasant army.[77]

Men were ruefully aware of the new assertiveness of women and their assumption of an ever-larger share of men's traditional roles. To judge from the quantity of material on this theme that Fedorchenko included in her collection, she clearly thought such anxiety was widely shared among soldiers, and that it impinged on their sexual identity. Soldiers said women had abandoned skirts and now strode about in trousers and boots, with cigarettes clenched in their teeth and shorn of their curls. Others regretted that "Girls have cut off their curls / And run off to Revolution."[78] Where that left men was unclear, although one ditty suggested that if women changed, men might be forced to as well:

> Soon we'll see some funny stuff,
> Changes on all sides.

---

[74] Stockdale, "'My Death,'" 113.

[75] Sanborn, *Drafting the Russian Nation*, 151.

[76] Quoted in Stockdale, "'My Death,'" 104.

[77] Sanborn, *Drafting the Russian Nation*, 151; Shcherbinin, *Voennyi faktor v povsednevnoi zhizni russkoi zhenshchiny*, 430–31; Stockdale, "'My Death,'" 102–04.

[78] Fedorchenko, *Narod na voine*, 141, 147. On the phenomenon of such "masculinized" women during and after the Revolution, see Healey, *Homosexual Desire*, 57–62, 143–44.

Blokes are getting up the duff,
And lads are blushing brides.[79]

Not only were men's prerogatives under siege from a phalanx of masculinized Amazons, but men themselves seemed poised to lose the final marker of their virility: the active sexual role that ultimately defined them as not-women.[80] The Bolsheviks allowed women to continue serving as combatants but disallowed women-only battalions; after 1917 many women-fighters transferred to nursing roles, evidently restoring the traditional gender norm of the nurturing female working alongside the fighting male.[81]

If literal and figurative inversions of femininity served certain military objectives and momentarily pointed toward a new gender order, the inversion of normally dominant masculinity could be an index of just how disordered the world had become. Sexual anxieties gave such inversions added power; men's loss of status might not merely put them on the bottom in the heterosexual dyad but lead to homoerotic humiliations too. Bourgeois observers imagined inversions of martial manliness that confirmed, for some, the depravity of revolutionary socialism. Arkadii Averchenko's satirical story "The Baltic Sailor" took aim at the famed sailors of the Baltic Fleet.[82] Nikita Shkliarenko, a boatswain, and his mate from the cruiser Aurora, Egor', were hard-drinking, rough-and-ready, broad-shouldered and decent seamen whom the Revolution had totally transformed. Like many of their comrades they became landlubbers and entered the curious new aristocracy of commissariats and Cheka:

> These strange sailors were powdered and strongly perfumed; on their crude paws one could see the results of an unsuccessful but deliberate manicure; on their feet they wore slippers with high heels and practically with ribbons; on their breasts they pinned a rose.... It was clear that they couldn't stop at half-measures: the newspapers said that in the capital's theaters the majority of the audience were sailors

---

[79] Fedorchenko, *Narod na voine*, 141. I am indebted to Nick Baron for this free translation of the original: "Teper' nado ozhidat', / Chto vse peremestitsia, / Muzhiki pochnut rozhat', / A parni nevestit'sia."

[80] For more representations of men's discomfort with women's assumption of active roles during the revolutionary 1917 and after, see Fedorchenko, *Narod na voine*, 141–47; and see a short story by Isaak Babel' about a man accepting payment for sex: "Moi pervyi gonorar," in Babel', *Sochineniia v 2-kh tomakh* (Moscow: Khudozhestvennaia literatura, 1990), 2: 245–53.

[81] Stockdale, "'My Death,'" 113; Sanborn, *Drafting the Russian Nation*, 157–60.

[82] Arkadii Averchenko, "Baltiiskii matros," in A. Averchenko, *Salat iz bulavok: Rasskazy i fel'etony* (New York: Russica Publishers, 1982), 219–26. From internal evidence, the story was written during or just after 1918. Thanks to Victor Oboin for bringing this story to my attention.

in décolletage, powdered, with eye-liner and touched-up lips; bracelets on their wrists and diamond broaches on their breasts.[83]

Taking a box in the Aleksandrinskii Theater, the two sailors peer through opera glasses at the audience, and mince and preen as they squabble over jewelry and Egor''s pilfering of Nikita's perfume. Only after encountering a revolutionary mob on Nevskii Prospekt, gathered around a dying young man, are the feminized sailors forced to confront their strange transformation. They donate their fine baubles to help the poor boy. A night of boozing and brawling shakes off the vestiges of their bizarre lifestyle, and they return to the sea to serve on new ships. A cartoon picked up the same theme in Averchenko's *Novyi Satirikon* magazine (fig. 40). The fantastic image of the Baltic Fleet's legendary sailors transformed into overripe society matrons—who themselves were a frequent target of *Novyi Satirikon* mockery before the Revolution—reveals Averchenko's reading of how far these helpmates of the Bolshevik takeover had crossed the boundaries of class, and from there, gender. As jumped-up representatives of the "new aristocracy," Baltic sailors Nikita and Egor' attempted to model the refinements of the old ruling class. The queerness of their comradeship was never made explicit in Averchenko's tale. Yet the parody of femininity they temporarily embodied was a comment not just on their perversion of the order of class but on their forgetting of the traditional sexual order as well: the joke was that two effeminate and implicitly passive "inverts" could hardly constitute a credible pair of lovers.

Whether Averchenko was aware of it or not, the sailor's place in Petrograd's homosexual subculture was firmly fixed well before 1914, and the continuing participation of seamen in the northern capital's clandestine parties thrown by male homosexuals was made vividly evident when police closed down one such assembly on 15 January 1921.[84] The raid netted a significant number of sailors and soldiers who frequented these regularly organized parties; the festivities included some men in women's dress and mock-wedding celebrations, and there was a "flying post" messaging system to help these men get acquainted. Such exotic behavior was apparently not confined to the capital. In June 1921 in Kamenets-Podol'skii, the Cheka arrested one flagrant drag queen using the *nomme de guerre* "Karolina Ivanovna" who reportedly denounced five men from the Petliurist forces to the Bolshevik secret police. The Reds sent "Karolina" for psychiatric assessment when they suspected he had had sexual relations with the Petliurists. He used the feminine gender in speech (*"ia poshla, sdelala"*; I went, I did), relied on male lovers to support

---

[83] Averchenko, "Baltiiskii matros," 220–21.

[84] The principal sources on this party and the police raid are V. M. Bekhterev, "O polovom izvrashchenii, kak osoboi ustanovke polovykh refleksov," in *Polovoi vopros v shkole i v zhizni*, ed. I. S. Simonov (Leningrad: Brokgauz-Efron, 1927); and Bekhterev, "Polovye ukloneniia i izvrashcheniia v svete refleksologii," *Voprosy izucheniia i vospitaniia lichnosti*, no. 4–5 (1922): 644–746. See Healey, *Homosexual Desire*, 44–46.

him, wore women's clothing frequently, and was notorious in Kamenets-Podol'skii.[85] Few revolutionaries if any expected that same-sex lovers would parade their desires as flagrantly as "Karolina Ivanovna" dared to do, but in the midst of a social world turned upside down, some queerly desiring Russians did expect that previously repressed sexualities might have a chance to speak more freely.[86]

Part II. Recasting Authority

Mobilizing Sex, 1914–17

The tsarist state, mistrustful of constructions of citizenship and concerned to protect its autocratic prerogatives, mobilized sexuality as a force in total war in a haphazard and usually only implicit fashion. One of the most direct measures adopted by the state even before the war, in 1912, was the welfare payment (*paek*) to soldiers' families; these payments were conferred on conscripts as the war erupted, although inflation reduced their value.[87] These transfers from the state into the hands of (usually) soldiers' wives were a complex and contested symbol of the tsar's support not just for the individual servicemen but arguably for the heterosexual families they left behind. "Family values were encoded into the relationship between the citizen, the army, and the state," in the *paek*, notes Joshua Sanborn.[88] The *paek* became an instrument in the tsarist army's increasingly futile attempts to control soldier behavior. Authorities revoked payments to families of deserters, and wives of the captured, wounded, or killed had trouble tapping their entitlements.[89] Little is known about the impact of these payments on lower-class women

---

[85] S. P. Vysotskii, "Sluchai prevratnogo polovogo chuvstva. (Bol'noi demonstrirovan v Obshchestve kurskikh vrachei 2-go iiunia 1921 goda)," *Vestnik Kurskogo gubernskogo otdela zdravookhraneniia*, no. 1 (1921): 9–11. On the use of Russian feminine grammatical forms by flagrantly effeminate homosexual men, see Dan Healey, "Comrades, Queers, and 'Oddballs': Sodomy, Masculinity, and Gendered Violence in Leningrad Province of the 1950s," *Journal of the History of Sexuality*, 21, 3 (2012): 496–522.

[86] For a contemporary plea for homophile emancipation by one Evgeniia Fedorovna M., see Healey, *Homosexual Desire*, 68–72. Note also the appearance of Englishman Edward Carpenter's *The Intermediate Sex*, a defense of same-sex love, in a Russian translation, intriguingly "passed by the military censor": *Promezhutochnyi pol* (Petrograd: M. V. Pirozhkov, 1916).

[87] Gatrell, *Russia's First World War*, 64.

[88] Sanborn, *Drafting the Russian Nation*, 110.

[89] Sanborn, *Drafting the Russian Nation*, 108; Alfred G. Meyer, "The Impact of World War I on Russian Women's Lives," in *Russia's Women: Accommodation, Resistance, Transformation*, ed. Barbara Evans Clements, Barbara Alpern Engel, and Christine D. Worobec (Berkeley: University of California Press, 1991), 211.

but they must have contributed to the much remarked confidence with which women now entered the public sphere.[90] The disappearance of the *paek* ruptured the implicit contractual triangle between state, soldier, and family. The collapse of these payments in revolutionary 1917 and their reinstatement by the Bolsheviks in 1918–19 had a direct impact on soldiers' motives and thus the fortunes of war, demonstrating just how deeply the state founded its appeals to loyalty on the basis of heterosexual familial ties.[91]

Wartime tsarist propaganda was comparatively weak and reflected the state's reliance on hoped-for loyalty to a patriarchal tsar and reluctance to appeal to ideals of national citizenship. Propaganda was generated by the army, government, and quasi-official organizations, notably the Skobelev Committee; the theme of Germany's threat to Russian women's honor was invoked in some of this material. Postcards featured less militaristic themes, concentrating instead on the soldier-nurse, or soldier–wife dyad; these attempts to arouse consoling heterosexual emotion seem ironic when one considers how the peasant-soldier viewed both nurses and wives with great suspicion, according to Astashov.[92] War-focused propaganda had to compete with the unbroken stream of popular fiction, non-fiction and cinema that vied for audience attention. In some accounts, sexuality figured heavily in this market-driven domain. Richard Stites asks if the popular taste for "sexual melodrama" of the early wartime films of Evgenii Bauer and Iakov Protazanov, in which poor women were victimized by wealthy men, helped to generate class resentment.[93] If the hypothesis remains unprovable, at least it is indisputable that a template of decadent bourgeois mores provided grist for the Bolshevik mill when the Soviet regime later devised its own "socialist" propaganda and enlightenment.[94]

Revolutions of Desire, 1917–22?

The Provisional Government had little time to demonstrate how sexuality might be revolutionized under a Russian liberal-democratic regime. Certainly no legislation reforming marriage and divorce, to say nothing of other, more

---

[90] Shcherbinin, *Voennyi faktor v povsednevnoi zhizni russkoi zhenshchiny*, 222–69.

[91] Sanborn, *Drafting the Russian Nation*, 109.

[92] Gatrell, *Russia's First World War*, 88–89; on patriarchal values in this material, see Karen Petrone, "Family, Masculinity, and Heroism in Russian War Posters of the First World War," in *Borderlines: Genders and Identities in War and Peace 1870–1930*, ed. Billie Melman (New York: Routledge, 1998); Astashov, "Seksual′nyi opyt russkogo soldata," 375–77.

[93] Stites, "Days and Nights," 16. Theater repertoire is discussed in Frame, "Cultural Mobilization."

[94] On Soviet sexual enlightenment, see Frances Lee Bernstein, *The Dictatorship of Sex: Lifestyle Advice for the Soviet Masses* (DeKalb: Northern Illinois University Press, 2007).

controversial, aspects of sexuality, was undertaken while the regime waited for the Constituent Assembly to pronounce on the future of the Russian republic.[95] Yet in these brief months with the declaration of equal suffrage for women, and the institution of women's death battalions, a turn to radical notions of gender equality and citizenship emerged. Under the Bolsheviks, from late 1917, radicalism accelerated. Sexuality was not apparently a first-rank priority for Lenin's Communist Party (as it renamed itself in 1918), but the record of activity in the midst of civil war showed how intimate life mattered to this strange new regime, the first in the world to capture a state with the avowed purpose of making it "socialist." The violence of civil war was integral to the ways in which the Communists shaped sexuality. Peter Holquist observes, "As fantastic utopian dreams fused with an experience of devastation and brutality, those employing violence invested it with a redemptive and purifying significance."[96] Where sexuality was concerned, Communist radicalism promised an all-or-nothing confrontation with old norms and values. Yet the forge of violence also transformed the blueprints inherited from a century of socialist thinkers.

The imprint of civil war can be seen in the first Code on Marriage, the Family and Guardianship, adopted in October 1918.[97] This code put flesh on the bones of two December 1917 decrees of the Soviet regime that secularized marriage (henceforth only civil weddings would be recognized) and legalized divorce at the request of either spouse. These early decrees contributed to the growing enmity between the socialist regime and Russia's Orthodox Church, a hostility that intensified in 1918 when the church anathematized Lenin's government while anticlerical Red violence grew. Many Soviet legislators and commentators considering the 1918 Marriage Code admired its radicalism but wished it could go further: they asked why the state should sanction marriage at all. The formal registration of any kind of marital bond struck some as contrary to their "socialist consciousness" and nothing less than "a bourgeois survival."[98] The bourgeois housewife dependent on a husband for her existence was a "labor deserter," little better than a prostitute, in the

---

[95] A commission to examine implementation of criminal code reform did sit during the last four months of the Provisional Government regime; V. D. Nabokov, *The Provisional Government*, ed. Andrew Field (Brisbane: University of Queensland Press, 1970), 95–96.

[96] Holquist, *Making War, Forging Revolution*, 287.

[97] On the code, see Wendy Z. Goldman, *Women, the State, and Revolution: Soviet Family Policy and Social Life* (Cambridge: Cambridge University Press, 1993), 48–57; Elizabeth Waters, "Family, Marriage, and Relations between the Sexes," in *Critical Companion to the Russian Revolution 1914–1921*, ed. Edward Acton, Vladimir Iu. Cherniaev, and William G. Rosenberg (London: Arnold, 1997).

[98] Goldman, *Women, the State, and Revolution*, 55, citing N. A. Roslavets, a woman from Ukraine and a non-Party delegate to the 1918 Central Executive Committee of

view of Aleksandra Kollontai.[99] In conferences of socialist women-activists in 1918 and 1919, the same arguments against the rule of husbands and capital in marriage were rehearsed.[100] Yet, as Wendy Goldman argues, in a society where the peasant household remained a productive nexus and not merely a site of consumption (as the urban family had become, Marxists alleged), the deconstruction of the family and sexual relations could only be taken so far. The allegiance of the peasantry in the Civil War might not hinge on such arcana, but there was little value in gratuitously antagonizing this potential ally, while also trying to reduce its attachment to religion. If the code refused to accept communal property in the marital alliance, it nevertheless recognized alimony and child support as necessary adjuncts to freer divorce provisions in the "transitional period" from capitalism to socialism. In Bolshevik deliberations about the code, its potential as "a strong weapon in the struggle with the church" was considered conclusive.[101] While at war with the Orthodox Church, Communists would have to offer the population civil marriage as an alternative to religious ceremonies, rituals that retained broad popular allegiance. The chief author of the 1918 Marriage Code, Aleksandr Goikhbarg, ruefully noted, "We must accept this [code] knowing that it is not a socialist measure"; war, poverty, and underdevelopment imposed limits on socialist ambition.[102]

If the new Soviet marriage provisions seemed to disappoint some radicals, even greater paradox surrounds the November 1920 legalization of abortion, in a joint decree of the health and justice commissariats. In retrospect, no other measure did as much to bring the Soviet "sexual revolution" to the notice of all Europeans regardless of political creed.[103] The resolute manner with which Bolsheviks made abortion legal and relatively freely available outraged religious moralists across Europe, moved political conservatives and fascists to flay "godless Bolshevism" and its local representatives, and inspired generations of 20th-century radicals and feminists. Nevertheless, any

---

the Soviet (VTsIK) that adopted the code. See also Waters, "Family, Marriage, and Relations between the Sexes," 362–65.

[99] A. M. Kollontai, *Prostitutsiia i mery bor′by s nei. (Rech′ na III Vserossiskom soveshchanii zaveduiushchikh gubzhenotdelami)* (Moscow: Gosudarstvennoe izdatel′stvo, 1921), 10–11.

[100] Waters, "Family, Marriage, and Relations between the Sexes," 365–68.

[101] Quoted in Goldman, *Women, the State, and Revolution*, 43–48, 54.

[102] Goldman, *Women, the State, and Revolution*, 56–57. On the continuing popularity of religious weddings, see Pavel Rogoznyi, "Rossiiskaia tserkov′ i 'Krasnaia smuta,'" *Neva*, no. 2 (2011): 157–73.

[103] Herzog, *Sexuality in Europe*, 49. On the decree, see Goldman, *Women, the State, and Revolution*, 254–57; Susan Gross Solomon, "The Demographic Argument in Soviet Debates over the Legalization of Abortion in the 1920′s," *Cahiers du Monde russe et soviétique* 33, 1 (1992): 59–82.

presumption that Lenin's Communists believed in a woman's right to manage her own fertility was misplaced. The law was the product of civil war and desperate deprivation. The health commissariat's medical experts realized that in the catastrophic wartime conditions, women persisted in terminating unwanted pregnancies regardless of any prohibition. They drank bleach and other irritants, or, turning to rural wise women and midwives, used crude mechanical means to achieve the result they desired.[104]

In conditions of wartime desperation, Soviet doctors and jurists argued that legal medical abortion conducted by doctors in clinics was safer for women's reproductive capacity than continuing to criminalize the problem. Soviet socialists widely viewed attempts to evade childbearing as antisocial; even the leading Bolshevik Kollontai, whose writing celebrated woman's capacity to master her own erotic destiny, could still declare "that *childbirth is a social obligation.*"[105] Leninists and medical experts conceived of reproductive capacity as a collective resource rather than an attribute over which an individual should exercise supreme control. Maternity was social, not personal: there was little space in the imagination of this "sexual revolution" for the late 20th-century notion of "a woman's right to choose." It was axiomatic of the Soviet understanding of the abortion law that by 1924, women's access to free abortion would be controlled by a *troika* of gatekeepers: a doctor, a social worker, and a woman-Communist. In making medical abortion available, the law explicitly referred to pregnancy termination as "this evil" and justified legalization by pointing to persistent backwardness in society and to the reigning dire socioeconomic conditions.[106]

That some women might *use* the revolutionary legislation to control their own sexual destiny as freely as men could, was of course possible. The full implications and contradictions of Soviet policies on women, family, and sexuality were not instantly apparent in the Civil War era. The Communist Party did not arrive in power with a single, monolithic "line" on sexuality. Instead debate raged over the "sexual revolution" and its meaning, in literature and culture, in politics, and of course in relations between the sexes; in a 1920 interview with German Communist Clara Zetkin, even Lenin struggled

---

[104] Goldman, *Women, the State, and Revolution*, 254, 281.

[105] Quotation in Goldman, *Women, the State, and Revolution*, 257. For Kollontai's celebration of women's right to erotic self-determination, see, for example, A. M. Kollontai, *Novaia moral´ i rabochii klass* (Moscow: Izd-vo VTsIK, 1919), 35, 44–47; and note also Alexandra Kollontai, *Selected Writings of Alexandra Kollontai*, trans. Alix Holt (London: Allison & Busby, 1977).

[106] On reproductive capacity as a collective resource under Soviet socialism, see Healey, *Bolshevik Sexual Forensics*, 164–65; on the *troika*, with its doctor, maternity health officer, and representative of the Party's Women's Section, see Goldman, *Women, the State, and Revolution*, 261–64; and Janet Hyer, "Fertility Control in Soviet Russia: A Case Study in Gender Control and Professionalization" (Ph.D. diss., University of Toronto, 2007).

to make his views on the subject heard.[107] For Bolsheviks trying to define a clear line on sexual politics, medicalization offered answers that seemed to dovetail with their brand of "scientific socialism," and frequently the regime turned to physicians and hygienists to solve the "sex question." The People's Commissariats of Public Health and Justice relied upon forensic gynecologists, psychiatrists, and other specialists to define sexual disorder and set sexual norms, and presumptions about gender, the social body, and national hierarchies adapted from European biomedicine permeated their science.[108]

The regime did adopt some sweeping measures that were genuinely radical, inspired perhaps by the challenging of hierarchies during the "continuum of crisis." In an apparent attempt to accommodate diverse social and physiological realities in a multiethnic polity, the regime abolished the age of consent in its criminal legislation on sexual relations, and adopted the vague biosocial marker of "sexual maturity" as the threshold of sexual citizenship.[109] The results of this experiment were tragic for victims and confusing for Soviet men and women.[110] The decriminalization of male homosexuality in 1922, which had been under discussion in the Commissariat of Justice since 1918, was a genuinely revolutionary move: it made Soviet Russia the first major European nation since newly unified Italy in the 1870s, and before that revolutionary France in 1791, to legalize sex between men.[111] The relaxation of this prohibition was interpreted by some as rational, socialist, and liberating.[112] It apparently also made it easier for Soviet doctors in the

---

[107] For the debate, see Naiman, *Sex in Public*, and Gregory Carleton, *Sexual Revolution in Bolshevik Russia* (Pittsburgh: University of Pittsburgh Press, 2005). For Lenin's views, see Clara Zetkin, *Lenin on the Woman Question* (New York: International Publishers, 1934).

[108] Healey, *Bolshevik Sexual Forensics*, 17–36. The convergence of interests between Bolsheviks and expert "modernizers" is explored in Daniel Beer, *Renovating Russia: The Human Sciences and the Fate of Liberal Modernity, 1880–1930* (Ithaca, NY: Cornell University Press, 2008).

[109] On this measure, see Dan Healey, "Defining Sexual Maturity as the Soviet Alternative to an Age of Consent," in *Soviet Medicine: Culture, Practice, and Science*, ed. Frances L. Bernstein, Christopher Burton, and Healey (DeKalb: Northern Illinois University Press, 2010).

[110] Healey, *Bolshevik Sexual Forensics*, 37–82.

[111] Healey, *Homosexual Desire in Revolutionary Russia*, 115–25. Germany, the United Kingdom, and the successor states of the Hapsburg Empire continued to criminalize homosexuality into the 1960s.

[112] For the text of a British Communist's 1934 letter to Stalin explaining the socialist principles behind the 1922 decriminalization of male homosexuality, see Glennys Young, *The Communist Experience in the Twentieth Century: A Global History through Sources* (New York: Oxford University Press, 2012), 88–89.

1920s to transform approaches to the intersex patient (hermaphrodite) from obscurantist ignorance to world-leading scientific and clinical treatment.[113] Another revolutionary step was in sexual enlightenment, where frank speaking and unvarnished hygiene messages stunned European visitors and perhaps yielded many unintended consequences for popular behavior.[114] Bolsheviks were also capable of confused and contradictory responses to sexual matters, as the case of heterosexual prostitution illustrates. The regime embraced the female prostitute as a victim of capitalist exploitation (sentiments embodied in an Interdepartmental Commission on the Struggle against Prostitution, established in 1919 and chaired by the health commissariat), while simultaneously arresting and confining uncounted thousands of urban women caught soliciting, citing "labor desertion," during the Civil War.[115]

Conclusion

The prewar idea that sexuality might provide the "keys to happiness" that could unlock the redemption of society was put to the test during Russia's long crisis. Hesitantly at first, sex was invested with increasing weight as the nation fought a total war that seemed to consume all of its internal resources. In a carnival of violence, sexuality's colors grew ever darker as degradation and violation became ubiquitous. When Bolsheviks finally reconstituted the state, they considered how sexuality might remake the social body and began erecting a legal framework that reflected not only socialist expectations, but also the biopolitical needs of a depleted and exhausted society.

In the long "continuum of crisis" a revolution in sexual cultures and behavior came well before 1917. For the elite and townspeople in the "business-as-usual" rear, it was slow to develop, but at the front for the vast peasant army, and the families from which it originated in the village, mobilization beginning in 1914 triggered new ways of living and dying that compelled soldiers (at least) to reevaluate their ideas about sex, women, and family. Detached from patriarchal village surveillance in the homosocial barracks world, it is hardly surprising that young peasant soldiers talked about sex, experimented with casual relations, and questioned authority in sexual terms—whether it be

---

[113] Healey, *Bolshevik Sexual Forensics*, 134–58.

[114] Bernstein, *The Dictatorship of Sex*.

[115] Waters, "Family, Marriage, and Relations between the Sexes," 366–67; see also Waters, "Victim or Villain: Prostitution in Post-Revolutionary Russia," in *Women and Society in Russia and the Soviet Union*; and Lebina, and Shkarovskii, *Prostitutsiia v Peterburge*, 60–85. "Prostitution" would be an exclusively heterosexual concept for early Bolsheviks; their attention did not turn to male prostitution until the 1933–34 recriminalization of male homosexuality; see Dan Healey, "Masculine Purity and 'Gentlemen's Mischief': Sexual Exchange, Barter and Prostitution between Russian Men," *Slavic Review* 60, 2 (2001): 233–65.

the authority of village patriarchs, of the "sisters of mercy," or the Romanov dynasty itself. Schooled in an ideology of misogyny in the village, for peasant soldiers the language of the parade-ground and the barracks only codified mistrust of women. That semiofficial misogyny was mirrored "from below" in soldiers' letters, songs, and verse. Boredom, cynicism, and daily violence further corroded habitual restraints, and the plunge into revolution and then civil war would seem to have made sexual violence a ubiquitous threat, where once it had been largely confined to the front and its proximate districts. For middle- and upper-class women, the threat of sexual violation drew ever nearer and more frighteningly real, bringing to the privileged classes danger that had already been experienced by many peasant women and girls living near the frontlines. Old standards of decorum disappeared rapidly in 1917, a consequence of the collapse of the tsarist state and the social contracts (like the soldier's *paek*) that upheld it. Love was no longer a sweet emotion "in [the] breast" but a physiological stirring "lower down," and nudity was no longer gentlemen's titillation but the actual condition of nakedness born of poverty and victimization.

At the same time, there were elements of hope in the revolution in sexual culture and behavior, even if such hopes could be corrosively contradictory on each side of the gender divide. Young peasant soldiers apparently yearned to return home not to the large patriarchal household but to a wife and hearth of their own, no longer willing to be subservient sons. The Imperial Army's disintegration in 1917 is usually attributed to the pull of the share-out of land seizures in the village, but arguably land was a vehicle to broader hopes; the desire to form new households and families lay behind this pull too. Yet many peasant and worker young women and wives, having tasted varying degrees of financial and personal independence, were no longer willing to enter into or revert to traditional subordination in the marital dyad. The stage was already set for transformations in sexual and marital life before 1917, and the traditional historical attention paid to "sexual revolution" as Bolshevik policy obscures this fact.

In the war between Reds and Whites, sexuality nevertheless became a symbol that boldly illustrated how distinctive were the two contending ideologies seeking to claim Russia. The Civil War ignited cultural battles around sexuality, religion, and nation that Russians continue to fight to this day. For the Whites, Russia was a female figure crucified or ravished, and the values she evidently stood for were those of Christian Orthodoxy. The religious iconography in much White propaganda that invoked women's sexuality (crucifixion, sacrifice, exhausted and terrified Madonna and child) bound sex to nation and religion in a tight construction. The gender inversion of a woman's body nailed to the cross instead of Christ's was instantly legible as proclaiming Russia in peril.[116] The Reds too viewed their revolutionary

---

[116] Eremeeva, "Woman and Violence," 728–33; for the White cartoon of a crucified woman symbolizing Russia, see 730.

approach to sexuality as one weapon in their battle with the Orthodox Church, the one truly national symbol that the fissiparous White movements could rally around, especially once the Romanovs had been executed. By stripping the church (and eventually all religious confessions) of authority over the regulation of sexuality, the Bolsheviks brought what they hoped to be "a remorseless, strictly scientific critique" to the issue.[117] In their drive to secularize and medicalize sexuality, they dreamt of love unchained from property and from religious moralizing. If White iconography bound women's sexuality to a "natural" order underpinning religion and nation, Red rhetoric conceptualized that order as a fraud perpetrated by patriarchal religion that collaborated deviously with capital, creating "family egoism, self-regard, and isolation."[118] Yet as the Bolsheviks soon showed, their ideology was simplistic when it approached sexual questions, and with their attention usually fixed elsewhere, they were content to let fellow-traveling policy-makers in medicine and law fill in many blank spots for them. Ironically some of the landmarks of the first Soviet "sexual revolution" were responses to desperate socioeconomic conditions, and others were the brainchildren of liberal experts with, in Daniel Beer's memorable phrase, "blueprints for change."[119]

The Soviet "sexual revolution" thus had its origins before Soviet power, in the social transformations of the First World War in Russia. Whoever prevailed in 1917 would have presided over a disrupted and contentious sex/gender order. Once in power, determined to secularize sex, the Bolsheviks set up a legislative framework that pitted their vision of marriage and family against that of the church. Yet they also partially outsourced the definition and regulation of the "sexual revolution" to legal and medical experts whose gender prejudices, embedded in their scientific and social-science disciplines, did much to undermine radical socialist visions for sexuality.

---

[117] Kollontai, *Prostitutsiia i mery bor'by s nei*, 21. It would take the Bolsheviks many more years to challenge sharia rule in Muslim societies under Soviet rule; see Douglas Northrop, *Veiled Empire: Gender & Power in Stalinist Central Asia* (Ithaca, NY: Cornell University Press, 2004).

[118] Kollontai, *Prostitutsiia i mery bor'by s nei*, 22.

[119] Daniel Beer, "Blueprints for Change: The Human Sciences and the Coercive Transformation of Deviants in Russia, 1890–1930," *Osiris* 22 (2007): 26–47.

Figure 1. Patriotic Demonstration on Palace Square, 20 July 1914. Political Poster collection, Poster RU/SU 1061, Hoover Institution Archives. Courtesy of Hoover Institution Library and Archives, Stanford University.

Figure 2. Lubok of Cossack Hero Koz'ma Kriuchkov, 1914. Political Poster collection, Poster RU/SU 83, Hoover Institution Archives. Courtesy of Hoover Institution Library and Archives, Stanford University.

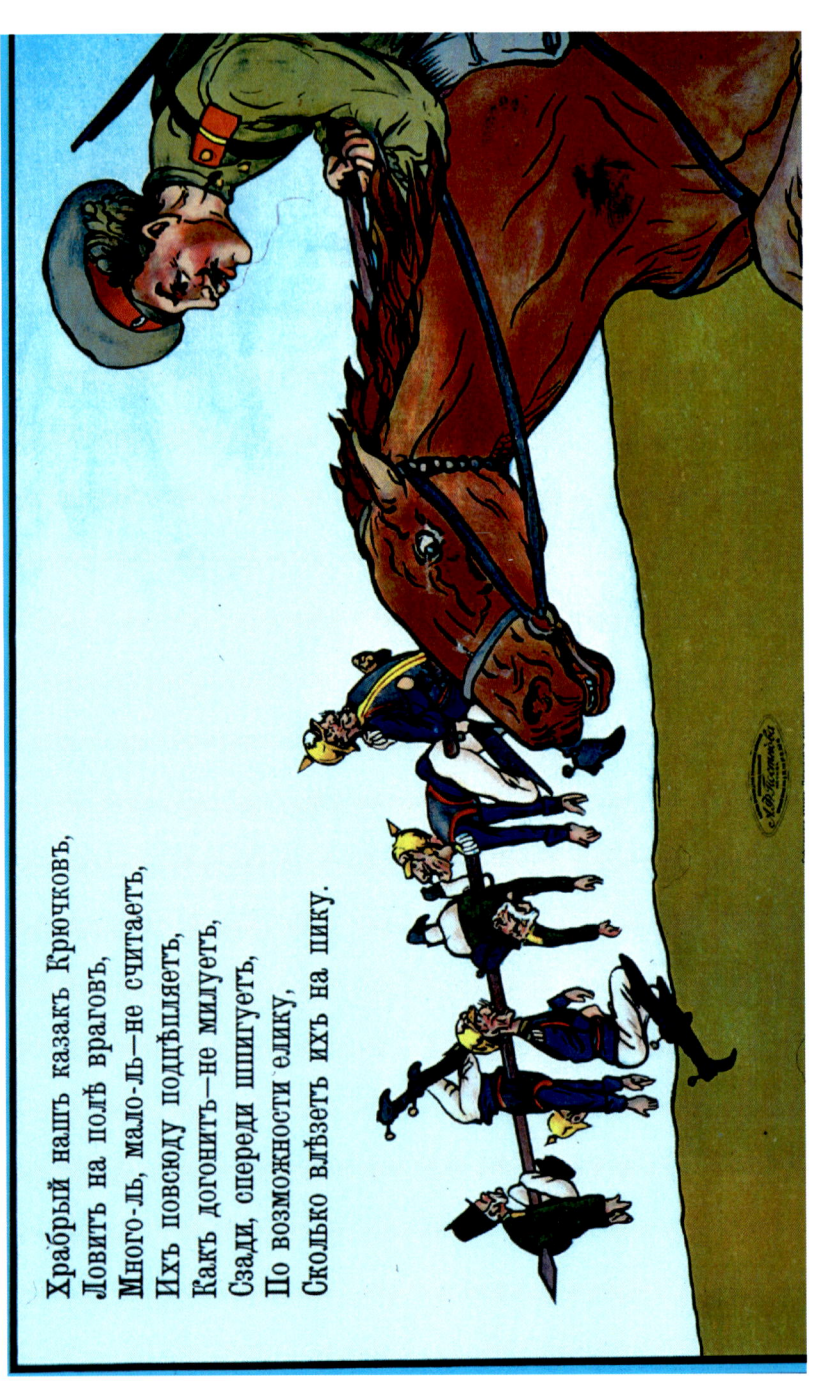

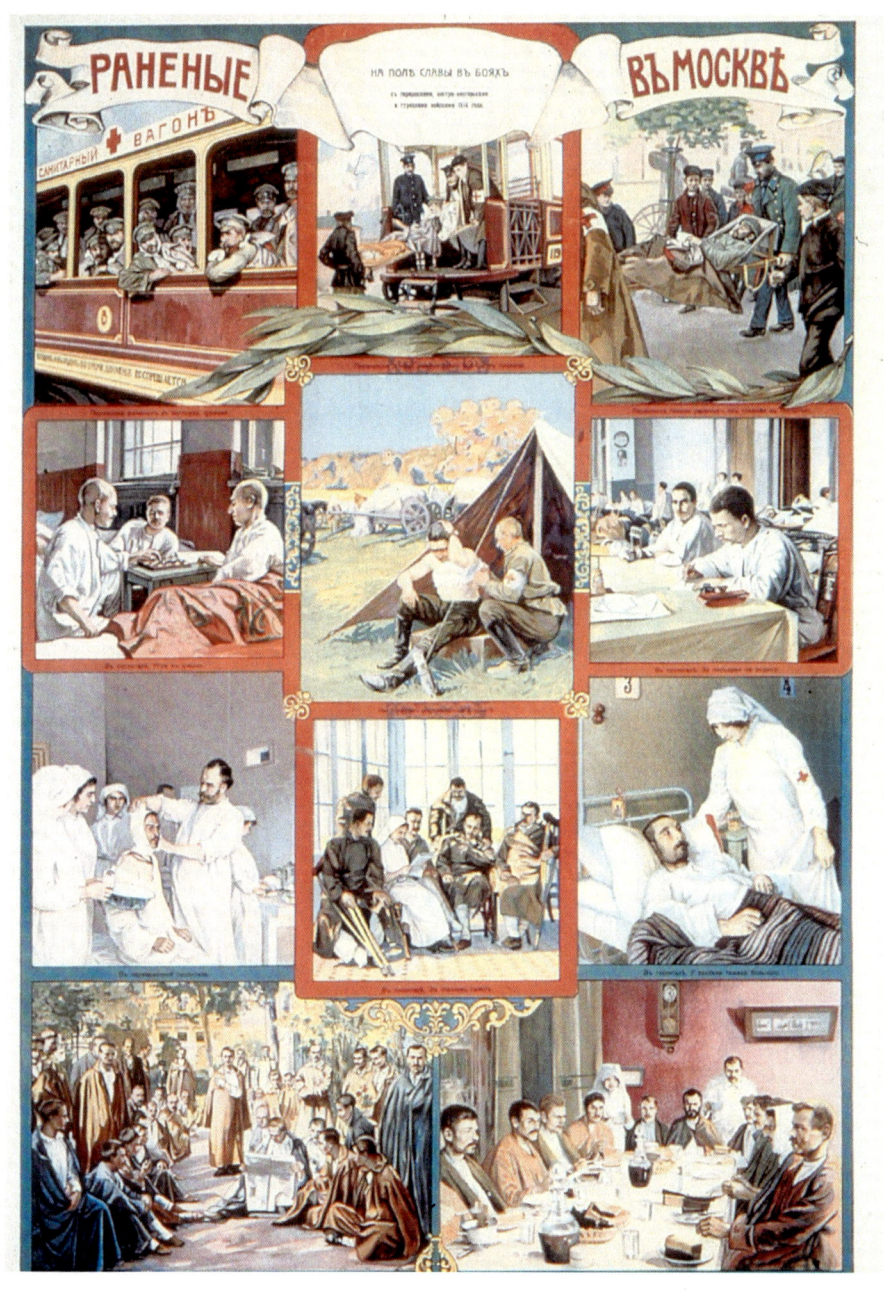

Figure 3. "The Wounded in Moscow." A 1914 poster showing the myriad ways Russians tended to the needs of wounded soldiers. Political Poster collection, Poster RU/SU 763, Hoover Institution Archives. Courtesy of Hoover Institution Library and Archives, Stanford University.

Figure 4. "The Great World War in Pictures." This 1916 poster was one of many free, war-related publications offered to subscribers of the rural newspaper *Sel´skii vestnik*. Political Poster collection, Poster RU/SU 1088, Hoover Institution Archives. Courtesy of Hoover Institution Library and Archives, Stanford University.

Figure 5. "No more discord between Brothers." This 1914 poster depicting Poles and a Russian soldier illustrates the national dimension of the narrative of "sacred union." Political Poster collection, Poster RU/SU 450, Hoover Institution Archives. Courtesy of Hoover Institution Library and Archives, Stanford University.

ЯВЛЮСЯ ЕМУ САМЪ

Figure 6. "He Himself Appears." This image speaks to the justness of Russia's war and the probability of ultimate victory, since God is on her side. Political Poster collection, Poster RU/SU 316, Hoover Institution Archives. Courtesy of Hoover Institution Library and Archives, Stanford University.

Figure 7. 1917 Liberty Loan Poster by Boris Kustodiev. Political Poster collection, Poster RU/SU 1225, Hoover Institution Archives. Courtesy of Hoover Institution Library and Archives, Stanford University.

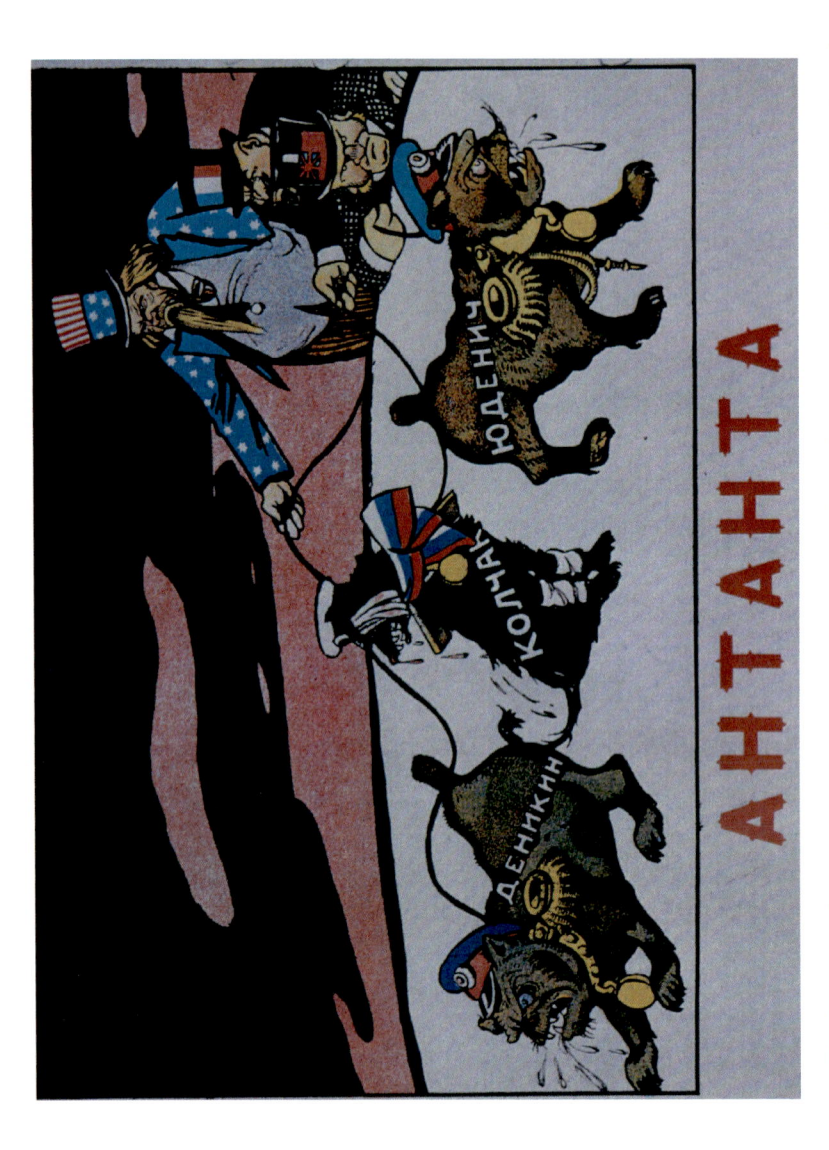

Figure 8. "The Entente." This civil war poster invokes nationalist feelings by depicting White generals as the creatures of foreign capitalists. Political Poster collection, Poster RU/SU 1257, Hoover Institution Archives. Courtesy of Hoover Institution Library and Archives, Stanford University.

Figure 9. "The Great European War. The Great Battle of the Russian Warrior (bogatyr) Russian with the German Serpent." Political Poster collection, Poster RU/SU 175, Hoover Institution Archives. Courtesy of Hoover Institution Library and Archives, Stanford University.

Figure 10. Fedor Petrovich Tolstoi, Narodnoe opolchenie. Fragment. *Medal´ony v pamiat´ voennykh sobytii 1812, 1813, 1814, 1815 gg.* (St. Petersburg, 1837).

Figure 11. Twenty-five ruble banknote (1899). http://commons.wikimedia.org/wiki/File:Russian_Empire-1899-Bill-25_rubles-Timashev-avers.jpg?uselang=ru

Figure 12. *Gore-okhotniki, Zhalo* 48 (1914): 5.

Figure 13. Kazimir Malevich, *Shel avstriets v Radzivili, da popal na bab'ivily*. From *Kazimir Malevich. Khudozhnik i teoretik: Al'bom* (Moscow: Sovetskii khudozhnik, 1990), 103.

Figure 14. Re-mi, *Vostochnyi bazar*, *Novyi satirikon*, no. 39 (1915).

Figure 15. Jahn, *Patriotic Culture* <<needs caption>>

Figure 16. *Rossiia i ee voin.* Victoria E. Bonnell, *Iconography of Power: Soviet Political Posters under Lenin and Stalin* (Berkeley: University of California Press, 1997), 89. <<needs caption>>

Figure 17. *Zaiavka evropeiskoi voiny*, *Zhalo*, no. 31 (1914): 1..

Figure 18. *Ulk*, no. 50 (1914): 1>

Figure 19. *Plody russkoi dobroty i doverchivosti*, Zhalo, no. 38 (1914): 4.

Figure 20. *Na Maslenoi, Zhalo, no. 5 (1915): 4.*

Figure 21. *Da zdravstvuet demokraticheskaia respublika i 8mi chasovoi rabochii den'. Znamia rabochikh Izhorskogo zavoda*, in Orest A. Pozdniakov, *Izhortsy: kratkii ocherk istorii Izhorskogoordena Lenina i ordena trudovogo krasnogo znameni zavoda imeni A. A. Zhdanova* (Leningrad: Lenizdat, 1960).

Figure 22. *Da zdravstvuet demokraticheskaia respublika,* in *Relikvii bor´by i truda: Katalog znamen. Gosudarstvennyi muzei Velikoi Okt´iabrskoi sotsialisticheskoi revoliutsii,* comp. P. K. Kornakov and E. F. Mudrina (Leningrad: Lenizdat, 1985), 32.

Figure 23. *Osvobozhdennaia Rossiia.* http://www.jetons.ru/jetons/s/317

Figure 24. Boris Antonovskii, *Roman Lenina i Rossii*, *Novyi satirikon*, no. 27 (1917): 16.

Figure 25. Bernard Partridge, "Betrayed," *Punch*, no. 153 (26 December 1917), http://www.gutenberg.org/files/11444/11444-h/images/399.png. ?.

Figure 26. 1000 ruble note, Don government, 1919, http://ru.wikipedia.org/wiki/Файл:Донские_деньги_-_1000_рублей._Реверс_1919_Ростов.jpg.

Figure 27. <<Marks fig. 1>>

Figure 28. <<Marks fig. 2>>

Figure 29. <<Marks fig. 3>>

Figure 30. <<Marks fig. 4>>

Figure 31. <<Marks fig. 5>>

Figure 32. <<Marks fig. 6>>

Figure 33. <<Marks fig. 7>>

Figure 34. <<Marks fig. 8>>

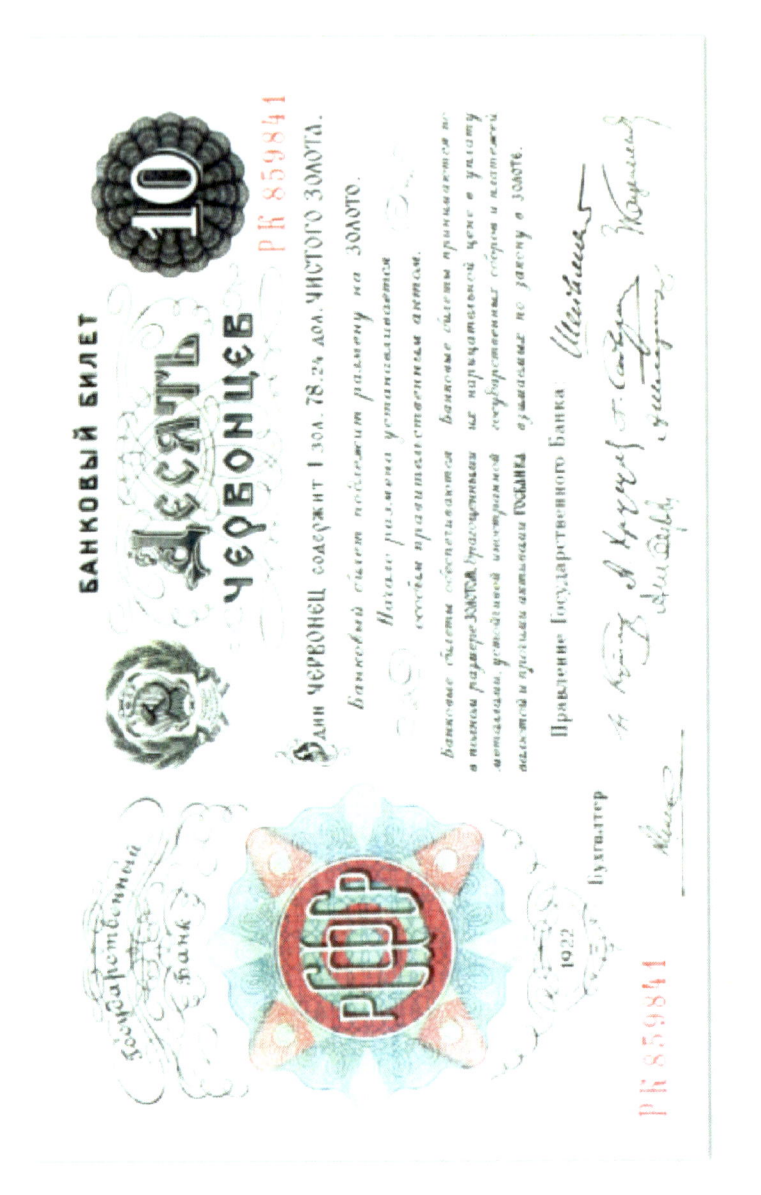

Figure 35. <<Marks fig. 9>>

Figure 36. <<Marks fig. 19>>

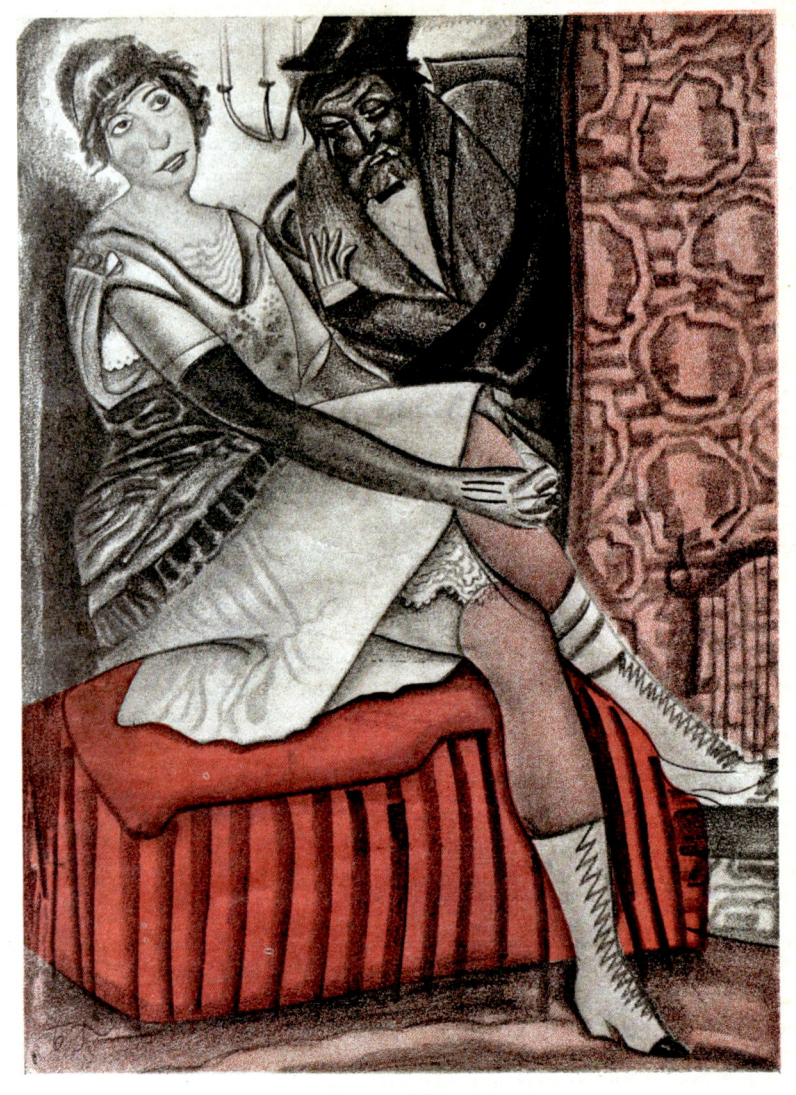

Figure 37. B. Grigor'ev, *Eia dokhody*, *Novyi Satirikon*, no. 11 (1916): 4. Author's collection.

Figure 38. A. Radakov, *Surrogat*, *Novyi Satirikon*, no. 45 (1916): 8. Author's collection.

Figure 39 (above and opposite). B. Grigor'ev, K. Grus, *U kazhdoi epokhi svoi vkusy*, *Novyi Satirikon*, no. 4 (1918): 8–9. Author's collection.

СВОИ ВКУСЫ.

Рис. Казиміра Груса.

„НЮ" нашихъ дней.

Figure 40. Re-Mi, *Mody vremen russkoi revoliutsii. (Istoricheskoe), Novyi Satirikon*, no. 13 (1918): 8. Author's collection.

Figure 41. French high fashion in 1915. The modest hat is modeled after the British Brodie helmet worn during the Great War. *Damskii mir,* no. 8 (1915): 5.

Figure 42. English wartime fashion, the Norwich coat. *Damskii mir,* no. 8 (1915): 13..

Figure 43. One of the fashions from the May 1916 fashion show sponsored by the Union of Russian Women. The designer has rather unsuccessfully placed Russian embroidered pockets and trim onto a European dress. N. Shebuev, *Modoborchestvo, Sol´ntse Rossii*, no. 328 (22) (May 1916): 13.

Figure 44. Student sketches from the May 1916 fashion show that far more effectively combine Russian and French design. N. Shebuev, *Modoborchestvo*, *Sol'ntse Rossii*, 328/22 (May 1916): 15.

Figure 45. A wartime portrait of a young couple almost certainly taken before the husband went off to the front. The woman's dark unadorned outfit reflects both wartime economic hardships and the critique of women's fashionable dress. Private collection.

Figure 46. A photograph of a tailors' congress in 1922 reveals the effects of the 1917 Revolution and Civil War on Soviet citizens' wardrobes. Private collection.

Figure 47. <<caption>>

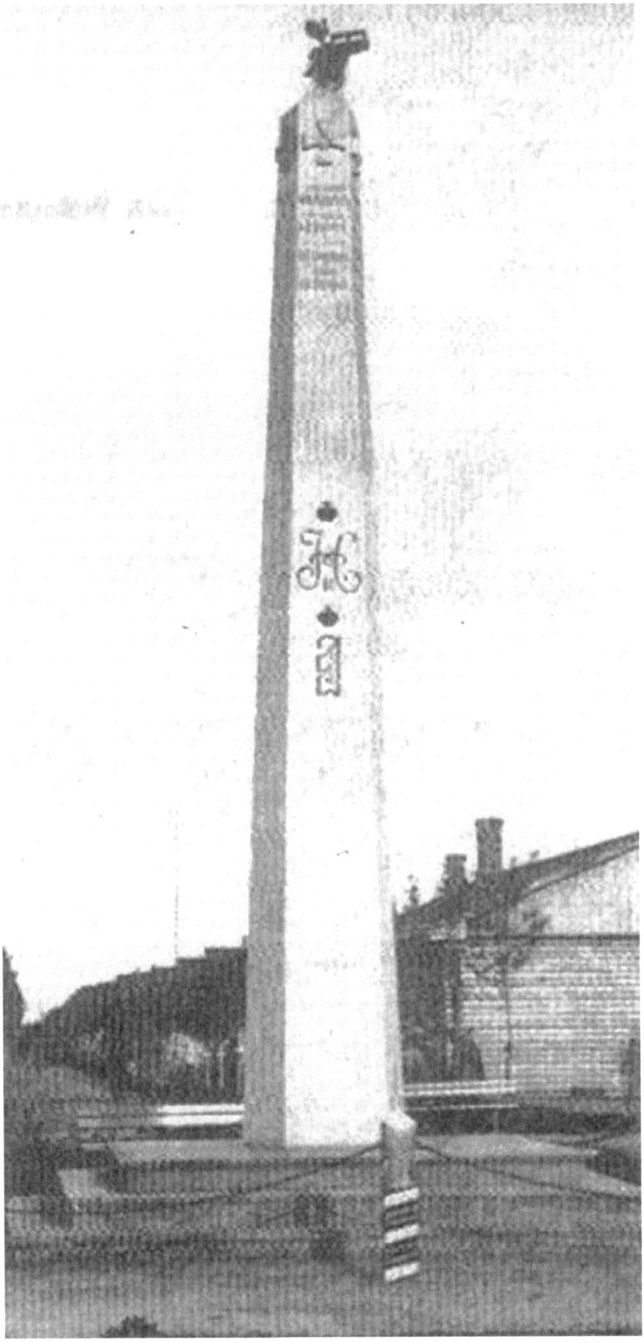

Figure 48. <<caption>>

Figure 49. <<caption?>>.

Figure 50. <<caption?>>.

Figure 51. <<caption?>>.

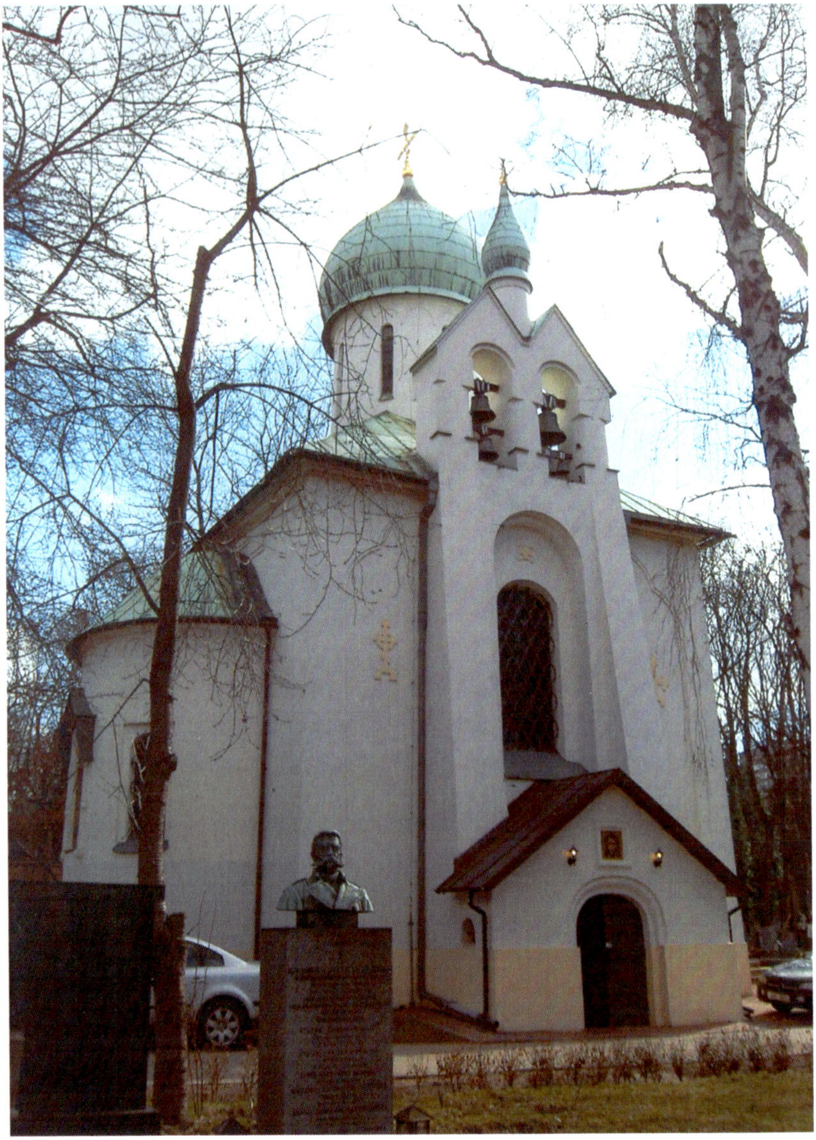

Figure 52. <<caption>>

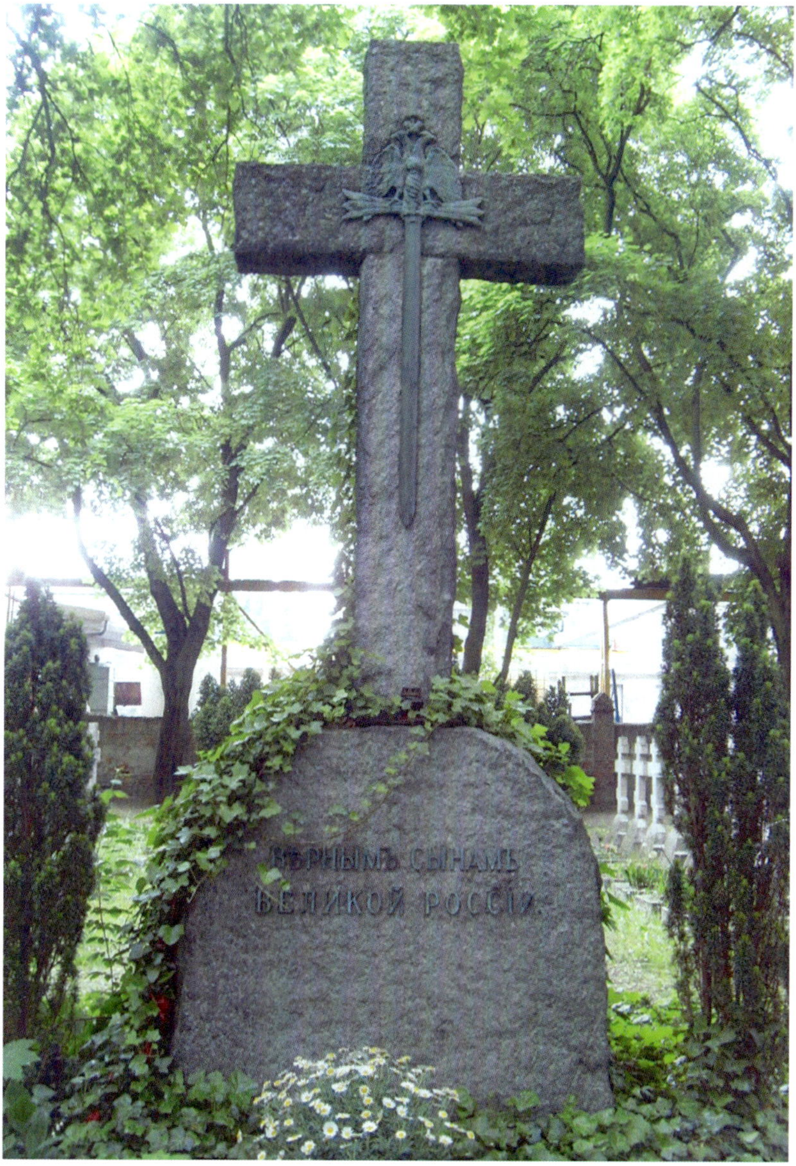

Figure 53. <<caption>>

Figure 54. <<caption>>

Figure 55. <<caption>>

Figure 56. <<caption?>>.

Fashion in Russia's War and Revolution

Christine Ruane

All societies use clothing as a social signifier. Gender, social status, and occupation are often revealed or disguised in an individual's garments. Consequently, clothing takes on critical importance during times of great social upheaval. Russia's revolutionary crisis was no exception, and yet, most fashion histories have tended to focus on the avant-garde designs of the mid-1920s while general histories ignore the subject altogether.[1] At the same time, fashion, like the other decorative arts, plays a different role in cultural production than the fine arts. People can survive without painting, sculpture, or literature, but everyone needs clothing, dishes, and furniture. It is precisely the role of the decorative arts in everyday life that allows them to serve as a locus of cultural debate. In revolutionary Russia, fashion became a flashpoint for debates about the nature of Russian identity as well as the business and consumer culture that created it. This chapter seeks to explore the complex role that clothing as a cultural image and material artifact played in Russia from 1914 to 1921.

Since the 18th century, European fashions had become the preferred clothing of the Russian court, bureaucracy, and urban society.[2] While the moneyed elites wore haute couture, other Russians donned what became known as "city clothes"—inexpensive copies of European styles—and even peasants tried to acquire these garments, if they could. These changes in Russia's sartorial landscape did not go unnoticed. Opposing fashion were two ideological enemies. One was the radical Right, which since the days of the Slavophiles had used traditional dress as a way of expressing its deep discontent with the government's Westernization program, especially its bourgeois consumer culture. The other ideological opponent was the radical Left. Long before

---

[1] Djurdja Bartlett, *Fashion East: The Spectre That Haunted Socialism* (Cambridge, MA: MIT Press, 2010); and Lidija Zaletova, Fabio Ciofi degli Atti, and Franco Panzini et al., eds., *Revolutionary Costume: Soviet Clothing and Textiles of the 1920s* (New York: Rizzoli, 1987).

[2] For more on the history of fashion, see Christine Ruane, *The Empire's New Clothes: A History of the Russian Fashion Industry, 1700–1917* (New Haven: Yale University Press, 2009).

Russian Culture in War and Revolution, 1914–22, Book 2: Political Culture, Identities, Mentalities, and Memory. Murray Frame, Boris Kolonitskii, Steven G. Marks, and Melissa K. Stockdale, eds. Bloomington, IN: Slavica Publishers, 2014, 179–97.

Thorstein Veblen had coined the phrase "conspicuous consumption,"[3] Russian populists, Marxists, and feminists had condemned luxury in dress. For them, elegant outfits worn by either sex represented the unrelenting toil and exploitation of the impoverished working classes. This ideological critique of capitalism became part of a radical asceticism that developed in Russia in the 19th century. From these two differing perspectives, each group carried out a war on fashion during World War I and the 1917 Russian Revolution.

The Attack from the Right

In the early months of 1914 Iulii L. Elets published *Epidemic Insanity: Toward the Overthrow of the Yoke of Fashion*. On the very first page, he declared:

> This book about the most burning and painful question in modern social and family life appears as a sincere howl of despair about how women disfigure themselves with ugly and absurd fashions, how they extort countless sums of money, how debauchery and disintegration are introduced into the family by constant yearnings for the newest fashionable nonsense, how colorful rags cultivate emptiness in women's minds and hearts, how many crimes are committed because of the mindless laws of fashion, and how many people perish because of them!![4]

Elets went on to argue that women's desire to attract men overpowered them. Not content with the admiration of their husbands, they sought to seduce other males as well. This led to a ceaseless search for the perfect outfit: "[Woman] spends [money] without purpose, spends it because it is in her nature, as it is a bird's nature to sing."[5] Consequently, their hapless husbands spent far more money than they had to keep female family members dressed in the latest fashions. This corruption, due to women's selfishness, led directly to the physical and moral breakdown of the Russian family.

To end fashion's tyranny, Elets proposed that all women should wear native dress. In his view, Russian clothing was modest, inexpensive, and suited to the country's climate. As a case in point, he publicized the work of the Union of Russian Women (URW), founded in 1909 as a women's auxiliary of two right-wing organizations, the Russian Assembly and the Union of the Russian People. Beginning in 1912, members of the URW had organized "evenings of our native land." At these gatherings, participants wore traditional clothing

---

[3] Thorstein Veblen, *The Theory of the Leisure Class: An Economic Study of Institutions* (London: Macmillan Company, 1899), 167–87.

[4] Iulii L. Elets, *Poval'noe bezumie: K sverzheniiu iga mod* (St. Petersburg: Tipografiia Shtaba voisk gvardii i Peterburgskogo voennogo okruga, 1914), i.

[5] Ibid., 6.

"to revitalize Russian costume."[6] Elets insisted that all Russian women should join with the URW in wearing national dress.[7]

Elets's book provoked a lively debate about fashion. On the one hand, dress reform advocates agreed with Elets that fashion played a detrimental role in women's lives, but they argued for a return to the values of the 1860s, when women were encouraged to fill their lives with civic responsibilities rather than spending money on frippery. Other commentators rejected Elets's views completely. They believed that fashion allowed women to express their individuality. In the winter and spring of 1914, Lev Bakst wrote two articles supporting this viewpoint. He insisted that those who lived in the 20th century must reject the dress of their ancestors. Instead, women should wear modern clothing that expressed their individuality in all of its complexity.[8] What was at stake in this debate was the role of women in Russian society. Were they going to cover their bodies in traditional robes and headdresses, or were they going to participate as equal members in modern Russian life? Before a definitive answer to that question could emerge, World War I began.

The outbreak of war in August 1914 presented the international fashion industry with a serious challenge. Fashion's purpose is to celebrate luxury and comfort, while wars inflict hardship and suffering. The mobilization of European armies transformed culture and society. If fashion were going to remain relevant, it needed to change with the times. By 1914 the fashion industry had developed clear strategies for adapting itself to wartime situations. Despite all the hardships that Paris experienced during the Great War, it remained the fashion capital. French designers continued to provide sketches of lovely outfits. (See fig. 41 in the gallery of illustrations following page 178.) What proved more challenging was to disseminate the designs and other fashion news to the wider world because the war was so disruptive of European economies. Thus, the problems facing the Russian fashion industry were similar to those faced by the other European nations. What made the Russian situation different was the inability of the Russian economy to provide the resources to keep the fashion industry going and the continued assault from the Russian right wing on European fashion and its industry.

---

[6] Soiuz russkikh zhenshchin, *Otchet o deiatel'nosti sostoiashchego pod Avgusteishim Ee Velichestva Gosudaryni Imperatritsy Aleksandry Fedorovny pokrovitel'stvom Soiuza russkikh zhenshchin* (St. Petersburg: Tipo-Litografiia Sankt-Peterburgskoi tiur'my, 1912), 2–3.

[7] Elets, *Poval'noe bezumie*, 301.

[8] E. Likhacheva, "Poval'noe bezumie," *Zhenskii vestnik*, no. 9 (1912): 76–79; Al. Khlebnikova, "K voprosu o *Poval'nom bezumii*—zhenskikh modakh," *Zhenskii vestnik*, no. 4 (1914): 112–13; Adov, "Bezumnoe povalie (*Otvet na knigu g. Eletsa*) (St. Petersburg: Tipografiia "A. Smolinskii," 1914); L. Bakst, "Moda," *Peterburgskaia gazeta*, 20 February 1914, 3; and Bakst, "Ob iskusstve segodniashnego dnia," *Stolitsa i usad'ba*, 20 April 1914, 18–19.

The first task that the Russian fashion industry undertook was to acknowledge the war. One magazine, *Women's Affair*, briefly renamed its bimonthly fashion column "Instead of Fashion." The author declared: "Scarcely any of our readers will be thinking about fashionable dress now when the entire country is anxiously living through events of such historic importance."[9] Having declared its solidarity with the war effort, the fashion press could then turn its attention to practical matters. The most serious issue was that Russia's enemy, Germany, stood between the Russians and Paris. To compensate for this, Russian fashion magazines ordered fashion plates from England since they could be shipped via neutral Sweden to Russia.[10] (See fig. 42.) Sketches by Russian artists and photographs also provided illustrations of the newest fashions. A quick perusal of the designs in the magazines shows changes that occurred as a result of the war—changes that emanated from Paris. After the bright colors introduced by Bakst in the previous decade, brown, gray, and black colors dominated the wartime palette. Skirts were shortened to just above the ankle to conserve fabric. To express solidarity with the soldiers, hats became smaller and imitated the different Allied helmet shapes. The overall impact of the outfits was one of subdued elegance. Advice columns recommended that everyone pay attention to their clothing, hair, and makeup even while dressing modestly and frugally. It was a way in which women could maintain their dignity and self-worth in troubled times. As a further nod to the changes that war had initiated, the magazines provided helpful tips on how to economize and information about women's wartime activities in Western Europe. As Russia's economic crisis intensified, many fashion magazines were forced to cease publication due to skyrocketing costs and a paper shortage, but those that remained took on the role of supporting women in their time of need in the hope that when the war was over they would remain loyal readers.

If the fashion magazines were able to provide designs during the war, it proved far more difficult to manufacture fashionable clothing as the economy shifted into wartime production. By the time the war was over 15 million men had served in the Imperial Army. Every serviceman needed uniforms, bedding, and boots. Infirmaries and hospitals also needed bedding, bandages, and blankets. The immediate question became: how was Russia to supply its fighting men with enough clothing so that they could be successful on the battlefield? In past wars, the Russian officer corps relied upon tailors who specialized in uniforms, while their men used the services of regimental tailors. By 1914 there were two factories that made military uniforms in Moscow, but the sheer scale of the mobilization quickly overwhelmed these manufacturers.

---

[9] Irma Laurent, "Vmesto mody," *Zhenskoe delo*, no. 15 (1 August 1914): 25. The name change lasted only two issues.

[10] N. Alovert, "Ot izdatelia," *Vestnik mody*, no. 37 (1914): 73; and "Ot redaktsii," *Modnyi kur'er*, no. 11 (1915): 119.

To meet the demand, ready-to-wear manufacturers converted their civilian operations into military workshops.

Other organizations also responded to the urgent need for military clothing. The Russian Red Cross, the Union of Towns, the Union of Zemstvos, and members of the royal family established sewing centers that distributed precut fabric and sewing instructions to home workers and then collected the finished garments. At first home workers only made shirts, underwear, and bed linen, but eventually they produced overcoats and trousers. These sewing shops made a considerable contribution to the war effort. Between August 1914 and January 1916, the 11,500 employees of the Union of Towns's workshop in Moscow produced over 12,000,000 garments, and this was only one of the many workshops scattered across the empire.[11]

World War I also brought about a significant change in the workforce in the clothing trades. As more men were called into the army, women replaced them. Beginning in the late 18th century, the Russian government and educated society had expended a great deal of effort to teach young women to sew, and now the war called upon them to perform this task for the greater glory of the motherland. In this way, wartime roles tried to reinforce traditional gender stereotypes—men fought their government's enemies while women sewed them clothes for battle—but the war also undermined gender roles by forcing women to seek work outside of the home in jobs formerly held by men. And even though women received praise for their war work, it was precisely this incorporation of women into the waged labor force that the Russian Right abhorred.

In the early months of the war, the Russian Right had another more pressing enemy that it was pursuing—German, Austrian, and Turkish businesses in Russia. What Russian entrepreneurs resented most was the business culture that foreigners introduced into Russia—their ability to produce high-quality merchandise, establish competitive pricing, and create a commercial infrastructure that emphasized the use of mail-order catalogues and advertising. These business practices meant that consumers preferred to purchase goods made by foreign firms rather than items of Russian manufacture, which had a reputation for indifferent construction and high prices.[12] Two manufacturers typified these concerns. The Austrian ready-

---

[11] Gosudarstvennyi arkhiv Rossiiskoi Federatsii (GARF) f. 6869 (Commission to Study the History of the Tailors' Union), op. 1, d. 35, l. 25; ibid., d. 34, ll. 321–22; and Paul Gronsky and Nicholas Astrov, *The War and the Russian Government* (New Haven: Yale University Press, 1929), 254.

[12] For more on this, see Ruth AmEnde Roosa, *Russian Industrialists in an Era of Revolution: The Association of Trade and Industry, 1906–1917*, ed. Thomas C. Owen (Armonk, NY: M. E. Sharpe, 1997); Thomas C. Owen, *Capitalism and Politics in Russia: A Social History of the Moscow Merchants, 1855–1905* (Cambridge: Cambridge University Press, 1981); Alfred J. Rieber, *Merchants and Entrepreneurs in Imperial Russia* (Chapel Hill: University of North Carolina Press, 1982); and Moskovskoe Kupecheskoe Obshchestvo, *Doklad*

to-wear manufacturer M. and I. Mandl' Company had established its first branch in Moscow in 1877, and in 1914 was Russia's largest producer of ready-to-wear. The arrival of the American Singer Sewing Machine Company introduced installment buying and easy credit to Russia, giving Singer a serious competitive advantage over other sewing machine producers. The entire retail experience of clothes shopping—elegant shops, fashion magazines, advertising, mail-order catalogues, and credit—had begun in foreign establishments in Russia. And, because of the industry's success in getting Russians to wear European clothing, it became an obvious target for those who would rid Russia of foreign cultural influences. Not content with condemning European fashion, they meant to destroy it.

Following the declaration of war against Germany and Austria, the radical Right and nationalist businessmen began a campaign to eliminate "German dominance" (*nemetskoe zasilie*) from Russian life. The campaign began with a boycott of German businesses, and in the spring of 1915 anti-German hostility in Moscow exploded into violence. On 26 May, women workers gathered to receive their sewing work at the distribution center of Grand Duchess Elizaveta Fedorovna. Told that there was no work that day because the center's fabrics had been sent to the Mandl' company, the women, who were mostly war widows and soldiers' wives, became deeply upset. Shouting erupted as onlookers confirmed that they had seen the fabric carted away. Before the women left, they declared that if the authorities would not rid Moscow of Germans, then they would do it themselves.[13] In an ominous sign of things to come, that night individuals broke into and destroyed the Sokolov ready-to-wear store.[14] The next day some tailors and dressmakers shut down their workshops and vanished from the city to avoid the angry mob.[15]

On the third day, patriotic demonstrations from all parts of the city converged on Red Square to pillage foreign stores. The Austrian Mandl' Company's three retail stores in central Moscow stood in the path of the raging mob. The stores were looted, business records destroyed, and the premises badly damaged. Onlookers complained bitterly about German insolence toward the Russians and how they oppressed their Russian employees.[16] The destruction

---

Kommissii po vyiasneniiu mer bor'by s germanskim i avstro-vengerskim vliianiem v oblasti torgovli i promyshlennosti (Moscow: Tipografiia A. N. Ivanova, 1915).

[13] Sergei Riabichenko, *Pogromy 1915 g.: Tri dnia iz zhizni neizvestnoi Moskvy* (Moscow: n.p., 2000), 5.

[14] *Moskovskie vedomosti*, 27 May 1915, 4.

[15] Rossiiskii gosudarstvennyi istoricheskii arkhiv (RGIA) f. 23 (Ministry of Trade and Industry), op. 28, dd. 2713, 2682, and 2802; and Eric Lohr, *Nationalizing the Russian Empire: The Campaign Against Enemy Aliens during World War I* (Cambridge, MA: Harvard University Press, 2003), 32–33.

[16] Riabichenko, *Pogromy*, 19–28.

of Mandl''s retail outlets forced the company to lay off its vast network of rural garment workers. Thousands lost their jobs in a matter of days.[17] The biggest blow to the company came with the government's seizure of its assets. On 1 June the government appointed a trustee to oversee the conversion of the company to a military workshop.[18] With the collapse of the Mandl' company, it was much more difficult for Russians to find ready-to-wear.

The Moscow pogrom marked the beginning of the Russian government's liquidation of businesses belonging to enemy aliens. Because wartime legislation specified that any company with even one enemy alien board member was subject to liquidation, this gave the government the power to interfere in the affairs of any firm located in the Russian Empire. One company that fell victim to this campaign was the Russian subsidiary of the American Singer Sewing Machine Company.

In 1915 articles began appearing in the Russian press claiming that Singer was a German business. The right-wing newspaper *Russkoe znamia* claimed that every employee was either German or German Jewish. Supposedly headquartered in Hamburg, Singer had established a "monopolistic exploitation of our consumers." Newspapers claimed that Singer sold German machines instead of American ones at exorbitant prices. "Singer agents travel primarily among the rural and working-class populations of the Empire, promising them wonders and selling machines on credit." When individuals fell behind, these same agents came back with the bailiff.[19] Over the course of the winter and into the spring, these false accusations continued to circulate.[20]

Meanwhile, the Russian military high command found the time to conduct its own investigation into the company and its business culture. They uncovered a number of disgruntled employees who claimed that Singer agents collected "military data."[21] Without any attempt to corroborate these accusations, the military high command (*stavka*), which had supreme authority over all aspects of life along Russia's western frontier, ordered local

---

[17] GARF f. 6869, op. 1, d. 60, l. 58; and RGIA f. 23, op. 28, d. 1312 (Government Supervision of Commercial Enterprises), l. 43.

[18] "Likvidatsiia T./D. M. i I. Mandl'," *Utro Rossii*, 28 May 1915, 4; and "Iskliuchenie L. Mandlia iz tsekha," *Utro Rossii*, 2 June 1915, 4.

[19] RGIA f. 23, op. 28, d. 805, l. 117 and l. 47. The Singer folders contain articles from *Novoe vremia*, *Za Rossiiu*, and other newspapers. For more on the image of the spider web in Russia, see Orlando Figes and Boris Kolonitskii, *Interpreting the Russian Revolution: The Languages and Symbols of 1917* (New Haven: Yale University Press, 1999), 169–71.

[20] Robert Bruce Davies, *Peacefully Working to Conquer the World: Singer Sewing Machines in Foreign Markets, 1854–1920* (New York: Arno Press, 1976), 284; and RGIA f. 23, op. 28, d. 805, l. 43.

[21] Ibid., l. 204.

government officials to begin shutting down Singer stores.[22] On 3 April, the company was placed under government inspection at the insistence of the military authorities.[23]

The company was now in deep crisis. On 8 August Singer representatives met with leaders of the Union of Zemstvos and Towns to try to save their company. After reviewing all of the evidence, the union leaders declared the charges against the company to be false. They sent a copy of their findings to the military authorities, recommending that Singer be allowed to resume normal operations.[24] On 18 September the Council of Ministers ruled that the military commanders could decide the fate of the stores in those areas near the front, but Singer should be allowed to reopen those retail outlets outside of the battle zones.[25] This decision only confirmed what was already the status quo and continued the company's precipitous decline. Provincial inspectors wrote to government officials that Singer's business practices baffled them.[26] The result was that it became much more difficult to purchase a sewing machine, at a time when demand had never been higher.

The liquidation of "German" firms had a disastrous effect. Prices for basic goods skyrocketed, and certain items became harder to find—textile shortages were of particular concern. There were also shortages of thread, buttons, and needles. In 1915 one government report warned: "The retail trade is beginning to feel the effects of the three months' decrease in output. The stock intended for the towns and for the peasant population will shortly be exhausted, and the warehouses are no longer overcrowded with goods as they used to be. In consequence of heavy demands from the Army Supply Department there is hardly any stock on hand." With 70 to 80 percent of cloth going to the army, there was very little for the civilian market.[27]

To try and stabilize the economy as the war dragged on, the Russian government enacted a series of price controls in the summer of 1915, but this simply led to speculation and profiteering. An amorphous social category, speculators, who had made handsome profits from government contracts and graft, flaunted their ill-gotten wealth by spending it lavishly on clothing, meals, and entertainment. Meanwhile, the rest of Russia struggled to put

---

[22] Ibid., ll. 37–38.

[23] Ibid., ll. 44 and 165.

[24] Ibid., ll. 164–72. For a discussion of company policies and secrecy about its operations, see Davies, *Peacefully Working*, 280–84.

[25] RGIA f. 23, op. 28, d. 805, ll. 251–53ob.

[26] Ibid., d. 806, ll. 26–27ob. and 42–42ob.

[27] Quoted in S. O. Zagorsky, *State Control of Industry in Russia during the War* (New Haven: Yale University Press, 1928), 61; and Michael Florinsky, *The End of the Russian Empire* (New York: Collier, 1971), 48.

food on the table. Never before had conspicuous consumption seemed more monstrous than it did in 1915 and 1916.

In the spring of 1916, Aleksandr A. Bublikov, a member of the Fourth Duma and future minister of transportation for the Provisional Government, proposed legislation to ban the importation of luxury goods. The list of goods was long. Women's and children's clothing was banned, but not men's wear. Since fashion was a female preoccupation, it made sense that women should be punished for their extravagant outfits in a time of war and hardship. The ban would begin on 1 June 1916 and remain in effect for three years.[28] Supporters of the proposed ban argued that it was "a 'wartime' measure directed against the extensive and intolerable expenditures on luxury goods by a certain part of the public at a difficult time in the survival of the motherland."[29] Consequently, fashionable women increasingly became scapegoats in the campaign to punish speculators. Even soldiers' wives were attacked for supposedly spending their government stipend on attractive clothing.[30]

As the Duma was considering the proposed ban, a fashion show organized by the Union of Russian Women took place in Petrograd's Palace Theater on 14 May 1916. The URW, in keeping with their goal of maintaining "the beauty of the national spirit," had sponsored a contest among the students at the Imperial Society for the Encouragement of the Arts to see who could draw the most attractive Russian fashions, offering a 500-ruble prize. The results of the contest were on view in the halls of the theater that night.[31] To further the celebration of Russian dress, artists collaborated to create a series of tableaux. The first was entitled "In a Dressmaker's Workshop," in which some of Russia's leading ballerinas appeared in various gowns and hats.[32]

Such an extravagant production immediately captured the attention of the press. A *Petersburgskaia gazeta* reporter protested, "Is now the time to create an entire spectacle devoted to women's fashionable dress and hats? Everywhere there is talk about the battle against luxury and the high cost-of-living." Another commentator, N. Shebuev, grumbled, "We thought we were going to see Russian beauties in costumes prepared by Russian dressmakers from sketches by Russian artists using Russian fabrics, taking care not to spend

---

[28] RGIA f. 32 (Council of the Congresses of Representatives of Trade and Industry), op. 1, d. 586, ll. 1–8; and *Stenograficheskie otchety*, no. 1 (4 May 1916): 1–8.

[29] V. G., "Zapreshchenie vvoza predmetov roskoshi," *Promyshlennost' i torgovlia*, no. 13 (26 March 1916): 375–76.

[30] Emily Pyle, "Village Social Relations and the Reception of Soldiers' Family Aid Policies in Russia, 1912–1921" (Ph.D. diss., University of Chicago, 1997), 218–25.

[31] N. Shebuev, "Modoborchestvo," *Solntse Rossii*, no. 329/23 (May 1916): 13–14.

[32] "Vecher mod," *Peterburgskaia gazeta*, 15 May 1916, 9.

large sums during wartime." Instead, the outfits on display cost between 250 rubles and 2,000 rubles.[33]

The journalists also attacked the design of the clothes. One journalist complained that the ugliest fashions of the entire show appeared in the Russian fashion portion of the program. The chief criticism of these garments was that Russian folk elements were too obviously grafted onto French fashions. (See fig. 43.) As Shebuev put it, despite the wartime alliance between France and Russia, French fashion did not harmonize well with folk costume. Nikolai Alovert, the publisher of Russia's leading fashion magazines, concurred, pointing out that "A sarafan, since it does not vary, will always be a sarafan," and could not be successfully combined with anything but other Russian folk elements.[34]

The one outfit that was declared a success was a Bakst dress.[35] Bakst had consistently integrated Russian concepts of beauty, line, and color with those of Parisian high fashion. Because his designs had revolutionized haute couture, Russian women had no need to parade around in folk costume as the URW advocated. Instead they could wear French fashion knowing that it reflected Russian sensibilities. The student sketches that lined the walls of the Palace Theater confirmed this—the designs gracefully integrated the Russian spirit with French fashion. (See fig. 44.)

If a consensus had been reached about what style of clothing Russian women should wear, nevertheless, Shebuev's article merged the prewar critique of fashion with the discourse about speculators and conspicuous consumption. He insisted that the war years were a time of "insane" bodily extravagance. The shortages of dress patterns and fabrics encouraged some Russian women to obsess about fashionable clothing to an unhealthy degree. He condemned fashionistas for wearing frippery when others of their sex wore mourning or nurses' uniforms, outfits that symbolized wartime sacrifice and patriotism. Women pursued fashion until they "lost consciousness." Dressmakers in Russia took advantage of their gullible clients and encouraged them to dress extravagantly. Meanwhile, the dressmakers pocketed the money.[36] Thus, Shebuev revived Elets's critique of fashion and blamed women for falling into the hands of those dreadful war profiteers, dressmakers, and their ugly business culture. The only way to stop these ruthless craftswomen and restore female modesty was to join the fight against speculation. (See fig. 45.)

While journalists were busy attacking fashion, the Council of Ministers set up a special subcommittee to study the ramifications of Bublikov's ban. One member of the subcommittee believed that the purpose of the war was

---

[33] Ibid.; Shebuev, "Modoborchestvo," 14.

[34] N. A., "Russkaia zhenskaia odezhda," *Modnyi kur'er*, no. 17 (1 August 1916): 265.

[35] Shebuev, "Modoborchestvo," 13.

[36] Ibid., 12–15.

to rid Russia of all foreigners.[37] Although the ban specifically violated prewar trade agreements, committee members saw it as an opportunity to create a favorable balance of trade with Western Europe by decreasing foreign imports and providing greater protection of certain Russian industries, particularly as Russia transitioned from a war to a peacetime economy.[38] The Council of Ministers approved the ban on 13 September 1916.[39]

The ban on imported luxury goods was the final salvo in the Russian right wing's war on fashion and its business and consumer culture. During World War I, government officials and a significant number of Russian industrialists worked to realize their goal of economic autarky, and the fashion industry became one of their victims. Egged on by the right-wing press and various sectors of the Russian business community, the government shut down or crippled thousands of clothing manufacturers. And while the ban on luxury goods presumably denied elite women and war profiteers the high fashions that they craved, the loss of ready-to-wear and sewing machines meant that "city clothes"—the unpretentious, ordinary garments that Russians wore to work and at home—were difficult to find.

The 1917 Revolution and Its Dress Code

The fashion industry faced a new assault in the winter of 1917—this time from the radical Left. The discourse on war profiteers and their elegantly dressed female companions was now merged with the antifashion views of the various socialist parties and quickly transformed itself into a virulent campaign against the bourgeoisie and the aristocracy as part of a larger redefinition of all social markers that occurred between 1917 and 1921. The clothing of the victors now symbolized the ardor and spirit of the triumphant revolutionaries while that of their opponents was condemned. At the same time, because clothing production came to an almost complete standstill during those years, the process of redefining the dress code in revolutionary Russia was fraught with difficulties.

The groups that brought down both the tsarist regime and the Provisional Government were the workers, soldiers, and sailors of Petrograd.[40] Consequently, it was their clothing that symbolized the new revolutionary spirit,

---

[37] Boris E. Nolde, *Russia in the Economic War* (New Haven: Yale University Press, 1928), 158–59.

[38] RGIA f. 32, op. 1, d. 586, ll. 9–29.

[39] See "Khronika—V Sovete ministrov," *Torgovo-promyshlennaia gazeta*, 14 September 1916, 2; and "Ob ogranichenii vvoza v Rossiiu predmetov roskoshi," *Sobranie uzakonenii i rasporiazhenii pravitel′stva izdavaemoe pri pravitel′stvuiushchem Senate*, no. 298 (28 October 1916), otd. 1, 2358.

[40] B. I. Kolonitskii, *Simvoly vlasti i bor′ba za vlast′: K izucheniiu politicheskoi kul′tury rossiiskoi revoliutsii 1917 goda* (St. Petersburg: Dmitrii Bulanin, 2001).

replacing the three-piece suits and civilian uniforms of the old order. Working-class men usually combined elements of peasant dress with inexpensive copies of European clothing. Peaked caps, peasant shirts, and pants worn with some kind of European-styled jacket or coat constituted everyday dress for male workers.[41] After October 1917, many, if not all, Bolshevik officials made this style of dress into an unofficial uniform. Leather jackets were often substituted for woolen ones. Many Bolshevik officials and Red Guards carried revolvers or rifles to complete their new "look." This combination of firearms and clothing helped to create a style of dress suitable for the tough, hyper-masculine image that the Bolsheviks wanted to project.

It is important to stress that the new Bolshevik dress code for men was a case of making a virtue out of necessity. The simple fact was that with clothing production virtually shut down, supporters of the new regime wore what clothing they had. Since so many men had recently served in the military, it meant that they incorporated elements of military dress with their civilian clothing, combining pieces from the different styles of dress as needed, just as workers had done previously. Rather than wear European jackets, the men could wear military greatcoats, to give one example. More than anything else, it was the widespread adoption of the firearm as the essential accessory to these worker/military outfits that quickly helped to militarize men's dress. While they took enormous pride in the tough, masculine authority that these outfits gave them, the civilian population felt fear and terror of this new ruling class.

Their comrades in the army also refashioned a new image for themselves. At the height of the February Revolution the Petrograd Soviet issued a series of decrees that were intended to democratize the Russian armed services through the elimination of titles and insignia.[42] Although these decrees did not discuss military dress explicitly, soldiers quickly abandoned the proper care of their uniforms. A Red Cross nurse described the crowds of soldiers found in Petrograd in April 1917:

> The streets are revolting—full of soldiers that have deserted the front and are supposedly on their way home.... They look horrible. They've let their hair grow, and wear it hanging over their foreheads in long, dirty, unkempt locks—they're unshaven, unwashed, and their clothes are the most slovenly things I've ever seen. They seem to glory in their appearance and do everything they can not to look like the soldier of the "old regime." With their caps set at a jaunty angle way back on their heads, their coats unbuttoned and soiled, the insolent expression

---

[41] Ia. N. Rivosh, *Vremia i veshchi: Ocherki po istorii material'noi kul'tury v Rossii nachala XX veka* (Moscow: Iskusstvo, 1990), 125–35.

[42] L. E. Shepelev, *Tituly, mundiry, ordena v Rossiiskoi imperii* (Leningrad: Nauka, 1991), 215–16.

on their faces, their loud coarse shouts and the eternal spitting of sunflower seeds, they present a sorry spectacle.[43]

Russian soldiers saw no reason to continue to follow the rules of an army and a government that no longer existed, and one way to show their contempt for the old regime was to defy the uniform regulations and create a new martial image for themselves.

When the Bolsheviks came to power, they commissioned designs for a new army uniform, but nothing came of this until the outbreak of the Civil War in May 1918. At that point, the Bolshevik forces needed new clothing to distinguish them from the Whites who continued to wear the old tsarist uniforms. At the same time, Red Army commanders hoped that a new uniform would help forge a more disciplined military force. In December 1918 the Revolutionary Military Council issued a khaki helmet with a red star, modeled after medieval Russian headgear, and a greatcoat with red trim and modest insignia. A few months later, new designs for shirts and shoes were announced as well as a redesigned greatcoat. Despite these efforts, many soldiers did not receive the garments because there was not enough fabric.[44] They continued to wear their old clothing and whatever else they could find, which sometimes meant stealing clothing and boots.[45] Nevertheless, Red soldiers projected a powerful, masculine image that together with that of workers was celebrated in Bolshevik propaganda. The two groups stood ready to defend the Bolshevik Revolution against all enemies.

If male workers and soldiers saw themselves as revolutionary heroes, what about their female counterparts? Working-class women's dress covered the spectrum from handmade traditional peasant outfits to ready-to-wear dresses, skirts, and blouses. What they wore depended on how long they had lived in urban or factory settings. While the inexpensive nature of these garments usually indicated the proletarian status of the wearers, working women often tried to incorporate stylish touches into their best outfits. This simple, utilitarian dress which had become commonplace during World War I as more women joined the workforce, now became the dress code for women in revolutionary Russia. Women could wear garments similar to those worn

---

[43] Irina Skariatina, *A World Can End* (New York: Jonathan Cape & Harrison Smith, 1931), 143–44.

[44] Tatiana Strizhenova, *Soviet Costume and Textiles, 1917–1945* (Paris: Flammarion, 1991), 27–30; and Mark von Hagen, *Soldiers in the Proletarian Dictatorship: The Red Army and the Soviet Socialist State, 1917–1930* (Ithaca, NY: Cornell University Press, 1990), 54.

[45] Iurii Vladimirovich Got'e, *Time of Troubles: The Diary of Iurii Vladimirovich Got'e*, trans. and ed. Terence Emmons (Princeton, NJ: Princeton University Press, 1988), 179; and Donald J. Raleigh, ed., *A Russian Civil War Diary: Alexis Babine in Saratov, 1917–1922* (Durham, NC: Duke University Press, 1988), 65.

in Western Europe, but all traces of elegance and luxury had to be removed for women to demonstrate their loyalty to the new regime.

Despite these attempts to create a new dress code for women, working women's dress was not endowed with the same heroic qualities as that of their male counterparts. As Victoria Bonnell has shown, Bolshevik propaganda rarely depicted women as revolutionaries, and when it did, it showed them in a subordinate position to their men folk.[46] It was men who had made the revolution with women serving as their helpmates. It was this gendered hierarchy of power that the Bolsheviks wanted to maintain in their new political iconography and in their dress codes for daily life.

At the same time that the Bolsheviks were creating appropriate dress for men and women in the new revolutionary state, they attacked the clothing of their enemies. If the radical Right had condemned fashion as a kind of foreign illness whose cure lay in elite women's adoption of Russian traditional dress, the radical Left declared that any elegance or luxury in dress was counter-revolutionary because it represented the exploitation of the working class by fashion's capitalist business culture. The beauty of fashionable clothes stood in sharp contrast to the awful working conditions that produced them.

The attacks on class enemies and their clothing took many forms. The historian Iurii Got′e confided to his diary that a fellow passenger on a trolley cursed him for wearing a bowler a few weeks before the October Revolution. In the fall of 1918, he mounted a "fur-coat cavalry" because the new regime initially refused to allow him to get the family's fur coats out of storage. It took six weeks of endless trips and arguments before Got′e was successful in retrieving the coats.[47] But rather quickly, more coercive measures were used to deprive former members of the aristocracy, merchantry, and professional classes of their property. Bolshevik officials and Red Guards conducted raids against "enemies of the people" in which household items and clothing were confiscated. In Saratov, a group of Red Army soldiers sent to break up a drunken brawl at a dance used the opportunity to steal clothing from the cloakroom.[48] Emma Cochran Ponafidine, the wife of a tsarist diplomat and landowner, recorded such a raid in her memoir. While searching through the family's possessions, an official found and put on her son's last civilian suit. Her son was dumbfounded as he walked home and realized that this man was wearing his clothes.[49] In Petrograd, a new form of hooliganism emerged as robbers forced pedestrians to hand over *all* of their clothing and make

---

[46] Victoria E. Bonnell, *Iconography of Power: Soviet Political Posters under Lenin and Stalin* (Berkeley: University of California Press, 1997), 65–79.

[47] Got′e, *Time of Troubles*, 64, 190, 198, and 203.

[48] Raleigh, *A Russian Civil War Diary*, 51.

[49] Emma Cochran Ponafidine, *Russia—My Home: An Intimate Record of Personal Experiences Before, During and After the Bolshevist Revolution* (Indianapolis: The Bobbs-Merrill Company, 1931), 180.

their way home naked on cold, snowy nights. If they protested, they were shot.[50] This close association between fashionable clothing and class enemies inevitably led to cases of mistaken identity. In March 1918, a Red Army soldier mistakenly killed a Bolshevik official in Saratov because he was wearing a fashionable suit. He mistook him for a class enemy rather than a comrade just because of what he was wearing.[51]

In this environment it was especially difficult for those classified as enemies to know what to wear. Since virtually no clothing was being produced, it was difficult to purchase garments of any kind, which meant that repairing old clothes was the only viable option. As Emma Ponafidine reported, "[D]ry-goods, soap, kerosene and the thousand and one little things without which the civilized woman is supposed not to be able to exist, were not to be had. How often has the want of a button, a needle, or a spool of thread faced us!"[52] Aleksei V. Babin wanted to donate a pair of underwear to a museum because by 1921 it was just a collection of patches.[53] Everyone did the best they could to mend their garments with whatever fabric and thread they could find and by making shoes out of carpets.[54] Individuals reported that they sometimes did not recognize friends or acquaintances in the street due to their shabby appearance.[55] Most hoped that their shabby appearance would protect them from arrest, which it sometimes did, but just as often, it served as a pretext for arrest.[56] Mariia Avinova observed in her memoir, "People would be picked up in the streets and whisked away without an arrest warrant, and without even knowing what crime they were charged with. Many were guilty merely of having a 'bourgeois' appearance; and what constituted such an appearance to Bolshevik eyes was undefinable. Anyone who didn't make rude noises in public was liable to be seized as a suspect."[57] Thus, all of the markers

---

[50] Skariatina, *A World Can End*, 223; and Raleigh, *A Russian Civil War Diary*, 210–11. American Relief Administration workers worried constantly about the theft of their clothing, especially trousers. Bertrand Patenaude, *The Big Show in Bololand: The American Relief Expedition to Soviet Russia in the Famine of 1921* (Stanford, CA: Stanford University Press, 2002), 250–53.

[51] Raleigh, *A Russian Civil War Diary*, 71.

[52] Ponafidine, *Russia—My Home*, 99.

[53] Raleigh, *A Russian Civil War Diary*, 182.

[54] E. M. Almedingen, *Tomorrow Will Come* (New York: Holt, Rinehart and Winston, 1968), 211–13; and Paul Chavchavadze, *Marie Avinov: Pilgrimage Through Hell* (Englewood Cliffs, NJ: Prentice Hall, 1968), 117–18.

[55] Raleigh, *A Russian Civil War Diary*, 153.

[56] Florence Farmborough, *With the Armies of the Tsar: A Nurse at the Russian Front, 1914–1918* (New York: Stein and Day, 1975), 374.

[57] Chavchavadze, *Marie Avinov*, 62.

of class and respectability—dress, even if it was old and worn, diction, and public behavior—could serve as a pretext for arrest. The only clothing that was reported to save lives was the nurse's uniform. Nurses who came from the upper and middle ranks of society reported that they felt "safe" in their uniforms and often wore them when they needed to protect themselves from the authorities and the Red Guards.[58]

This campaign against stylish dress also had some unintended consequences. By 1918 the Russian economy had virtually shut down, and prices were extremely high for the few goods that were for sale. To make matters worse, there were numerous different currencies in use during the Civil War, which complicated any retail transaction and very quickly led to the development of a barter economy. The final blow for Russian consumers was the ban on private trading in November 1918.[59] The paradoxical result was that old regime clothing became even more valuable in the chaos of the Civil War and War Communism. Confiscated garments were recycled among the victors of the Revolution. Destitute members of the old aristocracy and middle classes sold their clothes for food. Got'e reported one such transaction in 1919: "The whole morning was occupied with exchange: a felt jacket for potatoes, shoes for butter; we sold a lady's cloak for money and with the money bought flour."[60] Even though private trade was illegal, former aristocrats would stand on the street or gather at the marketplaces to surreptitiously sell their wares despite the constant danger from raids by the Red Guards.[61] Individuals who received clothing in these transactions could give it to family members, sell it to someone else, or use it to bribe officials. In an ironic twist, "bourgeois" dress during the Revolution and Civil War was worth more than it had been in tsarist times, serving as a kind of currency that all classes could use in different ways to keep themselves fed and clothed.

By 1920 clothing shortages affected the victors and the losers. Got'e mentioned mandatory clothing drives for the poor and the army, which further depleted the wardrobes of Moscow residents. Joseph Ponafidine told his mother that while he was in the nearest town on business, he happened upon some commotion in the street. A Red Army soldier had been captured and accused of stealing a suit from a local commissar. The accused was made to sign his own arrest warrant. At that point, a Bolshevik quickly stepped up and shot him in the back of the head right there on the street.[62] More gruesomely,

---

[58] Farmborough, *With the Armies of the Tsar*, 338–39, 345; Chavchavadze, *Marie Avinov*, 48–49; and Skariatina, *A World Can End*, passim.

[59] Julie Hessler, *A Social History of Soviet Trade* (Princeton, NJ: Princeton University Press, 2004), 25–26.

[60] Got'e, *Time of Troubles*, 307.

[61] Almedingen, *Tomorrow Will Come*, 111–12.

[62] Ponafidine, *Russia—My Home*, 110.

class enemies who had been executed and victims of the famine in the Lower Volga were buried naked, their clothing removed and redistributed.[63] No piece of clothing was too old or too ragged to be thrown away.

The situation was so dire that something had to be done. The Soviet government responded in several ways. Within the newly reorganized textile industry, new design institutes were set up under the supervision of Nadezhda P. Lamanova, a prerevolutionary fashion designer. The purpose of these institutes was to train a new generation of designers. However, none of the proposed designs could be made until there was more fabric.[64]

With few options available, the end result was the refashioning of "bourgeois" clothing on proletarian bodies. While Bolshevik propaganda continued to celebrate the martial images of soldiers and workers, Lenin and his top government officials continued to wear the bourgeois business suit and tie. Photographs taken of Bolshevik leaders from 1917 to 1921 show most of them wearing a suit or a military uniform. The wives of many members of the new Bolshevik government hired dressmakers to alter confiscated clothing to fit them or to create new confections from fabrics expropriated from the former elites.[65] Without any new designs, the reality was that the new governing elite and professionals had no other choice but to democratize bourgeois dress. In February 1921, Got'e noted in his diary:

> A dole has been issued by the soviet authorities to those who received the academic ration according to the list of March 1920. It consists of a jacket, three changes of shirts and underwear, six pairs of socks, and a pair of shoes and galoshes… The jacket they gave us was the kind that used to cost 25 or 30 rubles. It was strange to collect all of this in a store where I used to shop for the highest-quality goods. And it was all given free of charge![66]

By distributing garments that had been defined as counterrevolutionary, the Soviet government tacitly acknowledged that the war on bourgeois clothing was over. The business suit became an integral part of the male dress code in the Soviet Union, and modest, toned-down versions of European fashions were the expectation for women. The reasons for this are not hard to find. The new Bolshevik leaders and their female companions wanted to project a modern, urbane appearance for themselves and the regime they represented, so they chose to rehabilitate men's business suits and modest attire for women

---

[63] Pitirim A. Sorokin, *Leaves from a Russian Diary and Thirty Years After* (Boston: The Beacon Press, 1950), 204 and 269; Chavchavadze, *Marie Avinov*, 80; and Patenaude, *Big Show*, 323–27.

[64] Strizhenova, *Soviet Textiles*, 33–54.

[65] Almedingen, *Tomorrow Will Come*, 119.

[66] Got'e, *Time of Troubles*, 403.

as another expression of proletarian identity, thereby legitimating their new government in the eyes of the world. Meanwhile, at home these garments provided a social distance between the new urban class and the peasantry.

It was only with the announcement of the New Economic Policy in March 1921 that the clothing situation began to improve. Private trading was legalized again, allowing tailors and dressmakers to reopen their shops.[67] The end of the Civil War meant that the demand for military uniforms declined, so that there was a bit more fabric for use for civilian clothing. Finally, news of the latest fashion trends began to circulate as the fashion press was allowed to resume publication. It was now time to add color and comfort to ordinary life after almost a decade of unimaginable hardship.[68]

The results of the war on fashion were devastating and far-reaching for the fashion industry. All three regimes—tsarist, provisional, and Soviet—privileged the clothing needs of the military over the civilian population. Shops large and small converted to wartime production, and the army requisitioned such vast quantities of fabric, buttons, and thread that there was little left over for consumers. In addition to this, the campaign against enemy aliens resulted in the deportation of many of the fashion industry's leading businessmen and eventually led to the demise of foreign companies such as the Singer Sewing Machine Company. For Russian nationalists, the Moscow pogrom and the ban on luxury goods served as a Russian declaration of independence from fashion's cosmopolitan thrall. As the industry staggered under the weight of these blows, the new Soviet regime finished off what remained with its economic policies. With no current fashion magazines to provide information about the latest styles, no fabric to make the garments, or shops to sell clothing, the prerevolutionary industry and its business culture were dead.

The concept of fashion had a more complicated fate. Fashion, the idea of continually changing clothing styles, had been under attack long before World War I began. The radical Right condemned those who wore fashionable clothing as foreigners in their native land. The only way to rectify this intolerable situation was for Russian women, whose job it apparently was to preserve ethnic identity, to abandon French fashions in favor of Muscovite clothing while men were free to continue to wear European clothing with no compromise to their sense of Russianness. This sartorial shift in women's attire would presage the return of traditional cultural values. Meanwhile, the radical Left attacked fashion for its luxuriousness as well as its labor and business practices. Consequently, there was a rare moment of agreement between Russia's warring political factions that fashion must be eliminated, but what Russians would wear remained dependent upon the outcome of the political

---

[67] Some dressmakers had made clothing from confiscated fabrics for the wives of the Bolsheviks during the Civil War, but these retail transactions were illegal. See Almedingen, *Tomorrow Will Come*, 119.

[68] Strizhenova, *Soviet Textiles*, 33–54. For more on dress in the 1920s, see Bartlett, *Fashion East*, 13–62.

struggle for power. Once the Bolsheviks emerged victorious, they declared that working-class dress would become the standard for men's and women's dress in the new Soviet regime and led a vicious attack against fashion and its consumers. But, at the same time, Bolshevik leaders' reluctance to give up their suits and ties meant a gradual rehabilitation of men's fashionable dress. The bourgeois suit was symbolically proletarianized and democratized. In order to be seen as a modern representative of the first socialist state, men were expected to dress like their counterparts in the West—business suits, military uniforms, and clothing appropriate to their work had a place in Soviet men's wardrobes, while peasant dress was increasingly defined as backward and inappropriate.

Women's wear had a much harder time creating a legitimate alternative because it had been so closely associated with fashion. In the new Soviet state, luxury and impracticality were to be eliminated from women's clothing. Nevertheless, clothing styles continued within the rubric of European design vocabulary and followed Parisian trends in terms of the overall look of the clothing. In eliminating fashion's excesses, the government wanted to ensure that Soviet women would be seen as modern representatives of the democratic and proletarian future. In stripping fashion of its playfulness and excesses, however, the clothing lost much of its appeal. In the end, Soviet women's wear became modest and utilitarian copies of Western styles, but without the glamour and luxury of "real" fashion. (See fig. 46.)

Thus, the war on fashion played a key role in Russia's revolutionary upheaval. What began as a right-wing attack on women's greed, obsession with their looks, and supposed abandonment of traditional Russian values became a powerful weapon that the Bolsheviks used against their foes. The lower classes literally stripped their enemies of their clothing, forcing them to suffer the disrespect and sartorial discrimination that the lower classes had endured for years. At the same time, the war on fashion also reveals dimensions of a gender war that was taking place as well. One of the international fashion industry's greatest successes was the intertwining of physical appearance and clothing with modern femininity. And while fashionable dress was a feature of men's lives as well, modern men were supposed to focus on more important pursuits than the search for a perfect outfit. Consequently, women's supposed sartorial extravagance during wartime made them a scapegoat for Russia's economic collapse during the Great War. And while both sexes suffered equally during the clothing famine of 1917–21, it was the creation of the new Bolshevik dress codes that reveals the deep ambivalence that Bolshevik men had for their female comrades. At the same moment that women were gaining new rights and obligations as citizens, an intensive campaign to limit what they should wear was also underway. In the end, even though the Bolsheviks claimed to have liberated women from their enslavement to the cosmopolitan fashion industry, they simply replaced one form of dictatorship with another.

Thinking the Nation through Times of Trial: Russian Philosophy in War and Revolution

Christopher A. Stroop

In 1924, Fr. Sergius (Sergei) Bulgakov (1871–1944) observed that "the problem of a religious society is a typically Russian problem." He was right. An emerging leader in émigré Russian and ecumenical religious organizations, Bulgakov himself had given a great deal of thought to the problem, particularly after 1905. From that time, Bulgakov, like many other exponents of Russian idealism (or neo-idealism, as it is sometimes called), had become an opponent of revolutionary "cosmopolitanism" and a proponent of a religious society— but not just any society that defined itself as Christian. Unwilling to become a priest under the repressive conditions of the old regime, in which the state heavily interfered in church affairs, Bulgakov was ordained only in 1918.[1]

The concern with a religious society that Bulgakov identified in Russian thought penetrated well beyond the strand of Christian philosophy he represented—a strand that was nevertheless prominent and influential in Russia's Silver Age (c. 1890–1920) of cultural efflorescence, and that remained so in the Russian emigration. The problem is arguably inherent to Marxism-Leninism, which Bulgakov and other opponents of the Bolsheviks cast as an ersatz religion of this-worldly eschatology—a fruitful line of thinking that has been pursued and debated in later scholarship. And in the early 1920s the Bolsheviks still tolerated, however uneasily, a "God-Building" strain of

---

I would like to thank Shimshon Ayzenberg and the participants in the 2012 Stanford European History Workshop for their comments on earlier versions of this article. I would especially like to thank George L. Kline for his very detailed attention to multiple drafts and his immensely helpful suggestions for improvement. In addition, I thank the editors and the anonymous reviewers, who have also made this piece substantially better than it otherwise would have been.

[1] Sergius Bulgakov, "The Old and the New: A Study in Russian Religion," *The Slavonic Review* 2, 6 (1924): 509. S. N. Bulgakov, "Moe rukopolozhenie (24 goda)," in S. N. Bulgakov, *Avtobiograficheskie zametki. Dnevniki. Stat'i* (Orel: Izd-vo Orlovskoi gosudarstvennoi teleradioveshchatel'noi kompanii, 1998), 69.

Russian Culture in War and Revolution, 1914–22, Book 2: Political Culture, Identities, Mentalities, and Memory. Murray Frame, Boris Kolonitskii, Steven G. Marks, and Melissa K. Stockdale, eds. Bloomington, IN: Slavica Publishers, 2014, 199–220.

Marxism that sought to make the socialist project explicitly into a religion of humanity.[2]

Meanwhile, many of late imperial Russia's leading philosophers and public intellectuals had spent the years between the revolution of 1905–07 and the final Bolshevik triumph in the Russian Civil War becoming increasingly reticent toward revolution and urgently trying to cultivate a religious Russian national identity as the basis for unity and future development. The experience of living with and through this failed idealist social project is the tragic human story this article attempts to convey as it examines Russian philosophy in war and revolution. For many Russian idealists, including Bulgakov, this story ends with expulsion from the nascent Soviet Union in a handful of deportations that have come to be referred to collectively as "the Philosophers' Steamboat."[3]

To be sure, a handful of Russian idealists embraced revolution, and others of necessity reconciled themselves to it, temporarily or permanently. And so, for some, the story ends in the Soviet Union, where it generally does not end well. The intellectuals featured here were selected for their prominent presence in late imperial Russian civil society, and/or for their ability to illustrate the kinds of trajectories followed by Russian philosophers through some of the most turbulent events to take place in the most violent century in human history. In most cases they were closely associated with Russia's professional philosophical establishment, and their responses to war and revolution took place against a backdrop of the ascendancy of metaphysics in academic, as well as popular, Russian philosophy.[4]

Twentieth-century Russian idealism is closely associated with three paradigmatic symposia: *Problems of Idealism* (*Problemy idealizma*, 1902), edited by the legal philosopher Pavel Novgorodtsev (1866–1924); *Landmarks: A Collection of Articles about the Russian Intelligentsia* (*Vekhi: Sbornik statei o russkoi intelligentsii*, 1909), edited by the philosopher, public intellectual, and innovative literary critic Mikhail Gershenzon (1869–1925); and *Out of the Depths: A Collection of Articles on the Russian Revolution* (*Iz glubiny: Sbornik statei o russkoi*

---

[2] On God-Building, see Richard Stites, *Revolutionary Dreams: Utopian Vision and Experimental Life in the Russian Revolution* (New York: Oxford University Press, 1989), 101–05. For a typical Russian idealist treatment of Marxism as an ersatz religion, see S. N. Bulgakov, "Geroizm i podvizhnichestvo (Iz razmyshlenii o religioznoi prirode russkoi intelligentsii)," in *Vekhi: Sbornik statei o russkoi intelligentsii*, 2nd ed. (Frankfurt am Main: Posev, 1967), reprinted from *Vekhi: Sbornik statei o russkoi intelligentsii*, 2nd ed. (Moscow, 1909), 27–29.

[3] Stuart Finkel, *On the Ideological Front: The Russian Intelligentsia and the Making of the Soviet Public Sphere* (New Haven: Yale University Press, 2007), 8–10.

[4] Those seeking a more technical approach to the philosophy of the period should consult G. M. Hamburg and Randall A. Poole, eds., *A History of Russian Philosophy, 1830–1930: Faith, Reason, and the Defense of Human Dignity* (New York: Cambridge University Press, 2010).

revoliutsii, 1918), edited by the leading national liberal intellectual Petr Struve (1877–1944). These well-known symposia belonged to a broader genre of ideological anthology that was widespread in late imperial Russia, but these three intimately connected volumes, and especially *Landmarks*, have received more scholarly attention than most.[5] This article draws on *Landmarks* and *Out of the Depths*, but its analysis, based upon a much broader source base, takes into account the institutional, social, and intellectual contexts of Russian idealists. It is the first piece of scholarship in English to treat a wide variety of philosophical responses to the First World War and the revolutions of 1917 synthetically, identifying the war—often neglected in British and American scholarship—as an important episode in the story of Silver Age idealists and their unrealized social vision.

Russian historiography has been more apt to take philosophical responses to the war seriously. One scholar, for example, has argued that the beginning of the war is an episode "demanding special consideration," and that the early war years represent "a milestone in the history of the Russian cultural renaissance"—particularly with respect to intense thinking on the historical significance of nations in general and of the Russian nation in particular.[6] This view has much to recommend it, although it may exaggerate the uniqueness of Russian wartime thought. In addition, it is necessary to observe that what might be termed the "national turn" in Russian idealism, which was closely associated with Bulgakov's "problem of a religious society," had deeper roots. In the immediate context, the intellectual foundation for idealist responses to war was laid in the disappointing aftermath of the revolution of 1905–07, and idealist war commentary should be read in this light.

It was at this moment that leading Russian idealists came to advocate national renewal through the conversion of the Russian intelligentsia from "positivism" and cosmopolitanism to national and religious ways of thinking, prominently in *Landmarks*. Identifying with the intelligentsia as internal critics, Russian idealists pinned their hopes for national renewal and positive

---

[5] M. A. Kolerov, *Industriia idei: Russkie obshchestvenno-politicheskie i religiozno-filosofskie sborniki 1887–1947* (Moscow: OGI, 2000). On *Problems of Idealism*, see the thorough introduction to Randall A. Poole, trans., *Problems of Idealism: Essays in Russian Social Philosophy* (New Haven: Yale University Press, 2003). On the significance of *Landmarks*, see Christopher Read, *Religion, Revolution and the Russian Intelligentsia, 1900–1912: The Vekhi Debate and Its Intellectual Background* (London: Macmillan, 1979). On *Out of the Depths*, see William F. Woehrlin, "Introduction: Voices from *Out of the Depths*," in *Out of the Depths (De Profundis): A Collection of Articles on the Russian Revolution*, ed. and trans. William F. Woehrlin (Irvine, CA: Charles Schlacks, Jr., 1986), xvii–xxxiii, esp. xviii–xix, xxvii.

[6] V. V. Noskov, "'Voina, v kotoruiu my verim': Nachalo Pervoi mirovoi voiny v vospriiatii dukhovnoi elity Rossii," in *Rossiia i Pervaia mirovaia voina (materialy mezhdunarodnogo nauchnogo kollokviuma)*, ed. N. N. Smirnov (St. Petersburg: Dmitrii Bulanin, 1999), 326.

social transformation on the intelligentsia's ability to change. The Russian people, in their view, needed a national and religious, rather than "nihilistic," intelligentsia, one that would no longer be tragically alienated from the people.[7] This already existing tendency shaped Russian philosophical responses to the Great War as well as responses to the revolutions of 1917 and the Russian Civil War.

For most Russian idealists, the Great War represented a moment of optimism in which they believed their attempt to foster a unified, patriotic Russian national identity was being realized, and that this transformed Russia would come to play a leading role in the postwar international community. Their writings between the February and October Revolutions, which cannot be thoroughly assessed here, exhibit varying degrees of cautious optimism and an increasing foreboding that the revolutionary process might culminate with the Bolsheviks coming to power. Indeed, as one scholar has observed, the sense that the war was becoming a revolution can be observed among some of Russia's educated elite as early as 1915.[8] It is very clear, in retrospect, that by 1918 Russian idealists had lost the battle for hearts and minds, and that this loss was facilitated by Russia's failed effort in the war. But the idealists continued to preach national consciousness during the Civil War, a time when, according to one contributor to *Out of the Depths*, the words "national rebirth of Russia" were "on everyone's lips." They generally believed, as many observers did at the time, that Bolshevik power could not last long. The Bolsheviks' "service," as Aleksandr S. Izgoev (born Aron S. Lande, 1872–1935) ironically remarked, was to demonstrate to Russia and the world that the selfishness, arbitrariness, and disharmony prevailing in 1918 were the inevitable result of socialism. Izgoev gave two reasons for this conclusion: socialist ideology's internationalism was an empty utopian pipe dream, and its materialism and atheism led to ethical cynicism. On this point, he quoted Dostoevskii's famous characterization of nihilism: "If there is no God, then everything is permitted."[9]

To be sure, there were various interpretations of the idealist social alternative. For religious philosophers like Bulgakov and Prince Evgenii Trubetskoi (1863–1920), the idealist project had a clear confessional coloring, although it

---

[7] On Russian idealists as internal critics of the intelligentsia, see Woehrlin, *Out of the Depths*, xviii–xix, xxvii. For a typical prewar example of this argument, see N. A. Berdiaev, "K voprosu ob intelligentsii i natsii," in N. A. Berdiaev, *Dukhovnyi krizis intelligentsii* (Moscow: Kanon+, 2009), 135. Reprint from N. A. Berdiaev, *Dukhovnyi krizis intelligentsii: Stat'i po obshchestvennoi i religioznoi psikhologii (1907–09 g.)* (St. Petersburg: Obshchestvennaia pol'za, 1910).

[8] N. N. Smirnov, "Voina i rossiiskaia intelligentsiia," in *Rossiia i Pervaia mirovaia voina*, 265–66.

[9] S. A. Kotliarevskii, "Ozdorovlenie," in *Iz glubiny: Sbornik statei o russkoi revoliutsii* (Moscow: Russkaia mysl', 1918), 175. A. S. Izgoev, "O zaslugakh bol'shevikov," *Russkaia mysl'* 39, 1–2 (1918): 60–61.

entailed support for the liberal freedoms of conscience, speech, and the press. For others, such as Novgorodtsev and Struve, the project represented a less confessional attempt at the construction of a unifying civil religion, but one that was clearly meant to be grounded in a genuine shared faith in a higher power.[10] Among Russian idealists there were both Christians and Jews. The latter included prominent Jewish converts to Christianity such as Semen Frank (1877–1950) and Izgoev, whose pseudonym is derived from the Old Russian word *izgoi*, a legal category for *déclassé* persons in medieval Rus' whose loss of social status brought them under the protection of the church. There were also assimilated Jews, such as Gershenzon, who did not convert, which meant foregoing the possibility of university teaching.[11]

Juxtaposing a broadly religious national identity with godless revolutionary "cosmopolitanism," Russian idealists were overwhelmingly anti-Bolshevik and often came to define themselves as anti-socialist and/or anti-Communist. Even so, many readily countenanced left-wing economic policies. Bulgakov, a social justice Christian, refused to dissociate himself from the Russian progressive tradition even in the conservative Russian émigré atmosphere of the 1930s.[12] The general tendency within Russian idealism, especially after 1905, was to find that the values espoused by socialists were not supportable on the basis of what the idealists took to be socialism's positivist and utilitarian premises—that only a religious worldview could support these values. The bulk of the Russian intelligentsia refused to consider this message, and thus, in writing about the messengers, one cannot escape the feeling that one is writing about "doomed people, for they embodied a doomed milieu." The liberal theorist Sergei Kotliarevskii (1873–1939) wrote these words in *Out of the Depths*. He applied them to an older generation of the Russian intelligentsia, doomed by Russia's history of serfdom to an unhealthy "populist" mentality.[13] But he might well have been writing about his own generation of Russia's finest philosophical minds. Many of them contributed essays to *Out of the Depths*, which was printed but blocked from distribution, surviving in only

---

[10] For a study contrasting more and less confessional idealist visions by focusing on Bulgakov and Novgorodtsev, see George Putnam, *Russian Alternatives to Marxism: Christian Socialism and Idealistic Liberalism in Twentieth-Century Russia* (Knoxville: The University of Tennessee Press, 1977).

[11] On Frank's conversion, see Philip Boobbyer, *S. L. Frank: The Life and Work of a Russian Philosopher, 1877–1950* (Athens: Ohio University Press, 1995), 72–81. On Gershenzon's identity, see Brian Horowitz, "A Jewish-Christian Rift in Twentieth-Century Russian Philosophy: N. A. Berdiaev and M. O. Gershenzon," *Russian Review* 53, 4 (1994): 506 n. 27; and Horowitz, *The Myth of A. S. Pushkin in Russia's Silver Age: M. O. Gershenzon, Pushkinist*, Studies in Russian Literature and Theory (Evanston, IL: Northwestern University Press, 1996), 10–12.

[12] S. N. Bulgakov, "Moe bezbozhie," in Bulgakov, *Avtobiograficheskie zametki*, 28.

[13] Kotliarevskii, "Ozdorovlenie," in *Iz glubiny*, 170.

a handful of copies.[14] Although Russian idealism would develop in exile and eventually be resurrected in Russia, from 1918 to 1922 the Bolsheviks took measures that led to its effective suppression in Russia for decades.

The Mentality of the Doomed

Russian idealists put forth their turn to the nation and to religion as a reaction against nihilism, broadly defined. A leading scholar of Russian philosophy has characterized the imperial Russian intelligentsia's nihilism as primarily "instrumental nihilism," remarking that instrumental nihilists "do not say, 'Everything is permitted' (Dostoevskii's *vse dozvoleno*) but rather, 'Everything is permitted which serves the new order.'" But the early 20th-century Russian idealists, who frequently quoted precisely these words of Dostoevskii, blurred the line between varieties of nihilism, finding any distinction among types of nihilist worldviews ultimately inconsequential.[15] Philosophically, this move is related to what a prominent historian of Russian thought describes as a "return to the ontological reality of Kant's concept of the noumenal," which distinguished Russian idealism from contemporary German Neo-Kantianism.[16] For Kant, the noumenal referred to the spiritual reality that his philosophical system posited but left essentially unknowable. To 20th-century Russian idealists, this inaccessibility was unacceptable, as they believed that ethics could only be grounded in real, absolute values that were accessible to the human mind.

To understand how Russian idealists reached this conclusion, it is necessary to realize that they accepted the premise in the Kantian paradox that the empirical must be regarded as given and therefore determined. If empirical phenomena comprised the only knowable reality, even when it came to human experience, then humans would be reduced to animals, to unfree biological actors mechanically responding to stimuli. The inevitable result would be the elevation of material self-interest above all. Therefore nihilism—which Russian idealists identified with positivism and Neo-Kantianism in an abstract sense, as well as concretely with Russian socialism and with modern German thought and militarism—represented a grave threat to culture, morals, and society, and to the nation as the organic repository of cultural values.

---

[14] Woehrlin, *Out of the Depths*, xxiii–xxiv.

[15] George L. Kline, "The Varieties of Instrumental Nihilism" in *New Essays in Phenomenology: Studies in the Philosophy of Experience*, ed. James M. Edie (Chicago: Quadrangle Books, 1969), 177. For examples, see E. N. Trubetskoi, "Razvenchanie natsionalizma: Otkrytoe pis′mo P. B. Struve," *Russkaia mysl′* 37, 4 (1916): 85–86; N. A. Berdiaev, "Dukhi russkoi revoliutsii," in *Iz glubiny*, 50, 61; and I. A. Il′in, "Osnovnoe nravstvennoe protivorechie voiny," *Voprosy filosofii i psikhologii* 25, 5 (1914): 804.

[16] Randall A. Poole, "The Neo-Idealist Reception of Kant in the Moscow Psychological Society," *Journal of the History of Ideas* 60, 2 (1999): 323.

Applying this understanding of ethics to the lives of nations as well as to the lives of individuals, Russian idealists argued that a national actor would also inevitably raise its material self-interest to the level of an absolute value unless constrained by an absolute ethical principle higher than the nation-state itself.

Russian idealists' association of nihilism not only with the revolutionary intelligentsia, but also with German thought, can be observed in *Landmarks*. For example, the contribution of the religious philosopher Nikolai Berdiaev (1874–1948) demonstrates how the idealists' desire for a new, salvific national worldview is tied to the rejection of nihilism and to what one scholar identifies as the "anti-German feelings (often submerged in a generalized resentment of the West)" that were prevalent in Russian philosophers' war commentary.[17] Berdiaev's piece attacked the intelligentsia for rejecting absolute truth (*istina*) in favor of utilitarian criteria for determining truth (*pravda*). Declaring the advent of a period of "reevaluation of the old ideologies," Berdiaev argued that the way forward lay in developing the religious-philosophical direction of Vladimir Solov'ev (1853–1900), a major influence on younger Russian idealists. While Neo-Kantian thought had served as a "bridge to higher forms of philosophical consciousness" for Russians, a Russia "called to create in the sphere of religious philosophy" could not found a national philosophical tradition "around [Hermann] Cohen, [Wilhelm] Windelband or any other German, alien to the Russian soul."[18]

This dual association of nihilism with both the Russian intelligentsia and German thought was put succinctly by another Russian idealist in *Out of the Depths*. Contrasting "medieval religious culture" with "modern irreligious culture," he remarked, "The most logical expression of the latter in the spiritual sphere is the Russian intelligentsia ethos and attitude, and, in the material sphere, German militarism."[19] For Russian idealists, nihilism was, thus, at the root of the evils of both war and revolution. The solution they proffered to redress these evils—after 1905, during the First World War, and in response to the October Revolution—was the cultivation of a unified national identity grounded in absolute truth and values.

---

[17] Richard Stites, "Days and Nights in Wartime Russia: Cultural Life, 1914–1917," in *European Culture in the Great War: The Arts, Entertainment, and Propaganda, 1914–1918*, ed. Aviel Roshwald and Stites (Cambridge: Cambridge University Press, 1999), 16–17.

[18] Berdiaev, "Filosofskaia istina i intelligentskaia pravda," in *Vekhi*, 1, 15, 17, 19n.

[19] V. N. Murav'ev, "Rev plemeni," in *Iz glubiny*, 192, 197.

Interpreting the Great War in a Changing Institutional Landscape

In 1915, Berdiaev wrote, "The world war has sharply posed the question of Russian national self-consciousness."[20] Indeed it had, along with other questions about the role of nations in the postwar world, the place of nationalities within the Russian Empire, and the place of the Russian state in the postwar world. When the war broke out, even Russian journals and organizations devoted to academic philosophy felt compelled to address these issues, while Russian philosophers used existing institutions and created new institutions in order to address the concerns provoked by the war.

The Moscow Psychological Society was late imperial Russia's premier professional philosophical organization. Membership in the prestigious body, which had been chaired by Lev Lopatin (1855–1920) since 1900, was secured by nomination and a vote of the current members. A neo-Leibnizian speculative philosopher, Lopatin had begun co-editing the society's journal, *Questions of Philosophy and Psychology* (*Voprosy filosofii i psikhologii*), in 1894, becoming its sole editor in chief in 1905. The doyen of academic philosophy in the waning years of the old regime, Lopatin had taught numerous younger elite philosophers.[21] Unlike many of his protégés, Lopatin was hardly a public intellectual. Articles in *Questions of Philosophy and Psychology* often referenced current events, but the journal did not normally print articles dedicated solely to such commentary. Interestingly, it made an exception for the outbreak of war—the revolutions of 1917 received no such official nod—with a brief piece by Kotliarevskii.

"We are living through a great break [*velikii perelom*]," wrote Kotliarevskii, continuing:

> and not only in that sphere in which the war is directly occurring. New relations between states and nations are being created, new foundations are being laid down for the organization of these states, new paths for the development of these nations, but aside from all that the spiritual atmosphere in which humanity has lived, and to which it has been accustomed, is changing.[22]

---

[20] N. A. Berdiaev, *Dusha Rossii* (Leningrad: Skaz, 1990), 3. Reprinted from *Dusha Rossii: Voina i kul'tura* (Moscow: I. D. Sytin, 1915).

[21] On the Moscow Psychological Society, see Poole, "The Neo-Idealist Reception of Kant," and also Poole, trans., *Problems of Idealism*, 3–6. On Lopatin, see also James P. Scanlan, "Russian Panpsychism: Kozlov, Lopatin, Losskii," in *A History of Russian Philosophy*, 156–61. A prewar festschrift goes some way toward demonstrating the admiration Lopatin commanded: *Filosofskii sbornik L'vu Mikhailovichu Lopatinu k tridtsatiletiiu nauchno-pedagogicheskoi deiatel'nosti. Ot Moskovskogo Psikhologicheskogo Obshchestva (1881–1911)* (Moscow: Kushnerev, 1912).

[22] S. A. Kotliarevskii, "Voina," *Voprosy filosofii i psikhologii* 25, 4 (1914): i.

Russian idealists, by and large, heralded the war as ushering in the spiritual change they had already been advocating. This perceived transformation was regarded as civilizational or universal, but it was to be realized through nations. In Kotliarevskii's assessment, the war was "not only a trial of the material might of nations," but also of their "cultural principles." On this front, Russian intellectuals initially derived confidence from their sense that the Great War was proving to be a "national war," a war Russian soldiers would have the will to win, in a way that the Russo-Japanese War had not been.[23]

But Russian intellectuals also recognized the unprecedented horror of the conflagration. In Kotliarevskii's view, the realities of the war rendered "monstrous ... these praises of war that were sung in the latest literature, primarily, though not exclusively, German." While one could neither condemn all of German culture nor hold other national cultures guiltless, modern German culture exhibited especially strong tendencies toward the "perversion of ... moral sensibility." The result was the spread of "the principle of absolute self-affirmation," both with respect to individuals and to states (Hegel being culpable in the latter). Kotliarevskii spoke out against the absolutization of any particular interest—individual, national, religious, state, social class. Such interests had their place, but they must all be subordinated to "principles of justice" and to "the recognition of human dignity."[24]

Kotliarevskii accepted nationality as an especially powerful positive historical force. While he believed that the war heralded a "reevaluation" of European cultural principles and a "renewal of European culture" that would be grounded in "a new religious-moral understanding and experience," he expected the state to remain "the organizing power" and "the bearer of great material and spiritual tasks." Nationality was to be understood as "the reflection and embodiment of the universally human." After the February Revolution of 1917, Frank made a similar point while praising the patriotic war commentary of his sometime ideological nemesis, Vladimir Ern (1882–1917), who had died of chronic illness at the age of 34. "The path to general human brotherhood," Frank wrote, "proceeds not through the rejection, but through the strengthening of national cultures." Nationality as the means of realizing the universally human was a common trope at this time; in the Russian intellectual context, it can be traced immediately back to Solov'ev,

---

[23] Kotliarevskii, "Voina," iii. For Russian philosophers contrasting the Great War with the Russo-Japanese War, see N. A. Berdiaev, "Voina i vozrozhdenie," *Utro Rossii*, 17 August 1914; I. A. Il'in, *Dukhovnyi smysl voiny: Voina i kul'tura* (Moscow: I. D. Sytin, 1915), 35–36; and E. N. Trubetskoi, *Voina i mirovaia zadacha Rossii: Voina i kul'tura* (Moscow: I. D. Sytin, 1915), 3–6. These comparisons were part of a wider discourse. See William C. Fuller, Jr., *Strategy and Power in Russia: 1600–1914* (New York: The Free Press, 1992), 408–09.

[24] Kotliarevskii, "Voina," iv–vi.

who distinguished the positive historical force of nationality (*narodnost'*) from the unethical ideology of nationalism (*natsionalizm*).[25]

Early in the war, Russian idealists frequently expressed the belief that the war was bringing about imperial unity and transforming Russian national consciousness along the lines they had called for in *Landmarks*, but their wartime commentary and activism also belies an undercurrent of fear that this could be wishful thinking. One can observe this tension in Ivan A. Il'in (1883–1954), a young Hegel scholar and philosopher who joined other Russian idealists in urgently preaching patriotism on the home front. Il'in publicly asserted that in a national war, the "juridical division of the people into 'combatants' and 'non-combatants'" was of little meaning. Anyone committed to directing his or her "*will, thoughts, feelings* and *actions*" toward victory became a "*spiritual warrior,*" and the role of the "spiritual warrior" was critical. If Russians could achieve the "spiritual ascent" the nation had needed even prior to the war, this would represent "the beginning of our rebirth" and the road to victory.[26]

Il'in was not the only Russian philosopher fostering spiritual warfare on the home front.[27] Galvanized into action, Russian philosophers gave public speeches and lectures and published reams of commentary. Naturally, much less of it appeared in *Questions of Philosophy and Psychology* than in national liberalism's leading "thick" journal, *Russkaia mysl'*. Struve, who departed from most Russian idealists (who eschewed the term nationalism) by espousing a rather incoherent concept of "ethical nationalism," had been sole editor in chief of *Russkaia mysl'* since 1910.[28] But neither Lopatin's nor Struve's journal truly reached the masses, and both had occasion to double up issues during the war, most likely due to supply shortages and the increased costs of paper and ink.[29] Thus, much like they would respond to revolution by creating the

---

[25] Kotliarevskii, "Voina," iii–vi; S. L. Frank, "Pamiati V. F. Erna," printed in *V. F. Ern: Pro et Contra. Lichnost' i tvorchestva Vladimira Erna v otsenke russkikh myslitelei i issledovatelei*, ed. A. A. Ermichev (St. Petersburg: Izd-vo Russkoi Khristianskoi gumanitarnoi akademii, 2006), 638; V. S. Solov'ev, *Opravdanie dobra: Nravstvennaia filosofiia*, in *Sobranie sochinenii Vladimira Sergeevicha Solov'eva* (Brussels: Izd-vo Zhizn' s Bogom, 1966), 8: 308–31. For more information regarding Solov'ev's views on nationalism and the national question, see Greg Gaut, "Can a Christian be a Nationalist? Vladimir Solov'ev's Critique of Nationalism," *Slavic Review* 57, 1 (1998): 77–94.

[26] Il'in, *Dukhovnyi smysl voiny*, 41, 47.

[27] For another piece using the phrase "spiritual war" and declaring "the entire Russian nation" responsible for it, see N. A. Berdiaev, "O dremliushchikh silakh cheloveka," *Utro Rossii*, 5 November 1914.

[28] Richard Pipes, *Struve: Liberal on the Right, 1905–1944* (Cambridge, MA: Harvard University Press, 1980), 90–92, 169–98, 209–12, 449.

[29] On wartime publishing conditions, see Charles A. Ruud, *Russian Entrepreneur: Publisher Ivan Sytin of Moscow, 1851–1934* (Montreal: McGill-Queen's University Press,

League of Russian Culture in June 1917, Russian intellectuals created new institutions to promote patriotism and to address the issues raised by the war during the war years.[30] These institutions included the Committee on War and Culture (COWC) and the Russian Society for the Study of Jewish Life (RSSJL).

In their support for the war effort, Russian intellectuals were not unlike other European intellectuals.[31] Even many socialists, in both Russia and the West, could not countenance defeatism.[32] Russian intellectuals' strong early support would erode, in some cases after the Russian defeats in the spring of 1915.[33] But with some exceptions, leading Russian idealists generally supported the war until the bitter pill of Brest-Litovsk. The exceptions included many Symbolists. Andrei Belyi (1880–1934) never supported the war; Zinaida Gippius (1869–1945) was at first publicly supportive but privately doubtful; her husband, Dmitrii Merezhkovskii (1865–1941), was hesitant.[34] By late 1914, Merezhkovskii and Gippius were openly critical of Neo-Slavophiles who championed the war effort, accusing them of nationalism. Merezhkovskii attacked "Bulgakov, Berdiaev, Ern, Florenskii, and miscellaneous 'vekhovtsy,'" the latter term referring to contributors to the 1909 symposium *Landmarks*. The symposium's general orientation was certainly shared by Ern and the priest and polymath Pavel Florenskii (1882–1937), although neither had contributed to it. Gippius's slightly different list of nationalists included Struve, whom she distinguished from a Neo-Slavophile group she dubbed "the Muscovites." Among the latter were Bulgakov, Trubetskoi, Ern, Grigorii A. Rachinskii (1859–1939), and Viacheslav Ivanov (1866–1949).[35]

In contrast to the Symbolists mentioned above, Ivanov was indeed one of the staunchest consistent defenders of the Russian war effort. In a 1914 public speech, he described Germany as "entering into spiritual union with the elements of hell," but found the enemy nation "too spiritually petty and

---

1990), 148–55.

[30] On the League of Russian Culture, see Pipes, *Struve: Liberal on the Right*, 234–36.

[31] See *European Culture in the Great War*.

[32] Michael Melancon, *The Socialist Revolutionaries and the Russian Anti-War Movement, 1914–1917* (Columbus: Ohio State University Press, 1990), especially 2–3. For the international socialist context, see James Joll, *The Second International, 1889–1914*, 2nd rev. ed. (London: Routledge and Kegan Paul Books, 1974), 161–86.

[33] Smirnov, "Voina i rossiiskaia intelligentsiia," in *Rossiia i pervaia mirovaia voina*, traces this development thoroughly.

[34] Stites, "Days and Nights," 10–11. See also Ben Hellman, *Poets of Hope and Despair: The Russian Symbolists in War and Revolution (1914–1918)* (Helsinki: Institute for Russian and East European Studies, 1995).

[35] D. S. Merezhkovskii, "O religioznoi lzhi natsionalizma," in *V. F. Ern*, 455; Z. N. Gippius, "Skazhite priamo!" in *V. F. Ern*, 458.

small … to embody in itself the genuine spirit of the coming Anti-Christ."[36] Neo-Slavophile commentary often interpreted the war through an explicit framework of Christian providentialism and eschatology, proclaiming the downfall of modern godless civilization, and predicting victory and spiritual transformation—perhaps even the advent of the millennium—if Russia could prove repentant and pure.[37] Such commentary became sparser and more subdued in 1916 and 1917 than it had been in 1914 and 1915. In addition, Neo-Slavophile commentary came to place greater emphasis on Russia's British ally, putting forth a vision of a future imperial order in which Russia and Britain would cooperate in spreading freedom and Christian civilization. In warming to Britain as the war progressed, Neo-Slavophile intellectuals laid some of the groundwork for expanded Orthodox–Protestant interaction in a shaken interwar and postrevolutionary world.[38] While the Neo-Slavophiles must have wrestled with doubt, despite their changed tone and emphasis after 1915, they generally held on to their wartime illusions until the October Revolution changed everything.

One small but important institution closely associated with religious philosophy and Neo-Slavophilism was the Put' (The Way) Publishing House, founded in 1910. Its publication of books peaked in 1913 and fell off sharply after 1914, with none published in 1918 and 1919, despite the continued

---

[36] V. I. Ivanov, "Vselenskoe delo," *Russkaia mysl'* 35, 12 (1914): 104. On polemics between Belyi and Ivanov, see Heinrich A. Stammler, "Belyj's Conflict with Vjačeslav Ivanov over War and Revolution," *Slavic and East European Journal* 18, 3 (1974): 259–70.

[37] For examples of wartime concern with repentance and purity, and of representing the war as a source of purification, see V. F. Ern, "I na zemli mir. 25. dekabria," in V. F. Ern, *Mech i krest: Stat'i o sovremennykh sobytiiakh* (Moscow: I. D. Sytin, 1915); Berdiaev, "Voina i vozrozhdenie"; S. N. Bulgakov, "Rodine," *Utro Rossii*, 5 August 1914; Ivanov, "Vselenskoe delo," 105; E. N. Trubetskoi, *Natsional'nyi vopros, Konstantinopl' i sviataia Sofiia. (Publichnaia lektsiia). Voina i kul'tura* (Moscow: I. D. Sytin, 1915), 23, 29–31. For a more thorough assessment of Neo-Slavophile war commentary and what I call its "politics of Providentialism," see Christopher Stroop, "Nationalist War Commentary as Russian Religious Thought: The Religious Intelligentsia's Politics of Providentialism," *Russian Review* 72, 1 (2013): 94–115.

[38] Some important writings demonstrating this changed tone and increasing attention to Britain include S. N. Bulgakov, "Chelovechnost' protiv chelovekobozhiia: Istoricheskoe opravdanie anglo-russkogo sblizheniia. Publichnaia lektsiia," *Russkaia mysl'* 38, 5–6 (1917): 1–32; N. A. Berdiaev, "Rossiia, Angliia i Germaniia," *Birzhevye vedomosti*, 21 May 1916; N. A. Berdiaev, "Rossiia i zapadnaia Evropa," *Russkaia mysl'* 38, 5–6 (1917): 5–6; and V. I. Ivanov, "Rossiia, Angliia i Aziia," in Ivanov, *Rodnoe i vselenskoe: Stat'i (1914–1916)* (Moscow: Izdanie G. A. Lemana i S. I. Sakharova, 1917), 24–30, reprinted from *Birzhevye vedomosti*, 18 December 1915. On Ivanov's thoughts on Russia, Britain, and imperialism in Asia, see also Hellman, *Poets of Hope and Despair*, 197–201. On postwar ecumenism, see Bryn Geffert, *Eastern Orthodox and Anglicans: Diplomacy, Theology, and the Politics of Interwar Ecumenism* (Notre Dame, IN: University of Notre Dame Press, 2010).

official existence of the organization. But Put"s reduced production during the war seems to have been, at least initially, a decision the organization's leaders made not so much for lack of resources as because they felt called to more direct social action. The publishing of purely philosophical books now seemed an unjustifiable luxury. Society needed to be called to patriotism and to a reexamination of values, exhorted to recognize the spiritual significance of the moment and to stand firmly behind the war effort.[39] As Put"s owner Margarita Morozova (née Mamontova, 1873–1958) wrote to Trubetskoi, the war signaled that the time had come to proclaim the downfall of "the authority of *modern* Germanism" and "to hoist the banner of genuine, true, religious Russian culture."[40]

Interestingly, Morozova had also financially supported Put"s sometime ideological rival, the Russian version of the Tübingen-based Neo-Kantian journal *Logos*, which was published by Musaget. Edited on the Russian side by Fedor Stepun (1884–1965), Nikolai Bubnov (1880–1962), and Sergei Gessen (1887–1950), *Logos* was shut down in the Germanophobic climate of 1914, having existed only since 1910.[41] While neither Put' nor *Logos* was profitable, both had been intended to benefit the Russian nation by raising philosophical consciousness.[42] But if anti-German sentiment was already present among many Russian philosophers before the war—philosophers like Berdiaev, for example, and Ern, who in 1910 mockingly lamented Russian intellectuals' desire for German "philosophical goods of the very latest manufacture"—war against Germany probably made untenable the continuing publication of a journal with an explicit German orientation.[43]

---

[39] Evgenii Gollerbakh, *K nezrimomu gradu: Religiozno-filosofskaia gruppa "Put'" (1910–1919) v poiskakh novoi russkoi identichnosti*, Seriia issledovaniia po istorii russkoi mysli (St. Petersburg: Aleteiia, 2000), 246–49 and appendix (b), "Spisok izdanii 'Puti,'" 456–58. While Put' was important for Russian religious philosophy, Berdiaev considered it too narrow and tendered his resignation from its editorial board in April 1912, on which see ibid., 170–80.

[40] Quoted in Gollerbakh, *K nezrimomu gradu*, 248.

[41] For more on Stepun, a significant figure with respect to the topic of Russian philosophy and war, see Ben Hellman, "In Search of the Truth about the Great War: The Theme of War in the Works of Five Russian Writers," in book 1 of this volume.

[42] See Michael Meerson, "Put' against Logos: The Critique of Kant and Neo-Kantianism by Russian Religious Philosophers in the Beginning of the Twentieth Century," *Studies in East European Thought* 47, 3–4 (1995): 225–43. Morozova is treated in some detail throughout Gollerbakh, *K nezrimomu gradu*; see also Natal'ia Dumova, *Moskovskie metsenaty* (Moscow: Molodaia gvardiia, 1992), 97–107.

[43] V. F. Ern, "Nechto o Logose, russkoi filosofii, i nauchnosti: Po povodu novogo filosofskogo zhurnala 'Logos,'" in V. F. Ern, *Bor'ba za Logos: Opyty filosofskie i kriticheskie* (Moscow: Put', 1911), 73. On the folding of *Logos*, see Michail V. Bezrodnyj,

In their search for a means of taking direct action in response to the war, Put''s leaders became involved in the creation of a new institution, the COWC. The COWC could be characterized as a coalition of public intellectuals and liberal leaders in industry and philanthropy—there were other such partnerships in late imperial Russian society—that gave patriotic Russian philosophers a platform to promote their views on the war, through public talks and in print. The COWC's War and Culture (Voina i kul'tura) Series was published by Sytin and Co. Ivan Sytin (1851–1934), a towering figure in late imperial Russian publishing, was known for his efforts to spread literacy and to market to the peasant masses. He was good at what he did. Sytin and Co.'s revenues actually *increased* over previous years in 1914 and 1915, although in 1916 Sytin laid off 432 workers.[44] During the war, Russian philosophers also published in newspapers, and Berdiaev, Bulgakov, Ivanov, and Gershenzon did so extensively in national liberal newspapers with not insubstantial circulations, especially *Birzhevye vedomosti* and Pavel P. Riabushinskii's (1871–1924) *Utro Rossii*.[45]

A joint forum of the COWC and the Moscow Religious-Philosophical Society in Memory of Solov'ev (MRPS) that took place on 6 October 1914—Trubetskoi and Morozova seem to have been the primary initiators—provides examples of the sorts of public speeches and lectures the COWC hosted.[46] The event took place in the 1000-seat auditorium of the Moscow Polytechnic Museum, and proceeds from the tickets, which sold out easily, benefited

---

"Zur Geschichte des russischen Neukantianismus: Die Zeitschrift 'Logos' und ihre Redakteure," *Zeitschrift für Slawistik* 37, 4 (1992): 500.

[44] Ruud, *Russian Entrepreneur*, especially 148–64, and appendix 5, figure 1.

[45] For references to many of their newspaper articles, see Ben Khellman [Ben Hellman], "Kogda vremia slavianofil'stvovalo: Russkie filosofy i pervaia mirovaia voina," in *Problemy istorii russkoi literatury nachala XX veka*, ed. Lissa Byckling and Pekka Pesonen, Studia Russica Helsingiensia et Tartuensia 6 (Helsinki: Department of Slavonic Languages, University of Helsinki, 1989), 211–39. On Riabushinskii, see James L. West, "The Riabushinsky Circle: Burzhuaziia and Obshchestvennost'" in *Late Imperial Russia*," in *Between Tsar and People: Educated Society and the Quest for Public Identity in Late Imperial Russia*, ed. Edith W. Clowes, Samuel D. Kassow, and West (Princeton, NJ: Princeton University Press, 1991), 43–56. *Utro Rossii* had a circulation of 25,000 in 1910 and a circulation of 40,000 in 1913. *Birzhevye vedomosti* had a circulation of 228,000 in 1915 and 157,000 in 1916, in addition to annual street sales in St. Petersburg of almost 21 million in 1914 and over 29.8 million in 1915, taking the morning and evening editions together. These figures are found in Louise McReynolds, *The News Under Russia's Old Regime: The Development of a Mass-Circulation Press* (Princeton, NJ: Princeton University Press, 1991), appendix A, table 8.

[46] Gollerbakh, *K nezrimomu gradu*, 248–49. On the MRPS, see Kristiane Burchardi, *Die Moskauer "Religiös-Philosophische Vladimir-Solov'ev Gesellschaft" (1905–1918): Forschungen zur Osteuropäischen Geschichte* (Wiesbaden: Harrassowitz Verlag, 1998).

wounded soldiers.[47] The speakers included Rachinskii, Ivanov, Bulgakov, Trubetskoi, and Ern, whose speech, "From Kant to Krupp," has been described as "infamous."[48] While Ern was attacked for seeming to condemn all of German culture, he quickly clarified his position by pointing to what he took to be the "pure gold" in German culture (which included Bach, Mozart, and Schelling).[49]

Many objected vocally to Ern's "From Kant to Krupp," not least Il´in, who publicly and passionately confronted Ern with his objections.[50] Yet Il´in, though clearly considering himself an anti-nationalist, also made quite nationalist statements during the war, and likewise under the auspices of the COWC. For example, in a passage dripping with resentment, he remarked, "And after this war, our enemies and our allies will learn that they ought first and foremost to study Russian with the same attention and with the same love with which we study *their* languages." It was, after all, "the language of Pushkin and Lermontov, the language of Derzhavin and Tiutchev...."[51] In the same piece, Il´in argued that preemptive warfare could be considered defensive and therefore justified, while waxing poetic on "the *ethical beauty* constituting the spiritual image of the *hero*."[52] Apparently, Il´in saw no contradiction between this and his finding that "the fundamental ethical contradiction of war" lay in the fact that, while murder is a sin even in war, it is a necessary sin when undertaken selflessly in order to defend the nation's spiritual existence and cultural heritage, and in the hopes of bringing about a more ethical society in which such sin will cease to be necessary.[53]

His objections to "From Kant to Krupp" notwithstanding, Il´in found that German culture contained both "healthy" and "decayed" elements. He associated Germany with the ideology of "might makes right" and resented

---

[47] These details are found in Gollerbakh, *K nezrimomu gradu*, 249–55, including footnotes.

[48] See Robert Bird, "Imagination and Ideology in the New Religious Consciousness," in *A History of Russian Philosophy*, 281; and Randall A. Poole, "Religion, War and Revolution: E. N. Trubetskoi's Liberal Construction of Russian National Identity, 1912–20," *Kritika: Explorations in Russian and Eurasian History* 7, 2 (2006): 204. On initial reactions to the speech, see A. A. Ermichev, "Zhizn´ i dela Vladimira Frantsevicha Erna," in *V. F. Ern*, 52–54.

[49] V. F. Ern, "Nenuzhnye rydaniia," in Ern, *Mech i krest*, 82–83.

[50] On Il´in's response to "From Kant to Krupp," see M. Z., "Spor o germanskoi kul´ture. (V Religiozno-filosofskom obshchestve pamiati V. Solov´eva)," in *V. F. Ern*, 463–64.

[51] Il´in, *Dukhovnyi smysl voiny*, 38.

[52] Ibid., 21.

[53] Il´in, "Osnovnoe nravstvennoe protivorechie."

the scorn with which Germans regarded "our spiritual strengths."[54] The Great War spawned intense debate among Russian philosophers regarding the extent to which German culture and German thinkers were to blame for German militarism, but virtually all Russian philosophers ascribed to them some culpability. This culpability lay largely in the nihilism of German thought, the roots of which some Russian intellectuals, including Ern and Bulgakov, were inclined to find in German Protestantism.[55]

But if the war naturally occasioned Russian thought about Germany, it also occasioned thought about the nationalities of the Russian Empire, not least the Jews. Founded in response to pogroms carried out by Russian forces in Galicia, the RSSJL's most significant initiative was the publication of a volume called *The Shield: A Literary Anthology* (*Shchit: Literaturnyi sbornik*), a collection of essays and poetry by Russian intellectuals meant to advocate for Jewish civil rights.[56] Leaders in the society and its publishing activities included Maksim Gor'kii (1868–1936), Leonid Andreev (1871–1919), Fedor Sologub (1863–1927), and Solomon Pozner (1876–1946). *The Shield's* publication in July 1915 was timed to coincide with the opening of a new session of the State Duma, "at which," in the words of one scholar, "it was planned to raise once again the situation of Jewish refugees and the acts of violent anti-Semitism in the army, and to demand the abolition of the Pale of Settlement." Over the course of 1915–16, it went through three editions.[57] Among the contributors were Bulgakov and many leading Symbolists.

However well intentioned the project may have been, the Russian-Jewish community received it with ambivalence.[58] This is understandable, and all the more so in light of some of the contributions, including those of Ivanov and Bulgakov, which defined Jewish experience in Christian terms, exemplifying what is sometimes called theological anti-Judaism. Ivanov's essay is an example of Christian philo-Semitism that casts the Jews as "our Providential testers," suggesting that if Christians would only embody Christ-like love in relation to Jews, the Jews would convert. Bulgakov's contribution is an example

---

[54] Il'in, *Dukhovnyi smysl voiny*, 35–37.

[55] For more contemporary comments on and contributions to these debates, see S. L. Frank, "O poiskakh smysla voiny," *Russkaia mysl'* 35, 12 (1914): 125–32; N. A. Berdiaev, "K sporam o germanskoi filosofii," *Russkaia mysl'* 36, 5 (1915): 115–21; Berdiaev, "Sovremennaia Germaniia," *Utro Rossii*, 19 October 1914; Berdiaev, "Nitsshe i sovremennaia Germaniia," *Birzhevye vedomosti*, 4 February 1915; Berdiaev, "Kharakter germanskoi filosofii," *Utro Rossii*, 13 March 1915.

[56] On the devastation of Jewish communities in Galicia by Russian forces, see Gabriella Safran, *Wandering Soul: The Dybbuk's Creator, S. An-sky* (Cambridge, MA: Harvard University Press, 2010), 225–57.

[57] Viktor Kel'ner, "The Jewish Question and Russian Social Life During World War I," *Russian Studies in History* 43, 1 (2004): 25.

[58] Ibid., 35–37.

of Christian Zionism that ascribes Christian eschatological significance to Jewish migration to Palestine, and it also seems to hint at the possibility of Jewish conversion.[59]

On the Death of a Philosopher, or the Rise and Fall of Idealism in Russia

In January 1917, Lev Lopatin gave a commencement speech at Moscow University called "The Urgent Tasks of Contemporary Thought."[60] The bulk of his speech restated his previous arguments for what he called a "spiritualist" (as opposed to "geocentric" or materialist) worldview. But if Lopatin's arguments were not new, the degree of his urgency was, and the fact that he stressed the need for a spiritualist worldview in a commencement speech is significant. According to Lopatin (and not a few of his Russian and European contemporaries), the "struggle of nations," the "great war," represented nothing less than "the great wreck of European culture." The crisis of European philosophy was no longer a mere abstraction. The horrors of the times indicated that nothing less than a "review and ... reevaluation of all values of thought and life" was a "burning and urgent necessity."[61]

Lopatin argued that respect for the equality of human individuals as ends-in-themselves demanded a worldview that logically justified such respect. The modern European worldview that privileged empirical, scientific knowledge failed this test. A spiritual worldview, including a belief in individual immortality, was necessary for "higher morals," and if this worldview failed to take root, the consequences would be disastrous. Current events showed not only that human beings would not soon become incapable of war, but also that each future war would be more horrifying than the last. Yet, Lopatin mused, before the war, "We really did think that we stood on the verge of the bright

---

[59] V. I. Ivanov, "K ideologii evreiskogo voprosa," in *Shchit: Literaturnyi sbornik*, 3rd ed., ed. L. Andreev, M. Gor′kii, and F. Sologub, Russkoe Obshchestvo dlia izucheniia evreiskoi zhizni (Moscow: A. I. Mamontova, 1916), 98–99; S. N. Bulgakov, "Sion," in *Shchit*, 43–46. Bulgakov did publicly recognize Russian-Jewish patriotism and participation in the war effort; see "Rodine." For a brief assessment of Bulgakov's attitude toward Jews, see Rowan Williams, ed. and trans., *Sergii Bulgakov: Towards a Russian Political Theology* (Edinburgh: T&T Clark, 2001), 293–303. For more detailed commentary, see Dominic Rubin, *Holy Russia, Sacred Israel: Jewish-Christian Encounters in Russian Religious Thought* (Brighton, MA: Academic Studies Press, 2010), chap. 2, "Bulgakov and the Sacred Blood of Jewry," 61–152.

[60] L. M. Lopatin, *Neotlozhnye zadachi sovremennoi mysli* (Moscow: A. I. Snegireva, 1917). Also published as "Neotlozhnye zadachi sovremennoi mysli," *Voprosy filosofii i psikhologii* 28, 1 (1917): 1–80. The latter printing identifies the piece as a "Speech delivered at the commencement ceremony at Moscow University on 12 January, 1917," though it would have been very long if delivered in full. The two published versions differ slightly, for example in footnotes and punctuation.

[61] Lopatin, *Neotlozhnye zadachi*, 3–4.

completion of the historical process," that "the radiant, unshakeable kingdom of justice, reason, freedom, peace and harmonious all-human happiness" was almost at hand. Lopatin declared that the war, whatever its outcome, had dealt a fatal blow to this "modern religion of earthly progress and culture." He also maintained that the war heralded an end to the battle between materialism and spiritualism, with a return to metaphysics representing "the only way out of modern intellectual chaos."[62]

Three years after he stressed these points to a new crop of Moscow University graduates, Lopatin was dead. Still a bachelor at 65, he died, as one scholar describes it, "in the same family home he had occupied all his life, though the brilliant salons of earlier days were now replaced by crowds of needy strangers whom Bolshevik authorities had forcibly settled there." Privation was likely a factor in his death from influenza on 21 March 1920.[63] Trubetskoi died the same year at only 56, his death probably hastened by the trying times. He succumbed to typhus while aiding the Whites on the Southern Front in the Civil War, his faith in the meaning of life seemingly intact.[64]

Lopatin likewise kept the faith. He closed "The Urgent Tasks of Contemporary Thought" with an exhortation to believe "that there is no darkness that the rays of eternal light will not pierce!"[65] And in a 1919 letter to a friend, Lopatin wrote, "I am convinced that everything taking place is necessary, a painful, agonizing process of the rebirth of humanity."[66] According to a fellow idealist who visited him at his deathbed, some of the last words Lopatin spoke were: "There we will understand everything."[67] But as the dying Lopatin dreamt of understanding everything, the Bolsheviks—who believed they understood everything already—were trying to realize the Communist vision for humanity's rebirth by force. In the final two years of Lopatin's life, they went actively about the business of suppressing Russian idealism. While they continued to tolerate small private publishers that did not adhere to their ideology, in 1918 they shut down both Struve's *Russkaia mysl´* and Lopatin's *Questions of Philosophy and Psychology*, which Lenin denounced as "a

---

[62] Lopatin, *Neotlozhnye zadachi*, 4, 5–7, 10–11, 18–23, 61–62, 76–83.

[63] Scanlan, "Russian Panpsychism," 161. For the precise date, see A. I. Ognev, *Lev Mikhailovich Lopatin* (Petrograd: Kolos, 1922), 11. Despite the Bolshevik adoption of New Style dating in 1918, Ognev gives the date as 8/21 March.

[64] N. O. Lossky, *History of Russian Philosophy* (London: Allen and Unwin, 1952), 153. *The Meaning of Life* was the title of Trubetskoi's last work of systematic religious philosophy, in large part a theodicy. See E. N. Trubetskoi, *Smysl zhizni* (Moscow: I. D. Sytin, 1918).

[65] Lopatin, *Neotlozhnye zadachi*, 83.

[66] Quoted and translated in Scanlan, "Russian Panpsychism," 161.

[67] Ognev, *Lopatin*, 11.

platform for all kinds of idealism, metaphysics, and benighted clericalism."[68] Unsurprisingly, Lopatin was banned from teaching.[69]

Of course, he was not the only one. In the year Lopatin died, the State Academic Council set about transforming universities, implementing a Marxist curriculum, preventing ideologically "unreliable" professors from teaching, and disbanding "problematic" departments—not least philosophy departments, where, in the words of one scholar, "the popularity of courses taught by neo-idealist thinkers was a particular irritation." Berdiaev, Frank, and Il'in were among those banned from teaching in 1921. After they were all deported in late 1922, Il'in would distinguish himself as one of very few Russian intellectuals to stand with Struve in advocating the overthrow of Soviet power by military force, a position Berdiaev would violently oppose. But in the meantime, Russian idealists continued to conduct research and also to lecture, debate, and discuss their ideas openly through the Moscow Psychological Society, which Il'in headed after Lopatin's death; the Free Academy of Spiritual Culture that Berdiaev founded in 1918; and the Moscow University Institute of Scientific Philosophy.[70]

The prevailing chaos of the revolutionary years expressed itself among Russian philosophers in yet more profound ways. While it may be unsurprising that "ideologically incorrect" books continued to appear, it is still striking that at least one significant such publication, Gershenzon and Ivanov's *Correspondence from Two Corners* (*Perepiska iz dvukh uglov*), was written by prominent Russian idealists who were officially working for the regime. Gershenzon embraced the Revolution before the preparation of *Out of the Depths*, and was therefore notably absent from its roster of contributors. He would die in the Soviet Union, an official supporter of the regime, but disillusioned with it.[71] But even among the contributors to *Out of the Depths* there were those who would reconcile themselves to the Soviet project. Ivanov, whose brief contribution to *Out of the Depths* consisted of a denunciation of

---

[68] On the initial toleration of non-Marxist publishers, see George L. Kline, "The Rise and Fall of Soviet 'Orthographic Atheism,'" *Symposion: A Journal of Russian Thought* 14 (2009): 3. On the suppression of *Voprosy filosofii i psikhologii* and for the quotation from Lenin, see B. V. Emel'ianov, V. M. Russakov, and R. Ia. Shliapugina, *"Voprosy filosofii i psikhologii": Pervyi russkii filosofskii zhurnal, 1889–1918* (Ekaterinburg: Ural'skaia gosudarstvennaia Selkhoz. akademiia, 2001), 21–22.

[69] Scanlan, "Russian Panpsychism," in Hamburg and Poole, ed., *A History of Russian Philosophy*, 161.

[70] Finkel, *On the Ideological Front*, 46–47, 106, 221–22. On Struve and Il'in in emigration, see also Boobbyer, *S. L. Frank*, 134–47; and Pipes, *Struve: Liberal on the Right*, 361–66.

[71] On Gershenzon's revolutionary period, see Horowitz, *The Myth of A. S. Pushkin*, 77–93.

the new orthographic reform, did so temporarily, without ceasing to be a Christian idealist.[72]

After the Revolution, Old Bolshevik connections allowed both Ivanov and Gershenzon to take up work for the People's Commissariat of Enlightenment (Narkompros), headed by Anatolii Lunacharskii (1875–1933). As roommates in a sanitarium, the two produced their *Correspondence* in June and July 1920.[73] While Gershenzon asserted an impotent desire to escape from the entire cultural legacy of the past, and Ivanov argued for the importance of preserving and building on this cultural heritage, the correspondence reveals that both continued to believe in the transcendent and the immortality of the soul. Ivanov's contributions were laced with allusions to the Gospel. In the words of a leading Ivanov scholar, "Some, especially among the Bolsheviks, read the *Correspondence* as the swan song of the prerevolutionary intelligentsia."[74] In a way it was. Both correspondents' references to the Revolution were oblique and ambiguous. When Ivanov was at last allowed to leave the USSR for Italy in 1924, ostensibly for research, he never came back. On 17 March 1926, he converted to Catholicism. He subsequently set about arguing that Catholicism was the logical culmination of Symbolism.[75]

Among those who remained in the Soviet Union was Kotliarevskii. He was subjected to arrest and a revolutionary tribunal in connection with his work for anti-Bolshevik organizations, with which, however ineffective the organizations were, he was in fact involved. He was sentenced to death, had his sentence commuted, and made a career in the USSR until falling victim to the Great Terror in 1939. Kotliarevskii was rehabilitated in December 1956.[76] In connection with his arrest and interrogation by the Cheka, he has been

---

[72] V. I. Ivanov, "Nash iazyk," in *Iz glubiny*. For a brief treatment of Ivanov's officially prerevolutionary period, see Robert Bird, *The Russian Prospero: The Creative Universe of Viacheslav Ivanov* (Madison: The University of Wisconsin Press, 2006), 29–35. Bird suggests Ivanov was driven by hardship including the need of his wife for medical attention, and that he may have been trying to bring a religious coloring to the Soviet project.

[73] The *Correspondence* is reprinted in Mikhail Gershenzon, *Izbrannoe*, 4: *Troistvennyi obraz sovershenstva* (Moscow–Jerusalem: Universitetskaia kniga/Gesharim, 2000), 22–48.

[74] Bird, *The Russian Prospero*, 230. Interestingly, Sir Isaiah Berlin described the *Correspondence* precisely as "the swan song of the old intelligentsia." See his introduction to Marc Raeff, ed., *Russian Intellectual History: An Anthology* (1966; New York: Harcourt, Brace, & World, 1992), 11.

[75] Bird, *The Russian Prospero*, 29–41, 228–62.

[76] V. A. Tomsinov, "Sergei Andreevich Kotliarevskii (1873–1939)," in *Rossiiskie pravovedy XVIII–XX vekov: Ocherki zhizni i tvorchestva*, Russkoe iuridicheskoe nasledie (Moscow: Zertsalo, 2007), 2: 404–13. Other major Russian philosophers purged by Stalin include Florenskii and the phenomenologist Gustav G. Shpet (1879–1937).

portrayed as a traitorous coward.[77] His previous record indicates a cautious and hesitant nature. For example, after the government banned student gatherings in universities in January 1911, and then sent police to suppress a demonstration at Moscow University, Kotliarevskii refused to resign from his teaching post in protest, something that other leading Kadets did, including even Novgorodtsev and Bulgakov after some hesitation.[78]

But whatever ultimately motivated Kotliarevskii in these instances, he was not simply a self-serving coward. In his testimony before the revolutionary tribunal, he attempted to spin his answers in such a manner as to protect his fellow anti-Bolshevik conspirators.[79] And while it is impossible to say what became of Kotliarevskii's religious convictions, in his inner life he may have seen his teaching and research in the USSR as consistent with his prerevolutionary efforts to foster the rule of law in Russia.[80] While Kotliarevskii later claimed to have internalized Marxism-Leninism in a letter to Stalin, he clearly remained a Christian idealist in 1918. Not only did he hold the position of deputy oberprocurator of the Holy Synod and then deputy minister of confessions under the priest and historian Anton Kartashev (1875–1960), doing both legal and religious work for the Provisional Government and in connection with the All-Russian Council of the Orthodox Church of 1917–1918,[81] he also continued to speak out on the necessity of religious consciousness for ethics and national development. In his contribution to *Out of the Depths*, "Recovery," Kotliarevskii put it this way: only internal religious experience could transform "the cold and incomprehensible commands of the categorical imperative" into "a yoke that is easy and a burden that is light."[82]

Such sentiments could have essentially no place in the Soviet Union. Many prominent Bolsheviks and idealists understood this well before 1917. When the Bolsheviks gained the upper hand, they naturally acted to eliminate a way of thinking that was indeed incompatible with Marxism-Leninism's denial of the freedom of individual conscience, and with its brutal utilitarian implementation, which disregarded the human individual as an end-in-itself. After the 1920s, Russian idealism lived on in the Soviet Union almost exclusively in memories and restricted library collections, and, from

---

[77] See George Leggett, *The Cheka: Lenin's Political Police: The All-Russian Extraordinary Commission for Combating Counter-Revolution and Sabotage (December 1917 to February 1922)* (Oxford: Clarendon Press, 1981), 287.

[78] Tomsinov, "Sergei Andreevich Kotliarevskii," 373–75, 385–89.

[79] Ibid., 404–13.

[80] See Randall A. Poole, "Sergei Kotliarevskii and the Rule of Law in Russian Liberal Theory," *Dialogue and Universalism*, 1–2 (2006): 81–104.

[81] Tomsinov, "Sergei Andreevich Kotliarevskii," 395–400, 412.

[82] Kotliarevskii, "Ozdorovlenie," in *Iz glubiny*, 180. Here Kotliarevskii is not only alluding to Kant, but also paraphrasing a saying attributed to Jesus in Matthew 11: 30.

the 1960s, in the occasional public comment or university philosophy course, as well as in official encyclopedia articles and unofficial *samizdat*.[83]

Violently transforming society, the early Bolsheviks rendered Russian idealism an ethereal specter from a bygone age. To be sure, the phantasmal voice of the doomed would come back to haunt their successors in the form of late Soviet dissidence, but the philosophers exiled in 1922 would not live to see it. If they had, many of them would have been disturbed to see that the virulent nationalism among some dissident Christians excelled even their World War I era excesses. But the exiles could only carry on in a diaspora whose "mission was to preserve the values and traditions of Russian culture and to continue its creative efforts for the benefit and ongoing spiritual progress of the homeland."[84] In the 1930s, they generally came to accept the fact that they could never go home.

---

[83] On idealism in the Soviet Union and post-Soviet Russia, see Stanislav B. Dzhimbinov, "The Return of Russian Philosophy," in *Russian Thought After Communism: The Recovery of a Philosophical Heritage*, ed. James P. Scanlan (Armonk, NY: M. E. Sharpe, 1994). See also Dmitry Pospielovsky, "A Comparative Enquiry into Neo-Slavophilism and Its Antecedents in the Russian History of Ideas," *Soviet Studies* 31, 3 (1979): 323, 331–32; and James H. Billington, *Russia in Search of Itself* (Washington, DC: Woodrow Wilson Center Press, 2004).

[84] Marc Raeff, *Russia Abroad: A Cultural History of the Russian Emigration, 1919–1939* (New York: Oxford University Press, 1990), 4. On religious-philosophical publishing in emigration, see also Matthew Miller, "A Hunger for Books: The American YMCA Press and Russian Readers," *Religion, State and Society* 38, 1 (2010): 53–73.

Music and Russian Identity in War and Revolution, 1914–22

Rebecca Mitchell

In January 1915 the weekly Moscow journal *Muzyka* unveiled a new cover logo: an unsheathed sword whose upright hilt formed the shape of a Christian cross and whose blade was framed by a musical lyre. This single image provided a visual encapsulation of three interlocking themes that dominated Russian-language discourse in the early months of the Great War: music, battle, and the spiritual mission of Holy Russia.[1] (See fig. 47 in gallery of illustrations following page 178.) Immediately after the outbreak of war in 1914, *Muzyka*'s editor, Vladimir V. Derzhanovskii, asserted that music was to play an active role in the conflict. How, he asked, were his readers (as *Russian* musicians) to "react to these great events experienced by the motherland" and "fulfill their duty" to society? How would they defend "Russian national culture"? While some might be called to "exchange their lyre for a sword," Derzhanovskii intimated that the vast majority faced the difficult mission of redoubling their important cultural work amid total war.[2] The problem of Russian musical identity in the context of a multiethnic empire was to play a central role in defining just what that mission was to be.

While the role of nationalism in Russian music has long been a topic of study, the relationship between Russian national (*russkii*) and imperial (*rossiiskii*) identity, particularly in the midst of war and revolution, deserves closer consideration.[3] With the outbreak of war, loyalty to one's ethnic background, one's country of citizenship, or to a universal, shared culture of humanity emerged as an urgent problem for musicians, music critics, and audiences.[4]

---

[1] The original logo employed by *Muzyka* at the journal's inception in 1910 was a lyre; in 1914 this was altered to Russian folk instruments. The martial symbol of lyre-and-sword appeared after the outbreak of war.

[2] V. V. Derzhanovskii, "V buriu, vo grozu," *Muzyka*, no. 192 (26 July 1914): 453–55, here 454; "Ot redaktora," *Muzyka*, no. 194 (25 October 1914): 480.

[3] For a recent scholarly assessment of Russian nationalism in music, see Marina Frolova-Walker, *Russian Music and Nationalism: From Glinka to Stalin* (New Haven: Yale University Press, 2008).

[4] On the overlapping categories of "nationalism" and "patriotism" in France during the Great War, see Carlo Caballero, "Patriotism or Nationalism? Fauré and the Great

Russian Culture in War and Revolution, 1914–22, Book 2: Political Culture, Identities, Mentalities, and Memory. Murray Frame, Boris Kolonitskii, Steven G. Marks, and Melissa K. Stockdale, eds. Bloomington, IN: Slavica Publishers, 2014, 221–43.

Though the question of Russian national and imperial identity had long been an unresolved issue in the musical world, it was only in 1914 that the question took on pressing political significance. Similarly, the larger context of these wartime developments framed developing national musical styles in the early Soviet period.

Recent historical scholarship on musical life has generally used the 1917 revolutions as either a starting- or an end-point, without granting particular attention to the ways in which the experience of war and revolution impacted music's symbolic and practical status.[5] Although it has been argued that professional musicians showed little engagement with or interest in the war effort, analysis of Russian music periodicals of the time tells a different story.[6] In the first months of combat, the war was a common theme for discussion, and many musicians of various stripes (composers, performers, critics) actively sought to carve out a role for themselves in defending the motherland. These attempts at self-definition ushered in a darker development in musical life: the politicization of musical creativity shattered the multiethnic musical community that had begun to take root in the final years of the Russian Empire, replacing it with an exclusionary nationalist discourse focused on Russian (and Pan-Slav) ethnic identity. This nationalist politicization of music left a legacy that haunted Soviet-era interpretations of music and continues to influence music to the present day.

Through close analysis of textual discourse between 1905 and 1922, this chapter uncovers the ways in which both the concept and the practice of music were shaped by the experiences of the Great War and revolutions of 1917. At least initially, the war provided an opportunity for musicians to define their role and function as part of a larger, unified community in a time of conflict. While the idea that music had political implications was by no means new (as the forced resignation of Nikolai Rimskii-Korsakov from the St. Petersburg Conservatory in 1905 demonstrated), it was only with the lifting of censorship after 1905 that music's political meaning could be openly

---

War," *Journal of the American Musicological Society* 52, 3 (Autumn 1999): 593–625.

[5] Recent monographs dealing with musical life in this period include James Loeffler, *The Most Musical Nation: Jews and Culture in the Late Russian Empire* (New Haven: Yale University Press, 2010); Amy Nelson, *Music for the Revolution: Musicians and Power in Early Soviet Russia* (University Park: Pennsylvania State University Press, 2004); Lynn Sargeant, *Harmony and Discord: Music and the Transformation of Russian Cultural Life* (Oxford: Oxford University Press, 2011).

[6] Richard Stites, "Days and Nights in Wartime Russia: Cultural Life, 1914–1917," in *European Culture in the Great War: The Arts, Entertainment, and Propaganda, 1914–1918*, ed. Aviel Roshwald and Stites (Cambridge: Cambridge University Press, 1999), 8–31, here 14. Contemporary periodicals consulted for this chapter include *Golos Moskvy, Iuzhnyi muzykal'nyi vestnik, Moskovskii ezhenedel'nik, Muzyka, Muzykal'nyi sovremennik, Novoe zveno, Rampa i zhizn', Russkaia muzykal'naia gazeta, Russkaia mysl'*, and *Russkie vedomosti*.

debated in the public press.[7] For this reason, 1914 served as an important moment for open discussion defining music's purpose and delineating how musicians might be actively involved in contemporary social and political life. At the same time, however, the politicization of music along national lines alienated and ultimately excluded those individuals and groups not deemed part of "Russian" musical heritage. As Soviet musical institutions took root after 1917, they tended to follow nationalist assumptions introduced in the late imperial period.

Two fundamental concepts framed this discussion: *musical metaphysics* and *musical patriotism*. In the aftermath of the 1905 Revolution, Russian musicians and commentators commonly envisioned music as a unifying force, capable of transcending cultural, social, and political divisions that seemed to increasingly divide the Russian Empire. Music took on a tutelary role as a potential means of counteracting the divisive forces of the modern age and reuniting society. In my research, I refer to this symbolic interpretation as musical metaphysics.[8] The basis of this world view, together with contemporary attempts at its implementation, is given detailed attention in section 1. In the second section, I explore the ways in which the concept of musical metaphysics became enmeshed with attempts to define musical patriotism. With the outbreak of war in 1914, musical society by and large embraced the exuberant outpouring of patriotism that dominated all Russian society. Patriotic sentiment could feasibly be construed musically in various ways: in lyrics, compositional style, loyalty of the composer or musician to the Russian state, or by ethnic background. It was the last of these that gained sway in Russia in 1914. Russia, it was argued, faced spiritual as well as physical battle against its "Prussian" enemy, and music was conceived as a crucial weapon. The unifying goal of musical metaphysics, when interlocked with the debate over musical patriotism gave rise to an exclusivist narrative in which it was commonly assumed that only ethnically "pure" Russian music could advance the wartime effort.

As an image of "pure" Russian music was embraced, music became symbolically linked with the fate of Russia itself. Because of this collapsing of Russian music and the Russian nation, musical discourse took an increasingly dark turn as Russian losses in the war began to mount, the focus of section 3. The fate of Russia found expression not just in physical numbers of dead

---

[7] On the resolution by the Russian Music Society (RMO) to dismiss Rimskii-Korsakov (19 March 1905), together with the larger political implications of this event, see Lynn Sargeant, "Kashchei the Immortal: Liberal Politics, Cultural Memory, and the Rimsky-Korsakov Scandal of 1905," *Russian Review* 64, 1 (January 2004): 22–43.

[8] Rebecca Mitchell, "Nietzsche's Orphans: Music and the Search for Unity in Revolutionary Russia, 1905–1921" (Ph.D. diss., University of Illinois at Urbana-Champaign, 2011); Mitchell, "In Search of Orpheus: Music and Irrationality in Late Imperial Russia: 1905–1917," in *Irratsional'noe v russkoi istorii*, ed. Julia Mannherz (Moscow: Germanskii istoricheskii institut v Moskve, forthcoming).

and wounded but in the symbolic loss of Russian musical creativity itself, embodied perhaps most poignantly in the death of Aleksandr Skriabin in 1915. In this phase, the silencing of musical creativity and the dark mood expressed in many musical compositions from the time captured a sense of imminent destruction. Escapism rather than patriotic enthusiasm came to dominate the musical mood of the day. The final section investigates the impact of the revolutions of 1917 on Russian musical circles. In continuity with preceding trends, the search for a new national anthem emphasized the search for a unified "Russian" society after February 1917, just as after October 1917 earlier visions of music's potentially unifying power gained new force and relevance when reinterpreted through a Marxist lens. Having developed the argument that they were preservers of the cultural wealth of all humanity (as embodied in the "universal" values expressed in Western art music), many tsarist-era musicians took an active role in shaping the musical life and institutions of the early Soviet Union. Nevertheless, a heightened emphasis on national identity underpinned Soviet musical life—the Great War's final legacy to the musical world of the USSR.

Musical Metaphysics in Late Imperial Russia

By the early 20th century, the Russian Empire was increasingly strained by the effects of urbanization and modernization, which were destabilizing the very basis of social life. Observing that the outmoded system had proven unable to respond to rapid changes, many music commentators gave voice to a widespread desire for a unified basis upon which to rebuild the political and social order by proposing music as both a symbol of unity and a means through which to achieve social harmony. Inspired by the Greek concept of *harmonia* (referring both to musical consonances and the ordering of the cosmos) in correspondence with Nietzschean ideas of Dionysian unity, writers on music regularly employed the image of musical harmony as a metaphor for social unity.[9] In the words of music critic and social activist Aleksandr L. Maslov: "Music calls forth a harmony of feelings between various distinct individuals and is a means of making the heart beat in sympathy, just as the strings of a musical instrument or human voices sound in consonance.... music is an instrument of social unity and agreement."[10] Music, it was believed, might transcend both social and ethnic divisions. Thus, it was argued that, while classical music had evolved as entertainment for the upper class, its

---

[9] Such an idea was by no means limited to the Russian Empire. See, for instance, Sheramy Bundrick, *Music and Image in Classical Athens* (Cambridge: Cambridge University Press, 2005); Geoffrey Baker, *Imposing Harmony: Music and Society in Colonial Cuzco* (Durham, NC: Duke University Press, 2008).

[10] A. L. Maslov, "Narodnaia konservatoriia: Muzykal′no-teoreticheskii obshcheobrazovatel′nyi kurs. Stat′i i lektsiia," supplement of *Muzyka i zhizn′*, no. 1 (9 January 1909): 3.

ability to reach all people (regardless of social origin) through its direct appeal to emotion might provide the basis through which the very social fabric of the empire might be reforged.[11] At the same time, music was envisioned as a means of uniting different ethnic groups of the empire into a harmonious relationship. The director of the music school in Tiflis, N. D. Nikolaev, thus envisioned the future purpose of his institution to be providing the educational framework from which "the songs of the diverse peoples of the Caucasus / Will stream together into one harmonious chord."[12] United song would give rise to a unified imperial citizenship.

This focus on social harmony spread to musicians and music critics throughout the empire by means of a well-established institutional network of music societies and educational facilities. As Lynn Sargeant has shown, by the final years of the tsarist regime, musical life in Russia had expanded from the capital cities and penetrated deep into the provinces. The guiding force behind these developments was the Russian Music Society (RMO), which, from its modest beginnings in 1862, had grown by the early 20th century to include conservatories, schools, concert series, and local branches scattered throughout much of the European portion of the Russian Empire.[13] Graduates of the educational institutes associated with the RMO actively worked to bring musical knowledge to the provinces, spreading not only musical knowledge but also assumptions about the civilizing power of music and a historical narrative in which Russia was given pride of place as the newest country that had developed a distinct national voice. These institutional advancements were accompanied by a growing desire on behalf of musicians to clarify their own professional status.

The importance of the RMO began to wane in the aftermath of the 1905 Revolution that shook the Russian Empire. Angered in part by the response of the RMO to the crisis of student protests (culminating in the resignation of Rimskii-Korsakov from the St. Petersburg Conservatory) and in part by longstanding tensions between musical professionals and amateurs, professors and students at conservatories and music schools throughout the empire began to demand greater autonomy from the RMO, a goal that would not be

---

[11] Anonymous, "Zhizn' i muzykal'noe iskusstvo," *Muzyka i zhizn'*, no. 1 (10 February 1908): 1–2; A. L. Maslov, "Zadachi narodnykh konservatorii," *Muzykal'nyi truzhenik*, no. 17 (1 May 1907): 3–5; Pr. Neelov, "Rasprostranenie muzyki," *Muzykal'nyi truzhenik*, no. 19 (1908): 4–5; Fr. V. Lebedev, [untitled], *Baian*, no. 1 (28 January 1907): 2–4; Neelov, "Penie svetskogo kharaktera, kak odna iz funktsii deiatel'nosti narodnykh khorov," *Baian*, no. 4–5 (1907): 7–10; N. Ianchuk, "Muzyka i zhizn'," *Muzyka i zhizn'*, no. 1 (10 February 1908): 2–5.

[12] Sargeant, *Harmony and Discord*, 195–96.

[13] Sargeant, *Harmony and Discord*, 175–217; Gosudarstvennyi arkhiv Rossiiskoi Federatsii (GARF) f. 102, osobyi otdel (o.o.) 1915, op. 245, d. 307, t. 2, ll. 16–17.

fully achieved until 1918.[14] At the same time, new music journals, organizations, and concert societies were formed in the aftermath of 1905, giving new life and diversity to musical culture.[15] While there was not a centralized attempt to form a coherent interpretation of music at this time, the concept of musical metaphysics summarizes a central component that dominated discourse about music: the desire to overcome current social divisions through the art of music.

In the midst of such grandiose visions, the relationship between Russian national and imperial identity received limited analysis. The question as to whether the RMO's mission was to promote ethnically Russian music or the music of all the ethnic groups of the empire had never been clearly answered. In practice, with the expansion of the RMO into provincial centers, musicians involved in late imperial Russian musical life increasingly represented a range of ethnic backgrounds, including Jewish, Russian, German, Armenian, Georgian, and Ukrainian.[16] As James Loeffler has shown, the development of a Jewish national school of music in late imperial Russia was initially seen as a natural outgrowth of the same national sentiment informing the development of a Russian school of composition.[17] In this way, the work of the RMO and the loosely defined doctrine of musical metaphysics combined to create the possibility for the development of both a Russian national and a Russian imperial musical culture.

This is not to suggest that Russian cultural chauvinism was by any means absent before the war. Ethnic tensions were common in all spheres of life and musicians were not exempt.[18] All ethnicities were not created equal, either from the view of the Russian governmental bureaucracy or of its citizens. Music critic Boris Popov harshly condemned the Moscow composer Nikolai Medtner's piano compositions in a 1906 review with the racially-charged comment that "in Medtner, there is too much German blood."[19] Similarly, the argument that Russian music was more intuitive, natural, and spiritual, repeated often in published articles ranging from musical aesthetics to concert reviews and social commentaries, echoed Dostoevskii's famous speech on the death of Pushkin in which the Russian people were

---

[14] Sargeant, *Harmony and Discord*, 231–60, 267–73; Sargeant, "Kashchei the Immortal."

[15] New musical journals that appeared at this time included *Muzyka, Muzykal'nyi truzhenik, Orkestr, Muzyka i zhizn'*, and *Baian*.

[16] Sargeant, *Harmony and Discord*, 193–96.

[17] Loeffler, *Most Musical Nation*, 106–08.

[18] Emil Medtner's anti-Semitic outbursts are a good example of this. See Vol'fing [Emil Medtner], *Modernizm i muzyka: Stat'i kriticheskie i polemicheskie, 1907–1911* (Moscow: Musaget, 1912), esp. 87–122.

[19] Boris Popov, "Noiabr'skie rozy," *Pereval*, no. 2 (December 1906): 58–61.

identified as the "god-carriers" of the modern age.[20] Nevertheless, Russian national and imperial musical identities were seldom clearly differentiated in contemporary discourse. In this sense, musical metaphysics did not offer an accurate reflection of life or a blueprint for societal change, but rather an idealized image of an imagined future in which social, national, and imperial identity would somehow exist in communion rather than in conflict.

As a worldview, musical metaphysics was a rather nebulous concept, but it gave rise to numerous forms of social engagement, as well as providing a philosophical underpinning for the creative inspiration of composers like Skriabin, Vladimir I. Rebikov, Fedor S. Akimenko, and others. Though the ultimate goal in each case differed, Skriabin's envisioned *Mystery* and Rebikov's musical-dramatic "mysteries" both sought to overcome divisions between art and life.[21] For those involved in direct social engagement, musical metaphysics gave rise to a common assumption that the most effective means of achieving social unity was to fuse the people into a collective group or choir in which the individual human voice would find its place through performing as part of a greater whole. The stated task of the Moscow People's Conservatory, founded in 1906, was the creation of a genuine choir of the *narod*, a choir that would eventually prove able to collectively create its own "folk operas" in which each individual would compose a unique part. In this way, each individual's free creative potential would combine with others into a single, collective whole.[22] This focus on collective, communal creation through choral song was dwelt upon at length both in speeches presented at the People's Conservatory by one of its founders, Nadezhda Ia. Briusova, and in the periodical press of the day, with most authors embracing choral song as a necessary step in the education of the *narod*.[23] Through singing, individual differences might be

---

[20] See, for instance, K. R. Eiges, "Nauka o muzyke (po povodu lektsii Renchitskogo)," *Muzyka*, no. 154 (2 November 1913): 725–29; Eiges, "Krasota v iskusstve," *Zolotoe runo*, no. 11–12 (November–December 1909): 61–68; A. P. Koptiaev, "Skriabin (iz svobodnykh muzykal′nykh besed)," *Evterpe: Vtoroi sbornik muzykal′no-kriticheskikh statei* (St. Petersburg: Tipografiia glavnogo upravleniia udelov, 1908), 100–09; V. I. Rebikov, "Muzyka cherez 50 let," *Russkaia muzykal′naia gazeta*, no. 6 (February 1911): 151–52.

[21] O. M. Tompakova, *Vladimir Ivanovich Rebikov: Ocherki zhizni i tvorchestva* (Moscow: Muzyka, 1989); Simon Morrison, *Russian Opera and the Symbolist Movement* (Berkeley: University of California Press, 2002), 184–241; Richard Taruskin, *Defining Russia Musically: Historical and Hermeneutical Essays* (Princeton, NJ: Princeton University Press, 1997), 308–59.

[22] N. Ia. Briusova, "Muzyka dlia naroda," "Nasha narodnaia konservatoriia," Rossiiskii gosudarstvennyi arkhiv literatury i iskusstva (RGALI) f. 2009, op. 1, ed. khr. 86, ll. 20–83.

[23] See, for instance, F. Smirnov, "Narodnaia konservatoriia," *Baian*, no. 1 (28 January 1907): 10–11; anonymous, "Narodnaia konservatoriia," *Muzykal′nyi truzhenik*, no. 2 (15 September 1906): 10–11; A. Shepelevskii, "Korrespondentsiia," *Muzykal′nyi truzhenik*, no. 2 (15 January 1910): 21–22; anonymous, "O 'khudozhestvennom blagosostoianii

transformed into greater consonance. The spread of choirs, organized by both professional musicians and by social activists, was thereby a practical attempt to implement musical metaphysics and forge a unified Russian society.[24]

Redefining Musical Metaphysics after 1914

While the distinguishing line between Russian national and imperial music was blurred throughout most of the late 19th and early 20th centuries, the outbreak of war in 1914 led to explicit attempts to define patriotic sentiment on a purely ethnic basis. Patriotic sentiment in Russia's musical press (like the periodical press more generally) was increasingly expressed in anti-German tones. The popular press repeatedly attacked alleged "German bestiality" and "German dominance," exposing the latter in economic, political, and even musical spheres. Popular resentment of German success in farming, trade, and sales found expression in waves of violence perpetrated against anyone with suspected German heritage. Under pressure from the army leadership as well as popular sentiment, the Russian government gradually moved to repress the rights of German citizens and Russians of German descent, confiscating property, forcing entire communities to resettle, and removing legal rights. Jews were similarly targeted as a potentially disloyal ethnic group situated along the border.[25] Within this heightened mood of ethnic tension, musical society found itself in an awkward situation: in many ways, the very structure of musical life in the Russian Empire (not to mention a large percentage of the performance repertoire) was of German origin, while Jews had long predominated in Russian musical life in numbers disproportionate to their percentage of the larger population.[26] To demonstrate their loyalty to the empire, musicians increasingly had to fashion their creative work upon a "Russian" ethnic basis.

The early days of the war saw many members of Russia's musical community still emphasizing the central, unifying role of their art and proposing that music could transcend national divisions. Thus, N. N. Fatov insisted,

---

narodnykh mass,'" *Vestnik narodnogo obrazovaniia*, no. 1 (January 1916): 103–06; E. Linevaia, "Organizatsiia narodnykh khorov," *Vestnik narodnogo obrazovaniia*, no. 6–7 (June–July 1916): 721–22.

[24] Sargeant, *Harmony and Discord*, 208–10; N. N. Minor, *N. Ia. Briusova i ee shkola muzykal'nogo obrazovaniia* (Saratov: Izd-vo saratovskogo pedagogicheskogo instituta, 1994); Mitchell, "Nietzsche's Orphans," 62–69.

[25] Eric Lohr, *Nationalizing the Russian Empire: The Campaign against Enemy Aliens during World War I* (Cambridge, MA: Harvard University Press, 2003); Peter Gatrell, *A Whole Empire Walking: Refugees in Russia during World War I* (Bloomington: Indiana University Press, 2000).

[26] On the prevalence of Jews in musical life in imperial Russia, see Sargeant, *Harmony and Discord*, 136–40, 154–61; Loeffler, *Most Musical Nation*.

we must not forget the final goals of this war. It must bring us closer to the future brotherhood of nations [*narody*], and not to their division. We must destroy everything that interferes with that brotherhood, that disunites peoples, and all the more must we value that which enables unification. And truly is there anything that might unite people more than the fruits of spiritual culture, philosophical ideas, scientific discoveries, creations of art?[27]

Several new musical journals began publication in 1915, demonstrating the significance that music's unifying power was granted in the midst of wartime upheaval. The editor of the Odessa-based *Iuzhnyi muzykal′nyi vestnik* announced that his paper was devoted to reuniting the "connections between cultured peoples" at a time when the entire world, shaken by the events of war, seemed to have lost all unifying threads.[28] Rather than focusing on the unification of people of various nations, the Petrograd-based journal *Muzykal′nyi sovremennik*, also founded in 1915, highlighted the role of music in overcoming the societal divisions within Russia itself, which, argued the editor, had become ever more pronounced with the outbreak of war.[29] These ideals also found practical implementation: benefit concerts, the proceeds of which were devoted to victims of the war, were a common event by late 1914.[30] Underlying such arguments and actions was the assumption that music, as the most widespread of arts, was an expression of "universal human genius, universal spirit," a claim in keeping with the universalizing aspect of musical metaphysics developed in the prewar era.

However, it became increasingly difficult amid rising nationalist tensions to advocate a universal, progressive view of human history and music without an explicit embrace of Russia's unique, messianic role. In a 1913 series of articles dedicated to the "national particularities of Russian music," Iurii V. Kurdiumov argued that just as it was impossible for anyone to love "Russians, Germans, and Tatars" equally, it was human nature to prefer one's homeland (and, by extension, the art of that homeland). For this reason, he concluded, a "universal" art was possible *only* upon a national basis.[31] Russian

---

[27] N. Fatov, "Eshche po povodu 'Iskusstvo vragov,'" *Russkaia muzykal′naia gazeta*, no. 46 (16 November 1914): 843–45, here 844–45.

[28] [N. Martsenko], "Ot redaktsii," *Iuzhnyi muzykal′nyi vestnik*, no. 1 (March 1915): 2.

[29] "Ot redaktora," *Muzykal′nyi sovremennik*, no. 1 (September 1915): 1–21.

[30] Hubertus F. Jahn, *Patriotic Culture in Russia during World War I* (Ithaca, NY: Cornell University Press, 1995), 148.

[31] Iu. V. Kurdiumov, "O natsional′nykh osobennostiakh russkoi muzyki," *Russkaia muzykal′naia gazeta*, no. 13 (31 March 1913): 322–26, here 323. The series of articles appears in the following issues of *Russkaia muzykal′naia gazeta*, no. 13 (31 March 1913): 322–26; no. 14 (7 April 1913): 359–62; no. 40 (6 October 1913): 856–58; no. 41 (13 October 1913): 884–87; no. 43 (27 October 1913): 953–60.

composers would, by their very nature, write specifically Russian music, so long as they deeply loved their country, sharing its dreams, beliefs, joys and grief.[32] Underpinning this call for Russian music was the concern expressed by many that, although music in Russia "currently occupies a leading role [in the development of Russian culture], both in the range of its development, and in its content," most music performed in the empire was of foreign rather than Russian origin.[33] Russian audiences, it seemed, lacked sufficient patriotic content in their concerts.

In keeping with the above debates, and in correspondence with other boycotts of German products, public discussion turned to the question of banning German music. In early 1915, the journal *Rampa i zhizn'* posed two questions to its reading public: Would a ban on musical works of the nations battling against Russia be appropriate? If so, would such a ban harm the development of Russian music? While posing the issue as a question open to discussion, journalist M. Unigovskii made no secret of his own views, arguing that "in Rus' we have enough of our own great purely Russian composers.... Being freed from the influence of the Germans, there will appear among us Wagners and Beethovens in the Russian spirit, who have thus far, due to our love of everything foreign, not received their deserved attention."[34] The published responses covered the full spectrum of opinions, but a general boycott of German music was generally observed.[35] German and Austrian musicians performing in Russia were replaced by musicians from "friendly" countries such as Russia, Poland, and France. In some cases, German and Austrian musicians stranded in Russia at the outbreak of war were expelled or arrested.[36]

Such a rejection of all things German did not, however, receive universal approval among Russian musical society. In an attempt to reclaim the Germanic

---

[32] Kurdiumov, "O natsional'nykh osobennostiakh russkoi muzyki," 323.

[33] Ia. Karklin, "Chto nuzhno provintsii dlia uspeshnogo propagandirovaniia russkoi simfonicheskoi muzyki," *Bibliograficheskii listok Russkoi muzykal'noi gazety*, no. 1 (1914): 1–3; Manfred, "Letopis' provintsii," *Muzyka*, no. 223 (12 September 1915): 338–41.

[34] M. Unigovskii, "Voina i nemetskaia muzyka," *Rampa i zhizn'*, no. 4 (1915): 7.

[35] Ibid., 7; Unigovskii, "Voina i nemetskaia muzyka," *Rampa i zhizn'*, no. 5 (1915): 5–6; Stites, "Days and Nights," 361 n. 5; Nicolai Malko, *A Certain Art* (Toronto: George McLeod Publishers, 1966), 135. This boycott of German music, while commonly followed, was not absolute. For instance, at a concert on 12 December 1916, the conductor Sergei A. Kusevitskii included a performance of Mozart's op. 49 Symphony on the program. See "Kontserty S. Kusevitskogo," *Moskovskie vedomosti*, 14 December 1916, 4. Nevertheless, such programming choices occurred rarely.

[36] The ban on musicians seems to have started voluntarily and then culminated in a government policy that supported the expulsion of enemy musicians. See Zritel', "Muzykal'nyi mir," *Muzyka*, no. 194 (25 October 1914): 492–93; "Muzyka i voina," *Russkaia muzykal'naia gazeta*, no. 2 (1915): 44–46.

musical heritage, numerous contemporaries adopted an explicit contrast between modern-day "Prussia" and the cultural heritage of "Germany."[37] It was claimed that "Prussian" belligerence was of recent origin, which it was necessary to distinguish clearly from the great (and universal) achievements of past German culture. While the latter could continue to serve as a source of inspiration for contemporary Russia, the former deserved only hatred. Building on this distinction in 1914, Derzhanovskii claimed "only several decades ago [Prussia] transformed [Germany] into a spiritual desert, on the soil of which had grown the false empty blossoms of [Richard] Strauss and [Max] Reger."[38] It was the duty of all true Russian musicians, he concluded, to preserve the great German humanist traditions of the past, while struggling against the materialistic, warlike culture of modern-day Prussia.[39]

In contrast to "Prussia," "Germany" symbolized a lost world of culture that had once inspired the greatest products of human creativity. "Germany" was the world of Bach, Beethoven, Mozart, Goethe, and Kant, a world "of musicians, philosophers, and poets" to which Russian intellectuals and artists could continue to turn for inspiration.[40] In doing so, Russians would supposedly differentiate themselves from Prussia. Because the German people had proven deaf to the great humanistic message expressed by its past geniuses, the task of correct interpretation had fallen to Russia. The rhetorical thrust was obvious: through separating "cultural" Germany from the present-day military opponent, the Germanic musical and intellectual heritage could be preserved while simultaneously embracing Russian patriotism in support of the war.

Music itself emerged as a battlefield in which Russian spiritual victory was to be achieved over the German enemy. For many contemporary commentators, music expressed both the decline of German dominance and the birth of new, Russian creativity.[41] Germany's deterioration was allegedly embodied in the music of contemporary German composers like Max Reger and Richard Strauss. Contradictory interpretations emerged in particular

---

[37] Akimenko, "Iskusstvo i voina," 835–36. For a similar division made in the non-musical press, see A. Koral'nik, "Germanskaia ideia," *Russkaia mysl'*, no. 12 (December 1914): 42–60; Grigorii Rachinskii, "Bratstvo i svoboda," *Russkaia mysl'*, no. 12 (December 1914): 83–87; V. Buzeskul, "Sovremennaia Germaniia i nemetskaia istoricheskaia nauka XIX stoletiia," *Russkaia mysl'*, no. 2 (February 1915): 24–55; Petr Struve, "Sud' istorii," *Russkaia mysl'*, no. 11 (November 1914): 158–68, here 167.

[38] Derzhanovskii, "V buriu, vo grozu," 455. See also N. N. Fatov, "Iskusstvo vragov," *Russkaia muzykal'naia gazeta*, no. 38–39 (1914): 728–29.

[39] See, for instance, Iu. Shamurin, "Sviataia voina," *Muzyka*, no. 193 (2 August 1914): 462–72.

[40] Derzhanovskii, "V buriu, vo grozu," 455; Shamurin, "Sviataia voina," 468.

[41] A. Gorskii, "Germanizm i muzyka," *Iuzhnyi muzykal'nyi vestnik*, no. 6 (June 1915): 6–9, here 8; Shamurin, "Sviataia voina," 463.

around the figure of Richard Wagner, once the darling of the Russian Symbolist movement and a much-celebrated composer among Russian musical society in the early 20th century.[42] In the midst of wartime rhetoric, Wagner came to symbolize the intermingling of musical, metaphysical, and nationalist rhetoric. His creative output could be embraced now only in part, and only through specific explanation.[43] In defining the militarism of modern Germany, liberal philosopher Evgenii Trubetskoi turned to the music of Wagner, finding there an allegorical embodiment of "Prussianism" that was embraced by many contemporaries.[44] Vladimir Solov'ev's metaphorical adoption of the figure of Siegfried to symbolize contemporary Germany was revived for rhetorical effect in many musical commentaries.[45] Music critic A. Gorskii argued that, in order to understand the motivations of the German enemy, one must first study the creative output of Wagner. The character of Siegfried, Gorskii argued, had paved the way for future German actions, uniting them into a single, militaristic whole.[46] Nor was rhetoric limited to lofty, spiritual concerns. A. Kankarovich argued that Germany had lost, not merely economically, but also musically from the impacts of the war; in his view, the Wagner *Festspiel* in Bayreuth had been canceled because it operated primarily on money provided by Russian tourists who were no longer able to attend. Moreover, he argued, most concert halls, music stores, and publishers in Germany had suffered, since Russians had formed the most supportive market.[47] Underpinning such claims was the assumption that only Russians could truly appreciate the spiritual importance of arts such as music.

---

[42] Jahn, *Patriotic Culture*, 145–46; Rosamund Bartlett, *Wagner and Russia* (Cambridge: Cambridge University Press, 1995), 114, 117–217; Rebecca Mitchell, "How Russian was Wagner? Russian Campaigns to Defend or Destroy the German Composer during the Great War (1914–1917)," in *Wagner in Russia, Poland and the Czech Lands—Musical, Literary, and Cultural Perspectives*, ed. Anastasia Belina-Johnson and Stephen Muir (Farnham, UK: Ashgate Press, 2013), 51–71

[43] See, for instance, Viacheslav Ivanov, "Natsional'noe i vselenskoe," RGALI f. 225, op. 1, d. 38, ll. 46–49.

[44] Mikhael Baliasnyi, "Nibelungov shchit," *Novoe zveno*, no. 2 (December 1913): 63; Evgenii Trubetskoi, "Voina i mirovaia zadacha Rossii," *Russkaia mysl'*, no. 12 (December 1914): 88–96, here 91; Bulgakov, "Russkie dumy," 109; A. Smirnov (Kutacheskii), "Pochemu nam dorog Konstantinopol?" *Russkaia mysl'*, no. 4 (April 1915): 20–22, here 20.

[45] See, for instance, Ars. Avr., "Rikhard Vagner. Nibelungi," *Muzyka*, no. 218 (11 April 1915): 248; A. Moshchanskii, "Materialy po istorii russkoi literatury i kul'tury," *Russkaia mysl'*, no. 12 (December 1914): 140–45.

[46] A. Gorskii, "Germanizm i muzyka," *Iuzhnyi muzykal'nyi vestnik*, no. 12–13 (1915), 3–4; no. 5–6 (1916): 23.

[47] A. Kankarovich, "Chto poteriala muzykal'naia Germaniia ot voiny s Rossiei: Vpechatleniia pobyvshego v plenu u nemtsov muzykanta," *Rampa i zhizn'*, no. 8 (1915):

Such critique was not limited to patriotic sentiment, but extended to an attack on many of the values and practices that had emerged in the modern age. Moscow critic Iurii Shamurin argued that it was not Germany alone that had fashioned "Prussia," but that "all peoples spiritually created [Prussia]."[48] While Prussia was, in Shamurin's view, the birthplace of contemporary decay, all people and nations were equally guilty of adopting a "Prussian" worldview in their own lives and societies. For this reason, "in destroying Prussia, people will destroy a shameful page of their own past": the development of materialism, capitalism, rude strength, and "all the evils and devilishness of our century."[49] "Prussianism" in this sense was not a German, but a universal human, and specifically modern, concern. Since the "Teutons" had proven deaf to the great humanistic message expressed by its past geniuses, argued composer Fedor Akimenko in 1914, the task of correct interpretation had fallen to Russia.[50] Russia's mission was clear: the overcoming of the divisive, modern spirit and creation of a new, less individualistic society. This task was physically embodied in the current "holy war" (*sviataia voina*) Russia waged against the enemy. Russia could not merely defeat Germany by military might, as this would simply mark the shift of power from one people to another.[51] Rather, Russia's mission was to transform the spiritual basis of the world itself. Comparing the import of the current crisis with Christ's crucifixion, Shamurin envisioned the "birth of a new humanity, of a new life, of which it was impossible to even think before," through Russian victory over German forces.[52] Through Slavic intervention, the world would be transformed and "all will become brothers. Never before on the earth has such a flame of love and communality burned." By "throwing off its petty concerns," all humanity would emerge from the battle "united and wonderful!"[53] In this

---

5.

[48] Shamurin, "Sviataia voina," 466–67.

[49] Shamurin, "Sviataia voina," 466–67, 468. See also Gorskii, "Germanizm i muzyka," *Iuzhnyi muzykal'nyi vestnik*, no. 5–6 (1916): 24. For a similar discourse in the nonmusical press, see Sergei Bulgakov, "Russkie dumy," *Russkaia mysl'*, no. 12 (December 1914): 108–15.

[50] Akimenko, "Iskusstvo i voina," 836. For similar views in the general press, see also Nabliudatel', "Otvet na vozzvanie 'k kul'turnomu miru' predstavitelei germanskoi nauki i iskusstva," *Moskovskie vedomosti*, no. 26 (1 February 1915): 1.

[51] Shamurin, "Sviataia voina," 465–66; Gorskii, "Germanizm i muzyka," 24–25.

[52] Shamurin, "Sviataia voina," 463.

[53] Ibid., 466.

and similar narratives, Russia was often envisioned in the role of Christ, with contemporary Germany (or Prussia) cast as the Antichrist.[54]

As the war progressed, rhetoric surrounding music generally proved more ubiquitous than the production of actual musical works. Critics eagerly reinterpreted contemporary Russian composers in the public press to highlight their meaning amid military conflict. Aleksandr Brianchaninov, editor of the short-lived *Novoe zveno*, re-envisioned the musical significance of "universalist" composer Aleksandr Skriabin in Pan-Slavic terms.[55] Brianchaninov's journal trumpeted its preference for Slavic peoples, arguing that the only rational way to improve the human condition was to focus "first [upon] the good of Russia itself, then the good of Slavs, to whom the Russian people belong, then the good of Europe, from the culture of which humanity feeds, and only then the good of all humanity."[56] The collective Slavic soul, he argued, was in a desperate battle for survival with "Prussian" individualism and militarism.[57] Brianchaninov cited Skriabin as the artistic symbol of Russia's struggle, an ethnically pure composer whose message was not for the unification of all humanity, but for the unification of Slavic peoples under Russian leadership. This increasingly Slavophile interpretation of the composer was seconded by other authors.[58] Music, Skriabin, and military victory by an ethnically pure Russia were three parts of a single whole.

In comparison with the richness of public discourse about music's wartime significance, few new compositions explicitly addressed the wartime experience. Unity, however, remained as a musical ideal. Composer Vladimir Rebikov had celebrated the First Balkan War with a 1913 piece for piano,

---

[54] Ibid., 470; Bulgakov, "Russkie dumy," 115; Viacheslav Ivanov, "Vselenskoe delo," *Russkaia mysl'*, no. 12 (December 1914): 97–107, here 104.

[55] Skriabin himself explicitly rejected nationalism as a basis for musical creativity. See "A. Skriabin i I. Gofman o Shopen," *Russkaia muzykal'naia gazeta*, no. 13 (28 March 1910): 353–54. Brianchaninov was an intimate acquaintance of the composer and well-acquainted with the composer's views. See Gosudarstvennyi tsentral'nyi muzei muzykal'noi kul'tury (GTsMMK) f. 31, no. 649–51 (Brianchaninov to Skriabin).

[56] [A. N. Brianchaninov],"Ot izdatelia," *Novoe zveno*, no. 1 (14 December 1913): 2–3.

[57] This nationalist reinterpretation of Skriabin's role in history was aided by the composer's decision to publish his 1915 assessment of the significance of the war in the Petrograd journal *Novoe zveno*. Skriabin suggested that the military conflict was simply a sign that all nations of the world were preparing for the next stage of human history. He planned to usher it in with the composition of his *Mystery*—a magnum opus destined to unify all peoples in a final moment of ecstasy and bring about the end of the world.

[58] See, for instance, A. N. B[rianchaninov], "Zven'ia zhizni," *Novoe zveno*, no. 43 (18 October 1914): 1119–23; Iu. Osberg, "Pis'mo v redaktsiiu," *Novoe zveno*, no. 34 (1914): 939–40; Pavel Polianov, "Nekotorye motivy tvorchestva A. Skriabina," *Muzyka*, no. 214 (14 March 1915): 169–72.

entitled *For the Freedom of the Slavs*. The work celebrated the potential for Slavic unity and the victory of Christianity, the same basis upon which Russia was called to lead the struggle in its 1914 "holy war." The cover page depicted the rulers of Serbia, Bulgaria, Montenegro, and Greece side by side, part of a unified Slavic brotherhood.[59] The music itself was a military march subtitled "To Constantinople," written at a basic technical level and intended for wide circulation among the scores of less-skilled pianists in the Russian Empire searching for music that was accessible, relatively simple, and suitably "Slavic" in character. With Russia's direct involvement in war in 1914, composers like Sergei Vasilenko, Aleksandr Kastal'skii, and Aleksandr Glazunov were similarly inspired to create patriotic compositions celebrating the unified power of the Allied peoples.[60]

While Russia's position, both as leader of a united Slavic people, and as humanity's deliverer from the multiple evils of modernity, was celebrated both in word and sound, the fate of ethnic minorities in the Russian Empire demonstrated a policy of exclusion and open hostility. Germans and Jews, ethnic groups specifically targeted as potential enemies during the war, had played an important role in the development of Russian musical life since the very founding of the RMO.[61] Music conservatories throughout the empire had attracted frequent criticism, both from the general public and within the musical community, for providing an opportunity for Jews to evade military service.[62] One Jewish father, Sholom Berkov Goldin, attempted to circumvent limitations on Jewish enrollment in the Moscow Conservatory (and thereby assure the acceptance of his son) through explicit adoption of patriotic discourse. Emphasizing his own past military service, as well as another son's death in battle in East Prussia in 1914, Goldin insisted that the only way Russian society could distinguish itself from the "Teutonic barbarians" was through accepting Jews as loyal subjects of "our dear fatherland Russia" and its "Great Tsar."[63] Similarly, despite a successful musical career centered in Moscow, by fall 1914 the composer Nikolai Medtner found that his Baltic German background had become a source of continual suspicion and hostility. At a meeting of the Religious-Philosophical Society on 19 October 1914, at the home of his former piano student and patroness, Margarita Morozova, Medtner was deeply stricken by the anti-German sentiments expressed in a

---

[59] The leaders depicted were George I of Greece, Peter I of Serbia, Ferdinand I of Bulgaria, and Nicholas I of Montenegro. See V. I. Rebikov, *Za svobodu slavian* (Moscow: Jurgenson, [1913]).

[60] Jahn, *Patriotic Culture*, 141.

[61] On the specific targeting of Germans and Jews, see Lohr, *Nationalizing the Russian Empire*.

[62] Sargeant, *Harmony and Discord*, 263–65; Loeffler, *Most Musical Nation*, 176–77, 210–11.

[63] Goldin's petition had no effect. See Sargeant, *Harmony and Discord*, 265.

series of papers on the "German question" by such intellectual luminaries as Viacheslav Ivanov, Semen Frank, Sergei Bulgakov, and Trubetskoi.[64] He was equally hurt by Morozova's accusation that his failure to enlist in the army demonstrated a lack of patriotic feeling, a suspicion that similarly inspired police surveillance of his family and the confiscation of numerous letters.[65]

Growing ethnic tensions also sparked a backlash among some Jewish musicians. A 1915 polemic between the Moscow and Petrograd branches of the Jewish Musical Society centered upon the question of whether Jewish folk songs that showed the influence of non-Jewish musical styles should serve as a basis for Jewish composers. Composer Lazare Saminskii argued that only music from the synagogue should be taken as a source, as all other forms of folk music were contaminated by their association with non-Jewish groups. Despite vehement protest from Joel Engel (one of the founders of the society), several composers in the Petrograd group embraced Saminskii's call for a "reorientation in the direction of religious melodies."[66] The uneasy relationship between ethnic identity and music's unifying impulse, never clearly delineated in the concept of musical metaphysics that took hold in late imperial Russia, thus found sharp differentiation as a result of wartime rhetoric. The metaphorical sword with which Derzhanovskii had summoned his readers to fight for Russia (and all cultured humanity) through their musical creativity, instead cut through the very cultural ties that had allowed for the creation of a Russian imperial musical culture.

Russia's Musical Death: Disillusion in 1915

While many composers and performers were able to avoid direct military service, there were others who, voluntarily or involuntarily, were called up for service at the front. In early 1915, *Rampa i zhizn'*, which kept a regular column on "artists at war," requested biographical information and photographs for musicians or artists killed at the front for inclusion in future issues. The lists of wounded and killed artists and soldiers grew ever longer as the war dragged on, and patriotic sentiment gave way to war weariness.[67] The scarce letters sent from the front by members of the musical community tell a similar story. Writing home from his service as an officer, composer Nikolai Miaskovskii

---

[64] These talks were published in *Russkaia mysl'*, no. 12 (December 1914).

[65] GTsMMK f. 132, no. 4730 (Medtner to Ivan Il'in, 30 May 1915); Barrie Martyn, *Nicolas Medtner: His Life and Music* (London: Scolar Press, 1995); GARF f. 102 o.o. 1915 g., op. 245, d. 165, t. 3, ll. 65–66.

[66] Loeffler, *Most Musical Nation*, 177–85, esp. 180.

[67] "Artisty-voiny," *Rampa i zhizn'*, no. 13 (1915): 7. See also "Artisty-voiny," *Rampa i zhizn'*, no. 11 (1915): 8; "Pamiati N. I. Kazanli," *Russkaia muzykal'naia gazeta*, no. 32–33 (7–14 August 1916); K. Eiges, "Dve poteri russkoi muzyki," *Russkaia mysl'*, no. 12 (December 1915): 18–22.

stated simply that "everyone is fed up with the war."[68] This disillusion found expression not just with the war, but with music itself. Music critic Abaza-Grigor'ev wrote to his old companion Aleksandr Koptiaev from the front, describing "a completely different world, [one of] pistols, blood and fire." He mused that "not considering my organic connection with music, I cannot say that I even miss it. It is true that there is too little time left over here for anything other than the most elementary work for self-preservation."[69] Reflecting in December 1915 upon the significance of Christ's birth, Rebikov disconsolately concluded that the present age demonstrated the "victory of the material [realm]" over the spiritual. While insisting that at some future point in time humanity would once again remember Christ's teachings, he observed that such a time would come to pass perhaps only after another 20,000 years.[70] Dreams of Russian music's transformative, unifying and Christianizing power paled in the face of wartime reality.

For Russian educated society as a whole, however, it was the death of composer Aleksandr Skriabin from blood poisoning in 1915 that cast a dark shadow upon the fate of Russia. Mulling over the significance of the composer's death, music critic Evgenii Gunst passionately opined,

> Evil, merciless death! The sacrifices of this nightmarish war were not enough for you! You have come to the climax of your mad dance! You were not satisfied with the tens and hundreds of thousands of lives of people that you carry off each day.... Insatiable, you wanted to seize from the long-suffering Russia one of her greatest geniuses![71]

While, in the first throes of grief, Gunst insisted that Russia would "never let Skriabin go," discussion surrounding this popular figure soon took on a darker hue. In a brief article for *Rampa i zhizn'*, Skriabin's former piano student Mark Meichek hinted that the composer's death was caused by the intervention of supernatural forces, while in 1916 Leonid Sabaneev openly accused his former idol of "satanism." Rather than embodying the "Russian" traits of spirituality, harmony, and unity, Skriabin had, in Sabaneev's assessment, fallen prey to the "Prussian" elements of egoistic individuality and divisiveness.[72] The death of composer Sergei Taneev, a fixture of Moscow musical life, in summer 1915 (after allegedly catching a cold while attending Skriabin's funeral), together with the constant knell of military losses, contributed to the darkening of the

---

[68] Stites, "Days and Nights," 14.

[69] Rossiiskaia natsional'naia biblioteka (RNB) f. 371, op. 1, ed. khr. 1 (Abaza-Grigor'ev to A. P. Koptiaev, 6 August 1916), ll. 2ob.–4.

[70] GTsMMK f. 68, no. 102 (Rebikov, "1915 let tomu nazad rodilsia chelovek"), l. 2ob.

[71] E. Gunst, "Dlia genii net smerti," *Rampa i zhizn'*, no. 16 (19 April 1915): 3–4.

[72] L. L. Sabaneev, *Skriabin* (Moscow: Skorpion, 1916), especially 68–84.

musical landscape. Sergei Kusevitskii's orchestra, one of the few performing ensembles to have continued an active performance agenda in the midst of the war, dissolved in 1916 after more than half its members were drafted into active service.[73] Nikolai Medtner, shattered by the strains of the war and by attacks on his "German" background, found his creative abilities virtually paralyzed.[74] Picking up on this mood, Sergei Rachmaninoff's *Études-tableaux* op. 39, composed and premiered primarily in 1915, made extensive use of the *Dies Irae* chant from the Latin Requiem.[75]

While musical life did not fall silent entirely, the social and spiritual connotations that musical metaphysics had granted to it increasingly did. Music served ever more as a realm for escape rather than an active means through which to engage with current events. Russia's "holy war" had not progressed as envisioned. Politicization of the musical sphere, while claiming to awaken unifying patriotic sentiment, had succeeded only in deepening divisions. Ethnic tensions shattered musical society, while the association of Russia's fate with the triumphal growth of her musical life was turned into a mockery with the death of her representatives. By early 1917, Russia seemed to face defeat both militarily and musically.

In Search of a New Identity

In contrast to the gradual silencing of the musical landscape in the twilight of the tsarist empire, the February Revolution of 1917 was greeted with music. As Boris Kolonitskii has demonstrated, the singing of revolutionary songs was a key way in which crowds in Petrograd and elsewhere celebrated the end of the tsarist regime.[76] Many members of the musical elite responded with enthusiasm to the new political system. In a letter of 20 March from Perm', music critic Boris Popov rejoiced at the abdication of the tsar and the birth

---

[73] Nelson, *Music for the Revolution*, 13; Stites, "Days and Nights," 14.

[74] GTsMMK f. 132, no. 1826–41 (Nikolai Medtner to Emil Medtner, 8 November 1914), ll. 3–7; f. 132, no. 1826–41 (Nikolai Medtner to Emil Medtner, 2 February 1915), ll. 9–10; Library of Congress (LC) Medtner correspondence (Anna Medtner to Emil Medtner, 8 November 1914), l. 1ob.

[75] Eight of the nine op. 39 *Études-tableaux* (c-moll, a-moll, fis-moll, h-moll, es-moll, a-moll, c-moll, D-dur) were premiered on 5 December 1916 in the Theater of K. N. Nezlobin. *Étude-tableau* op. 39, no. 2 bears a 1917 date, but a version of the piece was performed on 5 December 1916. See RGALI f. 2985, op. 1, ed. khr. 624, ll. 30–32. On the presence of the *Dies irae* motif, see Mitchell, "Nietzsche's Orphans," 407–10.

[76] The "Marseillaise" was particularly popular. See B. I. Kolonitskii, *Simvoly vlasti i bor'ba za vlast': K izucheniiu politicheskoi kul'tury Rossiiskoi revoliutsii 1917 goda* (St. Petersburg: Dmitrii Bulanin, 2001), 14–37.

of a new, free Russia.[77] Writing from Rostov on 22 March, the pianist Matvei Presman declaimed "Long live Free, Mighty Russia!" and enthusiastically greeted the new political system as a time when one could finally "breathe deeply and freely."[78]

One of the central questions with which musical elites concerned themselves in the months after the February Revolution was the creation of a new anthem for Russia. While the Provisional Government recognized the need for a new state anthem to replace "God Save the Tsar," no practical measures were taken to adopt a new anthem.[79] Russian musical circles quickly sought to take measures into their own hands: in early March, members of the Mariinskii Theater approached Glazunov with a request to "quickly compose" a new anthem for performance on 13 March, while in early March, *Russkaia muzykal'naia gazeta* requested proposals for a temporary anthem.[80] Responses to this call demonstrate ongoing divisions over the question of how Russia's future should be represented musically. Various blends of the Russian national musical style were proposed: some suggested a competition to create an entirely new anthem, others insisted that the only appropriate anthem for the new Russia should employ a melody created by the Russian people itself, such as the "Song of the Volga Boatmen."[81] Attracted by the potential for popular recognition, Sergei Prokof'ev briefly toyed with the idea of submitting an anthem.[82] Boris Popov proposed the use of Modest Musorgskii's "Slava!" chorus from *Boris Godunov*; while recognizing the opera's unflattering historical context, he composed new words glorifying Russia's transformed political situation. These lyrics, he argued, reflected the legal formulation of the new state, with themes of territory, people (*narod*), and

---

[77] RNB f. 816, op. 2, no. 1722, ll. 65–69 (Popov to Nikolai Findeizen, 20 March 1917).

[78] RNB f. 816, op. 2, ed. khr. 1741, l. 32 (Presman to Nikolai Findeizen, 22 March 1917). Inspired by the events of February, Presman founded a new music conservatory in Rostov, which boasted an enrollment of almost 500 students after only a few months of existence. RNB f. 816, op. 2, ed. khr. 1741, ll. 33–38 (Presman to Nikolai Findeizen, 14 May 1926).

[79] Kolonitskii, *Simvoly vlasti*, 285–86; O. N. Znamenskii, *Intelligentsiia nakanune velikogo oktiabria* (Leningrad: Nauka, 1988), 183–85.

[80] Glazunov rejected this request but emphasized the need for the new anthem to represent the Russian *narod* as a whole. See Kolonitskii, *Simvoly vlasti*, 286; Znamenskii, *Intelligentsiia nakanune velikogo oktiabria*, 183–84.

[81] Kolonitskii, *Simvoly vlasti*, 286; Znamenskii, *Intelligentsiia nakanune velikogo oktiabria*, 184.

[82] Nevertheless, Prokof'ev concluded that the most fitting anthem would be Glinka's "Slava" chorus, which "only needs new words." See Sergei Prokof'ev, *Dnevnik 1907–1933*, 1: *Dnevnik 1907–1918* (Paris: SPRKFV, 2002), 645.

state power.[83] Other respondents suggested specific works by composers as diverse as Rimskii-Korsakov and Dmitrii Bortnianskii, while poet Konstantin Bal′mont offered his own rendition of an anthem set to music by Aleksandr Grechaninov. Many of these proposals emphasized the expression of ethnic Russianness as an inherent part of the new anthem.

While these debates provide insight into the worldview of Russian musical society after the February Revolution, they had little practical result. Events were moving too quickly for any unified sense of musical direction to develop, such that in the end the Provisional Government's unofficial anthem (the "Marseillaise") was selected by popular usage rather than by the musical elite.[84] It was only after the October Revolution that musical society began to exert greater influence on popular musical expression, in large part through cooperation with the new Soviet regime.

Continuity and Rupture after 1917

Despite dramatic political upheavals under Bolshevik rule after October, the musical realm experienced surprising continuity. Within the new political system, music and musical elites took on a lofty mission—the education of the masses in order to create the new Soviet citizen. In official rhetoric, musical metaphysics was reinterpreted to emphasize class rather than nationality as the predominant social factor. During the Civil War period (1918–21), the government sought to bring existing musical institutions under state control, expand their reach into provincial areas, and win over musical elites to the Communist cause. The goal was to employ music as an educational and propagandistic force for spreading revolution and transforming society.

To accomplish these tasks, early Soviet musical life built upon the institutions founded in the prerevolutionary era and the specialists who had staffed them. When the new government was formed on 26 October 1917, Anatolii Lunacharskii was chosen to head the Commissariat of Enlightenment (Narkompros), an institution that took over jurisdiction of the former ministries that had dealt with Public Education, the Imperial Theaters, and the Academy of Arts.[85] Most of the musical institutions of the former Russian Empire accordingly fell under its jurisdiction. In an attempt to win over musical elites, Lunacharskii spent the months after the Revolution forming temporary bodies such as the Moscow Musical Council, whose function was to unite the most important Moscow musicians into a single advisory

---

[83] RNB f. 816, op. 2, ed. khr. 1722, ll. 65–66ob. (Popov to Nikolai Findeizen, 20 March 1917).

[84] Kolonitskii, *Simvoly vlasti*, 287.

[85] Sheila Fitzpatrick, *The Commissariat of Enlightenment: Soviet Organization of Education and the Arts under Lunacharsky, October 1917–1921* (Cambridge: Cambridge University Press, 1970), 11.

body. Such local groups gradually disbanded with the formation of Muzo, the musical division of Narkompros, whose branches were founded in Petrograd in January 1918 and Moscow in June 1918.[86] Often their staff were the same leading musicians who had dominated musical life in late imperial Russia.[87]

Although Muzo held a dominant position by 1918, institutional plurality and overlap defined the landscape of postrevolutionary musical life.[88] October 1917 also witnessed the formation of Proletkul't: a cultural-educational organization dedicated to the promotion of "proletarian culture" which viewed itself as a distinct, independent entity.[89] Despite subsequent conflict that ultimately led to the subjugation of Proletkul't to Narkompros control in late 1920, the musical realm witnessed a considerable degree of overlap between the members of Proletkul't and Muzo. Similarly, music schools and conservatories often depended on the same prerevolutionary musical elites who also found employment in Muzo and/or Proletkul't. Despite institutional upheaval and the loss of a number of leading musical figures through emigration, the early years following the Revolution thus saw relatively little turnover in the realm of musical elites.

The philosophical realm likewise evinced significant continuities, as Marxist-Leninist ideology sustained music's role as a civilizing force destined to unify society. The concept of bringing music to the workers, both through open concerts and the creation of mass choirs, was an extension of ideals that had developed in the ferment after 1905, while the active work of Briusova and others in the People's Conservatory movement required only modest adaptation to serve the new system's ideological aims.[90] The years after the Revolution saw educational initiatives expand their reach into the provinces. Acting on the belief that the riches of musical culture should be available to all, Petrozavodsk (capital of Soviet Karelia) could already boast in 1918 of the establishment of a "small but active symphonic orchestra of some twenty

---

[86] In his diary, A. B. Gol'denveizer reports continued work for the Moscow Music Council in July 1918, though Muzo seems to have been in existence since 1 June 1918. See A. B. Gol'denveizer, *Dnevnik: Tetradi vtoraia–shestaia, 1905–1929* (Moscow: Turtuga, 1997), 26; Nelson, *Music for the Revolution*, 20–22, 251 n. 25. From a humble beginning of 12 staff, Muzo expanded to include 184 full-time staff, together with an additional 600 to 784 people under its jurisdiction by 1921. See Nelson, *Music for the Revolution*, 20.

[87] Nelson, *Music for the Revolution*, 21.

[88] Ibid., 13–40; Boris Schwarz, *Music and Musical Life in Soviet Russia, 1917–1970* (New York: Norton, 1972), 3–37; Susannah Lockwood Smith, "From Peasants to Professionals: The Socialist-Realist Transformation of a Russian Folk Choir," *Kritika: Explorations in Russian and Eurasian History* 3, 3 (Summer 2002): 393–425; Sargeant, *Harmony and Discord*, 267–83.

[89] Fitzpatrick, *Commissariat of Enlightenment*, 89–109.

[90] N. Ia. Briusova, *Zadachi narodnogo muzykal'nogo obrazovaniia* (Moscow: Narkompros, 1919); Sargeant, *Harmony and Discord*, 279.

players, an orchestra of Russian folk instruments, a choir, [and] a brass band."[91] Similarly, the town of Vitebsk, which "had not had a single music school" prior to the Revolution, saw the establishment of five music schools, a conservatory, choir, and music club, as well as a symphony orchestra that performed 240 times during its first two-and-a-half years of existence.[92]

Despite such overriding continuities, the October Revolution did introduce new trends and even ruptures into musical life, most notably an increased dependence upon (and desire to influence) governmental authority. The possibility of direct governmental involvement exacerbated pre-existing divisions within musical society at the same time that convoluted layers of institutional power produced confusion and contradiction, both within the government and among musicians. Although the nationalization of the RMO, music schools and conservatories moved forward with little difficulty in 1918, questions surrounding musical stores and instruments exposed an ongoing divide between musical elites and popular demand.[93] Not long after the Soviet government passed a resolution pertaining to the nationalization of musical stores on 23 November 1918, Muzo lodged a complaint against local government officials in the provinces who, without waiting for orders, had taken the nationalization process into their own hands.[94] The question of whether musical instruments ultimately belonged to local worker groups (who had spontaneously seized pianos and other instruments) or to central government agencies like Muzo was still unresolved in 1922.[95]

Ultimately, whether for good or ill, the possibility of an imperial Russian (*rossiiskii*) musical identity vanished after 1917, both inside and outside the

---

[91] Pekka Suutari, "Going beyond the Border: National Cultural Policy and the Development of Musical Life in Soviet Karelia, 1920–1940," in *Soviet Music and Society under Lenin and Stalin: The Baton and Sickle*, ed. Neil Edmunds (London: Routledge, 2004), 163–80, here 167.

[92] Malko, *A Certain Art*, 140. The Piatnitskii Choir (founded in 1911) similarly found new justification by performing for mass audiences in the Soviet Union. See Smith, "From Peasants to Professionals," 393–99.

[93] On the nationalization of local RMO branches and their reorganization, see GARF f. 130, op. 2, d. 1015, ll. 6; GARF f. 120, op. 2, d. 1051, ll. 34–44.

[94] Protokol 157 (Proekt dekreta o natsionalizatsii notnykh muzykal'nykh magazinov, skladov, notopechaten i notoizdatel'stv) was passed by the small inner council (*malyi sovet*) of the Council of People's Commissars (Sovnarkom) on 23 November 1918 and returned to Narkompros for preparation of its practical application in Moscow and the provinces. Insofar as numerous music stores included instrument sales as part of their business, this decision also influenced the nationalization of stores of instruments. See GARF f. 130, op. 2, d. 1040, l. 1; GARF f. 120, op. 2, d. 1051, ll. 31–39; GARF f. 130, op. 3, d. 883, ll. 30–31.

[95] GARF f. 130, op. 7, d. 2, ll. 154, 159; GARF f. 130, op. 7, d. 114, ll. 198, 203–05 ; GARF f. 130, op. 7, d. 144, l. 217; GARF f. 130, op. 7, d. 145, ll. 146, 155, 168.

Soviet Union. While the internationalist rhetoric underpinning Marxism led to the embrace of revolutionary songs from various ethnic milieux, musical elites trained in Moscow and Petrograd took on a tutelary role (particularly among non-Russian ethnic groups) and aided in the continuing formation of nationally-based compositional styles. In 1920, the local branch of Narkompros in Kazakhstan established a special commission tasked with identifying the "national musical forms" of the Kazakh people.[96] Similar processes were repeated in other Soviet republics, with the initial impetus generally coming from musicians with roots in the prerevolutionary period.[97] In musical émigré communities outside the USSR, artists tended to split into ethnically based "national" schools, rather than maintaining any sense of a Russian imperial heritage. Jewish émigrés gravitated toward communities in Palestine or the United States, where they laid the groundwork for a distinct "Jewish national" school, while those of Russian origin congregated primarily in France, founding a "Russian Music Conservatory" in Paris that lacked the multiethnic component of late imperial Russian musical life.[98] While the Soviet Union encouraged the development of national musical styles amongst its various ethnic groups, this was a worldview increasingly based upon the assumption of an inherent (and insurmountable) division between ethnic groups. In this manner, war and revolution had swept away the era of a complex, multivalent *rossiiskii* musical synthesis, leaving behind a musical realm marked by national differentiation.

---

[96] Michael Rouland, "Music and the 1936 Festival of Kazak Arts," in *Soviet Music and Society*, 181–208, here 186.

[97] Matthew O'Brien "Uzeyir Hajibeyov and His Role in the Development of Musical Life in Azerbaidzhan," in *Soviet Music and Society*, 209–27; Marina Frolova-Walker, "'National in Form, Socialist in Content': Musical Nation-Building in the Soviet Republics," *Journal of the American Musicological Society* 51, 2 (Summer 1998): 331–71.

[98] Bakhmeteff Archive (BAR) Gunst (Printed material): Université Populaire Russe: Section Musicale Conservatoire, "Statuts de la société denommée Institut Musical Russe a Paris (conservatoire Russe)."

Psychiatric Diagnosis as Political Critique: Russia in War and Revolution

Martin A. Miller

The association of revolution and political violence with qualities of madness has long been imbedded on the margins of the professional literature of psychiatric diagnosis. Philippe Pinel in revolutionary France, often considered the foundational figure in modern Western psychiatry, and Benjamin Rush in early 19th-century America, credited with establishing professional standards of psychiatric treatment in the United States, were both convinced that violent periods of revolution and war were responsible for triggering forms of insanity in individuals unable to cope with such politically unstable conditions. Although Pinel and Rush had each experienced revolutions in their respective countries, they were markedly cautious in the manner in which they interpreted these political events as medical specialists.

Pinel is justly acclaimed for publishing in 1806 one of the first textbooks on psychiatric treatment in the modern era. In spite of his acceptance of the notions of the polarities of reason and passion typical of his time, he developed a highly sophisticated diagnostic classification framework. His case studies also show that he was acutely aware of the impact that the revolutionary shift from monarchy to republic in the 1790s had on his patients. One example concerns an aristocrat who lost all his property and all his financial resources in the 1789 upheaval. The result was that "his calamities reduced him to a state of insanity." Pinel describes in vivid detail all the modes of treatment utilized to "subdue his passions" and remove him from his mental state of having been reduced to the status of an "incurable maniac."[1] In this and many similar cases in his writings, Pinel rarely strayed from the posture of the professional physician, succeeding in remaining apart from the conflicting political factions of the period. As a result, he managed to retain his position at the highest levels of the medical profession through the tumultuous changes in France from Robespierre to Napoleon.

Rush was actively involved in the American transition from a colonial outpost of the British crown to an independent republic, mainly as a moderate social reformer. He worried about "the excesses of democracy" as illustrated by

---

[1] Portions of Pinel's cases are reproduced in *The Faber Book of Madness*, ed. Roy Porter (London: Faber, 1991), 12–13, 52–54, 89–91.

Russian Culture in War and Revolution, 1914–22, Book 2: Political Culture, Identities, Mentalities, and Memory. Murray Frame, Boris Kolonitskii, Steven G. Marks, and Melissa K. Stockdale, eds. Bloomington, IN: Slavica Publishers, 2014, 245–55.

the insurgency of Daniel Shays and the "radical" Pennsylvania Constitution of 1776, which he feared would lead to "mobocracy" and "anarchia." He did not, however, attempt to formulate a psychiatric nomenclature based, as he put it, on these deranged forms of behavior stirred in stressful times by primitive passions instead of the civilized restraints of reason.[2]

The pathway from their work, in the early years of the 19th century, to a psychiatric nosology responsive to the psychological impact of violent political upheavals underwent another significant advance a century later. The important research in this area was done by Jean-Martin Charcot in the 1880s in Paris and by W. H. R. Rivers in London and Edinburgh during the Great War. Charcot is far better known for his attention to the symptomatology of hysteria, which dominated both his published work and his treatment modalities. However, he also developed a vast etiological canvas on the subject of psychiatric trauma, which turned out to be a crucial register from which post-traumatic stress disorders would later emerge and be applied to situations of wars and revolutions. Rather than choosing to emphasize one or another of the dominant etiological themes favored by his contemporaries, Charcot tried to demonstrate that mental traumas resulted from both endogenous forces as well as exogenous events. For example, he found that his traumatic patients traced their symptoms back not only to moments of extreme danger or fear of personal harm but also to the quotidian of workplace accidents.[3] One of Charcot's most famous students, Sigmund Freud, took this structural theory and transformed it into a comprehensive personality analysis in which the traumatic violence of childhood sexual abuse became the paramount theme.

Rivers headed a clinic during the First World War near London that specialized in treating wounded soldiers who had been sent home from the front by their commanders. The operating assumption of the time was that the battlefield wounds were triaged in treatment into the curable and the incurable. For the former, as soon as the patients were certified as fit for battle again, they were to be dispatched back to their units. Rivers was remarkable in that he discovered many of his patients were unfit to return to battle even after their physical wounds had healed because of their mental state. In his view, they had been traumatized in the trenches to the point that they had become incapable of resuming their role as violent defenders of king and country. They had lost the will and purpose to fight. Rivers diagnosed their condition as "shell shock" and perhaps unwittingly brought attention to the psychiatry of warfare, with his emphasis on the fact that the violence of battle

---

[2] Jason Frank, "Sympathy and Separation: Benjamin Rush and the Contagious Public," *Modern Intellectual History* 6, 1 (2009): 27–57. Rush was a signatory to the Declaration of Independence.

[3] Mark S. Micale, "Jean-Martin Charcot and *les nevroses traumatiques*: From Medicine to Culture in French Trauma Theory of the Late Nineteenth Century," in *Traumatic Pasts: History, Psychiatry and Trauma in the Modern Age, 1870–1930*, ed. Micale and Paul Lerner (Cambridge: Cambridge University Press, 2001), 115–39.

can wound the mind as severely as it can the body. Mental trauma in war, he sought to demonstrate, was a treatable condition, not a trait of shameful cowardice.[4]

However, neither Charcot nor Rivers sought to interpret their findings within the framework of a whole new field, one that we could now designate as *political psychiatry*. European and American psychiatrists were, on the whole, essentially supportive of their governments, whether monarchical or democratic. Even once Europe was plunged into war, there were no case studies in the medical journals linking psychological symptoms with opposition and criticism of domestic and international affairs. Political issues also rarely appeared in the annual congresses of specialists. To take one well-known example of this overall trend, Freud not only gave unambiguous support to his son's decision to enlist in the Austro-Hungarian army in 1915, but there are no important findings concerning political criticism in his work during the years of his classic studies.[5] In another instance, Emil Kraepelin, arguably the most prominent psychiatric specialist in Germany, criticized one of his patients for his political opposition to the war. He claimed his patient's pathology was his deficiency of will power to respond as a noble warrior for the nation's defense.[6]

---

[4] The term "shell shock" was already in the psychiatric literature in Russia, where it was employed as a diagnostic category during the Russo-Japanese War. On this, see the discussion in Paul Wanke, *Russian/Soviet Military Psychiatry: 1904–1945* (New York: Routledge, 2005), esp. chap. 2. On Rivers, see Richard Slobodin, *W. H. R. Rivers* (New York: Columbia University Press, 1978); and Elaine Showalter's interesting discussion in *The Female Malady* (New York: Pantheon, 1985), 167–94. See also Rivers' preface to John T. MacCurdy, *War Neuroses* (Cambridge: Cambridge University Press, 1918); and Rivers' own magnum opus, *Instinct and the Unconscious* (Cambridge: Cambridge University Press, 1922).

[5] Freud, in 1917, while the war was still raging and after his son's death at the front, wrote his very personal essay, "Mourning and Melancholy," in which he distinguished "normal" responses to the death of loved ones (mourning) from the pathology of being unable to overcome the period of grief (melancholy). On the general situation, see the following studies: Mark S. Micale and Paul Lerner, eds., *Traumatic Pasts: History, Psychiatry and Trauma in the Modern Age, 1870–1930* (Cambridge: Cambridge University Press, 2001); Ben Shephard, *A War of Nerves: Soldiers and Psychiatrists in the Twentieth Century* (Cambridge, MA: Harvard University Press, 2001); Peter Barham, *Forgotten Lunatics of the Great War* (New Haven: Yale University Press, 2004); Hans-Georg Hofer, Cay-Rüdiger Prüll, and Wolfgang U. Eckart, eds., *War, Trauma and Medicine in Germany and Central Europe, 1914–1939* (Freiburg: Centaurus Verlag & Media, 2011). While these books detail the great efforts made to psychologically understand the casualties from the war, there is little evidence of a political critique on the part of the psychiatrists.

[6] The Kraepelin response is discussed in Robert Weldon Whalen, *Bitter Wounds: German Victims of the Great War, 1914–1939* (Ithaca, NY: Cornell University Press, 1984), 64–65. For politically related issues in Western psychiatric history, see Jan Goldstein, "'Moral Contagion': A Professional Ideology of Medicine and Psychiatry in Eighteenth- and

The first truly politically oriented psychiatric critique emerged instead in tsarist Russia, particularly during the period between the 1905 revolutionary era and the Great War. To be sure, psychiatry in prerevolutionary Russia resembled its professional counterparts in Western Europe in many respects. Specialized diagnostic categories and institutional care for the insane developed intensively for the first time in the 18th century, though there is little evidence to suggest that the madhouses were more than detention centers for the exclusion of members of families whose behavior was considered irrational or blasphemous. In the 19th century, the moral management treatment modes begun by Pinel in France, William Tuke at the York Retreat in England, and Rush in Philadelphia were adopted by I. M. Balinskii and his successors at the Medical-Surgical Academy in St. Petersburg.[7]

Major hospitals for treating the insane were established also in Moscow, Kazan′, Odessa and Khar′kov. The main universities all had departments of psychiatry by the end of the 19th century and supported the research projects and studies of their faculty, the results of which were published in Russian as well as in international medical journals.

At the same time, Russian psychiatrists became involved in political activities in ways that were far more pronounced than was the case with their professional colleagues abroad.[8] Even before the revolution of 1905, which brought this trend indelibly into the medical mainstream, Russian psychiatrists were politically active. Part of this had to do with the nature of functioning professionally in an autocratic environment. Whether in the provinces, where the zemstvo boards administered staffing and patient intake in clinics, or in urban centers where larger medical facilities were the primary treatment institutions, virtually every request had to be submitted for government approval. Psychiatrists routinely complained about the lack of adequate facilities to accommodate the rising incidence of the patient population and the refusal of the central government to hire and train sufficient numbers of new graduates to meet this need.

Even more irritating and provocative to the psychiatric community was the increasingly important role that the police played in the hospital system. Because the authorities generally considered rebellion as extreme and irrational

---

Nineteenth-Century France," in *Professions and the French State, 1700–1900*, ed. Gerald Geison (Philadelphia: University of Pennsylvania Press, 1984), 181–222; and also Edward James Erikson, "The Anarchist Disorder: The Psychopathology of Terrorism in Late Nineteenth Century France" (Ph.D. diss., University of Iowa, 1998).

[7] Among the most prominent of these psychiatric reformers were I. P. Merzheevskii, P. I. Kovalevskii, Sergei Korsakov, and V. M. Bekhterev. See the comprehensive historical analysis in T. I. Iudin, *Ocherki istorii otechestvennoi psikhiatrii* (Moscow: Gosizdat, 1951).

[8] Martin A. Miller, "The Concept of Revolutionary Insanity in Russian History," in *Madness and the Mad in Russian Culture*, ed. Angela Brintlinger and Ilya Vinitsky (Toronto: University of Toronto Press, 2007), 105–16.

behavior, increasing numbers of prisoners arrested at demonstrations and strikes were brought to mental clinics during the 1905 uprising. However, the individuals in custody remained under police supervision, which meant that the psychiatrists' medical protocols were subordinated to the political and security interests of the state.[9]

In the years between the collapse of the 1905 rebellion and the Great War, the conflicted situation facing many psychiatrists in Russia only worsened. As one scholar has put it, "the position of psychiatrists, sandwiched between the requirements of the state and the needs of the population, contributed to the growth of a professional consciousness in very important and distinctive ways. Russian psychiatrists declared themselves advocates for Russia's insane population, even against state interests."[10] While the psychiatrists were politicized earlier and more widely than most of the other medical specializations, normally staid annual meetings of physicians at the Pirogov Society of Russian Physicians were filled with passionate outcries demanding resolutions expressing opposition to the government's resistance to reform similar to those that had come to dominate the meetings of the Russian neuropathologists and psychiatrists.[11]

One of the more public denunciators of the government among the psychiatrists was V. I. Iakovenko. After having spent years treating patients in the provinces as a zemstvo physician, he delivered a paper at the 1907 annual meeting of the Pirogov Society in Moscow which analyzed the mental condition of the nation within the framework of political activism. He tried to prove that different personality types gravitated toward progressive as opposed to conservative political movements. He also sought to distinguish neurasthenics and hysterics from "the morally depraved" individuals who were capable of committing barbaric acts of violence. Although his characterizations have questionable validity in terms of diagnostic science, he did

---

[9] Julie V. Brown, "Social Influences on Psychiatric Theory and Practice in Late Imperial Russia," in *Health and Society in Revolutionary Russia*, ed. John F. Hutchinson and Susan G. Solomon (Bloomington: Indiana University Press, 1990), 32–33.

[10] Irina Sirotkina, *Diagnosing Literary Genius: A Cultural History of Psychiatry in Russia, 1880–1930* (Baltimore: Johns Hopkins University Press, 2002), 12.

[11] See Nancy M. Frieden, *Russian Physicians in an Era of Reform and Revolution, 1865–1905* (Princeton, NJ: Princeton University Press, 1981); and Iudin, *Ocherki istorii otechestvennoi psikhiatrii*, especially 314–40. Zemstvo physicians were similarly undergoing a politicization process at this time, as John Hutchinson has shown in his book *Politics and Public Health in Revolutionary Russia, 1890–1918* (Baltimore: Johns Hopkins University Press, 1990). Also see Susan K. Morrissey, *Suicide and the Body Politic in Imperial Russia* (Cambridge: Cambridge University Press, 2006); and Marina B. Mogil'ner, *Mifologiia podpol'nogo cheloveka: Radikal'nyi mikrokosm v Rossii nachala XX veka kak predmet semioticheskogo analiza* (Moscow: Novoe literaturnoe obozrenie, 1999).

make clear his own moral stance on the need to challenge the autocracy's political authority from a professional perspective.[12]

Some psychiatrists were in fact members of radical political parties during this period. One example is P. P. Tutyshkin, who was attracted to the Bolshevik Party during the chaos of 1905. He made a number of public denunciations at professional meetings reflecting his political commitments. At the Third Congress of Russian Psychiatrists in 1911, he proclaimed that it was the professional responsibility of the clinical community to acknowledge "the pathological effects of the political repression we are enduring" which have led to "the disease-producing seeds of lawlessness and brute force being scattered throughout the country."[13] Another was L. M. Rozenshtein, who worked tirelessly both before and during the Great War to establish new forms of care for psychiatric patients who were poor or in rural areas without access to hospitals to compensate for the failure of the regime to provide these medical necessities.[14] In addition, there is evidence showing political activities by psychiatrists even inside the asylums and hospitals. Political meetings with patients led by anti-regime psychiatrists were held in the Kazan´ hospital, and, at the same time, members of the psychiatric staff at the Kharkov clinic admitted hunted radical activists under the guise of a false diagnosis to protect them from arrest. Other hospitals permitted illegal pamphlets to be published in basements, and some were engaged in networks smuggling radical newspapers as well as pistols and rifles for the insurgency.[15]

Other members of the profession, such as the prominent psychiatrist V. F. Chizh, were dedicated loyalists of the tsarist regime and found little worthwhile in the diagnostics of revolutionary violence produced by their colleagues on the left. Most, however, like N. A. Vigdorchik and F. E. Rybakov, did not publicly affiliate with either side of the extremes, although they were nonetheless deeply concerned about rising rates of "political suicide" and the increased incidence of psychoses due to the challenges of coping in a culture of violence for which the regime was seen as primarily responsible.[16]

The outbreak of the war in 1914 further aggravated these trends. The clinical journals were filled with articles describing cases of "shell shock" and "traumatic psychoses" as Russian psychiatrists sought to define the symptoms

---

[12] Julie V. Brown, "Revolution and Psychosis: The Mixing of Science and Politics in Russian Psychiatric Medicine, 1905–1913," *Russian Review* 46, 3 (1987): 283–302.

[13] Quoted by Angela Brintlinger in her introduction to *Madness and the Mad in Russian Culture*, 4–5.

[14] See the discussion in Sirotkina, *Diagnosing Literary Genius*, 149–56.

[15] Mogil´ner, *Mifologiia podpol´nogo cheloveka*, 85–86.

[16] N. A. Vigdorchik, "Politicheskie psikhozy i politicheskie samoubiistva," *Obrazovanie*, no. 12 (December 1907): 51–64; F. E. Rybakov, *Dushevnye rasstroistva v sviazi s poslednimi politicheskimi sobytiiami* (Moscow: Tip. V. Rikhter, 1906).

of pathological responses damaging the mental capacities of the affected soldiers. Although the mood was supportive of the war effort during the first year of fighting as a consequence of fears of invasion and even occupation, by 1915 professional opposition to the government's military involvement began to take shape and gain support. This was particularly visible at the annual medical meetings where specific case studies of psychiatric casualties of war were discussed. Faced with a continuing dependence on the state for hospital resources, Russian psychiatrists reacted with strongly critical responses, literally blaming the central government for the inadequate clinical facilities available to treat their patients. In some instances, they went even further, suggesting that the military administration bore responsibility for the deteriorated mental condition of some victimized soldiers in the field hospitals, and making clear their opposition to the prioritizing of war needs over the necessities of the mental health system.[17]

There was ample recognition of psychological damage from the violence of combat, most frequently referred to as "traumatic war psychoneuroses." In some cases, patients were described as suffering from "diffuse lesions of the central nervous system" as well as by hallucinations, delusions, and episodes of paranoid fears.[18] One study looked at two army officers who suffered from "complete mutism" and "bilateral deafness" which had occurred at the front; both made a recovery after treatment with hypnosis under difficult conditions.[19] Another examined the understudied subject of the impact of war violence on women left at home and who were dependent on their sons and absent husbands for support. The admission rate at two Moscow hospitals demonstrated that "the anticipated increase of insanity among those remaining at home has actually materialized." The patients suffered from attacks of "psychic trauma associated with war conditions," including severe manic and depressive states, with elevated levels of anxiety and intense fear "connected with wartime experiences."[20]

What was emerging in these case studies was the association of the psychiatric diagnosis of war traumas with criticism of the imperial regime. In

---

[17] Irina Sirotkina, "The Politics of Etiology: Shell Shock in the Russian Army, 1914–1918," in *Madness and the Mad*, 117–29. For a contrasting perspective, see Catherine Merridale, "The Collective Mind: Trauma and Shell-Shock in Twentieth-Century Russia," *Journal of Contemporary History* 35, 1 (2000): 39–55.

[18] See A. V. Gerver's medical report in *Russkii vrach*, no. 14 (1915): 793–800, 841–44.

[19] D. A. Smirnov, "Dva sluchaia travmaticheskogo nevrozisa," *Zhurnal nevropatologii i psikhiatrii* 14, 3 (1915): 312–24.

[20] A. A. Butenko, "Voina i psikhozy u zhenshchiny," *Obozrenie psikhiatricheskoi nevrologii*, no. 19 (1914–15): 521–42. See also A. B. Astashov, "Voina kak kul'turnyi shok: Analiz psikhopatologicheskogo sostoiania russkoi armii v Pervuiu mirovuiu voinu," ed. E. S. Seniavskaia, *Voenno-istoricheskaia antropologiia. Ezhegodnik* (Moscow: RossPEN, 2002): 268–81, which is based on archival holdings.

one exposé of psychiatric services in the army in the midst of the war, it was determined that transportation of the officers and enlisted men designated as psychiatric patients from Vilna, Warsaw, and Białystok to Moscow hospitals for treatment took so long that significant numbers of the patients either had their conditions worsen as a result or actually died before arrival.[21]

In another study, the author complained of inadequate provisions for insane patients, stating that "care of the insane in Russia is in a very primitive state," that the numbers of untreated cases of mentally disturbed people "reveal a very deplorable situation" in that estimates show over 60,000 people ought to be in hospitals who are not. The conclusion reached was that "the problems that the Russian government is facing as to its insane and defectives, especially with the additional burdens of the present war, are gigantic."[22]

At the same time, many of the articles in the journals point to a variety of problems complicating the effort to reach definite conclusions about the correlation between war violence and diagnosed psychoses. In one study, a psychiatrist spent three months in a general field hospital near the front and reported on 27 cases of mental disorders. His conclusion was that "the diagnoses of these cases were unsatisfactory because of lack of time for study and observation."[23]

While the government and the military administration were held responsible for many of these negative findings, other studies reflect problems of reliability on the part of the psychiatric investigators. A major statistical study of the diagnoses and treatment of the military insane was carried out by P. P. Kashchenko in 1915 with results that show questionable reliability. The sources for much of the data cited are not made clear, including the number of patients in treatment from which his rates of incidence were taken. Some data were unavailable due to the division of care between cases handled by the Red Cross and those of the army medical corps, with each keeping separate and often contradictory records. Further, symptoms that were somatic or neurological in origin were not clearly distinguished from those classified as "psychological."[24] Other studies reviewing the available psychiatric epi-

---

[21] N. N. Reformatskii, "Psikhiatricheskie sluzhby," *Russkii vrach*, no. 15 (1916): 230–34.

[22] V. A. Giliarovskii, "Voina i bezumnye," *Sovremennaia psikhiatriia*, no. 9 (1915): 287–97.

[23] D. A. Amenitskii, "Sumasshedshie na fronte," *Sovremennaia psikhiatriia*, no. 9 (1915): 325–33. For two more recent contributions to the study of the psychological problems in the Russian army at this time, see Jacqueline Friedlander, "Approaching War Trauma: Russian Psychiatrists Look at Battlefield Breakdown during World War I," *ISEEES Newsletter* (Institute of Slavic, East European, and Eurasian Studies, University of California at Berkeley) (Fall 2004): 3–4, 19–23; and Astashov, "Voina kak kul'turnyi shok." Neither, however, is concerned with the political implications for the psychiatrists of the disorders described.

[24] P. P. Kashchenko, "Statistiki o sumasshedshikh v armii," *Psikhiatricheskaia gazeta* 2, 5 (1915): 199–203.

demiologic data gathered from the mentally disturbed soldiers exhibiting symptoms of trauma from war violence were critical of the incomplete, and at times erroneous, nature of the material. A. V. Timofeev expressed serious doubts as to whether "war psychosis" had even been demonstrated, since so many of the patients had already been seen in hospitals and presented many of their symptoms of distress before the war.[25]

In many respects, the Russian story of fusing politics and psychiatry, or, the politicizing of the psychiatric profession in the late imperial period, was a singular moment in the evolving series of crises that beset the country at the time. Between 1905 and 1921, Russia underwent multiple upheavals leading to the collapse of authority and subsequent transfers of legitimacy that occurred in February and October of 1917, in addition to the earlier Russo-Japanese War, the Great War, and the postrevolutionary Civil War that convulsed the nation. Throughout these tumultuous experiences, the medical profession as a whole was presented with extraordinary challenges. Although the number of psychiatrists rose during the period, it was never sufficient to deal adequately with the momentous needs of the expanding patient population that emerged from these catastrophic events.[26]

With the assumption to power of the Bolsheviks, efforts to deal with the chaos of a devastated medical profession, hospital closures, as well as limited supplies of drugs and vaccines took two main forms. One was an argument for decentralized psychiatric care on the model of the prewar zemstvo facilities in the provinces, which would, in effect, have established a network of medical centers under the direction of local authorities, who were presumed to have been familiar with the treatment needs in their own areas. The other model centered on the centralization of medical diagnosis and care at the national level. According to this perspective, since the country was in the grip of a crisis of emergency proportions, only a single administrative system with directives from the center could deal responsibly with such huge problems. The inspiration in this case came from the soviets, which, while regionally responsive to localities, were organized as administrative cadres under supervision of central directives tied to national policy.[27]

The outcome was a victory for the centralists. One of the earliest directives of the new Bolshevik regime was to establish the People's Commissariat of

---

[25] See Timofeev's reports in *Psikhiatricheskaia gazeta*, 2 (1915): 261, 341.

[26] In 1916, there were around 350 registered psychiatrists in the empire while by 1932, according to the Soviet Commissar of Health, the number reached 538 trained psychiatrists and an additional 743 neuropathologists. See David Joravsky, *Russian Psychology: A Critical History* (Oxford: Blackwell, 1989), 420.

[27] These discussions had been in progress since at least April 1917, before the Bolshevik seizure of power, as the transcription of the meeting of the Russian Union of Psychiatrists and Neuropathologists clearly shows. See Sirotkina, *Diagnosing Literary Genius*, 146 ff.

Public Health, referred to by its Russian acronym, Narkomzdrav. With slogans proclaiming the need for national salvation under government auspices replete with utopian expectations of introducing measures designed to triumph over mental disorders, Narkomzdrav recruited psychiatrists across the country to respond to the extraordinary situation confronting the nation. Prominent psychiatrists such as P. B. Gannushkin, P. P. Kashchenko, and L. M. Rozenshtein, among others, played key roles in establishing the new system of care. Those like Rosenshtein, who brought revolutionary credentials with them from the imperial era, were in a particularly favorable position to assume responsible positions in setting up the world's first national health care system committed to socialist principles. Indeed, Rozenshtein became an enthusiastic supporter of the new socialist health care system where he worked to design an innovative "psychiatric synthesis" that would include community, family and social components as psychiatric priorities.[28]

The political involvement for psychiatrists was amplified under Bolshevik rule, but shifted from operating as an opposition to the government, as they had been during the reign of Nicholas II, to joining the central administration whereby they effectively became agents of the state. N. A. Semashko, who was appointed the first commissar of public health, emphasized the importance of improving living conditions for Soviet citizens. On the one hand, he encouraged the widespread distribution of posters and illustrations on billboards, in newspapers, and in cinemas on how to live more sanitary and healthy lives. In addition, journals and university courses dedicated to conquering mental as well as physical diseases were introduced. On the other hand, the notion of "social hygiene" was transformed into ideological appeals for the building of socialism.[29]

These measures further politicized the theory and practice of psychiatry in the Soviet Union, and they were all consciously designed to fuse with the general ideology of the new regime as it sought to consolidate its authority and legitimacy through the Civil War and into the transformative NEP era. In the process, psychiatry became increasingly state controlled, receiving all its support from the government, which, given the apparent absence of resistance within the profession, seemed to answer the primary demands of the prerevolutionary period when such demands had gone largely unheeded by the tsarist ministers responsible for health care. There was, of course, the political disagreement in the 1920s between Ivan Pavlov and several leading

---

[28] Rozenshtein had been detained by the police while a student at Novorossiiskii University in Odessa during the repression that followed the 1905 Revolution, and later resigned his position at the Moscow Psychiatric Clinic in 1911 in support of the dismissal of his mentor, V. P. Serbskii. Another prominent psychiatrist from the earlier period was Vigdorchik, who made important contributions to the fields of psychiatric epidemiology and public health throughout the Soviet era.

[29] See Frances Lee Bernstein, *The Dictatorship of Sex: Lifestyle Advice for the Soviet Masses* (DeKalb: Northern Illinois University Press, 2007), 100–28.

party authorities (mainly Nikolai Bukharin, but also, to a lesser extent, Trotskii and Grigorii Zinov'ev) about the validity of Marxism as a science, but these did not provoke widespread responses in the profession as a whole.[30]

As the Stalinist "revolution from above" gathered force toward the end of the 1920s, the psychiatric profession found itself caught in the same vise of repression and conformity that faced most other professions and the arts at the same time. The pluralism and experimentation of the early part of the decade, from the "psycho-hygiene" movement's emphasis on de-institutionalization to the efforts to establish a psychoanalytic theory consistent with Marxism, were silenced by what became known as the ruling party's "psycho-neurological offensive" against efforts to establish a "bourgeois restoration."[31] One of the main consequences of this wave of demands for conformity from the center was the collapse of the kind of political opposition within the psychiatric profession that was so vital in the years before the Revolution.

Psychiatry in Russia has been virtually inseparable from its political context, whether serving under tsars or commissars, in the main because of the overwhelming authority of the central state in both contexts. Although most of the profession practiced quietly within the legal framework in the imperial period, and a similar majority functioned the same way under the Soviet regime, the profession never lost its identity as a political opposition force. Although it lies beyond the present framework of discussion, it is important to be reminded that Soviet psychiatrists emerged as a distinctive voice of protest during the 1960s and 1970s in Moscow and Leningrad.[32] The climax of this long trajectory of political psychiatry, to which the Russians have contributed so much, may have been the field case studies of Frantz Fanon, whose work treating both "the colonists and the colonized" during the Algerian revolution advanced the infusion of politics into the profession of psychiatry to the point where it became synonymous with insurgent rebellion.[33]

---

[30] See Daniel P. Todes, "Pavlov and the Bolsheviks," *History and Philosophy of the Life Sciences* 17, 3 (1995): 379–418.

[31] See the discussion in Joravsky, *Russian Psychology*, 339–40; Alexander Etkind, *Eros nevozmozhnogo: Istoriia psikhoanaliza v Rossii* (St. Petersburg: Meduza, 1993); and Martin A. Miller, *Freud and the Bolsheviks: Psychoanalysis in Imperial Russia and the Soviet Union* (New Haven: Yale University Press, 1996).

[32] Among the leading psychiatrists in this resistance were Vladimir Bukovskii, Semen Gluzman, Anatolii Koriagin, and Aleksandr Voloshanovich.

[33] Frantz Fanon, "Colonial War and Mental Disorders," in *The Wretched of the Earth* (1961), trans. Richard Philcox (New York: Grove Press, 2004), 181–233.

Myths and Memory

The Great War and the Civil War in Russian Memory

Karen Petrone

In 1975, when literary scholar Paul Fussell wrote *The Great War and Modern Memory*, he paved the way for a new interdisciplinary field of literary and historical studies of war and memory. Using the works of war poets such as Siegfried Sassoon and Wilfred Owen, and memoirists such as Robert Graves, Fussell contended that the experience of World War I created a rupture in European thinking and a new "modern" ethos. He wrote, "I am saying that there seems to be one dominating form of modern understanding; that it is essentially ironic; and that it originates largely in the application of mind and memory to the events of the Great War."[1] The work of French historian Pierre Nora also fueled the study of memory in general, and, thereby, the study of World War I memory, though he emphasized continuities over ruptures. Nora theorized the conflict between history and memory in his studies of French nationhood and coined the notion of "sites of memory" through which one could access popular collective memory that had been obscured by dominant narratives of modern historical change.[2] This idea has become a powerful conceptual tool for historians of memory.

Historians of Britain, France, and Germany soon engaged with and contested the works of Fussell, Nora, and other scholars of war and memory. Historian Jay Winter challenged the notion that World War I ushered in a dominant modern mentality by showing how those memorializing and mourning World War I relied heavily on traditional and religious discourses. Historians such as George Mosse and Modris Eksteins probed the extent to which the commemoration of war led to the militarization of the nation and the normalization of violence, especially in Germany. Winter, historian Daniel Sherman, and other scholars of Britain and France suggested, on the other hand, that the commemoration of war could also lead to national and local debates in which some participants soberly acknowledged the costs of war,

---

[1] Paul Fussell, *The Great War and Modern Memory* (London: Oxford University Press, 1975), 35.

[2] Pierre Nora, "Between Memory and History: *Les Lieux de Mémoire*," *Representations*, no. 26 (Spring 1989): 7–24.

Russian Culture in War and Revolution, 1914–22, Book 2: Political Culture, Identities, Mentalities, and Memory. Murray Frame, Boris Kolonitskii, Steven G. Marks, and Melissa K. Stockdale, eds. Bloomington, IN: Slavica Publishers, 2014, 259–72.

rejected violence, and questioned the efficacy of militarization.[3] All of these scholars agreed, however, that war memory played a crucial role in interwar Western European politics and social life.

Implicit in almost all of the scholarship about memory is the notion of competition and contestation, an acknowledgment that memory is, in Jay Winter's words, "unstable, plastic, synthetic, and repeatedly reshaped."[4] Sites of memory are significant, according to Nora, because they capture and preserve what narrations of national history sought to destroy. Various institutional and individual actors within a given society, and also transnationally, work to construct and maintain particular versions of both "history" and "memory" and also to suppress or supersede alternative versions of the past. Historian Alon Confino usefully suggests that memory is "an outcome of the relationship between a distinct representation of the past and the full spectrum of symbolic representations available in a given culture."[5] War memory, then, is always and everywhere contested memory.

Soviet Memory of World War I

Despite the "memory craze" hitting Europe and the United States, only very recently has the Russian and Soviet memory of World War I become a topic for historical investigation. As historian Daniel Orlovsky aptly observed in 1999, the burgeoning European scholarship on World War I memory did not include "a single word about Russia and Russian memory about the fallen."[6] There were two major reasons for this omission. The first was the tendency of both European and Soviet historians to separate Russia and the Soviet Union from the rest of European history because of the great rupture of the October Revolution of 1917. The persistence of a notion of a Soviet special path discouraged historians from employing comparative trans-European frameworks across the Soviet borders. Recent work by historian Peter Holquist and others has encouraged scholars to view Russian and Soviet history within

---

[3] George L. Mosse, *Fallen Soldiers: Reshaping the Memory of the World Wars* (New York: Oxford University Press, 1990); Modris Eksteins, *Rites of Spring: The Great War and the Birth of the Modern Age* (New York: Anchor Books, 1989); Jay Winter, *Sites of Memory, Sites of Mourning: The Great War in European Cultural History* (Cambridge: Cambridge University Press, 1995); Daniel J. Sherman, *The Construction of Memory in Interwar France* (Chicago: University of Chicago Press, 2000).

[4] Jay Winter, *Remembering War: The Great War Between Memory and History in the Twentieth Century* (New Haven: Yale University Press, 2006), 3–4.

[5] Alon Confino, "Collective Memory and Cultural History: Problems of Method," *American Historical Review* 102, 5 (December 1997): 1391.

[6] Daniel Orlovsky, "Velikaia voina i rossiiskaia pamiat'" in *Rossiia i Pervaia mirovaia voina: Materialy mezhdunarodnogo nauchnogo kollokviuma*, ed. N. N. Smirnov (St. Petersburg: Dmitrii Bulanin, 1999), 56.

the framework of "the common European deluge" that occurred between 1914 and 1921, and the comparative study of memory is a critical aspect of understanding the aftermath of this "deluge."[7]

The second reason for the lack of scholarship on Soviet World War I memory was the attitude of the Soviet state toward the war. Because Soviet leaders believed that the World War (or the "world imperialist war," as they called it) tragically pitted the working classes of the different combatant countries against one another, they saw the war as profoundly illegitimate and unworthy of commemoration. While Soviet ideologues marked war anniversaries in the press and articulated their view that the war was an inevitable result of capitalist imperialism, "there were no major public monuments to the war, no great cemeteries for World War I fallen, and no Armistice or Remembrance Day."[8] On the contrary, sites that were dedicated to the remembrance of the war before the October Revolution, such as the Moscow City Fraternal Cemetery (also known as the All-Russian War Cemetery), were allowed to fall into disrepair, and many were ultimately demolished to make way for Soviet construction projects.[9]

Given these circumstances, most contemporary scholars have argued that the Soviet Union was marked by an absence of World War I memory. Peter Gatrell, for instance, in his recent social and economic history *Russia's First World War*, argued that the Bolsheviks "discouraged public reflection on the war as a compelling human struggle and did nothing to sustain its commemoration."[10] Cultural historian Richard Stites even used the absence of Soviet memory of World War I to construct an argument about Russia's "special path." He suggested that "the absence of a real historical memory [of World War I] in Russia" is "one of the many historical phenomena that have divided Russia from the West psychologically in our century."[11] Catherine Merridale's work on death and memory in 20th-century Russia also emphasized the "forgetting" of World War I and the displacement of the World War I dead by

---

[7] Peter Holquist, *Making War, Forging Revolution: Russia's Continuum of Crisis, 1914–1921* (Cambridge, MA: Harvard University Press, 2002), 2.

[8] Aaron J. Cohen, "Oh, That! Myth, Memory, and World War I in the Russian Emigration and the Soviet Union," *Slavic Review* 62, 1 (Spring 2003): 70.

[9] For a discussion of the Moscow City Fraternal Cemetery, see Karen Petrone, *The Great War in Russian Memory* (Bloomington: Indiana University Press, 2011), 1–4.

[10] Peter Gatrell, *Russia's First World War: A Social and Economic History* (Harlow, UK: Pearson, 2005), 260.

[11] Richard Stites, "Days and Nights in Wartime Russia: Cultural Life, 1914–1917," in *European Culture in the Great War: The Arts, Entertainment, and Propaganda, 1914–1918*, ed. Aviel Roshwald and Stites (Cambridge: Cambridge University Press, 1999), 8.

"millions of more important bodies—red heroes of the civil war—for the new state to honor."[12]

While the phenomenon of "memory studies" has reached Soviet history most recently through the pioneering work of Frederick Corney on the decade-long process of constructing a usable narrative of the October Revolution, and in Lisa Kirschenbaum's penetrating analysis of the remembrance of the Siege of Leningrad in World War II, until recently, the only scholar who had addressed World War I memory was Aaron Cohen.[13] In an important 2003 article in *Slavic Review*, Cohen identified Russian and Soviet World War I "sites of memory" in émigré commemorations outside of the Soviet Union and in Soviet newspaper coverage of the anniversary of the start of the war. He persuasively argued that "the public language of the military emigration was suffused with traditional images of military virtue and patriotism, a strong religious sensibility, and, less often, a nostalgic reverence for the monarchy." He suggested that Russian émigrés "organized the memory of World War I for a variety of reasons: to create a worthy, if idealized, war experience; to recreate the wartime alliance; and to support veterans and their organizations around the world."[14] Cohen effectively illustrated the existence of multiple and competing sites of Russian diasporic war memory.

Cohen also analyzed the rhetoric of Soviet newspapers and suggested that they juxtaposed "the good civil war" with "its antithesis: the bad imperialist world war." He concluded that in the Soviet Union, "the war's memory was not evoked to recall actual historical events for personal or public reasons; it instead represented and demonstrated the Soviet version of contemporary reality as a struggle between the Soviet Union and imperialist aggressors." Cohen suggested that Soviet memory denied "connections between the war experience and Soviet Russia."[15] His work on Soviet World War I memory, like that of other scholars, underscored the separation of the Soviet discourse from individuals' memory of World War I.

I have challenged both the absence of Soviet war memory and its lack of connection with individuals' war experience in my book *The Great War in Russian Memory*. I argue that previous scholars have conflated an absence of

---

[12] Catherine Merridale, *Night of Stone: Death and Memory in Twentieth-Century Russia* (New York: Viking Press, 2000), 99.

[13] Frederick C. Corney, *Telling October: Memory and the Making of the Bolshevik Revolution* (Ithaca, NY: Cornell University Press, 2004); Lisa A. Kirschenbaum, *The Legacy of the Siege of Leningrad, 1941–1945: Myth, Memories, and Monuments* (New York: Cambridge University Press, 2006). Other notable books on Soviet memory include Nina Tumarkin, *The Living and the Dead: The Rise and Fall of the Cult of World War II in Russia* (New York: Basic Books, 1994); Kathleen E. Smith, *Remembering Stalin's Victims: Popular Memory and the End of the USSR* (Ithaca, NY: Cornell University Press, 1996).

[14] Cohen, "Oh, That!" 75, 78.

[15] Ibid., 83.

official state commemoration with an absence of memory. The millions who suffered during the war (the families of the dead, the injured, the prisoners of war) did not forget World War I. Especially in the first decade after the war, Soviet individuals and institutions actively participated in a transnational discourse of war memory. One telling but often overlooked episode is the enthusiastic and warm reception of Erich Maria Remarque's *All Quiet on the Western Front* when it first appeared in the Soviet Union in Russian translation in 1929. The World War was, however, never a central part of the Soviet state's foundation myths or fundamental to its ideological framework. Earlier scholars have rightly pointed out that the circumstances of the World War were rather inconvenient for the early Soviet state, as it could plausibly be argued that the Revolution emerged out of tsarist military failures and not because of the superiority of communism. Although the memory of the World War remained on the margins of early Soviet ideology, it was nonetheless a significant aspect of Soviet interwar culture. While the memory of the war was not privileged, neither was it suppressed.

There are several reasons why it has been difficult for scholars to recover the vibrant and variegated early Soviet memory of the World War. Because of the overwhelming presence of the state in Soviet life, it has been hard for scholars to look beyond official state categories and pronouncements. In effect, scholars accepted the state's dominant narrative, which downplayed the war, as the only narrative; they did not seek alternative views. The mythology of the Revolution demanded an official narrative of profound rupture with the past. Soviet ideologues thus tended to suppress acknowledgment of the deep continuities between tsarist prosecution of the war effort and their own administrative and mobilizing structures. They also did not like to admit the extent to which Soviet ideals of masculinity, heroism, honor, sacred duty, sacrifice, and national belonging were based on tsarist military, political, and religious culture.

At the same time that most of Soviet officialdom downplayed or ignored the war, there were Soviet institutions and individuals that actively engaged with war memory. One such institution, the Red Army General Staff's Commission on the Research and Use of the Experience of the World War, populated in large part by former tsarist officers, worked actively for more than a decade to compile and publish both raw statistical data about the war and sustained analyses of the data for tactical and strategic purposes. These works also included treatises on military leadership such as Aleksandr Svechin's *The Art of Leading a Regiment*.[16] In the mid-1920s, the State Historical Museum also developed exhibits for the populace devoted to the World War and the history of warfare. Because Soviet doctrine posited that capitalism made war inevitable, these professionals sought to study and explain war both to soldiers and officers and to the general population in advance of the next

---

[16] A. A. Svechin, *Iskusstvo vozhdeniia polka po opytu voiny 1914–1918 gg.* (Moscow: Gosizdat, 1930; Moscow: Assotsiatsiia "Voennaia Kniga Kuchkovo Pole," 2005).

conflict. In doing so, they imported select aspects of tsarist military culture and Russian national tradition into early Soviet militarization efforts.

Although Soviet ideology did not celebrate the war itself, the plight of the individual rank-and-file soldier during the World War fit very well into Soviet ideological conceptions of class warfare. In the 1920s and early 1930s, there were a number of novels written from the point of view of the common soldier as well as memoirs written by actual soldiers. These works testified to the class struggle in the army by depicting the brutal behavior of officers who saw the common soldier as little more than "cannon meat." The memoirs of Dmitrii P. Os´kin, a soldier who rose through the ranks to become first a tsarist officer and then a Red Commander in the Civil War, detailed the many misdeeds of cowardly and abusive officers who punished soldiers arbitrarily and hid in the trenches while sending soldiers into attack.[17] While these works prefigured the overthrow of the officers in the revolutionary struggle of 1917, they also detailed the miseries of the soldiers' lives in the barracks or in the trenches.

In addition to these soldiers' testimonies, there were significant literary works and memoirs about the war published by prominent early Soviet authors. These include works by Il´ia Erenburg (Ehrenburg), Sof´ia Fedorchenko, Dmitrii Furmanov, Kirill Levin, Mikhail Sholokhov, and Lev Voitolovskii among others. While Mikhail Sholokhov's classic Soviet novel *Quiet Flows the Don* is usually thought of as a "Civil War" book, the World War portions of the work introduced complex moral themes such as the guilt of the soldier after killing his first enemy in battle, and the struggle of a father with grief over the loss of his soldier-son. The author of the paradigmatic Soviet novel *Chapaev*, Dmitrii Furmanov, also produced World War diaries that were published posthumously in 1929, but never republished, because they were too honest both about the horrors of war and about the callow nature of their author.[18]

The view of the war that emerged from these works, like the jaundiced view of barracks life in soldiers' memoirs and novels, posed challenges to Soviet narratives of militarization. While the future Soviet leader Lenin was uncompromisingly against the World War from its very first days, he and other Soviet leaders were emphatically not pacifists. In 1915, Lenin advised tsarist soldiers to "pay no heed to the mawkish snivelers who are afraid of war; too much still remains in the world that must be destroyed with fire and sword for the emancipation of the working class."[19] He urged soldiers to

---

[17] See, for example, D. Os´kin, *Zapiski soldata* (Moscow: Federatsiia, 1929), 110, 144, 167, 200–01, 215, 239, 244.

[18] Dmitrii Furmanov, *Dnevnik 1914–1915–1916* (Moscow–Leningrad: Moskovskii rabochii, 1929).

[19] V. I. Lenin, "The Collapse of the Second International," *Kommunist*, no. 1–2 (1915), translated in Lenin, *Collected Works* (Moscow: Progress Publishers, 1964), 21: 253–54.

keep their weapons and "turn the imperialist war into a civil war." He also advocated fraternization with enemy soldiers to encourage the proletariat on both sides to turn their guns against their officers.

But in the first decade after World War I, the best artistic and literary works about the war demonstrated ambivalence not just about "the world imperialist war" but about all wars. Building on Tolstoian and other religious pacifist traditions as well as on socialist internationalism, Soviet war memory questioned the need for war and detailed its horrifying effects on the bodies and minds of the men who fought. Il'ia Erenburg, who is far better known for his powerful rhetoric mobilizing citizens against the Germans during World War II, wrote a pacifist memoir in the wake of World War I. He lamented in *The Face of War*, "Only in the ancient book, not effaced by anything, and somewhere in the depths of each of our souls, not completely trampled, lives the prohibition 'Thou shalt not kill.'"[20] Erenburg's war memoir, detailing his experiences as a war reporter in France, was a self-contradictory work that in some places articulated militant atheism and in other places a religious pacifism that was completely out of step with both Soviet militarism and atheism.

Memoirist Lev Voitolovskii, a Marxist doctor who was mobilized into the tsarist army both during the Russo-Japanese War and the World War, penned an antiwar memoir that embraced a more secular pacifism. He defined war as "the greatest obstacle and the most repulsive exterminator of culture. It is the destruction of all that has been accumulated by the centuries in hearts and minds—and now hurled wastefully under the feet of the armed soldiers." According to Voitolovskii, "on every military banner, on the eagles, on the shoulder boards, the secret motto is imprinted: down with culture, long live destitution and the poverty of the spirit." War demanded of "the cultured person" that he abandon his "theories" and "commandments" and provide only "vacant endurance and uncomplaining submissiveness."[21] This way of thinking about civilization and warfare posed a direct challenge to the Bolshevik notion that war was necessary and even desirable in order to accomplish the goal of world revolution.

Some World War I memoirs chipped away at other key assumptions of Soviet militarism. For example, they emphasized the way in which war, far from affirming the manliness of the soldier, destroyed his body and his mind. The oft-reprinted memoir of Kirill Levin about his years in an Austrian POW camp lingered over the details of the suffering of his fellow prisoners. He depicted the despair of a soldier who had been shot in the genitals and who was "gradually turning into a eunuch." Levin showed him "delicately crying" and holding an icon of St. Nicholas to his wounded groin in the vain hope that he might be cured. When this miracle did not occur, the soldier went to

---

[20] Il'ia Erenburg, *Lik voiny* (Berlin: Gelikon, 1923), 72.

[21] L. Voitolovskii, *Po sledam voiny: Pokhodnye zapiski, 1914–1917* (Leningrad: Gos. izd-vo, 1925), 1: 68.

work in a home for blind veterans who would not be able to see his deformity. Levin also depicted the excruciating death of a bear-like hero of a man whose body disintegrated completely due to smallpox in "the most terrifying death imaginable." Levin described numerous cases of what came to be called "shell shock" in the West and brought to light the particularly horrific plight of soldiers robbed of their sanity by the war.[22] With his vivid and graphic depictions of damaged male bodies and minds, he undercut the notion that war could ever be a glorious or heroic event.

The hybrid ethnographic and literary work of Sof´ia Fedorchenko, who served as a nurse during the World War, created a very dark picture of war and the soldiers who participated in it. She attacked notions of soldierly heroism and honor by depicting the ways that, in wartime conditions, ordinary soldiers participated willingly in the most reprehensible kinds of violence against not only enemy soldiers but also civilian women and children, and how they brought this violence home with them in their treatment of their own families. Fedorchenko's *The People at War* was a collection of partially ethnographic and partially fictionalized first-person accounts purportedly from the wounded soldiers she had met while working as a war nurse.[23]

One of these soldiers described the effect of the war on his behavior by admitting that he now "gave no quarter" in battle and no longer asked for anything but simply took it. When he arrived in the destroyed town of Oprisheny there was nothing left to loot, so he seized a plump woman as his war booty: "Three days I kept her with me and amused myself. And I shared her with my platoon commander. Like I would share tobacco, I shared the woman. And then I became afraid and let her go in the field."[24] Both soldier and (no doubt) officer were well aware that their behavior broke every law of war and every moral precept connected to ideals of soldierly honor, but they nonetheless participated in this behavior without remorse and without concern for the welfare or the future of their victim. Fedorchenko showed how war produced moral corruption and destroyed honor rather than producing it.

Many of the Soviet works published in the first decade and a half after the war thus challenged some of the central tenets of Soviet militarization by depicting war not as a necessary tool in defeating capitalism, but as a force destroying the human spirit, world civilization, and the soul. War was shown to damage the soldier's body and his mind, emasculating him rather than making him stronger. Furthermore, in wartime, soldiers lost their moral

---

[22] Kirill Levin, *Zapiski iz plena* (Moscow: Federatsiia, 1931), 36–37, 104–05, 124.

[23] For a discussion of the controversy over Fedorchenko's work, see Petrone, *The Great War in Russian Memory*, 235–38.

[24] This passage is based on Petrone, *The Great War in Russian Memory*, 255. Sof´ia Fedorchenko, *Narod na voine* (Kiev: Tip. Vserossiiskago Zemskogo Soiuza Kom. Iugo-Zap. Fr., 1917), 45; Fedorchenko, *Narod na voine* (Moscow: Novaia Moskva, 1923), 94.

bearings and committed atrocities against the innocent. In these depictions, war was anything but a heroic event.

Disappearance of Anti-Heroic Discourse

Puzzled by why these fascinating works and powerful critiques of war remained largely unacknowledged by scholars, I set about examining how and when they disappeared from Soviet public life. By examining archival documents and tracing changes in various Soviet editions of the same works over time, I established that somewhere early in the 1930s, Soviet publishing houses and censors began systematically to suppress literature that cast any doubt on the heroic soldierly ideal or the efficacy of war. One notable example was the elimination from all post-1933 editions of Sholokhov's *Quiet Flows the Don* of a scene that depicted the protagonist, Grigorii Melekhov, becoming fearful in battle and wishing to throw himself on the ground to weep "childishly to the earth as if she were his mother."[25] Despite the fact that Melekhov was a complex character who eventually ended up as the novel's anti-hero rather than the hero, his wavering on the battlefield was nonetheless struck from the novel. The onset of both Stalin's "great break" and the purges also limited the discussion of the World War as several of the most prominent World War authors fell victim to repression and were prevented from publishing.

Yet the World War did not entirely disappear from view as the militarizing Soviet state in the mid-1930s became quite concerned with rebutting the notion that Russians were incapable of defeating a powerful German foe. One member of the Red Army's general staff, Colonel Aleksandr D. Pulko-Dmitriev candidly explained the rationale for publicizing "a series of examples when whole German corps ran from the field of battle in panic." He was concerned that "the absolute horror of World War" had left a powerful impression on the Soviet population: "The German heavy artillery created the common opinion, that, in battle, Germany knows how to use all means of fighting and all its forces very well. This pernicious influence has very likely penetrated the milieu of the rising generation as well." Pulko-Dmitriev suggested that current Red Army commanders seemed like "pygmies" when compared to "powerful and prepared" German commanders.[26] Because of these phenomena, it was imperative for military leaders to present Russia's participation in the World War in a more positive light.

---

[25] Mikhail Sholokhov, *Quiet Flows the Don*, trans. Robert Daglish, ed. Brian Murphy (New York: Carroll & Graf, 1996), 366–67; A. B. Murphy, V. P. Butt, and H. Ermolaev, eds., *Sholokhov's Tikhii Don: A Commentary in 2 Volumes* (Birmingham, UK: Birmingham Slavonic Monographs No. 27, 1997), 1: 75–76.

[26] Rossiiskii gosudarstvennyi voennyi arkhiv (RGVA) f. 39352 (Nauchnyi voenno-istoricheskii otdel general'nogo shtaba Krasnoi Armii), op. 1, d. 61, l. 31.

One way in which they did this in the second half of the 1930s was to publish long-delayed document collections (some originally commissioned in 1929) detailing Russian military participation in various World War operations. They also emphasized the most successful Russian offensives of the war, especially the one led by General Aleksei Brusilov. Military publishing houses featured this offensive in a number of publications in the late 1930s, first as "The Breakthrough on the Southwestern Front in 1916," or "The Lutsk Breakthrough," and then, by 1940, as "The Brusilov Breakthrough." The latter title returned the prominent tsarist (and later Soviet) general Brusilov to the Soviet public sphere, from which his name had been absent since the early 1930s. He was now held up to the Red Army officer corps as a successful military leader to be emulated. Other works praised the heroic "Russian soldier" whose accomplishments were betrayed by the "High Command" and positively depicted the use of heavy artillery and poison gas against the enemy, regardless of class.[27] After the German invasion in June 1941, the experience of fighting the Germans in the first war became an essential part of war propaganda, and any hint of ambivalence about the war disappeared. While, in 1929, memoirist V. Dmitriev could celebrate desertion to the Austrians as a heroic revolutionary act, in the 1943 novel *Brusilov's Breakthrough* by Sergei N. Sergeev-Tsenskii, Brusilov issued an order to shoot "to a man" deserters and those attempting to retreat, "even if this should involve ceasing fire against the enemy."[28] The memory of the First World War had come full circle; the original jingoism of 1914 was challenged by two decades of ambivalence about war, but after 1941 war memory returned to its heroic mode, underscoring the absolute necessity to fight and die for one's country.

Civil War Memory

One of the critical questions for further research is the relationship between the memory of World War I and the memory of the Civil War. Despite the fact that the Civil War is supposedly one of the central events in Soviet mythology, surprisingly there has not been, until very recently, much attention given to Civil War memory. There are a number of reasons for this. For one thing, the multiple fighting forces, mass destruction, peasant uprisings, famine, and disease that occurred in the years 1918–22, in short the chaos of the Civil War, cannot easily be put into a coherent narrative. It has been difficult for both Soviet propagandists and scholars to capture and analyze this fragmented kaleidoscope of a war narrative. Secondly, the leadership

---

[27] See, for example, E. A. Boltin, L. V. Zhigarev, and M. M. Kaplun, eds., *Artilleristy: Sbornik statei i rasskazov* (Moscow: Molodaia gvardiia, 1939).

[28] V. Dmitriev, *Dobrovolets: Vospominaniia o voine i plene* (Moscow–Leningrad: Gosizdat, 1929); S. Sergeyev-Tsensky, *Brusilov's Breakthrough: A Novel of the First World War*, trans. Helen Altschuler (London: Hutchinson, 1945), 26.

struggles that occurred in the mid-1920s, ending with Stalin's ascendancy to power, and the retribution against former oppositionists in the purges, have profoundly shaped the story of the Civil War as its events had to be narrated and re-narrated in the 1920s and 1930s in order to exclude enemies (here, one might think of Trotskii in particular) from the heroic drama. Yet the study of Civil War memory should be a central question on the agenda for Soviet cultural historians. While a number of scholars have linked a Civil War ethos to Bolshevik militancy during "the great break" and the violence of collectivization,[29] only recently have scholars such as Sean Guillory and Justus Hartzok begun to analyze the myth of the Civil War in depth.

Earlier scholars' generalizations about the heroic representations of the Civil War and the influence of the Civil War myth need to be interrogated. Catherine Merridale, quoted above, suggests a strong opposition between the valued Civil War dead and the neglected dead of the World War. I would suggest, however, that early Soviet leaders were generally resistant to commemorating the dead. While there were a few prominent civic places of commemoration of select victims and leaders of the Revolution, in particular graves (and later Lenin's mausoleum) in Red Square and on Mars Field in Petrograd, the Soviet government tended to be utilitarian about the burials of the majority of both heroes and enemies of the Revolution. In the case of the All-Russian War Cemetery in Moscow, World War dead, revolutionaries, and Whites were all buried together. In the late 1920s, all of these graves were neglected and in the 1930s all of them were destroyed. These events would suggest that the treatment of the vast majority of war dead from 1914–22 is more consistent across ideological and revolutionary lines than Merridale depicts it. Soviet discomfort with the religious aspects of burial seems to have prevailed over the impetus to commemorate the graves of revolutionary and Civil War heroes, and the vast majority of both World War and Civil War bodies were neglected.

Aaron Cohen is, of course, right in suggesting that the Civil War is generally understood as a "good war" in the 1920s and 1930s. There is a substantial amount of Soviet interwar rhetoric that creates a stark opposition between the heroic Reds of the Civil War era and the brutal Whites who, for example, committed all kinds of vile atrocities against innocent women and children. Yet in the 1920s there were many different narratives of the Civil War era, and not all of them depicted Reds and Whites as cardboard cut-out heroes or one-dimensional villains. Isaak Babel''s 1926 masterpiece *Red Cavalry* depicted the complexity of the Russian-Polish campaign of 1920 and ambivalently represented its Red heroes as cruel and violent. Babel' used multiple narrators to provide different perspectives on the violence of war. The Jewish journalist Liutov was anguished when he enacted symbolic violence, by killing a goose, in order to fit in with the Cossacks. The unapologetic Red Cossack Balmashov,

---

[29] See, for example, Anne E. Gorsuch, "NEP Be Damned! Young Militants in the 1920s and the Culture of the Civil War," *Russian Review* 56, 4 (October 1997): 564–80.

on the other hand, killed readily, and justified the rape and murder of innocent civilians.[30] The complex themes about the enactment of violence that appeared in World War discourse in the 1920s, thus also emerged in some treatments of the Civil War era.

A striking discussion of the personal cost of enacting violence occurred in Sholokhov's *Quiet Flows the Don*. Il'ia Bunchuk, the model Bolshevik character in the novel, headed the tribunal of the Don Revolutionary Committee and was in charge of executing the condemned every night. Within days, carrying out this horrible task had changed Bunchuk: "In one week his face grew gaunt and black, as if he had been buried under ground. His eyes hollowed out and the nervously twitching lids failed to hide their anguished brightness." The act of killing "buried" both Bunchuk and the dead. Bunchuk acknowledged the necessity of what he was doing: "before you plant out the flowerbeds and the trees, you've got to get rid of the filth! You've got to manure the ground! You've got to get your hands dirty!"[31] In spite of Bunchuk's convictions, however, enacting revolutionary justice took a physical and mental toll on him.

In a striking scene from the novel, Sholokhov showed that killing robbed Bunchuk of his manhood. When Anna, the woman whom Bunchuk loved, offered herself to him for the first time, he was not physically able to consummate the relationship because executing Whites had made him impotent.[32] When Bunchuk and Anna finally did have sex, Anna explained that she thought Bunchuk had been unable to perform the first time because he had been with another woman: "I thought you'd spent it all before. I didn't realise it was the work that had taken it out of you."[33] Here Sholokhov demonstrated that whether or not killing could be considered justified by revolutionary law, committing such violence still damaged the very manhood of the perpetrator. The novel problematized the valorization of revolutionary justice and revolutionary acts of violence. In the interwar period, Civil War narratives, like World War narratives, could be complex and contradictory.

An article by Sean Guillory that appeared in *Slavic Review* in Fall 2012 provides compelling new evidence that Civil War narratives were not always heroic. His analysis of Komsomol memoirs shows that "alongside a narrative that framed the war as a 'heroic epoch,' veterans voiced confusion, personal

---

[30] I. E. Babel', *Konarmiia* (Moscow: OGIZ, 1926).

[31] Sholokhov, *Quiet Flows the Don*, 567–68.

[32] Mikhail Sholokhov, *Tikhii Don*, bk. 2 (Moscow: Khudozhestvennaia literatura, 1933), 337.

[33] Murphy et al., *Sholokhov's Tikhii Don*, 130; Sholokhov, *Quiet Flows the Don*, 570.

loss, hardship, physical suffering, and fear in the face of death."[34] The image of the Civil War that emerged from these narratives in the late 1920s and early 1930s is as ambiguous as the image of the World War in narratives of the same era. Guillory emphasizes the traumatic legacies of the Civil War era evident in these memoirs and the shattered selves of the veteran-memoirists, struggling to cope with the aftermath of the war.

Justus Hartzok's 2009 dissertation "Children of Chapaev: The Russian Civil War Cult and the Creation of Soviet Identity, 1918–1941" also provides important new evidence about the ebb and flow of Civil War memory. Hartzok examines how the cult of the Civil War was used by Soviet ideologues to promote state authority and legitimacy, and how the Soviet population received and consumed this myth. Parallel to my work on the memory of the First World War, Hartzok's research on the Civil War suggests that multiple versions of the Civil War myth in the 1920s gave way to more determined attempts to forge a single overarching narrative in the 1930s. He argues that in works such as the blockbuster 1934 film *Chapaev*, "the regime's official language did not always transmit Soviet values in the way that leaders expected, but it often did make a powerful emotional impact on its intended audience."[35] Although Stalin's purges significantly interfered with the creation of heroes and the consolidation of the Civil War myth, aspects of this myth remained central to mobilizing the Red Army during World War II. Hartzok's work effectively uses archival materials to gain access to decision-making processes through which Civil War memory was constructed and destroyed.

Given this emerging research, I would like to pose a tentative hypothesis that the trajectory of Soviet Civil War memory has a great deal in common with the course of Soviet World War I memory. In the first 15 or so years of the Soviet period, this memory was particularly multivalent, allowing both for heroic episodes and for more traumatic memories that problematized and undercut that heroism. In the years preceding World War II, the possibilities for ambiguity were decreased and war memory became more fixed and canonical. I would argue, then, that there should not be as sharp a conceptual divide as has been previously thought between the World War and the Civil War in Soviet culture. Additional research is needed to test this hypothesis.

03 80

Future research on Soviet war memory should focus not only on the multiplicity of war myths of the World War and the Civil War (not to mention the fascinating legacy of World War II that has outlasted the existence of the Soviet

---

[34] Sean Guillory, "The Shattered Self of Komsomol Civil War Memoirs," *Slavic Review* 71, 3 (Fall 2012): 547.

[35] Justus Grant Hartzok, "Children of Chapaev: The Russian Civil War Cult and the Creation of Soviet Identity, 1918–1941" (Ph.D. diss., University of Iowa, 2009), 4–5.

Union and been propelled to new prominence in the post-Soviet Russian state), but also on myriad points of contradiction and contestation within these myths. More archival work that explores the contours of individual conflicts about the construction and dissemination of war memory will help scholars to understand what was at stake in promoting one version of war memory over another, and to identify the actors that shaped the narratives—both positively by creating them and negatively by seeking to prevent them from coming into existence. The struggle over memory and forgetting can offer tremendous insight into the nature of Soviet political culture and also into the emotional underpinnings of that culture, the deep psychic structures that facilitated and hindered political and social mobilization.

The Great War in Soviet Interwar Films: How to Forget (or Not)

Alexandre Sumpf

"The World War, we've seen it dozens of times on screen. The columns of soldiers sent to the front, the parades and processions, the cemeteries, the bits of human corpses—they have already shown them to us with great force, with anger, with artistic expressiveness. It is difficult to take up this theme yet again and to say anything new."[1] That was the reaction of a critic in November 1929 after a screening of *God of War*, one of five Soviet films that year to deal directly with the Great War. His statement might appear surprising to us, since it is a common misperception that for the most part Soviet Russia ignored the First World War, and that its interwar cinema focused instead on the October Revolution. But that neglects the fact that the war was then still a recent event that obviously remained present in the memory of artists, critics, and spectators. The production of 21 Soviet fictional and documentary films on the subject between 1919 and 1933 indicates the strength of this memory with which the new regime had to contend. Study of these films reveals a singular conjuncture between the Bolshevik shaping of history, cinematographic experimentation, and commercial interests. The films all shared the same goals: giving meaning to the trial endured by the public during the war; displaying technical and aesthetic mastery of filmmaking, which was in full renaissance; and providing a spectacle of contemporary genres that drew inspiration from the foreign filmmaking models admired by professionals and popular audiences alike.

It would hardly be fruitful to mention these cinematic productions in isolation, as if they were not part of a rich network of visual and literary representations, as if Soviet society was completely cut off from the rest of Europe. But everywhere the arts took the old cultural construct of war and overturned it.[2] If the Soviet public perhaps had not seen *All Quiet on the Western Front*

---

[1] *Bor´ba*, 28 November 1929; Rossiiskii gosudarstvennyi arkhiv literatury i iskusstva (RGALI) f. 3015 (Dzigan), op. 1, d. 537, l. 120.

[2] Laurent Véray, *La Grande Guerre au cinéma: De la gloire à la mémoire* (Paris: Ramsay, 2008); Denise J. Youngblood, *Russian War Films: On the Cinema Front, 1914–2005* (Lawrence: University Press of Kansas, 2007).

by Lewis Milestone (1930), it certainly debated the Remarque novel upon its release.[3] *J'accuse* by Abel Gance (1919) was shown in both Moscow and Petrograd.[4] Filmmakers had access to foreign productions and were conscious of the legacy of prerevolutionary Russian cinema.[5]

It would also be a mistake not to recognize that the Soviet state's demand for films had a variety of motives. Thus the film industry constantly sought new ways of staging and new genres, so as to reconcile ambivalent and sometimes implicit demands from the political authorities with the need to achieve public success, to both influence "the masses" and respond to popular taste.[6]

The political and aesthetic reconstruction of the experience of the Great War, necessarily unique in Russia given subsequent events, obeyed an internal logic in which the struggle for power after the death of Lenin was interlaced with the economics of the film industry and an intensification of Soviet mass mobilization. Memory of the First World War underwent oscillations in official discourse rather than a generalized neglect; power instrumentalized memory more than it silenced it. Cinema tackled the subject during a series of propaganda campaigns occasioned by the 1927 anniversary of the October Revolution, the antireligious campaign of 1929, and the rising crescendo of mobilization for the "future war" during 1927–40. Between the Russo-Japanese War (almost never depicted in cinema), a civil war that was overrepresented, and a Second World War that was regularly anticipated from 1931 on, the Great War, as the prototype of modern war, occupied a singular place in Soviet film and memory that was exceptional and foundational, capturing the resources and the attention of the public, at least before the turn towards victory in 1943. Far from the Bolshevik insistence on a complete distinction between "before" and "after" October 1917, we must view these years as a trajectory, a difficult transition that occurred with much suffering.

---

[3] Karen Petrone, *The Great War in Russian Memory* (Bloomington: Indiana University Press, 2011).

[4] The Management of Spectacles for the City of Moscow (Upravlenie Moskovskikh Zrelishchnykh Predpriiatii, UMZP) in July 1924 authorized *La Zone de la mort*, the art film that had brought the filmmaker to the public eye at the end of 1917. Tsentral'nyi arkhiv goroda Moskvy (TsAGM) f. 2238 (UMZP), op. 1, d. 24, l. 87.

[5] In March 1929, the office of the State Research Institute of Art (Gosudarstvennyi issledovatel'skii institut iskusstva) in Leningrad organized an evening of prerevolutionary Russian cinema. *Kino (Leningradskaia gazeta)*, no. 3 (1929): 12.

[6] On 17 November 1930, the Association of Workers of Revolutionary Cinematography (Assotsiatsiia Rabotnikov Revoliutsionnoi Kinematografii, ARRK) organized an evening of military films in Moscow *(Vecherniaia Moskva*, 19 November 1930, 2). On 21 February 1932 at the Moscow Publishers' House (Moskovskii Dom izdatelei) a debate, organized by the journal *Kino*, about the defense film *(oboronnyi fil'm)* took place between young Communists from the Red Army and Navy on the one side and members of the military branch of Soiuzkino on the other. *Letopis' rossiiskogo kino, 2: 1930–1945* (Moscow: Materik, 2007), 157.

This chapter concerns itself less with the cinematic representation of the Great War than with the emergence of the war experience as a *lieu de mémoire*, a site of memory in the terminology of Pierre Nora.[7] In the first place, it is incumbent upon us to draw up an unedited inventory of feature films on the Great War—an ever-present theme in the Soviet arts of the interwar period. We will then examine the documentary imperative in these films, in which the demand for "truth" in the depiction of politics or military action also had stylistic implications. Finally, we will examine how genre—history, revolution, adventure—combined with aesthetic debates, strategies of audience persuasion, and political maneuvers over national and international issues. One way or another, these films integrated Marxist concepts and participated in attempts to fashion the new Soviet society.

A Very Present War

While famous, *Outskirts* by Boris Barnet (1932) is not quite "the only movie made before World War II to deal exclusively with World War I."[8] In reality, many productions from interwar Soviet cinema did deal with it. Apart from canonical films of the 1927 jubilee by Vsevolod Pudovkin (*The End of St. Petersburg*), Sergei Eisenstein (*October*), or Esfir Shub (*The Fall of the Romanov Dynasty*), and the celebrated productions *A Fragment of the Empire* (Fridrikh Ermler, 1928), *Arsenal* (Aleksandr Dovzhenko, 1929), and *Outskirts*, no less than 16 films addressed the Great War, either wholly or in part. Most are preserved and available for consultation at Gosfilmofond (State Film Archives), while periodicals and archives offer additional information. The inventory is as follows: *Comrade Abram* (1919), *Enemies* (1924), *Iron and Blood* (1927), *The First Cornet Streshnev* (1928), *Zvenigora* (1928), the documentary *The World War* (1929), *Women of Riazan* (1929), *God of War* (1929), *Her Way* (1929), *Merchants of Glory* (1929), *Cities and Years* (1930), *Doomed* (1930), *Sniper* (1931), *Quiet Flows the Don* (1931), *Three Soldiers* (1932), and *The First Platoon* (1933).[9] These representations

---

[7] Pierre Nora, *Les Lieux de mémoire* (Paris: Gallimard, 1984).

[8] Youngblood, *Russian War Films*, 32.

[9] *Tovarishch Abram* (Aleksandr E. Razumnyi, Studio Ermol'ev, 1919, 20 minutes, Gosfilmofond [GFF]); *Vragi*, also known by the alternative titles *Otets i syn* and *Razrushennyi ochag* (Cheslav G. Sabinskii, Goskino, 1924, 75 minutes); *Zhelezom i krov'iu* (Vladimir N. Karin-Iakubovskii, Goskino-Kul'tkino, 1927, 1945 meters, not preserved); *Pervyi kornet Streshnev* (Efim L. Dzigan, Mikhail E. Chiaurelli, Goskinprom Gruzii, 1928, 64 minutes); *Zvenigora* (Aleksandr Dovzhenko, Vse-Ukrainskoe Foto-Kino Upravlenie [All-Ukrainian Direction for Photo and Cinema, VUFKU, 1928, 109 minutes, GFF); *Mirovaia voina* (Evgenii Iakushkin, Gosvoenkino, 1929, 60 minutes, Rossiiskii gosudarstvennyi arkhiv kino-foto dokumentov [RGAKFD]); *Baby riazanskie* (Ol'ga I. Preobrazhenskaia, Sovkino, 1927, 70 minutes, GFF); *Bog voiny*, also known by the alternative title *Belyi vsadnik* (Dzigan, Goskinprom Gruzii, 1929, 70 minutes, GFF);

of the Great War on the Russian screen corresponded to the boom years of this theme in Western film and the peak of pacifism in Europe. This rather limited group of productions nonetheless invalidates the perception of a "war that wasn't," a view that overlooks the use of this war in the Bolshevik discourse of mass mobilization or Soviet positioning in the international arena.

The First World War was far from "forgotten." There was a plan to commemorate the 15th anniversary of its outbreak, which sparked a response from every studio that was at once political, aesthetic, and commercial: obedience to official orders, a necessity to renovate the revolutionary film genre by returning to the "catalyzing event" (Lenin), and interest in capturing spectators. It is true, however, that production plans for 1928–29 did not intend to expend so much film stock on the subject, on top of which Sovkino (the state studio) was criticized for the excess of blood spilt on screen.[10]

In considering whether the Great War was "forgotten," it is also worth looking beyond the subject matter to the men who created these works, to the directors, screenwriters, cameramen, and actors. A fuller picture emerges of the collaborative process that yielded these films on the conflict. For example, the cameraman Aleksandr Dorn filmed *Iron and Blood*, then *Merchants of Glory*; Evgenii V. Cherviakov made *Cities and Years* before acting in *Three Soldiers*; Fedor M. Nikitin played a principal role in *A Fragment of the Empire* and in *The First Platoon*. Finally, Efim L. Dzigan and Ermler both directed films on each of the world wars. Most of these men were students in film schools during the First World War and thus belonged to the generation affected by it. However, the only one who could claim direct experience of war was Ermler, and his activities as a Jewish spy from Latvia with a good command of the German language placed him in a delicate position.[11]

Studios did not release their films in virgin territory but rather drew upon multiple representations of the war in literature. Thus, *A Fragment of the Empire* was drawn from *The Man from the Past*, a little known short story by Nikolai Pogodin, a renowned writer and future recipient of the Stalin Prize.

Ee put' (Aleksandr Z. Shtrizhak, Sovkino, 1929, 60 minutes, GFF); *Torgovtsy slavoi* (Leonid L. Obolenskii, Mezhrabpom-Fil'm, 1929, 53 minutes—the fourth part is missing, GFF); *Goroda i gody* (Evgenii V. Cherviakov, Soiuzkino-Derussa, 1930, 73 minutes, GFF); *Obrechennye*, also known by the alternative title *Russkie vo Frantsii* (Lev Push, Goskinprom Gruzii, 1931, 65 minutes, GFF); *Snaiper* (Semen A. Timoshenko, Sovkino Leningrad, 1931, 74 minutes, GFF); *Tikhii Don* (Preobrazhenskaia, Soiuzkino, 1931, 91 minutes, GFF); *Tri soldata*, also known by the alternative title *Zachem ty zdes'* (Aleksandr G. Ivanov, 1932; not preserved); *Pervyi vzvod*, also known by the alternative title *Zapadnyi front* (David G. Gutman, Boris L. Brodianskii, and Vladimir V. Korsh-Sablin, Belgoskino, 1933, 84 minutes, GFF).

[10] Gosudarstvennyi arkhiv Rossiiskoi Federatsii (GARF) f. 8326, op. 2 (Sovkino), d. 4, ll. 71–73 (Report).

[11] Tsentral'nyi gosudarstvennyi arkhiv literatury i iskusstva Sankt-Peterburga (TsGALI SPb) f. 166 (Ermler autobiographical documents), op. 1, d. 349.

Cities and Years brought to the screen the homonymic bestseller by Konstantin Fedin, published in 1924; *Quiet Flows the Don* also benefited from the aura of Sholokhov's novel, the first part of which appeared in 1928. *Merchants of Glory* extended the Russian revival of the satirical play by Marcel Pagnol and Paul Nivoix (1925), and *Her Way* grew out of a tale by Mikhail Nikitin.

The geographical distribution of filmmaking by the various studios dispels any notion of an unequivocal image of the First World War in Russian cinema. The year 1929 saw the basic disarray of the profession—Gosvoenkino (State Military Cinema Organization) was liquidated on 13 August 1929;[12] Derussa (German-Russian Film Alliance) went bankrupt three weeks later.[13] While the Workers' and Peasants' Inspectorate (Rabkrin) investigated Mezhrampom (the joint German-Russian film studio of the International Workers' Aid), the prominent role of the German film industry and its precious commercial outlets for Russian cinema was challenged, allowing a greater role for the domestic industry throughout Soviet Russia. However, as far as the films on the Great War were concerned, one discerns a certain balance between private and public studios, or among studios of the republics. Such distribution between studios in the 1920s is not explained by planning in a geographic sense but rather by competition at the heart of the new cadre established under the tutelage of the industry in the wake of the party conference on cinema in March 1928.[14]

Finally, we must specify the exact role of the war in these films. Sometimes the war served only as a backdrop for the action (*Women of Riazan, Golden Mountains*) or as the principal location for the plot (*God of War, Sniper, The First Platoon*). The conflict weighs heavily on the local community in *Comrade Abram, Her Way,* and *Outskirts*; it separates families in most of the 21 fictional productions; and it brings about class struggle in one manner or another by sharpening class consciousness. The classic Manichean structure of war films[15] is intensified: added to the traditional opposition between men and women or between the front and the rear is the opposition between classes. Finally, certain spaces beyond the front are given special attention: the countryside (including the Jewish shtetl); the artisanal or manufacturing city (*Iron and Blood, Outskirts,* and *Arsenal*); and France, in no less than three films (*Merchants of Glory, Doomed,* and *Sniper*).

In all, the Great War, as a test of tsarist society, which it undermined both militarily and financially, initially played the role of "historical catalyst"

---

[12] *Kino*, no. 33 (1929): 2.

[13] *Letopis' rossiiskogo kino*, 1: *1895–1928* (Moscow: Materik, 2004), 670.

[14] B. S. Ol'khovyi, *Puti kino: Pervoe partiinoe soveshchanie po kinematografii* (Moscow: TeaKinoPechat', 1929).

[15] Natacha Laurent, "Les traces de 1914–1918 dans le cinéma soviétique: Mémoire et oubli," in *Une guerre qui n'en finit pas: 1914–2008, à l'écran et sur scène*, ed. Christophe Gauthier, David Lescot, and Laurent Véray (Brussels: Complexe, 2008), 133–45.

(Lenin), a central emphasis of Soviet historiography. In other words, war led to revolution: on a large scale with the diptych of Shub, in a balanced manner by Eisenstein, and in the guise of a conclusion by Dovzhenko or Barnet. Some of the films led in the direction of revolution, others pacifism. Several of them mixed together the battles of the Great War and the Civil War (*A Fragment of the Empire*, *Her Way*, and *Cities and Years*), and some anticipated the war to come (*A Fragment of the Empire*, *The World War*, and *Sniper*). The hero of *Sniper* is a former soldier who becomes a worker and instructor at the shooting clubs of Osoaviakhim (Society of Friends of Defense and Avia-Chemical Construction). The scene of the final skirmish, where two veterans from the same elite unit of the Russian army confront each other on the border—one is a rank-and-file soldier who has become a Soviet worker, the other an officer who remained in exile—foreshadows many other war films to come, from *Maybe Tomorrow* (V. Dalskii, 1932) to *If Tomorrow Comes the War* (Dzigan, 1938).

The crucial choice of the *finale* was not only aesthetic or political. Originally Pudovkin had intended to present St. Petersburg across three successive eras to explain the history of the revolution in Russia.[16] Financial concerns and shortages of film stock forced him to center his attention on the years 1914–17 and abandon plans to multiply the characters, focusing instead only on the Peasant. He reintroduced historical progression by balancing images and commentary in each of the three periods: if the tsarist period is fluid and indeterminate, the war and the revolutions of 1917 are subjected to sophisticated editing and minutely positioned intertitles. The film elaborates an assertive pedagogic discourse that insists on the insufficiency of the first revolution: it makes a systematic comparison between the monarchical order and its continuation in republican guise after February. And between the defeat of the monarchy and the rise of the proletarian dictatorship, Pudovkin clearly positions the Leninist acceleration of the political and social revolution. But he does not depict either the Civil War or the violence of the Red Terror; nor does he suggest the inevitable comparison between the old and new autocracies: the film is about the end of St. Petersburg, that is, the fall of the tsarist empire and the collapse of capitalism, which Pudovkin explains as historical events.

The Documentary Imperative

Following the example of literature, and certainly more than the other visual arts, Soviet interwar cinema documented the principal aspects of the Great War on both the battlefield and the home front. With the exception of the most famous films, known for their intrinsic value or for the celebrity of their directors rather than because they are about the Great War,[17] most of the

---

[16] Vance Kepley, *The End of Saint-Petersburg* (London: I. B. Tauris, 2003).

[17] *Quiet Flows the Don* appears mainly to be about the Civil War in the Cossack region, but the work is as much about the First World War (Petrone, *Great War*, 141–49).

works discussed here have been forgotten and have never known a second release on screen or on video. However, the documentary imperative which flowed from the ideology imposed by the Party on the film studios found an echo in each of these productions and yielded some curiosities. Thus, one is surprised that an industry that was producing relatively few movies devoted two entire feature films to the Russian Expeditionary Force in France—which involved 40,000 combatants of the 13 million mobilized.[18] All these films, however, contain more than mere documentary value. They were conceived not to teach us today but to strike a chord of emotional memory in spectators of the period through the depiction of specific wartime episodes.

Only a few movies showed the moment of mobilization, though it was a crucial event in the common experience of Russians in 1914. In *Outskirts*, as in other films situated in urban settings, two images echo each other: the lugubrious whistle of the factory (which symbolically replaces church bells) and a gravely serious population running frenetically in response to the announcement of mobilization. Anti-capitalist and anti-bourgeois discourses are elements of fiction added for ideological reasons. The farewell scene on the train platform in *God of War* between the young Natasha and her fiancé Georgii is convincing, despite the romantic literary motif (the father of the heroine opposes this misalliance). Departure scenes in the "peasant" films went even further in verisimilitude. In *Zvenigora*, the disorganized departure of the men of the village, displaying something between pitiful joy and affliction, has parallels in similar scenes in *Women of Riazan* and *Her Way*. In *Her Way* Shtrizhak smartly reversed the farewell motif by balancing the dazed depression of those present with the moral discomfort of the wife who rejoices as her abusive husband is leaving for a long time. Even slower than those marching through the village to the assembly point is Praskovia, who covers the distance with her husband. In the film, it is the distance of Russia, deep with militarism and "Faith, Tsar, and Fatherland," that Emma Tsessarskaia evinces, an actress whom spectators knew for her roles as woman of the rebellious people.

We must consider the visual experience of Russian spectators to better appreciate the impact on these films of the theoretical debates that were taking place at the heart of the artistic world, as well as how the films were received. The Great War was the occasion for the Russian film industry to produce its own newsreels, intended initially for domestic audiences and later, as in the era of Pathé Russe (1904–13), for export abroad. As in other belligerent nations, two crucial issues needed to be addressed: the relationship film producers enjoyed with military authorities (authorizations to film; censorship of filmed images) and the mixture between live images and staged ones filmed either as spectacle or for propagandistic purposes.

---

[18] Jamie Cockfield, *With Snow on Their Boots: The Tragic Odyssey of the Russian Expeditionary Force in France During World War I* (New York: St. Martin's Press, 1999).

We are familiar with the growing role played in this domain by the cinematic section of the Skobelev Committee, to which the tsar granted a monopoly on filming at the front from the autumn of 1914 onwards. Its critical and public success was such that in the town of Lugansk the distributor, Skvirskii Brothers, showed fake copies, doubtlessly made from the original film rushes.[19] The newsreels of the Skobelev Committee certainly struck contemporaries:

> Our descendants, having experienced the historical moment through this film, will see the war and the misfortunes that result from it. Possessing this living and instructive representation of the carnage, they will no doubt fight so that such a thing will never happen again. Every spectator of the *Realities of War* can say with assurance—I have seen and I know war such as it is.[20]

Such sentiments, which the committee intended to mobilize for the Russian war effort, resulted from a cinematic sleight of hand. Petr K. Novitskii, one of the film operators working on their productions, revealed some years later an "interesting detail. As experience showed, filming under fire did not provoke as strong an impression as good staging"—principally for technical reasons: smoke interrupted filming, and the front had many dangers. "Some staging was performed under the supervision of military specialists... That offered a chance to film more closely and more precisely. However, the percentage of staged scenes was insignificant, exceptional really."[21] Yet the film reels conserved in the Russian State Documentary Film and Photo Archive at Krasnogorsk (RGAKFD) confirm the analysis by Laurent Véray of their French equivalent:[22] dramatization and the editing of rushes seem the rule, which is not surprising given the restrictions on filming at the front and persnickety censorship.[23]

Novitskii's point of view can be understood in the context of early aesthetic and political debates involving visual experience. Closely linked to the abstract experimentation of Aleksandr Rodchenko's journal *LEF* was Dziga Vertov, whose concept of Cinema Eye led to a visual reexamination of the everyday in film. The importance of the Vertov phenomenon must not

---

[19] *Kine-zhurnal*, no. 19–20 (1916): 101.

[20] Dzhim, "Voina na ekrane," *Kinematograf* (Rostov-on-Don), no. 4–5 (1915): 11.

[21] "Kino na voine: Iz lichnykh vospominanii operatora P. K. Novitskogo," *Sovetskii ekran*, no. 6 (1929): 12.

[22] Laurent Véray, *Les films d'actualités français de la Grande Guerre* (Paris: SIRPA/AFRHC, 1995).

[23] Rossiiskii gosudarstvennyi voenno-istoricheskii arkhiv (RGVIA) f. 13836, op. 1, d. 44 (Petrograd military censorship).

let us forget that from July 1924 Sovkino edited a weekly news publication, *Sovkinozhurnal*, whose editors took a different position than *LEF*'s.[24] There, a new model of authenticity emerged, concerned for the restoration of facts.[25] The theoretician Sergei M. Tret′iakov urged the exclusive use of raw material. Another leading theoretician, Viktor B. Shklovskii, attributed the idea of editing to old newsreels and tells of having assisted the young Esfir Shub in her quest for documentary matter.[26]

Although Shub obviously intervened in the presentation of her material, she considered herself a "factographic" filmmaker and "in editing I tried not to render the material of the newsreel abstract, but rather to reinforce its documentary principle. Everything was subjected to this idea."[27] Application of these principles is evident at several levels in *The Fall*: revolutionaries are filmed in a dynamic way and counterrevolutionaries are always static; here intertitles are explanatory, whereas in Eisenstein's *October* they are exhortatory; and the emphasis is on the logic of the images rather than an obviously superimposed directorial discourse. The tenth anniversary of the October Revolution reinforced the documentary tendency through the resurrection of national history.[28] Besides the ubiquitous assessment of "ten years of Soviet power" in every newspaper column and review, one can pick out numerous testimonies on the war and the Revolution, underscoring the work of the Institute of History of the Revolution directed by David B. Riazanov.

Shub writes in her autobiography about her intensive research in Moscow and Leningrad, where at the end of summer 1926 numerous reels of footage lay in storage in a humid basement on Sergievskaia Street.[29] A decade after the Great War, a certain Khmelnitskii helped her find 20,000 meters of film in the private archives of Nicholas II.[30] For two months in the Museum of the Revolution, she and the future author of the intertitles, Mark Z. Tseitlin (an employee of the museum), screened 60,000 meters of poorly identified films of varying quality and length. Between its advanced screening and its debut on 11 March 1917, Shub imbedded in this film—first named *February* and then *The*

---

[24] Copies are conserved at RGAKFD.

[25] Mikhail Yampolsky, "Reality at Second Hand," *Historical Journal of Film, Radio, and Television* 11, 2 (1991): 161.

[26] Viktor Shklovskii, "Ob Esfire Shub i ee kinematograficheskom opyte," *Za 60 let: Raboty o kino* (Moscow: Iskusstvo, 1985), 98–100.

[27] Ibid., 103.

[28] Frederick C. Corney, *Telling October: Memory and the Making of the Bolshevik Revolution* (Ithaca, NY: Cornell University Press, 2004).

[29] Esfir Shub, "Krupnym planom," in *Zhizn′ moia* (Moscow: Iskusstvo, 1972), 99–101, 113.

[30] Graham Roberts, *Forward Soviet! History and Non-Fiction Film in the USSR* (London: I. B. Tauris, 1999), 51–56.

Fall of the Romanov Dynasty—snippets of newsreels featuring Lenin that had been shot by Amtorg (American Trading Corporation). Sovkino finally agreed to grant Shub the status of the film's director, recognizing her creative input.

Shub did not intend to retrace the history of the war in textbook fashion; the assassination of Archduke Franz Ferdinand was not even mentioned. Marxist history, which privileges great socioeconomic trends, made its influence felt. Shub highlighted those who were economically or politically responsible (for example, Vtorov, the largest Russian producer of arms) and insisted less on the technical aspects of the conflict—despite endless shots of warships—than on its consequences. The horrifying sequence titled *Faces of War* shows the dead, the destruction, the prisoners, the wounded (the longest sequence), the refugees, the "scorched earth," and the women in factories. These side effects of combat, which were low-hanging fruit for the propaganda machine of the tsarist regime and its charitable institutions, constitute the largest part of the rediscovered film stock, and their editing presents the best-constructed passage in the film.

Other documentaries were also made from similar archival materials. *The World War*, a montage film by Evgenii Iakushkin intended for the 15th anniversary of the outbreak of war, was filmed soon after the appearance of *Verdun Visions of History* by Leon Poirier in France.[31] Overturning the concept of a film made retrospectively on the Great War, Poirier's movie traced a new horizon for Soviet filmmakers. The story follows the major steps of the battle but uses veterans as actors: "Verdun was not acted, but relived," Poirier claimed. This casting came from a preconceived idea of the period, namely that the "truth" of the conflict lay in the testimony of survivors, an idea, however, that did not preclude the inclusion of scenes filmed in 1927 and from archives of the *Service Cinématographique des Armées*. With a concern for realism mixed with an obvious didactic purpose, the filmmaker formulated a precise discourse across 70 intertitles, inserting detailed maps and animated diagrams to inform the spectator and detail the various military operations. The live wiring for sound by the audio engineers produced a very strong impression when the film was screened on 8 November 1928, signaling as well the ambition to achieve an authentic reproduction of the event—thus realism, albeit through artifice.

The thematic program of the Red Army's Gosvoenkino studio, specializing in pedagogical films (*kul'turfilmy*), granted Iakushkin, director of *Days of Struggle and Victories*, 15,000 rubles to "make a film as good as Shub's."[32] In the cinema warehouses of Lefortovo, Potylikha, and Donskoi Monastery, he screened 280,000 meters of film, from which he culled 7,000 meters of us-

---

[31] Clément Puget, "Verdun… de Léon Poirier," *1895*, no. 45 (April 2005): 5–29.

[32] RGALI f. 645, op. 1, d. 532, l. 15 (Tematicheskii plan Gosvoenkino na 1928–29).

able material, and integrated it in an 1,800-meter film.[33] To promote sales, emphasis was placed on the rarity of some of the images: the French Socialist minister Albert Thomas visiting Russia (taken from *Ikh tsarstvo* by Mikhail K. Kalatozov and produced by the State Film Studio of Georgia, Goskinprom Gruzii), or footage from several German film canisters found in Ukraine. Iakushkin also made clear his goal of overturning the heroic viewpoint of the Skobelev Committee and similar organizations, including foreign ones, in order to afford a "true sense" of the images.

The originality of Iakushkin's film resides in its presentation of the military experience of the Great War, elsewhere reduced to (countless) parades, armaments, and officers. The narrative also stresses conditions at the front—the deaths, the trains for the wounded, a scene of delousing in the snow—and conditions of women's work in the rear. If Kerenskii is mocked here (as usual) by association with the women's battalions defending the Winter Palace, suggesting his deficient virility, the fifth part of the film on October presents an unexpected cause of the Revolution, linked to the international context. Scenes of fraternization from 1917 segue to Lenin's speech, to scenes of the German revolution, then to negotiations at Versailles, and finally to a cardstock with "Peace" placed over images of ruins. "We know that only a worldwide October will save humanity from more war": the final intertitle, at once pacifist and revolutionary, is in keeping with the tone of that year (1929) and underscores the reproducibility of the first worldwide conflict, the universality of its causes, and its social and political consequences.

It is difficult to determine the impact of *The World War* on the Soviet public. The reviewer V. Solev would have liked "a little more pathos in the intertitles, indeed quotations from the best anti-militarist works."[34] He also surmised that "the first spectators would be adults who themselves experienced the war," and would have noticed such incongruous details as metal helmets in 1914, but who would have appreciated what Solev regarded as entertaining images: the elephant in the German zoo, French artillery on the water, female workers standing on a scale with artillery shells. This critic from the popular periodical *Sovetskii ekran* predicted a reactivation of the war experience while at the same time denying it: the interest in this lived past would be reduced to a few details and then lost in the ridiculous or touching aspects of the war. It is safe to wager, however, that the laughs flew during the screenings while comments and other emotional outbursts were also overheard.

---

[33] RGAKFD, film no. 2709. The film features 6 parts: the causes of the imperialist war; 1914 (leadership and patriotic demonstrations, refugees, prisoners); 1915 (generals and wounded); February 1917; October 1917; the USSR in 1929 and the threat of future war.

[34] V. Solev, "Mirovaia voina," *Sovetskii ekran*, no. 30 (1929): 4.

To the chagrin of Sovkino, the distributor, the film did not succeed as a work of propaganda.[35] The 600 soldiers invited to a special screening at the Central House of the Red Army only moderately appreciated this "reel of rather quickly made political agitation," which no doubt recalled all those films they suffered through during their political education. Despite everything, it was approved for distribution to army clubs, perhaps for want of something better.[36] *Krasnaia zvezda*, the official organ of the army, came out squarely in favor of the patriotic and heroic themes, and it criticized *The World War*. "One senses throughout the film a whiff of pacifism" not compatible either with the suffering of the Civil War or with the fact that the imperialist war, filled with capitalist horrors, had led to the Revolution.[37] Ordered by the army, well financed, and, as far as we can surmise today, rather well constructed, this film ostensibly intended for the troops did not seem either to provoke the intended response or to synthesize a military account of a conflict so misunderstood by its conscripts.

By contrast, *The Fall* enjoyed immediate success in the eyes of the greater public, which was usually partial to American adventure films. Shub claimed not to recall the preview before the elites of Russian cinema, except for the applause after the part entitled "First World War." The queues in front of movie theaters confirmed the commercial success of the film, praised by Shklovskii, given the modest cost of 5,000 rubles.[38] But the comparison with foreign productions, a strong incitement for the Russian and Soviet cultural industry, underscored the distance still to be covered in order to catch up. *Verdun Visions of History* relied on battle veterans, the music of the veteran André Petiot, and the publication of soldiers' reminiscences of war. In the USSR, critics regretted that such publicity and appeals to specific types of audiences did not accompany the 1927 jubilee.[39]

The Cinematic Genre of the Great War

Determining which genres these films belong to should help us to distinguish them from similar contemporary works, but also to appreciate more fully the strategies used to disseminate political messages. Besides the need for reenactments—provided by décor and costumes and indeed by the discursive strategies themselves—that influence the visual pact with the spectator, the historic film requires an epic mode of narration with a focus on "great men"

---

[35] RGALI f. 645, op. 1, d. 369, l. 13 (Orlikova in "Soveshchanie rabotnikov proizvodstva i prokata polit-prosvet kul'turfil'm pri Sovkino," 3–5 February 1930).

[36] RGALI f. 3015, op. 1, d. 537, l. 69.

[37] A. P. Palei, in *Krasnaia zvezda*, 20 November 1929; RGALI f. 3015, op. 1, d. 537, l. 65.

[38] "Temperatura kino," *Sovetskii ekran*, no. 13 (1927): 4.

[39] Iu. and V. Fefer, "Klassicheskaia propaganda," *Sovetskii ekran*, no. 31 (1929): 9.

in "historical moments" and the constant confrontation between Good and Evil. The genre of the revolutionary epic poem that periodically invaded the Soviet screen corresponded to this model in its relationship to the event (mythologized) and to history (revisited teleologically). However, it differed in the ideology it promoted (less nationalist than class-based, at least at the start) and the role of the individual (serving the interests of the masses, whenever the masses are not the motor of the action). Finally, the war film, a genre that has existed from the very beginning of cinema itself,[40] emphasizes the mechanical more than the body, action more than sentiment. The Soviet approach to cinema was further complicated by a reflection on characters and acting, a subject that will not be considered here in detail, but for which the notion of "type" played an important role.

In the Soviet Union, the representation of the Great War in the interwar period evolved rapidly from one that focused on past conflict to one that imagined combat in the war to come. The trenches and mechanized war were deeply rooted in the visual memory of the population. Photographs or newsreels from the earlier period were used by Shub and Iakushkin to show the uniqueness of the Russian trenches. They appeared simpler in organization and shallower than those on the Western front; the image of rifles aligned across the ground at chest height is a recurrent theme. Most of the works analyzed here show little inventiveness or only modest attention to reconstruction, with the exception of *Sniper*, which was in the privileged position of having been shown to the French communist writer Henri Barbusse on 28 September 1932 in Moscow.[41] Here, the reconstruction process is set in a *mise-en-abîme*, where one of the first scenes shows the construction of a fake battlefield for the training of elite marksmen, somewhere in the north of France. The excavation, the installation of barbed wire, the firing distances, and the visibility all give the spectator a lesson in ground-level tactics, minus the mud and the mortal pressure of enemy fire. The trench is always presented at moments of crisis in *The Fall* or *God of War*, including shots mowing down heads that poke over the top of the trenches. This recurring scene plays as much on the memory of omnipresent danger as it asserts the vainglorious and unjust character of this war. Aside from *The First Platoon*, the trench never really represents its other role, that of a place of safety and survival. It is shown only as a place of waiting; and that passivity in 1933 contrasted sharply to the mechanized movement that dominated the fictions of the future war.

The emphasis on mechanized warfare, evident with the fictional film *Tankists* (albeit unconvincingly portrayed given the absence of opposition in the field and the weakness of the tactics surrounding the mechanized war

---

[40] Emmanuel Vincenot, "Cuba, 1898: Le cinéma au service de la guerre," in *Une histoire mondiale des cinémas de propagande*, ed. Jean-Pierre Bertin-Maghit (Paris: Nouveau Monde Editions, 2008), 13–26.

[41] *Letopis' rossiiskogo kino*, 2: 185.

of movement), resulted in a slow evolution based on two commonplaces: the depiction of explosions and the role of machine guns. They too were inscribed in the collective Russian memory after 1905. The engagements are a mix of blind combat at a distance and hand-to-hand combat. The trio of cannon-smoke-explosion varies in angle and close-up but makes its way into every film, Soviet or not. War of position and attrition entails a new visual and sound/sonorous landscape. Space disappears, sucked up by explosions that spray clods of earth and sometimes even swallow up combatants.

The machine gun played a major role in experimentation with the visual "voicing" of combat, at a time when silent films were not really "soundless" but accompanied by standard and/or improvised tunes, and even with special scores.[42] Soviet filmmakers from Eisenstein to Barnet increased the close-ups on the muzzles of this weapon capable of mowing down an entire company in minutes, translating the implacable ferocity of mechanized warfare onto the screen. Yet this gun was mostly used in Russia during the Civil War by soldiers who salvaged foreign hardware from former French and British allies or from German troops. This false-bottomed memory found its echo in the famous scene of recollection elaborated by Ermler, in keeping with Freudian theories that he debated with Eisenstein.[43] In *A Fragment of the Empire*, the return of a repressed memory popped into the mind of Filimonov, a victim of auditory and visual concussion, triggered by his wife's outburst in 1928; he endured a physical as well as a psychological recollection. This sound obsession took shape through the motif of the high-speed mechanical clicking sound produced by a sewing machine or machine gun. The auditory evocation was made visible on screen by superimpositions and montages of shots tightly alternating between the sewing machine needle and the muzzle of the weapon. Despite this successful rendering, the scene appeared to please neither critics, irritated by the insistence that psychological shock had occurred, nor spectators in general. One of the latter went so far as to lament the "hardly comprehensible scenes, like those of tanks and other scenes of the imperialist war."[44]

Soviet filmmakers did not intend to represent the experience of the Great War in detail, or to use this theme in action movies. Rather, it became an

---

[42] Valérie Pozner, ed., *Le muet a la parole: Cinéma et performance au début du XXe siècle* (Paris: AFRHC, 2005); Alexandre Sumpf, "Le 'grand muet' à la campagne: Educateurs politiques, projectionnistes ambulants et paysans dans l'URSS des années 1920," *1895*, no. 52 (September 2007): 57–88.

[43] Alexandre Sumpf, "Trauma et amnésie: Grande Guerre et guerre civile russes dans *Un débris de l'empire* de Fridrikh Ermler," in *Les mises en scène de la guerre au XXe siècle: Théâtre et cinéma*, ed. Laurent Véray and David Lescot (Paris: Éditions Nouveau Monde, 2011), 63–80.

[44] TsGALI f. 166, op. 1, d. 337, l. 1 (Postcard dated 8 December 1928, sent from Nizhnii Novgorod and signed by Rakov and Shirin).

allegory of liberation from suffering and oppression. This insistence on the meaning of "imperialist" war stemmed either from contemporary European pacifism, or from its Soviet version, which advocated revolution as a remedy to the danger of future war. Of all the Soviet films about the First World War, *The First Platoon* is remarkable for its description of trench life, but only *God of War* stands out in its representation of "massive slaughter." Besides the scene described earlier, Dzigan created many novel images for the Soviet spectator that nonetheless still echoed recent memory: operational maps with small flags (an imitation of Western fictions, or the influence of documentaries?); the spontaneous returns from the front; and incomprehension on the home front. Furthermore, comparison with foreign productions underscores the recurrent use of night scenes in Soviet cinema. Film critics have in particular held forth on the lack of resources at Ermler's disposal, which explains his choice of minimalist staging in the confrontation between the German and Russian armies, incarnated in the two soldiers who share the name Ivan. But his expressionist inspiration denotes an aesthetic choice aimed at reinforcing the theater of clashes using contrasts between black and white, night and day. With the technique of spotlights, first experienced by Russian soldiers during the terrible siege of Port Arthur (1904), Ermler dramatizes the nightmarish dimension of the conflict.

Soviet filmmakers had to respond to the aesthetic challenge of crowd scenes, inaugurated by D. W. Griffith and the rest of American cinema in his wake, to which was added the role of the masses as a political force on the national stage. Eisenstein's *October* thus distinguished itself by its crowds, not in battle but at the protest that was suppressed on 3 July 1917 in Petrograd at the intersection of Nevskii Prospekt and Sadovaia Street. That scene, preferred by spectators of the period to the one of the storming of the Winter Palace famous today,[45] was filmed using a high-angle shot from a nearby apartment building, recalling photographs from the era. Eisenstein used montage, previously considered an "American" technique, alternating long shots and close-ups of the combatants in a quick rhythm from unnatural angles using a mobile camera. Soviet spectators were surely disappointed not to find these same dynamic techniques employed in films about the Great War. Critics found cause to reject *Cities and Years* as a "chamber" rather than a "symphonic" film—meaning it was on a less grand scale than anticipated; moreover it lacked the "little something" that was the working masses.[46] In its inspection of the script, Sovkino in June 1929 disapproved of the absence of October, of Social Democrats, of the German revolution, and the marginalization of one of the

---

[45] Alexandre Sumpf, "La vision de l'Histoire des spectateurs soviétiques: La Révolution à travers *Octobre* d'Eisenstein," *Communisme*, no. 90 (November–December 2007): 31–49.

[46] L. Nezhdanov, *Vecherniaia Moskva*, 22 October 1930, 3.

characters, the German painter Kurt Van, from his social milieu.[47] Because the film was criticized from every quarter, it is surprising that Amkino was able to distribute the film in the United States (as of 3 April 1931).[48] Undoubtedly this was due to the popularity of Fedin's novel and its internationalist topic.

A more pointed debate about the verisimilitude of combat and the didactic role of cinema took place among specialists in the cinema journal *Sovetskii ekran*. They deplored the lack of good popular military films in the USSR depicting "real combat" and the Red Army in the Civil War.[49] For M. Penzenskii, shoulder-to-shoulder infantry assaults did not capture the actual experience of combat, which had been carried out essentially by crawling flat on the ground. Participation of Red Army units produced an effect opposite to the one intended. Specifically, he criticized the repeated showing of cavalry attacks on screen, an experience more appropriate to the Civil War than the Great War.[50] It is revealing that for scenes filmed on site in the Donbass for *Iron and Blood*, 12,000 extras were called in, "veterans of the Civil War" as well as soldiers from a nearby garrison.[51] Denouncing "illiteracy in the military arts" and its "deplorable" effect on the spectator, Penzenskii proposed that a unit commander direct these particular scenes rather than an artistic director. Thus he made the case for the prioritization of consultants, who could bring to bear their experience of the battlefield, over filmmakers supposedly armed only with their imaginations.

These discussions show the difficulty of making sense of Soviet filmmaking on the First World War without also considering the ever-present Civil War, whether in general political discourse or the actors' own experience and understanding. Indeed, numerous films on the Civil War were made in the 1920s, with 11 productions in 1929 alone.[52] In those films, heroism is a matter of political conscience and individual sacrifice for the collective cause: not infrequently, the heroes die (Chapaev) or suffer the loss of dear ones (Praskovia in *Her Way*). In adapting Marcel Pagnol's play *Merchants of Glory* for the screen, Leonid L. Obolenskii offered a stunning reflection on the emptiness of the heroic figure of the (imperialistic) Great War. Pagnol and Obolenskii treat the economic and ideological profiteers of war, revealing the

---

[47] GFF f. 2, op. 1, d. 190 (*Goroda i gody*), ll. 47, 54.

[48] RGALI f. 2686 (Cherviakov), op. 1, d. 22 (Letter from L. Monoszon [Amkino] to Cherviakov).

[49] V.L., "Nashi zriteli—eto nasha armiia," *Sovetskii ekran*, no. 8 (1929): 4.

[50] M. Penzenskii, "O batal'nom fil'me," *Sovetskii ekran*, no. 20 (1929): 29.

[51] G.D., "*Zhelezom i krov'iu*: Beseda s rezhisserom V. I. Karinym," *Sovetskii ekran*, no. 18 (1925): 2.

[52] *Bol'shoe gore malen'koi zhenshchiny*; *V sugrobakh*; *Dva-buldi-dva*; *Zamallu*; *Znakomoe litso*; *Konnitsa skachet*; *Otel Savoi*; *Peregon smerti*; *Poslednii attraktsion*; *Piat' nevest*; *Sosny shumiat*.

underside of the military machine. The arts, cynically placed in the service of militarism and nationalism, broadcast a double illusion: the picture gives the illusion of the presence of someone who has become irremediably absent; the festive public celebration of the son's sacrifice forbids the private mourning of the father. Although the French context of the plot is evident, it could be risky to bring up such issues in the USSR after "the Seven-Year War." In other films, heroism begins when saying "no," rebelling, but also knowing how to remain constant through the tests of these troubled times, as shown by the soldier in *Sniper* or Kurt Van in *Cities and Years*.

If it is customary for us to emphasize the historical-revolutionary genre in the USSR, it was far from essential for studios, who worried about protecting their bottom line. Decision-makers perceived, from intuition, experience, or surveys, that the public preferred comedies, especially foreign ones, and adventure films that Soviet producers struggled to keep up with.[53] Was it necessarily a question of rejecting films about the Revolution or war? Was it due to a saturation of the market or the people's rejection of the Soviet regime? It is difficult to say for certain, but the introduction of certain foreign techniques suggests a serious consideration of this problem by Soviet filmmakers at a moment when the number of imported films declined significantly, and when movie theaters offered little that was new (though in those days, people were happy to watch the same film several times). Thus, in *God of War*, instead of staging the shocking abandonment of the wounded by the Orthodox bishop's Red Cross train by means of a panning shot of a field hospital surrendered to the enemy, Dzigan chose slapstick: a troupe of cripples with enormous bandages and crutches chasing train cars as they roll away. In Tiflis, the newspaper *Zaria vostoka* lamented this pale imitation of an American-style chase scene (*gon'ka*); in Ul'ianovsk, a film critic ironically commented on invalids who "run and collapse; it is nonsense, a failed imitation of Pudovkin and Eisenstein."[54] The filmmaker had rendered implausible an actual historical episode survived by some soldiers.

Another widespread method of reaching audiences during the interwar years was to target certain segments of the public, particularly spectators who were captives of their social institutions (army, school, Komsomol, unions, etc.). Soviet authorities demanded that the least commercially viable productions deliver propaganda content. By this yardstick, we can understand the role studios played in the propagation of particular images of the Great War to the detriment of a more universal vision of the conflict. *The World War* appears to be an educational film for conscripts participating in military or sports training. *Merchants of Glory*, filmed by a theater actor, undoubtedly

---

[53] Alexandre Sumpf, "Le public soviétique et *Octobre* d'Eisenstein: Enquête sur une enquête," *1895*, no. 42 (February 2004): 5–34.

[54] RGALI f. 3015, op. 1, d. 537, ll. 97, 114 (G.K.N., *Zaria vostoka*, 6 August 1929; G.C., *Proletarskii put'*, 17 November 1929).

attempted to profit from the worldwide success of the play by Pagnol. With *Cities and Years*, Soiuzkino (which replaced Sovkino in 1930) tried to imitate the methods and success of Mezhrabpom by allying itself with the German firm Derussa and seeking an international audience. Finally, *God of War* participated in the "cinema versus Church" campaign, in which Goskinprom Gruzii distinguished itself in 1929 with the first film by Mikhail E. Chiaurelli, *Saba*. The censorship agency governing moving pictures, Glavrepertkom (Glavnyi repertuarnyi komitet), strove to define these different audiences. It gave precise instructions on types of audience (four categories), how long a film would be available to theaters (from two years for *Doomed* to five years for *Cities and Years*), and which ones would be exported abroad. It rated certain films positively or negatively, in the case of the latter imposing restrictions more often than completely banning films.[55]

Press clippings indicate that in 1930 those two films were shown in the best movie theaters of the capital[56]—*Doomed* played at the Malaia Dmitrovka, the Forum, the Gorn, and the Taganskii.[57] The seven largest movie theaters in Moscow at that time charged prohibitive prices, from one to one-and-a-half rubles, as opposed to forty to eighty kopecks for the other downtown theaters.[58] The cost of seats determined the audience but also guaranteed a certain profitability that allowed studios to tolerate the price cut granted to workers' clubs and public institutions. Other clippings reveal that *God of War*, initially screened in the two capitals in August 1929, continued to be shown in November while also playing in Rostov-on-Don, Ul′ianovsk, or Stalinabad, then the Volga region in January 1930.[59] Out in theaters at the end of October 1929, *A Fragment of the Empire* was screened in Nizhnii Novgorod in early December, from where two spectators, Rakov and Shirin, sent a postcard

---

[55] GFF f. 2, op. 1, d. 606 (*Obrechennye*), l. 7, and d. 190 (*Goroda i gody*), l. 1.

[56] According to the 1930 guide *Teatral′naia Moskva* (which presented data for 1929), the Gorn had a 712-seat room with a 5 x 5.7 meter screen; the Malaia Dmitrovka had 750 seats and a 4.3 x 5 meter screen; the Forum, 1030 seats and a 5.7 x 8.6 meter screen. At the Gorn, the orchestra included 15 musicians, as did the Malaia Dmitrovka; at the Forum, there were 20 musicians plus 11 for the foyer orchestra; at the Sovkino, 30 musicians played in the auditorium and 10 in the foyer. *Teatral′naia Moskva* (Moscow: Mosreklampravsizdat, 1930), 178–86.

[57] GFF, f. 2, op. 1, d. 606, l. 11.

[58] According to the advertisements on the final page of *Pravda* for November 1927, cinema ticket prices were as follows: at the Sovkino No. 1, prices ranged from 35 kopecks to 1 ruble 10 kopecks; the cost of the first showing—the least expensive—at the Malaia Dmitrovka was 40 kopecks, 45 at the Forum, and 50 at the Kolizei. According to *Kino*, the average price for the Gorn was 60 kopecks. *Kino*, no. 3 (1927): 4.

[59] RGALI f. 3015, op. 1, d. 537, passim.

congratulating the director for having captivated them.[60] Given the limited scope of entertainments, it is unlikely that any restrictions were respected, especially outside Moscow and Leningrad: even if there was a target audience, it was likely that anyone who wanted to see the film could manage to do so. But in the absence of data on attendance and of the systematic collection of public feedback on the films, it remains difficult to determine whether and how these films affected Soviet spectators.[61]

Soviet films that pleased critics and public alike were rare, without speaking about the forms of censorship that affected the script, the number of final copies, or authorizations for screenings. The works of renowned directors, for instance Barnet or Ermler, passed muster more easily: both were more experienced than their competitors, and their exported films reaped profits.[62] Thus in *A Fragment of the Empire* the spectators easily recognized Ermler's distinct signature, with the original comedy of actor Fedor M. Nikitin and the hybrid nature of the film. Situated between war fiction and industrial film, it engaged a reflection on the "Seven-Year War" into the perspective of a decade of constructing socialism. However, even a film by Pudovkin, bearing the imprimatur of Mezhrabpom, struggled to achieve popularity. Although it was ready for the anniversary of the Revolution, *The End of St. Petersburg* was not released until 14 December 1927. Mezhrabpom's management meant to make a good impression on the authorities with this film, but without sacrificing its commercial appeal. And yet, the cinema that belonged to it, the Colossus (Koloss), showed the then-famous German film *Varieties* (A. Dupont, 1925) with great success. Pudovkin's film, by contrast, made only 325,000 rubles in several years, far from the 3.2 million of *Mess-Mend* or even the 500,000 rubles of *Mother*; its earnings covered only 88 percent of the distribution costs for 1929 (105,605 rubles versus 127,182).[63] Eisenstein's *October* did not fare any better—it was withdrawn from Moscow screens after two weeks—even though it was a production of Sovkino, the state trust which had a monopoly over film distribution from 1924 onwards. The critical reception of films commemorating the Revolution was all rather poor, which can be explained by the tense political situation created by the banishment of the "Trotskyite"

---

[60] TsGALI SPb. f. 366, op. 1, d. 337, l. 1.

[61] One audience survey was organized by Glaviskusstvo (the Narkompros organ established in 1928 to oversee the arts in the Soviet Union) for *Her Way* on 18 January 1929. RGALI f. 645, op. 1, d. 362, ll. 132–68.

[62] *A Fragment of the Empire* met with success in Holland (August 1930) and Germany. Ermler's film was applauded at the Kamera of Berlin movie theater in early March 1930 (*Letopis' rossiiskogo kino*, 2: 21) before being forbidden in June 1931 in Cologne (*Letopis' rossiiskogo kino*, 2: 110). Ermler had a successful career in Paris and the United States.

[63] RGALI f. 645, op. 1, d. 369, l. 55ob. (Svedeniia o rezul'tatakh prokata v Sovkino khudozhestvennykh fil'mov sovetskogo i zagranichnogo proizvedeniia).

opposition, as well as by the reluctance of spectators to watch films on revolutionary themes that offered little in the way of adventure or spectacle.

Conclusion

I would like to offer a few reflections on what the films discussed in this chapter reveal about the society and its perceptions in the time they were made—films that echoed the Russian experience of the Great War in very precise ways, while also assimilating and transforming it in response to the requirements of Soviet propaganda. For one, the films suggest that the social trauma of a lost war could in part explain the Revolution. In the Bolshevik view, that explanation involved the critique of former elites for betraying the people—career officers (Colonel Khrushchev in *Doomed*) or clerics (Bishop Arsen in *God of War*)—as well as denunciations of the capitalist system. The sequence at the stock market in *The End of St. Petersburg* suggests a parallel between the rising number of deaths and economic growth: the emotional crescendo ignores the fact that the parallel is based on false reasoning from the economic (capitalist) viewpoint while asserting its validity from the revolutionary political viewpoint. The denunciation of war profiteers in *Merchants of Glory* or *A Fragment of the Empire* could also be cited in this regard.

However the social critique could also be deeper and more violent. The falseness and dishonesty of bourgeois solidarity are ostentatiously revealed in the outward signs of charity. In *God of War*, an officer offers a toast "To the grey ones [i.e., the grey mass of soldiers in uniform], as they say, the heroes!" while at the same time scenes of the front roll across the upper part of the screen. The bottom of the screen shows the living, who congratulate themselves on their resolute action on their "front," while combatants hang on barbed wire, fingers spread in vain supplication. The fog of poisonous gasses symbolically envelops the do-gooders wearing sophisticated hats who converse in the shelter of their living rooms. The erasure of the once hermetic partition between their world and that of the exploited thus promises violence against the well-to-do. Authentic proletarian solidarity is expressed through fraternization at the front. In France, the trenches were said to have united social classes in an unexpected fraternity, whereas in Russia this specific war experience united the international proletariat against the dominant bourgeoisie. Episodes of fraternization (for example, in the finale of *Outskirts*) are an obligatory transition in the Soviet representation of the Great War—but also more complicated for political reasons than, say, depictions of soldier committees.

The destiny of soldiers wounded in the conflict and the supposed promotion of women in society were also significant issues in these films. After the war, the wounded constituted a social problem insofar as there were large numbers of them, they were not well compensated for their sacrifices, and their reintegration into society did not go smoothly.[64] Produced by the Drankov Studio in 1916, *The Care of the Committee for Wounded and Disabled Soldiers, Returned from the Front and from German Camps under the Patronage of the Princess Mariia Pavlovna*—also known as *Reborn to Life*—was unique in Russia and deeply impressed its contemporaries.[65] Entire sequences from that film found their way into *The World War*, but they were edited differently. Soldiers receive decorations but the intertitles—"in the place of their legs," "in lieu of eyes," etc.—underscore their derisory character. In *Quiet Flows the Don*, the visit of high-ranking officers to the hospital closes with the hero Grigorii's laughter, worthy of an insane person. He mocks the militarist faith in war and the doctors' faith in science that cures in order to send soldiers back to the front to die, faiths against which the soldiers strain to be heard and understood.[66] The physical consequences of the Great War are thrown in the spectators' faces in *Merchants of Glory*. The charity gala organized by Mr. Bachelet, Sr., turns into an ordeal for the severely wounded guests of honor, from their arrival at the private mansion whose steps are too steep to climb, right up to the meal that is more frugal than the one for the able-bodied, and which these "broken faces," played by amateurs, cannot consume without the help of nurses or tubes. *A Fragment of the Empire* exposes how soldiers suffered from psychological trauma, or "shell shock," a practically invisible injury that was therefore more easily overlooked or forgotten than physical maiming.

In contrast to the recurrent and sometimes shocking presence of the wounded, the image of women generally matched their status in tsarist society, a role from which they were unable to escape except by joining the medical services or engaging in combat. This theme was the subject of two fiction films from 1929 that pertained to the anti-religious campaign (*God of War*) and to the campaign for a new way of life in the village (*Her Way*). The year 1929 marked the beginning of the use of women on screen to convey emancipation from the "backwardness" of the tsarist regime. Praskovia in *Her Way* frees herself from control by village society and her violent husband by choosing love for a Czech war prisoner, Jan. The latter convinces the village to side with the Revolution, an act that costs him his life at the hands of Praskovia's husband, who has become a White "bandit." Praskovia then makes a second decision, namely to enlist in the Red Army. The actress Tsessarskaia (who

---

[64] Alexandre Sumpf, "Une société amputée: Le retour des invalides russes de la Grande Guerre, 1914–1929," *Cahiers du monde russe* 51, 1 (January–March 2010): 35–64.

[65] RGAKFD, film no. 786 (*Vozrozhdaemye k zhizni*). Alexandre Sumpf, "War Invalids on the Screen: Remembering and Forgetting the Great War in the Russian and Soviet Cinema, 1914–1940," in "Commemorating the Disabled Soldier: Comparative Approaches to the History of War, Disability and Remembrance, 1914–1940, special issue, *First World War Studies* (forthcoming).

[66] Sophie Delaporte, "Le corps et la parole des mutilés de la grande guerre," *Guerres mondiales et conflits contemporains*, no. 205 (2002): 5–14.

also appeared in *Women of Riazan*, *Quiet Flows the Don*, and *Love and Hate*) specialized in the role of female peasant soldier.[67] *Her Way* was a message addressed to housewives and "home front" workers. A film poster specifically addressing this idea established the connection between women soldiers in the Civil War and those ready in 1929 to defend the country.[68] But this heroism, as opposed to that of the Women's Death Battalion ridiculed by Eisenstein in *October*, remained less striking for spectators than Jan's transformation: the memory of Slavic war prisoners who became revolutionaries seems to have lasted longer than memory of the women who took up arms.

Another significant theme that emerges is that of the evident trauma from the Great War that foreshadows the psychological impact of the Civil War, the famine of 1921, and collectivization. The fourth part of *The World War* opens with the intertitle "FRONT" followed by clear images: a dead soldier in a trench, another exposed to the sun, and finally a wide shot of the trenches with detritus and dead bodies strewn about. In *God of War*, while the train carries off soldiers, graves are already being dug. In *Sniper*, Timoshenko inserts a close-up of a quick hand working an abacus that symbolizes both the scope and rapidity of the losses, and the increasing earnings of war profiteers. In *A Fragment of the Empire*, Filimonov falls victim not to a bullet, a collapsing trench, or shrapnel, but is completely crushed by a tank whose tracks destroy his flesh and leave behind only his clothes. In contrast to Abel Gance's *J'accuse*,[69] Ermler does not have a dead person come back to haunt the living. Russia was deprived of most war graves, which lay in the heart of Central European forests and beyond the reach of families, as did national war memorials or monuments to the dead in villages. Its sole war cemetery was hidden somewhere north of Moscow and disappeared little by little under other layers of memory and planned urban construction.[70]

Civilian populations suffered heavy losses from the occupation of the empire's western territories and their subsequent flight as war refugees. Their suffering forms part of the enemy's "atrocities" (*zverstva*) whose denunciation in cinema serves to mobilize Russian and international opinion. These films shift the blame for "brutalization" onto the Other, be it German or Cossack (always negative characters). Russian studios before 1917 illustrated this theme in the most off-color way—most notably the rape of women in *Under the Thunder of Cannons: Prussian Rapists*, produced as early as October 1914. Crimes against civilians were readily depicted, including those fueled by rumor or occurring on the ever-fascinating Western Front. Władysław Starewicz dedicated *The Lily of Belgium* "to the suffering and to the resurrection of

---

[67] Al'bert Gendelstein, *Liubov' i nenavist'*, 1935, GFF.

[68] GFF f. 2, op. 1, d. 283 (*Ee put'*), ll. 109–12.

[69] Laurent Véray, "Abel Gance, cinéaste à l'œuvre cicatricielle," *1895*, no. 31 (October 2000): 19–52.

[70] Petrone, *Great War*, 292–300.

Belgium," and Grigorii I. Libken showed a German officer raping a nurse on the altar of the cathedral in *The Horrors of Reims*.[71] And yet civilian victims quite rarely appeared in Soviet cinema, which mainly ignored the suffering endured by refugees or occupied populations. Then international pacifism somehow neutralized the accusation of barbarism against the Germans, and the renewed militarization of the "masses" taking place in Stalinist Russia voluntarily silenced the hardships of wartime.

Likewise, hardly a single war crime against military personnel, in combat or in prisoner camps (hardly ever depicted on screen), appears in a Soviet film. The only exceptions were the two Soviet fiction films about the 40,000 combatants of the Russian Expeditionary Corps in France—despite the corps' minimal impact and its absence from other war mobilization discourse in Russia. One could imagine that *Doomed* would exaggerate the role of the two special divisions of Russians fighting along the French "Chemin des Dames" in the mutinous spring of 1917, and dwell upon the armed liquidation of the revolt in the camp La Courtine, while also highlighting the collective refusal to fight for Denikin, etc. However, filmmakers chose instead to denounce the duplicity of officers and the rebellious instinct of these soldiers abroad.[72]

On the other hand, POWs detained in Russia appear several times on screen as converts to pacifism or carriers of revolutionary fever to the rest of Europe. Critics of *Her Way* (the archetype of this theme), and also audiences, viewed Soviet Russia as possessing a monopoly on internationalist pacifism.[73] For example, the Hungarian Mate Zalka, a war prisoner who later fought for the Reds during the Civil War, appreciated the way the film treated this issue. The favorable reception of *Her Way*, as well as the performance of its two actors, undoubtedly explains the decision to send it for screenings abroad, despite the fact that it is silent on the terrible treatment of Austrian prisoners by the Russians.[74] It was distributed in Germany, Denmark, and the United States, and was even reviewed positively by Mordaunt Hall, the New York film critic, in *The Screen*.[75]

ೞ ೞ

In the interwar period, at least 21 Soviet productions alluded to the Great War as experienced by Russian families. No doubt others exist that are

---

[71] Hubertus Jahn, *Patriotic Culture in Russia during World War I* (Ithaca, NY: Cornell University Press, 1995), 160, 164–66.

[72] GFF f. 2, op. 1, d. 606, l. 5.

[73] RGALI f. 645, op. 1, d. 362, ll. 133–66.

[74] Alon Rachamimov, *Prisoners of War and the Great War: Captivity on the Eastern Front* (Oxford: Berg, 2002).

[75] GFF, f. 2, op. 1, d. 283 (*Ee put'*).

worth including in our analysis. It would also be worthwhile to compare Polish or Baltic representations of the war and its role in the construction of a new national, postimperial identity. A study of the productions of Jewish filmmakers, starting from *Eyes that Saw* (*Glaza, kotorye videli*, V. Vilner, 1928), would also make for an interesting case-study. But the cinematic reference to this conflict was eclipsed by the mythology of the Civil War. The "Great Patriotic War" then buried memory of the First World War even deeper, to the point where Soviet or contemporary Russian fictional films of the conflict remain rare. For the time being, only new documentaries are attempting to revive this buried past.[76]

Translated by Victoria Steinberg

---

[76] Igor' Voitenko, *Gibel' Imperii* (Lennauchfil'm, 1998), 2,474 meters.

Russian Monuments to the First World War: Where Are They? Why Are They?

Aaron J. Cohen

The first major Russian public monument to the First World War opened in 1916 at the center of the new "Boulevard of Heroes" in the town of Viaz'ma (see fig. 48 in the gallery of illustrations following page 178). Destroyed in the 1920s, it was also the last major public monument to the First World War on the territory of Russia before the end of the Soviet Union.[1] As Daniel Orlovsky observed in 1999, "[T]he Great War fell into silence" in Russia after 1917.[2] With no public memorials and no cult of war dead in the Soviet Union, Russia has not attracted the attention of historians in Europe and the United States who began in the 1980s to study the memory of World War I. Yet Russians did plan memorials during the war itself, and in the interwar period Russian émigrés built numerous war monuments outside Russian borders, where many exist to this day.[3] Not only were Russian people not different from other Europeans in their desire to memorialize fallen war dead, their monuments played an important role in the politics and culture of the national community as in Europe and North America. But the fate of these émigré World War I monuments shows that the memory of the war was linked to the concept of an anti-Soviet alliance, and their construction depended on the agreement of the non-émigrés who controlled public space. Russian monuments to World War I thus made sense in certain areas outside Russia but not in the Soviet Union.

In late imperial Russia, the monarchy and the state took on the prime responsibility for the construction of war monuments. The government in tsarist Russia was determined to memorialize its leadership and events of

---

[1] K. G. Sokol, *Monumental´nye pamiatniki Rossiiskoi imperii: Katalog* (Moscow: Vagrius Plius, 2006), 306.

[2] Daniel Orlovsky, "Velikaia voina i Rossiiskaia pamiat´," in *Rossiia i Pervaia mirovaia voina: Materialy mezhdunarodnogo nauchnogo kollokviuma*, ed. N. N. Smirnov (St. Petersburg: D. Bulanin, 1999), 49.

[3] For more details and sources on Russian monuments in Europe, see Aaron J. Cohen, "'Our Russian Passport': World War I Monuments, Transnational Commemoration and the Russian Emigration in Europe, 1918–39," *Journal of Contemporary History* (forthcoming, December 2014).

Russian Culture in War and Revolution, 1914–22, Book 2: Political Culture, Identities, Mentalities, and Memory. Murray Frame, Boris Kolonitskii, Steven G. Marks, and Melissa K. Stockdale, eds. Bloomington, IN: Slavica Publishers, 2014, 297–312.

monarchical significance, and state officials exercised great control over public spaces, could intervene almost at will in local affairs, and commanded vast funds compared to grassroots organizations. Official public statues were designed to project imperial power, and official myths generally excluded educated society and the common people from the monarchy's "heroic narratives."[4] By contrast, public figures in civil society and the intelligentsia placed cultural leaders and events of educational, scientific, or antiautocratic political significance into a memorial pantheon that resembled the "institutionalized democratic pageantry" of republican France.[5] Local governments were more interested in funding schools or scholarships for veterans or survivors than expensive projects that glorified the military and the autocratic state. War monuments were not general sites of memory for the amelioration of suffering, the creation of national identity, or the reinforcement of masculinity; they served to explain the history of the monarchical state, demonstrate its power, and legitimize its rule.[6]

To judge by their wartime interest in monuments, Russian people would have devoted great time and energy to memorialize the war had it not been for the formation of the Soviet Union. In combat zones, soldiers built many small, informal memorials to mark mass and individual graves or to make the feats of their unit known to others. In October 1914, the popular weekly *Ogonek* published illustrations of such frontline grave markers, and later issues showed a variety of memorials, from the modest to the more developed.[7] These ad hoc monuments existed up and down the frontlines in uncounted numbers; many were still in East Prussia in the interwar period, cared for by local people and noted by passing journalists.[8] In Russia proper, the imperial state sponsored the semiofficial Aleksandrovskii Committee, which hoped to

---

[4] Richard S. Wortman, *Scenarios of Power: Myth and Ceremony in Russian Monarchy*, 2: *From Alexander II to the Abdication of Nicholas II* (Princeton, NJ: Princeton University Press, 2000), 5, 525.

[5] This characterization of the memorial policy of the Third Republic is in Sergiusz Michalski, *Public Monuments: Art in Political Bondage 1870–1997* (London: Reaktion Books, 1998), 27. For a list of writers, composers, public figures, and scientists proposed for memorialization in St. Petersburg by the city government, see "Uvekovechenie pamiati," *Rech'*, 28 October 1912, 5.

[6] The association between autocracy and monumental public sculpture was expressed openly after the February Revolution. See Aleksandr Benua [Benois], "O pamiatnikakh," in *Aleksandr Benua razmyshliaet...*, ed. I. S. Zil'bershtein and A. N. Savinov (Moscow: Sovetskii khudozhnik, 1968), 62–63; Aleksandr Rostislavov, "O pamiatnikakh," *Rech'*, 14 April 1917, 5.

[7] *Ogonek*, 26 October 1914; 7 June 1915; 28 August 1916; 2 October 1916.

[8] See, for example, "Mogily chestnykh," *Rul'*, 16 September 1928, 8.

aid local governments and organizations in efforts to erect war memorials.[9] In 1916, for example, the Petrograd city council discussed the creation of a monument for the victims of the hospital ship *Portugal*, sunk by a U-boat in the Black Sea.[10] The sculptor Ivan Shadr (pseudonym of Ivan D. Ivanov) designed a *Monument to World Suffering* to be a *Portugal* monument (fig. 49), and it was later slated for construction at the new Moscow City War Cemetery.[11] Also in 1916, the Russian Society for Remembrance of Soldiers of the Russian Army Who Fell in the War ran a competition that produced designs for major memorials.[12] In any non-Bolshevik postwar Russia, such projects would likely have become central places for a cult of Russian war dead.

The Bolshevik government that emerged after 1917 did place a high priority on monuments as a major component of revolutionary mobilization.[13] Its monument building program was one of the few personal cultural initiatives of Lenin, who in April 1918 signed a decree for the removal of statues "raised in honor of the tsars and their servants."[14] To replace them, the revolutionary government wanted new monuments that depicted "great people in the area of revolutionary and public [*obshchestvennyi*] activity," the revolutionaries, artists, writers, scientists, and other exemplary individuals who were worthy of display to the population.[15] In this policy, Lenin and others were following the prerevolutionary intelligentsia tradition in which monuments served as a means to educate the people. They explicitly rejected the tsarist practice that used public sculpture to display state power; the 1918 order, for example, removed only the most objectionable of imperial monuments and spared

---

[9] Melissa K. Stockdale, "United in Gratitude: Honoring Soldiers and Defining the Nation in Russia's Great War," *Kritika: Explorations in Russian and Eurasian History* 7, 3 (Summer 2006): 465.

[10] *Izvestiia S.-Peterburgskoi (Petrogradskoi) gorodskoi dumy* 54, 28 (1916): 1456–58.

[11] *Rech'*, 1 April 1916, 4; V. P. Tolstoi, ed., *Khudozhestvennaia zhizn' Sovetskoi Rossii 1917–1932: Sobytiia, fakty, kommentarii. Sbornik materialov i dokumentov* (Moscow: Galart, 2010), 72; A. A. Arsen'ev and M. S. Morozova, "Moskovskoe gorodskoe bratskoe kladbishche," *Voenno-istoricheskii arkhiv* 10 (70) (2005): 51.

[12] Stockdale, "United in Gratitude," 468. For some of the designs, see *Ogonek*, 29 May 1916.

[13] See Christina Lodder, "Lenin's Plan for Monumental Propaganda," in *Art of the Soviets: Painting, Sculpture, and Architecture in a One-Party State, 1917–1992*, ed. Matthew Cullerne Bown and Brandon Taylor (Manchester: Manchester University Press, 1993), 18–21.

[14] V. N. Kuchin, ed., *Iz istorii stroitel'stva Sovetskoi kul'tury: Moskva 1917–1918. Dokumenty i vospominaniia* (Moscow: Iskusstvo, 1964), 25–26.

[15] Ibid., 37. See also V. N. Perel'man, ed., *Bor'ba za realizm v izobrazitel'nom iskusstve 1920-kh godov: Materialy, dokumenty, vospominaniia* (Moscow: Sovetskii khudozhnik, 1962), 90; Lodder, "Lenin's Plan for Monumental Propaganda," 21.

those considered to have artistic value. For Lenin, the specific form of public sculpture did not matter as much as the need to fill tsarist public space with new symbolic artifacts.[16] His stipulation that such monuments be temporary and his angry impatience with the slow pace of construction show that the highest priority was to reoccupy public space as quickly as possible.

The Bolsheviks, though, showed no interest in war monuments, although the confusion and uncertainty of these early years meant that nothing was set in stone. For a time, the needs of invalids and veterans of the World War and Civil War were recognized as equally worthy of "the greatest attention of all of society, the population, and each individual citizen of the Soviet republic."[17] Shadr believed that his *Monument to World Suffering* was just as relevant to the Revolution as the war, and one commentator agreed that "the art of communist society could find its true expression in such all-encompassing monuments [*monumental'nye pamiatniki*]."[18] But the government did not build World War I monuments, and the Civil War was not well-memorialized outside the depiction of heroic individuals. No organized pilgrimages, memorial societies, or battlefield tourism seem to have existed for either conflict.[19] At its core, Bolshevik ideology was forward-looking and triumphalist, and it had little room for the religious, personal, and retrospective qualities associated with death, defeat, or grief.[20] Moreover, individual personal commemoration and certain popular ideas about World War I in the Soviet Union, especially those that involved religion, gendered heroism, or patriotism, did not sit well with official priorities in agitation.[21] In Soviet public culture, World War I was a symbol that showed the party's conception and ideas about imperialist war, not a concrete reference to a specific event for the personal use

---

[16] After February 1917 the act of substitution itself helped distance the new regime from the old. See Orlando Figes and Boris Kolonitskii, *Interpreting the Russian Revolution: The Language and Symbols of 1917* (New Haven: Yale University Press, 1999), 187–88.

[17] A. Prigradov-Kudrin, "Pomoshch' invalidu," *Izvestiia*, 22 January 1924, 8.

[18] Tolstoi, *Khudozhestvennaia zhizn'*, 70–72.

[19] One legal organization dealt with support for invalids and war veterans through most of NEP. Another was set up to inventory losses of the foreign intervention to organize claims against foreign governments. Curiously, a Society of Former Russian Officers of the 1st and 2nd Special Divisions in France and in the Balkans apparently existed in 1925. On the other hand, a Society of Active Russian Antimilitarists of the Imperialist War 1914–1917 was denied legal status in 1924 on account of its "unclear goals." See I. I. Il'ina, *Obshchestvennye organizatsii Rossii v 1920-e gody* (Moscow: RAN, 2001), 79, 130–31, 201, 206.

[20] Catherine Merridale, *Night of Stone: Death and Memory in Twentieth-Century Russia* (New York: Penguin, 2002), 115–17, 129.

[21] For a description of these expressions of Soviet war memory, see Karen Petrone, *The Great War in Russian Memory* (Bloomington: Indiana University Press, 2011), 30–32.

of individuals.[22] Official images represented the consequences of the war as generic and abstract; a photomontage in *Pravda*, for example, abstracted war from its specific context to emphasize an idea about the war as imperialist and capitalist (fig. 50). Shadr's memorial, with its gendered grief, nonrevolutionary connotations, and emotional appeal to individuals, did not fit Bolshevik commemorative priorities or conceptions of war (fig. 49).[23]

Russian World War I monuments were built instead by Russian émigrés, paradoxically in the absence of the conditions that most historians assume should be necessary for war memorial construction. Russians abroad did not have a state, legal power, or a lot of money to shape public space in a way necessary for the creation of monuments. They did not have Russian villages, towns, or cities with millions of grieving citizens who sought consolation, and there were no Russian commercial interests to profit from a war memory culture industry. With the exception of some areas in Eastern Europe, Russian battle sites were rare or nonexistent in the West, and long distances and multiple frontiers separated them from the vast majority of Russian people in the Soviet Union and in the emigration. Nonetheless, in France it is possible to find Russian monuments at an official military cemetery in Champagne, at memorial complexes in Soissons and Verdun, and in towns such as Valenciennes, Vanves, and Omont. War monuments are located in major city cemeteries in Warsaw, Belgrade, and Prague, and they are found in modest Czech towns, high in the Slovenian Alps, in the suburbs of Brussels, and at an Orthodox cemetery in Berlin. As a writer in the émigré newspaper *Vozrozhdenie* noted in 1927, "It seems there is no state in Europe where there are no Russian war cemeteries."[24] Indeed, memorials and commemorations for Russians soldiers killed during World War I and the Civil War appeared almost everywhere émigrés landed, whether in Tunisia, Ceylon, Malaysia, or Seattle.[25]

Such monuments were important for the émigrés because they served as a means for the creation of new social, political, and cultural relations between Russians abroad and their friends in various countries. Public leaders in the emigration believed that Russians needed to continue national culture in exile

---

[22] Aaron J. Cohen, "Oh, That! Myth, Memory, and World War I in the Russian Emigration and the Soviet Union," *Slavic Review* 62, 1 (2003): 81–82; S. Iu. Malysheva, *Sovetskaia prazdnichnaia kul'tura v provintsii: Prostranstvo, simvoly, istoricheskie mify (1917–1927)* (Kazan: Ruten, 2005), 171, 177.

[23] A later Soviet biographer argued that Shadr's work on this project showed that his talent was still under the influence of the "reactionary antirealist art" typical of the "mystical, symbolist, and formalist" trends in prerevolutionary Russian culture. Iu. D. Kolpinskii, *Ivan Dmitrievich Shadr, 1887–1941* (Moscow: Iskusstvo, 1954), 18.

[24] *Vozrozhdenie*, 20 July 1927, 3.

[25] For Malaysia, see *Izvestiia*, 20 February 2009, 4; and for Ceylon, *Illiustrirovannaia Rossiia*, 3 September 1938, 15. For Tunisia and Seattle, see below.

in order to prepare for a return to a new, non-Bolshevik Russia, and almost without exception considered themselves to be in a literal state of war with the Soviet Union. World War I was an experience understandable to people across Europe, and its international culture of memory gave émigrés the ability to explain their situation by means of public declarations of friendship and solidarity after the war. An editorialist in the conservative French daily *Figaro* reminded readers of the wartime alliance in his call for support for the émigrés. "They were never anything but our friends," he argued in 1920. "They fought for us, they left women and children in Paris whose misery was great, and ... they have sought refuge with us because they no longer had safety in their country and are completely dispossessed."[26] It was also important for host countries to show that Russian émigrés had supported them during the war. In Champagne, Russian soldiers died "for France," whereas in Belgrade they died "for Yugoslavia" or "for Serbia."[27] Russian war memorials therefore played a role in the creation of a culturally coherent émigré community that could also relate to non-Russians in host nations.

Expressions of grief played a role in the overcoming of divisions between individual loss and the loss of the community. Émigré memorials were built in places where Russians had some influence on public space, usually in Orthodox cemeteries or Orthodox areas of general cemeteries, almost always with help from prominent non-Russian supporters. In this way, families, friends, and communities of émigrés could show their respects to soldiers who died abroad. The French state, for example, brought the fallen of the Russian Expeditionary Force (REF) together at an official military cemetery not far from the village of St-Hilaire-le-Grand in Champagne on the Marne, and the émigrés built a memorial church (*khram-pamiatnik*) on private property adjacent to the cemetery in the late 1930s (fig. 51). In Czechoslovakia, a Russian civic group organized pilgrimages to memorials at cemeteries near former POW camps in the 1920s and built a memorial church to World War I dead in Prague's Olšanské cemetery in 1925 (fig. 52) with the help of the prominent Czech politician Karel Kramář. In 1934 the head of the Central European section of the main émigré military organization, the Russkii Obshche-Voinskii Soiuz (ROVS), organized the construction of a war monument at an Orthodox cemetery in Berlin (fig. 53). These monuments did provide some émigrés with a place to express personal grief. One "thin woman in black," for example, wept and prayed next to "the surviving Russian veterans of battle in Champagne" in the belief that "in the mass grave lies her son, an officer of the first regiment, missing in action."[28] More often, individual and social loss went together, as another writer observed during a pilgrimage to the REF

---

[26] Emile Berr, "D'autres Russes," *Figaro*, 2 November 1920, 1.

[27] See *Poslednie novosti*, 12 July 1922, 2; *Illiustrirovannaia Rossiia*, 3 May 1936, cover; *Politika* (Belgrade), 20 August 1934, 9.

[28] N.P.V., "Na mogilakh russkikh voinov," *Poslednie novosti*, 2 July 1929, 3.

cemetery: "We have lost everything—family, economic situation, personal happiness, the homeland.... Are our sufferings good to anyone? In truth—we have nothing, we have lost everything. Weep, weep."[29]

Émigré monuments to World War I were important as a means to maintain social and institutional cohesion among émigré military groups, who theoretically were preparing for battle against the Soviet Union.[30] In this milieu, memorials were seen as the physical manifestation of nationalism, patriotism, and military values such as duty and honor. The committee for the construction of a memorial church for Russian soldiers who fell on the French front, for example, wanted it to be "national, Orthodox, and military."[31] The war experience provided positive examples of military leadership, and war commemoration was a means for commanders in ROVS to claim a leading role among émigré veterans, especially in the 1930s. I. G. Barbovich, the head of the ROVS branch in Belgrade, reported to superiors in Paris that he was taking part in the public ceremonies for the 20th anniversary of the start of the war not out of sentimentality but to weaken competitors in the eyes of the public. "This celebration," he reported, "arose not by my wish to mark the event at core but only out of tactical considerations, since I don't want to give the initiative into the hands of any kind of unimportant and hostile groups (to us)."[32] Aleksei A. von Lampe, the leader of ROVS in Germany, organized the construction of the monument in Berlin in open competition with the extreme right for the attention of the émigré public: "The dedication of the monument was more than spectacular," he wrote, measuring his success in political terms, "and the unity around ROVS was greater. The Russian organizations that call themselves Russian national socialists like Vonsiatskii acted 'all high and mighty' (*prosnobirovali*) toward us politically but behaved like riff raff."[33] Both military commanders viewed war commemoration as an instrument of political mobilization rather than an expression of grief or means of personal consolation.

War monuments, however, also had some appeal to non-military members of the émigré community. On the left wing of émigré politics, a distrust of ROVS (and the military in general) did not prevent sympathy for wounded veterans and victims of war, and articles about war memorials in leftist and liberal newspapers emphasized those aspects. In the opinion of important members of the liberal intelligentsia, the creation of social connections was necessary to meet welfare goals in the absence of a state and other powerful social institutions. A group of prominent writers, for example, called on the

---

[29] N.R., "Na poliakh russkoi krovi," *Vozrozhdenie*, 9 July 1930, 3.

[30] Cohen, "Oh, That!" 73–76.

[31] *Vozrozhdenie*, 19 May 1928, 6.

[32] Bakhmeteff Archive, ROVS Papers, box 64.

[33] Ibid., box 62. Emphasis in the original.

émigré public to support veterans because there was no state to fulfill this function: "Russia can't do anything. It's our duty to act... It's the duty of our honor, of Russian honor. Just don't let them say they 'forgot their own!'"[34] An interest in war monuments therefore existed among non-military and more liberal members of the emigration, who used the memory of the war to mobilize support for war invalids and veterans from people in the émigré community and host nations. In the words of M. M. Fedorov, the committee to build a memorial church in Champagne was a "broadly social" organization whose "patriotic endeavor" (*delo*) was initiated by a small veterans group but expanded to "all the most powerful Russian organizations in Paris."[35] Other countries had built "great monuments to their heroes," he wrote. "Until now, only the memory of Russian heroes has remained forgotten." The memorial was intended to unite the emigration in France around a national, non-Bolshevik Russian culture that prized war heroes as much as other nations.

Through their participation in French public commemorations, Russian émigrés could demonstrate their links to France based on their status as allies during the war. A delegation of representatives of ROVS, the Union of Invalids, and the Union of Former Officer-Combatants on the French Front, for example, was "united with the delegation of French combatants" at the funeral of Marshall Foch in 1929.[36] The next year a French spectator exclaimed "Long live Russia" at a wreath-laying ceremony by émigré military units, who "had remained true allies to France," at the Tomb of the Unknown Soldier.[37] The mayor of St-Hilaire-le-Grand, for his part, was declared "a new friend of the Russians" at the dedication of the memorial church in Champagne in 1938.[38] Émigré journalists reported even small things that showed how the French and the émigrés remained allies: the fact, for example, that Russian crosses at French military cemeteries were white (the same as the French), while German crosses were black.[39] In 1929 a commentator recognized the role of the memory of the war on the French Day of the Dead.[40] His participation in this Catholic custom, he felt, made the lost Russian homeland real in France: "Our home [*rodnye*] graves have remained where Russia has remained. But walking around on this 'Day of the Dead' in foreign Parisian cemeteries you feel that they are not so foreign."[41]

---

[34] "K russkim liudiam," *Poslednie novosti*, 21 May 1930, 2.

[35] Hoover Institution Archive, Emel'ianov Papers, box 12, folder 20.

[36] *Poslednie novosti*, 25 March 1929, 1.

[37] *Poslednie novosti*, 7 September 1930, 1.

[38] *Poslednie novosti*, 7 June 1938, 4.

[39] *Poslednie novosti*, 8 July 1930, 3.

[40] Bor. Mirskii, "Den' usopshikh," *Poslednie novosti*, 7 November 1929, 2.

[41] "Dni usopshikh," *Poslednie novosti*, 2 November 1929, 3.

The experience of the emigration in the new states of Czechoslovakia and Yugoslavia shows that the memory of the war existed in an atmosphere of international philoslavism, a phenomenon that did not exist in France. In these countries, commemoration of the war was sometimes turned into a declaration of Czech, Serb, and Russian solidarity. The church in Prague was thus both "an artistic memorial church to Russian and Slavic warriors who fell in the World War" and a "symbol of Slavic mutuality [*vzaimnost'*] and Russian gratitude in the heart of the Czech land. This symbol has still greater value on account of the participation of Serbs."[42] Czechs and Russians organized pilgrimages to monuments to fallen Russians and Serbs at former POW camps in Czechoslovakia, often with the support of the Yugoslav Ministry of Religion.[43] Local people, Russian émigrés, and representatives of the Entente and other friendly Slavic nations all participated in memorial ceremonies. Representatives of Bulgaria and France, for example, took part in the ceremony that opened the memorial church in Prague.[44] In Belgrade, the memorial for the Russian soldiers who fell on the Macedonian Front became a place where officials and the public of Yugoslavia, Britain, Italy, and France conducted Armistice Day commemorations on 11 November. For these new Slavic states, World War I commemorations helped create public links to powerful allies in the unstable interwar period.

The conditions for the creation of a friendly alliance based on a common wartime experience were more complicated in Germany. Émigrés could count on some level of institutional and rhetorical friendship in France and the new Slavic countries, but they had limited support from the German state and people in the 1920s and became the object of political intrigue after 1933. Veterans groups in social democratic and left-liberal circles most often helped émigrés to commemorate war dead in Germany, but their pacifist aims did not find sympathy in the military organizations like ROVS who saw themselves as anti-Bolshevik warriors. The deeply conservative Von Lampe dryly remarked that it took an anti-Bolshevik German Social Democrat at a common German-Russian war commemorative ceremony to say that Germany had to show more hospitality vis-à-vis the émigrés.[45] Conservative newspapers, in contrast, wanted émigrés to return home "to certain death" in the USSR. "Typical," he wrote, "also in comparison to the attempts of German nationalists after Locarno to gravitate towards the Bolsheviks." In his opinion, German nationalists, not socialists, should be the natural allies of the Russian émigrés in their battle against Bolshevism. But he was convinced that it was useless to convince German rightists that Russians, be they émigrés

---

[42] Národní archiv, fond RUESO, karton 2, inv. č. 16, document 21, 1.

[43] Arhiv Jugoslavije, fond 69, fasc. 117.

[44] *Vozrozhdenie*, 25 November 1925, 3.

[45] Bakhmeteff Archive, ROVS Papers, box 44.

or Soviets, were anything but "hopelessly hostile to Germany" on account of their relationship with the French.[46]

Von Lampe's negative reaction to émigré participation in joint commemorations shows that war memorials served the goal of creating alliances between émigrés and their friends but could impede the cross-border unity of the emigration. He believed that émigrés stood to lose their broader anti-Soviet goal and their identity as Russians when they attempted to take up the culture of others. "In the pursuit of improving its position," he wrote to Mariia Dmitrievna Vrangel´ in 1929,

> the Russian emigration in several countries is forgetting its personality [*litso*] and is doing what in your work would be called "a tactless emigration"—that tactlessness, in my opinion, includes … the Russian celebration of the ten-year anniversary of the independence of Czechoslovakia, the participation in demonstrations at the grave of the Unknown Soldier in Paris, the appearance in the Russian flag [*sic*] of a group of Russians in Berlin at the time of the arrival of President Hindenburg, and so on.[47]

From Von Lampe's perspective, the emigration had to keep its own culture, for the adoption of diverse practices in various countries would only weaken the common struggle against Bolshevism. He disagreed with the participation of émigrés in war commemorations in France; such actions, in his view, would hinder his attempts to reach out to German nationalists, who suspected that the old friends from wartime would recreate an alliance against Germany.[48] For Von Lampe, war monuments could unify and mobilize the military forces of the emigration, but Russian participation in non-Russian commemorations threatened the cultural and political integrity of the emigration in its larger struggle against the USSR.

The role that World War I monuments played in delimiting friends from enemies can be seen in the case of the St. Nicholas memorial church on the grounds of the Washelli cemetery in Seattle (fig. 54). In 1926 the Russian Veterans Society of the World War decided to build an "enduring monument" to "the memory of their millions of slain comrades and to the greater glory of their ancient faith."[49] Its planners immediately became embroiled in a disagreement with the Russian Orthodox Church, whose Chicago diocese argued that such a memorial should not be built in Seattle nor by émigrés

---

[46] Bakhmeteff Archive, ROVS Papers, box 62.

[47] Hoover Institution Archive, Mariia Dmitrievna Vrangel´ Collection, box 7, folder 7. Emphasis in the original.

[48] Bakhmeteff Archive, ROVS Papers, box 14.

[49] "Russ Soldiers Plan Church. Will Build It as Memorial," *Seattle Times*, 11 July 1926, 11.

but "there, where their memory needs to be honored, and that the Russian People [*Narod*], freed of Bolshevism, will do."[50] The secretary of the Veterans Society, though, responded in anger that "monuments erected by 'peoples' do not exist" and equated the church's attitude to Soviet propaganda: "Our enemies also resort to the same method of references to 'the people' in their demagogic attacks."[51] He pointed out that the "monument is not necessary for the dead but for the ablution of the souls of those remaining," and that it "ought to be totally imbued with remembrance of continual suffering at the hands of the atheistic 'international' enemy of the human race." Although a poke in the Soviet eye, the memorial was also intended to speak to Americans as former wartime allies. Aleksandr Elshin, the main organizer, explained to the *Seattle Times* that "of all the Allied nations of the World War, Russia alone has no memorial to her soldier dead," and he suggested that Russian people would design and build the church but look for donations of material and money from their "American friends."[52] The monument was finally dedicated on 30 August 1936 in "memory of 1,700,000 soldiers of the Czar who died during the World War."[53] Memorial services were not held on Armistice Day 1937, since, as Elshin's son remarked, "the Armistice meant two more years of war to us—civil war," but Russian veterans did hold them on later Memorial or Armistice Days, often with American counterparts in attendance.[54]

These political meanings are one important reason why memorials for World War I did not exist in the USSR even though the conflict was present in Soviet public culture in the 1920s and 1930s. In Europe and the US, monuments united Russians with others who considered the war to be an important positive experience, but the memory of this war had the opposite purpose in the official discourse of the USSR: it was used to distance the Soviet regime from anti-Soviet politics and culture.[55] The USSR was something newer and better in world history; the World War, in contrast, was a part of the imperialist, capitalist, and tsarist world (fig. 50). "Tsarism," wrote one Soviet newspaper columnist in 1939, "conducted the war in complete agreement with the Russian bourgeoisie and in its own imperialist interests."[56] In bourgeois countries, war monuments served the interests of the ruling class; the memorial at Verdun, for

---

[50] Hoover Institution Archive, A. A. Kurenkov Papers, box 5, folder 1, page 1.

[51] Ibid., page 2.

[52] "Russ Soldiers Plan Church. Will Build It as Memorial."

[53] "Russ Here Honor Heroes of War," *Seattle Times*, 30 August 1936, 12.

[54] "No Armistice Services Held At Russ Shrine," *Seattle Times*, 11 November 1937, 5. See also *Seattle Times*, 29 May 1943, 6; 11 November 1949, 25; 29 May 1953, 4; 6 November 1959, 15.

[55] Cohen, "Oh, That!" 78–79.

[56] *Pravda*, 1 August 1939, 5.

example, was presented as a tool for French imperialists to stoke chauvinism.[57] This separation between Soviet and non- or anti-Soviet ideas of war was clear in newspaper articles that emphasized the uniqueness or specialness of the Bolshevik Party's steadfast rejection of the conflict: "Only one party remained true to the great banner of revolutionary internationalism.... Only one party led the working class to fight the imperialist war. That was the party of the Bolsheviks, the party of Lenin and Stalin," "at the beginning of the war ten years ago we Communists were alone in the literal sense of the word," and "the Bolsheviks were the only revolutionary party in the world that opposed the predatory war."[58] Since Soviet ideologists rejected World War I as imperialist and capitalist and ceded any positive war memory to their opponents in the emigration and in bourgeois countries, neither the Soviets nor the émigrés contested the notion that the war was a fundamentally anti-Soviet event. Ironically, they used different interpretations of the war aimed at different audiences for the same goal: to undermine the political legitimacy of the enemy.

The experience of Russian émigrés in China supports the idea that war memorials were a way to make friends, for there the emigration did not build memorials to the First World War. A China under imperialism created a different set of audiences and subjects for monuments than in Europe and the United States. Chinese people were not interested in the far-off European war, and monuments generally were not a useful means to make connections to the Chinese public; most showed warlord power or the martyrdom of soldiers and did not seem to have much local popular support.[59] The brutal warlord Zhang Zongchang, for example, built a monument in a Jinan cemetery for Russians killed fighting for his army in the late 1920s, but few Chinese sympathized with Zhang or his Russians.[60] By 1940 it was already "forgotten."[61] Foreign imperialists were a more important audience for Russian émigrés in China, since émigrés could justify their claims of material and cultural status to Westerners based on Russia's history as a former colonizer. The different priorities of these audiences from those in Europe and the United States made émigré World War I monuments less relevant in the Chinese context.

---

[57] *Ogonek*, 31 August 1932, 7.

[58] *Krasnaia zvezda*, 1 August 1939, 1; *Pravda*, 1 August 1924, 4; *Komsomol'skaia pravda*, 1 August 1939, 1.

[59] Henrietta Harrison, "Martyrs and Militarism in Early Republican China," *Twentieth-Century China* 12, 2 (April 1998): 64; James A. Flath, "Managing Historical Capital in Shandong: Museum, Monument, and Memory in Provincial China," *The Public Historian* 24, 2 (Spring 2002): 45–46; Madeleine Yue Dong, *Republican Beijing: The City and Its Histories* (Berkeley: University of California Press, 2003), 88.

[60] On the monument, see S. S. Balmasov, *Beloemigranty na voennoi sluzhbe v Kitae* (Moscow: Tsentrpoligraf, 2007), 75.

[61] "Na zabytykh russkikh mogilakh," *Rubezh*, 7 July 1940, 19.

In Manchuria, Japanese occupiers determined the experiences that émigrés would memorialize in the 1930s. Already-existing memorials to the Russo-Japanese War in particular became a means for the presentation of Russian-Japanese friendship.[62] Public respect for the former enemy seemed to be a way to build friendship in the interwar period. "The Russian military burial sites," remembered Elena Taskina, "were always visited by the Japanese official representatives on the days of remembrance of the fallen."[63] V. A. Kislitsin, the official head of the emigration in Japanese-occupied Manchuria, returned this feeling of official friendship in 1941: "to honor the memory of the former enemies ... fully reflects the greatness of the spirit of the noble Nipponese people and we Russians ... will indelibly keep in our hearts our deep recognition of our true friends."[64] The Japanese authorities and Russian émigré community also shared an interest in political anticommunism. Émigrés in Manchuria saw themselves as bitter opponents of the Soviet Union (and in some cases were involved in direct combat with Soviet forces), while the Japanese were intent on limiting Soviet and Chinese Communist encroachment. With significant Japanese support, the leaders of the emigration were able to build a major public monument to anti-Communists in Harbin in 1941.[65]

In Shanghai, émigré memorialization served to integrate Russians into Western expatriate communities. French, English, American, and other citizens from the wartime Entente had a common World War I memorial on the Bund (an area of central Shanghai), and Russian émigrés participated in common Armistice Day celebrations there in the 1930s. A separate Russian war memorial was not necessary in the context of the émigré existence inside an enclave of Europeans surrounded by Chinese. Russian people, however, needed good relations with authorities in the French Concession, where many had settled, and the French appreciated Russian contributions to the maintenance of European cultural life in a place where French people were a very small minority.[66] In 1936, a Russian émigré newspaper commentator held up the idea of a Pushkin monument in Shanghai as a way to assert the worth of the emigration to foreign audiences. Russians, he argued, were "not in a position equal to other foreigners in the sense of great material prosperity," but they were "not beggars in spirit."[67] Such a monument, he added, would

---

[62] Aaron J. Cohen, "Long Ago and Far Away: War Monuments, Public Relations, and the Memory of the Russo-Japanese War in Russia, 1907–1914," *Russian Review* 69, 3 (July 2010): 394–95.

[63] Elena Taskina, *Neizvestnyi Kharbin* (Moscow: Prometei, 1994), 57.

[64] V. A. Kislitsin, *Panteon voinskoi doblesti i chesti* (Harbin: Izd. GBREM, 1941), 9.

[65] *Rubezh*, 21 June 1941, 12–14.

[66] Van Chzhichen [Wang Zhicheng], *Istoriia russkoi emigratsii v Shankhae* (Moscow: Russkii put', 2008), 244–45.

[67] N.G., "Iubilei Pushkina," *Shankhaiskaia zaria*, 8 November 1936, 8.

have wide appeal in Shanghai because it would speak "not only to one Russian heart but to every foreign one [*chuzhestranets*]." At the statue's dedication in 1937, an influential French lawyer made the link between monument and Franco-Russian alliance explicit: "It is with respect and even with tenderness that the French will contemplate the monument that we have inaugurated today and which will stand as a symbol of the friendship that unites French and Russians."[68] The role of the Pushkin monument as a means of interethnic solidarity in the French Concession can be seen in the words of another French observer who called it a "monument of remembrance, a momentary communion that abolished divisions of race and politics."[69]

The selection bias that favored the appearance of Russian World War I monuments in the West can be seen in a comparison to the memorialization of the Civil War. Many Russians abroad were Civil War veterans who evacuated Russia in defeat in 1920, and in emigration they cultivated a distinctive memorial culture of the White movement. White culture commemorated certain important dates, individuals, groups, and events from the Civil War, and White veterans created monuments to their experience in places where they landed after the Crimean evacuation (on Gallipoli, for example). In Bizerte, Tunisia, they built a memorial chapel dedicated to the preservation of the White army (and its ships) in the fight against the Bolsheviks: "The Army saved, tens of thousands of Russian people saved, for the new struggle for the honor of the homeland—that is the deed of the Russian ships, and this deed should be immortalized in the glory of our Russia."[70] World War and Civil War often ran together in White memorial practices, for the movement's "stab in the back" myth linked the image of enemy Germans with traitorous Bolsheviks to salvage White military honor in defeat.[71] Von Lampe's World War I memorial thus contained the language of the White movement in its inscription "To the true sons of great Russia." But Civil War monuments were less common than World War I memorials in the emigration because the former spoke to a narrower audience. For leftist émigrés, White military culture was anathema, and for foreign hosts, it was inconvenient, subversive, or irrelevant.

The story of the only major memorial site for World War I in post-Soviet Russia shows that the old Soviet and anti-Soviet political meanings of the war can be resolved in modern Russian patriotic culture. In 2004, the site of the former Moscow City War Cemetery was dedicated as a "Memorial Park

---

[68] "L'allocution de Me. d'Auxion de Ruffé," *Journal de Shanghai*, 13 February 1937, 5.

[69] Claude Rivière, "Le centenaire d'un grand poète," *Journal de Shanghai*, 13 February 1937, 3.

[70] Bakhmeteff Archive, ROVS Papers, box 45.

[71] Cohen, "Oh, That!" 74–75.

Complex for the Heroes of World War I."[72] After 1932, the cemetery was destroyed and reconstructed as a local park, but after the end of the Soviet Union local church officials and neo-nationalist campaigners tried to revive the memory of its existence and, more broadly, that of Russia's World War I experience. Their difficulties attest to the war's continued uncertain place in Russian culture. In the 1990s, activists began to erect crosses, gravestones, and other memorial symbols on the site of the former war cemetery or the nearby church. Dedication ceremonies for these non-official monuments were often conducted as neo-White military ceremonies (sometimes accompanied by representatives from Allied countries and Germany), and repeated acts of vandalism show that such memorial practices remained contested for many years. Nationalist conspiracy theorists maintain that Communist or KGB dead-enders have made a coordinated effort through assassination and vandalism to prevent the rehabilitation of World War I.[73] Others suggest that local businesses vandalized memorials to forestall new restrictions on commercial activity if the park were to become an official memorial site.[74] The decision by the Moscow city government to organize a formal memorial complex with new monuments but maintain space for leisure activity represents a compromise between the realities of modern Russia over the controversies of the past (fig. 55). As Valerii Shantsev, vice mayor of Moscow, remarked, "opening the memorial, we solve historical, political, and public problems [obshchestvennye zadachi]."[75] The existence of the first official monuments for the war on Russian soil since 1916 also shows the potential for the full integration of World War I into post-Soviet Russian patriotism (fig. 56). In 2012, Vladimir Putin formally approved a law that added 1 August as the day of memory for Russian soldiers who fell during the 1914–18 war to the official list of Russian military holidays. He declared that Russia needed new monuments for a conflict that had been wrongly removed from the country's memory.[76]

Russian monuments to World War I were constructed where the memory of the war was considered important for the formation of social connections with specific audiences who valued the war experience. Political liberals and former soldiers in the emigration wanted to conserve the unity inside their community, and memorials were a means for the mobilization of national

---

[72] See Petrone, *The Great War in Russian Memory*, 306–12.

[73] "Letopis' Vserossiiskogo voennogo Bratskogo kladbishcha geroev Pervoi mirovoi voiny," http://lll22021918.livejournal.com/16763.html (accessed 8 October 2012). This material appears on several monarchist or nationalist websites in Russia.

[74] "Zapozdaloe pokaiania," *Novye Izvestiia*, 30 July 2004, http://www.newizv.ru/print/8713 (accessed 16 October 2012).

[75] "Geroiam Pervoi mirovoi," *Gudok*, 3 August 2004.

[76] "V Rossii uchredili Den' pamiati voinov, pogibshikh v gody Pervoi mirovoi," 31 December 2012, http://top.rbc.ru/society/31/12/2012/839185.shtml (accessed 13 June 2013).

identity and a point of contact with Western societies in the émigré struggle against the Soviet Union. The connection between war remembrance, institution-building inside the emigration, and public recognition from those outside was clear in a statement from a group of émigré intellectuals in 1930. "Peoples honor heroes," they argued, "To the living: care, to the dead: memory. We in a foreign land do not have a tomb of an 'unknown soldier,' but we do have thousands of suffering people. They are our honor and our justification [*opravdanie*] before the world. Their wounds and suffering are for Russia. They remained true to honor and obligation. That is our Russian passport."[77] Later Soviet politicians could recognize how World War I memory operated differently for different audiences. In 1959, for example, Nikita Khrushchev gave a speech before the Supreme Soviet that excluded the war from the Soviet experience in typical Soviet fashion: "the First World War was an imperialist war for the division of the world."[78] A mere five months later, however, he could express a non-Soviet Russian memory of the war to French "friends" while on a foreign trip to Reims: "I take off my hat and bow my head before the memory of those who fell for the greatness of France in the First World War. I bow my head before those Russian soldiers who together with the French fought the common enemy in the First World War and their remains that rest on French soil."[79] The émigré "passport" of war memory made sense in Europe and the United States, but it remained a symbol of anti-Soviet history in the Soviet Union and was not important for local people or foreign communities in China. In those countries, consequently, there were no Russian memorials to the Great War.

---

[77] "K russkim liudiam," *Poslednie novosti*, 21 May 1930, 2.

[78] *Izvestiia*, 1 November 1959, 2.

[79] *Izvestiia*, 30 March 1960, 1. The Soviet defense minister at the time, Rodion Ia. Malinovskii, was a veteran of the REF in World War I. He convinced Khrushchev to visit Champagne while on this official trip to France. It is rumored (but seems unlikely) that Malinovskii was present at an émigré memorial service at the cemetery in St-Hilaire-le-Grand and even saluted the tsarist flag. Jamie H. Cockfield, *With Snow on Their Boots: The Tragic Odyssey of the Russian Expeditionary Force in France during World War I* (New York: St. Martin's, 1998), 331.

"Twentieth-Century Apocalypse" or a "Grimace of Pain"? The Vanishing Traces of October

Frederick C. Corney

> I was a victim of the Revolution.
> I, esteemed comrade,
> was crushed by the engine of revolution.
> —Mikhail Zoshchenko, "A Victim of the Revolution," 1923

The Great October Socialist Revolution is over. It exists no longer, either as Communism's specter or as History's locomotive. This sentiment, if not these precise words, was trumpeted by historian Martin Malia, who in 1992, shortly after the demise of the USSR, wrote that "no one cares much any more" about celebrating the anniversary of October in the former Soviet Union.[1] In that same year, in a quixotic tilt at the actual state of affairs in Russia, *Pravda* imagined October's centenary. The newspaper's paean to October began with the shot heard round the world from the cruiser *Aurora* in 1917, praised the annual October celebrations for sustaining the population during the Great Patriotic War, and trumpeted the Soviet state's economic progress in the name of October after the war. The future centenary was contrasted favorably with the current 75th anniversary, when the "Russian [*Rossiiskie*] authorities in 1992 have not only repudiated the socialist choice in 1917, but have also reassured the world that Communism on this planet has been buried and will not be resurrected. Russia at that time was the center of world anti-Communism." Looking back from the vantage point of October's centenary, however, *Pravda* happily informed its still loyal readers (in 2017 of course) that in fact "socialism had passed the test of History," because its October roots had been planted so deeply and tended so carefully that Soviet Russia's brand of socialism had won the Second World War and the "restoration," and had ultimately managed to vanquish the "cult of commercialism, speculation, profiteering, the demon-

---

[1] Martin Malia, "Why Amalrik Was Right," *Times Literary Supplement*, 6 November 1992, 9.

Russian Culture in War and Revolution, 1914–22, Book 2: Political Culture, Identities, Mentalities, and Memory. Murray Frame, Boris Kolonitskii, Steven G. Marks, and Melissa K. Stockdale, eds. Bloomington, IN: Slavica Publishers, 2014, 313–39.

strated rejection of the tradition of our native [*otechestvennaia*] culture, the Yankification [*iankizatsiia*] of spiritual values."[2]

Malia would have been unsurprised to learn that in the intervening two decades October, and all that it had once been intended to stand for, had receded ever deeper into the recesses of popular memory. Not that October was without its defenders. The traditional pledges of fealty by local Communists to October's "world significance" certainly continued throughout this period (and not only from the head of the Communist Party of the Russian Federation, Gennadii Ziuganov, and president of Belarus, Aleksandr Lukashenko).[3] And for at least some older Communists, October still persisted as visceral memory. One Iurii Solonin, for example, argued that his life now felt somehow incomplete without October: "My childhood was spent among people who had gone to the Civil War.... My grandmother saw not only the tsar's family in their carriage trips around the Winter Palace, but also listened to a speech by Lev Davidovich Trotskii. My father, torn from a godforsaken little village in Poles′e in Belorussia by the stormy, social unrest, got a military political education.... Although his fate was hard, even tragic, he understood that he became somebody only because of the possibilities after October."[4] October could still find itself ranked among the major political or cultural caesuras such as the "discovery" of the New World, the fall of the Second Rome, and the storming of the Bastille.[5] Even dissident Andrei Siniavskii, in the wake of glasnost′, could liken the Russian Revolution to a "twentieth-century Apocalypse," which he acknowledged was a positive term in the minds of

---

[2] "Sotsializm vyderzhal ekzamen istorii," *Pravda*, 6 November 1992, 1.

[3] "Kommunisty prodolzhaiut verit′ v to, chto ikh delo pravoe i oni pobediat," *Novosti Praim*, 7 November 1997; "XXI vek budet vekom torzhestva idei Oktiabria," *Pravda*, 6 November 1998; "'Soiuz Sovetskikh Ofitserov Gruzii' otmetit ocherednuiu godovshchinu Oktiabr′skoi revoliutsii 1917 goda," *Novosti Praim*, 29 October 2000; "V Belorussii 7 noiabria otmechaetsia kak gosudarstvennyi prazdnik—Den′ Oktiabr′skoi revoliutsii," ITAR TASS, 6 November 2000; "V respublikakh SNG otmechaiut 7 noiabria," ITAR TASS, 7 November 2000; "Ziuganov optimistichno smotrit na budushchee kompartii," Interfaks Operativnye Soobshcheniia, 6 November 2001; "V regionakh Rossii proshli meropriatiia, posviashchennye 7 noiabria," ITAR TASS, 7 November 2001; "Levaia oppozitsiia otmechaet prazdnik 7 oktiabria," WPS: Monitoring TV i Radio. Politika, 8 November 2001; "1 tys. storonnikov Kompartii proveli v Sumakh miting pamiati Oktiabr′skoi revoliutsii," *Ukrainskie novosti*, 7 November 2002; "Aleksandr Lukashenko pozdravil belorusskikh grazhdan s dnem Oktiabr′skoi revoliutsii," BelTA, 7 November 2004; "600 storonnikov KPU proveli v Cherkassakh miting po sluchaiu godovshchiny Oktiabr′skoi revoliutsii," *Ukrainskie novosti*, 7 November 2005.

[4] Iurii Solonin, "Pravda i drama Oktiabria," *Rossiiskaia Federatsiia segodnia*, 14 November 2007.

[5] "Desiat′ dnei, kotorye potriasli poslednee tysiacheletie," *Nezavisimaia gazeta*, 30 December 2000.

"true believers."[6] Others argued that, despite its brutalities, the October Revolution had "saved Russia from a national catastrophe," because defeat of the Revolution would have laid the ground for a fascist regime.[7] Anti-Stalinist writer Aleksandr Zinov'ev argued in 2006 that, but for the October Revolution, "the West would have long since destroyed and seized this region."[8]

More often though, October found its once canonic status as Soviet Russia's foundation event increasingly in question in this period. Most directly, and unsuccessfully, President Boris Yeltsin sought in 1996 to replace the traditional annual celebration of October on 7 November with a new celebration of a Day of Reconciliation and Accord (*Den' primireniia i soglasiia*), in an effort, as one commentator put it, "to get the citizens out of the habit of celebrating the anniversary of the Great October Socialist Revolution."[9] This was recognized at the time as an effort to change the "symbolism" of 7 November.[10] It was doomed to fail, because, as *Nezavisimaia gazeta* put it in a clear indictment of the mixture of polarization and apathy in post-Soviet politics at that time, on the one hand, Communists would never reconcile themselves to this, and, on the other, "apolitical citizens, who had observed former November holidays as normal days off, required no accord and reconciliation, most of them (especially the young) having only the vaguest conceptions of the October Revolution or none at all."[11] In a sign of its failure, the Day of Reconciliation and Accord was replaced in 2005 by a Day of National Unity (*Den' narodnogo edinstva*) in celebration of 4 November, a commemoration of the "popular" uprising in 1612 that ended the Time of Troubles and ushered in the Romanov dynasty. This was a clear effort to replace a narrative of revolutionary rupture and renewal with a narrative of historical continuity and tradition.

In this period, October failed to cope with far more insidious challenges than this, challenges in the sense of fundamental reevaluations or rereadings of the historical and cultural meaning of the October narrative. The Great

---

[6] Andrei Sinyavsky, *Soviet Civilization: A Cultural History* (New York: Arcade Publishing, 1990), 5, 4.

[7] "Chto dlia nas Lenin segodnia?" *Izvestiia*, 20 January 2006.

[8] "Moguchee vliianie na vse chelovechestvo," *Sovetskaia Rossiia*, 21 January 2006.

[9] Dmitrii Pinsker, "God, kotorogo ne bylo," *Itogi*, 3 November 1997.

[10] "Pribavlenie smuty—kak eto bylo," *Rossiiskaia gazeta*, 4 November 2004; cf. Vladimir Dzaguto, "Den' narodnoi putanitsy," *Vremia novostei*, 4 November 2004. It might be argued that this effort to change the symbolic significance of this one day in fact led to a devaluation of the entire symbolism of national days of celebration in post-Soviet Russia. See O. Savel'ev, "Rossiianie ob izmeneniiakh prazdnichnykh dnei kalendaria," *Moskovskaia pravda*, 30 November 2004; "Narodnoe edinenie: Chto prazdnuem Rossiiane?" *Vedomosti*, 3 November 2005.

[11] "Oktiabr'skaia revoliutsiia byla neizbezhna," *Nezavisimaia gazeta*, 5 November 2000; also "Bystro zabyvaemyi prazdnik," *Belorusskaia delovaia gazeta*, 4 November 2003.

October Socialist Revolution, now shorn of revolutionary parties, Communist propaganda and agitation, or even of Lenin and Trotskii, now became "Russia's Golgotha," the blame for Russia's crucifixion lying with the Western Allies which had insisted on keeping Russia in the First World War despite clear evidence of its massive human losses, war fatigue, economic stress, and the poorly defined *raison d'être* for the war.[12] Approaches to October that had long been part of Western scholarly discourse now became part of post-Soviet discourse, including the argument that without the predations of the war, neither the February nor the October Revolution would have occurred, or that communism could be legitimately compared with fascism in terms of its human toll.[13] Now the once-iconic October Revolution could be cast as "the counterrevolution to the February Revolution," in the words of leading Russian academician Aleksandr Iakovlev, an event that bequeathed a "criminal state."[14] This kind of approach was a fundamental affront to the claims long made for the mythic Great October Socialist Revolution, which had relegated the First World War, February Revolution, and Civil War to prologue, interlude, and epilogue of its own grand narrative. Now the Civil War, for example, could be cast as the legitimate continuation of the tsarist General Staff's efforts to launch a necessary reaction to the "October Revolution of 1917—the violent seizure of power in Russia by the Bolshevik Party." Stripping October of its transcendent claims, this approach wondered how it was possible that "three-quarters of a century after the departure of General Vrangel'*'*s army from the Crimea, ... until now not a single biographical guide to the participants in the White movement had appeared (other than short treatments of its leaders) either in Russia or abroad."[15] The very cast of characters of the canonical October had changed, with the increasingly frequent reappearance in the post-Soviet press of historical actors whose past deeds had formerly rendered them anathema, most obviously Trotskii, or had relegated them to footnotes if they had been featured at all. Recollections of early chance encounters in New York with former Prime Minister of the Provisional Government, Aleksandr Kerenskii, and one of Rasputin's assassins, Feliks Iusupov, could now yield the conclusion that "now, long since dead, they belong not to themselves but

---

[12] "Vo vtoroi raz: V 1917 godu nazhim zapada na Rossiiu privel k revoliutsii, segodniashnee davlenie mozhet zavershit'sia eshche...," *Nezavisimaia gazeta*, 1 September 1998.

[13] "Oktiabr'skaia revoliutsiia byla neizbezhna," *Nezavisimaia gazeta*, 5 November 2000; "Professora Sorbony v poiskakh novogo 'svetlogo budushchego,'" *Obshchaia gazeta*, 2 April 1998.

[14] "Opasnosti vozvrata kommunizma v Evrope i v Rossii," ITAR TASS, 2 June 1999; also "Stoili li brat' Zimnii?" *Argumenty i fakty*, 8 November 2000.

[15] Ivan Smirnov and Aleksandr Utkin, "Kornilovtsy, Denikintsy, Vrangelevtsy," *Nezavisimoe voennoe obozrenie*, 14 March 2003.

to history."[16] Once upon a time, October had aspired to be History, relentless and final.

In short, the mythic status of October was at stake in such challenges, its once transcendent narrative diminished, now ranked alongside Muscovy's 17th-century Time of Troubles as little more than a "vicious civil war," just one more fateful episode in the ongoing cycle of the tragedy that is Russian history.[17] Even the brutality carried out in October's name, implied Boris Grebenshchikov, leader of the rock music group Akvarium, paled alongside the total brutality of the 20th century.[18] A 1998 article argued that despite Mikhail Gorbachev's effort to "resurrect" October as a vital force for the 1980s, the "mythological idol of the Revolution with a capital letter lives on somewhere in the depths of public memory, transporting some to ecstasy, others to horror." The author treated the October Revolution as near-fairytale with its "heroes and villains, sacrifices and heroic deeds," a history that "never stopped being sacred." The piece's ironic distance from the "magic word" *revolution* and from the entire "naïve" revolutionary metaphors of locomotives of history and inevitable Progress, would have been looked at askance even a decade earlier. So too would the author's point that the Bolsheviks, "the very creators of the idol of Revolution, became its hostages and victims—they repented and they confessed, abetting their own executioners and preserving the inhuman system of universal terror."[19] Such desacralization paved the way for new symbolic analogies of October, not so much with 1789, 1791, or even 1793, but with another year from Soviet history, 1937, when "the revolution began to devour its own children."[20]

In 1999, leading political, economic, and cultural figures in Russia would still name the October Revolution and Lenin respectively as the greatest event and greatest individual of the 20th century, although some also described October as a "catastrophe" and Lenin, enigmatically, as "the main experimenter

---

[16] "Aleksandr Kerenskii i Kniaz' Feliks Iusupov v N'iu-Iorke," *Vremia MN*, 15 December 2000.

[17] Respectively, Denis Babichenko, "Smutnye somneniia," *Itogi*, 2 November 2004; and Aleksandr Mekhanik, "Zhutkii khaos—zhestokii poriadok," *Ekspert*, 14 January 2002. For a broad treatment that cuts across Soviet Russia's own efforts to create a reductive canonical revolutionary narrative, see Peter Holquist, *Making War, Forging Revolution. Russia's Continuum of Crisis, 1914–1921* (Cambridge, MA: Harvard University Press, 2002).

[18] "Sobytie veka. Chelovek veka," *Kommersant Daily*, 25 December 1999.

[19] "Sud'ba magicheskogo slova," *Obshchaia gazeta*, 5 November 1998. By contrast, a textbook of Belorussian history could be criticized a year later for "wrongly and illegitimately" replacing the term "'October Revolution' with the words 'October events in Belarus'"; Andrei Makhovskii, "Delo istorikov," *Belorusskaia delovaia gazeta*, 25 February 1999.

[20] Iurii Taz'min, "1937 god: Iskuplenie grekhov?" *Khakasiia*, 6 December 2007.

of the age." Others favored the Great Patriotic War over October, and Napoleon Bonaparte, the writer Mikhail Sholokhov, or even Charlie Chaplin over Lenin. Still others praised the prerevolutionary economic reforms and Petr Stolypin or perestroika and Gorbachev as the seminal formative event and actor of the age.[21] The famous artist Ernst Neizvestnyi called the "collapse of the Soviet Union … [that] great empire," the most significant event of the 20th century, a sentiment echoed by Vladimir Putin several years later.[22] One article wryly invoked the fabled Cheshire Cat. After the "October overthrow" (*perevorot*), it observed, the Russian people (*narod*) disappeared, leaving only a "grimace of pain."[23] Opinion polls often asked people to imagine how they would have acted during the Revolution or what they would do if the October Revolution were to occur today. As recently as 2005, these and other polls still found that a majority of Russian citizens retained a positive view of the October Revolution as the beginning of a new era and a new form of Russian statehood.[24] "The Revolution is not over," proclaimed one such poll triumphantly, pointing out, apparently without irony, the high positive ratings for October and for the two individuals who evoked most sympathy in the population, Nicholas II and Lenin. Curiously, the "idea of revolution" in general, the poll noted, evoked majority feelings of "fear and resentment."[25] This sentiment perhaps explains the less encouraging findings among the young and the well-educated. Those in their early twenties were five times less likely than people in their mid-fifties to say that they would have fought on the side of the Bolsheviks, twice as likely to say they would have fought against the Bolsheviks, and six times more likely to say they would have emigrated.[26]

Even highly critical reevaluations at least preserved October as an object of scrutiny and debate. Far more perilous for October's mythic status was the disquieting level of ignorance about October in particular and Soviet history in general, particularly among the young. A 2006 survey of young people in

---

[21] "Sobytie veka. Chelovek veka," *Kommersant Daily*, 25 December 1999.

[22] Aleksei Berezhkov, "Samoe bol'shoe sobytie XX veka—raspad Sovetskogo Soiuza, schitaet Ernst Neizvestnyi," ITAR TASS, 29 December 2000; Putin called it "the biggest geopolitical catastrophe" of the 20th century (Michael Binyon, "Putin vs. the Bureaucrats—the Strong Man Struggles to Impose His Will," *The Times*, 26 April 2005, 18).

[23] Iakov Krotov, "Ten' Rossii," *Obshchaia gazeta*, 7 November 2001.

[24] "Khorosho ne zabytoe staroe," *Itogi*, 31 October 2005; see also "V sluchae povtoreniia sobytii Oktiabria 1917 goda, lish' kazhdyi desiatyi Rossiianin gotov byl by," Interfaks Operativnye Soobshcheniia, 5 November 2003.

[25] Leontii Byzov, "VTsIOMA," *Profil'*, 7 November 2005.

[26] Oleg Savel'ev, "Revoliutsiia: Velikaia ili uzhasnaia?" *Moskovskaia pravda*, 7 November 2005. Cf. for similar polls, "Vy—ochevidets," *Itogi*, 3 November 1997; Elena D'iakova, "Obshchestvo," *Novaia gazeta*, 6 November 2003.

Novosibirsk revealed that they could barely identify Lenin (or Gorbachev...), thought Brezhnev had launched perestroika, and could not date the October Revolution accurately. They were however able to recognize Victory Day, 9 May, as a commemoration of the "victory over the fascists ... in 1945." The problem, the reporter rued, lay in the content of their primary and secondary education.[27] In 2002, *Izvestiia* had earlier pointed out the problem of relying on Brezhnev-era textbooks which, as a "gift of deference," emphasized the experience of the Great Patriotic War, adding darkly that "other textbooks, as Iosif Vissarionovich would say, we don't have for you."[28] Of course, since 1991 the nature and function of history textbooks has been the subject of discussions that would have been unthinkable under Brezhnev.[29] Teachers wrote about how from the 1990s onwards, as the former constraints on their teaching loosened, they struggled with how to teach early Soviet history. They complained of having to deal now with the plethora of new fact-crammed textbooks in post-Soviet Russia, works that featured more and more historical figures from that era with a range of political outlooks, such as Trotskii and the White Admiral Aleksandr Kolchak, prompting one scholar to ask in 2005: "What happened in October 1917—revolution, mutiny, overthrow, plot?"[30]

October Bound

Malia had captured this equivocality at the heart of Russia's foundation event when he observed in 1992 at the birth of post-Soviet Russia that one's view of the meaning of the events of October 1917 "was really a debate about the legitimacy of the Soviet regime."[31] When François Furet declared in 1978, to much scholarly outcry, that the French Revolution was over, he was similarly attacking the role played by ideological credentials in sustaining a particular historiographic representation of the revolutionary narrative, a representation

---

[27] El'vira Novikova, "Lenin byl polkovodtsem, a Brezhnev nachal perestroiku...," *Sovetskaia Sibir'*, 21 January 2006. Cf. "Tema dnia," *Izvestiia*, 6 November 2002; Oleg Savel'ev, "Rossiiane ob Oktiabr'skoi revoliutsii," *Moskovskaia Pravda*, 6 November 2002.

[28] "S chego nachinaetsia Rodina," *Izvestiia*, 29 January 2002.

[29] Dar'ia Martynkina, "Istoriia—spravochnik, roman ili sbornik mnenii," *Argumenty i fakty*, 17 December 2003.

[30] Natal'ia Shiriaeva, "Uroki Oktiabria," *Profil'*, 7 November 2005.

[31] Malia, "Why Amalrik Was Right," 9. He developed his argument more fully in Martin Malia, *The Soviet Tragedy: A History of Socialism in Russia, 1917–1991* (New York: The Free Press, 1994). See also Malia, *History's Locomotives: Revolutions and the Making of the Modern World* (New Haven: Yale University Press, 2006). This same period witnessed other, more gleeful, celebrations of October's demise. See Richard Pipes, "Seventy-Five Years On: The Great October Revolution as a Clandestine *Coup d'État*," *Times Literary Supplement*, 6 November 1992, 3–4; and Robert Conquest, "I Told You So," *Encounter* 75, 2 (1990): 24–26.

that propagated the illusion that modern French history "began" in 1789 with its profound implications for the very periodization of French history. His problem with the French Revolution as national or imperial mission was, of course, in a sense the measure of the success of that project, for as he points out, "the Revolution does not simply 'explain' our contemporary history; it *is* our contemporary history." After the defeat of fascism, he added, "1789 disappeared from French politics," and "today the discourse of both Right and Left celebrates liberty and equality." He seemed to be saying that critical historical, ethical, and moral distance disappears when historians take "the revolutionary discourse at face value" and when "the Revolution has become history's protagonist." For both Furet and Malia, the real ethical and moral trouble began in October 1917 when Russia, having imbibed revolution at France's breast (first the examples of 1789 and 1791, and later that of the 1871 Commune), became the new "nation in the vanguard of history."[32] The claims made in the name of October by the young Soviet regime required rather than invited scholars of all stripes to hoist their moral and political colors in support of or opposition to the October Revolution.[33]

---

[32] François Furet, *Interpreting the French Revolution* (Cambridge: Cambridge University Press; Paris: Éditions de la Maison des Sciences de l'Homme, 1981), 3, 5, 16, 17, and 6, respectively. On this interpretation of the Revolution "in the shadow of the gulag," see Michael Scott Christofferson, "An Antitotalitarian History of the French Revolution: François Furet's *Penser la Révolution Française* in the Intellectual Politics of the Late 1970s," *French Historical Studies* 22, 4 (1999): 557.

[33] Studies of this political or moral polarization vis-à-vis the historiography of October are legion, and constitute their own subfield. For examples that chart changing conceptual approaches to this polarization over time, see Michael Karpovich, "The Russian Revolution of 1917," *Journal of Modern History* 2, 2 (1930): 258–80; Robert D. Warth, "On the Historiography of the Russian Revolution," *Slavic Review* 26, 2 (June 1967): 247–64; G. D. Alekseeva, *Oktiabr´skaia Revoliutsiia i istoricheskaia nauka 1917–1923* (Moscow: Nauka, 1968); Marc Ferro, "Pourquoi Février? Pourquoi Octobre?" *Annales. Économies. Sociétés. Civilisations* 23, 1 (1968): 31–48; John Keep, "The Bolshevik Revolution: Prototype or Myth?" *Studies on the Soviet Union* 11, 4 (1971): 46–60; George Enteen, "Marxists Vs. Non-Marxists: Soviet Historiography in the 1920s," *Slavic Review* 35, 1 (1976): 91–110; Ronald Grigor Suny, "Toward a Social History of the October Revolution," *American Historical Review* 88, 1 (1983): 31–52; James D. White, "Early Soviet Historical Interpretations of the Russian Revolution 1918–1924," *Soviet Studies* 37, 3 (1985): 330–52; "Izuchenie istorii Velikogo Oktiabria: Itogi i perspektivy," *Voprosy istorii*, no. 6 (1987): 51–72; V. I. Startsev, "Vopros o vlasti v Oktiabr´skie dni 1917 goda," *Istoriia SSSR*, no. 5 (1987): 36–55; *Revolution in Russia: Reassessments of 1917*, ed. J. Frankel and B. Knei-Paz (Cambridge: Cambridge University Press, 1992); Ronald Grigor Suny, "Revision and Retreat in the Historiography of 1917: Social History and Its Critics," *Russian Review* 53, 2 (1994): 165–82; Vladimir Bukharaev, "Istoriki pered zagadkoi 'Bol´shevistskoi Revoliutsii,'" in *Krasnyi Oktiabr´: Dvulikaia istoriia*, ed. Adgas Burganov, Vladimir Buldakov, and Bukharaev (Kazan: n.p., 1992), 48–65; Steve Smith, "Writing the History of the Russian Revolution after the Fall of Communism," *Europe-Asia Studies* 46, 4 (1994): 563–78; Adrian Jones, "Towards a New Structural Theory of

Unlike the October Revolution, however, the French Revolution, as an interwoven strand of the cultural DNA of modern French identity, was reaffirmed at the very moment it seemed most imperiled. When social and political groups in the late 1960s cast doubt on the integrity of the liberty and equality so publicly and insistently bequeathed to the world by the French Revolution, the scholar Pierre Nora responded to what he saw as a current crisis of French identity with a project to gather her sites of memory (*lieux de mémoire*) as a way of preserving historical continuity and stilling the troubled times. Where Furet (and Malia in the Russian case) had seen the absence of a critical historiography of the Revolution as the problem, Nora saw modern historiography as "iconoclastic and irreverent." Because of the historiography of the French Revolution in particular, he wrote, "we no longer unquestioningly identify with its heritage."[34] As Steven Englund notes, the *lieux* project essentially embodied the "*Sehnsucht* of the literati, this lament for 'the world we have lost'—or, rather, 'the patrimony we are losing.'"[35] These sentiments can certainly be found in the former Eastern Bloc in the form of Ostalgie and in post-Soviet Russia in an inchoate longing for the seeming stability of the Brezhnev era, although Putin has yet to find his Nora.[36]

Revolution: Universalism and Community in the French and Russian Revolutions," *English Historical Review* 107, 425 (1992): 862–900; John Eric Marot, "Class Conflict, Political Competition and Social Transformation: Critical Perspectives on the Social History of the Russian Revolution," *Revolutionary Russia* 7, 2 (December 1994): 111–63; Vera Tolz, *Russian Academicians and the Revolution: Combining Professionalism and Politics* (Houndmills, UK: Macmillan, 1997); Steve Smith, "Two Cheers for the 'Return of Ideology,'" *Revolutionary Russia* 17, 2 (2004): 119–35; R. K. Balandin, *Mify revoliutsii 1917 goda: Nauchno-populiarnoe izdanie* (Moscow: Veche, 2007); Wladislaw Hedeler and Klaus Kinner, eds., *"Die Wache ist Müde": Neue Sichten auf die Russische Revolution 1917 und Ihre Wirkungen* (Berlin: Karl Dietz, 2008).

[34] Pierre Nora, "Between Memory and History: Les Lieux de Mémoire," *Representations*, no. 26 (Spring 1989): 10.

[35] Steven Englund, "The Ghost of Nation Past," *Journal of Modern History* 64, 2 (June 1992): 303.

[36] Many nations in both Western and Eastern Europe have found their Nora, sometimes quite literally as he has featured as the guest speaker and totem at the founding events of similar national "sites of memory" projects, for example, in the Netherlands. H. L. Wesseling, *Plaatsen Van Herinnering. Een Historisch Succesverhaal*, ed. Wim Van den Doel (Amsterdam: Uitgeverij Bert Bakker, 2005). Nora himself has referred to this as an "age of ardent, embattled, almost fetishistic 'memorialism'"; Pierre Nora, "Reasons for the Current Upsurge in Memory," *Eurozine*, 8 October 2007, http://www.eurozine.com/articles/2002-04-19-nora-en.html. Post-Soviet scholars have shown interest in this "internationalization of memory." See *Pamiat´ o voine 60 let spustia. Rossiia, Germaniia, Evropa* (Moscow: Novoe Literaturnoe Obozrenie, 2005), 40–41 (2005); also T. Dzhadt, "'Mesta pamiati' P´era Nora: Ch´i mesta? Ch´ia pamiat?" *Ab Imperio*, no. 1 (2004): 44–72.

These issues of French Revolutionary historiography certainly resonate in the historiography of the October Revolution, and yet the fate of the October Revolution has been radically different from that of the French Revolution. The latter event persists today as a potent foundation narrative in France, even beyond. Similarly, the British war cult of the 20th century, created in the post-World War I period and rededicated after World War II, still manifests itself frequently in 21st-century Britain, although perhaps now more as part of a modern English identity.[37] These transcendent events are more than the sum of the individual episodes from which they were both consciously and unconsciously woven by their respective states. They lay claim to greater intrinsic or inherent "truths" about their nations, and are constantly being rededicated and reconsecrated in ever more innovative and accretive ways. Evidence of their continued persistence as constituent parts of these national cultures is their ability to accommodate troubling counternarratives in ways that do not threaten the integrity of that national or postimperial metanarrative.[38]

October Redux

When he launched perestroika and glasnost' in the mid-1980s at a crisis point in late Soviet history, Gorbachev was essentially engaged in a similar endeavor as Nora, if unknowingly. By explicitly invoking the narrative of the Great October Socialist Revolution, he sought to re-revolutionize the Revolution in troubled times and thereby reanimate the economic, political, social, and cultural body of a moribund Soviet state. Only later would this be seen as the last gasp of the official project to narrativize Soviet history as a revolutionary

---

[37] For example, Paul Fussell, *The Great War and Modern Memory* (New York: Oxford University Press, 1975); Fussell, *Wartime: Understanding and Behavior in the Second World War* (New York: Oxford University Press, 1990); George Mosse, *Fallen Soldiers: Reshaping the Memory of the World Wars* (New York: Oxford University Press, 1991).

[38] In the British case, for example, Winston Churchill's past conduct under the British Empire, in the public record for anyone to find, has always been overshadowed by his antifascist stance in the 1930s and his leadership role during World War II; Johann Hari, "The Two Churchills," *The New York Times*, 12 August 2010. His, and British, involvement in the brutal suppression of the Mau Mau in Kenya in the 1950s was catalogued in the Pulitzer Prize-winning Caroline Elkins, *Imperial Reckoning: The Untold Story of Britain's Gulag in Kenya* (New York: Owl Books, 2005). It has produced barely an eddy in the broader official or public narrative of postwar British triumph. Nor does the relatively recent "discovery" of Vichy, and the potential difficulties it raised for official and personal French postwar identity, seem to have had a fatal impact on France's own restorative postwar narrative of *La Résistance;* Robert O. Paxton, *Vichy France: Old Guard and New Order, 1940–1944* (New York: Columbia University Press, 1982); Henry Rousso, *The Vichy Syndrome: History and Memory in France since 1944* (Cambridge, MA: Harvard University Press, 1991).

foundation project. In his extended address to a joint session of the major party and state institutions in the Kremlin Palace in Moscow on the occasion of the 70th anniversary of October, Gorbachev explicitly invoked "the October days which shook the world" for their solid, spiritual (*dukhovnyi*) foundation and instructive lessons." The originary source of the narrative he laid out here was Lenin's personality and his revolutionary foresight in creating the "party of a new type" at the turn of the century, which would eventually raise up the *narod* to "storm the old world."[39]

Still, the February Revolution was the "most important historical stage on the road to October," he said, because it was the first victorious people's revolution in the age of imperialism when "workers and peasants, dressed in soldiers' greatcoats" took power. Only Lenin was able to see the contradictions inherent in the system bequeathed by February, and he now had the correct tools, the soviets, to force the socialist stage of the Revolution. The October Revolution was successful because it responded to the needs of multiple parts of the masses, "the basic interests of the working class, the eternal hopes of the peasants, the soldiers' and sailors' thirst for peace, the inexhaustible desire of the peoples of the multinational Russia for freedom and light." Lenin's supple revolutionary dialectic, Gorbachev argued, allowed him to realize the "political and moral feat of the Brest peace" that saved many thousands of lives, and to forego Marx's old call for a popular militia in favor of the Worker and Peasant Red Army that brought such "immortal glory" during the Civil War and in repelling the foreign intervention. Gorbachev praised the "legendary heroes" of that war, the sailors and cavalry, the young Red Army soldiers and commanders, the red partisans. Once the Civil War was over, Lenin's foresight was again in evidence with his New Economic Policy which ensured October's survival and thus October's transcendent significance. As he told the assembled, "the main meaning of October was the creation of a new life.... The greatest boost in the people's initiative and creativity could be observed at the start of the '20s. They became the true revolutionary laboratory of socialist innovation.... A new culture was born, which absorbed both the experience of the past and the multifarious richness, boldness, originality of talents, of lively individuality, which the Revolution had aroused and inspired."[40] Western observers might have found the near absence of the First World War in this speech jarring, but that had more to do with the West's rejection of Soviet Russia's ideological conception of that war. Others would have found encouraging the revised and upgraded place of the

---

[39] M. S. Gorbachev, "Oktiabr' i perestroika: Revoliutsiia prodolzhaetsia," *Kommunist*, no. 17 (1987): 4, 5.

[40] Ibid., 7, 8.

February Revolution in the revolutionary continuum, something that at least one Soviet historian had earlier attempted to his cost.[41]

Gorbachev might have chosen to press other parts of the Soviet historical narrative project into the service of the present. He might profitably have invoked the military-style campaigns for rapid industrialization and forced collectivization launched in the late 1920s. Indeed, in his speech he noted the many achievements of industrialization. He stressed, however, that it came about "under the leadership of the party, of its CC," implying that the creative popular energies he had so praised in the earlier period—and regarded as so urgent now—were less in evidence in this essentially top-down state-driven process.[42] He might even have called on the 1938 *Short Course of the History of the RCP(b)*, the form of the Soviet narrative that aspired to canonical status, although his October narrative cut against the *Short Course*'s representation in many important respects, not least in the relative roles ascribed to Stalin in the events.[43] Most plausibly, perhaps, he might have invoked the values of extraordinary self-sacrifice and stoic endurance enshrined in the Great Patriotic War myth (the spirit of Leningrad, Moscow, or Stalingrad, perhaps, to match Britain's "Blitz spirit"). But this myth contained many of the nationalist, tsarist, and religious icons that revolutionaries had sought to destroy in the name of October, and perhaps also had too much of the rearguard defense about it.[44] He chose none of these moments, perhaps because he truly was unable to conceive of Soviet Russia without October. He chose instead to in-

---

[41] E. N. Burdzhalov's attempted revision of the February Revolution in 1956 blurred the clear distinction between Bolshevism and Menshevism required by Soviet orthodoxy. Nancy Whittier Heer, *Politics and History in the Soviet Union* (Cambridge, MA: MIT Press, 1971), 91. Cf. E. N. Burdzhalov, *Russia's Second Revolution: The February 1917 Uprising in Petrograd* (Bloomington: Indiana University Press, 1987). For a broader take on the changing place of February, see D. A. Longley, "Iakovlev's Question, or the Historiography of the Problem of Spontaneity and Leadership in the Russian Revolution of February 1917," in *Revolution in Russia: Reassessments of 1917*, 365–87.

[42] Gorbachev, "Oktiabr' i perestroika," 12.

[43] The end of the short "ideological reign" of the *Short Course* had already been declared by Khrushchev in 1956, and at least one Soviet scholar in that same year had criticized its many factual errors, its diminution of the role of the party and the people in the Revolution, and of Lenin's role as the "great founder," and the elevation of its every proposition to "lifeless dogma." Paul H. Avrich, "The Short Course and Soviet Historiography," *Political Science Quarterly* 75, 4 (1960): 539; E. N. Burdzhalov, "XX s″ezd KPSS i zadachi issledovaniia istorii partii," *Voprosy istorii*, no. 3 (1956): 5. On the partial exhumation of its corpse under Putin and Dmitrii Medvedev, see David Brandenberger, "A New Short Course? A. V. Filippov and the Russian State's Search for a 'Usable Past,'" *Kritika: Explorations in Russian and Eurasian History* 10, 4 (2009): 825–33.

[44] Kevin M. F. Platt and David Brandenberger, eds., *Epic Revisionism: Russian History and Literature as Stalinist Propaganda* (Madison: University of Wisconsin Press, 2006).

voke the first years of the Great October Socialist Revolution, when it was in its most vital and engaging process of formation.

The successful construction of a foundation event must entail a broad cultural process that employs any and all usable media to draw the population into the process of construction.[45] Successful foundation narratives can never be simply politically imposed upon "society" by the "state." "Society" must be present in their very constitution. Indeed, in a sense, "society" itself must be reconstituted as part of any successful foundation narrative. Given that the Bolsheviks' early political measures (land, bread, and peace) clearly catered to the longstanding desires of various constituent elements of the popular classes, it seems reasonable to posit, as literary scholar Kevin Platt has, that even "setting aside the fictitious nature of the popular mandate of the Bolshevik Party (and the undeniable illegitimacy of its assumption of power), one may state unequivocally that the 'basic idea' of the October Revolution itself, conceived as a transformation of Russian society in some vaguely 'socialist' direction, enjoyed overwhelming popularity."[46]

The Bolsheviks drew on a range of media to argue their case for October as a revolutionary foundation event. Not all parts of society had to be touched by all media, but it would have been difficult for anyone to avoid at least some encounter with October in the first decade after 1917.[47] A new revolutionary statuary was created to eclipse the old tsarist statuary. Cities were rewritten with a new revolutionary toponymy, and in some cases topography. New Red Weddings and Red Funerals were intended to displace older rituals over time. Where feasible, revolutionary repertoires were played in the theaters, and Vsevolod Meierkhol'd conceived revolutionary theater as a veritable military-style assault on old attitudes and values. The anniversary celebrations of October in these first ten years were ritualized but by no means

---

[45] In the past two decades or so, the study of October as a cultural construct has received increased scholarly attention. For an early trailblazing work, see René Fülöp-Miller, *The Mind and Face of Bolshevism: An Examination of Cultural Life in Soviet Russia* (New York: Harper Torchbooks, 1965). See also Karl Schlögel, *Jenseits des Grossen Oktober: Das Laboratorium der moderne Petersburg 1909–1921* (Berlin: Siedler Verlag, 1988); Richard Stites, *Revolutionary Dreams: Utopian Vision and Experimental Life in the Russian Revolution* (New York: Oxford University Press, 1989); Orlando Figes and Boris Kolonitskii, *Interpreting the Russian Revolution: The Language and Symbols of 1917* (New Haven: Yale University Press, 1999); James von Geldern, *Bolshevik Festivals 1917–1920* (Berkeley: University of California Press, 1993); Frederick C. Corney, *Telling October: Memory and the Making of the Bolshevik Revolution* (Ithaca, NY: Cornell University Press, 2004); S. Iu. Malysheva, *Sovetskaia prazdnichnaia kul'tura v provintsii: Prostranstvo, simvoly, istoricheskie mify (1917–1927)* (Kazan: Ruten, 2005); Malte Rolf, *Das sowjetische Massenfest* (Hamburg: Hamburger Edition, 2006).

[46] Kevin M. F. Platt, *History in a Grotesque Key: Russian Literature and the Idea of Revolution* (Stanford, CA: Stanford University Press, 1997), 122–23.

[47] I develop the following at more length in my monograph. See Corney, *Telling October*.

routinized yet, and were tailored to the political exigencies and needs of a given year. Two celebrations, those in November 1920 and November 1927, stand out as the high points of this decade of construction of October. The mass spectacle staged on the square in front of the Winter Palace on the third anniversary—and intended for projection around the country as a short film—has long fascinated scholars for its scale, inventiveness, and reach.[48] The tenth anniversary celebrations saw the major filmmakers Vsevolod Pudovkin, Esfir' Shub, and Boris Barnet produce, respectively, *The End of St. Petersburg* (*Konets S.-Peterburga*), *The Great Way* (*Velikii put'*), and *Moscow in October* (*Moskva v Oktiabre*) specifically for the jubilee. But the truth is that even their earlier films for the twentieth anniversary of the 1905 Revolution or the tenth anniversary of the February Revolution, namely Pudovkin's *Mother* (*Mat'*) and Shub's *Fall of the Romanov Dynasty* (*Padenie dinastii Romanovykh*), were really in the service of the October narrative.

The most famous director of the age, Sergei Eisenstein, was in the process of making an epic seven-part cycle called *Towards the Dictatorship* (*K diktature*), of which only *Strike* (*Stachka*) was completed, and another intended seven-parter, of which only the famous *October* (*Oktiabr'*) was completed.[49] The revolutionary "truth," Eisenstein believed, was not the same as the literal "truth" and approvingly quoted Goethe: "For the sake of truthfulness one can afford to defy the truth." The October Revolution deserved an epic telling, and an appropriately grand effort to create a "socially useful emotional and psychological effect on the audience."[50] In keeping with the spirit and breadth of these early efforts to construct October as a foundation narrative, Eisenstein had drawn from a variety of sources for inspiration, notably American journalist John Reed's own romanticized epic, *Ten Days That Shook the World*, and the "participant" Nikolai Podvoiskii's memoirs about the "storming" of the Winter Palace on 25 October (indeed, Podvoiskii had served as the director's guide to the major "revolutionary sites" in St. Petersburg), to name but two inspirations. With his co-director, Grigorii Aleksandrov, Eisenstein had attended question-and-answer sessions with "participants" in October where the assembled had been gathered to reminisce about the events. He

---

[48] For the artist's own description of this spectacle within the context of the theatricalization of the politics of the time, see Nicolas Evreinoff, *Histoire du Théâtre Russe* (Paris: Éditions du Chêne, 1947), 408–30. See also František Deák, "Russian Mass Spectacles," *The Drama Review* 19, 2 (1975): 7–22; Christopher A. P. Binns, "The Changing Face of Power: Revolution and Accommodation in the Development of the Soviet Ceremonial System," pts. 1 and 2 in *Man*, n.s., no. 14 (1979): 585–606, and *Man*, n.s., no. 15 (1980): 170–87; Geldern, *Bolshevik Festivals 1917–1920*, 199–207.

[49] Corney, *Telling October*, 268 n. 48.

[50] Cited in ibid., 184.

thereby drew on a deeper, institutionalized layer of meaning-making in the early Soviet era.[51]

Museums of the October Revolution sprang up across the country, pictorially mapping the Revolution onto the former tsarist empire. Each of these required an active engagement with the October narrative and an active solicitation and collection of its artifacts. Countrywide, institutions were set up from 1920 on to gather and compile materials from which the history of October could be written for present and future generations: Istpart (the Commission on the History of the October Revolution and the Russian Communist Party [Bolsheviks]), Istprof (a similar commission to write the history of trade unions), and Istmol (for the history of Communist youth). In the process, these organizations, like all parts of the October project, sought to provide the broader narrative framework within which these materials would be articulated. Acutely aware of a paucity of extant materials, Istpart in particular sought to commission them in the form of sponsored reminiscences, offering as much of a revolutionary framework as they were able to potential "participants" (broadly conceived) in the Revolution. State publishing agencies were set up to immortalize the results in print.[52]

Given the Bolsheviks' transcendent claims in the name of October, it should not be surprising that both the First World War and the Civil War were subsumed in the state's broader efforts to construct a revolutionary foundation event. The Soviet state did not try to "forget" the First World War, nor did it lack a "real historical memory" of that war, as some scholars have suggested in contrasting the Soviet attitude to the war with the dominant attitude in the West.[53] In fact, the First World War was useful to Soviet Russia. State and party leaders articulated it as the imperialist war that had brought capitalism to the brink, had helped create the conditions to topple an ossified and repressive tsarist autocracy, and prepared the way for a mature socialist revolutionary takeover in Russia. There may well have been, as historian Karen Petrone argues, no "singular and agreed upon World War I 'memory'" in Soviet Russia.[54] Surely though this was because for Soviet Russia stressing the "senselessness" or "meaninglessness" of the First World War was as useful to the October foundation myth as was the "meaningful" and transcendent Storming of the Winter Palace.

Similarly, for the Bolsheviks the Civil War was the armed fulfillment of the promises of October, and absolutely necessary if the state were to overcome, as Trotskii put it in 1918, "every obstacle and resistance that hinders its survival and development…. It is obvious that Soviet power is organised civil war

---

[51] Cited in ibid.

[52] See ibid., 130–31.

[53] The latter quote is from Richard Stites, as cited in Karen Petrone, *The Great War in Russian Memory* (Bloomington: Indiana University Press, 2011), 5.

[54] Petrone, *The Great War in Russian Memory*, 7.

against the landlords, the bourgeoisie and the kulaks [rich peasants]."[55] In the early 1920s, though, it did not garner the resources or attention devoted to the events of 1917. Historian Justus Hartzok argues that only the "beginnings of a loosely structured Civil War cult" were in evidence during the early resource-rich stages of production of the October narrative. The "more concerted and deliberate effort to mythologize and formulate the Civil War," he adds, began in the early 1930s when "the Stalin regime deliberately invoked the Civil War years to catalyze its radical economic and cultural transformations."[56] This suggests that the Civil War myth had less to do with the efforts to fashion the October foundation narrative, at least in its earliest incarnation, and more to do with a time when Soviet party and state actors had abandoned a more flexible approach to their mythic foundations in favor of a more tightly imposed orthodoxy. Indeed, at that time, the party substituted other tropes for the revolutionary tropes it had floated in the 1920s. As historian David Brandenberger puts it, the party "rushed to embrace non-Marxist heroes drawn from the annals of the Russian national past," a move animated by the rising threat of Nazism.[57]

This new turn to orthodoxy was undoubtedly conceived as a more robust and decisive response to the particular needs of the time than the response offered in the first decade after October 1917. Brandenberger sees the initial formative decade of revolutionary Russia, of which the October foundation narrative was a major part, as essentially a failure in terms of its ability to mobilize the population, a failure particularly manifest in a "collapse of Soviet morale on the eve of the tenth anniversary of the Revolution.... Neither the party, nor the Revolution, nor the idea of the dictatorship of the proletariat appears to have enjoyed much sympathy."[58] Whether this was so or not, it is undeniable that this first decade represented a unique "laboratory of revolution," at least until the mid-1980s.[59] The process of construction of October was flexible, accretive, and broadly conceived. Unlike the later period, it was not as severely hampered by censorship and repression, at least after the "bourgeois" and the non-Bolshevik socialist press had all been outlawed by mid-1918 and large numbers of the old elites and the members of non-Bolshevik parties had either

---

[55] Leon Trotsky, "Two Roads," in *How the Revolution Armed*, 1: *1918* (New York: New Park Publications, 1979), 81.

[56] Justus Grant Hartzok, "Children of Chapaev: The Russian Civil War Cult and the Creation of Soviet Identity, 1918–1941" (Ph.D. diss., University of Iowa, 2009), 19–20.

[57] David Brandenberger, *Propaganda State in Crisis: Soviet Ideology, Indoctrination, and Terror under Stalin, 1927–1941*, The Yale-Hoover Series on Stalin, Stalinism, and the Cold War (New Haven: Yale University Press, 2012), 5.

[58] Brandenberger, *Propaganda State in Crisis*, 3, 23.

[59] See, for example, Schlögel, *Jenseits des Grossen Oktober*; Katerina Clark, *Petersburg: Crucible of Cultural Revolution* (Cambridge, MA: Harvard University Press, 1995).

been killed during the Civil War, left the country, or expelled. Revolutionaries of various stripes committed themselves to October. Of course, plenty of literature was being produced in praise of October, some of it by committed foreign socialists like Reed, but the project was such that the literature did not have to be uniformly positive in form or content. As Platt has pointed out in relation to early Soviet literature, works like Fedor Gladkov's *Cement* (*Tsement*, 1925) and Mikhail Bulgakov's *White Guard* (*Belaia gvardiia*, 1926, in a partial serialization of the novel) were by, respectively, an enthusiast of new revolutionary values and a nostalgist for older values: "Yet both of these works apply the standard idea of the revolutionary era—as a radical discontinuity in human affairs—to their contemporary scene. Thus they contribute equally to the establishment of the general 'contour' of the historical present, while they compete to propose a particular political evaluation of that paradigm. These texts not only 'manage' the Revolution but also 'create' the revolution and grant it specific ideologically charged features."[60]

October's Paradox

So Gorbachev chose to invoke October at its most formative, innovative, and evocative stage, and yet it proved woefully unfit for that challenge. This was not because October had suddenly been eclipsed or delegitimized by the "recovered memory" of the gulag experience and the new cult of "openness" in Soviet Russia from the mid-1980s. Nor did the formal end in 1991 of the ideological state that was October's *raison d'être* signal its deathknell, for the ideological essence of that state had long since dispersed. Aleksandr Zinov'ev has argued that during the Khrushchev and Brezhnev years, a "sharp divergence" could be observed between the "ideological picture of reality and reality itself.... Ideology had in fact ceased to be the guide to action for the authorities.... Millions of people studied it, but strictly formally."[61] Anthropologist Alexei Yurchak has brilliantly explored the paradoxes of living in "Late Socialism," a time when "the fundamental values, ideals, and realities of socialist life" were important to citizens at the same time as their routine navigations of Soviet life "transgressed, reinterpreted, or refused certain norms and rules represented in the official ideology of the socialist state."[62]

October had been in a state of decline for far longer, and by recalling that initial early period of enthusiasm and vitality, Gorbachev merely reminded the Soviet population how short-lived that period had been. Like Nora's response to France in crisis, Gorbachev's response to Soviet Russia in

---

[60] Platt, *History in a Grotesque Key*, 21.

[61] A. A. Zinov'ev, *Post-kommunisticheskaia Rossiia: Publitsistika 1991–1995 gg.* (Moscow: Respublika, 1996), 19.

[62] Alexei Yurchak, *Everything Was Forever, Until It Was No More: The Last Soviet Generation* (Princeton, NJ: Princeton University Press, 2005), 8.

(protracted) crisis sought to invoke the most innovative period of the Soviet state-in-the-making, the construction of the originary event. In so doing, he was also invoking October at its messiest and most contested. He seemed aware of this, tempering his revolutionary challenge to late Soviet Russia with deeply traditional cautions as well. By invoking Lenin as a *deus ex machina* and Lenin's pronouncements as unchallengeably canonical, he undercut his own argument for future reliance on the internal vitality of the Soviet people. He placed Lenin front and center, and then visited one by one the stages of the revolutionary cross that flanked him. He emphasized the dangers of factionalism, and singled out Trotskii the man (along with "oppositionists" Grigorii Zinov′ev and Lev Kamenev) and Trotskyism the "political tendency" as the worst examples of this in the 1920s, thereby further reinforcing the prescriptively orthodox in his speech.[63] Should the most conservative among the assembled in the hall need any further reassurances, Gorbachev left Stalin's persona largely intact, or at least in its post-1956 denunciation state. As historian Manfred Hildermeier put it in 1991,

> as much as perestroika has summoned criticism and new thinking, the fundamental switchpoints of Soviet history have been exempted from it as before…. Whoever raises doubt about Lenin's tactics together with their fulfillment in the October overthrow and the bloody self-assertion in the Civil War, places the self-conception of the Soviet Union in general in question. Every state with a certain tradition has a foundation myth; every society needs a basic consensus, which will as a rule be connected with the history of the origins of the state…. In the Soviet Union this connection was a particularly close one. In the past it had to bear the additional burden of the legitimation deficits, which grew from the unfulfilled promises of the official ideology.[64]

Indeed, from its inception the Great October Socialist Revolution was never *not* in a state of contestation. As one Russian newspaper put it in 2001, "the October Revolution was the first huge PR problem for the new Russia. The country was simply denied recognition."[65] In fact, its legitimacy was challenged both from within Soviet Russia and from without. Even before 25 October 1917 there had been considerable disagreement within the Bolshevik Party itself over what exactly would render a Bolshevik seizure of power from the Provisional Government legitimate. Central Committee members Zinov′ev and Kamenev found themselves in hot water for their public

---

[63] Gorbachev, "Oktiabr′ i perestroika," 11.

[64] Manfred Hildermeier, "Revolution und Revolutionsgeschichte," in *Die Umwertung der Sowjetischen Geschichte*, ed. Dietrich Geyer (Göttingen: Vandenhoeck & Ruprecht, 1991), 34.

[65] "Rupor revoliutsii," *Vedomosti*, 2 March 2001.

disagreement in mid-October with Lenin's call for an immediate seizure of power in Petrograd. Trotskii wondered whether the party should wait for the sanction of the Second Congress of Soviets on 25 October. Others wondered whether taking power in Petrograd and Moscow first could still be called a genuine revolution. These latter issues would be taken up in full force in the first weeks after 25 October, when, in the socialist and non-socialist press, competing representations of the events of late October 1917 were aired. Along with their loud proclamations of revolution, the Bolsheviks argued that while the "art of insurrection" had been practiced by the party, and that it had built upon the lessons learned in the earlier great revolutions, true revolutionary power lay with the energized soldier and peasant masses in whose name the Bolshevik Party worked. Non-socialist groups, along with socialist parties opposed to the Bolsheviks, like the Mensheviks and Socialist Revolutionaries, argued that the events of 25 October were like nothing more than the actions of a South American-style military junta with little or no mass support. Whether these critics regarded the Bolsheviks as power-hungry demagogues or hopeless dreamers depended on their position on the political spectrum, as did their assessment of the future trajectory of Bolshevik aspirations and plans.[66]

These opposing arguments could not be won through suasion, for they never constituted a debate or discussion. The critics of October and Bolshevism inside Soviet Russia were silenced by censorship and repression. But if the legitimacy of October was intended by the Bolsheviks to become an incontestable article of faith inside Soviet Russia, the illegitimacy of October served a similar function in the burgeoning Emigration. In three major waves, large numbers of people from all sections of the population (over a million people after October 1917 alone) were forced from their homeland, first in the wake of the revolutionary upheavals of 1917 and the Civil War, then during the tribulations of World War II, and finally the highly public expulsions of dissidents during the Brezhnev era.[67] The forced exile of political parties and groupings from which the most coherent counternarratives might have been expected to emerge certainly obviated the need for the October narrative to deal with them inside Soviet Russia. In the broad range of political and cultural views awkwardly yoked by the term "Emigration," however, a large part shared the basic assumption of October's illegitimacy and a deep animosity towards the Bolshevik regime. For some Western scholars, Russia Abroad

---

[66] Frederick C. Corney, "Narratives of October and the Issue of Legitimacy," in *Russian Modernity: Politics, Knowledges, Practices*, ed. David L. Hoffmann and Yanni Kotsonis (New York: St. Martin's Press, Inc., 2000), 185–203.

[67] On the numbers, see John Glad, *Russia Abroad: Writers, History, Politics* (Tenafly, NJ: Hermitage; Washington, DC: Birchbark Press, 1999), 105–08.

(*Zarubezhnaia Rossiia*) represented "a large part of the 'nation' [*natsiia*]."[68] For others, like historian Marc Raeff, "true" Russia resided not in the political emigration ("eclectic, muddled, and rather shallow") but in its cultural exiles, who were entrusted with the preservation and continuation of Russia's cultural heritage.[69] As the Civil War drew to a close, émigré groups on the left side of the political spectrum gradually abandoned their support for armed struggle against the Bolsheviks in favor of various alternative tactics, or even began to rethink their positions vis-à-vis the Soviet regime itself. Only a few, though, reconsidered their original opinions of October as a fundamentally illegitimate event.[70]

In many ways the Emigration, broadly conceived, came to stamp the ways in which Western nations perceived, indeed conceptualized, the Soviet Union and Russia's place in it, and hence enshrined this assumption of October's illegitimacy in much of the non-Communist West. The Menshevik Internationalists, for example, from their exile first in Berlin, then Paris, and ultimately New York City, sustained a 40-year critique of Communist Russia through their incessant writings, helping to shape the categories used in the West to conceive of the USSR, to make the terms "gulag" and "totalitarian" part of the dominant political lexicon, and to develop Kremlinology as "the tool of an entire profession."[71] This counternarrative of illegitimacy would find a home once more in Russia during glasnost′ and after the collapse of the Soviet Union, as émigrés (most famously Aleksandr Solzhenitsyn) returned, sure in the knowledge that the recent course of events in Russia was a confirmation of their lifelong beliefs. This found symbolic expression in Putin's official visit in 2000 to Ste-Geneviève-des-Bois near Paris, resting place of 10,000 émigrés. He made no acknowledgment of the countervailing views that had so animated their lives, preferring the anodyne comment: "We are all children of the same mother who is named Russia."[72]

For those in the Emigration, then, the a priori assumption of illegitimacy by definition divested October of any claims of transcendence, and so the First

---

[68] M. A. Kontenko and I. V. Domnin, comps., *Rossiiskii zarubezhnyi s″ezd, 1926, Parizh: Dokumenty i materialy* (Moscow: Russkii put′, 2006), 497–98.

[69] Marc Raeff, "Recent Perspectives on the History of the Russian Emigration (1920–1940)," *Kritika: Explorations in Russian and Eurasian History* 6, 2 (2005): 327, 331.

[70] The "Changing Signposts" (*smenovekhovtsy*) movement was the most prominent example of those émigrés who came to accept that October at some level expressed the will of the people. See Hilde Hardeman, *Coming to Terms with the Soviet Regime: The "Changing Signposts" Movement among Russian Émigrés in the Early 1920s* (DeKalb: Northern Illinois University Press, 1994).

[71] André Liebich, *From the Other Shore: Russian Social Democracy after 1921* (Cambridge, MA: Harvard University Press, 1997), 302.

[72] "Putin posetil memorial′noe russkoe kladbishche Sen Genev′ev-de-Bua," *Interfaks Operativnye Soobshcheniia*, 1 November 2000.

World War and the Civil War occupied quite different places in the narratives they fashioned from the events surrounding October 1917. Not surprisingly, those Black Hundreds, Octobrists, Kadets, and other monarchists who ended up in the Emigration had a very different view of the First World War and its optimal potential outcome than did the Socialist Revolutionaries and Mensheviks who had joined them in exile. Soviet Russia's departure from the war was an unmitigated disaster with the loss of former tsarist imperial territories and the national humiliation it brought, and Russian military émigrés in particular "organized the memory of World War I ... to create a worthy, if idealized, war experience," although they lacked the organizational and military resources to "create, organize, and impose that memory on a large scale."[73] So it was with the Civil War. For many émigrés the very viciousness of the Civil War after the October seizure of power represented the clearest expression of the deep illegitimacy of the Bolshevik coup as "patriotic" Russians rallied to the cause. In this view, the October seizure of power by the Bolsheviks had no transcendent value, only the very real and brutal result of Russians fighting Russians. Among these émigrés, the Civil War deserved to be remembered because it represented Russia's final defense against the Bolshevik onslaught. "In most of the memoirs of participants in and contemporaries of the Civil War that were written in emigration in the 1930s," historian Petr Grishanin observed

> a similarity of thematic content.... Almost everyone wrote about the early days after the Bolsheviks' accession to power (explaining the reasons for the October 1917 military coup in Petrograd), about the early mustering of the Volunteer Army (explaining how the White movement began to take shape), about the mood of the Russian people (explaining why the Bolsheviks were ultimately supported by the peasantry), about "preemptive terror" (explaining why violence won out over all the norms of community life), and so on.[74]

Émigré memoirs often referred to this entire period as a new Time of Troubles, with Russian civilization itself at stake.[75]

---

[73] Aaron J. Cohen, "Oh, That! Myth, Memory, and World War I in the Russian Emigration and the Soviet Union," *Slavic Review* 62, 1 (2003): 78.

[74] Petr I. Grishanin, "The White Movement and the Civil War," *Russian Studies in History* 49, 1 (Summer 2010): 34.

[75] See, of many examples, A. I. Denikin, *Ocherki russkoi smuty* (Paris: J. Povolozky, 1921–26); Alexander Kerensky, *Russia and History's Turning Point* (New York: Duell, Sloan and Pearce, 1965); Iurii Vladimirovich Got´e, *Time of Troubles: The Diary of Iurii Vladimirovich Got´e. Moscow. July 8, 1917–July 23, 1922*, trans. and ed. Terence Emmons (Princeton, NJ: Princeton University Press, 1988).

Inside Soviet Russia of course, as we have seen, October existed as a putatively mythic event. This did not mean however that the October narrative emerged full-blown on 25 October 1917. Although the construction of October was launched in a period of intense deprivation, disorder, and popular discontent, the real threat to its integrity came from within the Bolshevik Party rather than from without.[76] The threat of "Trotskyists" inside the Soviet body politic became a major political weapon in the battle waged by the Bolshevik Party for ideological "purity," part of which entailed the fashioning of the October foundation narrative.[77] Herein lay the problem, however, because the picture of October that emerged at the local level through the efforts of organizations like Istpart was neither expected nor desired by the Bolshevik Party. Surprised at the absence of local Bolshevik participation in preparing the revolutionary ground for Soviet power, at least as recalled by local activists, Bolshevik leaders became concerned about fashioning an October narrative that was missing the party.[78] This situation was not helped by perennial and highly public battles, particularly with Trotskii, a former hero of the Revolution and the Civil War.[79] These ideological clashes culminated—for the October narrative at least, if not yet for Trotskii's own personal fate—in the so-called "literary discussion" (*literaturnaia diskussiia*) in the final months of 1924.[80] This polemic—it was neither "literary" nor a "discussion"—revolved around Trotskii's particular telling of October in his pamphlet *The Lessons of October*. At a time when the actual role of the Bolshevik Party in the revolutionary events in Russia, broadly conceived, was by no means clear, he criticized the Central Committee for being out of step with Lenin's revolutionary foresight, singling out now very influential Bolshevik leaders, Zinov′ev and Kamenev in particular, for their failure to see the revolutionary writing on the wall in October 1917. Trotskii also barely mentioned Stalin at all in these events. At this point, the project to tell October as a foundation narrative for the new Soviet state came into direct conflict with the party's efforts to fashion itself,

---

[76] On the endemic but largely unfocused popular discontent in these years, see my review essay in *Kritika: Explorations in Russian and Eurasian History* 3, 1 (2002): 164–72.

[77] On the Soviet state's use of "Trotskyists" and the "Opposition" as political weapons, see Igal Halfin, *From Darkness to Light: Class, Consciousness, and Salvation in Revolutionary Russia* (Pittsburgh: University of Pittsburgh Press, 2000); Halfin, *Intimate Enemies: Demonizing the Bolshevik Opposition, 1918–1928* (Pittsburgh: University of Pittsburgh Press, 2007).

[78] See Corney, *Telling October*, especially 131–35.

[79] A special issue of a journal commemorating the Red Army in 1923 showcased Trotskii (among others) both for his role as "leader of the Red Army" and for his part in the Revolution and the Civil War (*Krasnaia niva*, no. 8 [23 February 1923]).

[80] Frederick Corney, trans., *Trotsky's Challenge: The "Literary Discussion" and the Fight for the Bolshevik Revolution* (forthcoming from Brill in 2015).

increasingly under Stalin's direction, as the sole arbiter of the past, the present, and the future.

Trotskii's political excommunication and physical banishment beginning in late 1927 was undoubtedly evidence of his ideological treason for some and of his political crucifixion for others. For all, however, it was surely evidence of a system in flux, a political system whose founding fathers were at each others' throats and whose foundational tale was not yet fully written. The desacralization of old icons of authority and the sacralization of new icons had been part and parcel of the revolutionary project long before and well after the events of October 1917. The cult of the tsars had given way to the new minor cults of Kerenskii and General Lavr Kornilov after the February Revolution, and to the cults of Mikhail Frunze and Trotskii from the Civil War period.[81] Most famously, of course, Lenin and Stalin would become the subjects of major cults in Soviet revolutionary culture. The periodic membership purges of the party and the agitation trials were clearly public "performances" of party and revolution, efforts to place critics of each, as Elizabeth Wood has written of the early agitation trials, before "the court of the people ... [and] ... the court of history."[82] This perception would have been merely reinforced by the show trials of leading "Trotskyists" in the late 1930s, a time of terror when, as Hartzok puts it,

> heroic images were shattered when newspapers suddenly branded as traitors and enemies of the people many of these revolutionary heroes. Only a select group of individuals, specifically Stalin and his closest associates, as well as deceased Civil War heroes like Chapaev, remained untarnished. Everyday people suddenly found themselves unsure of what to believe, as the political landscape changed dramatically on the eve of the Second World War.[83]

Erasures, omissions, and uncomfortable inclusions are part and parcel of any foundation event, of course, but such public erasures deeply undermined the Soviet project, surely adding to the public perception of the fundamental inconstancy of the October narrative, even in its initial stage of construction.

---

[81] Fülöp-Miller, *The Mind and Face of Bolshevism*, chap. 2; Figes and Kolonitskii, *Interpreting the Russian Revolution*, chap. 3; Balazs Apor et al., eds., *The Leader Cult in Communist Dictatorships: Stalin and the Eastern Bloc* (Basingstoke, UK: Palgrave Macmillan, 2005).

[82] Elizabeth A. Wood, "The Trial of Lenin: Legitimating the Revolution Through Political Theater, 1920–1923," *Russian Review* 61, 2 (2002): 248; also Wood, *Performing Justice: Agitation Trials in Early Soviet Russia* (Ithaca, NY: Cornell University Press, 2005).

[83] Hartzok, *Children of Chapaev*, 5–6.

October Eclipsed

Whether this lack of faith was a sudden development is debatable, and largely immaterial, for however well or poorly anchored the general belief in October, the population was urged during and after the Second World War to place its faith as a nation in a new foundation myth. This new narrative was forged from the immediate and visceral experiences of many millions of Soviet Russia's population during the war, and this alone would have given it the power to eclipse the more distant and far less widespread remembered experiences of October. The British war myth would be fashioned from Dunkirk, the Battle of Britain, and the Blitz—the terms themselves acquiring a totemic significance in the process.[84] So too would Soviet Russia fashion its postwar myth from those experiences in the war when it was faced with its most existential threats—Leningrad, Moscow, and Stalingrad, to name three such Soviet postwar totems—the very survival of such threats already lending a transcendent, mythic dimension to those experiences.[85]

Historian Amir Weiner has noted the similarity in aims of both the October and Great Patriotic War myths, namely the "ultimate goal of a homogeneous and harmonious society" (a function of all foundation myths perhaps?), arguing that for Soviet citizens the war was conceptually inextricable from the broader Soviet revolutionary project. In fact, he argued, the war signaled "the climax in the unfolding socialist revolution."[86] At the same time, however, faced with an existential threat, the Soviet authorities during the war had resurrected, in the service of national defense, prerevolutionary historical and religious tropes and conventions that were deeply incompatible with the iconoclasm of the October originary narrative. Where October and the Civil War "catered to the state of the workers and peasants," noted one article, by changing "national solidarity" to "class solidarity," May 1945 saw the return

---

[84] Malcolm Smith, *Britain and 1940: History, Myth, and Popular Memory* (London: Routledge, 2001).

[85] Scholars have recently focused well-deserved attention on these mythopoetic processes. See Peter Jahn, *Stalingrad erinnern: Stalingrad im deutschen und russischen Gedächtnis* (Berlin: Ch. Links, 2003); Lisa A. Kirschenbaum, *The Legacy of the Siege of Leningrad, 1941–1995: Myth, Memories, and Monuments* (Cambridge: Cambridge University Press, 2006); Steven Maddox, "Healing the Wounds: Commemorations, Myths, and the Restoration of Leningrad's Imperial Heritage, 1941–1950" (Ph.D. diss., University of Toronto, 2008); Arja Rozenholm and Bonner Withold, eds., *Recalling the Past, (Re)constructing the Past: Collective and Individual Memory of World War II in Russia and Germany* (Helsinki: Aleksanteri Institute, 2008).

[86] Amir Weiner, *Making Sense of War: The Second World War and the Fate of the Bolshevik Revolution* (Princeton, NJ: Princeton University Press, 2001), 7–8.

of the "Soviet people [*narod*], whose class nature was not so much scrapped as simply no longer mentioned."[87]

If potential ideological contradictions or political volte-faces were met with silence, the war myth also entailed the production of memory on a far grander and ambitious scale than was ever envisaged for October. October would, of course, continue to be perennially commemorated in the postwar period, most notably on its 50th jubilee. Even on that occasion, though, the journalist Harrison Salisbury described it picturesquely as rather tired and middle-aged, "a bit wheezy, inclined to sit back in an easy chair, turn on the TV and watch a good light programme. No speeches, please. No party exhortations!"[88] Weiner has written of the "tremendous power" of the elaborate (and often banal) rituals through which the war's "cataclysmic events are naturalized and integrated into the lives of men and women."[89] This power has produced the Great Patriotic War as the new Soviet totem. The Soviet postwar myth, largely unobjectionable to the Western Allies who were engaged in the construction of their own war myths cut to the terminally altered postimperial landscape, experienced none of the protracted crisis of legitimacy that had accompanied October. It now survives as the only part of the Soviet past that can be used by the Putin and Medvedev administrations for the post-Soviet present, and the resources deployed to this end still impress today.[90]

October is Over

Sic transit gloria mundi. A modern state can really sustain only one successful foundation myth at a time, and October slowly vanished into the shadow of the powerful war myth, leaving neither a smile nor a grimace. October faded because it had failed to become part of Soviet Russia's cultural fabric in the way

---

[87] Orkhan Dzhemal', "Novye russkie prazdniki," *Novaia gazeta*, 11 November 2004.

[88] Cited in Amir Weiner, "Robust Revolution to Retiring Revolution: The Life Cycle of the Soviet Revolution, 1945–1968," *Slavonic and East European Review* 86, 2 (2008): 228.

[89] Weiner, *Making Sense of War*, 20.

[90] Elizabeth A. Wood, "Performing Memory: Vladimir Putin and the Celebration of WWII in Russia," *Soviet and Post-Soviet Review*, no. 38 (2011): 172–200; also Mark von Hagen, "From 'Great Fatherland War' to the Second World War: New Perspectives and Future Prospects," in *Stalinism and Nazism: Dictatorships in Comparison*, ed. Ian Kershaw and Moshe Lewin (Cambridge: Cambridge University Press, 1997); Jacob Evan Lassin, "From the Trenches of Stalingrad to the Digital Front: The Myth and Memory of WWII in the Soviet Union and the New Russia" (Senior thesis, The College of William & Mary, 2012); Falk Bomsdorf and G. A. Bordiugov, eds., *60-letie okonchaniia Vtoroi Mirovoi i Velikoi Otechestvennoi: Pobediteli i pobezhdennye v kontekste politiki, mifologii i pamiati. Materialy k Mezhdunarodnomu Forumu (Moskva, sentiabr' 2005)* (Moscow: Fond Fridrikha Naumanna, AIRO-XXI, 2005); Mikhail Gabovich, ed., *Pamiat' o voine 60 let spustia: Rossiia, Germaniia, Evropa* (Moscow: Novoe literaturnoe obozrenie, 2005).

that successful foundation narratives by definition must. Only an internally robust and constantly resacralized foundation narrative, able to implicate and reimplicate subsequent generations of the population in its making, could have withstood or subsumed the counternarratives and contestations experienced by October throughout its precarious existence. Unlike the myth of the French Revolution for France, of the American Revolution for the United States, or of the war myth for modern Britain, October proved unable over the long term to withstand or accommodate serious challenges to the integrity of its narrative. Or to put it slightly differently, not enough people felt moved in their gut to come to its defense against these challenges, in the way that people in France or the USA or Britain are still moved today by their own foundation events.

Scarcely four years after Gorbachev's 1987 speech, the USSR formally ceased to exist, and with it Gorbachev's hopes for October. It is all but impossible today to conceive of a theme park in Moscow celebrating the October Revolution along the lines of the 1889 World Exposition in Paris with its replica of the Bastille, or the planned Napoleonland theme park dedicated to a French historical narrative built around the still divisive emperor.[91] An equivalent "Leninland" is more difficult to imagine today than a theme park centered on the Great Patriotic War, or, grotesquely, even on the gulag.[92] Today, the October Revolution seems a highly unlikely target of official commemoration (or, for most people, of private commemoration). The Presidential Commission to Counter Attempts to Falsify History to the Detriment of Russia's Interests (Komissiia po protivodeistviiu popytkam fal'sifikatsii istorii v ushcherb interesam Rossii), created in 2009 and recently dismantled, was really directed only at preserving the Great Patriotic War as a sacred site of memory for modern Russia. Even the recent intimations of possible tighter controls over the representation of the past seem unlikely to include October, as President Putin continues to seek a usable past for the new Russia.[93]

The October Revolution still features in textbooks and generates designated encyclopedias, but not as a transcendent event folding the First World War and Civil War and more into its grand narrative. It is more often described as an illegitimate Bolshevik coup d'état. In its laziest form, this narrative is reduced to the original sin of Lenin and Trotskii, who, as witting or unwitting

---

[91] Robert Zaretsky, "A Roller Coaster Ride of an Empire," *The New York Times*, 2 February 2012.

[92] Patrons can "experience" Soviet authoritarianism, replete with Soviet-uniformed guards, in a concrete bunker in Lithuania (http://www.sovietbunker.com/en/ [accessed 8 March 2014]). In what one can only hope was a hoax, the mayor of Vorkuta supposedly contemplated turning this former infamous gulag site into a tourist region where foreign tourists could pay to stay in a mock-up of a Soviet prison camp. Andrew Osborn, "Club Gulag: Tourists Are Offered Prison Camp Experience," *The Independent*, 4 August 2006.

[93] Amy Knight, "Putin's Propaganda Man," *The New York Review of Books. NYRBlog*, 31 May 2012.

tools of "Jewish-Masonic conspiracies" and backed by German and American gold, and, oddly, against the majority wishes of the Bolshevik Party, staged a coup that cost Russia its thousand-year empire and the imperial power that would have ensured its deserved place in the modern world.[94]

While America is readying itself for the inauguration in 2015 of a grand Museum of the American Revolution in Philadelphia, the symbolic heart of America's myth of liberty, Russia is planning no such Museum of the Great October Socialist Revolution, the likes of which were ubiquitous in Soviet Russia at one time. Were such a museum to be planned in Russia today, its design—in both senses of the word—would be dissected and interrogated both inside and outside of Russia. Not so the Museum of the American Revolution, which in an earlier design intended for Valley Forge was described as "Jacques Derrida over Fallingwater" and praised unironically as an example of "radical forms to commemorate a revolutionary past."[95] There is no better proof of the relative adaptive strengths of these two foundation myths.

---

[94] The "original sin" thesis is expounded in contentious and laborious form in a multipart DVD series entitled *Istoriia Rossii XX veka: Serial dokumental'nykh fil'mov na dvd* (Moscow: OOO "Novoe Vremia," 2010), episodes 29–31.

[95] Robin Pogrebin, "Design Shown for Museum of American Revolution," *The New York Times*, 11 June 2012; Herbert Muschamp, "Conjuring Histories at a Crucible of the Revolution," *The New York Times*, 25 February 2004, E1.

Conclusions

Summing Up: Culture(s) in a Time of Crisis

William G. Rosenberg

Collectively, the fine set of essays in these two books make three important points about cultural forms and practices during the devastating years of loss and revolutionary upheaval that began with the outbreak of war in 1914. They show, first, that a wide variety of cultural forms and practices did not exist in isolation from each other. Formal art as well as paper money reflected values; film, literature, theater, and fine art reflected traditions and perspectives increasingly under challenge by changing political and social conditions; religion, sexuality, and rumor all involved efforts to sort through the implications of real and imagined circumstance. In this respect, the diverse cultural forms discussed here constitute an appropriate unity, even as many of them also link to the important elements of culture in the anthropological sense—identity formation and reformation, household and community relations, social locations of power—that are beyond these books' purview.

These linkages to cultural anthropology are also essential, however, to sorting through the particular forms in which many cultural practices found expression in these years. Expectation, loss, deprivation, disorder—the conditions and sentiments that underlay the politics of war and revolution—underlay and affected art, literature, film, music, and other forms as well. The second collective point made by these essays is that what was perceived or represented during this period as "formal," "bourgeois," "high," or "proletarian" culture was not fundamentally removed from the social and cultural anthropological settings in which these cultural forms were situated. One must explore, for example, the anthropological meanings of "art for art's sake" in order to fully comprehend the implications of its aesthetic, just as we need to situate religious belief, rumor, even social memory within the community systems that nourished them in order to explore how and why the changes described in these books may have occurred, and evaluate them in terms of the broader and more familiar historical processes that define this period as well.

The effects these cultural forms may have had on these broader processes constitutes the third important point made collectively by the contributors to these books: that culture in the forms and practices described here helped shape the individual and collective historical experiences that the peoples of Russia's collapsing empire underwent during this fearsome period. They imbricated ideologies, politics, and social relations. They affected the nature and

Russian Culture in War and Revolution, 1914–22, Book 2: Political Culture, Identities, Mentalities, and Memory. Murray Frame, Boris Kolonitskii, Steven G. Marks, and Melissa K. Stockdale, eds. Bloomington, IN: Slavica Publishers, 2014, 343–56.

forms of economic exchange. They constituted in various ways the prisms of social and political understanding and the sources of contested values. The reverse is also true: the more common elements of historical explanation for this period—politics, ideology, social relations, economics, military policies—also need "cultural thickening" in order to carry convincing explanatory weight. In their insights and erudition, the essays collected here take a significant step forward in this direction, complicating assumptions and challenging established understandings.

Why Culture Mattered

Let us begin by asking *why* cultural forms and practices mattered so much during the last years of tsarism and the cataclysm that followed. The answer in short is that these years were ones in which beliefs, outlooks, values, and the wide range of representations through which they were expressed all came under increasing, and ultimately deadly challenge, just as they had during the French Revolution, which was often a point of reference for Russians in 1917, as well as more recently, during the social and political upheavals of 1968 and 1989. Revolutionary upheavals by their very nature shake cultural norms. This is partly because they imply that such norms are themselves in some way responsible for the deprivations and loss that fuel them. In its most naïve form, a commonplace argument is that cataclysms like the First World War (or the Vietnam War, or the collapse of the Soviet Union) were the direct consequence of "false" or "corrupt" cultural values, that "imperialism" was (and is) the logical (if not necessarily final) stage of diverse social and political orders that are commonly infused with certain sets of values. An equally naïve corollary is that radical changes in cultural norms will lead successfully to alternative outcomes. In its more sophisticated form, the argument can be expressed in terms of the ways in which revolutions feed on a growing awareness that existing cultural norms and practices are inadequate to explain or justify individual and collective loss and deprivation. As established cultural forms lose their social justification, the norms they reflect are undermined. The worse things get, challenges to their value become more cogent and persuasive.

Such challenges also characterize revolutionary moments, however, because all established orders are legitimized by certain sets of cultural practices, forms, and values, even if they are not universally acted upon or held, and even if they are maintained more by repression than consensus. In autocracies, the legitimizing values of religion, patriarchy, or class are undermined by collective or individual deprivation as well as social and political dysfunctionality, never mind the devastation brought on by unwinnable wars. "Proletarian" and other dictatorships are undermined when they seem to perpetuate "bourgeois" or otherwise contradictory cultural forms, especially if this contradiction itself seems to explain deprivation and dysfunction. In liberal democracies, too, well symbolized cultural values like the "consent of the governed" lose their legitimizing virtue when regimes or policies experience massive social protests, as was the case with Russia's Provisional Government in 1917. To be "patriotic," one needs a clear understanding of what the "patria" is and why it deserves reverence. Melissa Stockdale may be right in arguing that an enormous surge of patriotism swept the country in July 1914, but if so, and even if the depth of feeling it reflected may not have run very deep, the surge still reflected a culturally fixed notion of "tsar and country." In revolutionary moments like 1917, what have long been assumed to be legitimizing cultural forms, values, and practices can quickly become powerful agents of delegitimization if they appear to justify dysfunctional regimes. "Tsar and country" no longer carried cultural weight.

In this sense one can say that all culture is part of "political culture," despite the more specific way that term is commonly defined. The political culture of the tsarist regime involved religion, privileges tied to estates, formalized class distinctions, a distinct iconography, "respectable" sexualities, particular understandings of the sacred, and the supporting practices of social memory, memorialization, patrimony, and notions of hierarchy and subordination, among others. Not least was the idealistic and sometimes mystical anti-rationalism that stood at increasing odds with the processes of European "modernization." Some of the strongest supporters of autocratic traditions saw imperatives here for maintaining Russia's military strength and extending its empire, even after modernity found such awful expression in the new technologies of war, despite the resistance of cultural traditions. "Russians fight with God," one soldier wrote from the front in 1915, "the Germans fight with long range artillery."[1]

In 1917, the political culture of the Provisional Government embraced concepts of fairness, law, justice, elements of gender equality, local control over cultural (and other) institutions, and the images of leaders who represented "the people" and their interests. By early 1918, mass urban festivals and theatrical performances sought to create values through performance, while artists, writers, and musicians struggled along with architects and educators to create the rational foundations of a "scientific" communism. What these foundations actually were was initially less clear than what they were not, whether the issue was patrimony and gender relations, "classical" music, "bourgeois" fashion, or "art for art's sake."

The relationships between the legitimacy of Russia's successive regimes between 1914 and 1922 and their attendant cultural forms are amply revealed in these books, even if not always as explicitly as Pavel Rogoznyi does in his exploration of the Russian Orthodox Church. Catherine Evtuhov takes the argument further by positioning the church itself as a locus for revolution. What she illuminates is thus not simply an expression of aggression against the clergy or the church's vast land holdings at the end of the tsarist regime, but a democratic expression of religion itself as politics in 1917, one that almost

---

[1] A. Maksimova, ed., *Tsarskaia armiia v period mirovoi voiny i fevral'skoi revoliutsii* (Kazan': Tatizdat, 1932), 22.

certainly underlay the relative ease with which the Bolsheviks moved against the institutions of the church during the civil war. Anatolii Ivanov's and Evgenii Balashov's discussion of the Russian school system and its students is also relevant here. As they suggest, there was increasing expectation even before 1917 that the Russian educational system had to be, and therefore would be, reformed, if only to serve the larger purposes of the imperial state. This had in part to do with longer-term plans to simplify ("modernize") orthography and make non-Russian languages in the empire easier to learn and write, but even more so with the assumption that broader elements of social modernization required expanded curricula and even universal literacy. Balashov pays particular attention in this regard to the expectations of teachers and parents themselves, who sought increasing influence as Russia's social and economic conditions deteriorated. In their efforts to achieve direct local management of schools through local and municipal school committees, however, teachers and parents were also engaged in what can be called a "rights discourse" that related to the legitimacy of each successive regime. ("We must exercise our inalienable right," Balashov cites a speaker at the First All-Russian Congress of Parents' Organizations in 1917, "a right that is ours more than anyone else's—that is, the right to voice the demands that life is placing on school education."[2]) But as with the "needs" of the church, these demands were themselves subject to interpretations that related directly to political purpose. The "right" to a modern curriculum and the end to the teaching of religion challenged the legitimacy of tsarism. The simplification of orthography complemented and reinforced the democratic goals of the Provisional Government. And while Lunacharskii and other Bolsheviks carried democratization even further in these terms, emphasizing and strengthening the teaching of sciences as well, the question of who had the "right" to make these changes, and why, lay at the core of the party's monopolization of power in every area of life, perhaps especially those concerning "culture."

Here, the inverted commas around culture are necessary to distinguish the particular conception Bolshevik figures had of cultural forms and practices, one that linked them deliberately and directly to how they related to, and were fundamentally determined by, the sociopolitical orders in which they were produced. "High brow" (or "formalist") culture reflected social and political hierarchy. The independent theater discussed by Murray Frame was a reflection of detachment from contemporary experience precisely because "relatively little happened." It served in its continued amusement value to obscure social realities and dampen political protest. "Art for art's sake" could be construed as a "bourgeois" luxury, a criticism deeply rooted in the writings of Nikolai Chernyshevskii and other radical populists whose neglect the Bolsheviks soon addressed by reconstructing Russia's literary pantheon and constructing new monuments to honor its members. In a complementary

---

[2] Balashov, citing "Pervyi Vserossiiskii s"ezd roditel'skikh organizatsii," *Psikhologiia i deti*, no. 5 (1917): 50.

way, the mass urban spectacles discussed by Svetlana Malysheva and theatrical performances like Nikolai Evreinov's and Iurii Annenkov's *Storming of the Winter Palace* in 1920 were intended after 1917 to recreate the "lived" experience of revolution itself in ways that promoted both Soviet collectivity and the legitimacy of Leninist power. Never mind the actual experience of events themselves, like in the horrors of trench warfare or the awful depredations visited almost everywhere in these years as the tsarist empire and its successors slid into catastrophe. If "autocratic" and "bourgeois" culture served and was determined by autocratic and liberal democratic sociopolitical systems, "Soviet" culture had to reflect and be determined by the nature and forms of Bolshevik visions, if not social and economic realities.

And never mind, of course, that it was far easier to say what "proletarian" cultural forms and practices were not than to affirm what they were or should be, as the fate of Russia's brilliant artistic and musical avant garde would soon demonstrate. Literature and poetry, as Alex Ogden, Ben Hellman, and others suggest, could not be "formal" or reflect bourgeois values, but neither in the end could it be incomprehensible to its audiences. The same was true with music, even if the musical life of the factory whistle (*gudok*) was thankfully short lived. If the first years of the war saw musical performance emerge as a field of conflict over the relative merits of Russian as opposed to foreign composers, as Rebecca Mitchell details, and liberal thinkers like Evgenii Trubetskoi saw Wagner as an embodiment of Prussian militarism (engaging an issue which continues, of course, to this day), the question of whether and how music could become "proletarian" after 1918 connected directly to the issues of mass theater, "comprehensible" art, and the relationship between cultural forms, social differentiation, and stages of historical development.

For a while after 1917, some avant-garde artists like El Lisitskii could become more conventional in response to public tastes, as Aaron Cohen shows us; and some artists like Kuz'ma Petrov-Vodkin understood a "great obligation" to use art for the "public good," although its precise definition was too slippery to hold on for long. As Bolshevik power strengthened, however, and was entrenched in new and established institutions alike, non-objective art had increasingly to communicate didactically to a mass audience in ways that reflected the collectivist values and perspectives which ostensibly determined (and hence legitimized) Bolshevik rule in terms of history's "logic," and which Soviet culture thus necessarily had to reflect. The degree to which this also necessarily compromised artistic creativity generally and individual creative genius in particular was beside the point. Creativity for its own sake was art for its own sake: individualistic and liberal in all the ways that reflected the cultures and mentalities of socially hierarchical and historically outmoded (i.e., "bourgeois") regimes. The biographies of Soviet cultural greats like Shostakovich, Maiakovskii, Prokof'ev, Malevich, even Lisitskii and Gor'kii are testimonies to the difficulties here, as are those, of course, of many others.

The didacticism of Bolshevik cultural forms and practices was perhaps easiest in film and monuments. Intrinsically, these reflected technological as well as artistic modernity. But Page Herrlinger's review of workers' culture nicely shows how this mattered in broader class terms as well. However this culture was defined or expressed, it had to be "liberating" rather than merely "civilizing," as progressive and liberal enlighteners like Sof´ia Panina envisioned it even at the time of her arrest and trial shortly after Lenin came to power. In the case of films, as Alexandre Sumpf and Denise Youngblood discuss, their showings as well as their content could be designed to produce the cultural practices they ostensibly depicted, although here as well, the very medium itself also served to amaze "backward" peasants and others who sometimes regarded with incredulity this new "modern" wonder as symbolic, like electricity itself, of Bolshevik purpose and Soviet progress. In these instances content no doubt mattered less than performance, which might explain why, as Denise Youngblood's essay suggests, the trajectory of commercial filmmaking did not change significantly until late 1920, when many major filmmakers emigrated and "boulevard" films continued to circulate along with popular "agitprop" productions like *Overcrowding* and *The Frightened Bourgeoisie*. In this sense, as with pulp fiction after 1917, it was the cultural form itself that carried the message and achieved, through encouraging literacy or social awareness, the desired political goal. Films could be amusing and entertaining if they also brought Soviet modernity to the provinces; dance, music, and theater could be "classical" providing that the quality of the performance itself reflected an historical leap forward (as was soon the case with the productions of Konstantin Stanislavskii, Vasilii Tikhomirov, and at least to some extent, the youthful Dmitrii Shostakovich). Even popular *lubki* could spread primitive messages in primitive forms if they advanced literacy. In the broader terms of "workers' culture" reviewed by Herrlinger, the importance of developing its proletarian content was not only to relegate capitalist practices and bourgeois cultural forms to history's dustbin, but to create in all cultural mediums the active (if structurally derivative) agencies of social transformation.

Anthropological Linkages

Vladimir Buldakov understands the complex issues here primarily in terms of the way the revolution raised the question of how mass culture actually related to the culture of the masses, not in itself a new one for Russia. After the chauvinistic vulgarization of culture during 1914 and 1915, in his words, during which best-selling patriotic *lubki* complemented a commercialized and rapidly growing film industry where patriotic themes in largely romantic narratives competed in popularity with openly erotic ones and "high" art increasingly resonated to popular taste, 1917 saw open conflict about the nature and value of "aristocratic" as opposed to "democratic" art. Did stagehands have "equal rights" with soloists? Should a chorus go on strike? The historically ambivalent relationships between artists, intellectuals, and ordinary people took on a strong political valence, in which cultural "neutrality" was itself a political commentary. Buldakov is surely right to suggest that propaganda culture in any of its forms existed largely in isolation from ordinary people, who were focused overwhelmingly on survival after 1917, just as he cautions not to take the popularity of patriotic tropes before the revolution as clues to popular values or outlooks. The more important point, however, is that the relationship between cultural production and reception throughout this period was a function of the way people understood, valued, and conducted social relations in families, factories, and villages, that is, to the cultural anthropological forms and practices in which these relationships were set.

It is in these terms that we can particularly appreciate the imaginative work in these books of Corinne Gaudin, Boris Kolonitskii, Steven Marks, and, again, Page Herrlinger and Melissa Stockdale. When Herrlinger suggests that the concerns across the revolutionary divide about workers' general lack of cultural development underlay the civilizing missions of liberals like Sof′ia Panina as well as Aleksandr Bogdanov and the Bolsheviks' Proletkul′t enthusiasts, what she implies is that cultural forms created "from above" necessarily engage what were often quite different practices "from below." Herrlinger is surely correct to insist that what linked cultural activists on either side of 1917 was a belief in the transformative potential of culture. What this meant, in effect, was that the internalization of values and practices represented in "progressive" forms of art, literature, film, or theater, would not only produce "better," more socially and politically conscious, and hence more "enlightened" workers and peasants, but fundamental changes in the way ordinary people related to each other within and outside their families and communities. The political contest, of course, was about *which* values and practices, and implemented by *whom*, while the issue of cultural "strategies" (the construction of People's Houses, teaching "self-improvement," campaigns to encourage restraint or liberation in sexuality or gender relations, for example) not only mapped onto broader efforts at political change, but brought the civilizing "bearers" of culture directly into contact with the ways their cultural objects lived their everyday lives.

As Herrlinger shows, worker-intellectuals rejected elite assumptions, whether held by liberals or radicals, that workers' cultural development was as simple as moving them from the tavern to the tearoom, or cultivating the attraction of Tchaikovsky rather than primitive *chastushki*. If conservatives thought the crude level of peasant and worker lives and mentalities required discipline and control, and liberals argued that for Russia to modernize along European lines, popular "backwardness" had be addressed through vigorous social welfare institutions like the People's Houses, Bolshevik (and other) radicals thought that the cultural level of most workers was not yet sufficient for them to take such important matters into their own hands. In other words, there was no assurance anywhere in this period that ordinary people were yet "on the side of history" in cultural terms, however differently this was understood.

Consider, for example, the issue of fairness that Corinne Gaudin explores in her essay. The "moral economy" of the village was, of course, the reflection of embedded sociocultural practices that by their very nature are resistant to change. Such practices are always themselves in transition, but in ways and at a pace that is commonly quite different from those characterizing public political or sociopolitical interactions, especially at conjunctural moments like war and revolution. Well-intentioned efforts like those of the tsarist regime to "fairly" compensate soldiers' wives with special allowances during the war collided with village practices of shared sacrifice or collective rather than individual well being. "Enemies" were defined locally as much in terms of those responsible for the disappearance of goods or buying up the last salt or shoes as German and Austrian soldiers crossing the imperial Russian border. Particular meanings were found in the village for "speculation," rising prices, sacrifice, and loyalty that had little to do with the ways they were understood by state officials and public figures, or represented even in quite popular cultural forms like *lubki* or film. In a similar way, as Steven Marks shows us, money is also a symbolic representation of values, one that increasingly failed in this period to correspond to its formal designations. The crownless double-headed eagle on the Provisional Government's *dumki* notes did nothing to generate confidence in their worth. As Marks describes, the increasing popular reference to them as "Kerenki" as their purchasing power collapsed in 1917 connoted a popular devaluation of the republican government and its leader as much as its literal value as an instrument of exchange.

As with urban workers, religious belief and especially the institutions of the Orthodox Church in the countryside were also increasingly at odds with popular values and cultural practices in these years, which helps explain the rapid decline of their cultural roles after February. Stockdale shows neatly how both the issues and feelings of patriotism in 1914 were initially linked to the church and its language of sacrifice. Another way of saying this is that the institutions of Orthodoxy cultivated political faith as well as spiritual belief, the institutional forms of religious culture linking to the anthropological cultures of submission and hierarchy. This linkage itself, however, made both the regime and the church more vulnerable as either kind of faith or belief diminished, as seems to have been the case as the war dragged on. And in these terms as in others, as Gaudin makes clear (and Kolonitskii has explored elsewhere as well[3]), rumors—the culture of rumors, really—were not a world apart. They connected peasants and peasant soldiers to urban or official Russia, and influenced thinking and behavior precisely as a cultural form that often set peasant and peasant-soldier understandings in conflict with dominant official (or "urban") cultural representations. In other words, the practices and content of rumor as both a medium and a language were

---

[3] B. I. Kolonitskii, *"Tragicheskaia erotika": Obrazy imperatorskoi sem´i v gody pervoi mirovoi voiny* (Moscow: Novoe literaturnoe obozrenie, 2011).

increasingly, and with increasing sharpness, at odds with what more formal mediums and languages were attempting in this period to communicate.

The popular focus on "leaders" that Kolonitskii illuminates is also relevant here, especially if one uses inverted commas to signify differences in formal and informal ideas about what leadership meant. In terms of cultural anthropology, one might say that respect for village elders (*stariki*) infused power relations in the village, just as patriarchal notions of the "master" (*khoziain*), which anchored hierarchy in the family, were institutionalized in factories and elsewhere in the positions and roles of the *starosta* even if those holding these positions were not actually old. The roles and representations of political leaders like Nicholas II, Kerenskii, and Lenin, were thus set in a cultural context in which these representations were accepted, admired, distorted, or mocked in terms of the ways in which they corresponded to popular expectations. As Kolonitskii shows, images of leaders, once they gained purchase, were not readily controlled by their creators. How they were consumed is thus as important to understanding leader cultures as the ways they were produced.

An important additional question here, however, is why leader cults themselves were such a powerful part of Russia's political culture during these years. While the changing political situation evoked new forms of political personification, as Kolonitskii details, the veneration of leaders itself was a more constant cultural practice, albeit in various forms. If a democracy like the United States tends to idealize and venerate its presidents (each of whom since Franklin Roosevelt has been permanently memorialized in their own grandiose Presidential Libraries and Museums), why should not the Russian tendency toward "cults of personality" have similar anthropological foundations, especially in times of great stress. "Leaders" in whatever guise can reflect cultural practices of hierarchy, patriarchy, gender, and submission, just as they can reflect in moments of social upheaval and individual danger a wish for guidance, protection, or social order. The cultural meanings of monuments and memorials explored by Susan Smith and Aaron Cohen are similarly dependent on anthropologically "embedded" practices of behaviors and mindsets that may be far removed from the monuments' literal form or a memorial's symbolic representations. Oleg Riabov's thoughtful discussion of "Mother Russia" across these years is also particularly interesting in this regard. If the apparent inability of Nicholas to be a worthy husband demonstrated even for some loyalists his unsuitability as a spouse to Mother Russia, the eclipse of the "feminine" in Bolshevik thinking may well have resonated during and after 1917 to its relative absence in the mindsets of ordinary peasants and workers. As Melissa Stockdale has described elsewhere, the female soldiers grouped into Mariia Bochkareva's "Women's Battalion of Death," which Kerenskii among others hoped in 1917 would shame their reluctant male comrades into new acts of bravery at the front, bore qualities that were the very opposite of "feminine" as they were reflected in Christine Ruane's fashions, even if some aspects of their Rodina were still feminized. [4]

In my view, it is also useful to think in these terms about the range of expectations that Evgenii Balashov, Martin Miller, Ben Hellman, Dan Healey, Anke Hilbrenner, and others discuss as characterizing elements of culture during these tumultuous years. When Miller discusses the efforts of Narkomzdrav, the People's Commissariat of Public Health, to introduce measures to "triumph" over mental illness after 1917, and to recruit scores of psychiatrists for this purpose, he is also referring indirectly to culturally structured notions of science and scientific progress. Trotskii himself turned in this direction, as Julia Mannherz reminds us, when he presumed in 1923 that the "psycho-physical self-education" required in the process of creating new Soviet men and women presumed the ability to understand subconscious impulses and subordinate them to reason and rational human will. It is not only that the sciences, including psychiatry, were recognized here as the bearers of a different "truth" than that sought by Ben Hellman's writers, but that "science" and "truth" in these terms had little resonance with their cultural meanings elsewhere in Russia at the time. As Corinne Gaudin suggests, expectations in the countryside ranged from the coming of the end of time, reinforced by omens or by visions of the "Mother of God," to more practical (but no more realistic) notions that peasant soldiers would be rewarded with land after the war as just compensation for their sacrifice. The expectations of Jews and especially Jewish soldiers concerning political and civil rights that would ensue from their loyalty and service reflected similar cultural determinations, in this case the liberal emancipatory logic that was by now well rooted in Western Europe but whose values and principles were still distant from popular cultural practices. Indeed, the peasant soldiers who expected their own just rewards were often participants themselves in unspeakable brutalities against the Jews, especially (but not only) during the Civil War.

Issues relating to sexuality were especially fraught in this regard, as Dan Healey and others have argued. Sophisticated and often quite explicit debates about sexuality had brought the subject into broad public view well before 1914, and as Healey shows, utopias of sexual abstinence or gender fluidity as well as dreams of homogenic comradeship and same-sex love were all fresh in the popular mind as the war began. The war itself loosened sexual mores, as wars seem to do everywhere. Many discarded the religious and social restraints that, among other consequences, joined the fear of sexual violation to the dangers of assaults against landlords, factory administrators, or the "bourgeoisie" more generally. Still, Reds and Whites both linked political representations of sexuality that were at odds with changes in

---

[4] Melissa Stockdale, "'My Death for the Motherland is Happiness': Women, Patriotism, and Soldiering in Russia's Great War, 1914–1917," *American Historical Review* 109, 1 (February 2004): 78–116.

popular practice to the symbols of their causes: a religious iconography on the anti-Bolsheviks' part where Russia was female, crucified or ravished, the Madonna and Child terrified by the antichrists, the forceful end on the part of the Bolsheviks to the church's control over marriage, the "secularization" of sexuality, and the revolutionary state's own withdrawal from the task of regulating sexual behavior, at least until the consequences of this position clashed problematically with cultural notions of personal and family security.

Commonalities in Diversity

From all this it should now also be apparent that the wide variety of cultural subjects covered in these two books did not develop in isolation from each other, either in terms of their artifactual forms or their relationships to the broader cultural contexts in which they were practiced. They were mutually connected as well to the broader trajectories of Russian social and political change in this period, as their forms and meanings affected understandings of changing circumstances and helped define hopes and expectations for the future. Even such apparently disparate cultural fields as William Brumfield's architecture, the practices of hypnosis discussed by Julia Mannherz, the poets and poetry reviewed by Alex Ogden, the fashions explored by Christine Ruane, and Christopher Stolarski's press photography constituted interlocking cultural fields that collectively inflected Russia's revolutionary transitions. Art and poetry produced "for art's sake" bore the weight of social differentiation in ways that resembled the social and estate divisions between workers, peasants, educated urbanites and Russia's tradition-bound aristocracy. Architects like Ivan Fomin, Ivan Zholtovskii, and Konstantin Melnikov were moved to adapt recent modernisms to the familiar designs of traditional monumentalism that were easier to understand. And quite radical "proletarian" projects like Vladimir Tatlin's famous Third International Tower remained a model of unrealizable imagination appropriate only to museums. One of the roles of architects may have become the construction of practical and buildable "garden cities" for Soviet workers, reflecting other forms of utopian vision, but even here the "garden" part quickly yielded to the space and budget demands of large scale and ultra-functional apartment blocks.

Fashion, too, was increasingly symbolic of social difference during this period, and at times after 1917, fatally so, although some of the most memorable work of press photographers was not just focused on soldiers and workers in tattered uniforms and clothes or women demanding equal rights, but "bourgeois" women in furs lining the sidewalks to peddle what remained of their earthly possessions. Philosophers like Lev Lopatin could understand this as an extension of the "great wreck of European culture" reflected in the World War, as Christopher Stroop describes, and argue that the horrors of the times required nothing less than a full "reevaluation of all values of thought and life," but there was nothing that fundamentally differentiated formal phlosophy in this regard from the processes of reevaluating the traditions of social differentiation, religious values and practices, and issues of gender and sexuality, all of which also reflected the destabilization of cultural forms and practices. The "burning and urgent necessity" of philosophical rethinking insisted upon by Lopatin simply reflected in its way the burning and urgent necessity to relieve suffering and deprivation, cope with loss, and find one's individual or collective way through Russia's increasingly catastrophic circumstances. It is hardly surprising that hypnosis in these circumstances developed from a prewar technique for improving individual lives to a rhetorical explanation for disaster, something that helped explain the power of increasingly odious figures like Rasputin and even Kerenskii, rumored, as Julia Mannherz tells us, of mesmerizing his audiences into disaster, especially at the front.

Cultures Past and Present: The Implications of Conflict

As Christopher Read suggests, "cultural failure" may have been a primary cause of the collapse of the Soviet Union, although he (and others) seem less certain of this in terms of the end of tsarism. By cultural failure Read has in mind the ways a regime fails to maintain or win over a population to its values. Soviet "socialism" in the 1980s was manifestly at odds with the conditions, premises, and promises of the late Communist system, but can we say that the same held true with Orthodoxy, autocracy, and the "official nationality" of Russianness in the late tsarist empire? Certainly in the case of the "multitalented and vibrant intelligentsia" whose modern European mentalities, ideologies, values, and expectations largely contradicted the institutionalized premises of tsarism and whose cultural creativity, described so well in these books, pressed with increasing forcefulness against its varied resistances. Yet in some contrast to the moment of Soviet collapse, many of the most popular cultural mediums and practices described here strongly reinforced traditional values, especially (but not only) during the first years of the war. Loyalty, patriotism, faith, and even a patriarchal reverence for the tsar and his successors permeated film, poetry, literature, art, music, and theater in varying but significant degrees, and as far as one can tell, were supported by substantial (if also varying) degrees of conviction.

What was different about these two conjunctures has to do with the ways cultural forms are about answers as well as artifacts, about explanations as well as practices, forms, pleasures, expectations, and traditions. In the late Soviet period, cultural forms and practices answered with an increasingly resounding "no" to the question of whether Soviet socialism was desirable, sustainable, or capable of realizing its communist promise. Radical changes that would bring Soviet cultures into some degree of conformity with the values, practices, and institutions of a modern "Western" world were broadly thought to be the viable way forward, especially after Mikhail Gorbachev resurrected the faded hopes of the "sixties" generation. Between 1914 and 1922, however, there was neither conformity nor conviction about the reasons for Russia's disasters, and irreconcilable conflict about the appropriate ways forward. Cultural fields that became increasingly contested as the loss and deprivation increased soon became places of often violent conflict incapable of mediation.

It is precisely for this reason that the essays in these books are so valuable in terms of the cultural "thickening" one needs to understand the more familiar political and economic processes of this period. Relations of power are always inscribed with cultural meanings. Social relations and economic exchange always create and recreate cultural values. In the ways Russia's revolution challenged mentalities, hierarchies, beliefs, explanations, and instituted sociocultural relationships as well as political institutions, one can say it was fundamentally cultural in nature, in addition to its qualities as a political, social, and economic upheaval: all of its often brutal and more familiar political and social conflicts were affected and influenced in some way by a corresponding set of cultural ones. Cultural forms, symbols, practices, and institutions all refracted experience or otherwise inscribed meaning, in some cases "imagining the unimaginable" in Aaron Cohen's felicitous phrase.[5]

Here we come, finally, to an appreciation of how Karen Petrone and Frederick Corney have both dealt with the complexities of "remembering" these years, and the "vanishing traces of October." In important ways, of course, what Petrone describes as memory is not memory at all, but the effects of dominant political cultural narratives and their artifactual forms on the ways experiences were socially and politically processed after 1921. Both individual and social memories ascribe meaning, but it may be difficult in the extreme, even dangerous, for individuals to remember in ways that are radically at odds with meanings socially "remembered" in all of the many cultural mediums through which social memories are expressed. The decreasing "possibilities for ambiguity" over time in Soviet Russia, and the ways in which Petrone describes "memory " becoming "more fixed and canonical" reflected not only the decline of multiple and multivalent recollections of lived experience, but the ways in which increasingly institutionalized Soviet cultural forms and practices, like those in other societies, left increasingly little room for ambiguities about the past. If the American Civil War became all about preserving the union rather than slavery, and its first national commemoration in 1913 under a newly elected southern president brought whites from the North and South to celebrate a mutual heroism in which emancipated blacks were totally absent, it is not surprising that the formal Soviet reduction of Russia's First World War and its aftermath also reduced the awfulness of slaughter into more palatable ways of thinking and feeling, even for many who knew they were flawed.

---

[5] Aaron J. Cohen, *Imagining the Unimaginable: World War, Modern Art, and the Politics of Public Culture in Russia, 1914–1917* (Lincoln: University of Nebraska Press, 2008).

Little wonder as well, then, as Fred Corney has nicely described, that much of what was painful about the whole Soviet experience is also receding "ever deeper into the recesses of popular memory," save for the preservation in some forms of a generalized (and surely distorted) heroism with regard to World War II. Events like war and revolution become transcendent, to use Corney's word, in the service of the dominant narratives that come to describe them. In spite of, or perhaps even because of their awful depredations, their reductions thus serve as well to bring bitter cultural conflicts of the sort described so well in these books into some more tolerant, if not necessarily harmonious state of equilibrium, at least for a while.

The Great War and Russian Culture in Comparative Perspective

Aviel Roshwald

Stark contrast is a defining theme in many comparisons of Russian and Western European cultural history. Certainly under Communism, culture was political and politics were about culture, to a degree and in ways that marked the Soviet Union as fundamentally different from Western Europe. As Christopher Read's introductory chapter to these two books suggests, it is possible to trace this phenomenon back to the intense (and contentious) preoccupation of tsarist-era Russian political and social elites with shaping the masses' cultural values and identities.

Yet a perusal of the scholarship encompassed in these two books suggests that, even as telling differences continued to manifest themselves, the cultural trajectories of Russia and other European countries during the first three years of the Great War were marked by some striking elements of convergence that were cut short only by the radical rupture of the October Revolution.

Parallels and Convergences

In the course of the war—and particularly in its opening phase—the instrumentalization of cultural production in the service of the patriotic cause was a trend that cut across borders, even as the conflict undercut cosmopolitan commitments among European intellectual elites. When (as Christopher Stroop writes in his chapter on philosophy) Russian idealist philosophers depicted the war as a contest pitting Russian faith in moral absolutes against German (and German-inspired Russian-socialist) "nihilism" and Prusso-German militarism, they were actually engaging in a variation on a theme of national-cultural self-aggrandizement and high-flown justification of war that was common to writers, artists, and thinkers across wartime Europe. In the October 1914 "Manifesto of the 93" German intellectuals, some of that country's leading luminaries in the humanities and social sciences made a demonstrative Faustian commitment to their country's international propaganda effort. Many French academics, for their part, rallied around the flag of a French civilization that was facing down the soulless military industrial might of *les Boches*. Richard Stites (citing Jacques Barzun) noted one of the

---

Russian Culture in War and Revolution 1914–22, Book 2: Political Culture, Identities, Mentalities, and Memory. Murray Frame, Boris Kolonitskii, Steven G. Marks, and Melissa K. Stockdale, eds. Bloomington, IN: Slavica Publishers, 2014, 357–67.

more idiosyncratic cases in point: that of the French doctor of medicine who toured the country giving lectures about the allegedly bizarre and off-putting intestinal and digestive idiosyncracies of the German race.[1] In Britain, even an erstwhile pacifist such as the classicist Gilbert Murray was given to musing on the salutary aspects of war—if only for the non-intellectual classes of society:

> I do not forget the thousands left on the battlefield to die, or the groaning of the wounded sounding all day between the crashes of the guns. But there is a strange deep gladness as well....
> Human nature is a mysterious thing, and man finds his weal and his woe not in the obvious places. To have something before you, clearly seen, which you know you must do, and can do, and will spend your utmost strength and perhaps your life in doing, is one form at least of very high happiness.... Doubtless the few who are wise enough and have enough imagination may find opportunity for the same happiness in everyday life, but in war ordinary men find it. This is the inward triumph which lies at the heart of the great tragedy.[2]

When Christopher Nevinson (whose wartime work was largely state-funded) sought to highlight the horrors of war in his ironically titled painting "Paths of Glory," the censor prevented the public display of the canvas in 1917.[3]

The general wartime reversion to artistic realism in Russia was likewise part of a broad continental phenomenon, as the intelligibility of artistic representation took precedence over more purely aesthetic or philosophical considerations. The use of the traditional *lubok* format to disseminate chauvinistic narratives to the Russian peasant masses (see Aaron Cohen's chapter on the Russian art world)[4] found its parallel in the revival and retooling for propagandist purposes of *images d'Epinal* in France.[5] This trend was rein-

---

[1] Richard Stites in Aviel Roshwald and Richard Stites, "Conclusion," in *European Culture in the Great War: The Arts, Entertainment, and Propaganda, 1914–1918*, ed. Aviel Roshwald and Stites (Cambridge: Cambridge University Press, 1999), 349.

[2] Gilbert Murray, "How Can War Ever be Right?" [essay first published in September 1914], in *Faith, War, and Policy: Addresses and Essays on the European War* (Boston: Houghton Mifflin Company, 1917).

[3] Nevinson famously responded by hanging the painting with a banner reading "Censored" stretched across the canvas. Richard Cork, *A Bitter Truth: Avant-Garde Art and the Great War* (New Haven: Yale University Press, 1994), 169.

[4] See also Richard Stites, "Days and Nights in Wartime Russia: Cultural Life, 1914–1917," in *European Culture in the Great War*, 13; Hubertus F. Jahn, *Patriotic Culture in Russia during World War I* (Ithaca, NY: Cornell University Press, 1995), 12–28.

[5] Kenneth Silver, *Esprit de Corps: The Art of the Parisian Avant-Garde and the First World War, 1914–1925* (Princeton, NJ: Princeton University Press, 1989), chap. 2; Cork, *A Bitter*

forced in the French case by a perception of abstract art as an alien German innovation.[6] In Britain, wartime non-figurative creativity seemed largely confined to the design of camouflage "dazzle" patterns for warships.[7] The connection between science and war production was more obvious, and in this sphere as well general trends converged across the continent. Just as many Russian scientists turned their wartime research efforts to the needs of the military-industrial complex (see Anatolii Ivanov's chapter), so did the East European transplant Ezer Weizmann develop a technique for the synthetic production of acetone for Britain, while Germany's Fritz Haber pioneered the manufacture of chemical weapons.

There *is* a point of contrast in this context that is worth noting. In Russia, home to some of Europe's leading pioneers in modernist artistic experimentation, Kazimir Malevich felt comfortable bucking the general wartime trend by organizing the avant-garde 0.10 Exhibition in 1915, marking the birth of Suprematism. This does not appear to have exposed him or his peers to accusations of unpatriotic conduct. Indeed, Cohen observes that there were opportunities in Russia for the use of avant-garde forms to convey patriotic messages—partly bridging erstwhile chasms between modernist and traditional art worlds in ways that anticipated the later 20th-century commercialization of artistic modernism.[8]

As to internationalism, rare (especially in the early days of war) were the cases such as that of Romain Rolland and his tiny network of like-minded correspondents across Europe, who famously put their signatures to a peace manifesto within a few months of the war's outbreak.[9] Such dissident perspectives could normally be published only in neutral countries such as Switzerland and Spain. Indeed, where Russia proved exceptional in the realm of wartime cultural politics was not in the tub-thumping patriotism of its intellectual elite, but in its suspension of most forms of censorship under the Provisional Government in 1917 (see Melissa Stockdale's chapter).

Truth, chaps. 2 and 5; Jay Winter, *Sites of Memory, Sites of Mourning: The Great War in European Cultural History* (Cambridge: Cambridge University Press, 1995), 127–32.

[6] On early 20th-century German cultural production as the avant-garde of modernism, see Modris Eksteins, *Rites of Spring: The Great War and the Birth of the Modern Age* (New York: Doubleday, 1989).

[7] Cork, *A Bitter Truth*, 230–33.

[8] For a broader treatment of the global commercialization of Russian artistic modernism, see Steven G. Marks, *How Russia Shaped the Modern World: From Art to Anti-Semitism, Ballet to Bolshevism* (Princeton, NJ: Princeton University Press, 2003), chap. 7.

[9] "Manifesto of the Friends of the Moral Unity of Europe," dated Barcelona, 27 November 1914 and first published in *Journal de Genève*, 9 January 1915, reproduced in English translation (from original Spanish) in Romain Rolland, *Above the Battle* (La Salle, IL: The Open Court Publishing Company, 1916), 123–26. See also Rolland's original essay, "Au-dessus de la mêlée," *Supplement au Journal de Genève*, 22–23 September 1914.

Several chapters in these books point to a countertrend of escapism emerging in a variety of cultural spheres after the early flush of wartime patriotic enthusiasm had begun to give way to disinterest or disillusionment in many quarters. In this regard as well, the Russian experience was hardly unique. The flight from anything related to the war was particularly noticeable in the film industry, whose audiences grew exponentially across the continent during the war, perhaps precisely because of production studios' rapid turn to themes and plot lines that offered a distraction from the raging conflict. One characteristic that does seem idiosyncratic about much of the melodramatic fare churned out by Russian wartime cinema was its marked preoccupation with female sexual license as well as male predation on helpless young women (see Denise Youngblood's chapter on cinema).[10] In any case, the growing appetite for non-propagandist entertainment among a home-front public that was becoming all too familiar with the grimly unromantic material and human costs of total war spurred the growth of commercialized and popular culture as an autonomous sphere in Russia. In his chapter on mass culture, Vladimir Buldakov contends that:

> Popular culture, in the modern sense of leisure culture, was present in prewar Russia only to a small extent. Here, the very concept took on a rather different meaning than in the West. In a paternalistic social space, popular culture could not exist purely for relaxation. It had to be "public" culture, including actively spiritual and didactic elements and providing "healthy" entertainment.

Yet much of the material presented in these books, including by Buldakov himself, suggests that the quest for mental refuges from war was promoting the growth in Russia of just the sort of autonomous sphere of commercialized entertainment culture deemed typical of the West. Likewise, Page Herrlinger's chapter on worker culture draws our attention to the fact that, even in as heavily institutionalized a sphere as religion, wartime pressures were spurring many members of the industrial workforce to turn to unconventional sources of nourishment for their souls, such as lay preachers and Protestant congregations. One is immediately reminded of the wartime upsurge of the British public's interest in various forms of spiritualism, as documented by Jay Winter.[11]

Buldakov's chapter highlights the depth of Russian society's internal cultural divisions, especially between educated classes and "unwashed" masses. Across Europe, wartime served to bridge such gaps in some ways and accentuate them in others. The sentimental kitsch of songs such as "Roses of Picardy" might draw a tear from Oxbridge-educated officers and

---

[10] See also Stites, "Days and Nights in Wartime Russia," 16.

[11] Winter, *Sites of Memory, Sites of Mourning*, chap. 3.

"Other Ranks" alike, but there remained a world of difference between the culture of the music hall and the poetic sensibilities of Wilfred Owen and Edmund Blunden.[12] Moreover, even at the very onset of war, there was a marked difference between the widespread urban middle- and upper-class acceptance of the conflict as an unavoidable patriotic burden, and the apprehension and diffidence that marked the initial reception of war's outbreak by rural populations, in France just as in Russia.[13] It is true that, in Russia, the peasantry constituted a far higher proportion of the overall population—with higher rates of illiteracy—than in West European countries. But we should also take note of Melissa Stockdale's argument (in her chapter on Russian patriotic culture) that the Russian peasantry was not nearly as cut off from basic information about the war (often transmitted by the public reading of newspapers and other printed media) as stereotypes may lead us to believe. Conversely, Corrine Gaudin notes in her chapter that wartime rumor-mongering and preoccupations with far-fetched conspiracy theories were hardly less prevalent among Russia's educated urban elites than among unschooled rural masses. In their increasing alienation from official sources of information, Russians had much in common with the population of Austria-Hungary, where intrusive wartime censorship and ineffectual, poorly implemented propaganda efforts undercut the credibility of the political and military authorities.[14]

The tense dialectic between cohesion and division also played out in the field of gender relations. Across the European belligerents, the war thrust women into highly visible new roles in the public sphere. Vera Brittain recalls her surprise as a single young woman over her parents' lack of objection to her riding the train unaccompanied—something that would have furrowed bourgeois brows before the war, but that suddenly represented the new normalcy in a society where women were replacing men in the industrial workforce and volunteering to serve as nurses (in some cases, just behind the frontlines).[15] By the same token, soldiers groused over the prospect, upon their return from the war, of finding their jobs and social roles taken over by women. Frontline perceptions and portrayals of women tended to be bifurcated

---

[12] Jay Winter, "Popular Culture in Wartime Britain," in *European Culture in the Great War*, 334. On the enormous gulf in living standards that separated the British working classes of this era from their "social betters," see Adrian Gregory, *The Last Great War: British Society and the First World War* (Cambridge: Cambridge University Press, 2008), 278–80.

[13] Cf. Michael Neiberg, *Dance of the Furies: Europe and the Outbreak of World War I* (Cambridge, MA: Harvard University Press, 2011).

[14] Mark Cornwall, "Morale and Patriotism in the Austro-Hungarian Army, 1914–1918," in *State, Society and Mobilization in Europe during the First World War*, ed. John Horne (Cambridge: Cambridge University Press, 1997).

[15] Vera Brittain, *Testament of Youth* (1933; New York: Penguin Classics, 2005), 177.

between the images of patiently suffering wives, mothers, and angelic nurses on the one hand, and shameless harlots and double-crossing adulteresses on the other.[16] Such polarities seem to have been particularly acute in the Russian case. Alone among the regular armies, Russian forces under the Provisional Government of 1917 created several battalions of female combat troops, some of whom actually engaged in frontline fighting.[17] Conversely, Dan Healey's chapter on wartime sexualities documents the widespread preoccupation in the ranks of the Russian military with the supposed licentiousness of volunteer nurses—a prejudice that served to accentuate resentment and suspicion of the royal family when Romanov princesses opted to serve as "sisters of mercy." One is left to wonder whether there was a sociocultural connection between this hostile response to female medical care and the Russian film industry's wartime fixation on themes of sexual exploitation and misconduct.

Throughout Europe, women's postwar standing continued to be marked by ambiguities and paradoxes, as females gained access to the ballot box while being pushed out of the social and economic roles many of them had assumed during the conflict. Healey and Herrlinger both note that in Russia, even as the Revolution formally promoted women's equality under the law, the Civil War furthered the cult of militarized masculinity and broadened the behavioral and psychological gap between the sexes. This calls to mind Virginia Woolf's observation to the effect that literary men of postsuffragette Britain "are now writing only with the male side of their brains."[18] The notable exception in the realm of European gender relations in this era is not Russia but France, where women continued to be denied the vote until after the Second World War.

Caveats and Contrasts

Having pointed to some of the areas of convergence between Russian and other European wartime cultural trajectories, an observation is in order about an element of distortion that risks skewing any comparative assessment. Thus far, I have been discussing Russian culture as if the referent were the society of a nation-state. Even in the case of such "classic" European nation-states as Britain, France, or Germany, the use of a unidimensional national shorthand to designate what were in fact ethno-culturally heterogeneous and regionally diverse countries—whose governments, moreover, held sway over vast overseas territories—can be misleading and problematic. All the more so in the case of Russia, whose contiguous territories included major chunks

---

[16] John H. Morrow, Jr., *The Great War: An Imperial History* (Milton Park: Routledge, 2004), 159–62.

[17] Richard Stites, *The Women's Liberation Movement in Russia: Feminism, Nihilism, and Bolshevism, 1860–1930* (Princeton, NJ: Princeton University Press, 1978), 299.

[18] Virginia Woolf, *A Room of One's Own* (1929; Peterborough, Ontario: Broadview Press, 2001), 119.

of both Europe and Asia and over half of whose population in 1914 was ethno-linguistically, ethno-religiously, and in many cases juridically distinct from imperial subjects of Russian ethnicity (i.e., those identified as *russkii*, as distinct from politically Russian, or *rossiiskii*). Russia, as Andreas Kappeler reminded us, was a multinational empire.[19]

Of course, in and of itself, this characteristic did not make Russia *sui generis*; the Habsburg and Ottoman Empires were also structured as territorially contiguous, multinational polities. For that matter, the core territories of the United Kingdom included England, Scotland, Wales, and Ireland, pre-1914 Germany comprised a significant Polish minority, etc. The particular stumbling block in the Russian case is that there is a tendency in general and comparative works to treat the country in its pre-1917 configuration *as though* it were a nation-state with a significant minority population in its peripheries. It certainly came closer, in terms of its internal ethno-demographic ratios (especially if one chooses to think of ethnic Russians, Ukrainians, and Belorussians as part of an Eastern Slavic bloc) and the self-representation of its regime, to the characteristics of a nation-state or nationalizing empire than did either the Habsburg or Ottoman monarchies. But, viewed from the perspective of the *relatively* more culturally and linguistically homogeneous France or Germany, the Russian Empire still looks closer to the multinational than the nation-state end of the typological spectrum.

As our gaze shifts to intercultural relations within the Russian Empire, our attention is drawn to the surge of xenophobia, both official and unofficial, that marked the Russian government's policies as well as some popular attitudes towards a variety of nationalities during the war—most notably in the case of the Jews, who were forbidden to publish anything in Hebrew lettering and who were forced away from imperial borderlands into internal exile by the hundreds of thousands on suspicion of being a potential fifth column *avant la lettre*.[20] The First World War was a *khurbn* (Yiddish for destruction or devastation) for Jewish culture in the core areas of Jewish settlement, mitigated only by the relatively more tolerant policies of the invading German and Austro-Hungarian armies.[21] A number of chapters in these two books discuss the wartime paranoia, rumor-mongering, and violence in the Russian core territories directed towards people and establishments identified (correctly or incorrectly) as Jewish or German. Noting this element of internal intolerance towards some of the non-*russkii* peoples (be they Russian subjects or "enemy

---

[19] Andreas Kappeler, *Russland als Vielvölkerreich* (Munich: C. H. Beck, 1993).

[20] Eric Lohr, *Nationalizing the Russian Empire: The Campaign Against Enemy Aliens during World War I* (Cambridge, MA: Harvard University Press, 2003), 139–45.

[21] S. An-sky, *Der yiddisher khurbn fun Poylin, Galitsye un Bukovine* [The Jewish Catastrophe of Poland, Galicia, and Bukovina] (Wilno: Farlag An-ski, 1921); Aviel Roshwald, "Jewish Cultural Identity in Eastern and Central Europe during the Great War," in *European Culture in the Great War*, 89–126.

aliens") is important to a balanced understanding of the evolution of Russian culture itself during the war.

Having made that point, we can also note that here too there is potential for placing Russia in a comparative context alongside cases ranging from the Prussian army's politically loaded census of Jews serving in the frontlines (the *Judenzählung*, whose results were suppressed when they failed to confirm anti-Semitic assumptions about Jewish underrepresentation),[22] to Britain's violent confrontation with Irish nationalists in the Easter Uprising as well as the London anti-German riots that paralleled the May 1915 Moscow riots,[23] to the outright genocide that the Ottoman leadership orchestrated against that empire's Armenian population. Did the relative ratios of nationalities identifying with their respective states versus those alienated from them give Russia a comparative advantage over Austria-Hungary in maintaining a wartime culture of patriotism, whereas it disadvantaged Russia in its confrontation with a more cohesive Germany? Did, indeed, the multinational composition of the Russian Empire contribute significantly to the fragmentation of an early patriotic consensus and to what Hubertus Jahn has termed "the dispersion of loyalties in Russian society" on the eve of the Revolution?[24] Did the fact that the extensive Russian Empire territories occupied by the Germans from 1915 were predominantly populated by non-Russian speakers contribute to a perception of the conflict that was qualitatively different from that of French society? These are among the questions for a future research agenda that are raised by a contemplation of the present books' findings in comparative perspective.

One point of contrast that emerges strikingly from these books is the marked lack of direct engagement with the war on the part of Russian writers and artists following their early spurt of patriotic enthusiasm. While, as noted earlier, Russia's commercialized popular culture came to share the thirst for escapism prevalent across much of the continent, Russian intellectuals do not appear to have turned to the ironic or cynical modes of cultural expression that marked the work of an influential minority, at least, of their West European counterparts. The essays in these volumes indicate that most Russian purveyors of high culture either ignored the war or maintained a patriotic mode of engagement, writing about the suffering and sacrifice of the troops in a distinctly non-ironic register. As Cohen observes, there was no Russian literary equivalent to the sardonically, tragically, and/or critically

---

[22] Saul Friedländer, "Die politischen Veränderungen der Kriegszeit und ihre Auswirkungen auf die Judenfrage"; Werner Jochmann, "Die Ausbreitung des Antisemitismus"; and Eva G. Reichmann, "Der Bewusstseinswandel der deutschen Juden," in *Deutsches Judentum in Krieg und Revolution, 1916–1923*, ed. Werner Mosse (Tübingen: J. C. B. Mohr, 1971).

[23] Lohr, *Nationalizing the Russian Empire*, chap. 2.

[24] Jahn, *Patriotic Culture*, 177.

war-fixated works of the likes of Wilfred Owen, Christopher Nevinson, Ernest Hemingway, Otto Dix, or—one might add—Henri Barbusse. Some poets did write about the futility and horrors of warfare as the country's mood darkened. But in his chapter on poetry, Alex Ogden notes that these were generally people who had no direct experience of the frontline, as a much smaller percentage of Russian writers participated in combat than was the case among their counterparts in the West; only with the outbreak of civil war did armed conflict come to the cultural elite. In his chapter, Ben Hellman likewise observes that most Russian writers on the Great War had no firsthand experience of it upon which to draw. (Of the five exceptions he does identify, three—writing in 1915—tended to focus on patriotic themes if not clichés.[25])

By way of accounting for this dearth of combat exposure, Ogden explains that highly educated Russians found it easier to obtain exemptions from military service than did their counterparts in other countries.[26] But we should recall that in Britain, there was no conscription at all until 1916, yet male members of the country's intelligentsia volunteered in overwhelming numbers for service on the frontlines. This seems like a suggestive discrepancy, although exactly what it suggests remains a matter of speculation. At first blush, it would seem to call into question whether the patriotic enthusiasm of the war's early days was experienced as deeply and personally by members of the Russian educated classes as it appears to have been by their British counterparts. Conversely, to the extent that much of it remained sheltered from the disillusioning horrors of combat, the Russian intelligentsia may have found it easier to remain wedded to a naïve belief in their country's intrinsic capacity for victory if only the regime would allow the full potential of Russian civil society to be realized. And this in turn may have contributed to the conundrum of a Provisional Government that redoubled Russia's commitment to the war effort in the face of all indications that society's material and moral forces were spent, thus leading the country straight over the precipice of October.[27]

---

[25] It is worth noting, however, that Marc Ferro concludes that France's high literary culture was largely reduced to the repetition of patriotic clichés during the war precisely *because* such a high percentage of French writers were mobilized to fight on the frontlines (Ferro, "Cultural Life in France," in *European Culture in the Great War*, 295–307).

[26] Joshua Sanborn has noted that one way of evading conscription or at least being spared a frontline posting was to obtain a job in the state service—a prospect that was open only to those with at least a modicum of education. Joshua Sanborn, *Drafting the Russian Nation: Military Conscription, Total War, and Mass Politics, 1905–1925* (DeKalb: Northern Illinois University Press, 2003), 36–37.

[27] It is also worth considering that the ironic mode of response to the war may have been a peculiar artifact of the particularly stark and incongruous contrast between the astronomically large number of lives lost and the absurdly minimal amount of territory gained or lost on the Western Front between late 1914 and early 1918. The Eastern Front was more mobile, though no less homicidal, over the course of the war.

There was another side to this coin, of course: Russia may not have had its Wilfred Owen, but it did have its Lenin. Revolutionaries may deploy sarcasm against their enemies, but the ironic mode of expression does not lend itself readily to radical forms of political engagement. Indeed, wartime irony can be understood as a quasi-fatalistic response to the shattering of romantically patriotic and militaristic illusions among writers who nonetheless remained committed to staying in the frontlines out of a deep personal sense of loyalty to their comrades in arms. Russia's most strident critics of the war had, by and large, no direct experience of the trenches and indeed had no objections in principle to the massive use of violence for political purposes. They merely sought to shift the field of battle from the international to the domestic arenas—a task in which they succeeded admirably in Russia's case.

Memory

It was indeed the Bolshevik Revolution and Russia's pivot towards civil war ending in Communist victory that changed the relationship of Russian culture to the First World War in ways that had no counterparts elsewhere in Europe. In her chapter on memory, Karen Petrone succeeds in documenting the persistence of popular memory of the Great War through the 1920s, and indeed it should come as no surprise to find that Vasilii Grossman was occasionally to hear isolated snippets of First World War recollections from older Soviet combatants in the Great Patriotic War.[28] But Aaron Cohen's chapter on monuments and Petrone's contribution also serve to highlight the anemic quality of Soviet commemoration of Russian losses in the Great War, and the pedantic, doctrinally prescribed character of Soviet historical interpretations of the conflict—first casting it in the role of an imperialistic Götterdämmerung whose only function was to set the stage for the Bolshevik Revolution, and then turning back in the 1930s and 1940s to the "heroic mode, underscoring the absolute necessity to fight and die for one's country" (Petrone). Cohen's essay emphasizes that in the Soviet Union, personal recollections of the war—and mourning for its victims—had little in the way of evocative, state-sponsored rituals of remembering, emotionally resonant mythical narratives, or richly textured frameworks of meaning to which they could attach themselves. A Russian popular memory of the war that was thus cast adrift, bereft of a consistently evoked culture of interpretive commemoration, constituted an exceptional phenomenon, set apart from the widespread German perception

---

My thanks to Mordecai Roshwald for this observation. On the literary experience of the Western Front as the point of origin for 20th-century English literature's ironic mode of understanding, see Paul Fussell, *The Great War and Modern Memory* (New York: Oxford University Press, 1975).

[28] Antony Beevor and Luba Vinogradova, eds. and trans., *A Writer at War: Vasily Grossman with the Red Army, 1941–1945* (2005; London: Pimlico, 2006), 19.

of having suffered a defeat snatched from the jaws of victory, the growing British (and eventually to a degree also French) sense of having won a Pyrrhic victory in a war whose only meaning could lie in a recognition by all future generations of war's futility,[29] the Italian right-wing myth of a mutilated victory, and Atatürk's narrative of a national Phoenix (foreshadowed at Gallipoli) arisen from the ashes of imperial defeat.

If the realm of memory is where the differences between the Great War cultures of Russia/USSR and the rest of Europe are most striking, we should hasten to note that this serves not only to mark a form of Russian/Soviet exceptionalism, but also to set in bold relief some of the distinguishing characteristics of the cultural history of the war in the West. The contrast alerts us to the fact that much of what we commonly think of as the distinctive cultural impact of the war in Western and Central Europe has at least as much to do with the ways in which its memory was shaped and legacies defined in the postwar years as with wartime experiences *per se*. As Ben Hellman points out, many of the "truths" we impute to the First World War did not crystallize in Western culture until years after the conflict. Works by the likes of Erich Maria Remarque, Ernst Jünger, Robert Graves, Vera Brittain, Jean Renoir, and Stefan Zweig that have played a disproportionate role in shaping our understanding of the war and of its indelible impact on European civilization are themselves all postwar representations of the great cataclysm.

Conversely, Russian émigrés' very active and self-aware commemorations of the Great War draw our attention to another, less obvious feature of European—and ultimately global—war-memory culture that might otherwise have escaped our notice. Aaron Cohen reveals how diplomatically significant were émigré organizations' choices of venues for the construction of monuments to Russia's war dead. The selection of memorial sites was conditioned not only by the presence of a critical mass of locally resident émigrés but also by the political agenda of using what Cohen terms "the international culture of memory" to win sympathy and support for the anti-Soviet cause in countries where commemoration of the Allied war effort enjoyed broad resonance. The use of monuments and memory as instruments of alliance building and transnational bonding is a fascinating theme that merits further study. This is just one of the many ways in which the essays in these books lead us not only to think in new ways about Russian cultural history, but to see the cultural history of the modern world in a new light.

---

[29] See Gregory, *The Last Great War*, 266–71.

Notes on Contributors

Aaron J. Cohen is a Professor of History at California State University Sacramento.

Frederick C. Corney is an Associate Professor of History at the College of William and Mary, Virginia.

Murray Frame is a Senior Lecturer in History at the University of Dundee.

Corinne Gaudin is an Associate Professor of History at the University of Ottawa.

Dan Healey is a Professor of Modern Russian History at the University of Oxford.

Anthony Heywood is a Professor of History at the University of Aberdeen.

Boris Kolonitskii is a Professor at the European University at St. Petersburg and a Senior Research Fellow at the St. Petersburg Institute of History, Russian Academy of Sciences, St. Petersburg.

Svetlana Malysheva is a Professor of History at Kazan' (Volga Region) Federal University.

Steven G. Marks is a Professor of History at Clemson University, South Carolina.

David MacLaren McDonald is the Alice D. Mortenson/Petrovich Professor of Russian History at the University of Wisconsin-Madison.

Martin A. Miller is a Professor of Modern Russian History at Duke University, North Carolina.

Rebecca Mitchell is a Visiting Assistant Professor of History at Oberlin College, Ohio.

Russian Culture in War and Revolution, 1914–22, Book 2: Political Culture, Identities, Mentalities, and Memory. Murray Frame, Boris Kolonitskii, Steven G. Marks, and Melissa K. Stockdale, eds. Bloomington, IN: Slavica Publishers, 2014, 369–70.

Karen Petrone is a Professor of History at the University of Kentucky.

Oleg V. Riabov is a Professor of History at Ivanovo State University.

William G. Rosenberg is a Professor Emeritus of History at the University of Michigan.

Aviel Roshwald is a Professor of History at Georgetown University, Washington, DC.

Christine Ruane is a Professor of History at the University of Tulsa, Oklahoma.

John W. Steinberg is a Professor of History at Austin Peay State University, Tennessee.

Melissa K. Stockdale is an Associate Professor of History at the University of Oklahoma.

Christopher A. Stroop is a Senior Lecturer in the Humanities at the Russian Presidential Academy of National Economy and Public Administration (RANEPA), Moscow.

Alexandre Sumpf is a Lecturer in Modern History at the University of Strasbourg.